ABOUT THE CO\

JAVANESE DANCERS AT THE 1889 PARIS WORLD'S FAIR.

The 1889 World's Fair commemorated the centenary of the French Revolution, with the newly constructed Eiffel Tower as one centerpiece. This world's fair, like those that followed, also showed off the blessings of an empire, including Javanese and North African dancers, Vietnamese theater, and African village life to name a few attractions. The "backwardness" or "traditional" nature of their performances made empires look "modern" by comparison, even though Western composers and dancers came to integrate the forms of Indonesian, Egyptian, Indian, and the arts of others into what come to be celebrated as modern dance and music. The colonized performers for world fairs sometimes rebelled against their conditions, but nowhere to be seen was the incredible violence of empire. The fairs were about showing off and entertainment—or were they about something more?

Modern Empires

Modern Empires

A Reader

BONNIE G. SMITH

New York   Oxford

OXFORD UNIVERSITY PRESS

Oxford University Press is a department of the University of Oxford.
It furthers the University's objective of excellence in research, scholarship,
and education by publishing worldwide. Oxford is a registered trade mark
of Oxford University Press in the UK and certain other countries.

Published in the United States of America by Oxford University Press
198 Madison Avenue, New York, NY 10016, United States of America.

For titles covered by Section 112 of the US Higher Education Opportunity
Act, please visit www.oup.com/us/he for the latest information about pricing
and alternate formats.

Library of Congress Cataloging-in-Publication Data

Names: Smith, Bonnie G., 1940- author.
Title: Modern empires : a reader / Bonnie G. Smith.
Description: New York, NY : Oxford University Press, 2018. | Includes
    bibliographical references.
Identifiers: LCCN 2016059391| ISBN 9780199375929 (paperback) | ISBN
    9780190647650 (e-book)
Subjects: LCSH: History, Modern--Sources. | Imperialism—History—Sources. |
    World history—Sources.
Classification: LCC D5 .S63 2018 | DDC 909/.09712—dc23
LC record available at https://lccn.loc.gov/2016059391

9 8 7 6 5 4 3 2 1
Printed by Sheridan Books, Inc. in the United States of America.

TABLE OF CONTENTS

PREFACE

Modern Empires focuses on the diverse aspects of empire: its chaotic and unpredictable nature; its wide-ranging cast of characters; and its global power brokers. Coming from many imperial centers, the primary documents show the entanglement of empires beyond the usual European players. Thus, selections from China, Japan, Afghanistan, and Congo are interwoven not just with one another but with those from the more conventional European players. Testimony from those often marginalized in the story of empire stand side by side with pronouncement from rulers and other imperial celebrities. Primary sources from soldiers, women, slaves, and other subalterns provide a balanced and expansive resource from which readers can construct a more up-to-date imperial history. They offer the material for an understanding of globalization, attempts at world governance, and imperialism's lasting legacy in today's world. These original sources encourage the reader to analyze the various actions of individuals and evaluate the impact of their decisions on imperial systems and historical outcomes. It shows what it was like to live in a world of empires and to shape them.

Modern Empires consists of an Introduction and 12 chapters. The chapters are organized chronologically, and each chapter focuses on a theme that animates the period being examined. Chapters begin with a general introduction, with each document preceded by a headnote. To help readers approach the documents, headnotes pose questions for them to consider, while review questions that ask for comparisons of several documents end each chapter. The final review question in each chapter asks for an evaluation of a visual source found on the web. The URLs where the images reside can also be found at www.oup.com/us/smith

This reader aims to bring students an up-close view of 500 years of interactions not only among empires and other political regimes but among a selection of the world's diverse peoples. Students will also find justifications for conquest along with the bitter effects and aftereffects of imperial rule. Anonymous reviewers of the collection have offered sage advice on the composition of this collection, for which I am especially grateful. That advice is reflected in the pages ahead. Several decades of undergraduate and graduate students in my courses on imperial expansion and rule and on global interactions showered their teacher with ideas, insights, references, and critiques that were formative in the shaping of this book's interpretation. More than that, their own books on empire and global interactions and their integration of global themes into national histories or those of radio, television, sports, and other topics have critically informed this text. Heartfelt thanks go out to these dozens, even hundreds, of contributors.

Nancy Toff of Oxford University Press encouraged my first effort in the history of empires, and this current work owes a great deal to the many lessons in writing and thinking she has provided over the decades. Charles Cavaliere inherited that volume and has enthusiastically guided its revision into a more comprehensive look at the imperial contours of world history. Despite his incredibly busy schedule, Charles has edited, photo-researched, brain-stormed, and performed any number of high- and low-level tasks to improve the quality of *Modern Empires: A Reader*. Rowan Wixted capably and cheerfully pushed this volume to completion, capping the years of benefits I have received from Oxford's titanic editorial team. Debbie Ruel and Patricia Berube fixed editorial problems and infelicities on a tight schedule. Many thanks to both of them and to Donna Snyder for her help with the Index and with life.

Five longstanding colleagues and friends, experienced in writing about empires, have also helped, though in different ways: Michael Adas, Al Howard, Susan Kingsley Kent, Karen Ordahl Kupperman, and Mark Wasserman. It would be hard to express sufficient gratitude for their direct and indirect participation in this work. Donald R. Kelley has read the manuscript, translated documents, and as always provided astute comments from his wealth of historical wisdom.

Finally, I wish to thank Kris Alexanderson, University of the Pacific; Darcie Fontaine, University of South Florida–Tampa; Kenneth Orosz, Buffalo State College; Rebecca Scales, Rochester Institute of Technology; and Trevor Getz, San Francisco State University, who shared their helpful feedback with me.

ABOUT THE AUTHOR

Bonnie G. Smith is Board of Governors Distinguished Professor Emerita, Rutgers University. She is the author of books and articles in world, European, French, and women's and gender history and has taught survey, upper-level, and graduate courses in these fields. In addition to the *Modern Empires* reader, her latest publications include *Critical Readings in Gender History* and new editions of *Crossroads and Cultures: A History of the World's People, Europe in the Contemporary World since 1900*, and *Women's Studies: The Basics*. She is currently finishing a history of women in world history, in part related to *The Oxford Encyclopedia of Women in World History* (4 vols., 2008) of which she was general editor. She is also the editor and co-editor of book series in world history, including the New Oxford World History.

LIST OF MAPS

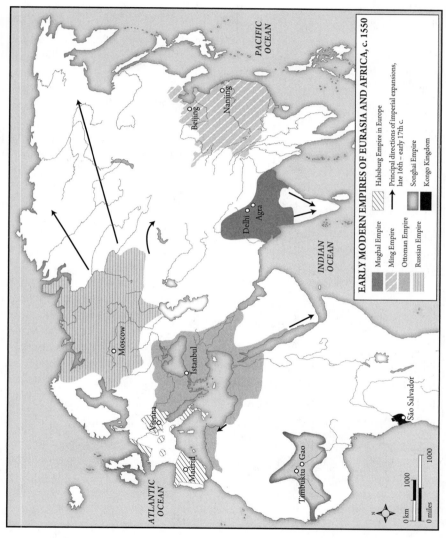

Map 1. Early Modern Empires of Eurasia and Africa, c. 1550

ATLANTIC
OCEAN

Tenochtitlan

Santiago

Santo Domingo

Caribbean Sea

PACIFIC
OCEAN

Cuzco

N

0 km   1000

0 miles   1000

EMPIRES OF THE AMERICAS, c. 1519

Aztec Core State

States paying tribute to the Aztecs

Allied States

Empire of the Inca

★ Important Spanish settlements

Map 2. Empires of the Americas, c. 1519

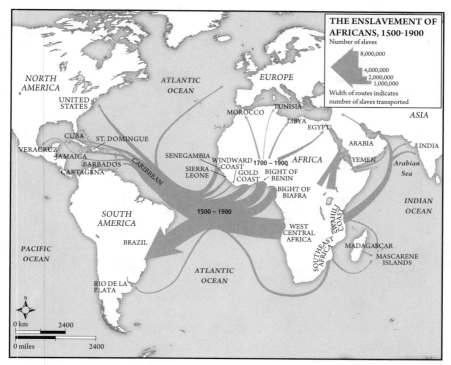

THE ENSLAVEMENT OF
AFRICANS, 1500-1900
Number of slaves
8,000,000
4,000,000
2,000,000
1,000,000
Width of routes indicates
number of slaves transported

NORTH
AMERICA
UNITED
STATES

ATLANTIC
OCEAN

EUROPE

ASIA

CUBA
VERACRUZ
JAMAICA
BARBADOS
CARTAGENA
ST. DOMINGUE

CARIBBEAN

MOROCCO
TUNISIA
LIBYA
EGYPT

ARABIA

INDIA

SENEGAMBIA
SIERRA
LEONE
WINDWARD
COAST
GOLD
COAST
BIGHT OF
BENIN
1700 – 1900
AFRICA

YEMEN
Arabian
Sea

BIGHT OF
BIAFRA

INDIAN
OCEAN

SOUTH
AMERICA

1500 – 1900

BRAZIL

WEST
CENTRAL
AFRICA

SWAHILI COAST

MADAGASCAR
MASCARENE
ISLANDS

PACIFIC
OCEAN

SOUTHEAST AFRICA

RIO DE LA
PLATA

ATLANTIC
OCEAN

N

0 km   2400

0 miles   2400

Map 3. The Enslavement of Africans, 1500–1900

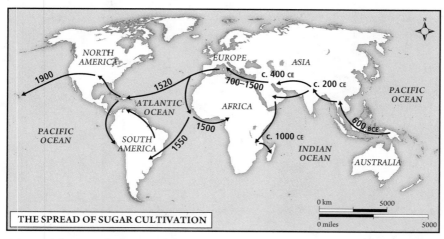

NORTH
AMERICA

EUROPE
ASIA

N

1900

1520

700–1500

c. 400 CE

c. 200 CE

PACIFIC
OCEAN

ATLANTIC
OCEAN

AFRICA

PACIFIC
OCEAN

SOUTH
AMERICA

1550

1500

c. 1000 CE

INDIAN
OCEAN

600 BCE

AUSTRALIA

0 km   5000

0 miles   5000

THE SPREAD OF SUGAR CULTIVATION

Map 4. The Spread of Sugar Cultivation

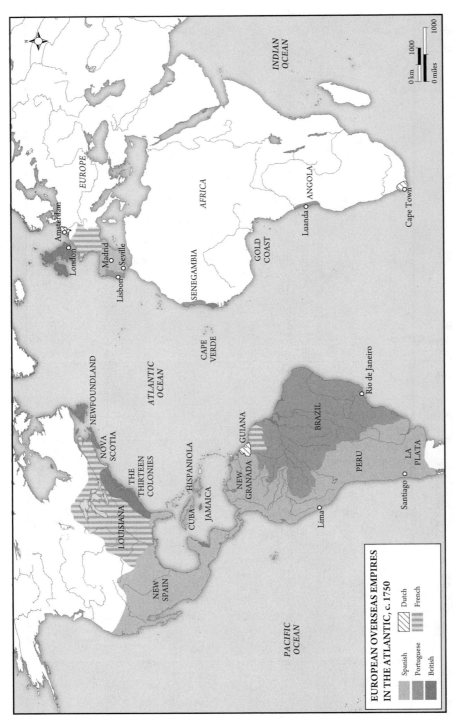

Map 5. *European Overseas Empires in the Atlantic, c. 1750*

**EUROPEAN OVERSEAS EMPIRES
IN THE ATLANTIC, c. 1750**

Spanish	Dutch
Portuguese	French
British	

INDIAN
OCEAN

EUROPE

AFRICA

Amsterdam

London

Madrid   Seville

Lisbon

SENEGAMBIA

GOLD
COAST

ANGOLA

Luanda

Cape Town

CAPE
VERDE

ATLANTIC
OCEAN

NEWFOUNDLAND

NOVA
SCOTIA

THE
THIRTEEN
COLONIES

LOUISIANA

CUBA   HISPANIOLA

JAMAICA

NEW
SPAIN

NEW
GRANADA   GUIANA

BRAZIL

Rio de Janeiro

PERU

LA
PLATA

Lima

Santiago

PACIFIC
OCEAN

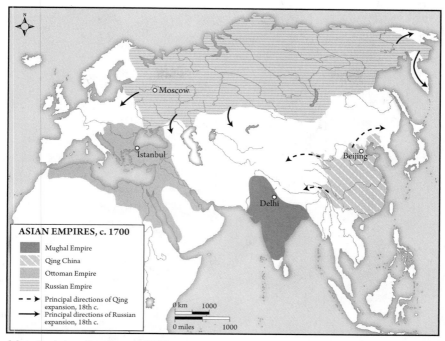

Map 6. *Asian Empires, c. 1700*

ASIAN EMPIRES, c. 1700

- Mughal Empire
- Qing China
- Ottoman Empire
- Russian Empire
- ▶ Principal directions of Qing expansion, 18th c.
- → Principal directions of Russian expansion, 18th c.

Moscow

Istanbul

Delhi

Beijing

0 km 1000

0 miles 1000

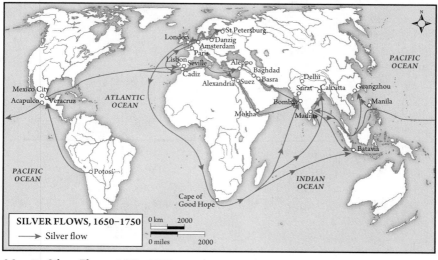

Map 7. *Silver Flows, 1650–1750*

SILVER FLOWS, 1650–1750

→ Silver flow

St Petersburg
London
Danzig
Amsterdam
Paris
Lisbon
Seville
Cadiz
Aleppo
Baghdad
Alexandria
Suez
Basra
Delhi
Surat
Calcutta
Guangzhou
Mokha
Bombay
Madras
Manila

Mexico City
Acapulco
Veracruz

ATLANTIC OCEAN

PACIFIC OCEAN

Potosí

PACIFIC OCEAN

Batavia

Cape of Good Hope

INDIAN OCEAN

0 km 2000

0 miles 2000

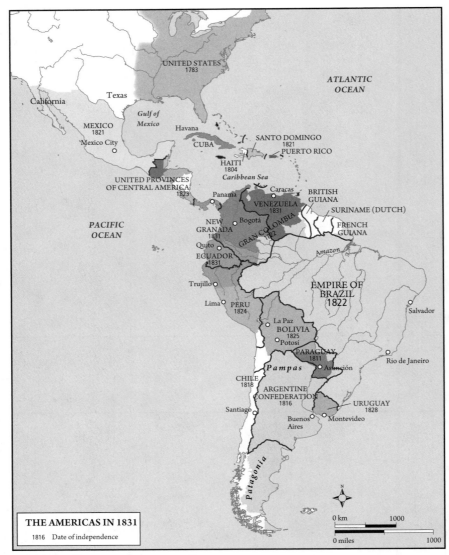

Map 8. *The Americas in 1831*

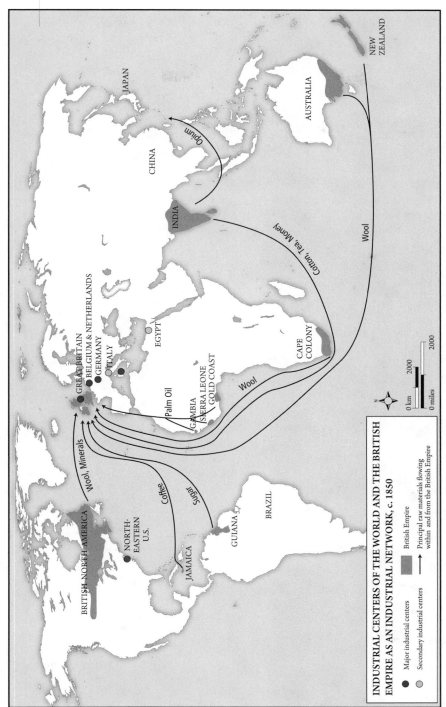

INDUSTRIAL CENTERS OF THE WORLD AND THE BRITISH
EMPIRE AS AN INDUSTRIAL NETWORK, c. 1850

● Major industrial centers
○ Secondary industrial centers

British Empire

→ Principal raw materials flowing
within and from the British Empire

0 km   2000
0 miles   2000

JAPAN

CHINA

Opium

INDIA

NEW
ZEALAND

AUSTRALIA

Wool

Cotton, Tea, Money

CAPE
COLONY

Wool

Wool

GREAT BRITAIN
BELGIUM & NETHERLANDS
GERMANY
ITALY
EGYPT

Palm Oil

GAMBIA
SIERRA LEONE
GOLD COAST

Wool, Minerals

Coffee

Sugar

NORTH-
EASTERN
U.S.

BRITISH NORTH AMERICA

JAMAICA

GUIANA

BRAZIL

Map 9. Industrial Centers of the World and the British Empire as an Industrial Network, c. 1850

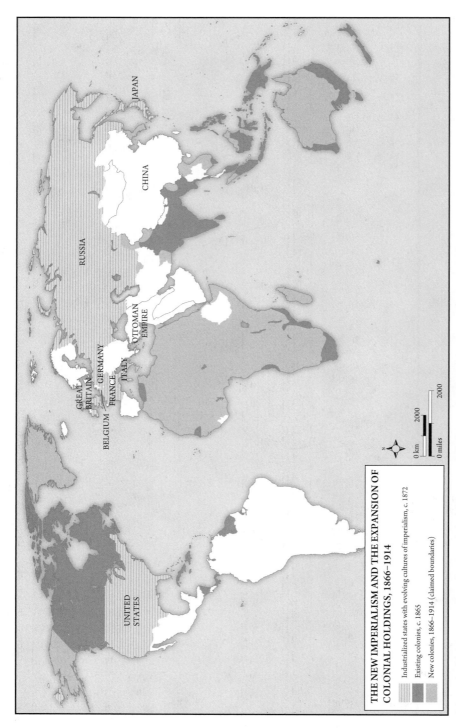

THE NEW IMPERIALISM AND THE EXPANSION OF
COLONIAL HOLDINGS, 1866–1914

Industrialized states with evolving cultures of imperialism, c. 1872

Existing colonies, c. 1865

New colonies, 1866–1914 (claimed boundaries)

JAPAN

CHINA

RUSSIA

OTTOMAN
EMPIRE

GREAT
BRITAIN

GERMANY

FRANCE

ITALY

BELGIUM

UNITED
STATES

N

0 km   2000

0 miles   2000

Map 10. The New Imperialism and the Expansion of Colonial Holdings, 1866–1914

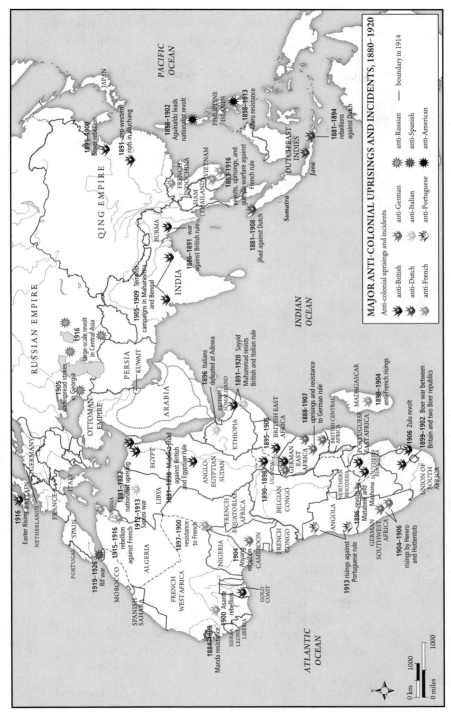

Map 11. Major Anti-Colonial Uprisings and Incidents, 1880–1920

MAJOR ANTI-COLONIAL UPRISINGS AND INCIDENTS, 1880–1920

Anti-colonial uprisings and incidents — boundary in 1914

- anti-British
- anti-Dutch
- anti-French
- anti-German
- anti-Italian
- anti-Portuguese
- anti-Russian
- anti-Spanish
- anti-American

1916 Easter Rising, BRITAIN

1919–1926 Rif war

1915–1916 rebellion against French, ALGERIA

1912–1913 Sanusi war, TUNISIA

1881–1882 nationalist uprising

1897–1900 resistance to French, FRENCH WEST AFRICA

1904 Anyang rebellion, CAMEROON

1884–1898 Manda resistance

1900 Asante rebellion, GOLD COAST

1896 revolt by Matabele and Mashona, SOUTHERN RHODESIA

1904–1906 risings by Herero and Hottentots, GERMAN SOUTHWEST AFRICA

1913 risings against Portuguese rule

1906 Zulu revolt

1899–1902 Boer war between Britain and two Boer republics, UNION OF SOUTH AFRICA

1898–1904 anti-French risings, MADAGASCAR

1888–1907 uprisings and resistance to German rule

1891–1920 Sayyid Muhammad resists British and Italian rule

1896 Italians defeated at Adowa, ETHIOPIA

1895–1905 BRITISH EAST AFRICA

1890–1898 UGANDA

1881–1898 Mahdist jihad against British and Egyptian rule, ANGLO-EGYPTIAN SUDAN

1905 widespread strikes in Georgia

1916 Large-scale revolt in Central Asia, RUSSIAN EMPIRE

1905–1909 Terrorist campaigns in Maharashtra and Bengal, INDIA

1886–1891 war against British rule, BURMA

1891 anti-western riots in Wuchang

1899–1900 Boxer rebellion, QING EMPIRE

1898–1902 Aguinaldo leads nationalist revolt, PHILIPPINE ISLANDS

1883–1916 revolts, uprisings, and guerilla warfare against French rule, VIETNAM, FRENCH INDOCHINA

1881–1908 jihad against Dutch, SUMATRA

1898–1913 Acehnese resistance

1881–1894 rebellions against Dutch, Java, DUTCH EAST INDIES

PACIFIC OCEAN

INDIAN OCEAN

ATLANTIC OCEAN

0 km 1000
0 miles 1000

NETHERLANDS · GERMANY · FRANCE · SPAIN · PORTUGAL · ITALY · OTTOMAN EMPIRE · PERSIA · ARABIA · KUWAIT · LIBYA · EGYPT · SPANISH SAHARA · MOROCCO · SIERRA LEONE · LIBERIA · NIGERIA · FRENCH EQUATORIAL AFRICA · FRENCH CONGO · ANGOLA · NORTHERN RHODESIA · BELGIAN CONGO · GERMAN EAST AFRICA · PORTUGUESE EAST AFRICA · BRITISH CENTRAL AFRICA · BRITISH SOMALILAND · SIAM (THAILAND) · JAPAN

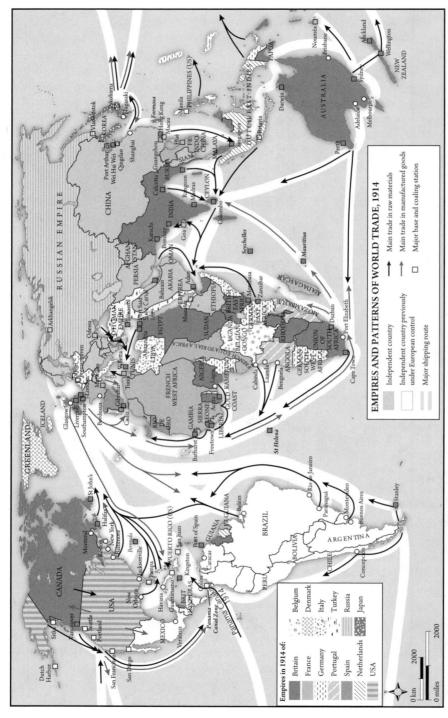

EMPIRES AND PATTERNS OF WORLD TRADE, 1914

Independent country

Independent country previously under European control

Major shipping route

Main trade in raw materials

Main trade in manufactured goods

Major base and coaling station

Empires in 1914 of:

Britain

France

Germany

Portugal

Spain

Netherlands

USA

Belgium

Denmark

Italy

Turkey

Russia

Japan

0 km   2000

0 miles   2000

Map 12. Empires and Patterns of World Trade, 1914

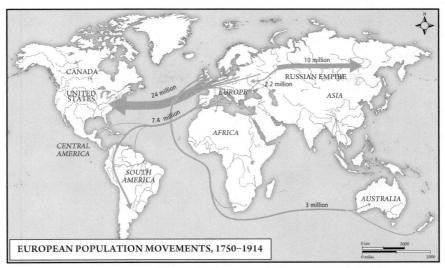

Map 13. *European Population Movements, 1750–1914*

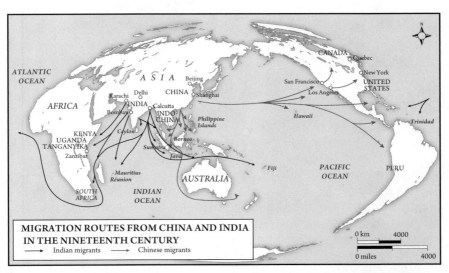

Map 14. *Migration Routes from China and India in the Nineteenth Century*

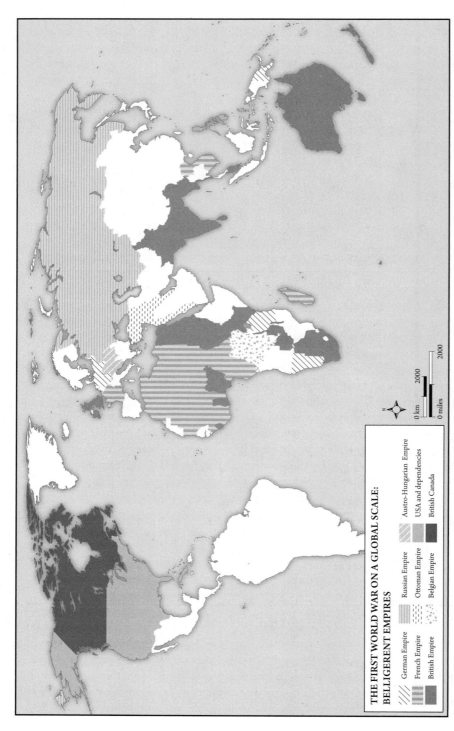

THE FIRST WORLD WAR ON A GLOBAL SCALE:
BELLIGERENT EMPIRES

German Empire   Russian Empire   Austro-Hungarian Empire

French Empire   Ottoman Empire   USA and dependencies

British Empire   Belgian Empire   British Canada

N

0 km   2000
0 miles   2000

Map 15. The First World War on a Global Scale: Belligerent Empires

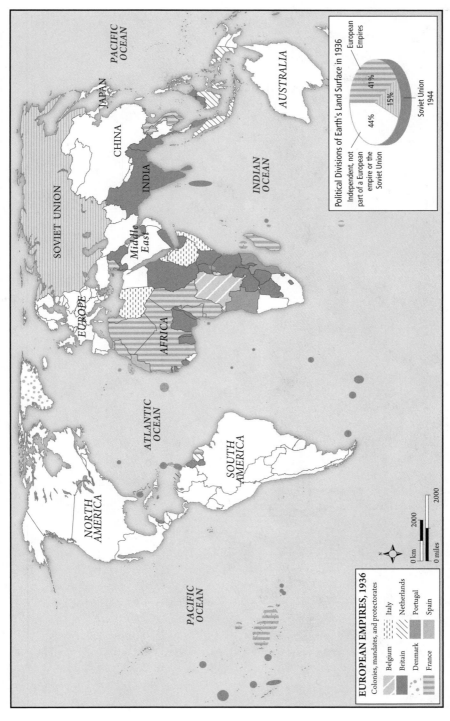

EUROPEAN EMPIRES, 1936

Colonies, mandates, and protectorates

Belgium
Britain
Denmark
France
Italy
Netherlands
Portugal
Spain

Political Divisions of Earth's Land Surface in 1936

European Empires
41%

Soviet Union 1944
15%

Independent, not part of a European empire or the Soviet Union
44%

Map 16. European Empires, 1936

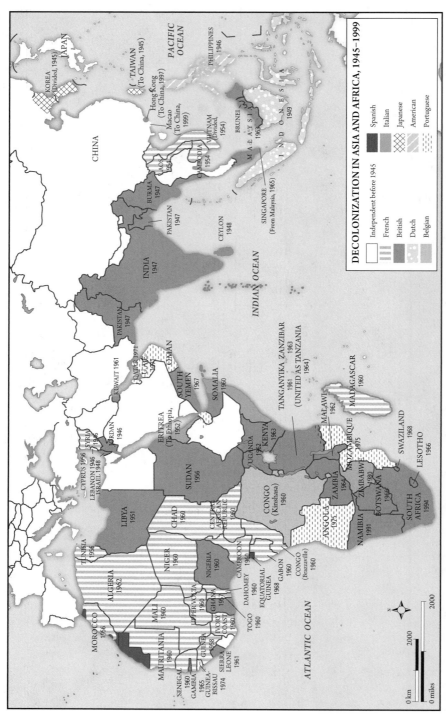

DECOLONIZATION IN ASIA AND AFRICA, 1945–1999

- Independent before 1945
- French
- British
- Dutch
- Belgian
- Spanish
- Italian
- Japanese
- American
- Portuguese

KOREA (Divided, 1945)

JAPAN

TAIWAN (To China, 1945)

PACIFIC OCEAN

PHILIPPINES 1946

Hong Kong (To China, 1997)

Macao (To China, 1999)

CHINA

VIETNAM (Divided, 1954)

BRUNEI 1963

LAOS 1954

CAMBODIA 1954

BURMA 1947

M A L A Y S I A

PAKISTAN 1947

I N D O N E S I A 1949

SINGAPORE (From Malaysia, 1965)

INDIA 1947

PAKISTAN 1947

CEYLON 1948

INDIAN OCEAN

CYPRUS 1956

SYRIA 1946

LEBANON 1946

ISRAEL 1948

JORDAN 1946

KUWAIT 1961

QATAR 1971

U.A.E. 1971

OMAN

SOUTH YEMEN 1967

ERITREA (To Ethiopia, 1952)

SOMALIA 1960

TANGANYIKA 1961 ZANZIBAR 1963 (UNITED AS TANZANIA 1964)

MADAGASCAR 1960

MALAWI 1962

SWAZILAND 1968

LESOTHO 1966

LIBYA 1951

SUDAN 1956

UGANDA 1962

KENYA 1963

CONGO (Kinshasa) 1960

MOZAMBIQUE 1975

ZAMBIA 1964

ZIMBABWE 1980

BOTSWANA 1966

SOUTH AFRICA 1994

TUNISIA 1956

CHAD 1960

CENTRAL AFRICAN REPUBLIC 1960

ANGOLA 1975

NAMIBIA 1991

MOROCCO 1956

ALGERIA 1962

NIGER 1960

NIGERIA 1960

CAMEROON 1960

GABON 1960

CONGO (Brazzaville) 1960

EQUATORIAL GUINEA 1968

MAURITANIA 1960

MALI 1960

UPPER VOLTA 1960

GHANA 1957

DAHOMEY 1960

TOGO 1960

SENEGAL 1960

GAMBIA 1965

GUINEA-BISSAU 1974

GUINEA 1958

SIERRA LEONE 1961

IVORY COAST 1960

ATLANTIC OCEAN

N

0 km 2000

0 miles 2000

Map 17. Decolonization in Asia and Africa, 1945–1999

Modern Empires

Introduction

Empires have molded our present world. The rise, expansion, and fall of empires span continents and centuries, and the effects of those empires circle the globe, dramatically shaping the saga of world history. A diverse host of history's most well-known players, from Spanish conquistador Hernan Cortes to Mughal emperor Akbar, Captain John Smith, the Kangxi emperor of China, British imperialist Cecil Rhodes, and German dictator Adolf Hitler, though living in different times, all undertook the building of empires. The pursuit of new and distant lands and the clashes involved in that pursuit led to some of humanity's most lethal wars as well as the slow drip of everyday violence that continues to determine contemporary events. Today's shared cultures and global interactions among peoples—both for good and for ill—frequently stem from earlier global contacts brought about by empire building. Given the vast influence of empire then and now, a closer study of empires past and present is called for. Primary accounts found in government reports, propaganda supporting expansion or opposing it, the words of conquerors, soldiers in imperial armies, migrants, and those subject to imperial rule provide a vivid portrait of empires.

EMPIRES: WHAT ARE THEY?

Over the centuries empires have taken many shapes and forms, and they have been defined in various ways. One standard definition is that an empire consists of dominion over foreign regions both close to and distant from the center of power or "metropole." The Roman Empire in ancient times and the British Empire more recently held sway over neighboring realms such as central Europe in the case of Rome and Ireland in the case of Britain. At the same time, Rome eventually ruled over Britain, and Britain, many centuries later, ruled over India. Empires can be either land-based, as in the Mongol or Russian cases, or oceanic, entailing the use of ships to conquer and rule as in the case British domination in India. They can also encompass vast territory—almost 13 million square miles for the Mongols—or far less—.5 million for the Songhay empire in Africa.

The ways that empires rule over these foreign territories have also varied. Portugal established its comparatively short-lived dominance in the Indian Ocean by fortifying strategic points all along the vast Indian Ocean coast and setting up strongholds. From those strongholds it controlled shipping through taxation of those using its shipping lanes. Because of its exclusively coastal supremacy, it has been called the Portuguese "sea-borne empire." As a result, people in the interior of India or East Africa, for example, might not even have been aware of the Portuguese presence. Imperial powers often selected local leaders among those conquered to govern the territories that constituted the empire, thus cutting costs and letting these "chiefs" bear the burden of rule. These local officers were tasked with collecting tribute or taxes, organizing forced labor, and maintaining order. In other instances settlers moved in to secure the position of the home country by directly ruling the territory and reaping wealth for themselves, as they stripped local peoples of their land, resources, and even their freedom. The settlement of the Western Hemisphere by Europeans, who first depended on Incan and Aztec governmental structures and knowledge followed by the subjugation of Native Americans, is one early example. Later settler colonies arose in such places as Australia, Algeria, and Kenya. In these colonies large numbers of people from the metropole confiscated land and settled it to farm, raise cattle, or set up mines and other enterprises to their own benefit. After being so robbed, local people became their badly paid day laborers and domestic servants. In one way or another, empires exercised dominion over other people.

In some empires, overlap and competition in administration occurred, with imperial governing structures having to compromise with local political structures and with free-booting adventurers from many parts of the world taking up residence and disrupting local or imperial order. Competitors such as religious personnel, mercenaries, and refugees sought power, opportunity, and influence on their own terms in the confusion of imperial rule. Britain's control of India is an example of this complexity: Mercenaries and missionaries from different countries settled alongside business people and civil servants; independent princes prospered in their own territories while surrendering their foreign policy prerogatives to Britain. Empires had no single form of domination: Even a single state such as Germany employed entirely different strategies in ruling regions stretching from Africa to the South Pacific. To that extent, empires may be seen as inconsistent and even chaotic entities.

A final kind of empire arose in the nineteenth century, when empires were overthrown in South and Central America, the Caribbean, and eventually across Asia and Africa. From the ashes of the old Spanish dominion, this type of domination is called business or informal imperialism and at other times new or neo-imperialism. In Latin America, where it first unfolded, the official grip Spain held on politics, trade, religion, law, and status in an all-encompassing imperial system of direct rule was replaced by the economic domination over the newly established, independent states first of Great Britain and then of the United States. Instead of taking full responsibility for government and military occupation, these countries successively gave loans for improvements ultimately repaid by taxpayers; their citizens were given or built businesses including major mining and agricultural operations in foreign lands; and their military or officials influenced the course of political events, sometimes by direct intervention and even occupation. In Mexico the government stripped local peasants of their land and gave it to U.S. citizens to keep American support. Both Britain and the United States found cause to threaten and actually invade client states on a temporary basis when policies were not beneficial enough to their own citizens and their property appeared to be under threat. Some maintain that a related type of imperial power remains active today, only in even less visible, non-territorial forms of domination. The power of the wealthiest and best equipped nations militarily—the United States, Russia, China, and a consortium of former imperial powers in the European Union—can determine the course of supposedly independent nations. Thus imperial domination is said to have transformed itself to be modern and almost invisible to the eye but nonetheless effective in controlling other countries and their wealth.

Finally, most empires claimed some kind of overarching cause or superiority driving expansion and justifying their rulership over distant, foreign, or simply different peoples. At the beginning of the early modern period in the mid-fifteenth century, justifications were most often religious: the spread of one or another form of Islam and thus the defeat of blasphemy; the spread of Christianity and the defeat of infidels, pagans, and other people of Satan; the conquest and blood sacrifice of defeated warriors to insure the continued workings of the universe; exercise of the mandate of heaven. Closer to our own age, justifications of imperial conquest have included the spread of "civilization," "civilized values," democracy, and progress, including the defeat of "barbarism"; the wider spread of prosperity through modernization of agriculture, which came to be called "development"; the strengthening of superior races, for example European ones; and the defeat of inferior "racial" enemies such as Jews, Native Americans, and Arabs. In other words, empires had unifying themes, which over time were developed and advertised by imperial administrations.

THE CREATION OF MODERN EMPIRES SINCE 1450

Empires have proliferated since 1450, causing increasing pride among the conquerors and suffering for the conquered. From the beginning of that proliferation, the destinies of both have become increasingly interlocked. In 1453, the Ottomans, a Turkic ethnic group originally from the northeastern ranges of Asia, conquered the Byzantine empire by taking its powerful capital city of Constantinople. Straddling Asia and Europe, Constantinople's fall consolidated the Islamic power of the Ottomans, who had been moving across Asia and into eastern Europe for several centuries. Over the next two centuries, the Ottomans conquered Syria, Lebanon, and Egypt, and North Africa and secured much of the rest of West Asia.

One justification for this drive was to defeat Shi'a Muslims, whom they saw as heretical. The wealth from these regions financed an expanding administrative apparatus and a final push to the gates of Vienna in 1683, where the Habsburg Empire repulsed the Ottomans. Even so, Ottomans felt that they had preserved large swaths of southeastern Europe from the Christian infidels.

By this time, the Ottoman empire controlled much of southeastern Europe, the Crimea, and Muslim lands in the Caucasus, where its influence would lead to struggles with Russia. Although looking like a nomadic, land-based empire, the Ottomans developed their own sea-going fleet after 1453 to the point of challenging a variety of competitors—especially Christian ones—on the water. The administration supported agriculture and commerce alike and, to ensure prosperity, did not systematically persecute people of other faiths. Instead it allowed Christians, Jews, and others to use their skills and flourish as "protected people." Eventually Russia, England, France, and Germany eyed Ottoman holdings greedily and eventually took over Egypt in 1882 as well as much of the Middle East after World War I. Despite these ups and downs, the Ottoman empire would be the longest lived of all modern empires, officially giving way to the state of Turkey in 1923.

The Ottomans were just one among various northeastern nomadic peoples forging empires. The Persians/Iranians and the Mughals also expanded and drew under their administration diverse peoples, welding them into imperial states composed of different tribal, ethnic, and religious groups. From 1501, Ismail founded the Persian Safavid dynasty that would compete for surrounding territories with the Ottomans, Russians, and Mughals. Ismail used his warrior commitment to spread Shia Islam, thereby enhancing his appeal to the individual tribes that followed him into the empire. His own religious drive against the Ottomans and others and his literary accomplishments passed down through the Safavid line, reaching its height with the rule of Shah Abbas (1571–1629), who was not only a successful religious warrior but a practitioner of the arts. Shah Abbas heightened the renown of Persian imperial culture by creating the splendid capital at Isfahan. "Few cities in the world surpass it," one admiring global traveler wrote later in the seventeenth century, "and none come near it for . . . stately buildings."[1] Claims to cultural and religious superiority galvanized attempts at further Savafid expansion across the region, including South Asia.

Other empire builders followed the traditions of the Mongols and the Turkic leader Tamerlane (Timur, 1336–1405), whose stunning conquests stirred up warrior competition in West, Central, and South Asia. The ambition as warrior to gain more land stirred Zahir al-Din Babur (1483–1530), the young and vigorous leader of the Mughals who would begin to take over India piecemeal and establish an empire in the 1500s. The name Mughal is a modification of the term *Mongol*, reflecting the linkages among the Asian groups. Yet the Mughals were less sea-faring than many other imperial groups. The conqueror Babur never saw the sea, and his grandson

---

[1] John Fryer, *A New Account of East India and Persia, Being Nine Years' Travels, 1672–1681*, William Crooke ed. (London: Hakluyt Society, 1911) 3:19.

and successor Akbar (1542–1605), perhaps the most accomplished sultan, was stunned to see it for the first time at the age of thirty.

These empire-builders were Muslim armed adventurers, but as they fought their way down the South Asian subcontinent, they settled into the cultures—most notably Hindu traditions—that were already in place, allowing religions, customs, and economic ways of life to thrive alongside one another. The peoples of India were prosperous because of skill in crafts, metallurgy, and agriculture, and this prosperity was tempting not only to the Mughals and Safavids but also to the Europeans. Amid competition, the Mughals conquered more of the subcontinent, even as mounting wealth led to a weakening of warrior discipline. Crumbling leadership after 1700 made India's talented people and productive wealth a tasty target. After centuries of warfare, by the late nineteenth century Britain claimed India as its own, declaring Queen Victoria empress of the region in 1877.

In Babur's time Ottoman strength also made trade in the eastern Mediterranean uncertain, intensifying competition for new routes and markets. Iberians found trade with Asia via the Middle East more difficult to access. In the early fifteenth century, sponsored by ambitious Portuguese Prince Henry, a naval school took shape to advance cartography, ship technology, and general knowledge of the seas, ships, and naval instruments. The Portuguese moved into the Atlantic islands off the Iberian coast where they set up wheat and sugar plantations to supplement the weak agricultural sector back home. They made forays along coastal Africa, whose reputation for wealth in gold, salt, and slaves had long spurred the comparatively poor Iberians to venture forth. Sailing in an ever more southerly route, the captain Bartolomeu Dias had reached the southern tip of the African continent in 1488, with Vasco da Gama rounding the Cape of Good Hope in 1497. As his and subsequent ships traveled the East African coast and then, with the help of local pilots, over to India and ultimately to the Straits of Malacca and to Macau, the Portuguese set up their forts that allowed some to reap fortunes from monitoring trade and profiting from carrying cottons and porcelain to European and other ports. Even as these developments were taking place, other captains located the eastern coast of South America, gradually populating present-day Brazil and setting up sugar plantations and trade in wood and eventually the mining of gold and diamonds. In the process of building an empire, the Portuguese clashed with peoples and empires—including African, West Asian, Chinese, and other imperial states—around the world.

By 1485, Genoese sailor Christopher Columbus was in Portugal, learning from the accumulation of navigational knowledge and attempting to join the quest for wealth that was already underway. Columbus had sailed for Genoese merchants but settled for a time in Lisbon, where he continued his habit of reading widely in history and geography. His reading made him eager to find a westward route to China and its vast wealth, and he petitioned the Portuguese king for support. Rebuffed by the king, whose ships were already making profitable discoveries, Columbus turned to Spain, where after a lengthy time lobbying, his efforts met with success. The Spanish monarchs Ferdinand and Isabella needed new sources of wealth to drive Muslims from the kingdom and to build a more effective state apparatus. They pinned slight hopes on Columbus's assurance of finding a way to access the riches of China by sailing westward, but they sponsored him nonetheless. Thus 1492 became a crucial date in the development of modern empires, as Columbus's four voyages into the Caribbean helped Spain join the ranks of empires that were being born.

Columbus and other adventurers like Hernando Cortes and Francisco Pizarro were part of a movement during which rising empires destroyed more established ones. Between 1519 and the 1530s, the remarkable Aztec and Inca empires in Mexico and Peru, respectively, were among those defeated, as the Spanish moved into the Western Hemisphere, taking over stretches of both continents and organizing a transoceanic empire that would last into the nineteenth century. Both the Aztecs and Incas were wealthy, highly organized societies, skilled in building infrastructure and in the techniques of domination. The Spanish made use of the institutional assets that were in place, but like the Portuguese they also found untapped resources—gold, silver, diamonds, and emeralds to mention a few. Both Portuguese and Spanish persecuted those under their dominion who did not convert to Catholicism, even using torture and execution. Their rule, riddled with exploitation and enslavement for the many and benefits for the few, provoked constant uprisings in addition to competition from newcomers for the Western Hemisphere's wealth.

Spain's Latin American empire was only an ocean away from Ming China, which came into being in 1368, securing territory in the southwest and integrating non-Chinese people at about the same time as the Ottomans and Portuguese were venturing into other lands. Although reputedly "closed" to outsiders, the empire was engaged globally. In 1405, emperor Chengzu send out the most massive fleet ever launched to expand the tribute system by which states acknowledged Chinese sovereignty with goods and payments. In seven voyages the fleet under the direction of Admiral Zheng He reached the Middle East and the coast of East Africa, engaging with the Mamluks and other leaders across the Indian Ocean world. By 1433 imperial advisors found such voyages unprofitable despite the massive amounts of treasure with which returning ships were laden. The Ming began its decline, as emperors more or less turned away from governing and maintaining infrastructure, all the while raising taxes. Banditry and smuggling increased, and the borders were hardly stable, with constant in- and out-migration. In the middle of the seventeenth century, troops of Manchu fighters from outside China's northeast borders ousted the Ming. Under the Manchu-born Kangxi emperor and his successors, the Qing moved across thousands of miles to expand and secure China's borders. They ultimately defeated ethnic groups to the north, northwest, and west of the country as well as taking over Tibet and the island of Taiwan. The conquest and incorporation of Xinjiang (and the Uighurs and other ethnic groups living there) enlarged the empire by millions of square miles.

Building on excellence in crafts and its division of labor in manufacturing as well as its productive agriculture, China had the largest economy in the world down to the end of the nineteenth century and was engaged in global trade. Its growth was stabilized by infusions of silver from the Western Hemisphere, once the Spanish had discovered mines and mastered the Pacific enough to fund the purchase of prized Chinese products, including silk, cotton textiles, lacquerware, porcelain, tea, and metal goods—to name a few. Its inventiveness was envied and its wealth coveted not by just one or two but the entire roster of global powers. The costs of such a vast empire were more than could be borne at the time, however, as the constant attacks by pirates, weakening of central control of commerce by the junk trade, inroads by Westerners, destabilization by the circulation of massive new amounts of South American precious metals, and rebellions against imperial government all injured social and political order. In the nineteenth century the vast Qing Empire appeared to the Europeans and Japanese like a golden apple ready to be picked.

While the discovery of silver and gold in both North and South America upset prices globally and fueled the drive for colonies, piracy thrived as a way of seizing new global wealth, especially the treasure carried on Spanish, Portuguese, and other ships. Piracy attracted both freelance adventurers and government agents, with weaker kingdoms such as England beginning their imperial efforts through the capture of wealth-laden ships. In 1592, British courtier and pirate Walter Raleigh seized the Portuguese ship "Madre de Deus" containing hundreds of tons of gold, silver, pearls, fine textiles, spices, and other valuable commodities, including a secret document on trade in China and Japan—all of which, once sold, could finance British expansion. Not only did sea-farers in the cause of their country's empire face dangers from the elements and from their own comparatively fragile ships, they also faced other privateers operating worldwide. Pirates plagued the wealthy coastline of Ming China. Europeans and Ottomans faced off through piracy in the Mediterranean with three objectives: gaining territorial advantage; finding wealth in slaves, goods, and ransom money to finance ship-building and expansion; conquering long-hated infidels, whether Christian or Muslim. Out-and-out warfare on the seas among contestants for empire and for personal wealth was a constant across the globe right through World War II in the twentieth century.

Counter to this trend, the Russian empire made huge land-based gains from the sixteenth century on. In 1552, it captured the Muslim city of Kazan "with the aid of our Almighty Lord Jesus Christ and the prayers of the Mother of God. . . ."[2] It had expanded from its base in Kiev with the aim of taking over various khanates which surrounded its southern and eastern borders before they could erode Russian security. In so doing the Russian empire came to comprise so many ethnic groups that by the nineteenth century it had over 100 different peoples, with vastly disparate customs, religions, and languages. Although the Russians hoped to integrate everyone so that they spoke the same language, embraced the Russian

[2]Quoted in Geoffrey Hosking, *Russia: People and Empire* (Cambridge: Harvard University Press, 1997)

Orthodox faith, and rejected the nomadic way of life, across the centuries officials had to acknowledge that in many cases homogenization of ethnic, clan, and tribal groups into a cohesive empire was impossible. They acknowledged that a more or less live-and-let-live attitude had to be adopted. This did not stop constant resistance to Russian takeover, as nomadic peoples contested the flood of land-hungry Russian peasants who moved eastward across Siberia to pursue settled farming and as clan groups acted against the centralizing state. While the Russian empire expanded to the south and east across Asia, its actions, like those of so many other empires, were intertwined with those of its competitors. It attempted to take lands from the Ottomans, Persians, and the many Muslim ethnic and nomadic groups in central Asia and often succeeded. Into the twentieth century Russia nipped into China and clashed with an expanding Japan over empire in East Asia

In the nineteenth century, Russian forces ran into British expansionists in Central Asia, who were already trading from South Asia as well as attempting to stake out northern frontier regions prized by the Russians. From being latecomers to empire because of religious and political turmoil in the sixteenth century, the British, Dutch, and French had become the vanguard of combined oceanic expansion from the seventeenth century on. Using trading companies to finance and accomplish the work of colonization, they initially competed in North America, the Caribbean, across South and Southeast Asia, and along the coasts of Africa to profit from its lucrative trade, above all in slaves. By the time the trade in African slaves to the Western Hemisphere began to subside in the nineteenth century, Britain and secondarily France were on their way to securing control of distant societies around the world. Despite constant competition with one another, Britain was a dominant force in India and Burma, Egypt, South and other African regions, Canada, Australia and New Zealand, and the Caribbean, while France dominated in north and west Africa, Southeast Asia, and some Pacific islands. These major powers also eyed China from the late eighteenth century into the twentieth and conducted business imperialism wherever they saw opportunity for profit. After World War I, Britain and France increased their holdings even more as they seized the possessions of the defeated Central Powers, notably the Ottoman and German empires in the 1920s.

For a long stretch of time, the United States was, like Russia, a land-based empire, taking over and often eradicating Native Americans in the name of bringing "civilized" people to "develop" the country. (Some 90 percent of the Native American population, estimated to be between 70 and 90 million on the eve of Columbus's voyages, was killed either by disease or by murder in the process of white settlement. The United States continued this trend, though mostly killing Native Americans outright through warfare and starvation as they lost their lands.) Developing their own oceanic trade after gaining independence from the British Empire in 1776, Americans were often at the mercy of suppliers in China, India, Japan, and other distant ports. Only after the middle of the nineteenth century did the United States government pursue overseas conquest, toppling the Hawaiian monarchy, helping to foment revolution against Spain by Caribbean and Pacific countries, taking over the Philippines after the Spanish American War, participating in smashing the Boxer Rebellion in China, and practicing business imperialism, often including military invasion, in the Caribbean, Mexico, and central America. In the late nineteenth century it was the American Alfred Thayer Mahon who devised what came to be the twentieth-century justification for naval buildup as a corollary of empire: control of the seas, Mahon theorized, was necessary for national well-being. Given the increasing firepower of modern weaponry, the stage was set for further and ever more destructive imperial warfare.

Japan and Germany conquered significant territory from the late nineteenth into the twentieth century, as each saw its newly modernized and centralized government as a latecomer to the development of empire. As such, both nations looked for opportunity abroad. In the sixteenth century, the Japanese leader Hideyoshi failed in his attempt to expand into Korea and China, showing that empire-building could be a start-and-stop undertaking. Some three centuries later, Japan integrated islands of the archipelago after the Meiji regime came to power in 1858. Eying the practices of the more established imperial powers at the time, it additionally took over Taiwan and Korea—even having the Korean queen who opposed Japan murdered—with the idea that expansion would prevent it from being gobbled up by the Europeans as was happening to the Southeast and South Asian regions. In 1894–1895 the Japanese fought China and actually invaded its mainland in the 1930s in hopes of adding it to its holdings. For its part, the new German empire, which had come into being in 1871, took over islands in the Pacific and in southwest and southeast Africa. Like the United States and Great Britain elsewhere, Germany practiced business imperialism in the Ottoman Empire, building railroads and loaning funds for a range of enterprises. By the early twentieth century, the German military and some officials began to develop a theory of European-based German empire in which Germany would expand into central Europe as well as overseas. This theory guided German aims in World War I and those of Adolf Hitler in the 1930s and during World War II.

Modern empires rose and fell over the course of centuries, developing unevenly in antagonism with one another, distant peoples, and even their own citizens who became divided by the twentieth century over the costs and deeds that empire entailed. Over the course of time, different aims and ideas surrounding the development of empire evolved and distinctive patterns of rule and imperial structures manifested themselves across the globe. The rise and fall of empires resulting from their interactions with one another and with conquered peoples whom they aimed to rule and plunder shaped modern history as much as any other single development, including the rise of industrial production or the nation-state. The Spanish Empire in the Western Hemisphere suffered an almost entire collapse in just a few decades, causing an enduring new kind of informal or business imperialism to arise alongside emerging nation-states. The aftermath of the Spanish and other empires across the globe remains to be studied from the point of view of collapse. The fall and afterlife of empires can be as interesting and eventful as their rise.

Empires' histories were interwoven with one another: The battles of Rhodes, Malta, and Lepanto in the seventeenth century, for example, constituted a clash of empires in a series of brutal encounters that, while taxing both sides to the utmost, had the dramatic effect of helping shift trade away from the Mediterranean and intensifying conquest and settlement of the Western Hemisphere by Europeans. The Ottomans fought the Byzantine, Safavid, Russian, British, and French empires, to name a few of its opponents, all the while connecting the fate of those opponents. To some extent the collapse of the Spanish resulted from independence leaders watching the fate of other empires and sensing its rulers' vulnerability. More than that, as imperial leaders were often well aware, competitors were always probing the health of existing empires in hopes of opportunity for their own expansion. A global panorama of empires allows us to see the wide-ranging impact of individual states upon one another as well as on the unfolding history of interactions around the world and among its peoples.

NATIONS, STATES, AND THE POLITICS OF EMPIRE

Across the globe, empire builders dreamed big dreams, filled with visions of triumph over thousands of local communities and global resources. Until recently the main attraction in modern history, however, has been the story of heroes associated with rising nation-states, the competition among those nations, and the struggles and victories of individual countries. The triumphs and agonies of nation-states grip us, and their development is often seen as the sole engine of history in modern times. We believe that our identities as humans are situated in that of our nation and its fortunes. Still, in the past empires were far more common as a political form than nations and they remained active until almost our own time. Many nations actually began within or as empires: Austria, Poland, and Turkey, for example, emerged from empires. The United States, Russia, and China aggressively expanded their borders—both near and far—in what is seen as the normal imperial effort at growth by conquering other people. Their identities as nations have superseded their imperial activities in many people's minds.

There are said to be differences between empires and the nation-state, however. Nation-states usually came to have explicit constitutions and the rule of law unlike empires, which may be lawful but which often discriminate against those outside the core boundaries of the dominant state. The imperial United States did not treat Native Americans or Filipinos it had conquered by the same rules it applied to whites. The Ottomans, whose Turkic peoples were mostly Muslim, did not persecute Christians and Jews but taxed them differently. Imperial rulers and officials often felt justified in treating those over whom they ruled in lawless ways, even killing them on a whim. Empires do not have the same need to view the conquered as equal or to treat them as such. The nation-state in theory marks all citizens as deserving of rights, while empires often develop ideologies based on racial, ethnic, or religious hierarchies. Nations have also discriminated against their own citizens—Native Americans, African Americans, and women, in the

United States, for example—but they almost uniformly treat imperial subjects as lesser people. The English treatment of the Irish is another example. Despite the attention to the positive values of the nation-state, evidence for the relationship between the nations and empires is ripe for new analysis. The plusses and minuses of empire need in fact need to be discussed, with full attention to who is advantaged, who is disadvantaged, and who might experience empire as complex and even inconsistent.

Government officials of empires aimed to squelch the competing capacities of other powers and to replace those capacities with the spread of their own way of life, including their own religion. Commitment to advancing Catholicism— and thus saving pagan souls from hell—motivated the expansion of Portugal and Spain in large part, just as Arab expansion in the early Middle Ages took its energy from commitment to extend Islam. Iberian sailors—agents of Portuguese and Spanish states—no matter how hardened, believed their mission to be a kind of crusade, and this belief fortified them during the often horrific conditions of charting unknown waters and stormy seas. Still, it is impossible, many believe, to disentangle religious fervor from the quest for gold and glory on behalf of themselves and the imperial rulers they served.

Thus, each state that participated did so to extend its territoriality in the quest for wealth and resources that would empower its religious and other commitments and in turn cement the empire. There were simultaneously serious state-building concerns in the modern period no matter what part of the globe. Confident in its financial future based on controlling resources beyond its shores, a state could build an administration staffed with government bureaucrats and advisors who would supervise the increasing tasks of government, from raising funds, collecting taxes, and overseeing the creation of roads, harbors, canals, and other public works to the expensive job of maintaining military forces and spreading systems of belief to ensure control. The modern state faced rising costs in the midst of rising complexity of rule; obtaining an empire was supposed to supply the wealth to cover those costs.

There is a complex politics to empire. On the one hand, empires can result from perceived national needs, concerns, consolidation, ambitions, ideologies, and economies. Thus empires can be studied from the perspective of the internal dynamics of individual states. In this case their political and economic needs come to the fore, as mentioned previously. On the other hand, empires in the modern period have interacted with one another as allies, competitors, or deadly enemies: The Safavid and European empires joined to retard the advance of the Ottomans, for example. In other words, state politics were intertwined with the international politics among imperial powers. In fact, it is possible that the unity of citizens at the core of the modern nation-state grew from seeing themselves as different from those they conquered and from other empires. From 1500 onward, interconnections among empires and the resulting growth of nations were at the core of the development, progress, and collapse of empires—threads in modern history that this anthology will provide in its sample of documents. The goal is to present empires from the perspective of both national and international politics, as historical actors addressed the question of empire from multiple points of view.

Chaos, disagreement, and vulnerability characterize large swaths of the politics of empire. Too often, discussions of the political course of empires interpret these entities as somehow sturdy and even omnipotent, because of their supposedly clever administrators, superior weaponry, and systematic governance. More recently, however, historians have demonstrated that the politics of empire can be chaotic and based on whimsical ideas and entirely inconsistent practices. In fact, agents of empire are often out of control and hardly rational or even successful. One example is the German empire in the nineteenth and early twentieth centuries whose policies were inconsistent across its holdings. Similar evidence exists for all empires. French politicians, for example, allowed Islam to flourish in West Africa but could be as violently intolerant of colonized peoples' religions as any other country. The French celebrated their lofty cultural values alongside their army's lethal acts in Algeria. Local conditions and varying local knowledge had a countervailing force of their own. The paradoxical and chaotic politics of empire, including the violence of its "civilizing mission," were spotted by colonial freedom fighters as well as by political opponents in the metropole.

EMPIRES: WORLD GOVERNANCE OR WORLD CHAOS?

As imperial politics produced competition and ever more chaos, plans for controlling expansion took shape. One of the earliest was a treaty sponsored by the Church to adjudicate permanently conflicts between Spain and Portugal over territory worldwide that each was claiming. Signed in 1494, the Treaty of Tordesillas provided a permanent line of demarcation 370 leagues west of the Cape Verde islands off the Atlantic coast of Africa. Thirty-five years later another treaty set bounds for each country in the Indian Ocean and Pacific regions. Disputes raged nonetheless, and there were constant adjustments to these and other would-be peacekeeping agreements. Moreover, as England, the Netherlands, France, and other European countries entered the imperial fray, they disregarded such regulations entirely, scouting the eastern coast of South America, allocated by the Pope to Portugal, for territory they might claim and colonize.

Wars constantly erupted over empire, followed by peace treaties dividing and aiming to regulate competition for the globe. These included treaties to arrange peace between the English and the Dutch between 1650 and 1674, the Peace of Paris after the French and Indian War in the eighteenth century, further treaties and proclamations after the American, Haitian, and Latin American revolutions at the turn of the eighteenth century, and a series of U.S. treaties made with various countries as the new nation expanded its control. The Monroe Doctrine, announced in 1823, set limits on the business of other nations in the Western Hemisphere. Still, the confusion of warfare was always imminent on the competitive imperial stage, as nations wielded arms to gain more.

Such was the case during the "scramble" for Africa after the middle of the nineteenth century. There, the European powers, fortified by quinine and steamships, fought to conquer local peoples and to seize their territory not just along the coasts but in the interior of the African continent. Simultaneously, they were fighting one another for the same territory or threatening to do so. On the initiative of German Chancellor Otto von Bismarck, a conference met in Berlin in 1884 to set the terms for empire-building in Africa. Agreeing among themselves to rules for taking over Africa, the imperial nations determined that the interior of the continent would be divided according to holdings on the coasts. Firearms and alcohol were not to be sold to local people, said to be the cause of violence. Those who actually lived in sub-Saharan Africa had no say in the agreements. The idea was to make takeover of their lands, labor, and natural resources go as smoothly as possible for expansionists. Although suggested here as a form of world governance, the example also shows that such governance was hardly beneficial for the people of Africa but instead was a tool of conquest.

The Peace of Paris after World War I (1914–1918) also envisioned a system of world governance. This post–World War I settlement produced the treaties of Versailles, Sèvres, St. Germain, and Trianon which dealt with the collapse of German, Habsburg, Ottoman, and Russian empires as a result of that war. The varying treaties redistributed the defeated empires' lands and resources and adjusted their borders, leaving an atmosphere of mistrust, resentment, and rage. The aftermath of these treaties and the organization of states in the League of Nations contributed mightily to the outbreak of yet another imperial war—World War II—and to the local and national angry determination behind decolonization after 1945. The question to consider is whether world governance could possibly have worked to benefit humanity when imperial rule was the force behind it.

The Peace of Paris poses the issue starkly. Even as some analysts at the peace conference in Paris in 1918–1918 warned that the terms of the Treaty of Versailles would make for resentments and future wars, leaders and special interests went ahead with its punishing terms against Germany and the former Austria Hungary. Moreover, during the war U.S. President Woodrow Wilson called for the "self-determination" of peoples in his Fourteen Points. Few, if any, imperial leaders believed it applied to the colonized. Although to many Wilson's proposal seemed on the one hand too idealistic, as a principle for anti-imperial world governance it turned out to pit ethnicities against one another—a condition that has caused bloodshed up to the present. Forced and chaotic migration occurred at the end of World War I as dominant ethnicities drove minorities from their homes, farms, and business in the name of ethnic self-rule at the end of four empires. Moreover, the League-of-Nations system of cooperative world governance actually extended the rule of empire when it handed the colonies of Germany and the territories of the defeated Ottoman Empire over to Britain, France, and several other imperial nations. As Germany, Italy, and Japan in addition to France and Britain acquired vast stretches of territory, the interwar years marked a high point of modern empires.

During World War II, U.S. President Franklin Roosevelt envisioned the end of formal empires and the beginning of effective world governance in the United Nations, organized in 1945 as the war came to an end. Roosevelt also believed that U.S. values would dominate the United Nations and that its statesmen would provide anti-imperial leadership. However, the United Nations arose in the climate of cold war, when the United States and the Soviet Union competed for world influence both in an old-fashioned imperial drive to control the political and economic development of distant lands and in the somewhat newer strategy of dominating world governance. Both based their claims for dominance on an updated version of imperialism's "civilizing mission." That is, both proposed to introduce their client states to the blessings of communism or of capitalism, often by force.

These two "superpowers" waged wars across the globe after World War II in hopes of triumph for their world-systems, just as empires had done before. U.S. troops engaged in Korea, Vietnam, Lebanon, Grenada, Afghanistan, and Iraq, among other places, and stationed their forces in more than 1,500 military bases around the world in 1989.[3] From these, somewhat like the Portuguese in the sixteenth-century Indian Ocean, they could dominate considerable territory, launching missiles, drones, troops, and other tactical instruments. The Soviet Union backed military action in eastern Europe, Korea, China, Vietnam, Cuba, and Afghanistan with military advisors also liberally spread across the globe, though without the reach of the far wealthier United States. With the collapse of the Soviet holdings in eastern Europe and in central Asia in 1989 and the 1990s, some observers believed the United States to control a single empire across the globe, albeit in a new form.

EMPIRES AND GLOBALIZATION

Empires have been a major player—some would say *the* major player—in the phenomenon we call globalization. They have fostered the interconnected movement of crops, manufactured goods, institutions, ideas, and cultural styles. Because of empire, people have been migrating globally for some five hundred years now, bringing their habits and ways of life to other parts of the world more rapidly than before. Empires have fought one another globally because of competition for worldwide power and for a larger share of the world's resources. To accomplish all of this, they have fostered innovation in transportation, science, and the creation of any number of products—especially weaponry—that would advance global influence if not total domination. Military people and even civilians involved in imperial projects have become more globally knowledgeable because of increasing worldwide experience. In this interpretation, empires, not nations, are seen as a driving force of globalization and thus of modern history.

---

[3]This number is one reduced from several thousand a decade earlier and then to 800 by 2016 after the fall of the Soviet Empire. The 800 figure does not include the growing number of "lily pads"—that is, small, secret bases that are replacing the large ones across the globe.

All of these in turn have motivated humans to adapt and integrate a variety of new ingredients into their everyday lives. Under empire people have developed modes of accommodation and resistance, global theories of political rule, systems of global interaction, and economic institutions for maximum extraction of goods to be deployed around the world. Religions such as Buddhism, Islam, and Christianity have spread globally and developed global bureaucracies as have institutions supporting capitalism, communism, anarchism, and other systems and theories. In the name of empire, historical actors in the drive for expansion, whether Columbus or Francis Drake or Heinrich Himmler, have exploited and even murdered those they controlled and thus have shaped the course of global history in the name of imperial domination.

Amid the imperial exploitation of peoples and natural resources, science has paradoxically advanced worldwide because of access to the global array of life forms. These include herbs and other plants from which scientists have devised formulae to synthesize into healing and even life-saving medicines. Rulers in China and the Ottoman empires collected foreign dishware, textiles, works of art, and other goods from around the world as a sign of their own magnificence. The array of products from any one locality led people elsewhere to emulate the crafts of distant lands and thus innovate. The Industrial Revolution was in large part based on figuring out the methods for making bright, lightweight cottons, whose production flourished in India and China. In Europe, botanical and horticultural studies began to flourish because of the many plants collected during trips to distant places that were often sponsored by imperial rulers. Local knowledge became global, as empire sparked global innovation.

Full of wonder at what the world had to offer, others set up special buildings to house their collections of odd or magnificent or novel items coming from conquered regions. They established museums to house these collections and opened them to visitors from across the globe; these institutions, though criticized, permit the interaction of cultures. Scholars interested in understanding the world's peoples developed ethnographic and anthropological mindsets and created these disciplines. Meanwhile, the pursuit of empire led medical personnel to study Chinese and other medical practices, including copying the Ottoman customs of inoculating children against small pox even in the early modern period. Peoples confronted new diseases, which have continued to travel the world up to the present day. Initially in the modern period these diseases spread globally because of imperial expansion, bringing death to millions but also building immunities. However, imperialists also used the knowledge gained in other countries to combat diseases like malaria and yellow fever. Before the use of quinine developed from South American know-how, diseases precluded empire not just for Europeans but for the Manchus who, for example, lacked immunity to malaria and smallpox and whose armies were terrified of falling victim to them. As we have seen, disease had an agency all its own: It often prevented European advances in the case of initial movement into the Western world when diseases made empire possible; simultaneously, it could work against foreign empire, as in the case of Africa before the widespread development of quinine. Gradually, however, local knowledge gained from contact became global science and the foundation of preventive medicine.

Empire was thus one mechanism by which globalization occurred, both for good and for ill. Advances by imperial powers destroyed many people's livelihoods—including the Indian crafts which for long had dominated cotton textile production. Globalization brought about by empire forced artisans to go in search of new jobs and often take up agricultural work that worsened their condition. As part of imperial control, slavery and other forms of forced labor moved people away from their homes to crushing jobs on sugar, rubber, cotton, coffee, and tobacco plantations. The mixture of peoples and traditions occurred worldwide, yet the globalization of culture provoked backlash such as racism, hypernationalism, and genocide even as new knowledge helped improve the lifespans of many.

Technology such as transportation, communications, and weaponry moved around the globe, yielding a wide range of complicated results. Railroads moved troops intended for conquest, and they moved crops and products out of a colony—sometimes starving the people who produced them. Colonial officials and colonized peoples often gained a wider sense of the world; often without their knowledge they were enmeshed in globalization. European languages and culture were forced on them, as were those of the Japanese and Chinese—all of this done in the name of providing a "superior" civilization to a "backward," distant land. Complicated forms of contact and conquest made for subsequent migrations of peoples, ideas, commodities, and innovation across regions, continents, and oceans.

THE TOOLS OF EMPIRE

When the Portuguese entered the Indian Ocean in 1498, markets along the coast of East Africa and South Asia were flourishing. Traders of varying ethnicities and creeds dealt in relative peace with one another and with local rulers who controlled ports and got their wealth from taxing trade. It was a sophisticated if highly competitive system that the Portuguese confronted, covering thousands of miles of interconnected trading posts. Having less knowledge of age-old practices in the region, although somewhat informed of overland Asian trade, and showing themselves the enemy of Muslims, who played a major role in commerce, the Portuguese held few cards. Their ships were smaller than those of established traders in the Indian Ocean; they did not know the geography, customs, or languages; and they were weighted down with a history of warfare against non-Christians. Instead of initially dealing and developing skills, the Portuguese turned to their accustomed responses: the murder and conquest of Muslims and other "infidels." Their initial tools of empire were surprise, arrogance, and hand-held guns. Ottomans and Manchus had the same conviction and to some extent similar weaponry.

The same tools—surprise, guns, and a conviction of their own Christian perfection—helped carry the day in the Western Hemisphere, allowing small groups of Spanish and Portuguese to overtake two mighty empires—the Aztecs and the Incas. Threatening leaders of communities should they not help, European invaders gathered up allies to make conquest possible across the hemispheres. Mughals and Ottomans joined in, sending emissaries to centers of power and thriving cities in advance of their arrival. The emissaries offered rewards for cooperation and threatened mass murder in case of resistance. When they carried out such threats, one tactic was to leave a few people alive to pass on horrific stories of empire builders' might in order to make the next conquest easier. Thus a sort of violent diplomacy formed another tool of conquest. The tools of empire were not simply technological.

Know-how and experience played a large role too in the fortunes of empire, being used by all sides in the contest for control. The Mongols, Mughals, and Ottomans were skilled horsemen and used their knowledge in conquest over land before conquest over the seas unfolded. Afghans developed techniques of retreat, evasion, and surprise returns to defend their territory on central Asian steppes from centuries of invaders. Allying with would-be conquerors allowed various local groups to gain the upper hand over enemies, as in the case of the Native Americans who allied with the Spanish horsemen in conquering the Aztecs and other local peoples of Central America. Still, too many demands from imperialists led people simply to disappear, locking up shops, swiftly escaping with animals and stores of food, and other "weapons of the weak" that might trick or discourage conquerors.

That said, other tools were more concrete. The Portuguese borrowed the use of triangular sails from the Arabs, often combining them with square-rigged ones to make better use of the winds. They created the caravel, a swift-moving and nimble sea-craft that aided them in policing Indian Ocean trade. Iberians also employed a range of navigational instruments in determining latitude, while their on-board cartographers created portolan maps indicating coastal dangers, good harbors, and other details important to seafarers. Astrolabes, quadrants, compasses, and other instruments gave good indications of location and direction, but it was not until the eighteenth-century development of the chronometer that seamen could chart longitudinal location. Knowledge of the seas was never a monopoly of one imperial power or set of powers, but there were regions and even empires that for different reasons did not take to the seas.

No single group monopolized the ongoing development of weaponry either, but some states were better than others at making constant technological improvements that both increased firepower and gave overall advantages to some invaders. The caravel gave Iberians an early advantage over galleys, while Iberian ships were able to support guns to be aimed at distant targets. Their competitors at first did not have naval firepower. The Ottomans used the latest in cannons to blast open the thick walls of Constantinople. This was the result of bad decision-making on the part of the Byzantine emperor and a forward-looking choice of Ottoman leader Mehmet II. He quickly engaged Hungarian engineer Orban to make a large number of massive cannons when the Byzantine emperor lagged in supporting the crafting of these weapons. The result was that not only were the walls pounded but stones were hurled into the center of the capital, ultimately forcing its surrender despite heroic resistance. Late in the eighteenth century, the French devised interchangeability of parts in the manufacture of guns, which had many benefits to armies in the field or in distant regions of the world. They could repair damaged weapons on the spot, which cut down on having to carry around spare weaponry and prevented the catastrophe of suddenly lacking replacements altogether.

Evolving firepower gave would-be imperialists the temporary advantage of surprise. The cannons of Mehmet II were shocking in their untested abilities, as were the cannons on Portuguese ships and the hand-held guns of invaders. To protect themselves, societies at risk quickly mimicked imperialists' inventions. In the first instance, the newest, most powerful innovations carried the day. The nineteenth-century machine gun and "repeater" firearms had the element of surprise, but even as they struck down their victims ever more powerful machines were in the making. Rivals and those targeted by imperial invaders were swift to produce their own muskets, cannons, rifles with interchangeable parts, and machine guns. Often, however, they were not experienced enough to manufacture in sufficient quantities to outgun imperial forces. Some evaluated the situation quickly: The Japanese enlisted the skilled German army in the second half of the nineteenth century to train and discipline their own soldiers into a modern fighting force.

Alongside guns, Europeans used the development of steam and the internal combustion engine in the nineteenth century to overpower other regions of the world economically and militarily. By later in the century the United States and Japan had joined the march toward efficient extraction and circulation of resources with steamships and railroads. Militarily, railroads and steamships helped in the rapid movement of troops. Although ships had carried weapons before for use in battles on the ocean, steamships could more effectively go up rivers to the interior of countries in Africa, Asia, and South America to enforce policies and to create internal strongholds. In the twentieth century engines powered airplanes and motorized vehicles including tanks. The development of the chemical industry and modern physics produced the powerful weapons of the twentieth and twenty-first centuries: poisonous gases, nuclear weapons, rocketry, and communications from space including remote deployment of precision, bomb-carrying rockets with which dominant powers were well supplied.

THE PEOPLE OF EMPIRE

Even though empire provoked thinking and sparked creativity, again with widely differing aims and outcomes, it was also the product of actual people inflicting horrific violence on victims both from the outset and right through the course of an empire's history. Perpetuating imperial rule within societies and in the face of competition made violence, including warfare, virtually continuous down through the centuries but also historically diverse because of the variety of people inflicting that violence. Spanish conquistadors marveled at "residences so marvelous that it is almost impossible to speak of their excellence and grandeur," but the gold and other precious items easily led to brutal methods to get such wealth for themselves.[4] Invaders such as the English or French in North America wanted Native Americans to help them find gold, and they needed the Native American know-how to help them farm. They simply could not survive on their own. Native Americans demanded that Europeans follow their customs in order to get furs to protect against the cold in winter. Never were furs so wanted as during the "little ice age" of the seventeenth century when for decades temperatures plummeted. In such situations trade and negotiations could go well for a time until one individual or another suddenly took offense, didn't get his or her way, or misinterpreted signs. Then violence and warfare erupted, as in the sudden, unpredictable death of Aztec leader Monteczuma or the breakdown of relations between the Inca Atahualpa and Francisco Pizarro that led to the death of the Inca. Individuals often mediated, but others might whimsically or wantonly turn mediation into aggression. Because individuals played an important role in the course of empire, outcomes were never foreordained or inevitable despite the fact that history can tend to make the unfolding of events appear predictable and easily understandable.

Empire flourished because of human needs and desires, their drives, misjudgments, and lethal greed. In the 1400s, the Europeans were comparatively poor and, as the preceding example shows, suffering cold as the "little ice age"—the name for a period of climate change lasting into the nineteenth century—unfolded. Empire in Asia and North America solved the problem with furs from native trappers. To build powerful states, monarchs, whether Spanish rulers Isabella and Ferdinand, Ottoman sultan Selim, Mughal emperor Akbar, or the kings of France, needed resources; tales of the wealth elsewhere across Eurasia and Africa sparked such interest that concerns for violence receded. Individuals such as Ferdinand Magellan expressed sincere beliefs in spreading Catholic glory, and he became increasingly prone to violence in the cause. Vasco da Gama met up with individual traders rich with goods but also with their own Muslim faith and their determination that the Christians would not take over their networks, linking Muslims to one another via trade and the spread of religious fervor. Da Gama was ruthless in his treatment of those in the way. In the nineteenth century, German imperialist Karl Peters shot East Africans to death whenever they slightly crossed him and even when they didn't, depending on his whim.

Human skill created empires as did the lure of imperial relationships. Not only was British sea captain and map-maker James Cook intent on charting coastlines and the oceans, he tried skillfully to get along with local peoples, though from time to time he erupted in rash action to get his way, ultimately resulting in his death. Other skills were those of go-betweens and local guides—that is, the skill of those being conquered: Malinche, the translator and go-between for the Spanish conquer Cortes; Sacagawea, the guide of explorers of North America

---

[4]Benjamin Keen, *The Aztec Image in Western Thought* (New Brunswick: Rutgers University Press, 1990), 59.

Lewis and Clark; and Nain Singh, the school-principal-turned-guide-and-spy for the British in nineteenth-central Central Asia all worked for those whose goal was empire. Such people—called "collaborators" by some—represented the vast knowledge that colonizers simply did not have.

Imperial history is about people, their aspirations, experiences, crimes, skills, and endurance. Slavery ripped apart families and transported individuals away from their homes. Armies composed of slaves, common in Asia and Africa, produced towering leaders, however, such as those in the Ottoman sultan's household or Malik Ambar (1548–1626), the African slave who came to command an army in southern India that successfully fought expansion of the Mughal Empire. Most slaves suffered, as did indentured servants drawn into imperial plantation life. At the same time, like the escaped maroons across the Caribbean and South America, they resisted; or like the armed slaves in the Haitian Revolution, led by freed slave Toussaint Louverture, they overthrew governments; they created important hybrid cultures that infused, for example, the Caribbean with Indian sagas such as the Mahabharata—a tale of titanic military struggles among cousins dating from some 2,000 years ago; and even, like Bermuda-born slave Mary Prince, wrote their own biographies that helped empires to fight slavery in their own realms.

IMPERIAL MENTALITIES

Empires have mutated during the past 500 years from their initial impetus in state-building, religious conquest, and financial gain. Today our contemporary world has been shaped by the aftermath of decolonization and the power of nation-states, global migration, indigenous rights movements, and neoimperialism. When empires in the modern period were taking shape, warriors and ordinary people alike experienced tedium, exhaustion, and fears of death and disease. Many were also filled with wonder and greed sparked by the vision of wealth that they might seize from the conquered. Racism and sexism flourished in tandem with empire and as part of its structure. Conquered women were raped and impregnated as a sign of conquest. The conquered were seen as racially or ethnically inferior and thus deserving to be ruled by "superior" people. Many colonized people, however, maintained their social values and structures, as the Incan uprisings show. There was variety across colonial mentalities.

Empire was the product of sentiments and beliefs and simultaneously produced attitudes and feelings. Ambition, religious fervor, and perceived need set people on the course of empire, and those emotions often determined the shape that empire took. Mongol leader Genghis Khan felt a confidence born of his belief that the sacred force of nature had destined him for conquest. Like him, Iberians—from monarchs to sailors—believed the creation of empire to be a religious crusade, whose success was accomplished with the blessings of Mary, Mother of God. The visible manifestation of success was gold and riches, testifying to the glory of God and the men who built wealth in the name of the Catholic Church. Gradually confidence in God's blessings on one's empire was transformed into a belief in the superiority of one's nation and one's race—even though empire also grew from a desire to capture the benefits of other's superior civilization and wealth. It is important to see that the quest for empire and the conduct of empire produced what today we see as contradictions: greed and violence, for example, alongside spiritual fervor.

In the nineteenth century, Charles Darwin and others announced that evolutionary science showed the superior intelligence and culture of white men and the inferiority of white women and all people of other races. Such theories—said to rest on factual evidence—became the new justification for empire along with white male dominance across societies. Because white men had this superior intelligence, according to Darwin and even more so his followers, it was their responsibility both to preserve their own civilization through fighting off savages and to spread the values of their superior civilization to others. The rise of racial thinking in this pseudo-scientific form spread to leaders outside of Europe who had imperial ambitions. Such racial thinking virtually demanded expansion and empire. More than that, it survived long after outright conquest diminished and even after DNA analysis in our own times showed that racial difference barely exists and is hardly meaningful in scientific terms.

Individuals involved in the course of empire often challenged those favoring conquest and exploitation of local peoples. Bartolomé de Las Casas, a sixteenth-century Dominican friar who had been an early colonizer and slave owner in the Caribbean, wrote a scathing condemnation of the brutal treatment of Native Americans after initially favoring enslavement. Native Americans constantly rose up against the savagery and greed of whites, fearing that they themselves were becoming too much like them. Or, like the Sioux, they upheld their own values including a warrior ethos. In the eighteenth century, Tupac Amaru righteously led an uprising against Spanish rule over the former Inca lands. Understanding the unfairness of their suffering, slaves imported to European societies constantly protested their condition, most prominent among them the eloquent Olauduh Equiano. In the nineteenth century, some white Europeans challenged slavery in abolitionist organizations and from the late nineteenth century objected to the existence of empire entirely, as they watched events such as the South African War, with its concentration camps, unfold. In the twentieth century, Mohandas Gandhi became a valued and even celebrated opponent of empire. He pointed out that imperial powers such as Britain and the United States hardly had superior values or a superior civilization to those of Indians. Britain's main values, he stated, were greed and materialism, and the United States was even worse. Gandhi's unmasking of empire's motivation and his and many others' commitment to civil disobedience spread to shape anti-imperial activism specifically and a range of other activisms more generally. By the mid-twentieth century proponents of U.S. and Soviet domination pointed to their superiority in technology, which was supposed to indicate a superior civilization and superior values. Their opponents pointed to the constant warfare against other countries as in fact indicating a lack of any concern for values other than greed and domination.

At the same time, some of those overtaken by imperial force and living under imperial domination had an array of attitudes toward newcomers and conquerors, beyond the powerful opposition discussed previously. Some were ambitious themselves, and in fact their ambition to profit from empire drew these colonized adventurers into the imperial commercial orbit, whether it was to acquire textiles, slaves, or precious minerals and commodities such as ivory. It would be virtually impossible to enforce imperial control of vast regions of the world without some cooperation from local peoples and the especially the passing on of their knowledge. Various rajas and sultans of South and Southeast Asia gained support against local rivals by allying themselves with Europeans and profiting from the connection. There came to be admiration among some local people for English campaigns against the immolation of widows or the marriage of children in nineteenth-century India. Imperial courts of law clamped down on criticism of empire, but some people also saw in such foreign institutions a chance to gain justice against violent spouses or occasionally against abusers. Women from other cultures found that Islam offered important protections not found in their own societies. There were differing attitudes at work among conquerors and conquered alike.

Technology and education in the sciences also gathered advocates among those who lived under colonial rule. With a range of outcomes, the exchange of knowledge, modern science, and Western styles of education spread, and many of those subjected to imperial rule sought a different education for their children and themselves: The young Berber girl Fadhma Amrouche was educated in Catholic religious schools in Algeria. An Indonesian businessman marveled at Western technology. Even as Japan threatened to conquer China, Chinese young people of both sexes traveled there, again with the idea that imperialists had a more modern and wide-ranging culture. Thus, Chinese-born Qiu Jin as a young woman sought out schooling in Japan because it was more advanced. In these and other cases the mentality of the conqueror was seen as desirable to obtain or at least to understand. Those East Africans who were forced to learn lessons in German history or the Native American author Zitkala Sa, who was taught against her will in a missionary school, engaged in the debate—pro or con—over hybrid cultures and the power of the conqueror.

There were others who experienced empire only as direct oppression. Sometimes the resistance was immediate: Muslim traders fought back against encroachments on their business when the Portuguese tried to bully their way in. Moreover they harbored grievances over centuries of Christian crusading against Muslims in the Mediterranean. For them, experience showed that Christians meant only destruction of property, torture, and death; their anger was long-lasting, passing down through generations. Resistance, as in the case of the Belgian Congo, also took the form of mental retreat away from the realities of empire: Religious sects countering imperial values grew, and people tinkered with the Western medical procedures they were supposed to follow. African traditions of worship migrated with slaves to create entirely new religious faiths in both South and North America.

Still others hardly sensed the imperialist presence, if they felt it at all, but this was increasingly difficult. Over the entire course of empire, however, the conqueror's violence was met as often as possible with rage from the oppressed. By the twentieth century, empire brought a range of taxes that needed to be paid in currency, not in goods and produce. People on self-sufficient farms, who had thought themselves immune to taxation, were increasingly faced with taxation that they could not meet. Lands were seized and turned into plantations on which those who had become landless because of such confiscations labored. Thus people felt the ups and downs of the global economy even when they might be somewhat immune from colonial conquest. Non-violent protest and political organizing arose alongside the outbursts of violent rage, revealing a different, more long-term channeling of rage and discontent into pragmatic movements. Imperialists reacted with rage too and with weapons to actualize that rage. While in the twentieth century violent uprisings and strikes occurred, the non-violence of Gandhi's movement or the Women's War of 1928 displayed the diversity of oppositional mentalities under empire. Imperial officials often had a difficult time dissecting this diversity of opposition and tended brutally to put down any opposition, revealing empire's persistently violent mentality and the dominance of emotion over intelligence.

Empire also can exist in the vivid memories of all those involved. The meaning of empire to the mentality of ordinary people comes alive and in the sources we find their reflections on the conditions of conquest and of living under empire. Activists call out for reparations—educational, emotional, and financial—for the suffering empire and its institutions has caused. Post-imperial commentators still have empire embedded in their psyches, and their essays and fiction display the legacy of empire. That literature pours from publishing houses globally. The world's peoples have not left empire behind, whether they know it or not. In fact, an important term—post-colonial—has arisen to inspire a consideration of what empire has meant. The term *post-colonial* does not just describe a condition after formal empires have more or less disappeared. It also calls for a mentality constantly rethinking both the past and present of empire and asking what the heavy presence of empire meant and continues to mean for economies, nations, ethnic groups and clans, and ordinary people's lives today. This reader presents the intertwined histories of modern empires across the globe from the late fifteenth century to the present in hopes of inspiring and informing reflection on that history.

CHAPTER 1

The Ferment of Empires, c. 1400–1550

The fifteenth and early sixteenth centuries saw several older empires such as the Ming in China flourish and new ones rapidly born. After the death in 1227 of the great nomadic conqueror, Ghenghis Kahn, the Mongol Empire was divided up among his sons and slowly lost its verve until it dissolved around 1370. Soon after, the Tatar Timur (Tamerlane) claimed to be the heir to Ghenghis, and using similar nomadic tactics created another nomadic empire, somewhat reduced in size from that of the Mongols. His death in 1405 brought the age of vast land-based, nomadic empires to a close. As Timur expanded his reach, he challenged and often temporarily defeated rising new empires such as that of the Ottomans, a Turkic group that moved across Asia to settle in Anatolia or Asia Minor. In the fourteenth century the Ottomans came to control areas of the Balkans. Coming up against the waning Byzantine Empire that had succeeded Rome as a religious and imperial center, the Ottoman leader Mehmet II captured Constantinople, its capital, in 1453. He and his successors continued their conquests and attempted expansion in the Middle East, across North Africa, and in Europe.

Simultaneously in Central and South Asia, Central Asian horsemen eventually known as the Mughals (related to the term *Mongol*) began moving southward, conquering individual small states and princedoms. The great and determined military leader in these campaigns was Zahir al-Din Babur, a descendant of both Tamerlane and Ghenghis Kahn. Babur not only conquered portions of the Indian subcontinent but also left his memoirs of military campaigns and his intimate life. He recorded the bad along with the good: his defeats and overuse of drugs and alcohol along with his successes in building an empire. The earlier empires of Ghenghis Kahn and Timur were land-based, dependent on horses and horsemanship and increasingly on guns. Later, Mughal campaigns in South Asia displayed the additional virtues of heavy weaponry, elephants, and massive armies. Later Mughals, however, added shipping capacity to their repertoire of imperial tools.

African and the Aztec empires were much smaller but also land-based. Africans were known for their great wealth, especially from goldmining and also from trading of salt and slaves across the Sahara Desert. In North America, the Aztecs conquered the competing groups surrounding them in what would become today's Mexico. The Aztecs too were known among their neighbors for their wealth and prosperous way of life but also feared for the murderous nature of their regime, which captured soldiers from other regions and made living sacrifices of them. South of them, stretching several thousand miles, was the South American empire of the Incas, similarly wealthy and powerful. They took over competing small groups of South American neighbors and more distant communities. The Incas integrated even the farthest towns, using well-organized systems of communication, trade, and religious practices along some 28,000 miles of roads. Like the Mongols, they demanded tribute, and like the Aztecs, human sacrifice. In the Incan case, the sacrifice was of children, who were pampered, feted, and then killed on behalf of the gods.

Imperial worldviews justifying what seem today brutal practices of imperial leaders in the fifteenth and early sixteenth centuries varied. Empires had different understandings of the universe, ranging from the benign to the murderous. Ghenghis Kahn, for example, had announced, "It is the will of God that we take the earth and maintain order."[1] Myths developed about sacred spaces in northeastern Asia where Ghenghis had made special decisions and meditated. In this large area of Mongolia, Ghenghis was said to have endured his many trials but also found his inspiration and direction from the God of the mountains and of nature. According to their beliefs, Aztecs needed a constant supply of living youth whose sacrifice of fresh blood would keep the universe functioning. Thus they waged constant warfare in a universal cause. The fortunes of empires during this period also varied, as ambitions soared to tap the wealth of others and to overturn competitors and seize their land. The Mongols had ridden with as many as 200,000 men to accomplish their ends, while the Incas searched over hundreds if not thousands of miles for the most perfect girls to sacrifice to ensure the well-being of their realm.

In 1405, the Ming emperor in China began a project of oceanic discovery, sending massive ships and crews, sometimes numbering 30,000, to travel the Indian Ocean. Under the command of Zheng He (1371–1433), some seven voyages took the imposing Chinese fleet to all the main cities and ports of the Indian Ocean world. A protegé and protector of the emperor, Zheng He gathered animals, notable people, precious jewelry and crafts, and many other goods in the tens of thousands to return to the emperor. The idea was that this sample of what the world had to offer would validate the emperor's standing as having the mandate of heaven. In the process of expanding China's imperial standing, the Chinese stirred up troubles in the Arabian and Red seas, forcing the leaders of Mamluk armies that controlled much of the region to fend off incursions and disorder. The Mamluk hold of territories in the Middle East thus weakened during the disturbances caused by the voyages of the Chinese fleet.

---

[1]Jack Weatherford, *Ghenghis Kahn and the Making of the Modern World* (New York: Crown, 2004), 111.

As in the case of the Mamluks and the Chinese, the interlocking of imperial ambitions resulted in disorder. The adventurous ruler of the Ottomans, Selim I (1470–1520), took advantage of the situation: he saw the Mamluk grip on ethnic groups in the region weakening because of distractions and faced off with another ambitious empire-builder—Shah Ismail (1487–1524). Selim also continued to advance Ottoman sea-power. Their trade hampered by rising Ottoman power, the Portuguese were likewise forced to devise new pathways to success, leading them to scout out western North Africa and the Atlantic coastline in the fifteenth century for new resources and markets after the Ottomans gained sway in the Middle East. At the time, inhabitants of the Iberian Peninsula were poor compared to Africans and Asians, and they ventured forth to improve their situation. They were cramped, and began looking to access legendary African wealth and spread Christianity to the pagans there. This was an age of state-building, and the weaponry and personnel for it took cash. These conditions inspired plans among many imperial rulers for the expansion of trade, communication, and conquest—often in the name of religion.

At the time of the Ottomans and Europeans taking to the sea, many rulers but by no means all in the Eastern Hemisphere used gunpowder-based weaponry. It gave an advantage to those who could afford it: for example, the Ottomans who in 1453 used heavy cannons to breech the sturdy walls of Constantinople and bring down the Byzantine Empire. This new and improving technology was not invincible and did not always conquer, but the cost of it was great, sparking even greater demand for resources. The flash of gunpowder from powerful Ottoman cannons and Portuguese sea-borne cannons and hand-held guns came to instill the same terror that the pounding sound of Mongol horses' hooves once did. However, as gunpowder spread as a technology, so too did violence against individuals, clans, and states. Even then, as with the Mongols, the Ottomans, Mughals, Ming, and others brought the world's peoples closer together under centralized administrative units. Cultures had spread under the Mongols along with the mingling of races, ethnicities, and religions. They would intertwine even more under these empires after 1500.

1. 'AKA-AD-DIN 'ATA-MALIK JUVAINI, *HISTORY OF THE WORLD CONQUEROR* (1200s)

Ghenghis Khan was the legendary "world conqueror" who united territories from East Asia into Europe in the Mongol Empire of the thirteenth century. The Mongol Empire was the work of tens of thousands of men and their families on horseback. These warriors carried dried meat and milk with them but needed fresh horses, which also accompanied their armies. Under the leadership of Ghengis Khan, the Mongols became known as bloodthirsty killers who would slaughter tens of thousands in a day if they resisted Mongol rule. That was the way Mongols wanted to be known, and in fact, one of their tactics was to drive people out of their homes and cities into the next area they wanted to conquer, thus cutting down on resistance.

Cruel as conquest and their rule often were, Mongol leaders sponsored craftspeople and engineers, helped revitalize trade and the spread of religion along the Silk Road, and advanced other contacts along thousands of miles. This document describes the conquest of Merv, probably the largest city in the world at the time, by Toli, a son of Ghenghis Khan.

. . . On the next day, which was the first of Muharram, 618 [25th of February, 1221], and the last of the lives of most of the inhabitants of Merv, Toli, that furious lion, arrived with an army like unto a dark night and a raging sea and in multitude exceeding the sands of the desert, "all warriors of great renown."

He advanced in person to the Gate of Victory together with some five hundred horse and rode right round the town; and for six days they inspected the outworks, walls, moat and minaret [*sic*] and reached the conclusion that the townspeople's supplies would suffice to defend them and that the walls were a stout bastion that would withstand their attack.

On the seventh day,

When the shining sun sought to cast his glittering lasso from the
   lofty citadel,

the armies gathered together and halted before the Shahristan Gate. They joined battle, some two hundred men issuing from the gate and attacking. Toli dismounted in person—

He uttered a roar like a furious elephant, raised his shield above his head and
   showed his hand

—and advanced upon them. And the Mongols attacked in his company driving them back into the town. Others issued forth from another gate but the Mongols stationed there repelled the attack. And so the townspeople were nowhere able to achieve any result and could not even put their heads out of the gates. Finally the world donned garments of mourning, and the Mongols took up positions in several rings around the fortifications and kept watch throughout the night, so that none had any means of egress.

Mujir-al-Mulk saw no way out save surrender and submission. In the morning, therefore, when the sun had raised the black veil from his moonlike face, he dispatched Jamal-ad-Din, one of the chief *imams* of Merv, as his ambassador and sued for quarter. Being reassured by fair words and promises, he got together presents from the quadrupeds in the town—horses, camels and mules—and went to Toli [in person]. Toli questioned him about the town and asked for details regarding the wealthy and notable. Mujir-al-Mulk gave him a list of two hundred persons, and Toli ordered them to be brought into his presence. Of the questioning of these persons one might have said that "*the Earth quaked with her quaking*" and the digging up of their buried possessions, both money and goods, that "*the Earth cast forth her burdens.*"

The Mongols now entered the town and drove all the inhabitants, nobles and commoners, out on the plain. For four days and nights the people continued to come out of the town; the Mongols detained them all, separating the women from the men. Alas! how many peri-like ones did they drag from the bosoms of their husbands! How many sisters did they separate from their brothers! How many parents were distraught at the ravishment of their virgin daughters!

The Mongols ordered that, apart from four hundred artisans whom they specified and selected from amongst the men and some children, girls and boys, whom they bore off into captivity, the whole population, including the women and children, should be killed, and no one, whether woman or man, be spared. The people of Merv were then distributed among the soldiers and levies, and, in short, to each man was allotted the execution of three or four hundred persons. . . . So many had been killed by nightfall that the mountains became hillocks, and the plain was soaked with the blood of the mighty.

We have grown old in a land in whose expanses one treads on nought but the cheeks of maidens and the breasts of striplings.

Then, at Toli's command, the outworks were destroyed, the citadel leveled with the ground and the *maqsura* of the mosque belonging to the sect of the greatest *imam* Abu-Hanifa (*God have mercy on him!*) set on fire.

When the Mongols had finished plundering and leading captive and massacring, Ziya-ad-Din ʿAli, one of the notables of Merv, who had been spared by reason of his retirement, received orders to enter the town and be emir and governor of those that reassembled out of the nooks and crannies. The Mongols also left Barmas as *sbabna*.

When the army departed, those that had sought refuge in holes and cavities came out again, and there were gathered together some five thousand persons. A party of Mongols belonging to the rearguard then arrived and wished to have their share of slaughter. They commanded therefore that each person should bring a skirtful of grain out on to the plain for the Mongols; and in this way they cast into the well of annihilation most of those that had previously escaped. Then they proceeded along the road to Nishapur and slew all they found of those who had turned back from the plain and fled from the Mongols when half way out to meet them.

By God, we live in violent times: if we saw them in a dream we should be terrified.
The people are in such an evil plight that he that has died deserves to rejoice.

Now the *sayyid* ʿIzz-ad-Din Nassaba was one of the great *sayyids* and renowned for his piety and virtue. He now together with some other persons passed thirteen days and nights in counting people slain within the town. Taking into account only those that were plain to see and leaving aside those that had been killed in holes and cavities and in the villages and deserts, they arrived at a figure more than one million three hundred thousand.

Source: ʿAla-ad-Din ʿAta-Malik Juvaini, *The History of the World-Conqueror*, John Andrew Boyle, trans. (Cambridge: Harvard University Press, 1958), 160–164.

2. SHIHAB AL-'UMARI, ACCOUNT OF MANSA MUSA'S PILGRIMAGE c. LATE 1320s–1330s

Renowned like Ghenghis, Mansa (King) Musa (1280–1337) was a larger-than-life ruler of the kingdom of Mali, whose pilgrimage to Mecca, the birthplace of Mohammed and the holiest city in the Islamic world, was legendary. The pilgrimage was one of the five "pillars" of Islam, which constituted the obligations of a practicing Muslim. To make this voyage across Africa to the Arabian Peninsula in 1324, Mansa Musa drew on the immense wealth of his kingdom, derived from its gold and developed by its skilled rulers. Damascus-born scholar Shihab al-'Umari (1300–1384) visited Cairo several years after the Mansa Musa's own trip. Reports on the pilgrimage, such as the one by al-'Umari, resonated across the Eurafrican world, eventually luring adventurers to try to tap that wealth. By the time of later Portuguese intruders on the West African coast in the fifteenth century, however, less skilled rulers had caused the kingdom to weaken and be overtaken by outside leaders and their forces.

From the beginning of my coming to stay in Egypt I heard talk of the arrival of this sultan Musa on his Pilgrimage and found the Cairenes eager to recount what they had seen of the Africans' prodigal spending. I asked the emir Abu . . . and he told me of the opulence, manly virtues, and piety of his sultan. "When I went out to meet him [he said] that is, on behalf of the mighty sultan al-Malik al-Nasir, he did me extreme honour and treated me with the greatest courtesy. He addressed me, however, only through an interpreter despite his perfect ability to speak in the Arabic tongue. Then he forwarded to the royal treasury many loads of unworked native gold and other valuables. I tried to persuade him to go up to the Citadel to meet the sultan, but he refused persistently saying: "I came for the Pilgrimage and nothing else. I do not wish to mix anything else with my Pilgrimage." He had begun to use this argument but I realized that the audience was repugnant to him because he would be obliged to kiss the ground and the sultan's hand. I continued to cajole him and he continued to make excuses but the sultan's protocol demanded that I should bring him into the royal presence, so I kept on at him till he agreed.

When we came in the sultan's presence we said to him: "Kiss the ground!" but he refused outright saying: "How may this be?" Then an intelligent man who was with him whispered to him something we could not understand and he said: "I make obeisance to God who created me!" then he prostrated himself and went forward to the sultan. The sultan half rose to greet him and sat him by his side. They conversed together for a long time, then sultan Musa went out. The sultan sent to him several complete suits of honour for himself, his courtiers, and all those who had come with him, and saddled and bridled horses for himself and his chief courtiers. . . .

This man [Mansa Musa] flooded Cairo with his benefactions. He left no court emir nor holder of a royal office without the gift of a load of gold. The Cairenes made incalculable profits out of him and his suite in buying and selling and giving and taking. They exchanged gold until they depressed its value in Egypt and caused its price to fall." . . .

Gold was at a high price in Egypt until they came in that year. The mithqal [a unit of measure for precious metals] did not go below 25 *dirhams* and was generally above, but from that time its value fell and it cheapened in price and has remained cheap till now. The mithqal does not exceed 22 *dirhams* or less. This has been the state of affairs for about twelve years until this day by reason of the large amount of gold which they brought into Egypt and spent there. . . .

Source: Shihab al-'Umari, in N. Levitzion and J. Hopkins, *Corpus of Early Arabic Sources for West African History* (Cambridge: Cambridge University Press 1981), 269–273.

3. MA HUAN, *OVERALL SURVEY OF THE OCEAN'S SHORES* (1433)

The eunuch Admiral Zheng He (1371–1433) was China's great voyager in the first third of the fifteenth century, leading hundreds of ships as far as the Middle East to explore the "Western Ocean." When but ten years old Zheng He was kidnapped and castrated by forces of the Ming, a group that had taken over the rulership of China. He became a major advisor to the future Ming emperor and helped him militarily to gain the imperial throne in 1402. Zheng He was ferocious as a military man both on land and sea, renowned among many other feats for putting down the worst of the piracy that plagued the China coast under the Ming. At the behest of the emperor, in 1405 Admiral Zheng He's first of seven voyages consisted of some 27,000 men and more than 250 ships of varying sizes. Over almost twenty years, he charted the Indian Ocean world, traveling around Southeast Asian waters, the East African coast, and the Arab shores to the point of reaching Mecca. The overt imperial designs of the Chinese stirred up fears along the fleet's route and threw some—for example the Mamluk rulers in the Middle East—off balance. A Muslim like Zheng He, Ma Huan recorded the knowledge gained—perhaps for exploitation of future tributary lands—from three of these far-reaching journeys. In so doing Ma Huan showed himself to be the forerunner of present-day ethnographers. How does such recording of peoples and places count as part of imperial ambition?

Setting sail from the country of Calicut, you go towards the north-west; [and] you can reach [this place] after travelling with a fair wind for twenty-five days. The capital lies beside the sea and up against the mountains.

Foreign ships from every place and foreign merchants travelling by land all come to this country to attend the market and trade; hence the people of the country are all rich.

The king of the country and the people of the country all profess the Muslim religion; they are reverent, meticulous, and sincere believers; every day they pray five times, [and] they bathe and practise abstinence. The customs are pure and honest. There are no poor families; if a family meets with misfortune resulting in poverty, everyone gives them clothes and food and capital, and relieves their distress.

The limbs and faces of the people are refined and fair, and they are stalwart and fine-looking. Their clothing and hats are handsome, distinctive, and elegant.

In their marriage- and funeral-rites they all obey the regulations of the Muslim religion.

When a man marries a wife, he first employs a go-between, and after the rites have been complied with, the man' family arranges a feast, to which he invites the *chia-ti*—the *chia-ti* is the official who superintends the regulations of the religion—and the people in charge of the wedding, and the go-between, [and] the eldest of the relatives. The two families inform each other about their local origin and antecendents for three generations back, and after the execution of the marriage-documents has been settled, they later choose a day for concluding the marriage. Were not this done, the authorities would regard it as adultery and punish them.

In their diet the people must use butter; it is mixed and cooked in with their food. In the market roast mutton, roast chicken, roast meat, wafer-cakes, *ha-la-sa*, and all kinds of cereal foods—all these are for sale. Many families of two or three persons do not make up a fire to prepare a meal—they merely buy food cooked to eat.

The king uses silver to cast a coin named a *ti-na-erh*; the diameter, [in terms of] our official *ts'un*, is six *fen*; on the reverse side it has lines; the weight is four *fen* on our official steelyard; it is in universal use.

Their writing is all in Muslim characters.

Their market-places have all kinds of shops, with articles of every description; only they have no wine-shops; [for] according to the law of the country wine-drinkers are executed.

Civil and military officials, physicians, and diviners are decidedly superior to those of other places. Experts in every kind of art and craft—all these they have.

They have one large mountain, the four faces of which produce four kinds of articles. One face produces salt, like that of the sea-side—red in colour; the people chisel out a lump with an iron hoe—like quarrying stone; some lumps weigh thirty or forty *chin*; moreover, it is not damp, and when they want to eat it, they pound it into powder for use. One face produces red earth—like the red colour of vermil-ion. One face produces white earth—like lime; it can be used for white-washing walls. One face produces yellow earth—like the yellow colour of turmeric.

In all cases chiefs are ordered to superintend [the quarrying]. Of course they have travelling merchants who come from every place to purchase [these products] and sell them to be used.

The land produces rice and wheat, [but] not much; it is all bought in different places and comes here to be sold; the price is extremely cheap.

For fruits they have walnuts, *pa-tan* fruit, pine-nuts, pomegranates, raisins, dried peaches, apples, Persian dates, water-melons, cucumbers, onions, leeks, shal-lots, garlic, carrots, melons, and other such things. The carrots—red, and as large as a lotus-root—are very plentiful. The melons are very large; some [stand] two *ch'ih* high. The walnuts have a thin white shell, which breaks when you squeeze in the hand. The pine-nuts are about a *ts'un* long.

The raisins are of three or four kinds; one kind resembles a dried date, and is purple; one kind is as large as a lotus-seed, has no pips, and is candied; [and] one kind is round, as large as a white bean, and rather white in colour. The *pa-tan* fruit resembles a walnut; it is pointed, long, and white; [and] inside there is a kernel which in flavor surpasses the flesh of the walnut. The pomegranates are as large as tea-cups. The apples are as big as [one's] fist—very fragrant and delicious.

Further, there are blue, red, and yellow *ya-ku* stones, and red *la, tsu-pa-pi, tsu-mu-la,* "cat's-eyes," diamonds, and large pearls—as big as longan fruits, and one *ch'ien* two or three *fen* in weight—, coral-tree beads, branches, and sterns, and golden amber, amber beads, rosary beads, wax amber, black amber (of which the foreign name is *sa-pai-chih*), all kinds of beautiful jade utensils, crystal utensils, and ten kinds of flowered pieces of brocaded velvet (on which the nap rises one or two *fen,* the length being two *chang* and the breadth one *chang*), woolens of every kind, *sa-ha-la* [cloth], felt, *mo* crepe, *mo* gauze, all kinds of foreign kerchiefs with blue and red silk embroidery, and other such kinds of things—all these are for sale. Camels, horses, mules, oxen, and goats are plentiful.

Source: J. V. G. Mills, *Ma Huan Ying-Yai Sheng-Lan "The Overall Survey of the Ocean's Shores"* (Cambridge: Cambridge University Press, 1970), 165–171.

4. NESTOR-ISKANDER, "NICOLO BARBARO SURGEON, DIARY" (1500)

The Ottomans, a nomadic Turkic group originating in East Asia, had gradually moved to West Asia and Anatolia or Asia Minor. They also settled in southeastern Europe, which at the time was part of the Byzantine Empire—the heir to the eastern Roman Empire. The Ottomans were expansionists and would construct the longest lived empire in modern times, lasting until 1923. In 1453, under the rule of Mehmet II, they used the most up-to-date and powerful cannons to pound the heavily fortified capital, Constantinople. Even so, its inhabitants resisted for almost two months by repairing damage and fighting back. Their ultimate defeat marked the end of the Byzantine regime, as its capital became that of the Ottomans and as one empire gave way to a more powerful, newer one. Here is the description, from one point of view, of Constantinople's defeat. What is the point of view of this report?

The godless Sultan Mohammed [Mehmet II, r. 1451–1481], son of Murad [Murad II, r. 1421–1451], who at the time ruled the Turks, took note of all the problems that plagued Constantinople. And, although he professed peace, he wanted to put an end to Emperor Constantine XI [r. 1449–1453]. Towards that end he assembled a large army and, by land and by sea, suddenly appeared with that large force before the city and laid siege to it. The Emperor, his nobles, and the rest of the population did not know what to do. . . . The Emperor . . . sent his envoys to Sultan Mehmed in order to discuss peace and past relations. But Mehmed did not trust them, and as soon as the envoys departed, he ordered cannons and guns to fire at the city. Others were commanded to make ready wall-scaling equipment and build assault structures. Such city inhabitants as Greeks, Venetians, and Genoese left because they did not want to fight the Turks. . . .

When the Emperor saw this exodus, he ordered his nobles and high officials to assign the remaining soldiers to each sector of the city's wall, to main gates, and to windows. The entire population was mobilized and alarm bells were hoisted throughout the city. Each person was informed of his assignment and each was told to defend his country. . . . Meanwhile, day and night, the Turks bombarded all parts of the city without stopping, and gave its defenders no time to rest. They also made preparations for the final assault. This activity went on for thirteen days.

On the fourteenth day, after they had said their heathen prayers, the Turks sounded trumpets, beat their drums, and played on all other of their musical instruments. Then they brought many cannons and guns closer to the walls and began to bombard the city. They also fired their muskets and thousands of arrows. Because of continued heavy shooting, city defenders could not stand safely on the wall. Some crouched down awaiting the attack; others fired their cannons and guns as much as they could, killing many Turks. The Patriarch, bishops, and all clergy prayed constantly, pleading for God's mercy and for His help in saving the city.

When the Turks surmised that they had killed all the defenders on the wall, they ordered their forces to give a loud shout. Some soldiers carried incendiary devices, others ladders, still others wall-destroying equipment, and the rest many other instruments of destruction. They were ordered to attack and capture the city. City defenders, too, cried out and shouted back and engaged them in fierce battle. The Emperor toured the city, encouraging his people, promising them God's help and ordering the ringing of church bells so as to summon all the inhabitants to defend their city. When the Turks heard the ringing of church bells, they ordered their trumpets, flutes, and thousands of other musical instruments to sound out. And there was a great and terrible slaughter! . . .

Deploying all of these forces the Turks concentrated their assault on the Poloe Mesto. When city defenders retreated from the Poloe Mesto, Turkish foot soldiers hurriedly cleared the way for other units to advance. Turkish units broke through and their light cavalry units overwhelmed city defenders. All city inhabitants came to the rescue of city commanders, dignitaries, and the regular forces, and they engaged the Turks. The Emperor joined the battle with all of his nobles, his special cavalry units, and his foot soldiers. They attacked the Turks inside the city, engaged them in fierce hand-to-hand combat, and drove them away from the Poloe Mesto.

When Mehmed learned about the death of his eastern military commander, he wept profusely because he admired the commander's bravery and wisdom. He also became very angry and led all of his forces to the Sublime Porte. He ordered that the Emperor's positions be bombarded with cannons and guns, being concerned that the Emperor's forces might attack him. Then, the godless Mehmed appeared opposite the Poloe Mesto and ordered his forces to fire cannons and guns at defenders in order to induce them to retreat. He also instructed the Turkish admiral Balta-Oghlu, in charge of many regiments and a select force of 3,000, to capture the Emperor dead or alive.

When they noticed the determination of the godless Mehmed, the Byzantine military commanders, officials, and nobles joined the battle and implored the Emperor to leave in order to escape death. He wept bitterly and told them, "Remember the words I said earlier! Do not try to protect me! I want to die with you!" And they replied, "All of us will die for God's church and for you!" . . .

The impious Mehmed then ordered all of his forces to occupy all city streets and gates in order to capture the Emperor. In his camp he retained only the Janissaries, who readied their cannons and guns in fear of a sudden attack by the emperor. Sensing God's command, the Emperor went to the Great Church [Hagia Sophia], where he fell to the ground pleading for God's mercy and forgiveness for his sins. Then he bade farewell to the Patriarch, the clergy, and the Empress, bowed to those who were present and left the church. Then all the clergy, indeed the entire people, countless women and children, cried and moaned, hoping that their plea would reach heaven. As he left the church the Emperor said, "If you want to suffer for God's church and the Orthodox faith, then follow me!"

Then he mounted his horse and went to the Golden Gate, hoping to encounter there the godless. He was able to attract some 3,000 soldiers. Near the Gate they met a multitude of Turks whom they defeated. The Emperor wanted to reach the Turkish force and they fought till darkness. In this manner the Orthodox Emperor Constantine suffered for God's churches and for the Orthodox faith. On May 29, according to eyewitnesses, he killed more than 600 Turks with his own hand. And the saying was fulfilled: "It started with Constantine, and it ended with Constantine." . . .

[After the capture of the city, the sultan, accompanied by his high officials,] went from the Sublime Porte to the Gate of St. Romanus to a church where the Patriarch, his clergy, and a multitude of people, including women and children, were assembled. He came to the square before the church, dismounted his horse, prostrated himself against the ground, put a handful of dust on his head, and thanked God. And, as he admired the wonderful structure, he said, "Truly no one can transcend the people who are here and who were here before!"

Then he went inside the church. The holy place resembled a wasteland. He stopped at a place reserved for the highest dignitaries. The Patriarch, his clergy, stopped and all who were present there cried, sobbed, and knelt before him. With his hands he motioned for them to rise and then said, "Athanasius! I am telling you, your suite and all of your people: From now on, do not fear my anger. Henceforth neither killing nor enslavement will be permitted!" . . .

Then [the sultan] went to the imperial palace. There he met a certain Serb who handed him the Emperor's [Constantine's] head. Mehmed was pleased with it and called Byzantine nobles and military commanders and asked them to verify whether or not the head was really the Emperor's. Because they were afraid, they all said, "It is the Emperor's head!" He examined it and said, "It is clear that God is the creator of all, including emperors. Why then does everyone have to die?"

Then he sent the head to the Patriarch, instructing him to inlay it with gold and silver and to preserve it the best he knew how. The Patriarch placed it in a silver chest, gilded it, and hid it under the altar of the great church. I have heard from others that the survivors of the battle at the Golden Gate where the Emperor was killed took the Emperor's corpse that night and buried it in Galati. . . .

All this happened as a consequence of our sins, that the godless Mehmed ascended the imperial throne. . . . Yet, those who know history also know that all of this was prophesied by Methodius of Patera and by Leo the Wise concerning the destiny of this city. Its past has been fulfilled and so will be its future. For it is written: "A nation of Rus, as has been prophesied in the vision of St. Daniel, will triumph. And they will inherit the traditions of the seven hills [Rome], as well as its laws, and will disseminate them among five or six nations that comprise Rus, and they will implant seeds among them and will harvest many benefits."

Source: A. Stender-Petersen, ed., *Anthology of Old Russian Literature* (New York: Columbia University Press, 1954).

5. SULTAN SELIM OF OTTOMAN EMPIRE, LETTER TO SHAH ISMAIL (1514)

Though born after the fall of Constantinople, Sultan Selim (c. 1465-70–1520) was pivotal in the expansion of the Ottoman empire by tripling its size. Selim came to power by overthrowing his father and killing his brothers and nephews, who might have contested his rule. Meanwhile, from their base in Persia (present-day Iran), the Safavids were external competitors to the Ottomans, who previously had mostly concentrated on taking lands in the Balkans and eastern Europe. Persian culture and the Persian system of bureaucratic rule were imitated across Central and West Asia. In this letter, the Sunni Muslim Selim warns his competitor, Shah Ismail, whose country had gone over to the Shi'ia form of Islam, that he is about to attack Persia. What followed the defiant response from Shah Ismail was the Battle of Caldiran, in which the Ottomans crushed the Safavids. As a result, the Ottomans began their march through the Middle East, taking the vast Egyptian territories, including the holy places of Mecca and Medina, and gaining the wealth necessary to imperial rule.

The Supreme Being who is at once the sovereign arbiter of the destinies of men and the source of all light and knowledge, declares in the holy book[2] that the true faith is that of the Muslims, and that whoever professes another religion, far from being hearkened to and saved, will on the contrary be cast out among the rejected on the great day of the Last Judgment; He says further, this God of truth, that His designs and decrees are unalterable, that all human acts are perforce reported to Him, and that he who abandons the good way will be condemned to hell-fire and eternal torments. Place yourself, O Prince, among the true believers, those who walk in the path of salvation, and who turn aside with care from vice and infidelity. . . .

[2]The Quran.

I, sovereign chief of the Ottomans, master of the heroes of the age; . . . I, the exterminator of idolators, destroyer of the enemies of the true faith, the terror of the tyrants and pharaohs of the age; I, before whom proud and unjust kings have humbled themselves, and whose hand breaks the strongest sceptres; I, the great Sultan-Khan, son of Sultan Bayezid-Khan, son of Sultan Muhammad-Khan, son of Sultan Murad-Khan, I address myself graciously to you, Emir Ismail, chief of the troops of Persia, comparable in tyranny to Sohak and Afrasiab,[3] and pre-destined to perish . . . in order to make known to you that the works emanating from the Almighty are not the fragile products of caprice or folly, but make up an infinity of mysteries impenetrable to the human mind. The Lord Himself says in his holy book: "We have not created the heavens and the earth in order to play a game" [Quran, 21:16]. Man, who is the noblest of the creatures and the summary of the marvels of God, is in consequence on earth the living image of the Creator. It is He who has set up Caliphs[4] on earth, because, joining faculties of soul with perfection of body, man is the only being who can comprehend the attributes of the divinity and adore its sublime beauties; but he possesses this rare intelligence, he attains this divine knowledge only in our religion and by observing the precepts of the prince of prophets . . . the right arm of the God of Mercy [Muhammad]; it is then only by practicing the true religion that man will prosper in this world and merit eternal life in the other. As to you, Emir Ismail, such a recompense will not be your lot; because you have denied the sanctity of the divine laws; because you have deserted the path of salvation and the sacred commandments; because you have impaired the purity of the dogmas of Islam; because you have dishonored, soiled, and destroyed the altars of the Lord, usurped the sceptre of the East by unlawful and tyrannical means; because coming forth from the dust, you have raised yourself by odious devices to a place shining with splendor and magnificence; because you have opened to Muslims the gates of tyranny and oppression; because you have joined iniq-uity, perjury, and blasphemy to your sectarian impiety; because under the cloak of the hypocrite, you have sowed everywhere trouble and sedition; because you have raised the standard of irreligion and heresy; because yielding to the impulse of your evil passions, and giving yourself up without rein to the most infamous disorders, you have dared to throw off the control of Muslim laws and to permit lust and rape, the massacre of the most virtuous and respectable men, the destruction of pulpits and temples, the profanation of tombs, the ill-treatment of the *ulama,* the doctors and emirs[5] descended from the Prophet, the

---

[3]Legendary kings of central Asia.

[4]Deputies, or political successors, of the Prophet Muhammad who lead the Muslim community on earth.

[5]Shias originally broke away from mainstream Islam over disagreements concerning the early caliphate. They believe that Ali, Muhammad's cousin and son-in-law (the fourth caliph), should have been the first. As a result, the Shias believe that the first three caliphs (all legitimate according to the Sunnis) are illegitimate.

repudiation of the Quran, the cursing of the legitimate Caliphs.[6] Now as the first duty of a Muslim and above all of a pious prince is to obey the commandment, "O, you faithful who believe, be the executors of the decrees of God!" the *ulama* and our doctors have pronounced sentence of death against you, perjurer and blasphemer, and have imposed on every Muslim the sacred obligation to arm in defense of religion and destroy heresy and impiety in your person and that of all your partisans.

Animated by the spirit of this *fatwa*,[7] conforming to the Quran, the code of divine laws, and wishing on one side to strengthen Islam, on the other to liberate the lands and peoples who writhe under your yoke, we have resolved to lay aside our imperial robes in order to put on the shield and coat of mail [armor], to raise our ever victorious banner, to assemble our invincible armies, to take up the gauntlet of the avenger, to march with our soldiers, whose sword strikes mortal blows, and whose point will pierce the enemy even to the constellation of Sagittarius. In pursuit of this noble resolution, we have entered upon the campaign, and guided by the hand of the Almighty, we hope soon to strike down your tyrannous arm, blow away the clouds of glory and grandeur which trouble your head and cause your fatal blindness, release from your despotism your trembling subjects, smother you in the end in the very mass of flames which your infernal *jinn*[8] raises everywhere along your passage, accomplishing in this way on you the maxim which says: "He who sows discord can only reap evils and afflictions." However, anxious to conform to the spirit of the law of the Prophet, we come, before commencing war, to set out before you the words of the Quran, in place of the sword, and to exhort you to embrace the true faith; this is why we address this letter to you. . . .

We urge you to look into yourself, to renounce your errors, and to march towards the good with a firm and courageous step; we ask further that you give up possession of the territory violently seized from our state and to which you have only illegitimate pretensions, that you deliver it back into the hands of our lieutenants and officers; and if you value your safety and repose, this should be done without delay.

But if, to your misfortune, you persist in your past conduct, puffed up with the idea of your power and your foolish bravado, you wish to pursue the course of your iniquities, you will see in a few days your plains covered with our tents and inundated with our battalions. Then prodigies of valor will be done, and we shall see the decrees of the Almighty, Who is the God of Armies, and sovereign judge of the actions of men, accomplished. For the rest, victory to him who follows the path of salvation!

Source: John J. Saunders, *The Muslim World on the Eve of Europe's Expansion* (Englewood Cliffs, NJ: Prentice Hall, 1966), 41–43.

---

[6]Ulama were bodies of religious teachers and interpreters of Muslim law; doctors here means teachers; emirs were military commanders and princes.

[7]Religious decree.

[8]Supernatural spirit.

6. MUHAMMED IBN AHMED IBN IYĀS, *AN ACCOUNT OF THE OTTOMAN CONQUEST OF EGYPT IN THE YEAR A.H. 922 (A.D. 1516)* (1520)

Ottoman sultan Selim took advantage of the momentum he gained from his victory over Persia. He began his attacks on the fragmented rule of the Mamluks in West Asia, taking Syria and finally defeating Egypt. Since the thirteenth century Mamluk armies had ruled Egypt and other parts of West Asia in addition to serving as military power for local rulers and notables. Formed as early as the ninth century, these armies were composed exclusively of slaves chosen for their fighting potential, as they put an end to the expansion of both Mongols and Christian crusaders in the Middle East. By the early sixteenth century, however, Mamluk forces had become disorganized, competitive, and demanding of prerogatives and pay before fighting. Moreover, they had also faced the Chinese in the early fifteenth century and later the Portuguese who threatened their access to trade in the Indian Ocean and their control of West Asian ports. The Mamluks faced the gun-wielding Ottomans in the region, as they took Syria and then moved into Egypt—a prosperous agricultural region. In 1517, the Ottomans, backed by dozens of supply ships, defeated the Mamluk Sultanate of Egypt and consolidated their control of the lucrative trade in the region and beyond. Compare Ottoman and Mamluk strategy in this confrontation.

Then the [Mamluk] Sultan sent for the letters brought by the emissaries, Whom he had not given an interview. Amongst them were a number addressed to the Amirs, executive officials, and Egyptian notables. It appeared after the Sultan's perusal of the letters that they were mostly expressed in Turkish, the purport of them being as follows: "From his Majesty to Amir Tfiman Bai. It has been revealed to me that I shall become the possessor of the east and west, like Alexander the Great." Much of the 'letter consisted of threats and violent language, as for example: "You are a Memlook, who is bought and sold, you are not fit to govern. I am a king, descended through twenty generations of kings, and have taken possession of the country by agreement with the Khalifah and the judges." After many similar expressions, the letter continued: "If you wish to escape violent treatment let an issue of coinage be struck in our name in Egypt, and let the Khutbah be delivered also in our name; and become our governor from Gaza to Egypt, while we will rule from Syria to the Euphrates. But if you do not obey us, then I will enter Egypt, and kill all the Circassians [Mamluk families] there, ripping open those with child and destroying the unborn." He made so great a display of grandeur and power that may be God will desert him on account of his excessive presumption.

When this letter was read to the [Mamluk] Sultan he wept and was terrified. The imported Memlooks had agreed that if the emissary came up to the citadel they would fall upon him with their swords, so he did not appear there. The contents of Ibn 'Othman's [the Ottoman sultan's] communication soon became known among the people, and led to great confusion. Everyone was on the watch for Ibn 'Othman, saying: "As his emissaries came to us when we did not expect them, so he may fall upon us unexpectedly." People began to make strongholds for themselves in the neighbourhood of the city, where they might be hidden if Ibn 'Othman entered Cairo. Others decided to take their families to Upper Egypt, should his approach be confirmed. A story was circulated that Khair Bey, Governor of Aleppo, who had rebelled and submitted to Ibn 'Othman, had written to some of the chief Amirs urging them to tender their submission to Ibn 'Othman, extolling his virtues and just treatment of his subjects, and assuring them that if he came into Egypt they might all retain their posts and salaries. All this was mere trickery and deceit to facilitate Ibn 'Othman's entry into Egypt. Then the Sultan proclaimed that the next issue of pay would take place on Wednesday, the 23rd; he sat on the dais in his courtyard and the troops came up to receive it. Each Memlook had thirty dinars and three months' pay, amounting to twenty dinars; but they threw it down before him and said, We will not start until we have received one hundred dinars apiece; moreover, we have neither horses, nor clothing, nor equipment." They left the citadel in anger. The Sultan, extremely displeased, left the dais. . . . He said "that he could not manage to pay one hundred dinars to each Memlook, for the state coffers were empty; that if they were not content they might elect whom they chose to be Sultan, and he would go to Mecca or elsewhere." So there were disturbances that day. It was reported that some Memlooks said to the Sultan himself, "If you are Sultan follow the custom of the former Sultans; if you resign, may the curse of Allah be upon you, and another will succeed you." The Sultan said to the troops, "You received thirty dinars from the Sultan al-Ghi'iri, and then you did not fight, but forsook him and left him to his death." The troops went away in anger, and some said they quarrelled among themselves. . . . On Thursday, the 24th, the Sultan took his seat again on the dais, and all the Amirs and troops assembled. Seyyid Muhammed Ibn al-Sultan al-Ghfiri also attended, and the Sultan said: " Here is your Master's son, ask him if his father left any money in the Treasury; he will tell you, and if you like to make him Sultan, I will be the first to kiss the ground before him." To this the imported Memlooks replied, "We will march without pay, to avenge our Master." But the Karanisah Memlooks said, "We will not march unless we receive one hundred and thirty dinars, like those who went on the former expedition." Then the meeting dispersed, many still murmuring, and there was much irresponsible talk that day.

Source: *An Account of the Ottoman Conquest of Egypt in the year A.H. 922*, W. H. Salmon, trans. (London: Royal Asiatic Society, 1921), 91–93. Hathi Trust online access available: http://catalog .hathitrust.org/Record/100029137.

7. KONSTANTIN MIHAILOVIC, *MEMOIRS OF A JANISSARY* (1462)

Konstantin Mihailovic (1435–1501) was a slave soldier in the Ottoman army from his capture in 1455 until the Hungarian defeat of the Ottomans in 1463. During those years he learned the history of both the Ottomans and Christians in their struggle for the control of the Mediterranean and West Asia. When he wrote his memoirs as a Christian, he was dead-set against Muslims and any other non-Christian people and described the "heathens" in entirely negative terms. As a former slave soldier, however, he provides a glimpse of the organization in the slave armies, which in a major part of the globe fought the battles for empire. This is a brief description of the capture, training, and conditions of janissaries. Evaluate this as a system for creating an effective fighting force and public servants.

Whenever the Turks invade foreign lands and capture their people an imperial scribe follows immediately behind them, and whatever boys there are, he takes them all into the Janissaries and gives five gold pieces for each one and sends them across the sea. There are about two thousand of these boys. If, however, the number of them from enemy peoples does not suffice, then he takes from the Christians in every village in his land who have boys, having established what is the most every village can give so that the quota will always be full. And the boys whom he takes in his own land are called *cilik*. Each one of them can leave his property to whom ever he wants after death. And those whom he takes among the enemies are called *pendik*. These latter after their deaths can leave nothing; rather, it goes to the emperor, except that if someone comports himself well and is so deserving that he be freed, he may leave it to whomever he wants. And on the boys who are across the sea the emperor spends nothing; rather, those to whom they are entrusted must maintain them and send them where he orders. Then they take those who are suited for it on ships and there they study and train to skirmish in battle. There the emperor already provides for them and gives them a wage. From there he chooses for his own court those who are trained and then raises their wages. The younger must serve the older, and those who come of age and attain manhood he assigns to the fortress so that they will look after them, as mentioned earlier.

And at the court there are about four thousand Janissaries, and among them there is the following organization. They have over them a senior hetman called an *aga*, a great lord. He receives ten gold pieces a day, and his steward, one gold piece a day. To each centurion they give a gold piece every two days, and to their stewards, a gold piece every four days. And all their sons who grow out of boyhood have a wage from the emperor. And no courtier who permits himself something will be punished by the honest ones by fine, but rather by death; they dare not, however, punish any courtier publicly, but secretly, because of the other courtiers, for they would revolt. And no Janissary nor any Decurion of theirs dare ride a horse, save the hetman himself and the steward. And among them it is so arranged that some are archers who shoot bows, some are gunners who shoot mortars, others muskets, and still others crossbows. And every day they must appear with their weapons before their hetmans. And he gives each one a gold piece per year for a bow, and in addition a tunic, a shirt, and large trousers made, as is their fashion, of three ells of cloth, and a shirt of eight ells. And this I myself distributed to them for two years from the imperial court.

Source: Konstantin Mihailovic, *Memoirs of a Janissary*, Benjamin Stolz, trans. (Ann Arbor: University of Michigan, 1975), 157–158.

8. ZAHIR AL-DIN BABUR, *MEMOIRS OF BABUR* OR *THE BABURNAMA* (1530)

The first of the Mughal emperors, Babur (1483–1530) became leader of the region of Ferghana in central Asia at the age of twelve on the death of his father. Though a descendant of both Ghengis Kahn and Tamerlane, he faced challenges to his leadership from the competing groups fighting one another in the region. Defeats never crushed his powerful ambition to be a conqueror however. In his teens and twenties, he overtook Samarkand, Kabul, and other important cities, but also lost them in fierce battles with rivals. Finally in 1525, he began his push into South Asia, driving to acquire its agricultural and other wealth as had many tribal and nomadic leaders before him. As a result of the stream of migrations and conquerors, the subcontinent became a mixture of cultures and customs from across Asia. More than a military leader alone, Babur wrote poetry, adopted Persian culture and helped it thrive, and filled his memoirs with self-reflection and observations of the lands and peoples he had conquered—like a true imperialist. Under the leadership of his descendants, the Mughal Empire began its impressive rise. To whom or what does Babur attribute his victories?

. . . Sultan Ibrahim's army was estimated at one hundred thousand. He and his commanders were said to have nearly a thousand elephants. Moreover, he possessed the treasury left over from two generations of his fathers. The custom in Hindustan is to hire liege men for money before major battles. Such people are called *badhandi*. If Sultan Ibrahim had had a mind to, he could have hired one hundred thousand to two hundred thousand troops. Thank God he was able neither to satisfy his warriors nor to part with his treasury. How was he to please his men when his nature was so overwhelmingly dominated by miserliness? He himself was an inexperienced young man who craved beyond all things the acquisition of money—neither his oncoming nor his stand was calculated to have a good end, and neither his march nor his fighting was energetic.

The Battle of Panipat

On Friday the eight of Rajab [April 20] news came at dawn from the scouts that the enemy was coming in battle array. We put on our armor, armed ourselves, and got to horse.

The sun was one lance high when battle was enjoined. The fighting continued until midday. At noon the enemy was overcome and vanquished to the delight of our friends. By God's grace and generosity such a difficult action was made easy for us, and such a numerous army was ground into the dust in half a day. Five or six thousand men were killed in one place near Ibrahim. All told, the dead of this battle were estimated at between fifteen and sixteen thousand. Later, when we came to Agra, we learned from reports by the people of Hindustan that forty to fifty thousand men had died in the battle. With the enemy defeated and felled, we proceeded. Along the way, the men began to capture the fallen commanders and Afghans and bring them in. Droves of elephants were caught and presented by the elephant keepers. Thinking that Ibrahim may have escaped, we assigned Qïsïmtay Mirza, Baba Chuhra, and Böchkä's troops from the royal tabin to pursue him behind the enemy lines and move with all speed to Agra. Crossing through the midst of Ibrahim's camp, we inspected the tents and pavilions and then camped beside a still river. It was midafternoon when Tahir the Axman, Khalifa's brother-in-law, discovered Sultan Ibrahim's body amidst many corpses and brought in his head.

That very day we assigned Humayun Mirza, Khwaja Kalan, Muhammadi, Shah-Mansur Barlas, Yunus Ali, Abdullah, and Wali Khazin to proceed swiftly and unencumbered, get hold of Agra, and confiscate the treasury. We appointed Mahdi Khwaja, Muhammad-Sultan Mirza, Adil Sultan, Sultan-Junayd Barlas, and Qutlugh-Qadam to separate themselves from the baggage and ride fast, enter the Delhi fortress, and guard the treasuries.

Babur Enters Delhi

On, Tuesday, after two bivouacs, I circumambulated Shaykh Nizam Awliya's tomb and camped beside the Jumna directly opposite Delhi. That evening I toured the Delhi fortress, where I spent the night; the next morning, Wednesday, I circum- ambulated Khwaja Qutbuddin's tomb and toured Sultan Ghiyasuddin Balban's and Sultan Alauddin Khalji's tombs, buildings, and minaret, the Shamsi pool, the Khass pool, and Sultan Bahlul's and Sultan Iskandar's tombs and gardens. After the tour I returned to the camp, got on a boat, and drank spirits.

I made Wali Qïzïl the provost of Delhi; I made Dost the divan of the prov- ince of Delhi; and I had the treasuries there sealed and turned over to them for safekeeping.

On Thursday we marched out and camped beside the Jumna directly opposite Tughluqabad.

On Friday we stayed in camp. Mawalana Mahmud, Shaykh Zayn, and some others went to perform the Friday prayer in Delhi and read the proclamation in my name. Having distributed some money to the poor and unfortunate, they returned to camp.

On Saturday the army proceeded by forced march toward Agra. I went for a tour of Tughluqabad and returned to camp.

On Friday the twenty-second of Rajab [May 4] we stopped in Sulayman Farmuli's quarters in the suburbs of Agra. Since this site was far from the fortress, we moved the next mornings to Jalal Khan Jighat's palace. Humayun had gone on ahead, but the men inside the fortress made excuses to keep him out. When they noticed how unruly the people were, they maintained watch over the exit, afraid someone might pilfer the treasury, until we should get there.

The ancestors of Bikramajit the Hindu, the rajah of Gwalior, had been ruling Gwalior for more than a hundred years. Iskandar stayed in Agra for several years planning the taking of Gwalior. Afterward, during Ibrahim's time, A'zam-Humayun Sarwani had kept up serious fighting for a period of time. Finally [in 1518]

Gwalior was taken by truce, and the rajah was given Shamsabad. Bikramajit died and went to hell when Sultan Ibrahim was defeated. His sons and clan were in Agra. When Humayun got to Agra, the people of Bikramajit's clan were thinking of fleeing, but the men Humayun had stationed there seized them and held them under guard. Humayun did not let them be plundered, and by their own agreement they presented Humayun with many jewels and gems, among which was a famous diamond Sultan Alauddin had acquired. It is well known that a gem merchant once assessed its worth at the whole world's expenditure for half a day. It must weigh eight mithcals. When I came, Humayun presented it to me, but I gave it right back to him.

One of the knowledgeable people from among the soldiers in the fortress was Malikdad of Kara. Another was Malli Surduk, and another Firoz Khan of Mewat. They had engaged in some dishonesty and were sent to be executed. When Malikdad of Kara was taken out for execution, some people pleaded on his behalf. With the coming and going it was four or five days before a decision could be made. We showed him great favor and granted his wishes, exempting all his possessions, Ibrahim's mother and her retinue were granted a one-crore estate in cash, and she was taken out of Agra with her baggage and settled a league downstream.

On Wednesday afternoon the twenty-eighth of Rajab [May 10], I entered Agra and camped in Sultan Ibrahim's quarters.

From the year 910 [1504–05], when Kabul was conquered, until this date I had craved Hindustan. Sometimes because my begs had poor opinions, and sometimes because my brothers lacked cooperation, the Hindustan campaign had not been possible and the realm had not been conquered. Finally all such impediments had been removed. None of my little begs and officers was able any longer to speak out in opposition to my purpose. In 925 [1519] we led the army and took Bajaur by force in two or three gharis, massacred the people, and came to Bhera. The people of Bhera paid ransom to keep their property from being plundered and pillaged, and we took four hundred thousand shahrkhis worth of cash and goods, distributed it to the army according to the number of liege men, and returned to Kabul.

From that date until 932 [1525–26], we led the army to Hindustan five times within seven or eight years. The fifth time, God through his great grace vanquished and reduced a foe like Sultan Ibrahim and made possible for us a realm like Hindustan.

. . . Never before had I had such an army on a Hinsutan campaign. What with liege men, merchants, servants, and all those with the army, twelve thousand persons were registered. The provinces that belonged to me were Badakhshan, Konduz, Kabul, and Kandahar, but no substantial assistance was forthcoming from them— in fact, since some of them were so close to the enemy, it was necessary to send much assistance there. Moreover, the whole of Transoxiana was in the hands of an old enemy, the Uzbek khans and princes, who had nearly one hundred thousand soldiers. The kingdom of Hindustan, from Bhera to Bihar, was under the control of Afghans, whose padishah was Sultan Ibrahim. By land calculation he should have had an army five hundred thousand. However, just then the amirs of Purab were in rebellion, and his standing army was estimated at one hundred thousand. He and his commanders were said to have one thousand elephants. In such a state of affairs and with such strength, we put our trust in God, turned our backs on one hundred thousand old Uzbek enemies, and faced a ruler with a huge army and vast realm like Sultan Ibrahim. In recognition of our trust, God did not let our pains and difficulties go for naught and defeated such a powerful opponent and conquered a vast kingdom like Hindustan. We do not consider this good fortune to have emanated from our own strength and force but from God's pure loving-kindness; we do not think that this felicity is from our endeavor but from God's generosity and favor.

Description of Hindustan

. . . Fifth was Nusrat Shah in Bengal. His father became padishah in Bengal and was a sayyid known as Sultan Alauddin.

Nusrat Shah ruled by hereditary succession. There is an amazing custom born in Bengal: rule is seldom achieved by hereditary succession. Instead, there is a specific royal throne, and each of the amirs, viziers, or officeholders has an established place. It is that throne that is of importance to the people of Bengal. For every place, a group of obedient servants is established. When the ruler desires to dismiss anyone, all the obedient servants then belong to whomever he puts in that person's place. The royal throne, however, has a peculiarity: anyone who succeeds in killing the king and sitting on the throne becomes the king. Amirs, viziers, soldiers, and civilians all submit to him, and he becomes the padishah and ruler like the former ruler. The people of Bengal say, "We are the legal property of the throne, and we obey anyone who is on it." For instance, before Nusrat Shah's father, Sultan Alauddin, an Abyssinian killed the king, took the throne, and reigned for a time. The Abyssinian was killed by Sultan Alauddin, who then became king. Sultan Alauddin's son has now become king by hereditary succession. Another custom in Bengal is that it is considered disgraceful for anyone who becomes king to spend the treasuries of former kings. Whoever becomes king must accumulate a new treasury, which is a source of pride for the people. In addition, the salaries and stipends of all the institutions of the rulers, treasury, military, and civilian are absolutely fixed from long ago and cannot be spent anywhere else.

The five great Muslim padishahs with vast realms and huge armies are the five who have been mentioned.

Of the infidels, the greater in domain and army is the rajah of Vijayanagar. The other is Rana Sanga, who had recently grown so great by his audacity and sword. His original province was Chitor. When the sultans of Mandu grew weak, he seized many provinces belonging to Mandu, such as Ranthambhor, Sarangpur, Bhilsan, and Chanderi. Chanderi had been in the *daru'l-harb* for some years and held by Sanga's highest-ranking officer, Medini Rao, with four or five thousand infidels, but in 934 [1528], through the grace of God, I took it by force within a ghari or two, massacred the infidels, and brought it into the bosom of Islam, as will be mentioned.

All around Hindustan are many rays and rajahs. Some are obedient to Islam, while others, because they are so far away and their places impregnable, do not render obedience to Muslim rulers.

Source: *The Baburnama: Memoirs of Babur, Prince and Emperor*, Wheeler M. Thackston, trans. and ed. (Oxford University Press, 1996), 324–330.

9. GOMES EANES DE ZURARA, *THE CHRONICLE OF THE DISCOVERY AND CONQUEST OF GUINEA* (1450)

As the Ottomans began building their own navy, merchants from southern Europe found new stumbling blocks to their trading prosperity in the eastern Mediterranean. In the fifteenth century the Portuguese sent spies overland into western Asia, Egypt, and even to the reaches of the Indian Ocean bordering on Arabia in order to gauge the conditions of trade. Simultaneously they began building naval capacity, venturing out into the Atlantic and along the west coast of Africa. The region was known for its incredible wealth, as stories of Mansa Musa circulated and as the trans-Saharan trade in slaves, gold, and goods reached North Africa and ultimately Europe. The Portuguese, inspired by the prince known as Henry the Navigator for his demanding sponsorship of sea-faring, at first made hesitant trips toward the coast of Africa, which offered the best possibility for thwarting Ottoman power, finding wealth, and converting any African peoples to Christianity. Beyond that were the early attempts to take a few captives who might be sold into the Mediterranean slave market, thus subverting the Trans-Saharan monopoly in the slave trade. Here the ship captain, Antam Gonçalvez, commissioned by Prince Henry, kidnaps two Africans in 1441. How would you describe these efforts at capturing and selling Africans?

Antam Gonçalvez called to him Affonso Goterres, another groom of the chamber, who was with him, and all the others that were in the ship, being one and twenty in all, and spoke to them in this wise: "Friends and brethren! We have already got our cargo, as you perceive, by the which the chief part of our ordinance is accomplished, and we may well turn back, if we wish not to toil beyond that which was principally commanded of us; but I would know from all whether it seemeth to you well that we should attempt something further, that he [Prince Henry] who sent us here may have some example of our good wills; for I think it would be shameful if we went back into his presence just as we are, having done such small service. And in truth I think we ought to labour the more strenuously to achieve something like this as it was the less laid upon us as a charge by the Infant our lord. O How fair a thing it would be if we, who have come to this land for a cargo of such petty merchandise, were to meet with the good luck to bring the first captives before the face of our Prince. And now I will tell you of my thoughts that I may receive your advice thereon. I would fain go myself this next night with nine men of you (those who are most ready for the business), and prove a part of this land along the river, to see if I find any inhabitants; for

I think we of right ought to meet with some, since 'tis certain there are people here, who traffic with camels and other animals that bear their freights. Now the traffic of these men must chiefly be to the seaboard; and since they have as yet no knowledge of us, their gathering cannot be too large for us to try their strength; and, if God grant us to encounter them, the very least part of our victory will be the capture of one of them, with the which the Infant will feel no small content, getting knowledge by that means of what kind are the other dwellers of this land. And as to our reward, you can estimate what it will be by the great expenses and toil he has undertaken in years past, only for this end." "See what you do," replied the others, "for since you are our captain we needs must obey your orders, not as Antam Gonçalvez but as our lord; for you must understand that we who are here, of the Household of the Infant our lord, have both the will and desire to serve him, even to the laying down of our lives in the event of the last danger. But we think your purpose to be good, if only you will introduce no other novelty to increase the peril, which would be little to the service of our lord." And finally they determined to do his bidding, and follow him as far as they could make their way. And as soon as it was night Antam Gonçalvez chose nine men who seemed to him most fitted for the undertaking, and made his voyage with them as he had before determined. And when they were about a league distant from the sea they came on a path which they kept, thinking some man or woman might come by there whom they could capture; but it happened otherwise; so Antam Gonçalvez asked the others to consent to go forward and follow out his purpose; for, as they had already come so far, it would not do to return to the ship in vain like that. And the others being content they departed thence, and, journeying through that inner land for the space of three leagues, they found the footmarks of men and youths, the number of whom, according to their estimate, would be from forty to fifty, and these led the opposite way from where our men were going. The heat was very intense, and so by reason of this and of the toil they had undergone in watching by night and travelling thus on foot, and also because of the want of water, of which there was none, Antam Gonçalvez perceived their weariness that it was already very great, as he could easily judge from his own sufferings: So he said, "My friends, there is nothing more to do here; our toil is great, while the profit to arise from following up this path meseemeth small, for these men are travelling to the place whence we have come, and our best course would be to turn back towards them, and perchance, on their return, some will separate themselves, or may be, we shall come up with them when they are laid down to rest, and then, if we attack them lustily, peradventure they will flee, and, if they flee, someone there will be less swift, whom we can lay hold of according to our intent; or may be our luck will be even better, and we shall find fourteen or fifteen of them, of whom we shall make a more profitable booty." Now this advice was not such as to give rise to any wavering in the will of those men, for each desired that very thing. And, returning towards the sea, when they had gone a short part of the way, they saw a naked man following a camel, with two assegais in his hand, and as our men pursued him there was not one who felt aught of his great fatigue.

But though he was only one, and saw the others that they were many; yet he had a mind to prove those arms of his right worthily and began to defend himself as best he could, shewing a bolder front than his strength warranted. But Affonso Goterres wounded him with a javelin, and this put the Moor in such fear that he threw down his arms like a beaten thing. And after they had captured him, to their no small delight, and had gone on further, they espied, on the top of a hill, the company whose tracks they were following, and their captive pertained to the number of these. And they failed not to reach them through any lack of will, but the sun was now low, and they wearied, so they determined to return to their ship, considering that such enterprise might bring greater injury than profit. And, as they were going on their way, they saw a black Mooress come along (who was slave of those on the hill), and though some of our men were in favour of letting her pass to avoid a fresh skirmish, to which the enemy did not invite them,—for, since they were in sight and their number more than doubled ours, they could not be of such faint hearts as to allow a chattel of theirs to be thus carried off:—despite this, Antam Gonçalvez bade them go at her; for if (he said) they scorned that encounter, it might make their foes pluck up courage against them. And now you see how the word of a captain prevaileth among men used to obey; for, following his will, they seized the Mooress. And those on the hill had a mind to come to the rescue, but when they perceived our people ready to receive them, they not only retreated to their former position, but departed elsewhere, turning their backs to their enemies.

Source: Gomes Eanes de Azurara, *The Chronicle of the Discovery and Conquest of Guinea*, Charles Raymond Beazley and Edgar Prestage, trans. (London: Hakluyt Society, 1899), 40–43. Also available on Project Gutenberg, https://www.gutenberg.org/files/35738/35738-h/35738-h.htm.

10. DUARTE PACHECO PEREIRA, *ESMERALDO DE SITU ORBIS (GUIDE TO GLOBAL NAVIGATION)* (1505)

By 1490, the Portuguese had descended the West African coast far enough to assess its wealth and the possibilities for trade in gold and other commodities and for the collection of slaves to work on their plantations in the Madeira, Azores, and other islands they had claimed earlier. The aim was to divert the Trans-Saharan trade to West Africa and the Atlantic Ocean and to harvest other African riches, including delicately crafted jewelry, from a region increasingly seen as rich agriculturally as well. In this way they would make up for lost possibilities in the eastern Mediterranean due to the rise of the Ottomans. Duarte Pacheco Pereira (1460–1533) provided navigational and geographical calculations, in addition to what he had discovered of economic possibilities on his voyages around Africa and during the months when he was stranded there after a shipwreck late in the 1480s. Pacheco became the official court geographer and made other oceanic voyages, including to India, as the Portuguese empire was being born. Knowledge like his was much needed. What kind of information seems important to the author? What exactly is the relationship between knowledge as described in this document and empire?

Concerning Serra Lyoa and how the virtuous Prince Henry's discoveries began at Cabo de Nam and ended there.

Following the plan of this work, we must tell of the character of the inhabitants of Serra Lyoa and of their way of living. The greater part of the inhabitants of this land are called Boulooes, a very warlike people and rarely at peace; they call gold "emloan" and water "men." Sometimes these negroes eat one another, but this is less usual here than in other parts of Ethiopia; they are all idolaters and sorcerers and are ruled by witchcraft, placing implicit faith in oracles and omens. In this country there is salt in small quantity, which the Boulooes barter for gold. They take the salt to a place called Coya, whence the gold comes; it is very fine, of nearly twenty-three carats. We obtain it in exchange for brass bracelets and basins of the size barbers use, linen, red cloth, bloodstones, cotton cloths and other articles. The teeth of these negroes are filed and sharp as those of a dog. In this land they make ivory necklaces more delicately carved than in any other country, also very fine and beautiful mats of palm-leaf which they call "bicas." In this country are many elephants and ounces and many other animals such as are not to be found in Spain nor in any other country of Europe.

Item. Serra Lyoa has a point called Cabo Ledo, where there is a shoal of rock, a good gunshot or more from the shore, which rises one . . . or more above the water; between this shoal and the land there is a channel with seven or eight fathoms of water. Hard by this shoal there are four fathoms of water and any ship can sail up this channel without danger. If when you are in front of Cabo Ledo you steer inland ENE a league along the coast, you will discover a bay with reddish sand. Here there is a very tall large tree and close at hand a stream of excellent fresh water. To the right there is a bay which has a creek with black sand; here is a good flat beach with room for fifteen or twenty ships to be repaired. In all this Serra there is much fish, rice, maize, hens, capons, and a few cows and other cattle; but whoever comes here must guard against the negroes, for they are very bad people and shoot with poisoned arrows. Serra Lyoa is 8° north of the Equator; these degrees are the number of degrees the Artic Pole is above the horizon. As there is a more direct route from Cabo Verde to this Serra, by the open sea, we will describe it here.

Item. He who leaves Cabo Verde for Serra Lyoa must sail south eighty leagues; he will then be opposite the shallows of Rio Grande and 11° north of the Equator, and the mouth of Rio Grande will be to the ENE 35 leagues off; here he will find depths of from 50 to 60 fathoms and a bottom of a very fine ash-coloured sand. From here he must sail ESE 120 leagues when he will arrive at Serra Lyoa. Twenty leagues before reaching it, the soundings reveal red coarse sand mixed with small pebbles, the bottom of the sea all round the Serra being of this kind; there is good fishing of sea-bream here. The pilot who goes to this country should have a stout sail on his ship, since there are frequently heavy thunderstorms here, accompanied by very strong winds; the best course is to furl sail till the storm passes. In this country there are large canoes made from a single tree, many of which carry fifteen men; they use them for war and other purposes. The country is full of woods which extend for nearly a thousand leagues along the coast; it is also very hot all the year round, and in this connection we may note that Alfragano states that winter and summer with the Ethiopians are of the same character. At this point the discoveries undertaken by the virtuous Prince Henry came to an end.

Many are the benefits conferred upon this realm of Portugal by the virtuous Prince Henry, for in the year of Our Lord 1420 he discovered the island of Madeira and ordered it to be peopled, and he sent to Sicily for sugar-canes and planted them in Madeira, and for skilled men to teach the Portuguese how to make sugar, as a result of which this island now yields thirty thousand gold crusados to the Order of Christ. Further, he sent to Majorca for Master Jacome, a skilled maker of charts—it was in this island that these charts were first made—and by many gifts and favours brought him to these realms, where he taught his skill to men who in turn taught men who are alive at the present time. Further, he ordered the peopling of the islands of Azores, which of old were called Guorguonas, were done by this virtuous prince, besides discovering Guinea as far as Serra Lyoa. We must therefore pray God for his soul; he died on the 13th of November in the year 1460 and is buried in the monastery of Santa Maria da Vitoria da Batalha, in the chapel of King John his father. The benefits conferred on Portugal by the virtuous Prince Henry are such that its kings and people are greatly indebted to him, for in the country which he discovered a great part of the Portuguese people now earn their livelihood and the Kings of Portugal derive great profit from this commerce; for, from the Rio de Çanaguá on the frontier of the kingdom of Jalofo, where are the first negroes (as we have stated at the end of the 27th chapter of this book) to Serra Lyoa inclusive, when the trade of this country was well ordered, it yielded yearly 3,500 slaves and more, many tusks of ivory, gold, fine cotton clothes and much other merchandise. Therefore we must pray God for the soul of Prince Henry, for his discovery of this land led to the discovery of the other Guinea beyond Serra Lyoa and to the discovery of India, whose commerce brings us an abundance of wealth. *Aqui mapa.*

Source: Duarte Pacheco Pereira, *Esmeraldo de situ orbis*, George H. T. Kimble, trans. and ed. (London: Hakluyt Society, 1936), 97–101.

11. BERNARDINO DE SAHAGUN, *FLORENTINE CODEX: GENERAL HISTORY OF THE THINGS IN SPAIN* (1545)

The Aztec Empire was both limited in size and highly organized, its society structured around waging war as a noble, essential duty to maintain the universe. Equipped with neither horses nor gunpowder weaponry, the Aztec army was a disciplined and greatly feared fighting force whose goals were both to collect tribute and to capture warriors alive to sacrifice ceremonially during one of the eighteen important moments in the calendar. Sacrifice was central to the Aztecs and other groups in the region as it was in fact to Christianity. The common idea was that the gods had sacrificed themselves for humans and that to keep the universe functioning human blood needed to be sacrificed as well. In fact, Aztec society as a whole emphasized sacrifice of animals, goods, food, and even oneself as important to entering the House of the Sun. Given the centrality of sacrifice, impeccable military organization was a major concern of the Aztec empire.

The ruler was known as the lord of men. His charge was war. Hence, he determined, disposed, and arranged how the war would be made. First he commanded masters of the youths and seasoned warriors to scan the [enemy] city and to study all the roads—where [they were] difficult, where entry could be made through them. This done, the ruler first determined, by means of a painted [plan], how was placed the city which they were to destroy. Then the chief noted all the roads—where [they were] difficult, and in what places entry could be made.

Then he summoned the general and the commanding general, and the brave warriors, and he commanded them how they were to take the road, what places the warriors were to enter, for how many days they would march, and how they would arrange the battle. And he commanded that these would announce war and send forth all the men dexterous in war to be arrayed, and to be supplied with provisions for war and insignia.

The ruler then consulted with all the majordomos. . . . He ordered them to take out all their [goods held in] storage, the tributes, costly articles—insignia of gold, and with quetzal feathers, and all the shields of great price.

And when the majordomos had delivered all the costly devices, the ruler then adorned and presented with insignia all the princes who were already able in war, and all the brave warriors, the men [at arms], the seasoned warriors, the fearless warriors, the Otomí, and the noblemen who dwelt in the young men's houses.

And when it had come to pass that the ruler adorned them, when he had done this to the brave warriors, then the ruler ordered all the majordomos to bear their goods, all the costly devices, and all the valuable capes there to battle, that the ruler might offer and endow with favors all the [other] rulers, and the noblemen, and the brave warriors, the men [at arms] who were about to go to war, who were to be extended as if made into a wall of men dexterous with arms. And the ruler forthwith called upon the rulers of Texcoco and Tlacopan and the rulers in the swamp lands, and notified them to proclaim war in order to destroy a [certain] city. He presented them all with costly capes, and he gave them all insignia of great price. Then he also ordered the common folk to rise to go forth to war. Before them would go marching the brave warriors, the men [at arms], the lord general, and the commanding general.

The lords of the sun, it was said, took charge and directed in war. All the priests, the keepers of the gods, took the lead; they bore their gods upon their backs, and, by the space of one day, marched ahead of all the brave warriors and the seasoned warriors. These also marched one day ahead of all the men of Acolhuacan, who likewise marched one day ahead of all the Tepaneca, who similarly marched one day ahead of the men of Xilotepec; and these also marched one day ahead of all the so-called Quaquata. In like manner the [men of] other cities were disposed. They followed the road slowly and carefully.

And when the warlike lands were reached, the brave warrior generals and commanding generals then showed the others the way and arranged them in order. No one might break ranks or crowd in among the others; they would then and there slay or beat whoever would bring confusion or crowd in among the others. All the warriors were extended there, until the moment that Yacauitztli, [god of] the night, would descend—that darkness would fall. And when they already were to rise against the city to destroy it, first was awaited tensely the moment when fire flared up—when the priests brought [new] fire—and for the blowing of shell trumpets, when the priests blew them.

And when the fire flared up, then as one arose all the warriors. War cries were raised; there was fighting. They shot fiery arrows into the temples.

And when they first took captive, one fated to die, forthwith they slew him there before the gods; they slashed his breast open with a flint knife.

And when the city had been overcome, thereupon were counted as many captives as there were, and as many Mexicans and Tlatilulcans as had died. Then they apprised the ruler that they had been orphaned for the sake of Uitzilopochtli; that men had been taken captive and been slain. And the ruler then commanded the high judges to go to tell and inform all the homes of those who had gone to die in war, that there might be weeping in the homes of those who had gone to war to die. And they informed those in the homes of as many as had gone to take captives in war that they received honors there because of their valor. And they were rewarded according to their merits; the ruler accorded favors to all—costly capes, breech clouts, chocolate, food, and devices, and lip rods and ear plugs. Even more did the ruler accord favors to the princes if they had taken captives. He gave them the offices of stewards, and all wealth without price—honor, fame, renown.

And if some had done wrong in battle, they then and there slew them on the battlefield; they beat them, they stoned them.

And if several claimed one captive, and one man said, "He is my captive," and another man also said, "He is my captive": if no man verified it, and also if no one saw how they had taken the captive, the lord of the sun decided between them. If neither had an advantage of the two who claimed the captive, then those who had taken four captives, the masters of the captives, decided that to neither one would the captive belong. He was dedicated to the Uitzcalco [or] they left him to the tribal temple, the house of the devil.

And when the city which they had destroyed was attained, at once was set the tribute, the impost. [To the ruler who had conquered them] they gave that which was there made. And likewise, forthwith a steward was placed in office, who would watch over and levy the tribute.

Source: Fray Bernardino de Sahagún, *The Florentine Codex: General History of the Things in Spain.* Book 8: *Kings and Lords*, Arthur J. O. Andersen and Charles E. Dibble, trans. (Santa Fe: School of American Research, 1954) as cited in Benjamin Keen, ed., *Latin American Civilization: History and Society, 1492 to the Present* (Boulder: Westview, 1996), 4–6.

12. PEDRO DE CIEZA DE LEÓN,
CHRONICLES OF THE INCAS, 1540

By reputation, the Incas were similarly well organized as an empire, spreading gener-
ally good levels of prosperity and order across great distances. As the Spanish con-
quistadores fought among themselves in the 1530s, Inca institutions remained to
fortify conflict-ridden Spanish governance. In fact, Cieza de León was impressed by
many aspects of Incan organization, especially in comparison with what he had seen
as a youth along the docks of Seville. This testimonial was written less than a decade
after the Spanish conquest of the empire when the Incan order was still functioning
but also very fresh in the memory of ordinary people. As with many empires, old and
new imperial structures were intertwined—in this case Incan and Spanish.

It is told for a fact of the rulers of this kingdom that in the days of their rule
they had their representatives in the capitals of all the provinces, for in all these
places there were larger and finer lodgings than in most of the other cities of this
great kingdom, and many storehouses. They served as the head of the provinces or
regions, and from every so many leagues around the tributes were brought to one
of these capitals, and from so many others, to another. This was so well-organized
that there was not a village that did not know where it was to send its tribute. In
all these capitals the Incas had temples of the Sun, mints, and many silversmiths
who did nothing but work rich pieces of gold or fair vessels of silver; large garrisons were stationed there, and a steward who was in command of them all, to
whom an accounting of everything that was brought in was made, and who, in
turn, had to give one of all that was issued. . . . The tribute paid by each of these
provinces, whether gold, silver, clothing, arms and all else they gave, was entered
in the accounts of those who kept the *quipus* [an instrument of multiple, multicol-
ored cords used for recording numbers and events] and did everything ordered by
the governor in the matter of finding the soldiers or supplying whomever the Inca
ordered, or making delivery to Cuzco; but when they came from the city of Cuzco
to go over the accounts, or they were ordered to go to Cuzco to give an accounting, the accountants themselves gave it by the *quipus*, or went to give it where
there could be no fraud, but everything had to come out right. Few years went by
in which an accounting was not made. . . .

At the beginning of the new year the rulers of each village came to Cuzco,
bringing their *quipus*, which told how many births there had been during the year,
and how many deaths. In this way the Inca and the governors knew which of the
Indians were poor, the women who had been widowed, whether they were able to
pay their taxes, and how many men they could count on in the event of war, and
many other things they considered highly important. The Incas took care to see
that justice was meted out, so much so that nobody ventured to commit a felony
or theft. This was to deal with thieves, rapists, or conspirators against the Inca.

As this kingdom was so vast, in each of the many provinces there were many
storehouses filled with supplies and other needful things; thus, in times of war,

wherever the armies went they drew upon the contents of these storehouses, without ever touching the supplies of their confederates or laying a finger on what they had in their settlements. . . . Then the storehouses were filled up once more with the tributes paid the Inca. If there came a lean year, the storehouses were opened and the provinces were lent what they needed in the way of supplies; then, in a year of abundance, they paid back all they had received. No one who was lazy or tried to live by the work of others was tolerated; everyone had to work. Thus on certain days each lord went to his lands and took the plow in hand and cultivated the earth, and did other things. Even the Incas themselves did this to set an example. And under their system there was none such in all the kingdom, for, if he had his health, he worked and lacked for nothing; and if he was ill, he received what he needed from the storehouses. And no rich man could deck himself out in more finery than the poor, or wear different clothing, except the rulers and the headmen, who, to maintain their dignity, were allowed great freedom and privilege.

Source: Pedro Cieza de Léon, *The Second Part of the Chronicle of Peru*, Clements R. Markham, trans. & ed. (London: Hakluyt Society, 1883), 36–50, passim.

REVIEW QUESTIONS

1. How do the documents describe the aims of the adventurers and empire-builders? In what ways are these aims similar and in what ways do they differ?
2. In what ways would you say that the descriptions or reputations of empire-builders and their exploits influenced the course of empire?
3. Compare and contrast the religious ingredients of empire building. How would you rank religion as a motive for empire as seen in the documents?
4. The Chinese Admiral Zheng He spent close to two decades in the first third of the fifteenth century taking a vast fleet of some 319 "treasure ships" across the Indian Ocean, to African and Middle Eastern shores. See the comparison of one of Zheng He's treasure ships to an Iberian ship of the 1490s at http://www.arscives.com/antonio/macau.thespell.htm, and describe what it can tell us about imperial power and accomplishment in the fifteenth century.

CHAPTER 2

Iberians and Others
Take to the Seas

From the mid-fifteenth century on, adventurers sailing under the flags of Spain and Portugal ventured farther from their homelands than ever before, traveling along the coasts of Africa, landing in the Caribbean, and reaching the west coast of India. Soon thereafter the Portuguese sailed into the Strait of Malacca and onward toward China and Japan, where the opportunity to gain incredible products lay. The spices, porcelain, silks, and other goods began almost immediately to make huge profits for the Portuguese, whereas the Spanish initially found far less wealth. Only in 1540 with the discovery of the mines at Potosi in South America did the Spanish find their own quite different sources of wealth—precious metals. A few decades later, precious metals were found in New Spain (present-day Mexico) as well. The Spanish had literally struck it rich. A new force had entered the drive for empire.

Those oceanic voyages led to encounters—many of them violent—between Europeans and local and long-distance traders, farmers, fishers, and agriculturalists often from more sophisticated, experienced societies. Portuguese sailors ran up against networks of Muslim merchants, who had long worked the Indian Ocean world from the east coast of Africa over to Southeast Asian island economies. These experienced traders not to mention government officials often resisted the incursions of the Portuguese and those Europeans who came much later, in many cases seeing the intruders as Christian enemies not just random entrants into a well-established trading scene. The Spanish faced off with small-scale communities in both hemispheres as well as Native American empires based on complex worldviews, efficient officials, and established rules for securing the prosperity of their societies. The contacts or encounters were mutually shocking both for good and for ill: For the Europeans a world of wealth and wonder opened to them; for traders based in Africa and Asia there were riches to be gained from dealing with the newcomers; for some Native Americans there were deals and conquests to be made; for most others there was only death and enslavement. "God, gold, and glory" was the Iberians' motto, and while they did not immediately find great mines of gold, they found new agricultural products, cotton textiles, porcelain, and sources for obtaining slaves. This last would become two centuries later a huge source of profit for them.

At the time, however, Asian traders in textiles, pearls, porcelain, and other luxury items had the upper hand in terms of skill. There was an asymmetry in favor of the Asians, who could make dazzling products and harvest spices to which the Europeans had no access except through local people. In addition, traders outside of Europe had traded the world, while European traders besides experience of the Mediterranean had age-old customs and a knowledge base that was pretty limited. Going outside the continent and the declining trade in the Mediterranean was shocking to the early sailors in many ways. In the Western Hemisphere, while searching for gold, the Europeans saw dazzling kingdoms—those of the Aztecs and the Incas—of which these sailors and soldiers had only dreamt. They saw magnificent porcelains and gadgets like umbrellas in East Asia. Initially European voyagers were motivated by the quest for gold and luxury goods and for the conversion of heathens around the world. Lacking skill in manufacturing, they sought gold to help in the conquest of markets and peoples.

Although handicapped by their own poverty and lack of manufacturing skills, the Iberians had sailing prowess. Along the coasts of Africa and in the Western Hemisphere they also had weaponry on their side at first. Communities in the Western Hemisphere were not generally oceanic groups, while in the Indian Ocean seamanship was excellent and ships were in fact larger than those of the Iberians. However, the Iberian caravels were nimble and they could be loaded with cannons, which the design of the Indian Ocean ships did not initially permit.

Local traders were intermediaries between the workers in porcelain, cotton, and other crafted products and the overseas buyers. Through them Europeans slowly learned about trading procedures, sources of goods, and the means for judging quality, as initially the Iberians were not well acquainted with dealing in the coastal regions. There were other go-betweens—for example translators such as Malinche (or Dona Maria, as the Spanish called her)—connecting Europeans and local people. She facilitated the passage of Hernando Cortes and his small army across Mexico and into the capital of the Aztec empire, gathering allies for him and warning him of impending danger. Because of hostility among different groups, go-betweens could thus help mobilize support for the Europeans among local peoples, even to the point where one local group would lead the charge against another, as in the conquest of both Central America in the 1520s after the fall of the Aztecs and in the Inca Empire in the 1530s. In the Central American case military groups who had helped defeat the Aztecs proceeded southward to facilitate Spanish occupation of present-day Honduras and Guatemala. The work of go-betweens would remain pivotal in trade relations and the politics of empire as well. Intermarriage along with co-habitation among Europeans and the daughters of the nobility, officials, and traders helped integrate conquerors and the conquered into a single society, however imperfectly.

Disastrous consequences such as death at the hands of European weaponry and diseases followed. In the Western Hemisphere, the local inhabitants' lack of resistance to European diseases may have been a more important factor in conquest than weaponry. Still, weapons were powerful in decimating, destabilizing, and weakening populations so that they could not mobilize their normal healing and health care resources. In the long run, weaponry, enslavement, and European diseases such as smallpox, measles, and others decimated perhaps as much as ninety percent of the Amerindian population, easing conquest for Europeans.

A great benefit to the European empires occurred between 1519 and 1522, when Ferdinand Magellan's ships navigated the globe under the auspices of Spain. Having developed enemies at the Portuguese royal court that he served, Magellan found no backing for his proposed trip and instead sailed under the Spanish flag. The voyage was brutal, causing mutinies and other problems which initially Magellan handled well, if at times harshly. His ships found the straits at the tip of South America and set out across the Pacific, eventually returning to Spain. Magellan's voyage transformed the quest for empire, hastening the development of global settlements and global contests for trade and bringing the benefits and harms that globalization entailed. It could market its precious metals via both oceans and more rapidly access the Chinese market across the Pacific. The final result was the new global reach of modern European empires and the simultaneous globalization of trade, societies, and warfare.

1. CHRISTOPHER COLUMBUS, LETTER TO THE KING AND QUEEN OF SPAIN (1494)

Christopher Columbus, an unemployed but experienced sailor from Genoa, succeeded in gaining the backing of Spanish monarchs Ferdinand and Isabella for a voyage across the Atlantic to the "Indies." Instead, he landed in the Caribbean islands, ultimately making four voyages to the region and setting Spain on the path to empire in the Western Hemisphere. Columbus's letters to their majesties were masterpieces, always focused on the massive treasure to be collected of which there was actually very little at first. In European eyes, Caribbean island people only wanted worthless trifles, accepting bits of broken glass, scraps of leather, and trinkets such as beads; in exchange they gave "a piece of gold weighing two and a half castellanos and others received even more for things of even less value."[1] The letters were full of advice for expansion and colonization as well as visions of the glory shining on the Spanish monarchy and the Catholic Church. At the time, Columbus's descriptions were full of exaggeration, which ultimately proved prophetic. The global expansion of the Spanish empire and with it the development of a global bureaucracy were underway. Great wealth ultimately followed.

Most High and Mighty Sovereigns,

In obedience to your Highnesses' commands, and with submission to superior judgment, I will say whatever occurs to me in reference to the colonization

---

[1]Christopher Columbus, "Letter on the New World" (1493) in Jon Cowans, ed. *Early Modern Spain: A Documentary History* (Philadelphia: University of Pennsylvania Press, 2003), 30.

and commerce of the Island of Espanola, and of the other islands, both those already discovered and those that may be discovered hereafter.

In the first place, as regards the Island of Espanola: Inasmuch as the number of colonists who desire to go thither amounts to two thousand, owing to the land being safer and better for farming and trading, and because it will serve as a place to which they can return and from which they can carry on trade with the neighboring islands:

[1.] That in the said island there shall be founded three or four towns, situated in the most convenient places, and that the settlers who are there be assigned to the aforesaid places and towns.

[2.] That for the better and more speedy colonization of the said island, no one shall have liberty to collect gold in it except those who have taken out colonists' papers, and have built houses for their abode, in the town in which they are, that they may live united and in greater safety.

[3.] That each town shall have its alcalde [Mayor] . . . and its notary public, as is the use and custom in Castile.

[4.] That there shall be a church, and parish priests or friars to administer the sacraments, to perform divine worship, and for the conversion of the Indians.

[5.] That none of the colonists shall go to seek gold without a license from the governor or alcalde of the town where he lives; and that he must first take oath to return to the place whence he sets out, for the purpose of registering faithfully all the gold he may have found, and to return once a month, or once a week, as the time may have been set for him, to render account and show the quantity of said gold; and that this shall be written down by the notary before the alcalde, or, if it seems better, that a friar or priest, deputed for the purpose, shall be also present.

[6.] That all the gold thus brought in shall be smelted immediately, and stamped with some mark that shall distinguish each town; and that the portion which belongs to your Highnesses shall be weighed, and given and consigned to each alcalde in his own town, and registered by the above-mentioned priest or friar, so that it shall not pass through the hands of only one person, and there shall he no opportunity to conceal the truth.

[7.] That all gold that may be found without the mark of one of the said towns in the possession of any one who has once registered in accordance with the above order shall be taken as forfeited, and that the accuser shall have one portion of it and your Highnesses the other.

[8.] That one per centum of all the gold that may be found shall be set aside for building churches and adorning the same, and for the support of the priests or friars belonging to them; and, if it should be thought proper to pay any thing to the alcaldes or notaries for their services, or for ensuring the faithful perforce of their duties, that this amount shall be sent to the governor or treasurer who may be appointed there by your Highnesses.

[9.] As regards the division of the gold, and the share that ought to be reserved for your Highnesses, this, in my opinion, must be left to the aforesaid governor and treasurer, because it will have to be greater or less according to the quantity of gold that may be found. Or, should it seem preferable, your Highnesses might, for the space of one year, take one half, and the collector the other, and a better arrangement for the division be made afterward.

[10.] That if the said alcaldes or notaries shall commit or be privy to any fraud, punishment shall be provided, and the same for the colonists who shall not have declared all the gold they have.

[11.] That in the said island there shall be a treasurer, with a clerk to assist him, who shall receive all the gold belonging to your Highnesses, and the alcaldes and notaries of the towns shall each keep a record of what they deliver to the said treasurer.

[12.] As, in the eagerness to get gold, every one will wish, naturally, to engage in its search in preference to any other employment, it seems to me that the privilege of going to look for gold ought to be withheld during some portion of each year, that there may be opportunity to have the other business necessary for the island performed.

[13.] In regard to the discovery of new countries, I think permission should be granted to all that wish to go, and more liberality used in the matter of the fifth, making the tax easier, in some fair way, in order that many may be disposed to go on voyages.

I will now give my opinion about ships going to the said Island of Espanola, and the order that should be maintained; and that is, that the said ships should only be allowed to discharge in one or two ports designated for the purpose, and should register there whatever cargo they bring or unload; and when the time for their departure comes, that they should sail from these same ports, and register all the cargo they take in, that nothing may be concealed.

• In reference to the transportation of gold from the island to Castile, that all of it should be taken on board the ship, both that belonging to your Highnesses and the property of every one else; that it should all be placed in one chest with two locks, with their keys, and that the master of the vessel keep one key and some person selected by the governor and treasurer the other; that there should come with the gold, for a testimony, a list of all that has been put into the said chest, properly marked, so that each owner may receive his own; and that, for the faithful performance of this duty, if any gold whatsoever is found outside of the said chest in any way, be it little or much, it shall be forfeited to your Highnesses.

• That all the ships that come from the said island shall be obliged to make their proper discharge in the port of Cadiz, and that no person shall disembark or other person be permitted to go on board until the ship has been visited by the person or persons deputed for that purpose, in the said city, by your Highnesses, to whom the master shall show all that he carries, and exhibit the manifest of all the cargo, it may be seen and examined if the said ship brings any thing hidden and not known at the time of lading.

• That the chest in which the said gold has been carried shall be opened in the presence of the magistrates of the said city of Cadiz, and of the person deputed for that purpose by your Highnesses, and his own property be given to each owner. -

I beg your Highnesses to hold me in your protection; and I remain, praying our Lord God for your Highnesses' lives and the increase of much greater States.

Source: Fordham Medieval Source Book online. http://legacy.fordham.edu/halsall/source/columbus2 .asp (accessed October 20, 2015). Available on many websites with no original attribution.

2. POPE ALEXANDER VI, TREATY OF TORDESILLAS (1494)

Early on in the Iberian Atlantic voyages it was clear that the Iberian states, besides fighting Muslims, were fighting one another over territory. One early document of world governance was the Treaty of Tordesillas (1494), which divided the globe in two between the rulers of Spain and Portugal. These two emerging powers had many disputes over territories, as their ships began to chart the seas and establish footholds on the eastern islands of the Atlantic, the North and West African shores, and the Caribbean islands and South America. Of the two, the Spanish at the time had less prowess than the Portuguese and did not like some of the earlier agreements, including those made with the help of the Pope. The Portuguese, however, did not make a spectacular touchdown in the Caribbean like Columbus. Thus regulation by treaty appeared to be the answer to rivalries, this one endorsed by Pope Alexander VI. What potential problems does the treaty ignore?

Don Ferdinand and Dona Isabella, by the grace of God king and queen of Castile, Leon, Aragon, Sicily, Granada, Toledo, Valencia, Galiciaj Majorca Seville, Sardinia, Cordova, Corsica, Murcia, Jaen, Algarve, Algeciras, Gibraltar, and the Canary Islands . . . together with the Prince Don John, our very dear and very beloved first-born son, heir of our aforesaid kingdoms and lordships . . . and . . . with the most serene Dom John, by the grace of God, king of Portugal and of the Algarves on this side and beyond the sea in Africa, lord of Guinea, our very dear and very beloved brother . . . ordered the said instrument of the aforesaid agreement and treaty to be brought before us that we might see and examine it, the tenor of which, word for word, is as follows. . . .

[1.] That, whereas a certain controversy exists between the said lords, their constituents, as to what lands, of all those discovered in the ocean sea up to the present day, the date of this treaty, pertain to each one of the said parts respectively; therefore, for the sake of peace and concord, and for the preservation of the relationship and love of the said King of Portugal for the said King and Queen of Castile, Aragon, etc., it being the pleasure of their Highnesses, they, their said representatives, acting in their name and by virtue of their powers herein described, covenanted and agreed that a boundary or straight line be determined and drawn north and south, from pole to pole, on the said ocean sea, from the Arctic to the Antarctic pole. This boundary or line shall be drawn straight, as aforesaid, at a distance of three hundred and seventy leagues west of the Cape Verde Islands, being calculated by degrees, or by any other manner as may be considered the best and readiest, provided the distance shall be no greater than abovesaid. And all lands, both islands and mainlands, found and discovered already, or to be found and discovered hereafter, by the said King of Portugal and by his vessels on this side of the said line and bound determined as above, toward the east, in either north or south latitude, on the eastern side of the said bound provided the said bound is not crossed, shall belong to, and remain in the possession of, and pertain forever to, the said King of Portugal and his successors. And all other lands, both islands and mainlands, found or to be found hereafter, discovered or to be discovered hereafter, which have been discovered or shall be discovered by the said King and Queen of Castile, Aragon, etc., and by their vessels, on the western side of the said bound, determined as above, after having passed the said bound toward the west, in either its north or south latitude, shall belong to, and remain in the possession of, and pertain forever to, the said King and Queen of Castile, Leon, etc., and to their successors.

[2.] Item, the said representatives promise and affirm by virtue of the powers aforesaid, that from this date no ships shall be despatched—namely as follows: the said King and Queen of Castile, Leon, Aragon, etc., for this part of the bound, and its eastern side, on this side the said bound, which pertains to the said King of Portugal and the Algarves, etc.; nor the said King of Portugal to the other part of the said bound which pertains to the said King and Queen of Castile, Aragon, etc.—for the purpose of discovering and seeking any mainlands or islands, or for the purpose of trade, barter, or conquest of any kind. But should it come to pass that the said ships of the said King and Queen of Castile, Leon, Aragon, etc., on sailing thus on this side of the said bound, should discover any mainlands or islands in the region pertaining, as abovesaid, to the said King of Portugal, such mainlands or islands shall pertain to and belong forever to the said King of Portugal and his heirs, and their Highnesses shall order them to be surrendered to him immediately. And if the said ships of the said King of Portugal discover any islands and mainlands in the regions of the said King and Queen of Castile, Leon, Aragon, etc., all such lands shall belong to and remain forever in the possession of the said King and Queen of Castile, Leon, Aragon, etc., and their heirs, and the said King of Portugal shall cause such lands to be surrendered immediately.

[3.] Item, in order that the said line or bound of the said division may be made straight and as nearly as possible the said distance of three hundred and seventy leagues west of the Cape Verde Islands, as hereinbefore stated, the said representatives of both the said parties agree and assent that within the ten months immediately following the date of this treaty their said constituent lords shall despatch two or four caravels, namely, one or two by each one of them, a greater or less number, as they may mutually consider necessary. These vessels shall meet at the Grand Canary Island during this time, and each one of the said parties shall send certain persons in them, to wit, pilots, astrologers, sailors, and any others they may deem desirable. But there must be as many on one side as on the other, and certain of the said pilots, astrologers, sailors, and others of those sent by the said King and Queen of Castile, Aragon, etc., and who are experienced, shall embark in the ships of the said King of Portugal and the Algarves; in like manner certain of the said persons sent by the said King of Portugal shall embark in the ship or ships of the said King and Queen of Castile, Aragon, etc.; a like number in each case, so that they may jointly study and examine to better advantage the sea, courses, winds, and the degrees of the sun or of north latitude, and lay out the leagues aforesaid, in order that, in determining the line and boundary, all sent and empowered by both the said parties in the said vessels, shall jointly concur. These said vessels shall continue their course together to the said Cape Verde Islands, from whence they shall lay a direct course to the west, to the distance of the said three hundred and seventy degrees, measured as the said persons shall agree, and measured without prejudice to the said parties. When this point is reached, such point will constitute the place and mark for measuring degrees of the sun or of north latitude either by daily runs measured in leagues, or in any other manner that shall mutually be deemed better. This said line shall be drawn north and south as aforesaid, from the said Arctic pole to the said Antarctic pole. And when this line has been deter-mined as abovesaid, those sent by each of the aforesaid parties, to whom each one of the said parties must delegate his own authority and power, to determine the said mark and bound, shall draw up a writing concerning it and affix thereto their signatures. And when determined by the mutual consent of all of them, this line shall be considered as a perpetual mark and bound, in such wise that the said par-ties, or either of them, or their future successors, shall be unable to deny it, or erase or remove it, at any time or in any manner whatsoever. And should, perchance, the said line and bound from pole to pole, as aforesaid, intersect any island or mainland, at the first point of such intersection of such island or mainland by the said line, some kind of mark or tower shall be erected, and a succession of similar marks shall be erected in a straight line from such mark or tower, in a line identi-cal with the above-mentioned bound. These marks shall separate those portions of such land belonging to each one of the said parties; and the subjects of the said parties shall not dare, on either side, to enter the territory of the other, by crossing the said mark or bound in such island or mainland.

[4.] Item, inasmuch as the said ships of the said King and Queen of Castile, Leon, Aragon, etc., sailing as before declared, from their kingdoms and seigniories to their said possessions on the other side of the said line, must cross the seas on this side of the line, pertaining to the said King of Portugal, it is therefore con-certed and agreed that the said ships of the said King and Queen of Castile, Leon, Aragon, etc., shall, at any time and without any hindrance, sail in either direction, freely, securely, and peacefully, over the said seas of the said King of Portugal, and within the said line. And whenever their Highnesses and their successors wish to do so, and deem it expedient, their said ships may take their courses and routes direct from their kingdoms to any region within their line and bound to which they desire to despatch expeditions of discovery, conquest, and trade. They shall take their courses direct to the desired region and for any purpose desired therein, and shall not leave their course, unless compelled to do so by contrary weather. They shall do this provided that, before crossing the said line, they shall not seize or take possession of anything discovered in his said region by the said King of Portugal; and should their said ships find anything before crossing the said line, as aforesaid, it shall belong to the said King of Portugal, and their Highnesses shall order it surrendered immediately. And since it is possible that the ships and subjects of the said King and Queen of Castile, Leon, etc., or those acting in their name, may discover before the twentieth day of this present month of June, following the date of this treaty, some islands and mainlands within the said line, drawn straight from pole to pole, that is to say, inside the said three hundred and seventy leagues west of the Cape Verde Islands, as aforesaid, it is hereby agreed and determined, in order to remove all doubt, that all such islands and mainlands found and discovered in any manner whatsoever up to the said twentieth day of this said month of June, although found by ships and subjects of the said King and Queen of Castile, Aragon, etc., shall pertain to and remain forever in the possession of the said King of Portugal and the Algarves, and of his successors and kingdoms, provided that they lie within the first two hundred and fifty leagues of the said three hundred and seventy leagues reckoned west of the Cape Verde Islands to the above-mentioned line-in whatsoever part, even to the said poles, of the said two hundred and fifty leagues they may be found, determining a boundary or straight line from pole to pole, where the said two hundred and fifty leagues end. Likewise all the islands and mainlands found and discovered up to the said twentieth day of this present month of June by the ships and subjects of the said King and Queen of Castile, Aragon, etc., or in any other manner, within the other one hundred and twenty leagues that still remain of the said three hundred and seventy leagues where the said bound that is to be drawn from pole to pole, as aforesaid, must be determined, and in whatever part of the said one hundred and twenty leagues, even to the said poles,—they that are found up to the said day shall pertain to and remain forever in the possession of the said King and Queen of Castile, Aragon, etc., and of their successors and kingdoms; just as whatever is or shall be found on the other side of the said three hundred and seventy leagues pertaining to their Highnesses, as aforesaid, is and must be theirs, although the said one hundred and twenty leagues are within the said bound of the said three hundred and seventy leagues pertaining to the said King of Portugal, the Algarves, etc., as aforesaid.

And if, up to the said twentieth day of this said month of June, no lands are discovered by the said ships of their Highnesses within the said one hundred and twenty leagues, and are discovered after the expiration of that time, then they shall pertain to the said King of Portugal as is set forth in the above.

The said Don Enrique Enriques, chief steward, Don Gutierre de Cardenas, chief auditor, and Doctor Rodrigo Maldonado, representatives of the said very exalted and very mighty princes, the lord and lady, the king and queen of Castile,

Leon, Aragon, Sicily, Granada, etc., by virtue of their said power, which is incorporated above, and the said Ruy de Sousa, Dom Joao de Sousa, his son, and Arias de Almadana, representatives and ambassadors of the said very exalted and very excellent prince, the lord king of Portugal and of the Algarves on this side and beyond the sea in Africa, lord of Guinea, by virtue of their said power, which is incorporated above, promised, and affirmed, in the name of their said constituents, saying that they and their successors and kingdoms and lordships, forever and ever, would keep, observe, and fulfill, really and effectively, renouncing all fraud, evasion, deceit, falsehood, and pretense, everything set forth in this treaty, and each part and parcel of it; and they desired and authorized that everything set forth in this said agreement and every part and parcel of it be observed, fulfilled, and performed as everything which is set forth in the treaty of peace concluded and ratified between the said lord and lady, the king and queen of Castile, Aragon, etc., and the lord Dom Alfonso, king of Portugal (may he rest in glory) and the said king, the present ruler of Portugal, his son, then prince in the former year of 1479, must be observed, fulfilled, and performed, and under those same penalties, bonds, securities, and obligations, in accordance with and in the manner set forth in the said treaty of peace. Also they bound themselves [by the promise]that neither the said parties nor any of them nor their successors forever should violate or oppose that which is above said and specified, nor any part or parcel of it, directly or indirectly, or in any other manner at any time, or in any manner whatsoever, premeditated or not premeditated, or that may or can be, under the penalties set forth in the said agreement of the said peace; and whether the fine be paid or not paid, or graciously remitted, that this obligation, agreement, and treaty shall continue in force and remain firm, stable, and valid forever and ever. . . .

Source: Frances Gardiner Davenport, European Treaties Bearing on the History of the United States to 1648 (Washington, DC: The Carnegie Institution of Washington, 1917). On Yale Project Avalon, http://avalon.law.yale.edu/15th_century/mod001.asp (accessed October 19, 2015).

3. ALBRECHT DÜRER, *JOURNAL OF A VOYAGE TO VENICE AND THE LOW COUNTRIES* (1520)

Albrecht Dürer (1471–1528) was a noted German artist, who while traveling the continent sought out some of the earliest displays of objects flowing into Europe from the conquered areas of the Western Hemisphere. Keeping a diary of his voyage, he remarks on the wonders before him that Spanish conquistadors had brought back to Charles V, King of Spain and also Holy Roman emperor. Dürer's appreciation of Native American art and culture was an early example of the fascination that creators in the arts found in the accomplishments of people in distant lands. It went beyond lust roused in others at the sight of gold existing in Africa or the New World. Out of wonder and curiosity large collections took shape of foreign animals, objects used in everyday life, plants, textiles, religious items, and many other artefacts came to fill both royal collections—as in the case of the Chinese and other emperors—and those of personal and public museums. Beyond fascination, artists, musicians, and writers often copied from works found around the globe, integrating the globe into what has been falsely seen as a style of "Western" art stemming from Greece and Rome alone. What sense of European culture at the time does this document convey?

Also I have seen the things which they have brought to the King out of the new land of gold: a sun all of gold, a whole fathom broad, and a moon, too, of silver, of the same size, also two rooms full of armour, and the people there with all manner of wondrous weapons, harness, darts, wonderful shields, extraordinary clothing, beds, and all kinds of wonderful things for human use, much finer to look at than prodigies. These things are all so precious that they are valued at 100,000 gulden, and all the days of my life I have seen nothing that reaches my heart so much as these, for among them I have seen wonderfully artistic things and have admired the subtle ingenuity of men in foreign lands; indeed, I don't know how to express what I there found.

Source: Albrecht Dürer, *Journal of a Voyage to Venice and the Low Countries* (1913) as reproduced from Project Gutenberg, http://www.gutenberg.org/files/3226/3226.txt (accessed October 19, 2015).

4. BARTOLOMÉ DE LAS CASAS, "THIRTY VERY JURIDICAL PROPOSITIONS" (1552)

Bartolomé de Las Casas (1484–1566) was a Catholic missionary who was an early settler in the Caribbean, even being awarded the grant of an encomienda for his bravery. An encomienda was usually a considerable piece of land, granted along with the right to the forced labor of the local people who resided on the land. Having participated in the brutal takeover of Cuba in 1513, Las Casas then heard sermons by a Dominican friar against the enslavement and savage treatment of these Indians. "Among these gentle sheep . . . the Spaniards entered . . . like wolves, tigers, and lions which have been starving for many days. . . ,"[2] Las Casas came to realize. In 1515, he returned to Spain in hopes of inspiring the monarchs to prohibit the institutionalization of this treatment as counter to Christian values and the goal of spreading the faith. Once back in the Caribbean he sought out remedies to the humanitarian crisis in addition to writing and preaching both there and in Spain on behalf of native peoples.

Proposition I: The Pontiff of Rome, the canonically elected Vicar of Christ, successor of St. Peter, has the authority and power of Christ Himself, the Son of God, over all the people of the world, faithful or not, insofar as he sees it necessary to guide men and set them upon the road to the eternal life, and to remove the impediments therefrom. He uses and must use such power, however, in one way

---

[2] *Bartolome de Las Casas: A Selection of His Writings*, trans. George Sanderlin (New York: Knopf, 1971), 166.

with the unfaithful who have never undergone holy baptism in the holy Church, particularly those who have never heard of Christ or His faith, and in another way with those who are faithful or once were so.

Proposition II: St. Peter and his successors are by divine law under the necessary obligation of attempting to see that the word and faith of Christ are preached throughout the world with the greatest diligence to all the unfaithful, *who it may be supposed will not resist the spread of the Gospels and Christian teachings. . . .*

Proposition IV: Among ministers for the propagation and maintenance of the faith and Christian religion and for conversion of the unfaithful, the Christian monarchs occupy a position most necessary for the Church; for by means of their power, royal forces and worldly riches they can aid, shelter, preserve and defend the churchly and spiritual ministers, and the end mentioned above can be sought and obtained without confusion or hindrance. . . .

Proposition VII: The Vicar of Christ, by divine authority and to avoid confusion, can and did most wisely, providently and justly divide among Christian princes the kingdoms and provinces of all the unfaithful of every disbelief or sect, thus committing and entrusting to the former the spreading of the holy faith, the extension of the Universal Church and the Christian faith and the conversion and spiritual welfare of those people as an ultimate aim.

Proposition VIII: The Supreme Pontiff did not make, nor does he or should he make, such a division, commission or concession *with the principle and final purpose of bringing the Christian princes into grace or enlarging with honor and more titles and riches their possessions.* His end is the spread of the divine religion, the honor of God and the conversion and salvation of the unfaithful, which is the intent and final aim of the King of Kings and Lord of Lords, Jesus Christ. *At the outset there is imposed upon the princes a most perilous duty and office,* for which they must give a complete accounting at the end of their days before the final judgment. *The aforesaid division and trust is therefore more for the good and benefit of the unfaithful than for that of the Christian princes. . . .*

Proposition X: Among the unfaithful who live in distant kingdoms, who have never heard speak of Christ or received the faith, there are true kings and princes. *Royal dominion, dignity and preeminence belong to them by virtue of natural law and the law of peoples* insofar as such dominion leads to the rule and governance of their kingdoms as sanctioned by divine and evangelical law and in the manner that superior persons have dominion over inferior things. With the advent of Jesus Christ, therefore, such dominions, honors, royal prerogatives and the rest were not abolished either universally or individually, *ipso facto nec ipso jure.*

Proposition XI: An opinion contrary to the preceding proposition is erroneous and most pernicious and *whoever defends it vigorously will incur formal heresy.* It would at the same time be most impious, harmful and productive of innumerable thefts, acts of violence, tyrannies, ravages and robberies, irreparable damages and grievous sins, infamy, stench and hatred of the name of Christ and of the Christian religion, and a most effective impediment to our Catholic faith. It would be death, perdition and vainglory for the greater part of mankind, the most certain damnation of infinite souls and, finally, the cruel and foremost enemy of piety, meekness and Christian evangelical custom.

Proposition XII: For no sin of idolatry *or any other sin, grave as it may be,* are the said unfaithful, masters or subjects, to be deprived of their dominions, dignity or other possessions, *ipso facto vel ipso jure.*

Proposition XIII: Merely for the sin of idolatry or for any other sin, however enormous, grave and heinous, which was committed during the whole period of their unfaithfulness, before they had received holy baptism of their own free will, the unfaithful, particularly those whose lack of faith is simple ignorance, *cannot be punished by any judge in the world*—unless it be a case of those who directly impede the propagation of the faith and, having been sufficiently warned, maliciously persist in their actions. . . .

Proposition XIX: All kings and natural rulers, cities, communities and villages in the Indies shall recognize the monarchs of Castile as their universal and sovereign rulers and emperors in the following manner: *after having received our holy faith and sacred baptism of their own free will; and if before receiving these they do not do so or wish to do so, they cannot be punished by any judge or court.*

Proposition XXII: The rulers of Castile are obliged by divine law to see that the faith of Christ is preached in the form which the Son of God left established in His Church. His apostles adhered to this form effectively and without any slack or failure; the universal Church has always by custom and decrees ordained and constituted it, and the holy sages have explained and enlarged upon it in their books. The form consists in attracting the unfaithful and particularly the Indians, who are by nature very meek, humble and pacific, in a peaceful, loving, sweet and charitable manner, with gentleness, humility and good examples, and in giving them gifts and grants from our part rather than by taking anything of theirs away from them. In this way they will consider the God of the Christians to be a good, gentle and just God and will wish to belong to Him and to receive His Catholic faith and holy doctrine.

Proposition XXIII: To subject them first by warlike means is a form and procedure contrary to the law, gentle yoke, easy burden and gentleness of Jesus Christ. It was the same method used by Mahomet and the Romans to upset and despoil the world. It is that used today by the Turks and the Moors and which the Sherif is beginning to use. Therefore it is most evil, tyrannical, libelous of the sweet name of Christ, and the cause of infinite new blasphemies against the true God and the Christian religion. We have had very extensive experience with what has been done and is being done today in the Indies; because of it, the Indians consider God to be the most cruel, unjust and pitiless of gods, and consequently it impedes the conversion of many unfaithful, giving rise to the impossibility of infinite people in the new world ever to become Christians. This is, moreover, most clearly the infernal path to all the irreparable and distressing evils and damages set forth in *Proposition XI.*

Proposition XXVIII: Satan could not have invented any more effective pestilence with which to destroy the whole new world, to consume and kill off all its people and to depopulate it as such large and populous lands have been depopulated, than the inventions of the *repartimiento* and *encomiendas,* by which those peoples were divided and assigned to Spaniards as if to all the devils put together, or like herds of cattle delivered to hungry wolves. (This means would have sufficed to depopulate the whole world.) By the *encomienda* or *repartimiento,* which was the cruelest form of tyranny and the one most worthy of hell-fire that could have been invented, all those peoples are prevented from receiving the Christian faith and religion, being held night and day by their wretched and tyrannical overlords, the Spaniards, in the mines, at personal labors and under incredible tributes; forced to carry loads one and two hundred leagues as if they were beasts or worse; and with clerics who preach the faith and give the Indians instruction and a knowledge of God persecuted and driven out of the Indian villages, leaving no witnesses to the acts of violence, cruelties and continual robberies and murders. Because of the *encomiendas* and *repartimiento* the Indians have suffered and still suffer continual tortures, thefts and injustices to their persons and to their children, women and worldly goods. Because of the *encomiendas* and *repartimiento* there have perished in the space of forty-six years (and I was present) more than fifteen million souls without faith or sacraments, and more than three thousand leagues of land have been depopulated. I have been present, as I say, and as long as these *encomiendas* last, I ask that God be a witness and judge of what I say: the power of the monarchs, even were they on the scene, will not suffice to keep all the Indians from perishing, dying off and being consumed; and in this way a thousand worlds might end, without any remedy.

Proposition XXX and the last: From all the aforesaid, by dint of necessary consequence, it follows that, *without prejudice to the title and royal sovereignty which the monarchs of Castile exercise over the new world of the Indies, everything which has been done there—both by the unjust and tyrannical conquests and by the* repartimientos *and* encomiendas—*is null, void and without value or sanction of any right,* for everything has been done by absolute tyrants, without just cause or reason or the authority of their natural prince and monarch. . . .[A *repartimiento* was an allocation of forced Indian labor. An *encomienda* was a conferred right to Indian tribute or labor; the grantee was responsible, though often only in theory, for the Indians' catechization and welfare.]

Source: *Apologética historia de las Indias* (Madrid, 1909), originally translated for *Introduction to Contemporary Civilization in the West* (New York: Columbia University Press, 1946, 1954, 1961). Online at http://www.columbia.edu/acis/ets/CCREAD/lascasa2.htm (accessed October 19, 2015).

5. BERNAL DÍAZ DEL CASTILLO, *THE TRUE HISTORY OF THE CONQUEST OF NEW SPAIN* (1568)

Born to a modest family, Bernard Díaz del Castillo (c. 1495–1584) left Spain in 1514 to find opportunity with other fortune seekers in the New World. First landing in Panama, where conditions were dangerous because of disease and rebellions, he moved around the Caribbean world, finally accompanying Hernando Cortes on his conquest of Mexico between 1519 and 1521. Díaz del Castillo lacked the advantage of wealth but he knew how to write, allowing him to compose what he believed to be an accurate history. This account captures the life of his fellow soldiers as well as the lives of both the great Aztec emperor Monteczuma and Malinche, the transla- tor and facilitator of Spanish inroads into the various states surrounding the Aztec empire. Díaz del Castillo became the Spanish governor of Guatemala after its con- quest, which followed that of the Aztecs. Malinche (also known as Doña Marina) became a controversial figure in Mexican history. What are Diaz del Castillo's views of Malinche, Monteczuma, and Aztec society?

On Malinche or Doña Marina

Previous to going into any details here respecting the powerful Motecusuma, his immense kingdom of Mexico, and its inhabitants, I must relate what I know of Doña Marina. She was born a ruler over a people and country,—for her parents had the dominion of a township called Painala, to which several other townships were subject, lying about twenty-four miles from the town of Guacasualco. Her father died when she was very young, and her mother married another young cazique [also cacique, a local chief]. By him she had a son, of whom it appears they were both very fond, and to whom, after their death, they designed to leave their territories. In order, however, that the daughter of the first marriage might not stand in his way, she was conveyed secretly during night-time to an Indian family in Xicalango, they spreading the rumour she had died, which gained further belief from the circumstance that a daughter of one of her female slaves happened to die at the time. The Indians of Xicalango did not keep the young girl themselves, but gave her to the inhabitants of Tabasco, by whom she was presented to Cortes. I knew her mother and half-brother myself, the latter having already reached man- hood, and governed the township jointly with his mother. When they were subse- quently both converted to Christianity, the latter was named Martha and her son Lazaro. I was well acquainted with the whole of this circumstance; for in the year 1523, when Mexico and several other provinces had been subdued, and Chris- tobal de Oli had rebelled in the Higueras, Cortes came to Guacasualco, and on that occasion visited Marina's birth-place. Most of the inhabitants of Guacasualco accompanied Cortes on this expedition; I myself was also among the number. As Doña Marina, in all the wars of New Spain, Tlascalla, and at the siege of Mexico, had rendered the greatest services in capacity of an interpretress, Cortes carried her everywhere with him. During this journey it also was that he married her to a cavalier of the township of Orizava, named Juan Xaramillo. Among others, there was present as a witness a certain Aranda of Tabasco, through whom this circumstance became immediately known. These are the true particulars of the whole case, not, however, as related by Gomara. For the rest, Marina had the most extensive influence in New Spain, and did with the Indians what she pleased.

While Cortes was staying in Guacasualco, he ordered all the caziques of the province to assemble, and advised them to adopt our holy religion. On this occasion the mother and brother of Doña Marina also made their appearance with the other caziques. They recognized each other immediately; the former, however, appeared to be in the greatest anxiety, thinking that they had merely been called there to be killed. Doña Marina, however, desired them to dry away their tears, and comforted them by saying they were unconscious of what they were doing when they had sent her away to the inhabitants of Xicalango, and that she freely forgave the past. By this means God certainly directed everything for her best, turned her away from the errors of heathenism, and converted her to Christianity.

Thus destined, she likewise bore a son unto her master Cortes, and then married a cavalier named Juan Xaramillo. All this I consider of much greater importance than if she had been presented with the sole dominion of the whole of New Spain. She likewise gave presents to her relatives on their return home. What I have related is the strict truth, and can swear to it. Gomara's account respecting this is wholly erroneous, and he adds many other circumstances which I shall leave without comment. This, however, is certain, that the whole affair reminds one of the history of Joseph and his brethren in Egypt, when they came into his power. After this diversion into matters which subsequently took place, I must relate how we first managed to understand Doña Marina. She was conversant with the language of Guacasualco, which is the Mexican, and with that of Tabasco. Aguilar, however, merely understood the latter, which is spoken throughout the whole of Yucatan. Doña Marina had, therefore, first to make herself understood to Aguilar, who then translated what she said into Spanish. This woman was a valuable instrument to us in the conquest of New Spain. It was, through her only, under the protection of the Almighty, that many things were accomplished by us: without her we never should have understood the Mexican language, and, upon the whole, have been unable to surmount many difficulties.

On Monteczuma

The mighty Motecusuma may have been about this time in the fortieth year of his age. He was tall of stature, of slender make, and rather thin, but the symmetry of his body was beautiful. His complexion was not very brown, merely approaching to that of the inhabitants in general. The hair of his head was not very long, excepting where it hung thickly down over his ears, which were quite hidden by it. His black beard, though thin, looked handsome. His countenance was rather of an elongated form, but cheerful; and his fine eyes had the expression of love or severity, at the proper moments. He was particularly clean in his person, and took a bath every evening. Besides a number of concubines, who were all daughters of persons of rank and quality, he had two lawful wives of royal extraction, whom, however, he visited secretly without any one daring to observe it, save his most confidential servants. He was perfectly innocent of any unnatural crimes. The dress he had on one day was not worn again until four days had elapsed. In the halls adjoining his own private apartments there was always a guard of 2000 men of quality, in waiting: with whom, however, he never held any conversation unless to give them orders or to receive some intelligence from them. Whenever for this purpose they entered his apartment, they had first to take off their rich costumes and put on meaner garments, though these were always neat and clean; and were only allowed to enter into his presence barefooted, with eyes cast down. No person durst look at him full in the face, and during the three prostrations which they were obliged to make before they could approach him, they pronounced these words: "Lord! my Lord! sublime Lord!" Everything that was communicated to him was to be said in few words, the eyes of the speaker being constantly cast down, and on leaving the monarch's presence he walked backwards out of the room. I also remarked that even princes and other great personages who come to Mexico respecting lawsuits, or on other business from the interior of the country, always took off their shoes and changed their whole dress for one of a meaner appearance when they entered his palace. Neither were they allowed to enter the palace straightway, but had to show themselves for a considerable time outside the doors; as it would have been considered want of respect to the monarch if this had been omitted.

Above 300 kinds of dishes were served up for Motecusuma's dinner from his kitchen, underneath which were placed pans of porcelain filled with fire, to keep them warm. Three hundred dishes of various kinds were served up for him alone, and above 1000 for the persons in waiting. He sometimes, but very seldom, accompanied by the chief officers of his household, ordered the dinner himself, and desired that the best dishes and various kinds of birds should be called over to him. We were told that the flesh of young children, as a very dainty bit, was also set before him sometimes by way of a relish. Whether there was any truth in this we could not possibly discover; on account of the great variety of dishes, consisting in fowls, turkeys, pheasants, partridges, quails, tame and wild geese, venison, musk swine, pigeons, hares, rabbits, and of numerous other birds and beasts; besides which there were various other kinds of provisions, indeed it would have been no easy task to call them all over by name. This I know, however, for certain, that after Cortes had reproached him for the human sacrifices and the eating of human flesh, he issued orders that no dishes of that nature should again be brought to his table. I will, however, drop this subject, and rather relate how the monarch was waited on while he sat at dinner. If the weather was cold a large fire was made with a kind of charcoal made of the bark of trees, which emitted no smoke, but threw out a delicious perfume; and that his majesty might not feel any inconvenience from too great a heat, a screen was placed between his person and the fire, made of gold, and adorned with all manner of figures of their gods. The chair on which he sat was rather low, but supplied with soft cushions, and was beautifully carved; the table was very little higher than this, but perfectly corresponded with his seat. It was covered with white cloths, and one of a larger size.

Four very neat and pretty young women held before the monarch a species of round pitcher, called by them Xicales, filled with water to wash his hands in. The water was caught in other vessels, and then the young women presented him with towels to dry his hands. Two other women brought him maise-bread baked with eggs. Before, however, Motecusuma began his dinner, a kind of wooden screen, strongly gilt, was placed before him, that no one might see him while eating, and the young women stood at a distance. Next four elderly men, of high rank, were admitted to his table; whom he addressed from time to time, or put some questions to them. Sometimes he would offer them a plate of some of his viands, which was considered a mark of great favour. These grey-headed old men, who were so highly honoured, were, as we subsequently learnt, his nearest relations, most trustworthy counsellors and chief justices. Whenever he ordered any victuals to be presented them, they ate it standing, in the deepest veneration, though without daring to look at him full in the face. The dishes in which the dinner was served up were of variegated and black porcelain, made at Cholulla. While the monarch was at table, his courtiers, and those who were in waiting in the halls adjoining, had to maintain strict silence.

After the hot dishes had been removed, every kind of fruit which the country produced was set on the table; of which, however, Motecusuma ate very little. Every now and then was handed to him a golden pitcher filled with a kind of liquor made from the cacao [seeds from which chocolate and cocoa are made], which is of a very exciting nature. Though we did not pay any particular attention to the circumstance at the time, yet I saw about fifty large pitchers filled with the same liquor brought in all frothy. This beverage was also presented to the monarch by women, but all with the profoundest veneration.

. . . As soon as he had finished his dinner the four women cleared the cloths and brought him water to wash his hands. During this interval he discoursed a little with the four old men, and then left table to enjoy his afternoon's nap.

After the monarch had dined, dinner was served up for the men on duty and the other officers of his household, and I have often counted more than 1000 dishes on the table, of the kinds above mentioned. These were then followed, according to the Mexican custom, by the frothing jugs of cacao liquor; certainly 2000 of them, after which came different kinds of fruit in great abundance.

Next the women dined, who superintended the baking department; and those who made the cacao liquor, with the young women who waited upon the monarch. Indeed, the daily expense of these dinners alone must have been very great!

Besides these servants there were numerous butlers, house-stewards, treasurers, cooks, and superintendents of maise-magazines. Indeed there is so much to be said about these that I scarcely knew where to commence, and we could not help wondering that everything was done with such perfect order. I had almost forgotten to mention, that during dinner-time, two other young women of great beauty brought the monarch small cakes, as white as snow, made of eggs and other very nourishing ingredients, on plates covered with clean napkins; also a kind of long-shaped bread, likewise made of very substantial things, and some pachol, which is a kind of wafer-cake. They then presented him with three beautifully painted and gilt tubes, which were filled with liquid amber, and a herb called by the Indians tabaco. After the dinner had been cleared away and the singing and dancing done, one of these tubes was lighted, and the monarch took the smoke into his mouth, and after he had done this a short time, he fell asleep.

About this time a celebrated cazique, whom we called Tapia, was Motecusuma's chief steward: he kept an account of the whole of Motecusuma's revenue, in large books of paper which the Mexicans call *Amatl*. A whole house was filled with such large books of accounts.

Source: Bernal Diaz del Castillo, *The Memoirs of the Conquistador Bernal Diaz del Castillo*, tr. John Ingram Lockhart (London: J. Hatchhard and Son, 1894), I: 84–86, 229–231. Also on Project Gutenberg, http://www.gutenberg.org/files/32474/32474-h/32474-h.htm#CHAPTER_XCI (accessed October 19, 2015).

6. ANTONIO PIGAFETTA, *THE FIRST VOYAGE AROUND THE WORLD BY MAGELLAN* (1534)

Ferdinand Magellan furthered Spanish expansion when he accomplished what appeared to be the impossible: He led a fleet of ships from Spain between 1519 and 1522 to circle the world by ocean. At a time of dangerous travel and uncertain and difficult conditions, it is hardly surprising that Magellan often faced unruly passengers and crews, often of various ethnicities, aboard his ships. He dealt with them harshly, even leaving mutinous aristocrats and high clergy on deserted islands for having threatened the mission. That said, Magellan had staunch admirers as he remained determined to circumnavigate the globe and brought all his skills to bear on the task. Only as he reached islands in the western Pacific did he seem to lose his steadiness, becoming haughty and provoking local peoples so unwisely that he was murdered. Antonio Pigafetta, an Italian on board, recorded the journey, reporting the good and the bad in his account. This excerpt ends just before Magellan was murdered. The completion of the route, however, gave Spain the first global trade route in modern times and made the Philippines an emporium for goods and precious metals from the New World.

Antonio Pigafetta, patrician of Vicenza and Knight of Rhodes, to the most illustrious and excellent Lord, Philipe Villiers de l'Isle-Adam, renowned Grand Master of Rhodes, his most honoured lord.

. . . having obtained much information from many books I had read, as well as from various persons, who discussed the great and marvellous things of the Ocean Sea with his Lordship, I determined, with the good grace of His Caesarean Majesty, and of his Lordship above said, to experience myself and to see those things that might satisfy me somewhat, and that might grant me some renown with posterity.

Having heard that a fleet of five vessels had been fitted out in the city of Seville for the purpose of going to discover the spicery in the islands of Molucca, under command of Captain-General Ferdinand Magellan, a Portuguese gentleman, *comendador* of the Order of Santiago de la Spada, [who] had many times travelled the Ocean Sea in various capacities, acquiring great praise, I set out from the city of Barcelona, where His Majesty was then residing, . . .

Some days after, the captain-general, with his other captains, descended the river in the small boats belonging to their ship, and we remained there for a considerable number of days in order to finish [providing] the fleet with some things that it needed. Every day we went ashore to hear mass in a village called Our Lady of Barrameda, near Sanlúcar. Before the departure, the captain-general wished all the men to go to confession, and he would not allow any woman to sail in the fleet for the sake of better order.

After fifteen days we saw four of those giants without their weapons for they had hidden them in certain bushes as the two whom we captured showed us. Each one was painted differently. The captain-general detained two of them, the youngest and best proportioned, by means of a very cunning trick, in order to take them to Spain; had he used any other means [than those he employed], they could easily have killed some of us. The trick that he employed to capture them was as follows: he gave them many knives, scissors, mirrors, bells, and glass beads. And those two having their hands filled with those things, the captain-general had two pairs of iron manacles brought, such as are fastened on the feet, and made motions as if to make a gift of them, whereat they were very pleased, since those manacles were of iron, but they did not know how to carry them, and they were grieved at leaving them behind. They had no place to put those gifts; for they had to hold the skin wrapped about them with their hands. The other two giants wished to help them, but the captain refused. Seeing that they were loath to leave those manacles behind, the captain made them a sign that he would put them on their feet, and that they could carry them away. They nodded assent with the head. Immediately, the captain had the manacles put on both of them at the same time, and when our men were driving home the cross bolt, the giants began to suspect something, but since the captain reassured them, they nevertheless remained still. When they then saw that they were deceived, they raged like bulls, calling loudly for [the god] Setebos to aid them. . . .

We remained in that port, which we called "Port St Julian," about five months where many things happened. In order that your most illustrious Lordship may know some of them, it happened that as soon as we had entered the port, the captains of the other four ships plotted treason in order that they might kill the captain-general; and these men were the overseer of the fleet, one Juan de Cartagena, the treasurer, Luis de Mendoza, the accountant, Antonio Coca, and Gaspar de Quesada; and when the treason was discovered, the overseer of the men was quartered, and the treasurer was killed by dagger blows. Some days after that, Gaspar de Quesada was banished with a priest in that land of Patagonia for planning another plot. The captain-general did not wish to have him killed, because the emperor, Don Carlo, had appointed him captain. . . .

At dawn on Saturday, 16 March 1521, we came upon a high land at a distance of three hundred leagues from the Islands of Thieves, an island named Samar. The following day, the captain-general desired to land on another island, which was uninhabited and lay to the right of the above mentioned island, in order to be more secure, and to get water and have some rest. He had two tents set up on the shore for the sick and had a sow slaughtered for them . . . .

On Thursday morning, 28 March, as we had seen a fire on an island the night before, we anchored near it. We saw a small boat that the natives call *boloto* with eight men in it, approaching the flagship. A slave belonging to the captain-general who was a native of Sumatra, which was formerly called Taprobane, spoke to them, and they immediately understood him. They came alongside the ship, but were unwilling to come aboard, taking a position at some little distance. When the captain saw that they would not trust us, he threw them a red cap and other things tied to a bit of wood. They received them very gladly, and went away quickly to advise their king. About two hours later we saw two *balanghai* coming (which are large boats and are so called by those people), full of men. Their king was in the larger of them, being seated under an awning of mats. When the king came near the flagship, the slave spoke to him. The king understood him, for in those districts the kings know more languages than the other people; he ordered some of his men to enter the ships. But he always remained in his *balanghai*, at some little distance from the ship, until his own men returned; and as soon as they returned he departed. The captain-general showed great honour to the men who entered the ship, and gave them some presents, and for this reason the king wished before his departure to give the captain a large bar of gold and a basketful of ginger; however, the latter thanked the king heartily but would not accept it. In the afternoon we went in the ships [and anchored] near the dwellings of the king.

The next day, Good Friday, the captain-general sent his slave, who acted as our interpreter, ashore in a small boat to say to the king that if he had any food that he should have it carried to the ships, for they would be well compensated by us, and that we had come to the island as friends and not as enemies. . . .

. . . Then we all approached the platform joyfully. The captain and the king sat in chairs of red and violet velvet, the chiefs on cushions, and the others on mats. The captain told the king through the interpreter that he thanked God for inspiring him to become a Christian, and that [now] he would more easily conquer his enemies than before. The king replied that he wished to become a Christian, but that some of his chiefs did not wish to obey, because they said that they were as good men as he. Then our captain had all the chiefs of the king called, and told them that, unless they obeyed the king as their king, he would have them killed and would give their possessions to the king. They replied that they would obey him. The captain told the king that he was going to Spain, but that he would return again with so many forces that he would make him the greatest king of those regions, as he had been the first to desire to become a Christian. The king, lifting his hands to the sky, thanked the captain, and requested him to let some of his men remain [with him], so that he and his people might be better instructed in the faith. The captain replied that he would leave two men to satisfy him, but that he would like to take two of the children of the chiefs with him, so that they might learn our language, who afterward on their return would be able to tell the others about Spain.

A large cross was set up in the middle of the square; the captain told them that if they wished to become Christians as they had declared on the previous days, they must burn all their idols and set up a cross in their place, they were to adore that cross daily with clasped hands, and every morning they were to make the sign of the cross (which the captain showed them how to make); and they ought to come hourly, at least in the morning, to that cross, and adore it kneeling; the intention that they had already declared, they were to confirm with good works. The king and all the others wished to confirm all this. The captain-general told the king that he was clad all in white to demonstrate his sincere love toward them; they replied that they knew not how to respond to his sweet words.

Source: Antonio Pigafetta, *The First Voyage around the World 1519–1522. An Account of Magellan's Expedition*, Theodore J. Cachey, Jr., ed. (Toronto: University of Toronto Press, 2007), 3–4, 6, 14–15, 17, 30, 34, 39.

7. GARCILASO DE LA VEGA (EL INCA), "THE ORIGINS OF THE INCAS," FROM *ROYAL COMMENTARIES OF THE INCAS* (1609)

In the 1530s Francisco Pizarro, a Spanish conquistador, finally gained a strong foothold in the Inca Empire in South America after executing the emperor Altahualpa in 1533. Pizarro and his small company of men entered an efficient system with excellent roads along which tax, tribute, and communication systems functioned. For a decade, however, the Spanish quarreled among themselves and in 1541 Pizarro himself was assassinated. Born in present-day Peru in 1539 in the midst of upheavals, Garcilaso de la Vega was known as the Inca because his mother was an Inca princess and his father a Spanish aristocrat, albeit a Spaniard who did not acknowledge the legitimate birth of his son. Pizarro himself had taken as mistresses the sister and a wife of Altahualpa. De la Vega lived the first years of his life with his mother and her Inca family, learning Inca history and lore from an oral tradition that was powerful. Later he also received a Spanish education when his father took him into his home for a time. At twenty-one, De la Vega moved to Spain, where he wrote important books on the Inca way of life and the Spanish conquest based on his Inca relatives' accounts even as he served in the Spanish army. This extract shows that arranging a marriage between an Incan noble woman and a conquistador was not always done on Spanish terms. It also questions whether the Spanish (or later imperialists) were ever fully in control of people they were said to have "conquered." How would you characterize the attitudes of the Incan upper classes toward the Spanish?

. . . Many of the colonists who had Indians had been killed in the later wars, and their widows had duly inherited the Indians. In order that they should not make second marriages among those who had not served His Majesty, the governors arranged marriages for them. This occurred throughout Peru, and many widows were so treated. Moreover many were the losers, since they found themselves wedded to husbands much older than the ones they had lost. The former wife of Alonso de Toro, Gonzalo Pizarro's commander, who had a great allocation of Indians, was married to Pedro López Cazalla, President La Gasca's secretary.

Martín de Bustincia's wife, who was the daughter of Huaina Cápac and herself (not her husband) the owner of the Indians, was married to a very good soldier called Diego Hernández, a very worthy man, who was said in his youth to have been a tailor—though it is more likely that this was false than true. The princess learned this and refused the match, saying that it was unjust to wed the daughter of Huaina Cápac with a *ciracamayo*, meaning tailor. Although the bishop of Cuzco and Captain Diego Centeno, as well as other personages who went to attend the ceremony of betrothal, begged and pleaded with her, it was all to no purpose. They then sent to fetch her brother Don Cristóbal Paullu, whom we have already mentioned. When he came, he took his sister into a corner of the room and told her privately that it was impolitic for her to refuse the match, for by so doing she would render the whole of the royal line odious in the eyes of the Spaniards, who would consider them mortal enemies and never accept their friendship again. She agreed, though reluctantly, to her brother's demands, and so appeared before the bishop, who wished to honor the betrothed by officiating at the ceremony.

When the bride was asked through an Indian interpreter if she consented to become the bride and spouse of the aforesaid, the interpreter said "did she want to be that man's wife?" for the Indian language had no verb for consent or for spouse, and he could therefore not have asked anything else.

The bride replied in her own tongue: *"Ichach munani, ichach manamunani,"* meaning: "Maybe I will, maybe I won't." Whereupon the ceremony continued. It was held in the house of Diego de los Ríos, a *vecino* of Cuzco They were still alive and living as man and wife when I left Cuzco.

Other marriages of this kind took place throughout the empire, and were arranged so as to give allocations of Indians to claimants and reward them with other people's properties. Many, however, were dissatisfied, some because their income was small and others because their wives were ugly: there is no perfect satisfaction in this world. . . .

Source: Garcilaso de la Vega, El Inca, *Royal Commentaries of the Incas and General History of Peru,* Harold V. Livermore, trans. (Austin: University of Texas Press, 1965), 2: 1229–1230. ACLS ebook http://quod.lib.umich.edu/cgi/t/text/text-idx?c=acls;cc=acls;view=toc;idno=heb02750.0001.001. Reprinted by permission.

8. JOSÉ DE ACOSTA, *NATURAL AND MORAL HISTORY OF THE INDIES* (1590)

Another step in the advance of empire came 1545, when the Spanish found the silver mines at Potosi high in the mountains of the Inca lands. News of the mines further sparked the rush to the New World and the massive transport of silver from the mines across the Pacific to the Philippines, which Magellan had claimed for Spain in 1521. Merchants from China, Japan, and other regions flocked to the Spanish port there with goods for the Spanish to purchase with their silver, boosting prices around the world and causing some back in Europe to worry about the moral and economic consequences of this boom. Potosi itself became a city of some 100,000 people, including African slaves and Indian forced laborers, described here by the Jesuit José de Acosta, who joined a growing number of researchers interested in the geography, plant life and minerals, and other scientific findings to be made in the New World. What was the purpose of de Acosta's account? What might have been its results?

It appears from the royal accounts of the House of Trade of Potosí, and it is affirmed by venerable and trustworthy men, that during the time of the government of the licentiate Polo, which was many years after the discovery of the hill, silver was registered every Saturday to the value of 150 to 200,000 pesos, of which the King's fifth (quinto) came to 30 to 40,000 pesos, making a yearly total of about 1,500,000 pesos. According to this calculation, the value of the daily output of the mine was 30,000 pesos, of which the King's share amounted to 6,000 pesos. One more thing should be noted in estimating the wealth of Potosí; namely, that accounts have been kept of only the silver that was marked and taxed. But it is well known in Peru that for a long time the people of that country used the silver called "current," which was neither marked nor taxed. And those who know the mines well conclude that at that time the bulk of the silver mined at Potosí paid no tax, and that this included all the silver in circulation among the Indians, and much of that in use among the Spaniards, as I could observe during my stay in that country. This leads me to believe that a third—if not one half—of the silver production of Potosí was neither registered nor taxed. . . . [It should also be noted that] although the mines of Potosí have been dug to a depth of two hundred estados [one estado is approximately six feet], the miners have never encountered water, which is the greatest possible obstacle to profitable operations, whereas the mines of Porco, so rich in silver ore, have been abandoned because of the great quantity of water. For there are two intolerable burdens connected with the search for silver: the labor of digging and breaking the rock, and that of getting out the water—and the first of these is more than enough. In fine, at the present time His Catholic Majesty receives on the average a million pesos a year from his fifth of the silver of Potosí, not counting the considerable revenue he derives from quicksilver and other royal perquisites. . . .

The hill of Potosí contains four principal veins: the Rich vein, that of Centeno, the vein called "of Tin," and that of Mendieta. All these veins are in the eastern part of the hill, as if facing the sunrise; there is no vein to the west. These veins run from north to south, or from pole to pole. They measure six feet at their greatest width, and a palmo at the narrowest point. From these veins issue others, as smaller branches grow out of the arms of trees. Each vein has different mines that have been claimed and divided among different owners, whose names they usually bear. The largest mine is eighty yards in size, the legal maximum; the smallest is four yards. By now all these mines are very deep. In the Rich vein there are seventy-eight mines; they are as deep as one hundred and eighty and even two hundred estados in some places. In the Centeno vein there are twenty-four mines. Such are as much as sixty and even eighty estados deep, and the same is true of the other veins and mines of that hill. In order to work the mines at such great depths, tunnels (socavones) were devised; these are caves, made at the foot of the mountain, that cross it until they meet the veins. Although the veins run north to south, they descend from the top to the foot of the mountain—a distance calculated at more than 1200 estados. And by this calculation, although the mines run so deep it is six times as far again to their root and bottom, which some believe must be extremely rich, being the trunk and source of all the veins. But so far experience has proven the contrary, for the higher the vein the richer it is, and the deeper it runs the poorer the yield. Be that as it may, in order to work the mines with less cost, labor, and risk, they invented the tunnels, by means of which they can easily enter and leave the mines. They are eight feet wide and one estado high, and are closed off with doors. With the aid of these tunnels they get out the silver ore without difficulty, paying the owner of the tunnel a fifth of all the metal that is obtained. Nine tunnels have already been made, and others are being dug. A tunnel called "of the Poison" (del Veneno), which enters the Rich vein, was twenty-nine years in the making, for it was begun in 1556 (eleven years after the discovery of those mines) and was completed on April 11, 1585. This tunnel crossed the vein at a point thirty-five estados from its root or source, and from there to the mouth of the mine was 135 estados; such was the depth of that they had to descend to work those mines. This tunnel (called the Crucero) is 250 yards in length, and its construction took twenty-nine years; this shows how much effort men will make to get silver from the bowels of the earth. They labor there in perpetual darkness, not knowing day from night; and since the sun never penetrates these places, they are not only always dark but very cold, and the air is very thick and alien to the nature of men. And that is why those who enter there for the first time get seasick, as it were, being seized with nausea and stomach cramps, as I was. The miners always carry candles, and they divide their labor so that some work by day and rest by night and others work at night and rest during the day. The silver ore is generally of a flinty hardness, and they break it up with bars. Then they carry the ore on their backs up ladders made of three cords of twisted cowhide, joined by pieces of wood that serve as rungs, so that one man can climb up and another come down at the same time. These ladders are ten estados long, and at the top and bottom of each there is a wooden platform where the men may rest, because there are so many ladders to climb. Each man usually carries on his back a load of two arrobas of silver ore tied in a cloth, knapsack fashion; thus they ascend, three at a time. The one who goes first carries a candle tied to his thumb, because, as I mentioned, they receive no light from above; thus, holding with both hands, they climb that great distance, often more than 150 estados—a fearful thing, the mere thought of which inspires dread. So great is the love of silver, which men suffer such great pains to obtain.

Source: José de Acosta, *Natural and Moral History of the Indies*, 1590 in Benjamin Keen, *Latin American Civilization: History and Society, 1492 to the Present* (Boulder: Westview, 1996), 84–86, Keen's translation.

9. SEYYIDI (SEYDI) 'ALI RE'IS, *THE MIRROR OF KINGDOMS* (1550S)

By the sixteenth century the Ottomans had developed a mighty sea-going fleet, along-side of that of Portugal. After the voyages of Vasco da Gama to India beginning in 1498, the Portuguese temporarily used their naval skills in trade and collecting trib-ute in the Indian Ocean. Increasingly empires depended on sea-faring, for accessing new regions, maintaining their holdings, and fighting off contenders. In the case of the Ottomans, their main seaborne enemies were the Iberians in the Mediterranean and the Portuguese in the Indian Ocean, where they conducted offensives against rival ships. The fierce competition was for resources, including territory, but also for the triumph of competing religions—especially Islam and Christianity. Ottoman admiral Seydi Ali Re'is faced the Portuguese in 1552 as he attempted to move some ships of the Sultan from Basra and return them to Suez. The offensives of the Portuguese were fierce, but the stormy conditions of the Indian Ocean were more so. Moreover, there were many shifting alliances and forces at work as Seydi Ali Re'is describes in this excerpt from one of his books on naval history and navigation. From this account, how might we describe empire as an enterprise of oceans and seas?

The Beginning of the Story [1552]

I must here mention that Piri Bey, the late Admiral of the Egyptian fleet, had, some time previous to this, been dispatched with about 30 ships (galleys and galleons) from Suez, through the Red Sea, touching Jedda and Yemen, and through the straits of Bab-i-Mandeb, past Aden and along the coast of Shahar. Through fogs and foul weather his fleet became dispersed, some ships were lost, and with the remainder he pro-ceeded from Oman to Muscat, took the fortress and made all the inhabitants prison-ers; he also made an incursion into the islands of Ormuz and Barkhat, after which he returned to Muscat. There he learned from the captive infidel captain that the Chris-tian [Portuguese] fleet was on its way, that therefore any further delay was inadvisable, as in case it arrived he would not be able to leave the harbor at all. As a matter of fact it was already too late to save all the ships; he therefore took only three, and with these just managed to make his escape before the arrival of the Portuguese. One of his gal-leys was wrecked near Bahrein, so he brought only two vessels back to Egypt. . . .

When this became known in Constantinople the command of the fleet had been given to Murad Bey. . . . He was ordered to leave two ships, five galleys, and one galleon at Basrah, and with the rest, i.e., 15 galleys (one galley had been burned in Basrah) and two boats, he was to return to Egypt. Murad Bey did start as arranged, but opposite Ormuz he came upon the Portuguese fleet, a terrible battle followed in which Suleiman Reis, Rejeb Reis, and several of the men, died a martyr's death. Many more were wounded and the ships terribly battered by the cannon-balls. At last, night put a stop to the fight. One boat was wrecked off the Persian coast, part of the crew escaped, the rest were taken prisoners by the infidels, and the boat itself captured.

When all this sad news reached the capital, toward the end of Zilhija of the said year 960 (1552), the author of these pages was appointed Admiral of the Egyptian fleet.

I, humble Sidi Ali bin Husein, also known as Kiatibi-Rumi [the writer of the West, i.e., of Turkey], most gladly accepted the post. I had always been very fond of the sea, had taken part in the expedition against Rhodes under the Sultan Suleiman, and had since had a share in almost all engagements, both by land and by sea. I had fought under Khaireddin Pasha, Sinan Pasha, and other captains, and had cruised about on the Western [Mediterranean] sea, so that I knew every nook and corner of it. I had written several books on astronomy, nautical science, and other matters bearing upon navigation. My father and grandfather, since the conquest of Constantinople, had had charge of the arsenal at Galata; they had both been eminent in their profession, and their skill had come down to me as an heirloom.

The post now entrusted to me was much to my taste, and I started from Aleppo for Basrah, on the first of Moharram of the year 961 (7 Dec. 1553). I crossed the Euphrates at Biredjik and when in Reka (i.e., Orfah), I undertook a pilgrimage to the tomb of Abraham. . . . [C]rossing the Euphrates near the little town of Wasib, I reached Kerbela (Azwie), where I made a pilgrimage to the graves of the martyrs Hasan and Husein. . . .

About What Happened in Basra

On the day after my arrival (February 1554) I had an interview with Mustafa Pasha, who, after seeing my credentials, made over to me the 15 galleys which were needing a great deal of repair. As far as could be, they were put in order, calked and provided with guns, which, however, were not to be had in sufficient quantity either from the stores there or from Ormuz. . . . [I]t was yet five months before the time of the monsoon. . . . One night I dreamed that I lost my sword, and as I remembered that a similar thing had happened to Sheik Muhieddin and had resulted in a defeat, I became greatly alarmed, and, just as I was about to pray to the Almighty for the victory of the Islam arms, I awoke. I kept this dream a secret, but it troubled me for a long time, and when later on Mustafa Pasha sent a detachment of soldiers to take the island of Huweiza (in which expedition I took part with five of my galleys), and the undertaking resulted in our losing about a hundred men all through the fickleness of the Egyptian troops, I fully believed this to be the fulfilment of my dream. But alas! there was more to follow—for "What is decreed must come to pass, No matter, whether you are joyful or anxious."

When at last the time of the monsoon came, the Pasha sent a trusty sailor with a frigate to Ormuz, to explore the neighborhood. After cruising about for a month he returned with the news that, except for four boats, there was no sign of any ships of the infidels in those waters. The troops therefore embarked and we started for Egypt.

What Took Place in the Sea of Ormuz

On the first of Shavval we left the harbor of Basrah, accompanied, as far as Ormuz, by the frigate of Sherifi Pasha. We visited on the way from Mehzari the grave of Khidr, and proceeding along the coast of Duspul (Dizful), and Shushter in Charik, I made pilgrimages to the graves of Imam Mohammed, Hanifi, and other saints. . . . I proceeded to Katif, situated near Lahsa and Hadjar on the Arabian coast. Unable to learn anything there, I went on to Bahrein, where I interviewed the commander of the place, Reis Murad. But neither could he give me any information about the fleet of the infidels.

Next we came to Kis, i.e., old Ormuz, and Barhata, and several other small islands in the Green Sea, i.e., the waters of Ormuz, but nowhere could we get any news of the fleet. So we dismissed the vessel, which Mustafa Pasha had sent as an escort, with the message that Ormuz was safely passed. We proceeded by the coasts . . . and forty days after our departure, i.e., on the tenth of Ramazan, in the forenoon, we suddenly saw coming toward us the Christian fleet, consisting of four large ships, three galleons, six Portuguese guard ships, and twelve galleys, 25 vessels in all. I immediately ordered the canopy to be taken down, the anchor weighed, the guns put in readiness, and then, trusting to the help of the Almighty, we fastened the lilandra to the mainmast, the flags were unfurled, and, full of courage and calling upon Allah, we commenced to fight. The volley from the guns and cannon was tremendous, and with God's help we sank and utterly destroyed one of the enemy's galleons. Never before within the annals of history has such a battle been fought, and words fail me to describe it.

The battle continued till sunset, and only then the Admiral of the infidel fleet began to show some signs of fear. He ordered the signal-gun to fire a retreat, and the fleet turned in the direction of Ormuz. With the help of Allah, and under the lucky star of the Padishah, the enemies of Islam had been defeated. Night came at last; we were becalmed for awhile, then the wind rose, the sails were set and as the shore was near . . . until daybreak. The next day we continued our previous course. On the day after we passed Khorfakan, where we took in water, and soon after reached Oman, or rather Sohar. Thus we cruised about for nearly 17 days. When on the sixth of Ramazan, i.e., the day of Kadr-Ghedjesi, a night in the month of Ramazan, we arrived in the vicinity of Maskat and Kalhat, we saw in the morning, issuing from the harbor of Maskat, 12 large boats and 22 gurabs, 32 vessels in all, commanded by Captain Kuya, the son of the Governor. They carried a large number of troops.

The boats and galleons obscured the horizon with their mizzen sails and Peneta all set; the guard-ships spread their round sails (Chember-yelken), and, gay with bunting, they advanced toward us. Full of confidence in God's protection we awaited them. Their boats attacked our galleys; the battle raged, cannon and guns, arrows and swords made terrible slaughter on both sides. The Badjoalushka penetrated the boats and the Shaikas and tore large holes in their hulls, while our galleys were riddled through by the Darda thrown down upon us from the enemy's turrets, which gave them the appearance of bristling porcupines; and they showered down upon us. . . . The stones which they threw at us created quite a whirlpool as they fell into the sea.

One of our galleys was set on fire by a bomb, but strange to say the boat from which it issued shared the like fate. God is merciful! Five of our galleys and as many of the enemy's boats were sunk and utterly wrecked, one of theirs went to the bottom with all sails set. In a word, there was great loss on both sides; our rowers were now insufficient in number to manage the oars, while running against the current, and to fire the cannon. We were compelled to drop anchor (at the stern) and to continue to fight as best we might. The boats had also to be abandoned.

. . . [C]aptains of some of the foundered ships . . . with the remainder of the Egyptian soldiers and 200 carpenters, had landed on the Arabian shore, and as the rowers were Arabs they had been hospitably treated by the Arabs of Nedjd. The ships (gurabs) of the infidel fleet had likewise taken on board the crews of their sunken vessels, and as there were Arabs amongst them, they also had found shelter on the Arabian coast. God is our witness. Even in the war between Khaiveddin Pasha and Andreas Doria no such naval action as this has ever taken place. When night came, and we were approaching the bay of Ormuz, the wind began to rise . . . we neared the shore while the galleys, dragging their anchors, followed. However, we were not allowed to touch the shore, and had to set sail again. During that night we drifted away from the Arabian coast into the open sea, and finally reached the coasts of Djash, in the province of Kerman. This is a long coast, but we could find no harbor, and we roamed about. . . . After unheard-of troubles and difficulties, we approached the harbor of Sheba.

Here we came upon a Notak, i.e, a brigantine, laden with spoils, and when the watchman sighted us they hailed us. We told them that we were Muslims, whereupon their captain came on board our vessel; he kindly supplied us with water, for we had not a drop left, and thus our exhausted soldiers were invigorated. . . .

Escorted by the said captain we entered the harbor of Guador. The people there were Beluchistanis and their chief was Malik Djelaleddin, the son of Malik Dinar. The Governor of Guador came on board our ship and assured us of his unalterable devotion to our glorious Padishah. He promised that henceforth, if at any time our fleet should come to Ormuz, he would undertake to send 50 or 60 boats to supply us with provisions, and in every possible way to be of service to us. . . .

What We Suffered in the Indian Ocean

God is merciful! With a favorable wind we left the port of Guador and again steered for Yemen. We had been at sea for several days, and had arrived nearly opposite to Zofar and Shar, when suddenly from the west arose a great storm known as fil Tofani. We were driven back, but were unable to set the sails, not even the trinquetla (stormsail). The tempest raged with increasing fury. As compared to these awful tempests the foul weather in the western seas is mere child's play, and their towering billows are as drops of water compared to those of the Indian sea. Night and day were both alike, and because of the frailty of our craft all ballast had to be thrown overboard. In this frightful predicament our only consolation was our unwavering trust in the power of the Almighty. For ten days the storm raged continuously and the rain came down in torrents. We never once saw the blue sky.

I did all I could to encourage and cheer my companions, and advised them above all things to be brave, and never to doubt but that all would end well. A welcome diversion occurred in the appearance of a fish about the size of two galley lengths, or more perhaps, which the pilot declared to be a good omen. The tide being very strong here and the ebb slow, we had an opportunity of seeing many sea-monsters in the neighbor-hood of the bay of Djugd, sea-horses, large sea-serpents, turtles in great quantities, and eels.

The color of the water suddenly changed to pure white, and at sight of it the pilot broke forth into loud lamentations; he declared we were approaching whirl-pools and eddies. . . . [I]t is generally believed that they are only found on the coasts of Abyssinia and in the neighborhood of Sind in the bay of Djugd, and hardly ever a ship has been known to escape their fury. So, . . . we drifted about all night and all day until at last, in God's mercy, the water rose, the storm somewhat abated, and the ship veered right round. . . .

Meanwhile, the wind had risen again, and as the men had no control over the rudder, large handles had to be affixed with long double ropes fastened to them. Each rope was taken hold of by four men, and so with great exertion they managed to control the rudder. No one could keep on his feet on deck, so of course it was impossible to walk across. The noise of the . . . and the . . . was deafening; we could not hear our own voices. The only means of communication with the sailors was by inarticulate words, and neither captain nor boatswain could for a single instant leave his post. The ammunition was secured in the storeroom, and after cutting the . . . from the . . . we continued our way.

It was truly a terrible day, but at last we reached Gujarat in India, which part of it, however, we knew not, when the pilot suddenly exclaimed: "On your guard! a whirlpool in front!" Quickly the anchors were lowered, but the ship was dragged down with great force and nearly submerged. The rowers had left their seats, the panic-stricken crew threw off their clothes, and, clinging some to casks and some to jacks, had taken leave of one another. I also stripped entirely, gave my slaves their liberty, and vowed to give 100 florins to the poor of Mecca. Presently one of the anchors broke from its crook and another at the podjuz; two more were lost, the ship gave a terrible jerk—and in another instant we were clear of the breakers. . . . So we commenced to examine the hold of the ship and found that the storeroom was submerged, in some places up to the walls, in some places higher still. We had shipped much water, and all hands set to work at once to bale it out. In one or two places the bottom had to be ripped up to find the outlet so as to reduce the water. . . .

What Happened in the Province of Gujarat

After five days, in God's mercy, the wind somewhat abated. All that was saved of the wreckage, cannon and other armament we left with the Governor of Daman, Malik Esed, who, since the time of Sultan Ahmed, the ruler of Gujarat, had held office there. In the harbor were some Junk's, i.e., monsoon ships belonging to Samiri, the ruler of Calcutta. The captains came on board our ship and assured us of the devotion of their chief to the Padishah [a superlative for the ruler, in other words Great Shah, in this case the Ottoman Sultan]. They brought us a letter which said that Samiri was waging war day and night against the Portuguese infidels, and that he was expecting the arrival of an Imperial fleet from Egypt under the guidance of the pilot Ali, which was to put the Portuguese to flight. Melik Esed, the Governor, gave me to understand that the fleet of the infidels was on its way, that it behooved us to avoid it and, if possible, to reach the fortress of Surat. This news frightened the crew. Some of them immediately took service under Melik Esed, and some went ashore in the boats and proceeded by land to Surat.

I remained on board with a few faithful of the men, and after procuring a Dindjuy, or pilot-boat, for each vessel, we set out for the harbor of Surat. After great difficulties we reached the open. Presently the Sutwal, Aga Hamsa, hailed us with a letter from Umad-el-mulk, the Grand Vizier of Sultan Ahmed, who informed us that there were large numbers of infidels about, and that Daman being a free port we had better be careful. He would allow us to come to Surat if we liked, as we were now in most perilous waters. This was exactly what we wanted to do, so we struggled on for five days longer, sailing at the flow, riding at anchor at the ebb of the tide, until at last we reached the harbor of Surat, fully three months after our departure from Basrah.

Great was the joy of the Mohammedans at Surat when they saw us come; they hailed us as their deliverers, and said: "You have come to Gujarat in troublous times; never since the days of Noah has there been a flood like unto this last, but neither is it within the memory of man that a ship from Rum has landed on these coasts. We fervently hoped that God in his mercy would soon send an Ottoman fleet to Gujarat, to save this land for the Ottoman Empire and to deliver us from the Indian unbelievers."

[[More disturbances occur in the complex political scene of Gujarat. There are assassination attempts against Seydi Ali Re'is as the Portuguese declare that they want him turned over, but eventually order is restored. The admiral returns to the Ottoman capital overland more than two years after selling the remainder of the fleet and leaving Gujarat in India.]]

Source: Seydi AliRe'is, *Mirror of Countries* in *The Sacred Books and Early Literature of the East*, Charles Francis Horne, ed. (New York: Parke, Austin, and Lipscomb, 1917), VI: 325–396.

10. AURELIO SCETTI, *JOURNAL OF AURELIO SCETTI: A FLORENTINE GALLEY SLAVE AT LEPANTO* (1565)

As in the Indian Ocean, so in the Mediterranean Sea imperial fleets clashed with one another. Aurelio Scetti had been a musician in Florence, when in 1565 his sentence to beheading for killing his wife was commuted to life in the galleys. These galleys were major weapons in the battle of imperial titans for control of the Mediterranean in the sixteenth and seventeenth centuries, but they were also places of suffering for those like Scetti condemned to man them. The Mediterranean was an arena for the war of empires and religions in those days, cutting into trading traditions across the Middle East, North Africa, and southern Europe. The Ottomans and Habsburgs ruling Spain, the Low Countries, and Austria came to blows and their agents— pirates and otherwise—damaged the lives of ordinary citizens who were captured and often enslaved into the galleys or domestic, sexual, and other service. The more important captives were ransomed by one side or another. The clashes were both small and large, the most significant being the Battle of Lepanto in 1571—costly in terms of lives and destruction on both sides. Here is Scetti's version of this legendary struggle among the Muslim Ottoman empire and the Catholic Spanish empire and allied powers for imperial control of the seas.

Each galley moved slightly away from the others, some on one side and some on the other, putting on stern lights to avoid collisions and stretching out the awnings while sailing, for fear of the rain. All the galleys sailed their way, using their oars and trying to continue on their own path with great pain, for the contrary winds made sailing very difficult. Aurelio, feeling particularly tired, since he was crippled and wet from the seawater and the rain, kept telling himself: "O father, if you could see me now, wouldn't you do your very best to beseech your lord and help me get out of this trouble? Dear God, move the heart of my prince so that he will take pity on me!" That night Aurelio's heart was heavy with tears and his sobbings were stronger than they had ever been before.

Sailing then towards Lepanto, with the sea and weather unfavorable, he [Don John of Austria, the illegitimate son of Charles V ruler of Spain, the Low countries, and Austria] was not afraid, but wanted to show the Turks his might. The next morning, at dawn, as he entered the sea between the mainland and the Curzolare Islands, on his way to the gulf of Lepanto, his watch on the mast spotted the Turkish fleet, which was sailing with favorable winds towards the Christians.

The Turks had left 30 *passacavalli* in Cyprus; they had sent to Modone six *maone* and seven galleys with two small ships that they had captured from the Venetians. They had also sent 25 galleys to Negroponte to support their fleet. They had a total of 225 *galere grosse* and four *brigantini*, as witnessed by the sailors of that fleet. As soon as they discovered the Christian ships, they divided their 225 galleys into four squadrons, as the Christians had previously done.

Meanwhile, His Highness Don John prepared for battle, according to the plan. He did not want the enemy to discover his rescue squadron before the start of the battle, so he left it near the mountain. He then boarded his *fregata* and ran along the ships of his fleet, exhorting the captains of the galleys and the infantry to fight courageously, doing the same for soldiers and sailors of the galleys. He told them that that was the day all Christendom should show its power by destroying that damned sect and achieving a great victory. Meanwhile the enemies were laughing at the Christians, saying that they were going to kill them all; they could not, however, see all the Christian ships. In fact, they kept mocking them just because they thought that the Christians had fewer galleys. As we said, after Caraguggia went to Messina to check on the number of the Christian galleys, he told Alì Bascià that the Christians had no more than 150 galleys, and failed to mention the *galeazze*. For this reason Alì Bascià kept mocking the Christians, saying: "This herd of Christian animals came here to be slaughtered by us!" And they were ordered to kill all Christians and avoid taking any prisoners.

The two fleets approached each other and eventually stopped. Don John fired his cannon, calling his enemies to fight. Alì Bascià answered with a shot, calling his squadron to battle. Then Uciali, a very experienced and astute corsair, reached the "Reale" and told Alì Bascià that it would be better not to fight, for, although the Christians seemed to be weak, in fact they were much stronger. Would he, please, look at the *maon* of Don John's squadron, and the other squadrons which had as many. Moreover, if he looked carefully, he would notice that there was another squadron behind, close to the mountain. If he decided to fight, he would not have as easy a victory as he thought. Alì Bascià did not want to listen, and told him that the *Gran Sultano* had ordered him to fight, and he was going to obey, with his own galleys, fighting as hard as he could. Hearing this answer, Uciali went back to his "Capitana." Then the "Capitana" of the *galeazze* of Don John's squadron approached with a mighty push of her oars, ahead of the squadron, and fired a cannon against the enemies. As a sign of God's will to give the victory to the Christians, that shot hit an enemy galley and sank it. When they saw this, the Christians started shouting very loudly: "Victory! victory!" and courageously pushed their galleys ahead and greeted the enemy with a furious volley of cannonballs and arquebuses.

[The battle continued, however.]

. . . Don John and *signor* Marcantonio, each with his own "Reale," hit at high speed the "Reale" of Alì Bascià, which had on board 300 janissaries ready to fight, all chosen from among the best in the galleys of their fleet.

When a violent battle started, many people died on both sides, in part because *signor* Gianandrea's squadron at first found itself separated from the others; he was in more trouble than the others, because the Turkish galleys, running away from the thick of the battle, attacked him. But he was wise enough not to get involved directly with any Turkish ship, but ran here and there, injuring the enemy. At this point the rescue squadron arrived, helping the wings that were more at risk. At that moment, if you could paint a picture of the shooting from the *galeazze*, you would portray a horrible and fierce scene of the Christians sinking this or that enemy galley, striking the Turks with such force that the Turks would have liked to be elsewhere. . . . In spite of that, Alì Basha's "Reale" kept defending itself with courage against our fury, . . . The Christians proved to be much stronger than their enemies, for in a short time they killed all the 300 janissaries. A terrific wrath overtook Alì Bascià. When he saw himself overwhelmed and his galley destroyed, he killed himself, slashing his own throat, choosing to die rather than to be taken prisoner by the Christians. But the astute and experienced Ucciali ran away with his 25 galleys, . . .

Since the Christians could not keep up with him, Uciali was saved for the Christians were still fighting to achieve a complete victory [and did not pursue him]. In fact, the crew of the Christian galleys was so inspired against these enemies of God that our captains had freed many prisoners from their chains so that they could fight. Several of them showed great courage that day, especially since they hoped, through their determination, to regain their freedom, as promised them by their captains, if they won that battle. Thus there was a high number of deaths among the Turks when the Christian prisoners jumped aboard the enemy ships, telling themselves: "Today either we die or we earn our freedom!" . . . Many of our prisoners who jumped aboard enemy ships were considering their own interest, for they feared being chained again. Others trusted the promises their captains had made to them and returned to their galleys.

That is what Aurelio did, for he trusted his captain's promise, God's help and his Prince's kindness, thinking: "It cannot be that after such a victory we will not get what we have been promised!"

Source: Aurelio Scetti, *Journal of Aurelio Scetti: A Florentine Galley Slave at Lepanto, 1565–1577*, Luigi Monga, trans. and ed. (Tempe: Arizona Center for Medieval and Renaissance Studies, 2004), 116–122.

11. TOYOTOMI HIDEYOSHI, MEMORANDUM ON THE KOREAN EXPEDITION (1582)

Attempts at empire could fail. At the same time as Lepanto, Toyotomi Hideyoshi (1536–1598), leader of Japan in the last third of the sixteenth century, was a self-made ruler, coming from low levels of society. Gradually through patronage, military success, and the ability to negotiate reforms, he unified the regions of Japan. In the process he became wealthy and powerful, full of ambitions for himself and his country. "I mean to do glorious deeds . . . and leave a great name behind me," he wrote to his wife. "I desire you to understand this and to tell it to everybody."[3] The drive to conquer foreign lands flourished in the sixteenth century, but in Hideyoshi's case dreams of empire did not lead to success. After making a successful landing in Korea in 1592 with a massive force of several hundred thousand men, he continued plotting his takeover of China—his ultimate ambition. On that occasion, he issued further instructions on how to proceed with that success—a success that never materialized as his forces were bogged down because of attacks by Korean guerrillas and Ming forces. In 1598 the Japanese began their withdrawal from the East Asian

---

[3]Sansom, George, *Japan. A Short Cultural History* (Palo Alto: Stanford University Press, 1952 (1931) 410.

mainland. What insights about empire can be drawn from Hideyoshi's plans and their failure?

[1] Your Lordship [Hidetsugu] must not relax preparations for the campaign. The departure must be made by the First or Second Month of the coming year.

[2] The Capital of Korea fell on the second day of this month. Thus, the time has come to make the sea crossing and to bring the length and breadth of the Great Ming under our control. My desire is that Your Lordship make the crossing to become the Civil Dictator of Great China.

[3] Thirty thousand men should accompany you. The departure should be by boat from Hyōgo. Horses should be sent by land.

[4] Although no hostility is expected in the Three Kingdoms [Korea], armed preparedness is of the utmost importance, not only for the maintenance of our reputation but also in the event of an emergency. All subordinates shall be so instructed. . . .

[The next thirteen items deal with supplying, equipping, and staffing the expeditionary force.]

[18] Since His Majesty is to be transferred to the Chinese capital, due preparation is necessary. The imperial visit will take place the year after next. On that occasion, ten provinces adjacent to the Capital shall be presented to him. In time instructions will be issued for the enfeoffment of all courtiers. Subordinates will receive ten times as much [as their present holdings]. The enfeoffment of those in the upper ranks shall be according to personal qualifications.

[19] The post of Civil Dictator of China shall be assigned, as aforementioned, to Hidetsugu who will be given 100 provinces adjacent to the Capital. The post of Civil Dictator of Japan will go to either the Middle Counsellor Yamato [Hideyoshi's half-brother], or to the Bizen Minister Hideyoshi's relative by marriage], upon declaration by either of his readiness.

[20] As for the position of Sovereign of Japan, the young Prince or Prince Hachijō shall be the choice.

[21] As for Korea, the Gifu Minister3 or Bizen Minister shall be assigned. In that event the Middle Counsellor Tamba shall be assigned to Kyūshū.

[22] As for His Majesty's visit to China, arrangements shall be made according to established practices for Imperial tours of inspection. His Majesty's itinerary shall follow the route of the present campaign. Men and horses necessary for the occasion shall be requisitioned from each country involved.

[23] Korea and China are within easy reach, and no inconvenience is anticipated for any concerned, high or low. It is not expected that anyone in those countries will attempt to flee. Therefore, recall all commissioners in the provinces to assist in preparation for the expedition. . . .

Source: Toyotomi Hideyoshi, "Memorandum on the Korean Expedition," in *Sources of Japanese Tradition*, Ryusaku Tsunoda, Wm. Theodore de Bary, and Donald Keene, eds. (New York: Columbia University Press, 1958), 318–319.

12. MANOEL SEVERIM DE FARIA, "SUGGESTION FOR HANDLING ORPHANS" (1655)

Empire gobbled up lives on all sides and thus had costs beyond financial ones. The hazards of sailing for ordinary hands and leaders of expeditions included not just death in battle but also sickness from lack of sanitation and scurvy and debilitation from lack of nourishment. Sailing in the early modern period brought accidents, including storms, lack of wind, and lethal encounters with rocks and other impediments in the ocean. Local peoples resisted incursions, slaughtering imperial invaders when they felt threatened. On board ship, deadly arguments and mutiny added to casualties. These conditions lasted almost as long as imperialism did. As empire took its toll, officials in tiny Portugal felt the lack of manpower early on in this age of overseas conquest. On the one hand, rulers and the middle classes with financial interests seemed impervious to the costs of empire in human lives; on the other there was a constant need to fill ships with unskilled and skilled labor. Additionally, empire drew people away from the home country, potentially causing population problems. In part, then, empire was also a quest for labor, often forced but sometimes free. Here is one proposal for righting the situation. How does this history of orphans fit into the history of state-building through empire?

In this regard it is convenient and of great value to Portugal, given the great multitude of foundlings and [male] orphans that exist in this Realm, who could be of great utility to the Republic, [if] raised in proper doctrine and placed in trades. It is more expedient to use this remedy in maritime regions, such as Lisbon, Setúbal, Porto, Viana, and in the Algarve; for in these [places], orphans and the abandoned once taken into custody could supply ships with cabin-boys, and swabbers for vessels, and sailors, all of whom there is a great shortage in this Realm. The proper teaching and training would be of great profit to our navigations, for there is a common lack of breeding geared toward men of the sea, as we have seen in so many shipwrecks and losses, of which there are many complaints. With this remedy we will also stop many of those who pretend to be poor, or who are vagabonds in this Realm, and they will occupy themselves in honest work. This will be of benefit to the Republic, and with this the number of residents in those locations would increase, and the population in the Realm.

This way of recruiting the orphans is so well-known that already in 1641 the members of the *Cortes* [the Portuguese parliament] asked His Majesty with these words: "It would be greatly advantageous that in the amassing of young orphans we recruit many boys, and that an amount be applied for their sustenance, for they will be taught the art of seafaring, with which there will always be an abundance of mariners, of whom there is a great lack in this Realm." [They gave] the example of the hospital that the Queen of Castile set up in Madrid to train boys to be mariners due to the existing shortage of them. And the response from His Majesty is that he would order that which they asked of him.

The same that has been said for the relief and remedy of orphaned boys can be said of orphaned girls. This is better yet, [because] much more care must be given to them, for lack of support is a greater danger to them, for women have much less means of making a living than men. Thus it is appropriate that a remedy be found for them, by applying all the means that can exist to have these [female] orphans of the people get married: for besides the great service [this will provide] to Our Lord by removing the occasion for them to disgrace themselves, we will attain our aim of increasing the number of people with the multiplication of marriages. The City of Milan, which is the most populous in Europe, serves as an example of this; one of the reasons for its growth is the dowry it provides each year to 800 [female] orphans. The same can be seen in the increase that the city of Seville has had for some years; for whereas much of it was caused by the commerce with the Indies, we can also attribute it to the marriages that take place each year of a great number of [female] orphans. In that city there are chapels . . . founded exclusively with large endowments to marry many [female] orphans: besides this there are many hospitals . . . that each marry many young women, and there are many more [public and private charities] that with the surplus from their revenues carry out this act of charity.

To put this means to work: we say that some portion of municipal revenues could be used, where a surplus exists, or some revenue from the head tax could be assigned to this, which income could be used solely for this pious work. We would also ask all municipal judges and officials that whenever they find money or bequests left to spend on pious works that were not named by the testators, they order [this money] spent entirely on these weddings. And likewise other similar things could be found for this purpose.

Source: An official for the bishop of Evora in Portugal. Severim de Faria, Manoel. *Noticias de Portugal*, 3rd ed., Darlene Abreu-Ferreira, trans. (Lisbon: Na Offic. De Antonio Gomes, 1791 [1655]), 57–63. Manoel Severim de Faria, "Manoel Severim de Faria, Noticias de Portugal [Book Excerpt]," in *Children and Youth in History*, Item #59, http://chnm.gmu.edu/cyh/primary-sources/59 (accessed February 12, 2013).

REVIEW QUESTIONS

1. What reasons for empire do these documents provide?
2. Describe the ways in which empires are connected.
3. What tensions and problems does empire create, both for individuals and societies?
4. Find an example of Indian cotton textiles before 1800 on the Internet and explain why they helped India prosper and led European states to wage trade wars. http://www.vam.ac.uk/content/exhibitions/the-fabric-of-india/about-the-exhibition/

CHAPTER 3

Competition for Empire Expands

In the late 1500s, the Netherlands, Britain, France, Denmark, and others seriously joined the quest to utilize if not control trade routes and to discover precious metals across the globe. Asian products and resources from the Western Hemisphere were more plentiful in European markets in the 1600s, but by then it was already evident that the Iberians had become wealthy because of their global reach. The first Europeans to venture out across the oceans, they were launched in many corners of the world by the 1520s when Protestantism started to become a divisive force. As Protestantism confronted Catholicism, the politics and expense of the conflict retarded a full-blown global undertaking, despite the lure of great rewards. In fact, Phillip II of Spain (1527–1598) was so wealthy from New World silver and gold that in 1588 he launched a massive armada of ships in order to defeat the Protestant Queen Elizabeth of England (1533–1603), whose own birth was part of the Protestant–Catholic divide.

Phillip's costly attempt was unsuccessful, but he continued to squander imperial wealth in persecuting other Protestants. Such efforts with little to show exposed Spain's weaknesses and provoked challenges to the Iberians across the globe. Elizabeth I of England began sponsoring voyages across the Atlantic, beyond those of fishermen and the adventurer John Cabot. In 1600, she chartered the East India Company to undertake business in the Indian Ocean and the seas of Southeast and East Asia. The Dutch also took advantage of Spanish vulnerabilities and followed suit, chartering its own East India Company in 1602 for imperial pursuit in the eastern stretches of the Indian Ocean and through the Strait of Malacca. These companies grew powerful, especially when they cornered trade and made deals to perform government tasks such as tax collecting. Some have called these companies states within states, because of the way they enforced their own political and economic rule just as a government would. The companies lasted several centuries, and under company rule overseas imperial systems often remained experimental until the companies failed. In the process, by the middle of the seventeenth century Dutch shipping became dominant as the country's wealth grew from imperial trade, replacing the Portuguese in the Indian Ocean and challenging everyone else in the Western Hemisphere. The entanglement of empires grew thicker.

Setting up companies for profitable expansion such as the Dutch, English, and French did, the fledgling European empires waged war among themselves and with local states—whether Native American, South African, or Indonesian. They were, like the Iberians, quick to use their main advantages—sailing technology that allowed for good weapons on board ship—against distant peoples but also against one another. The Iberians began their decline by neither keeping up technologically nor investing their wealth in the development of trade and manufacturing. There were other disadvantages that all of them faced, notably that inhabitants of Africa and Asia were more immune to a range of diseases. Even as they too fought one another, those local peoples were quick to build their own weaponry and sailing capacity. At the beginning, in fact, all across the Indian Ocean local traders often had ships that were far more capacious than were European vessels.

Mughals, Ottomans, and the Manchus—a powerful new group that eventually conquered China—were also advancing over the course of the sixteenth and seventeenth centuries and constantly engaged in warfare. The Mughals pushed southward toward the tip of the Asian subcontinent, while the Ottomans were driving into West Asia and across North Africa. Around the Mediterranean, they made alliances with local leaders in the fight against competition from European Christians. The Mediterranean remained a place of deadly struggle of Muslims against Christians, as coastal people and those traveling on ships remained fair game. On all sides, pirates captured, traded, enslaved, ransomed, and even executed rich and poor alike. After several decades of struggle against bandits and the Manchus—an ethnic group on its borders—the Chinese empire of the Ming collapsed in 1644. As with the collapse of old empires and the takeover by newcomers, the Manchu conquest was ragged. Adopting many Chinese customs, the Manchu mopped up resistance, pursuing an expansive policy westward that included putting down Ming loyalists, securing borders, and capturing millions of square miles filled with still other ethnic groups, the vast Qing empire—the name of the Manchu dynasty—came into being.

The English, as had the Spanish before them, found disease a potent weapon and a powerful enemy globally beginning with their North American settlements in 1607. The Chinese faced the same complex situation, being aided in their westward expansion by the lack of immunity of ethnic groups deep in the Asian interior to some of their illnesses. Yet the Manchus and Chinese soldiers working for them, like Europeans, were blocked by their own lack of immunity to malaria and yellow fever. For the Manchu armies these diseases meant high casualties when they attempted full control of Yunnan; for the Europeans the perils of malaria and yellow fever took a toll in the Caribbean, while in these early modern centuries they blocked settlements in the interior of sub-Saharan Africa and confined traders and adventurers to the coast.

The late sixteenth and seventeenth centuries were still times of violent trial and error in the forging of modern empires, even though almost a century had elapsed since the first settlements of the Iberians, the arrival of the Mughals, and the Ottoman expansion. In 1577–1580, Francis Drake made what was only the second circumnavigation of the globe, using the voyage to make geographical and navigational records and to capture Spanish treasure. Before this historical voyage, the pirate Drake had attacked Spanish strongholds, Iberian shipping, and mule trains to loot them, while on the circumnavigations he had killed mutineers and tangled with local people. Across the centuries, English seamen went out expressly to hunt for the regular Spanish convoys going back to Europe and to the Philippines but especially so from the mid-sixteenth into the seventeenth century. The English and other sailing peoples were so far behind in their quest for global wealth that simply capturing Spanish ships and stealing gold and silver became their way of catching up.

Soon, a range of books appeared to guide would-be adventurers, which is not that some such as Columbus had not scoured available sources of information a century earlier. In general, however, travel and advice books now abounded because most Europeans had little if any practical knowledge of the world. These books were prized and were widely circulated unrevised and even translated. They provided much-needed information about geography, the conditions for sailing, and the ways of inhabitants of distant lands. Though the Portuguese had early on controlled important points on the Indian Ocean coastline, their grip was weakening. Adventurers therefore sought facts about access to spices, textiles, and other goods and advice about how to prepare and conduct themselves to replace the Portuguese. In Brazil and the Caribbean the production of sugar expanded, opening up the possibility of wealth for striving Europeans and making data on climate and agricultural techniques crucial. They exchanged ideas on how to beat the competition in trade. In fact, would-be settlers and entrepreneurs needed details of every sort, as many of them were city folk or people without experience of farming, trading, or supplying themselves in distant regions.

Wherever attempts at expansion materialized, some local people continued to take note of new opportunities for trade and for providing service as intermediaries. As with the Incas and Aztecs, ruling families across the Eastern Hemisphere allied with Europeans for the political advantages it could bring them and their relatives. There were alliances of women with Europeans and other foreign representatives for sexual relations, the exchange of information and skills such as language acquisition, and for domestic services. It was also a common practice for children to be swapped in order to have translators, messengers, and possibly even spies. For example, in the 1520s Francisco Pizarro had exchanged boys from groups along the eastern South American coast; a century later, two young boys at Jamestown went to live with Native Americans, while similarly young Native Americans spent time in Jamestown.

Still, many people in the Western Hemisphere, across Asia, and along the West African coast were subjugated in a variety of ways with little reciprocity.

Conquered people often saw the invaders as inferior in their values and laws. In the face of imperial enforcement of new values, protest became violent rebellion. As labor shortages increased because of disease and violence toward Native Americans in the Western Hemisphere and as European lack of know-how became apparent, the Atlantic slave trade expanded, especially from the late sixteenth century onward. Slavery in fact flourished around the world—across the Sahara, in the Mediterranean, across Asia, and in the Western Hemisphere. At its beginning in the fifteenth century, enslavement of Africans by the Iberians was small compared to what it would become; by the early nineteenth century, the Atlantic slave trade stood out for its devastation of individuals, populations, and local life. It had brought some eleven million Africans to North and South America, the majority of them to the mines, sugar plantations, and other workplaces of the Spanish and Portuguese; a much smaller number went to North America. Conditions were horrendous and mortality was sky high. Such treatment was not only cruel but misplaced: As one historian has said, the Africans were "needed for their brains not their brawn," so ignorant were imperial adventurers of agricultural, mining, and manufacturing skills.

1. CORNELIS MATELIEFF DE JONGE, *DISCOURSE ON THE STATE AND TRADE OF THE INDIES* (1607)

Late in the sixteenth century, Dutch and other adventurers sailed to Southeast Asia in an attempt to discover Portuguese trade secrets and to embark upon the spice trade for the Netherlands. They surveyed the Indonesian islands and other oceanic areas, publishing informative accounts, and providing so much encouragement that the government authorized the creation of the Dutch East India Company. Ship captains' instructions went from picking up spices to the additional charge of waging war against Portuguese and Spanish ships and strongholds. The Dutch targeted those of the Spanish from whom they were striving to gain true independence and those of the Portuguese because of their stranglehold on Southeast Asian ports—especially that of Melaka. One authority in the forging of Dutch overseas policy was Admiral Cornelis Matelieff de Jonge (1569–1632), who first went to Southeast Asia in 1605 and fought the Portuguese there. He came up with the strategy for establishing permanent bases and for cornering trade in spices through what is today a common practice of dumping excess goods to drive out other competitors—in this case other Europeans. Would you describe the document as a program for trade or one for empire and why? The global entanglement of traders, speculators, and empires would only increase.

Surveying the state of our fatherland—where we are troubled by so great a war within the country, dealing with so powerful an enemy as Albert of Austria, who is supported by the House of Spain and his own House of Austria—I believe that we will not be able to sustain the cause of the East Indies by letting it be governed by the Gentlemen Directors alone. For I do not see that they will gain sufficient authority here in the Indies to bring the matter to a good end, since we are dealing with [the] Spanish and Portuguese. They started here over a hundred years ago and have taken root very firmly in the country, having many strongholds, a multitude of people and an established government, so that they can carry out all their business from a firmer ground than we can. We have to bring people from Holland half exhausted from the long journey, whereas they get them all fresh from their territories nearby. For although here in the Portuguese Indies they do not have enough people to manage their business and protect themselves from our nation's fleets, they nonetheless find it much easier to bring in people than we do, because the ships coming from Portugal only have to put the men ashore at Goa. From there their armadas are equipped which then are fresh again, just like the Spaniards arriving from Manila.

Therefore, if we want to do anything useful here in the Indies, we have to see to it that we obtain a place as well, where we can rest when we come from Holland. This will bring us much profit, such as the restoration of our people and ships in the first place, and secondly the increase of our reputation with the Indian princes and peoples who thus far do not place much trust in us, saying: "It's true that the Dutch are good people, better than Spanish and Portuguese, but what use is it? They come here in passing only, and once they have their ships full they leave again. Without help we are unable to defend ourselves against the Spanish and the Portuguese, who come and ruin us once the Dutch are gone because we have traded with them. The Spanish and Portuguese on the other hand protect us, and the Dutch (although they could overpower us) do not harm us even though we trade with the Spanish and Portuguese. Therefore, it is better for us to stay friends with the Portuguese: in that way, we are not destroyed completely."

These must be their deliberations, and moreover the Portuguese are doing their utmost to make it clear to the Indians that we do not have any power, but are just a disorganised people because we do not choose a permanent residence here in the Indies as they do. So we have to obtain one, or all our business is worth nothing.

The entire trade in the East Indies consists in the following parts.

1. Pepper, to be obtained at Banten, Johor, Patani, Kedah and Aceh.
2. Cloves, to be obtained at Ambon and the Malukus.
3. Nutmeg and mace, to be obtained at Banda.
4. The Cambay trade.
5. The Coromandel trade with pieces of cloth, and the Bengal trade, unknown so far.
6. The China trade, and attached to it Japan.

If these goods are not all in one party's hands, either those of the Portuguese or ours, we will ruin each other and give the goods a high price here in the Indies but a low price in Europe.

Now as regards to pepper: it is not well feasible for us to get it into our hands alone, for apart from the Portuguese the English sail to Banten as well, and they also have their house and factory there. The English are trading completely at ease while we wage war against the Portuguese, so that both they and the people of Banten are protected by us without having to bear any costs. It is not feasible either to make the king of Banten, who is still a child, make a solid decision to trade with us alone, or it would have to cost big money. Indeed, that would still achieve nothing, for I am convinced that he and all other Indian princes, no matter how strong a treaty they had made with us or anybody else, will break it as soon as they are in a bit of trouble or can make a better profit. Therefore, we should not aim for that, but try to ensure that the English do not obtain any other spices besides pepper, and that we bring pepper over as well, as ballast, putting such a price on it that they cannot make a profit on it, and that the other goods alone can give us our profit.

Getting all the nutmeg and mace into our hands is, in my view, something that can be achieved. To avoid having to take the island of Banda and build a fortress there (which, apart from the cost which is high, would give us a bad name with the Indian princes), one should take the matter in hand as follows.

The king of Makassar is a ruler mighty in people, who has a country rich in rice and all kinds of foodstuffs, so that Melaka's food mostly comes from his country; the same is true of Banda, where he sends rice every year. I would make an agreement with him and send three ships which would put ashore 200 men (combined with the Makassarese, that would be enough for Banda). We should also promise to help him take the land and to surrender it to him without claiming any of it for ourselves. We would make it a condition, however, that no one be allowed to come and take on cargo there but we, and that we purchase the mace and nutmeg from him at a certain price, namely the one current at this moment. I do not doubt that he would enter upon such an agreement, and then one could further stipulate that he build a house for us there at his expense, as big and strong as we wish, to keep our wares in it and to be secure from any attacks by enemies. We could then have it built at any location and as well-positioned as we liked, . . . As a consequence, a great enemy would have arisen for the Portuguese, and a great friend to us. One could make other conditions with him as well to secure the land, for example that he would take all Banda's nobility into his country and give them a place to live there, while bringing some of his own noblemen to Banda. That all the nobility would live in just one place on Banda, and that instead of the four or five cities there are now, a single city would be made, where we would have our house. That they— the people living in the country, that is—would be obliged to come to the market there every fortnight and deliver their goods to the factory. That as soon as the produce was harvested and treated, they would deliver them to the merchant and be paid immediately as well. To avoid the disorder of the great debts the Bandanese tend to incur and which they cannot pay afterward: that it would be forbidden to issue loans to each other, at a certain penalty. I believe that in this way, we would have Banda in our grip, and the king of Makassar bound to us in the best way.

Source: *Journal, Memorials and Letters of Cornelis Matelieff de Jonge: Security, Diplomacy and Commerce in 17th-Century Southeast Asia*, Peter Borschberg, ed. (Singapore: National University of Singapore, 2015), 335–342 passim.

2. INSTRUCTIONS FOR THE VIRGINIA COLONY (1606)

Britain, France, and other countries used corporations or companies to fund the expensive task of colonization. The English government issued charters to corporations which had gathered funds to sponsor ships, supplies, and colonists for developing trade or settlements. In the 1550s, it had issued a charter for the Muscovite Company to trade with Russia and somewhat later with the Levant Company to trade in the Middle East. The charter issued to a corporation of investors in 1606 was for colonies on the eastern shores of North America, including the colony ultimately established at Jamestown. Because most would-be colonists were entirely inexperienced as well as generally ignorant of the North American coast, explicit instructions served to educate and direct them in the interests of the business people financing the expedition. Despite these instructions, the establishment of European colonies such as Jamestown was tumultuous, their future uncertain. How would you evaluate the practicality of these directions as guidelines for empire?

As We Doubt not but you will have especial Care to Observe the Ordinances [i.e., the charter] set Down by the Kings Majestie and Delivered unto you under the privy Seal So for your better Directions upon your first Landing we have thought Good to recommend unto your care these Instructions and articles following. When it Shall please God to Send you on the Coast of Virginia, you shall Do your best Endeavour to find out a Safe port in the Entrance of Some navigable River, making Choise of Such a one as runneth farthest into the Land, and if you happen to Discover Divers portable Rivers, and amongst them any one that hath two main branches, if the Difference be not Great, make Choise of that which bendeth most toward the Northwest for that way shall You soonest find the Other Sea[.] When you have made Choise of the river on which you mean to Settle, be not hasty in Landing your Victuals and munitions but first Let Captain Newport Discover how far that River may be found navigable that you make Election of the Strongest, most Fertile and wholesome place for if you make many Removes besides the Loss of time You Shall greatly Spoil your Victuals and Your cask[s] and with Great pain transport it in Small boats But if you choose your place so far up as A Bark of fifty tuns will fleet then you may Lay all Your provisions a Shore with Ease, and the better Receive the trade of all the Countries about you in the Land and Such A place you may perchance find a hundred miles from the Rivers mouth, and the further up the better for if you sit Down near the Entrance Except it be in Some Island that is Strong by nature An Enemy that may approach you on Even Ground, may Easily pull You Out and if he be Driven to Seek You a hundred miles within the Land in boats, you shall from both sides of your River where it is Narrowest So beat them with Your muskets as they shall never be Able to prevail Against You. And to the end That You be not Surprised as the French were in Florida by Melindus and the Spaniard in the same place by the French you shall Do Well to make this Double provision first Erect a Little Sconce at the Mouth of the River that may Lodge Some ten men With Whom you Shall Leave a Light boat that when any fleet shall be in Sight they may Come with Speed to Give You Warning. Secondly you must in no Case Suffer any of the natural people of the Country to inhabit between You and the Sea Coast for you Cannot Carry Your Selves so towards them but they will Grow Discontented with Your habitation and be ready to guide and assist any Nation that Shall Come to invade You and if You neglect this You neglect Your Safety. When You have Discovered as far up the river as you mean to plant Your Selves, and Landed your victuals and munitions to the End that Every man may know his Charge you Shall Do well to Divide your Six Score men into three parts whereof one party of them you may appoint to fortifie and build of which your first work must be your Storehouse for Victual 30 Others you may imploy in preparing your Ground and Sowing your Corn and Roots the Other ten of these forty you must Leave as Centinel at the havens mouth The Other forty you may imploy for two Months in Discovery of the River above you and on the Country about you which Charge Captain Newport and Captain Gosnold may undertake[.] of these forty Discoverers when they Do Espie any high Lands or hills Captain Gosnold may take 20 of the Company to Cross Over the Lands and Carrying a half Dozen pickaxes to try if they Can find any mineral. The Other twenty may go on by River and pitch up boughs upon the Banks Side by which the Other boats Shall follow them by the Same turnings You may also take with them a Wherry Such as is used here in the Thames by Which you may Send back to the President for supply of munition or any Other want that you may not be Driven to Return for Every Small Defect.

You must Observe if you Can Whether the River on which you Plant Doth spring out of Mountains or out of Lakes[;] if it be out of any Lake the passage to the Other Sea will be more Easy and it is Like Enough that Out of the same Lake you shall find Some Spring which run the Contrary way toward the East India Sea for the Great and famous Rivers of Volga, Tan[a]is and Dwina have three heads near joynd and Yet the One falleth into the Caspian Sea the Other into the Euxine Sea and the third into the Polonian Sea. In all Your Passages you must have Great Care not to Offend the naturals if You Can Eschew it and imploy Some few of your Company to trade with them for Corn and all Other lasting Victuals if you [they?] have any and this you must Do before that they perceive you mean to plant among them for not being Sure how your own Seed Corn will prosper the first Year to avoid the Danger of famine use and Endeavour to Store yourselves of the Country Corn. Your Discoverers that passes Over Land with hired Guides must Look well to them that they Slip not from them and for more Assurance let them take a Compass with them and Write Down how far they Go upon Every point of the Compass for that Country having no way nor path if that Your Guides Run from You in the Great Woods or Deserts you Shall hardly Ever find a Passage back. And how Weary Soever your Soldiers be Let them never trust the Country people with the Carriage of their Weapons for if they Run from You with Your Shott, which they only fear they will Easily kill them all with their arrows And whensoever any of Yours Shoots before them be sure they be Chosen out of your best Markesmen for if they See Your Learners miss what they aim at they will think the Weapon not so terrible and thereby will be bould to Assault You. Above all things Do not advertize the killing of any of your men that the Country people may know it if they Perceive they are but Common men and that with the Loss of many of theirs they Deminish any part of Yours they will make many Adventures upon You if the country be populous[.] you Shall Do well also not to Let them See or know of Your Sick men if you have any which may also Encourage them to many Enterprizes. You must take Especial Care that you Choose a Seat for habitation that Shall not be over burthened with Woods near your town for all the men You have Shall not be able to Cleanse twenty acres in a Year besides that it may Serve for a Covert for Your Enimies round about You[,] neither must You plant in a low or moist place because it will prove unhealthful[.] You shall Judge of the Good Air by the People for Some part of that Coast where the Lands are Low have their people blear Eyed and with Swollen bellies and Legs but if the naturals be Strong and Clean made it is a true sign of wholesome Soil. You must take Order to Draw up the Pinnace that is Left with You under your fort and take her Sails and Anchors A Shore all but a Small Kedge [i.e., a small anchor] to ride by Least Some ill Disposed Persons Slip away with her. You must take Care that your Mariners that Go for wages Do not mar your trade for those that mind not to inhabite for a Little Gain will Debase the Estimation of Exchange and hinder the trade for Ever after and there fore you Shall not admit or Suffer any person whatsoever other than Such as Shall be appointed by the President and Councel there, to buy any Merchandizes or Other things whatsoever. It Were Necessary that all Your Carpenters and Other such like Workmen about building Do first build Your Storehouse and those Other Rooms of Publick and necessary Use before any house be Set up for any private person and though the Workman may belong to any private persons yet Let them all Work together first for the Company and then for private men And Seeing order is at the same price with Confusion it shall be adviceably done to Set your houses Even and by a line that You[r] Streets may have a Good breadth and be carried Square about your market place and Every Streets End opening into it that from thence with a few feild peices you may Command Every street throughout which marketplace you may also fortify if you think it needful. You Shall do well to Send a perfect relation by Captain Newport of all that is Done of what height you are Seated how far into the Land what Commodities you find what Soil Woods and their Several Kinds and so of all Other things Else to advertise particularly and to Suffer no man to return but by pasport from the president and Councel nor to write any Letter of any thing that may Discourage others. Lastly and Chiefly the way to prosper and Obtain Good Success is to make yourselves all of one mind for the Good of your Country and your own and to Serve and fear God the Giver of all Goodness for every Plantation which our heavenly father hath not planted shall be rooted out.

Source: University of Groningen, Department of Humanities Computing http://odur.let.rug .nl/~usa/D/1601-1650/virginia/chart02.htm see also, Library of Congress, American Memory Project, Thomas Jefferson Papers Series 8, Virginia Records Manuscripts, 1606-1737, Records of the Virginia Company, Volume I http://lcweb2.loc.gov/cgi-bin/ampage?collId=mtj8&fileName=mtj8pagevc01 .db&recNum=358

3. FERNANDES VIEIRA, INSTRUCTIONS ON HOW TO MANAGE A SUGAR MILL AND ESTATE (1663)

The production of sugar moved globally with the movement of empires. From South Asia, Muslim conquerors installed sugar plantations on Mediterranean islands and to some degree in Spain several centuries before Iberian settlement in the Western Hemisphere. The Spanish and Portuguese then transported sugar first to the Atlantic islands closest to Europe and then to the "new world" as part of their quest for wealth: Cortes, for example, set up sugar production in Mexico; later in the sixteenth century the Portuguese grew wealthier than all others through their huge sugar enterprises in Brazil and remained so until the English and French developed the sugar industry in the Caribbean. Brazilian sugar production was usually associated with forced labor, both of local people and of imported slaves from Africa. While both resident and absentee owners grew rich, the processing of sugar was one of the most dangerous jobs for slaves. Because of the wealth involved and the ignorance of Europeans in the processing and management, instructions for managing a sugar plantation were crucial not just for the owner's profits but for securing empire. How exactly do these instructions for the administration of private enterprise fit into the history of empire?

Regiment that the Administrator of the Engenho [[sugar mill]][should follow to satisfy his obligations and unburden his conscience, and doing otherwise, he must explain himself to God and is obliged to give restitution to the owner of the estate.

Confess the Slaves [*negros*] – He will be obligated every year to order everyone under his control to confess each Sunday and on saint's days, and he will order them to hear mass, and the children born he will order to be baptized in their time, and if any sick slave [is] in need of a confessor, he will send for one, and every Saturday and at night he will order the slaves to be instructed in their prayers.

Slaves Who Become Ill – As the blacks become ill, he will try to heal their bodies and provide whatever is lacking on the estate, and if the illness is dangerous, he will send the slave to the person who handles my affairs in Recife, if he believes that the slave cannot be cured on the estate.

Housing the Slaves – He will be obligated to go each morning to the slave quarters to see if the slaves are ill and to provide to them anything that is lacking and he will require that their houses be well swept with their sleeping platforms and mats in order; and he will require them to plant their gardens on saint's days and when the engenho is not milling, he will give them Saturdays for their planting in the winter.

Punishing the Slaves – Punishment of slaves should not be done with a stick nor should slaves be struck with rocks or bricks but when deserving of punishment, they should be tied to an oxcart and punished with a whip, and after being well-lashed, they should be cut with a razor or knife and then treated with salt, lemon juice, and urine and then placed for some days in chains; and if it is a woman being punished, she will be whipped in a shirt of baize and it should be done inside a house [privately] with the same whip.

Rationing the Slaves – In the winter, he should not awake the slaves before daybreak for any reason and only after daylight he should give them their ration of cane juice when it is available without fail.

Care with Slave Fights – He will take the greatest care to prevent hatreds among the slaves to prevent them from killing each other and try to promote friendships and when this does not occur, they should be sent to another estate. He should not permit them to eat meat of animals that have died and must be especially careful when oxen have died that they do not eat them.

Care for the Sick – When slaves develop a fever, he should wait forty-eight hours before ordering them bled. He should try to relieve them of the illness and get rid of it by ordinary means; and he should ask them what they have eaten or drunk in order to see if poison may be involved, and he should take them promptly to someone who knows about these things to see if they should be bled. And if a swelling of any kind appears and there is a suspicion that it may be a carbuncle, he should send the slave immediately to the house of Baltesar Leitão de Vasconcelos on my behalf to do me the favor of curing him. In similar cases, avoid using Master João or barbers because they do not know how to cure this and often have said it is a carbuncle and have killed the slave.

Count the Slaves – the slaves should be counted every day and those missing found by all means.

Care of the Oxen – He will take great care with the ox herd of the estate and send them to pasture with the best herdsmen and count the herd each day and look immediately for any that are missing. In the same manner, cure them of any illness or infestation [*bicheira*] that they may have and take care that those that work one day do not work the next and he will pay attention that they do not suffer the work too greatly and that young oxen are broken in slowly and prepared for the carts so that all are ready to work. To each cart, man give two, three, or four teams of oxen according to their availability so that each carter knows the teams he has to work, and he who holds the office of captain or the cart men should have all needed to control them, and whoever disobeys him should be punished.

Visit the Woodlands – He will be obliged to visit the woods of the estate and defend them, to go there and see where the boundary markers are placed and not allow anyone to remove wood without permission; and to know this, he should have the woods inspected each week by an overseer or a slave of his confidence, and if anyone is found cutting wood, he should seize their tools and stop them from transporting the wood, and if they are caught a second time, a complaint of theft should be initiated with justice officials.

Visit the Waterworks – The same obligations apply to inspect the water tanks (*açudes*) and channels and keep all in good repair as necessary and he should never trust only in ordering that this be done but in going himself to make sure it is done.

Take Charge of the Firewood – When firewood is prepared for the mill, he must turn over a measure of six palms high by six palms wide and twelve palms in length and he will go every week to see the firewood that is prepared and that it is of the proper measure and mix of thick and thin pieces and even if there is an assistant overseer assigned this task, the administrator will do this to make sure.

Source: Stuart B. Schwartz, ed., *Early Brazil, A Documentary Collection to 1700* (Cambridge: Cambridge University Press, 2010), 224–226.

4. RICHARD LIGON, *A TRUE AND EXACT HISTORY OF THE ISLAND OF BARBADOS* (1657)

Instructions such as the Charter of 1606 promoted the formation of colonial communities, but individuals also needed guidance in participating in distant enterprises. Richard Ligon (1585–1662) was on the losing side in the English civil war, leading him to seek his fortune in the sugar islands in 1647. From hard experience in Barbados, which he left in 1650, he wrote a major book describing the island and its enterprises, mostly sugar, of which, as he described, the first planters knew virtually nothing. For would-be adventurers, his history of and guide to Barbados provided warnings and practical advice for migrating whether to become a planter or a merchant. Such works assisted the tens of thousands of Europeans, ever growing in number, who were ignorant of the terrain they would be entering and had only heard from promoters of the quick riches awaiting them.

The voluptuous nor lazy persons are not Fit to inhabit on this Island

Some men I have known in England, whose bodies are so strong and able to endure cold, as no weather fits them so well as frost and snow; such Iron bodies would be for a Plantation in Russia: For, there is no traceing Hares under the Line, nor sliding on the Ice under either Tropick. Others there are that have heard of the pleasures of Barbadoes, but are loath to leave the pleasures of England behind them. These are of a sluggish humour, and are altogether unfit for so noble an undertaking; but if any such shall happen to come there, he shall be transmitted to the innumerable Armie of Pismires, and Ants, to sting him with such a reproof, as he shall with himselfe any where rather then amongst them. So much is a sluggard detested in a Countrey, where Industry and Activity is to be exercised. . . .

The Voluptuous man, who thinks the day not long enough for him to take his pleasure. Nor the sleepie man who thinks the longest night too short for him to dreame out his delights, are not fit to repose and solace themselves upon this Iland; . . .

Such may here find moderate delights, with moderate labour, and those taken moderately will conduce much to their healths, and they that have industry, to imploy that well, may make it the Ladder to clyme to a high degree, of Wealth and opulencie, in this sweet Negotiation of Sugar, provided they have a competent stock to begin with; such I mean as may settle them in a Sugar-work, and lesse then £ 4000 sterling, will not do that: in a Plantation of 500 acres of land, with a proportionable stock of Servants, Slaves, Horses, Camels, Cattle, Assinigoes, with an Ingenio, and all other houseing, thereunto belonging; such as I have formerly nam'd.

The value of a Plantation Stock't, of five hundred acres of Land, whereof two hundred for Canes, to be sold for £14000 . . .

But one wil say, why should any man that has £ 14000 in his purse, need to runne so long a Risco [risk], as from hence to the Barbadoes: when he may live ith ease and plenty at home: to such a one I answer, that every drone can sit and eate the Honey of his own Hive: But he that can by his own Industry, and activity, (having youth and strength to friends,) raise his fortune, from a small beginning to a very great one, and in his passage to that, doe good to the publique, and be charitable to the poor, and this to be accomplished in a few years, deserves much more commenda-tion and applause. And shall find his bread, gotten by his painfull and honest labour and industry, eate sweeter by much, than his that onely minds his ease, and his belly.

How this purchase of £14000 by providence and good husbandry, may be made with £3000

Now having said this much, I hold it my duty, to give what directions I can, to further any one that shall go about to improve his stock, in this way of Adventure; and if he please to hearken to my directions, he shall find they are no Impos-sibilities, upon which I ground my Computations: the greatest will be, to find a friend for a Correspondent, that can be really honest, faithful and Industrious, and having arriv'd at that happinesse, (which is the chiefest,) all the rest will be easie; and I shall let you see that without the help of Magick or Inchantment, this great Purchase of £ 14000 will be made with £ 3000 stock, and thus to be ordered.

One thousand pound, is enough to venture at first, because we that are here in England, know not what commodities they want most in the Barbadoes, and to send a great Cargo of unnecessary things, were to have them lye upon our hands to losse. This £ 1000, I would have thus laid out: £ 100 in Linnen Cloth, as Canvas and Kentings, which you may buy here in London, of French Marchants, at rea-sonable rates; and you may hire poor Journy-men Taylers, here in the Citty, that will for very small wages, make that Canvas into Drawers, and Petticoats, for men and women Negres. And part of the Canvas, and the whole of the Kentings, for shirts and drawers for the Christian men Servants, and smocks and peticoates for the women. Some other sorts of Linnen, as Holland or Dowlace, will be there very usefull, for shirts and smocks for the Planters themselves, with their Wives and Children. One hundred pounds more, I would have bestow'd, part on wollen cloath, both ne and coarse, part on Devonshire Carsies, and other fashionable stuffes, such as will well endure wearing. Upon Monmoth Capps I would have bestowed £25 you may bespeak them there in Wales, and have them sent up to London, by the waynes at easie rates. Forty pound I think fit to bestow on Irish Ruggs [a garment] such as are made at Killkennie, and Irish stockings, and these are to be had at St. James's faire at Bristow; the stockings are to be worne in the day, by the Christian servants, the Ruggs to cast about them when they come home at night, sweating and wearied, with their labour; to lap about them, when they rest themselves on their Hamacks at night, than which nothing is more needfull, for the reasons I have formerly given. And these may either be shipt at Bristow, if a ship be ready bound for Barbadoes, or sent to London by waynes which is a cheap way of conveyance. Fifty pound I wish may be bestowed on shooes, and some bootes, to be made at Northampton and sent to London in dry fatts, by Carts; but a speciall care must be taken, that they may be made large, for they will shrink very much when they come into hot Climats. They are to be made of severall sises, for men women and children; they must be kept dry and close, or else the moistnesse of the Ayre will cause them to mould. Gloves will sell well there, and I would have of all kinds, and all sises, that are thinne; but the most usefull, are those of tann'd leather, for they will wash and not shrinke in the wetting, and weare very long and soople; you may provide your selfe of these, at Evill, Ilemister and Ilchester, in Somerset-shire; at reasonable rates. Fifteen pound I would bestow in these Commodities. In fashionable Hats and Bands, both black and coloured, of severall sises and qualities, I would have thirty pounds bestowed. Black Ribbon for mourning, is much worn there, by reason their mortality is greater; and therefore upon that commodity I would bestow twenty pound; and as much in Coloured, of severall sises and colours. For Silkes and Sattins, with gold and silver-Lace, we will leave that alone, till we have better advice; for they are casuall Commodities.

Having now made provision for the back, it is fit to consider the belly, which having no ears, is to be done for, then talkt to; and therefore we will do the best we can, to fill it with such provisions, as will best brook the Sea, and hot Climates: Such are Beefe, well pickled, and well conditioned, in which I would bestow £100 in Pork £50, in Pease for the voyage, £10 in Fish, as Ling, Haberdine, Green-fish, and Stock-fish, £40 in Bisket for the voyage, £10 Cases of Spirits, £40 Wine, £150 Strong Beer, £50 Oyle, Olive £30, Butter £30. And Candles must not be forgotten, because they light us to our suppers, and our beds.

The next thing to be thought on, is Utensills, and working Tooles, such are whip-Sawes, two-handed Sawes, hand-Sawes, Files of severall sises and shapes; Axes, for felling and for hewing; Hatchets, that will fit Carpenters, Joyners, and Coopers; Chisells, but no Mallets, for the wood is harder there to make them: Adzes, of severall sises, Pick-axes, and Mat-hooks; Howes of all sises. butchiefly small ones, to be used with one hand, for with them, the small Negres weed the ground: Plains. Gouges. and Augurs of all sises; hand-Bills, for the Negres to cut the Canes; drawing-Knives, for Joyners. Upon these Utensills I would bestow £60. Upon Iron, Steel, and small Iron pots. for the Negres to boyl their meat, I would bestow £40. And those are to be had in Southsex very cheap, and sent to London in Carts, at time of year, when the waies are drie and hard. Nailes of all sorts, with Hooks, Hinges, and Cramps of Iron; and they are to be had at Bromigham in Staffordship, much cheaper then in London. And upon that Commodity I would bestow £30. In Sowes[1], of Lead £20, in

---

[1] "bars"

Powder and Shot £20. If you can get Servants to go with you, they will turn to good accompt, but chiefly if they be Trades-men, as, Carpenters, Joyners, Masons, Smiths, Paviers, and Coopers. The Ballast of the Ship, as also of all Ships that trade there, I would have of Sea-coales, well chosen, for it is a commodity was much wanting when I was there, and will be every day more and more, as the Wood decayes: The value I would have bestowed on that, is £50 which will buy 45 Chauldron, or more, according to the burthen of the Ship. And now upon the whole, I have outstript my computation of £145 but there will be no losse in that; for, I doubt not, (if it please God to give a blessing to our endeavours) but in twelve or fourteen months, to sell the goods, and double the Cargo; and, if you can stay to make the best of your Market, you may make three for one.

This Cargo, well got together, I could wish to be ship't in good order, about the beginning of November, and then by the grace of God, the Ship may arrive at the Barbadoes (if she make no stay by the way) about the middle of December; and it is an ordinary course to sail thither in six weeks: Comming thither in that cool time of the year, your Victualls will be in good condition to be removed into a Store-house, which your Correspondent (who, I account, goes along with it) must provide as speedily as he can, before the Sun makes his return from the Southern Tropick; for then the weather will grow hot, and some of your Goods, as, Butter, Oyle, Candles, and all your Liquors, will take harme in the remove.

The Goods being stowed in a Ware house, or Ware houses, your Correspondent must reserve a handsome room for a Shop, where his servants must attend; . . .

Source: Richard Ligon, *A True and Exact History of the Island of Barbados* (London: Humphrey Moseley, 1657). Available as an e-book, *A True and Exact History of the Island of Barbados*, 1657, David C. Smith, ed. http://media.wix.com/ugd/f295da_e1cc09fda4524e6aab26e7e904e43a30.pdf

5. "OATH OF ALLEGIANCE RUSSIANS ADMINISTERED TO BRATSK NATIVE LEADERS" (1642)

Economics drove the enlargement of the Russian empire too. Tsar Ivan IV (1530–1584) expanded Russian boundaries by conquering the Kazan Khanate—a division of Chinggis Khan's heritage and then by directing further expansion into Siberia. In 1582, the Cossack Yermak Timofeevich led some 900 fighters down the riverways into the heart of Siberia where he defeated regional forces. This drive, begun a century earlier, then took the Russians to the Pacific into the seventeenth century. There young warriors were awarded land and peasants rushed to the opening of new territory—the century's most extensive land-based, trade and agricultural expansion. The impetus for this takeover also came from merchants and trappers already operating on the Siberian borders, but without government protection. Like the fur traders advancing from many corners of Europe on the hunting lands of local people, they were eager for a protected market in the sable, beaver, and other pelts that the nomadic hunters could provide. The central government made provision for handing pelts over in the oath that the leaders of conquered peoples were forced to take so that the monarchy too could profit. In what ways is this oath important to the development of empire? Or is it unimportant?

I, Bului, a man of the Bratsk tribe, hereby give my firm oath of allegiance to my Sovereign Tsar and Grand Prince Mikhail Fedorovich, Autocrat of all Russia, and to his Sovereign Lordship, the Tsarevich and Grand Prince Aleksei Mikhailovich. I, Bului, and my brother Bura and our other brothers and tribesmen, and all my ulus [local/community] people, swear on our faith, by the sun, by the earth, by fire, by the Russian sword, and by guns, that we will come under His Tsarist Majesty's mighty authority, in eternal servitude, without treason, undeviatingly, for all time. I will serve my Sovereign in every way, loyally and gladly.

I will not commit any treason against his Sovereign servitors or against any other Russians or against his Sovereign people in the Verkholensk ostrozhek, or against agricultural settlers, in any places where the Sovereign's servitors and Russians may be working, nor will I come in war or in secret to kill them or harm them or commit treason against them. Neither I, Bului, personally, nor my brother, nor any of my ulus people will incite other hostile Bratsk people to commit treason against the Sovereign's people, nor incite them or guide them to come to kill.

Likewise, I, Bului, will encourage other Bratsk leaders and their ulus people to come under His Tsarist Majesty's mighty hand in eternal servitude and to pay iasak and pominki to the Sovereign, in large amounts and in full every year, for themselves and for their brothers, and in every way to be in complete concord with the Sovereign's people.

When the Sovereign's men come to collect Iasak [fur tribute] in my ulus, I will protect them, and will not allow them to be killed. If any Bratsk leaders and their ulus people become disloyal to the Sovereign, then I, Bului, will report about these disloyal persons to the Sovereign's prikaschiks [representative in charge of goods] in Verkholensk ostrog [community center], and I will join the Sovereign's forces in war against these disloyal people, and will try to pacify them by means of war and bring them back under your Sovereign Tsarist mighty hand, and will collect iasak from them for the Sovereign.

If I, Bului, do not carry out all these promises for my Sovereign Tsar, the Grand Prince Mikhail Fedorovich of all Russia, and for the Lord Tsarevich and Grand Prince Aleksei Mikhailovich, as written in this document, and if I do not serve loyally for all time, and gladly, or if I commit any treason against the Sovereign's servitors and go to war against the Russian people near Verkholensk ostrog, or against the agricultural settlers, or in other places where the Sovereign's people may come, or if I commit murder, or do not pay iasak in full for myself and for all my ulus people, or if I commit some foolish act, then, in accordance with my faith, the sun will not shine on me, Bului, I will not walk on the earth, I will not eat bread, the Russian sword will cut me down, the gun will kill me, and fire will destroy all our uluses on our land.

And if I commit treason, the final punishment will be that the Sovereign's anger will be loosed on me and I will be put to death without mercy and without pity.

Source: *Medieval Russia: A Source Book, 850–1700*, Basil Dmytryshyn, ed., 3rd ed. (Fort Worth: Harcourt Brace Jovanovich, 1991), 345–346.

6. MANCHU HEAD-SHAVING DECREE (1644)

Other aspects of imperial rule had little obvious connection to economics and much more to do with domination. The Mughals in their conquest of India and the Ottomans in their expansion across North Africa generally did not demand uniformity of behavior even as they took over entire communities. Initially at least, they often allowed pluralism, even marveling at some buildings, culture, and customs of those they conquered. The Manchus who gradually took over China over the course of the seventeenth century did the same, using Chinese soldiers and officers, adopting the examination system for government officials and promoting the study of Chinese classics. Still, enforcing some of their own ways was central to signaling imperial power in empires, as in this decree about hair styles. Europeans, somewhat later, would try to force Native Americans, Africans, and Asians to adopt Western dress. Compare the decree below to other forms of imperial domination.

The various decrees relating to head shaving have been purposefully inconsistent in some respects in order to meet a variety of situations that once all of China is pacified, a decree will be issued to end all the inconsistencies. Now that all of China has become one family, it is mandatory that the emperor and his subjects be united as one, as a subject's disloyalty to his emperor can no more be tolerated than that of a son to his own father. To be otherwise is to regard the emperor and his subjects as strangers to each other—an absurdity so obvious that you must know it fully well without any of my elaborations.

It is therefore decreed that within ten days after this public announcement all the men in the capital and its adjacent areas must shave their heads and that all the men in the provinces must shave their heads within ten days after the arrival of this announcement in their respective provinces. Only those who shave their heads are to be considered loyal subjects of this empire; those who hesitate or refuse to do it are to be regarded as traitors and will be punished severely. No excuses for evasion, however cunning or clever, are to be tolerated.

It is further decreed that all the local officials, civilian as well as military, must see to it that the above order relating to head shaving is to be implemented without fail and that any official who is impudent enough to petition the government to delay or relax the enforcement of this order will be condemned to death without mercy. The same penalty will also be imposed upon those officials who are impudent enough to petition the government for the maintenance of those Ming customs that are at variance with those of the present dynasty. However, a reasonable length of time will be allowed for people to change from their old Ming attire to that of the present dynasty. From now on all people in China must obey the laws of this dynasty, and defiance in whatever form is not to be tolerated.

The Board of Rites is hereby ordered to proclaim this decree in all the provinces, districts, and other administrative units, as well as the capital and its adjacent areas, to assure its observance by all officials, civilian as well as military, teachers, and students, and all other people in the empire.

Source: David G. Atwill and Yurong Y. Atwill, *Sources in Chinese History: Diverse Perspectives from 1644 to Present* (Upper Saddle River: Pearson, 2010), 6.

7. DZENGSEO, "MY SERVICE IN THE ARMY" (1680)

Despite expansion and policies to establish imperial rule, rebellions were legion and vast unconquered areas remained to be brought under imperial control. For the Manchus and their young Kangxi emperor, conquering the South and Southwest of China (and soon the adjacent regions to the northwest) became a major undertaking. In this undertaking that took years, imperial soldiers faced disease and fatigue, with huge casualties from malaria and yellow fever striking down as many or more than did the weapons of the resisters. The excerpt from the unique diary of a Manchu soldier in these years also shows the toll taken from a hot, humid climate and swampy but also mountainous terrain—all in the cause of imperial expansion. Because modern imperialists were most often from the global north invading the global south, these particular vulnerabilities provided those being invaded some small protection until the late nineteenth century when quinine and improved sanitary measures became available.

[January 31, 1680]

On the twelfth we received a written order to advance, and set out. Because the road was a cramped pass in a narrow mountain ravine, and because of the swampy rice fields, the march was extremely hard and distressing and the horses' loads fell off or got stuck. We proceeded [in this way] for eight nights, covering 290 li [a Chinese unit of distance varying over the centuries, now c. 1640 feet].

[February 7]

On the nineteenth we were ordered not to drink the water of the Badu river because there was a bad smell. In a message sent by Hife and others it was ordered that gifts should be entrusted to the officers to be delivered in person [by them] to the Field Marshal. After this order reached our Banner Ganduhai handed [the gifts] over to me and I presented them.

[February 8]

On the twentieth we set out from Yanyangtang and marched through a forest where sunlight could not be seen. After marching in close order for 15 li we set up camp.

[February 18]

On New Year's Day of the twentieth year of Kangxi, year of the White-Gray Rooster, we left Xilongzhou, and built a pontoon bridge [across the Badu River]. One could see that the river water looked greenish, the current was fast, and the track on the bank of the river, along the mountainside, was only two feet wide. Soldiers and horses were all pressed one against the other in a single row. We had not proceeded 10 li when it became dark. Because it was impossible to find a [suitable] place to camp, we pitched our tents in the sand on a bend of the river. The sand was being lifted up in the wind. We bought a few pints of water and spirits, and one pig to celebrate the New Year. In my heart I felt sad and disconsolate and, longing for my old people, I wept under the blanket. The Field Marshal issued an order: "The road is narrow; there is no place to set up the encampment. Pitch the tents one after the other as you see fit." We brought in some local people and questioned them [about the road]. They replied: [In this place] since ancient times there has never been a road for a marching army. After the hangsi festival, peacocks, snakes, and worms fill the river. Because the river is muddy, when the water overflows the road becomes submerged and people cannot get through. If they are struck by foul vapors, they will die. Therefore we build our houses on the top of the mountain. Upon observation, one could often detect movements on the riverbed and in the branches of trees. On the next day we departed and, as soon as night started to fall, we filed into a place where only one or two tents could stand, and set up camp.

[February 25]

Not until the eighth we reached and set camp at Bandunteng. Squeezed tight, we stopped at Shimen Ridge for eight days. Then we were ordered to cover the road with grass when marching.

[March 4]

On the fifteenth we set out again, and because it was raining and hailing lightly, we strapped leather and iron cleats [to our shoes] and walked on foot on the narrow mountain road for 15 li. Then we set up camp at the foot of Shimen Ridge.

[March 5]

On the sixteenth crawling and slipping along the way, we climbed up to the first level of Shimen Ridge. We spread grass on the slippery moss, and fetching the horses one by one, we crossed with great effort that swampy and hideous place. One could see that many horses had fallen into the precipice and died. The men's feet were covered with blisters, and could not go any further. After we had walked for 3 li it was getting dark. Staggering and stumbling, we struggled on crossing over the rock layer of the second ridge, and set up camp. One could see one by one the bodies of the rebels who had been killed.

[March 6]

On the seventeenth we marched 20 li on foot. With aching feet we struggled to cross over the third level ridge, where we rejoiced for being able to ride horses [again]. So we proceeded [on horseback] until we reached Anlongsuo.

[March 22]

On the third day we rested. When officers and soldiers were reassigned and squadrons were formed Ganduhai assigned me again to the first squadron.

[March 23]

On the fourth we marched for 40 li, and then set up camp at night.

[March 24]

On the fifth we marched 40 li and crossed the Huangni River.

[March 25]

On the sixth we climbed over a mountain ridge and, marching overnight, covered 30 li.

[March 26]

On the seventh, as we were climbing on foot the great mountain ridge of Yunnanbao, a formidable wind rose, and because the sand was getting into our eyes, it became impossible to proceed. Having marched 30 li, it got dark for the night, and a heavy fog rose up.

[March 27]

On the eighth [still] a strong wind blew, and it was impossible to open our eyes because of the dust. We passed Yizuo county covering 60 li.

[May 24]

On the seventh I fell ill with fever. The Generalissimo Conqueror of the South Mujan came to Yunnan from Guizhou at the head of a force of two soldiers from each company.

[June 20]

On the fifth of the fifth month [we] built a two-layer wall rampart around Yunnanfu. After a very heavy rain our camp was flushed away by the water, and there was no place to pitch [our] tents. My illness grew worse. Since my servant had also taken ill, the Hanjun Adjutant Li Dezan had me carried to his tent. . . .

[July 20]

On the sixth day of the sixth month it was reported that Provincial Commander Sangge had inflicted a crushing defeat on the rebel general Ma Bao. The servants of the soldiers of the Beise and the Green Standard soldiers went to the Desheng Bridge, on the outskirts [of the city], to collect plum-tree stakes.

When they went to pull down the houses [to get the timber], over 300 of them were cut off [and captured] by the rebels inside the city. Because the people besieged had nothing to eat, over 400 men, women, and children came venturing out of the suburbs. The Field Marshal established their price, and then sold them to the wounded soldiers of the Eight Banners. On the same day a loud noise was heard from inside the ramparts. With effort [due to the illness] I got up to see [what had happened]. An enemy patrol coming down from the mountain had captured our servants who had gone out to collect grass.

[October 16]

On the sixth of the ninth month, upon examination, those among the servants and the armored soldiers who were weak and could not proceed further were allowed to stop. The officers and soldiers who were ill or disabled were also

examined. All the corpses of dead officers and soldiers were removed by one officer from each wing and five armored soldiers from each banner. Then [the bodies]
were sent to the capital.
[October 19]

On the ninth Lieutenant-general Jihari died. Heroic Strategist General Zhao
Liangdong and others, with a force of three soldiers from each company and
20,000 Green Standard troops, arrived in Yunnan from the prefectural city of
Suiyi, in Sichuan. Looking at them, their faces showed an emaciated complexion, and many soldiers were on foot. Asked about their condition, they replied
that they had had nothing to eat, had been struck by foul vapors, and people and
horses had become ill and died in great numbers.

Source: *The Diary of a Manchu Soldier in Seventeenth-Century China*, Nicola di Cosma ed. and trans.
(London: Routledge, 2006), 59, 61–62, 64, 68, 69, 70.

8. MI'KMAQ OBSERVATIONS ON THE FRENCH (1677)

*Local peoples took any occasion to report their reactions to newcomers, whether from
northeast Asia, Anatolia, or Europe. A Mi'kmaq leader in Newfoundland expressed
his opinion of Catholic missionaries and of the French adventurers, who flocked to
Canada to establish bases for trading furs. Other Native Americans used competition among the French and English across North America by allying with one side or
another and showing skill in diplomatic maneuvering. There was little acquiescence
to empire or easy acceptance of imperial values in their case. None of the northern
European would-be empires had a solid foothold on the North American continent
at the time. How do you interpret Mi'kmaq comments on the French way of life?*

I am greatly astonished that the French have so little cleverness, as they seem
to exhibit in the matter of which thou hast just told me on their behalf, in the
effort to persuade us to convert our poles, our barks, and our wigwams into those
houses of stone and of wood which are tall and lofty, according to their account,
as these trees. Very well! But why now, . . . do men of five to six feet in height need
houses which are sixty to eighty? For, in fact, as thou knowest very well thyself,
Patriarch—do we not find in our own all the conveniences and the advantages
that you have with yours, such as reposing, drinking, sleeping, eating, and amus-
ing ourselves with our friends when we wish? This is not all, . . . my brother, hast
thou as much ingenuity and cleverness as the Indians, who carry their houses and
their wigwams with them so that they may lodge wheresoever they please, independently of any seignior whatsoever? Thou art not as bold nor as stout as we,
because when thou goest on a voyage thou canst not carry upon thy shoulders thy
buildings and thy edifices. Therefore it is necessary that thou preparest as many
lodgings as thou makest changes of residence, or else thou lodgest in a hired house
which does not belong to thee. As for us, we find ourselves secure from all these
inconveniences, and we can always say, more truly than thou, that we are at home

everywhere, because we set up our wigwams with ease wheresoever we go, and without asking permission of anybody. Thou reproachest us, very inappropriately, that our country is a little hell in contrast with France, which thou comparest to a terrestrial paradise, inasmuch as it yields thee, so thou sayest, every kind of provision in abundance. Thou sayest of us also that we are the most miserable and most unhappy of all men, living without religion, without manners, without honour, without social order, and, in a word, without any rules, like the beasts in our woods and our forests, lacking bread, wine, and a thousand other comforts which thou hast in superfluity in Europe. Well, my brother, if thou dost not yet know the real feelings which our Indians have towards thy country and towards all thy nation, it is proper that I inform thee at once. I beg thee now to believe that, all miserable as we seem in thine eyes, we consider ourselves nevertheless much happier than thou in this, that we are very content with the little that we have; and believe also once for all, I pray, that thou deceivest thyself greatly if thou thinkest to persuade us that thy country is better than ours. For if France, as thou sayest, is a little terrestrial paradise, art thou sensible to leave it? And why abandon wives, children, relatives, and friends? Why risk thy life and thy property every year, and why venture thyself with such risk, in any season whatsoever, to the storms and tempests of the sea in order to come to a strange and barbarous country which thou considerest the poorest and least fortunate of the world? Besides, since we are wholly convinced of the contrary, we scarcely take the trouble to go to France, because we fear, with good reason, lest we find little satisfaction there, seeing, in our own experience, that those who are natives thereof leave it every year in order to enrich themselves on our shores. We believe, further, that you are also incomparably poorer than we, and that you are only simple journeymen, valets, servants, and slaves, all masters and grand captains though you may appear, seeing that you glory in our old rags and in our miserable suits of beaver which can no longer be of use to us, and that you find among us, in the fishery for cod which you make in these parts, the wherewithal to comfort your misery and the poverty which oppresses you. As to us, we find all our riches and all our conveniences among ourselves, without trouble and without exposing our lives to the dangers in which you find yourselves constantly through your long voyages. And, whilst feeling compassion for you in the sweetness of our repose, we wonder at the anxieties and cares which you give yourselves night and day in order to load your ship. We see also that all your people live, as a rule, only upon cod which you catch among us. It is everlastingly nothing but cod—cod in the morning, cod at midday, cod at evening, and always cod, until things come to such a pass that if you wish some good morsels, it is at our expense; and you are obliged to have recourse to the Indians, whom you despise so much, and to beg them to go a-hunting that you may be regaled. Now tell me this one little thing, if thou hast any sense: Which of these two is the wisest and happiest—he who labours without ceasing and only obtains, and that with great trouble, enough to live on, or he who rests in comfort and finds all that he needs in the pleasure of hunting and fishing? It is true, . . . that we have not always had the use of bread and of wine which your France produces; but, in fact, before the arrival of the French in these parts, did not the Gaspesians [Native Americans of the Gaspé Peninsula in present-day Canada] live much longer than now? And if we have not any longer among us any of those old men of a hundred and thirty to forty years, it is only because we are gradually adopting your manner of living, for experience is making it very plain that those of us live longest who, despising your bread, your wine, and your brandy, are content with their natural food of beaver, of moose, of waterfowl, and fish, in accord with the custom of our ancestors and of all the Gaspesian nation. Learn now, my brother, once for all, because I must open to thee my heart: there is no Indian who does not consider himself infinitely more happy and more powerful than the French.

Source: Chrestien LeClerq, *New Relation of Gaspesia, with the Customs and Religion of the Gaspesian Indians*, William F. Ganong, ed. and trans. (Toronto: Champlain Society, 1910), 104–106. Reprinted with permission of the Champlain Society.

9. "DECLARATION OF THE INDIAN JUAN" (1681)

Colonized people often adapted by merging aspects of imperial culture with their own beliefs and behaviors. Devotion to "Our Lady of Guadelupe" developed around a version of the Virgin Mary garbed in Aztec clothing enlivened with Aztec design. They also devised well-organized protests besides the everyday modifications they gained in conditions of work through negotiation or small obstructive acts. In the 1670s, Pueblo Indians in the North American Southwest met increased Spanish demands amid difficult agricultural conditions with outbursts of violence against officials and priests. In 1680, however, they organized a mass rebellion, executing priests and officials who had tried to replace Pueblo religious rituals with Catholic ones and whose very presence had brought death and disease. Some eighty percent of the Pueblo population had died since the Spanish invasion. The Spanish finally put down the uprising, but they were forced to lessen their demands and loosen the grip of priests on communities. Here is one Pueblo version given at an official Spanish investigation of the independence movement.

Declaration of Pedro Naranjo of the Queres Nation. December 1, 1681.

. . . on the said day, month, and year, for the prosecution of the judicial proceedings of this case his lordship caused to appear before him an Indian prisoner named Pedro Naranjo, a native of the pueblo of San Felipe, of the Queres nation, who was captured in the advance and attack upon the pueblo of La Isleta. He makes himself understood very well in the Castilian language and speaks his mother tongue and the Tegua. He took the oath in due legal form in the name of God, our Lord, and a sign of the cross, under charge of which he promised to tell the truth concerning what he knows. . . .

Asked whether he knows the reason or motives which the Indians of this kingdom had for rebelling, forsaking the law of God and obedience to his Majesty, and committing such grave and atrocious crimes, and who were the leaders and principal movers, and by whom and how it was ordered; and why they burned the images, temples, crosses, rosaries, and things of divine worship, committing such atrocities as killing priests, Spaniards, women, and children, and the rest that he might know touching the question, he said that since the government of Senor General Hernando Ugarte y la Concha they have planned to rebel on various occasions through conspiracies of the Indian sorcerers, and that although in some pueblos the messages were accepted, in other parts they would not agree to it; and that it is true that during the government of the said senor general seven or eight Indians were hanged for this same cause, whereupon the unrest subsided. Some time thereafter they [the conspirators] sent from the pueblo of Los Taos through the pueblos of the custodia two deerskins with some pictures on them signifying conspiracy after their manner, in order to convoke the people to a new rebellion, and the said deerskins passed to the province of Moqui, where they refused to accept them. The pact which they had been forming ceased for the time being, but they always kept in their hearts the desire to carry it out, so as to live as they are living to-day. Finally, in the past years, at the summons of an Indian named Pope who is said to have communication with the devil, it happened that in an estufa [an underground assembly room of the Pueble] of the pueblo of Los Taos there appeared to the said Pope three figures of Indians who never came out of the estufa. They gave the said Pope to understand that they were going underground to the lake of Copala. He saw these figures emit fire from all the extremities of their bodies, and that one of them was called Caudi, another Tilini, and the other Tleume; and these three beings spoke to the said Pope, who was in hiding from the secretary, Francisco Xavier, who wished to punish him as a sorcerer. They told him to make a cord of maguey fiber and tie some knots in it which would signify the number of days that they must wait before the rebellion. He said that the cord was passed through all the pueblos of the kingdom so that the ones which agreed to it [the rebellion] might untie one knot in sign of obedience, and by the other knots they would know the days which were lacking; and this was to be done on pain of death to those who refused to agree to it. As a sign of agreement and notice of having concurred in the treason and perfidy they were to send up smoke signals to that effect in each one of the pueblos singly. The said cord was taken from pueblo to pueblo by the swiftest youths under the penalty of death if they revealed the secret. Everything being thus arranged, two days before the time set for its execution, because his lordship had learned of it and had imprisoned two Indian accomplices from the pueblo of Tesuque, it was carried out prematurely that night, because it seemed to them that they were now discovered; and they killed religious, Spaniards, women, and children. This being done, it was proclaimed in all the pueblos that everyone in common should obey the commands of their father whom they did not know, which would be given through El Caydi or El Pope. This was heard by Alonso Catiti, who came to the pueblo of this declarant to say that everyone must unite to go to the villa to kill the governor and the Spaniards who had remained with him, and that he who did not obey would, on their return, be beheaded; and in fear of this they agreed to it. Finally the senor governor and those who were with him escaped from the siege, and later this declarant saw that as soon as the Spaniards had left the kingdom an order came from the said Indian, Pope, in which he commanded all the Indians to break the lands and enlarge their cultivated fields, saying that now they were as they had been in ancient times, free from the labor they had performed for the religious and the Spaniards, who could not now be alive. He said that this is the legitimate cause and the reason they had for rebelling, because they had always desired to live as they had when they came out of the lake of Copala.

Asked for what reason they so blindly burned the images, temples, crosses, and other things of divine worship, he stated that the said Indian, Pope, came down in person, and with him El Saca and El Chato from the pueblo of Los Taos, and other captains and leaders and many people who were in his train, and he ordered in all the pueblos through which he passed that they instantly break up and burn the images of the holy Christ, the Virgin Mary and the other saints, the crosses, and everything pertaining to Christianity, and that they burn the temples, break up the bells, and separate from the wives whom God had given them in marriage and take those whom they desired. In order to take away their baptismal names, the water, and the holy oils, they were to plunge into the rivers and wash themselves with amole, which is a root native to the country, washing even their clothing, with the understanding that there would thus be taken from them the character of the holy sacraments. They did this, and also many other things . . .

Source: Charles Wilson Hackett, ed., and Charmion Clair Shelby, trans., *Revolt of the Pueblo Indians of New Mexico and Otermin's Attempted Reconquest, 1680–1682* (Albuquerque: University of New Mexico Press, 1942), 9: 247–248. Also available on Wisconsin Historical Society, www.americanjourneys.org/aj-009.

10. CHIEFS OF THE SIX NATIONS, *THE LAWS OF THE CONFEDERACY* (1900)

Empire-building invaders often marveled at the economic or political sophistication of the peoples they aimed to take over even as they came to call them "savages" to justify their own violence. The Confederacy of Iroquois nations in present-day upstate New York had been established before the arrival of the French, Dutch, and English in the region as a way of ending a cycle of retribution among individuals and individual nations and of maintaining a union of peace. The set of laws and procedures for keeping peace grew from the dilemma of Hiawatha (Hayenwatha) who did not want to engage in such a killing and his meeting with the Huron lawgiver Deganawidah who helped find a permanent solution to the system. Handed down through a sturdy oral tradition, the Laws of the Confederacy were first written down in the mid-nineteenth century, but they were wellknown to framers of the U.S. Constitution such as

Benjamin Franklin who asked "could not a dozen or so colonies" follow the Iroquois lead.[2] This excerpt is from a written version of 1900. How do the values expressed in this document differ from those of empire builders?

Then Dekanahwideh again said: "We have completed the Confederation of the Five Nations, now therefore it shall be that hereafter the lords who shall be appointed in the future to fill vacancies caused by death or removals shall be appointed from the same families and clans from which the first lords were created, and from which families the hereditary title of lordships shall descend."

Then Dekanahwideh further said: "I now transfer and set over to the women who have the lordships' title vested in them, that they shall in the future have the power to appoint the successors from time to time to fill vacancies caused by death or removals from whatever cause."

Then Dekanahwideh continued and said: "We shall now build a confederate council fire from which the smoke shall arise and pierce the skies and all nations and people shall see this smoke. And now to you, Thadodahho, your brother and cousin colleagues shall be left the care and protection of the confederate council fire, by the Confederate Nations."

Then Dekanahwideh further said: "The lords have unanimously decided to spread before you on the ground this great white wampum belt Skano-dah-ken-rah-ko-wah and Ka-yah-ne-renh-kowah, which respectfully signify purity and great peace, and the lords have also laid before you this great wing, Ska-weh-yeh-seh-ko-wah, and whenever any dust or stain of any description falls upon the great belt of white wampum, then you shall take this great wing and sweep it clean." (Dust or stain means evil of any description which might have a tendency to cause trouble in the Confederate Council.)

Then Dekanahwideh said: "The lords of this confederacy have unanimously decided to lay by you this rod (Ska-nah-ka-res) and whenever you see any creeping thing which might have a tendency to harm our grandchildren or see a thing creeping toward the great white wampum belt (meaning the Great Peace), then shall take this rod and pry it away with it, and if you and your colleagues fail to pry the creeping, evil thing out, you shall then call out loudly that all the Confederate Nations may hear and they will come immediately to your assistance."

Then Dekanahwideh said: "Now you, the lords of the several Confederate Nations, shall divide yourselves and sit on opposite sides of the council fire as follows: You and your brother colleagues shall sit on one side of the council fire (this was said to the Mohawks and the Senecas), and your sons, the Oneidas and Cayugas, shall sit on the opposite side of the council fire. Thus you will begin to work and carry out the principles of the Great Peace (Ka-yah-ne-renh-ko-wah)

---

[2]Quoted in Colin G. Calloway, *First Peoples: A Documentary Survey of American Indian History*, 4th ed. (Boston: Bedford/St. Martins, 2012), 57.

and you will be guided in this by the great white wampum belt (Ska-no-dah-ke-rah-ko-wah) which signifies Great Peace."

Then Dekanahwideh said: "You, Thadodahho, shall be the fire keeper, and your duty shall be to open the Confederate Council with praise and thanksgiving to the Great Ruler and close the same."

Then Dekanahwideh also said: "When the council is opened, Hahyonhwatha and his colleagues shall be the first to consider and give their opinion upon any subject which may come before the council for consideration, and when they have arrived at a decision, then shall they transfer the matter to their brethren, the Senecas, for their consideration, and when they, the Senecas, shall have arrived at a decision on the matter then they shall refer it back to Hahyonhwatha and his colleagues. Then Hahyonhwatha will announce the decision to the opposite side of the council fire.

"Then Ohdahtshedeh and his colleagues will consider the matter in question and when they have arrived at a decision they will refer the matter to their brethren, the Cayugas, for their consideration and after they have arrived at a decision, they will refer the matter back to Ohdahtshedeh and his colleagues. Then Ohdahtshedeh will announce their decision to the opposite side of the council fire. Then Hahyonhwatha will refer the matter to Thadodahho and his colleagues for their careful consideration and opinion of the matter in question and if Thadodahho and his colleagues find that the matter has not been well considered or decided, then they shall refer the matter back again to the two sides of the council fire, and they shall point out where, in their estimation, the decision was faulty and the question not fully considered, and then the two sides of the council will take up the question again and reconsider the matter, and after the two sides of the council have fully reconsidered the question, then Hahyonhwatha will again refer it to Thadodahho and his colleagues, then they will again consider the matter and if they see that the decision of the two sides of the council is correct, then Thadodahho and his colleagues will confirm the decision."

Then Dekanahwideh further said: "If the brethren of the Mohawks and the Senecas are divided in their opinion and can not agree on any matter which they may have for their consideration, then Hahyonhwatha shall announce the two decisions to the opposite of the council fire. Then Ohdahtshedeh and his brother colleagues, after they have considered the matter, and if they also are divided in their decision, shall so report, but if the divided factions each agree with the decision announced from the opposite side of the council, then Ohdahtshedeh shall also announce their two decisions to the other side of the council fire; then Hahyonhwatha shall refer the matter to Thadodahho and his colleagues who are the fire keepers. They will fully consider the matter and whichever decision they consider correct they will confirm."

Then Dekanahwideh said: "If it should so happen that the lords of the Mohawks and the lords of the Senecas disagree on any matter and also on the opposite side of the council fire, the lords of the Oneidas and the lords of the Cayugas disagree among themselves and do not agree with either of the two decisions of the opposite side of the council fire but of themselves give two decisions which are diverse from each other, then Hahyonhwatha shall refer the four decisions to Thadodahho and his colleagues who shall consider the matter and give their decision and their decision shall be final."

Then Dekanahwideh said: "We have now completed the system for our Confederate Council."

Then Dekanahwideh further said: "We now, each nation, shall adopt all the rules and regulations governing the Confederate Council which we have here made and we shall apply them to all our respective settlements and thereby we shall carry out the principles set forth in the message of Good Tidings of Peace and Power, and in dealing with the affairs of our people of the various dominions, thus we shall secure to them contentment and happiness."

Then Dekanahwideh again said: "We shall now combine our individual power into one great power which is this confederacy and we shall therefore symbolize the union of these powers by each nation contributing one arrow, which we shall tie up together in a bundle which, when it is made and completely tied together, no one can bend or break."

Then Dekanahwideh further said: "We have now completed this union by securing one arrow from each nation. It is not good that one should be lacking or taken from the bundle, for it would weaken our power and it would be still worse if two arrows were taken from the bundle. And if three arrows were taken any one could break the remaining arrows in the bundle."

Then Dekanahwideh said: "We have now completed our power so that we the Five Nations' Confederacy shall in the future have one body, one head and one heart."

Then he (Dekanahwideh) further said: "If any evil should befall us in the future, we shall stand or fall united as one man."

Source: Arthur C. Parker, *The Constitution of the Five Nations or The Iroquois Book of the Great Law* (Albany, NY: University of the State of New York, 1916), No. 184, 97–113.
Colin G. Calloway, *First Peoples: A Documentary Survey of American Indian History*, 4th ed. (Boston, MA: Bedford/St. Martins, 2012), 58–61.

11. EVLIYA ÇEBILI, NARRATIVE OF TRAVELS (1850)

Evliya Çebili Çelebi was born into a prosperous and well-connected Ottoman family in c. 1611. He might have advanced its well-being further because his extensive education made him successful at the court. His father, for example, had been court jeweler. Evliya, however, wanted to travel and be an observer of places and people. In fact, he traveled across the empire, employed by several patrons and recounting its riches. Threats in the form of uprisings against imperial conditions also appear, especially as inflation and the high cost of maintaining an empire took a bite out of ordinary people's daily budget. He went to places the Ottomans had conquered or hoped to subdue, even fighting in the war to capture Vienna. Evliya's detailed accounts are said to be inaccurate, but this has not stopped historians from using them extensively because of

their descriptions of the Islamic faith, of conditions across the empire, and their histo-
ries of Ottoman struggles and enormous successes. Reading of Ottoman wealth makes
for an interesting comparison with imperial conditions elsewhere—in Jamestown or
the East Indies, for example. What comparisons does this document encourage?

Súleimán was brought up at Trebisonde [city on the Black Sea], which has been
the seat of four Ottoman Emperors. In remembrance of his youth spent here, he
sent his mother to this place and raised it to a separate province. . . .

The whole [garrison] including the officers amounts to three thousand men.
They hold villages and land on condition that they should go to war under the
command of the Páshá, which if they do not they forfeit their leases.

Description of the Mosques.

In the centre of the castle was an old Christian church, Mohammed H. having conquered the town in the year 865, turned the mihráb (niche in wall of mosque] from
the east towards the Kiblah. Its mihráb and minber [stairs for preaching) are of
ancient workmanship, and on the east side is an oratory (mahfil) of most elegant
carving. The wood is cypress, nut, and box; it is always closed, and reserved entirely
for the Emperor's use. There are besides three other mahfils or oratories supported
by pillars in this mosque, where people are also allowed to pray when there is a great
crowd. It has two gates, an elegant mináreh and cells for students in the courtyard
outside; it is covered with lead. In the west suburb are also four mosques, and two
in the eastern; the mosque of the tower castle is a beautiful structure with a mináreh
much ornamented. The mosque of Khatúnieh was built by the mother of Selím I. who
was born here, it is extremely well endowed, the market called Púlta-bazárí belongs
to its foundation, with many cultivated villages. The cupola is illuminated by candles
every night, its elegant mináreh pierces the sky. The gate and walls of this mosque are
built of black polished stone, and white marble, in alternate rows; it was built in the
year 920. The mosque of Súleimán Beg on the west of the mosque of Khatúnieh, but
at a mile distance from it on the place of Kawák, has one mináreh covered with lead.

Description of the Scientific Colleges, Baths, Market-places, &c.

Outside of the courtyard of the mosque of the middle castle is the college of
Mohammed II. with a great number of cells and students. There is a general lec-
ture (Dersí-a'ám), the lecturer holds the degree of a Molla; it is a mine of poets,
and meeting-place of wits. The college of Katúnieh is adorned with cells on four
sides; the students receive fixed quantities of meat and wax for their subsistence.
The college of Iskender Páshá on the north side of the mosque, that bears the
same name, is richly endowed with stipends for the students. The reading-houses
of Trebisonde are those of the middle castle, at the mosque of Mohammed II. . . .

The abecedarian schools for boys are that of Mohammed II in the middle
castle; the school of the new mosque, a school so blessed, that a boy who has been
taught here to read the Bismillah (in God's name!) cannot fail to be a learned

man; the elegant school of Khatúnich on the west side of the mosque is built of stone, with a cupola, where orphans are supplied with mental and bodily food, with dresses on great festivals and presents besides.

There is a pleasant double bath for the use of both sexes, in the middle castle near the gate which leads to the lower castle.

The bath of the tower is on the north wall of the innermost or tower castle; it is a single one, and is said to have existed in the time of the Infidels. The bath of the Imáret, built by Khatúnieh mother of Selím I. The bath of the lower castle is a single one, that of Iskender Páshá is double; the bath of the Infidels is between the New Friday quarter and the Infidels' place. . . . There are besides at Trebisonde two hundred and forty-five private baths, and a great number of Kháns.

Description of the Principal Arts and Handicrafts.

The goldsmiths of Trebisonde are the first in the world. Selím I. being brought up in this town was taught the art of a goldsmith, and cut dies for the coin of his father Báyazíd, so skilfully, that they appeared as if engraved in marble; I saw some of this coin at Trebisonde. Súleimán (the great) himself was the apprentice of a Greek called Constantine. . . . From this time the goldsmiths of Trebisonde became the most famous in the world, and work vases for rose-water and incense, swords, daggers and knife-handles in most wonderful perfection. The knives of Ghorghúr-oghlí are the most famous of all; the hatchets of Trebisonde are a new and clever invention. The inlaid work of pearl-shells, with which tables, pulpits, inkstands, sand-boxes and chairs are ornamented in such perfection, that they cannot be equalled in any country, except it be by the pearl-shell work of India.

Eatables and Beverages.

The water of Trebisonde is fresh as the spring of life; the must of the raisins of Bozdepeh is sweet, and gives no headache to those who drink it; the sherbets called the triple, the muscat, and the clove wine are the best. The gardens produce most exquisite fruit; fine flavoured grapes, cherries red as woman's lips, pears of different kinds, apples called Sinope, figs called Bádinjián-Injúr, which are not found so sweet any where else, different kinds of lemons, oranges of a deep purple colour, pomegranates and olives, of which alone there are seven sorts to be found nowhere else except at Damascus and Jerusalem. One of the small sorts is eaten before it is quite ripe and resembles a black cherry; this is also an exclusive production of Trebisonde. Another fruit, which is called the date of Trebisonde is roasted on stoves, and is exported to many places; it is a sweet fruit, and has two or three kernels. The ruby-coloured pink which grows here, is peculiar to this place, each blossom is like a red rose, and perfumes the brain with the sweetest scent, and weighs, without the stalk, from five to six drachms.

The fish which are worthy of mention are Lorek-bálighí, Kefál-bálighí (Cephalus), the Kalkán-balighí (Rhombus), which if eaten by women renders them prolific; the fish called Kiziljeh-tekerbálik, with a red head and delicious to taste; the gold fish, the Sgombro which is taken in the season Erbain (forty days). But the most precious of all, which frequently causes bloody strifes and quarrels in the Market-place, is the Khamsí-bálighí taken in the season of Khamsan, (the fifty days when southerly winds blow); these fish were formerly thrown on the shore at Trebisonde by virtue of a talisman erected, as is said, by Alexander.

Of the Market-places, the first is outside of the gate of the wax-manufactory. There is a well-built Bezestan where the Arabian and Persian merchants reside, who are extremely rich and wealthy. In the middle castle the market called the small market, is furnished with every thing; its shops amount to the number of eighty.

The Imárets [public kitchens] are those of Mohammed II. in the middle castle, accommodating both rich and poor. The Imáret of Khátúnich, close to the mosque, is not to be equalled, even at Trebisonde; passengers and boatmen may dine here at their pleasure; there is an oven for baking white bread, and a cellar (kílar) for keeping the provisions of the Imáret. Near the kitchen is the eating-place for the poor, and the students have a proper dining-hall. Every day, in the morning, and at noon a dish of soup and a piece of bread is provided for each, and every Friday a Zerde Pilaw, and Yákhní (stewed meat); these regulations are to remain in force, as long as it pleases God.

Occupations, Guilds, &c.

The inhabitants are divided from the earliest period into seven classes. The first are the great and mighty Princes and sons of Princes (Beg and Beg-zadeh), who are dressed in magnificent pelisses of sables. The second are the Ulemás, the sheikhs and pious men, who dress according to their condition and live on endowments. The third are the merchants, who trade by sea and land to Ozakov, into the country of the Cossacks, into Mingrelia, Circassia, Abaza and the Crimea; they dress in ferrájís of cloth and dolimáns called kontosh. The fourth are the handicraftsmen, who dress themselves in ferrájís of cloth and bogássín. The fifth are the boatmen of the Black Sea; they have their peculiar dress, with iron buckles, shalwárs, dolimáns of clotli, and a kind of lining (astár) wrapped round the head, ready, thus accoutred, to trade or to fight at sea. The sixth class are the men of the vineyards, because the mountains of Bozdepeh are all planted with vines, and in the register are set down no less than thirty-one thousand gardens and vineyards, so that if only one man is reckoned to each garden, there are thirty-one thousand gardeners, but in some there are two and three. The seventh class are the fishermen, a calling in which many thousand men are employed.

Source: Evliya Effendi, *Narrative of Travels: Europe, Asia, and Africa, the Seventeenth Century*, Joseph von Hammer, trans., 2 vols. (London: William H. Allen, 1850), II: 42, 45–48 passim. Also found online: https://ia600402.us.archive.org/28/items/narrativeoftrave02evli/narrativeoftrave02evli.pdf.

12. ANTERA DUKE, DIARY (1788)

Antera Duke (c. 1735–as late as 1809) was a chief and trader in slaves working in precolonial Africa. This is the only known diary of an African slave merchant describing his daily business habits, his companions in the slave trade, and his deal-making with

*whites on the Atlantic coast. Antera Duke plied his trade at the height of the com-
merce in Africans, and his journals describe daily interactions with white ship captains as well as the everyday lives of his fellow dealers in human beings. The tactics for
the enslavement of Africans into the Atlantic slave trade varied. Rulers systematically
sold defeated enemy soldiers and the people of captured villages into slavery. Simultaneously there were freelance entrepreneurs bound up into societies or fraternities
of African slavers, who were known to European ship captains. These freelance merchants found among rival ethnic groups people to sell, taking their "merchandise" out
to ships for appraisal by the captain or agents of sponsoring shippers. In the eighteenth
century, the British merchants in slaves came to outstrip the Dutch and French, who
themselves had outstripped the early Portuguese slave merchants. How does Antera
Duke's description change understandings of the slave trade?*

April 21, 1785
At 5 a.m. at Aqua Landing, a fine morning. At 12 o'clock noon we 3 went on board
Burrows's ship. We begged him to "trust" for slaves but he would not. After that we
came back. Esien Duke came home from Orroup [Ododop] with 7 slaves. My fish-
erman came home with a slave, and Robin sent me 1 girl. And my first boy [head
slave] came from Curcock [Ikot Offiong] with a slave. And at 12 o'clock at night we
went [downriver] to Savage's ship.

April 22, 1785
At 5 a.m. in Coffee Duke's canoe. We got alongside Captain Savage's ship. We got
together to settle everything we owed him. He "dashed" Crim [Esien] I big great
gun and "dashed" us. We came away and left for Parrot Island.

May 26, 1785
At 5 a.m. at Aqua Landing, a fine morning. I went down to the landing. Afterwards I came up to work at my cabin. Soon after I saw Esien Duke bringing a new
captain with him to my cabin. He was Captain Comberbach and he said his ship
was at Parrot Island. Then we 3 dressed as white men [in European clothes] and
went down in his boat with one big canoe to bring up his ship.

June 14, 1785
About 6 a.m. at Aqua Landing, a fine morning. Duke Ephraim sent to call us to go
to Crim's [Esien's] house to see what he paid to Commrown Backsider Bakassey's
headman for slaves, 560 coppers for all. So they "chopped doctor" [took an oath]
to agree to obtain slaves for Duke. We made one canoe carry them home. All the
obong men went to Willy Honesty's Town.

July? 1, 1785
About 5 a.m. at Aqua Landing, a fine morning. I saw Duke Ephraim's son run
to tell us that the Andoni people were "catching wives" and won't let any market
canoes go past. They wanted to stop [seize] men until the Old Town palaver was

settled. I sent Esien down to the landing and Esien got his canoe. Then I got Coffee Duke. We went down in two great canoes and Egbo Young [Antera's] little canoe and two of Cobham's little canoes. Soon afterwards we saw them at 7 Fathoms Point. They ran. My canoe being first ran at them and they got away into the bush. My canoe got there at the same time, and my people ran into the bush. They caught 1 man and two slaves in the canoe and I took the canoe. Esien's canoe caught 1 man, Egbo Young's canoe and Ephraim Coffee's brother caught 1 man. Then we came home. After we got to town Ebrow Potter had occasion to go to look for those 7 men in the bush.

July? 2, 1785
At 5 a.m. at Aqua Landing, a fine morning. I went to the landing. Afterwards we went to Duke Ephraim. Duke had a discussion with [Commrown Backsider] Bakassey, and at 9 o'clock two new captains came ashore. We went on board Potter's ship with 7 canoes to collect "comey (anchorage fee given by ship captains to chief of town)." Awa Ofiong came home with a dead slave from Orroup.

July? 9, 1785
At 5 a.m. we were in Archibong Duke's yard and we had people make a grave in the same yard. After 10 o'clock we put her [Mbong] in the ground and fired 3 great guns, and we saw Willy Honesty come to collect "comey" on board Potter's ship and Cooper's ship.

July? 15, 1785
About 5 I was lying in my bed. Then I heard Egbo Young [Antera] call out for me. Then we 3 went aboard . . . Cooper's ship. I got goods for 50 slaves for the 3 of us. Soon after we came back.

July? 17, 1785
At 5 a.m. at Aqua Landing, a fine morning. I went on board Cooper's ship and came ashore. I "broke book" for 2 slaves with Captain Tatem. After 9 o'clock at night I sent 5 of my people to go to Yellow Belly's daughter, the mother of Dick Ebrow's sister, to seize one of her house women to give to the ship, because her brother gave one of my fine girls, whom I had given to my wife, to Captain Fairweather, and Yellow Belly's daughter's brother did not pay me. That's why I seized the house woman.

July? 21, 1785
At 6 a.m. at Aqua Landing, a fine morning. I went on board Cooper's ship and Esien went on board Comberbach's ship. We came ashore at 3 o'clock in the

Source: Antera Duke, *The Diary of Antera Duke, an Eighteenth-Century African Slave Trader*, Stephen D. Behrendt, A. J. H. Latham, and David Northrup (New York: Oxford University Press, 2010), 147, 149, 151, 153, 155, 157, 167.

afternoon. I sent a pawn [a person given as security for a debt] with Esien to give Comberbach to get 8 slaves to pay Captain Tatem. So I have paid Tatem for all I owed, and at 7 o'clock I sent my brother Egbo Young [Antera] to Boostam to trade for slaves.

November? 10, 1785

At about 5 a.m. in Curcock town, a fine morning. I went down to the landing. I gave Andam Curcock goods for 1 slave to leave at his place. After 3 o'clock in the afternoon I saw our Boostam canoe come down with 5 slaves and yams. At the same time I sailed away to come home with the slaves in my canoe, and there were 3 small canoes besides mine.

REVIEW QUESTIONS

1. In what ways did would-be conquerors among the newcomers resemble one another? In what ways did they differ from one another and from older imperial leaders?
2. Describe the variety among those facing the imperial invaders.
3. How would you describe attitudes of imperial conquerors toward those they wanted to subdue? How did those whose lands and livelihoods were overtaken view the conquerors?
4. Go to http://www.virtualjamestown.org/images/white_debry_html/debry47 .html, and describe and analyze this late-sixteenth-century depiction of Native Americans of North America from the point of view of the artist who drew them and the Native Americans' self-presentation.

CHAPTER 4

Everyday Life Amid Imperial Growth

Empire shaped the lives of millions by 1700. Settlers in the Western Hemisphere had come to direct the large-scale production of crops such as sugar cane and tobacco on plantations and to profit from the market in a range of commodities. Traders across the Indian Ocean prospered as well, with the exchange of multiple goods slowly building commercial networks worldwide. Knowledge, cultural forms, and commodities thus expanded the global foodscape, extended the pool of information, and often spread religious practices among peoples, altering everyday experience. For example, where Christianity was imposed, some local people integrated their old patterns of worship and systems of belief into Catholicism. Diversity in food made those who could benefit from it have longer lives—a pattern that continues to this day. There was worldwide interest in the constant arrival of new consumable goods. Alongside the disasters of death from novel diseases came the potential for longer, healthier lives for those who did not suffer the oppression of slavery and indenture or the growing violence inflicted by colonial rule. Only in Africa did population decline instead of rising, mostly because of the 11–12 million taken captive and sold into the Atlantic slave trade as well as tens of thousands more enslaved along Mediterranean and Indian Ocean networks.

Imperial violence and coercion accompanied new practices. If some local people still pulled out bows and arrows and knives at the sight of foreign ships, Ottomans, Mughals, Qing, Europeans and other imperialists fired their cannons and other guns. More often invaders faced a similar barrage from those under attack, as guns became the weapon of choice worldwide. Massive numbers of local canoes threatened the comparatively sparse crews of incoming foreign ships, especially when these crews might be weakened from scurvy and other diseases, not to mention shortages of food and water. Ship captains wanted peace with local people in order to gain water, wood, and food. Theft by local people who boarded these ships was often part of local customs signaling exchange, but it could elicit violent responses from uncomprehending Europeans, for whom theft was often a capital crime, not the first move in a trade. Both sides in this newly globalizing

world shared misunderstandings of others' political, social, and economic relationships. By the eighteenth century those whose lands were marked out for
seizure could still sign away their rights to land and resources while simultaneously violently resisting European crimes against their traditions. It remained the
case that many local people controlled food supplies, transportation routes, and
trade such as that in fur. In 1700, many confident empire-building governments
remained at the mercy of local people, their superior organization, and skills.

The number of would-be imperialists grew nonetheless, and migration
picked up around the world as people took the opportunity to become traders,
agriculturalists, and soldiers. Among these were officials sent by governments to
organize colonies and enforce colonial law—most notably in South and Central
America. In many cases, settlers resented the intrusion of these bureaucrats from
the metropole who had a higher social status. Although representing a foreign
power such as Spain, the rule of law that some bureaucrats enforced was highly
valued by colonial subjects, who brought disputes over property and power in
families to colonial courts. These, to some local people, appeared more predictable because cases were adjudicated in these imperial courts according to ruling
principles and written laws. Some, like the nun Sister Juana in Mexico City, even
thrived in this new world of intellectual mixture and adventure. Many migrants,
however, struggled to learn how to exploit and adapt to local conditions, while
many local people faced far greater difficulties adapting to the chaos, oppression,
and deprivation that also accompanied the onslaught of empire.

Social structure became more layered, as the influx of voluntary migrants and
forced laborers added diverse peoples, making social arrangements more complex. The arrival of single men in the early days of empire often upset kinship
arrangements and family values: These men, mostly starved for female compan-
ionship and sex, sought out sexual relationships in whatever society they landed.
Casual sex and rape were associated with empire. The distinguished amateur
scientist Joseph Banks, who traveled on important expeditions in the name of
eighteenth-century British science and imperial expansion, was energetic in finding sexual partners wherever the ships he traveled on landed. These casual cou-
plings sought out by sailors and adventurers spread sexually transmitted diseases
around the world. More permanently, traders and settlers from the imperial
metropole intermarried with local women, setting up hybrid families far from
their homeland. This happened across the globe—from West Africa to India and
into the Western Hemisphere. Spanish imperialists created terms defining various
forms of hybrid or "mixed" families depending on place of origin: Spanish with
Indians, Spanish/Indians with Africans, Spanish/Indian/African with Africans,
and so on. These alliances were often precisely defined by law and served as the
basis for social and economic roles.

Meanwhile, the geographic reach of empires expanded through conquest
and further expeditions across the globe. In the eighteenth century English
seaman James Cook traveled extensively, mapping the Canadian coast and the
Pacific Ocean better than anyone before him. The English also gained ground in

India, expanding their grip on resources as well as knowledge. Piracy continued to flourish as a career for individuals wanting to tap into seaborne wealth and for governments that still commissioned their navies to capture treasure-laden ships of rivals. In the Mediterranean the Barbary pirates of the eighteenth and early nineteenth centuries made shipping a nightmare for French and other ships, including those of the new United States of America. Despite multiple agreements, piracy has continued into the twenty-first century, though increasingly repressed by nations cooperating globally. More people experienced the rough conditions of life on the ocean, whether as slaves, indentured servants, sailors, investors, or adventurers, with death a constant outcome for many.

Some empires struggled after the mid-seventeenth century, in part because of climate change, famine, and general lawlessness, but these empires also adapted. The Jurchens, or Manchus, took advantage of increased banditry that had weakened the Ming regime in China. They pulled Mongol tribes into their empire, married into a variety of Han Chinese families, including those of the high-ranging military and the Ming bureaucracy, and incorporated Ming officials into their government. The Kangxi emperor (1662–1722), after decades of turmoil, consolidated the Qing empire and spread not only its influence but its territorial, military, and bureaucratic reach into vast new lands. The Kangxi emperor was curious about the world—an enlightened leader, he came to be called, and thus someone in stark contrast to European military men, including rulers, who generally hunted and waged war to the exclusion of other pursuits. He had come to power as a boy and took up the arts, followed scientific discoveries, and appeared eager to learn about new findings of almost any sort. Simultaneously, however, he exercised good leadership while waging war against those harboring loyalties to the Ming. He and his successors pursued conquests into western lands such as Tibet, part of a complicated maneuvering with Russia over the Asian interior. Western writers were stirred by his example and soon called for European readers to be more like Chinese rulers.

1. TASTING THE NEW FOOD

Empires gathered up all that the world had to offer, not just gold and silver. The appearance of new products challenged all people to rethink their world and determine the value of what it had to offer. Across the globe they seized on novel foods, figuring out how to use them and integrate them into their lives. The anti-slavery friar Las Casas was one of the first to write about peanuts in the mid-sixteenth century, and soon peanuts were circling the oceans, giving a distinctive cuisine to Indonesia, Malaysia, and other regions. Francisco López de Gómara fixed on potatoes at about the same time, while French aristocrat the Marquise de Sevigné, more than a century later, in 1671, announced her love of chocolate even if it might be bad for the health— or so some people believed. These were just the tiniest of fractions of the novelties that aroused curiosity and thought. What does the circulation and mixture of foodstuffs, as shown in these two documents, have to do with the domination of empire?

Bartolomé Las Casas, *History of the Indies*, 1647

They had another fruit [the peanut] which was sown, and grew beneath the soil, which were not roots, but which resembled the meat of the filbert nut of Castille. I say, that they were neither more nor less than filbert nut without the shells, and these had thin shells or pods in which they grew, and were covered in a different fashion than filbert nuts because they were in a manner similar to how beans are found in the pods, because these pods were not green nor soft, but were dried in a manner of the sweet pea or chick pea of Castille at the time they were ready for harvest, they are called maní, with an acute accent on the last syllable, and were so tasty that neither hazelnuts not walnuts, not any other fruit of those in Castille whatsoever could compare for taste. And because still if you ate too much of them for their good taste, then you got a headache from them, but not eating too much does not hurt the head nor cause other damage; it is always eaten, for they know it very well, with cassava bread, or wheat if they have it.

Marquise de Sevigné, Letter to her Daughter, October 25, 1671

But what shall we say of chocolate! Are you under no apprehensions of burning up your blood with it? May not all its boasted effects conceal some latent fire at the bottom? Make me easy on this subject, my dear, for in your present condition [her daughter was pregnant] I fear everything. You know I was very fond of chocolate; and besides, I thought it was too hot for me; I heard a very bad characterization of it. But from your account of it and the wonders that you say it has wrought upon you, I don't know what to think. . . .

I wanted to reconcile myself with chocolate; I took some the day before yesterday to help digest my dinner in order to be able to have a good supper; and I took some yesterday for a little nourishment in order to be able to fast until evening; it worked as I had hoped; that is what I find agreeable: when it works according to plan.

Source: Bartolomé Las Casas, *Apologética historia de las Indias*; Marie Rabutin Chantal, Marquise do Sevigné, *Letters from the Marchioness de Sévigné, to her Daughter the Countess de Grignan. 2: 212–213; Lettres de Madame de Sévigné, de Sa Famille et de Ses Amis*, M. Monmerqué, ed., 8 vols. (Paris: Hachette, 1862) 2: 398–400.

2. PEDRO DE CIEZA DE LEÓN, "TAXATION AND THE INCAS," FROM *CHRONICLES OF THE INCAS* (1540)

Pedro de Cieza de León observed the wealth arriving from the New World when he lived near the ports of Seville, Spain, as an early teen. Still a teenager, in 1536 he accompanied an expedition to northeastern South America and later served with military forces to put down a rebellion by Francisco Pizarro's brother against the Spanish government in the Inca lands. All the while, Cieza took notes on his travels, including descriptions of the countryside and its people. More important to his book he conversed with Inca luminaries to learn how the empire had been governed and how its infrastructure functioned. In this part of the book, the Incas compare very well with Spain and offer a model for better government. To some historians today, Spain, like Britain after it, never really conquered an empire but remained dependent on values and practices of those they supposedly ruled. Later in Cieza's study, Spain's role as a pillar of Christianity takes center stage as providing a major institution for the "New World." Arriving in Europe, such works provided food for thought about government, society, culture, and the economy. How would you describe Incan imperial values?

Which treats of the order they adopted in the payments of tribute by the provinces to the Kings, and of the system by which the tribute was regulated.

As in the last chapter I wrote of the method adopted by the Incas in their conquests, it will be well in this one to relate how they levied tribute from so many nations. It is a thing very well understood that there was no village, either in the mountains or in the valleys of the coast, which did not pay such tribute as was imposed by those who were in charge. It is said that when, in one province, the people represented that they had nothing wherewith to pay the tribute, the king ordered that each inhabitant should be obliged, every four months, to give a rather large cane full of live lice, which was a sign of the care taken by the Inca to make every subject contribute something. Thus we know that they paid their tribute of lice until such time as, having been supplied with flocks, they had been industrious enough to multiply them, and to make cloth wherewith to pay more suitable tribute in the time to come.

The system which the Orejones of Cuzco and the other native lords of the land say that the Incas adopted in imposing tribute was as follows: He who reigned in Cuzco, sent some of his principal officers to visit the empire, one by each of the four royal roads of which I have already written. One was called Chincha Suyo, which included all the provinces as far as Quito, with all the valleys of Chincha towards the north. The second was Conde Suyo, which includes the provinces on the sea coast, and many in the mountains. The third was called Colla Suyo, including all the provinces to the south as far as Chile. The last road led to Ande Suyo, which included the lands covered with forests at the foot of mountains of the Andes.

So it was that when the lord desired to know what tribute would be due from all the provinces between Cuzco and Chile, along a road of such great length, as I have often explained, he ordered faithful persons whom he could trust, to go from village to village, examining the condition of the people and their capacity for payment. They also took note of the productiveness of the land, the quantity of flocks, the yield of metals, and of other things which they required and valued. Having performed this service with great diligence they returned to the lord to submit their reports. He then ordered a general assembly of the principal persons of the kingdom to meet. The lords of the provinces which had to pay the tribute being present, he addressed them lovingly, saying that as they received him as their sole lord and monarch of so many and such vast districts, they should take it in good part, without feeling it burdensome, to give the tribute that was due to the royal person, who would take care that it was moderate, and so light that they could easily pay it. Having been answered in conformity with his wishes, the lords of provinces returned to their homes, accompanied by certain Orejones who fixed the tribute. In some parts it was higher than is paid to the Spaniards at present. But, seeing that the system of the Incas was so perfect, the people did not feel the burden, rather increasing and multiplying in numbers and well being. On the other hand, the disorder introduced by the Spaniards, and their extreme covetousness, have caused the prosperity of the country to decrease in such sort that a great part of the population has disappeared. Their greed and avarice will destroy the remainder, unless the mercy of God should grant a remedy by causing the wars to cease. Those wars have certainly been permitted as a just scourge. The country can only be saved by the taxation being fixed by moderate rules, so that the Indians may enjoy liberty and be masters of their own persons and estates, without other duty than the payment by each village of what has been fixed by rule. I shall treat of this subject a little more fully further on.

When the officers sent by the Incas made their inspection, they entered a province and ascertained, by means of the *quipus*, the number of men and women, of old and young. Then they took account of the mines of gold and silver, and, with so many thousand Indians at work, the quantity that should be extracted was fixed. An order was given that such quantity should be delivered to the overseers. As those who were employed to work at the extraction of silver could not attend to the cultivation of their fields, the Inca imposed the duty upon the neighbouring province to find labour for the sowing and reaping of the crops of the miners. If the mining province was large, its own inhabitants were able both to carry on the mining works and to cultivate the ground. In case one of the miners fell ill, it was arranged that he should return to his home, and that another should take his place. No one was employed in the mines who was not married, because the wives had to supply their food and liquor; besides which, arrangements were made to send sufficient provisions to the mines. In this manner, although men might be at the mines all their lives, they were not overworked. Besides, there was provision to rest for certain days in each month, for their festivals and for pleasure. But in fact the same Indians did not always remain at the mines; for there were periodical reliefs.

The Incas so arranged the mining industry, that they extracted great abundance of gold and silver throughout the empire, and there must have been years when more than fifty thousand *arrobas* of silver and fifteen thousand of gold were produced. It was always used for the royal service. The metal was brought to the principal place of the province, and in the manner that the mines were worked in one district in the same way were they ordered in all the others throughout the empire. If there were provinces where no metal could be extracted as a tribute, the people paid taxes in smaller things, and in women and boys, who were taken from the villages without causing any discontent. For if a man had an only child it was not taken, but if he had three or four children, one was required in payment of his dues.

Other provinces made their contributions in the form of so many thousand loads of maize, at each harvest. Others provided, on the same scale, a certain number of loads of dried *chuñus*, in the same way as the maize, and others again paid in *quinua*, or other products. In other provinces the tribute consisted of so many cloth mantles, and in others of shirts, according to the number of inhabitants. Another form of tribute was the supply of so many thousand loads of lances, another of slings and *ayllos*, and all other kinds of weapons that they used. Other provinces were required to send so many thousand labourers to Cuzco, to be employed on the public edifices of the city and of the kings, with supplies of their needful provisions. Other provinces contributed cables to move the great stones, while others paid tribute in coca. The system was so arranged that all the provinces of Peru paid something to the Incas in tribute, from the smallest to the most important. Such perfect regularity was maintained that while the people did not fail to provide what was required, those who made the collections never took even a grain of maize too much. All the provision and warlike stores that were contributed, were served out to the soldiers, or supplied to the garrisons which were formed in different parts, for the defence of the empire.

When there was no war, a large proportion was eaten and used by the poor; for when the kings were at Cuzco they were served by the *anaconas*, which is the name for perpetual servants who sufficed to till the royal fields, and do service in the palaces. Besides which, there was always brought for the royal table, from the provinces, many lambs and birds, fish, maize, coca, edible roots, and all kinds of fruits.

Such order was maintained in the tribute paid by the Indians that the Incas became very powerful, and never entered upon any war which did not extend their dominions.

To understand how, and in what manner, the tributes were paid, and the other taxes were collected, it must be known that in each *huata*, for a year, certain Orejones were sent as judges, but only with powers to inspect the provinces, and give notice to the inhabitants that if any felt aggrieved he was to state his complaints, in order that the officer who had done him the injury might be punished. Having received the complaints, and also ascertained whether any tribute had not been paid, the judges returned to Cuzco; whence others set out with power to inflict punishment on those who were in fault. Besides this, it was the rule that, from time to time, the principal men of the provinces should be permitted to appear before the lord, and report upon the condition of the provinces, on their needs, and on the incidence of taxation. Their representations then received attention, the Lords Incas being certain that they did not lie, but spoke the truth; for any deceit was severely punished, and in that case the tribute was increased. The women contributed by the provinces were divided between the service of the kings, and that of the temples of the Sun.

Source: Pedro de Cieza de León, *The Second Part of the Chronicle of Peru*. Clements R. Markham, trans. and ed. (London: Hakyluyt Society, 1884), 87–91. Also available at Project Gutenberg, http://www .gutenberg.org/files/48785/48785-h/48785-h.htm (accessed August 4, 2015).

3. ALONZO ORTIZ, LETTER TO HIS WIFE (1571)

From the arrival of Columbus in the Western Hemisphere down to the present, it is estimated that one-third of all Europeans migrated to other parts of the world. Alonzo Ortiz, a craftsman in Mexico City in the late sixteenth century, was one of these. In this letter, he details his life and asks his wife in Spain to join him, offering a picture of life's difficulties in the empire even for a Spanish person but also outlining the gradual improvement of his situation. He notes the people who work for him and their jobs. Ortiz's communications contrast with the fate of many single and other people who never made it to their destination or who simply disappear from the historical record. It also contrasts with the silences in the lives of slaves and colonized peoples.

Milady:

This will be to give you an account of what is happening here and how I am doing up to the day this letter is dated. For about a year now I have been in good health and working at my trade, though I had few Indian helpers. I couldn't find any who were trained, since the other tanners had them, and it was not for me to take them away from them. In this year I must have made 500 pesos profit, and if I said 600 I wouldn't be lying; it's about the same as 500 ducats of Castile. But I no longer have to take off my shoes to work, because now I have eight Indians who work steadily, and a black belonging to my partner who aids me very well, and all I do is give instructions, buy, and sell. That is enough work, and indeed it is not little, though it seems little for me; actually I don't want to work at more than supervision so I won't get some sickness that would be the end of me, because great is my desire to see you again.

. . . my partner has decided to send for you, and is sending you 150 pesos just for your sustenance, and the rest can be paid when you get here. You will find this money in Seville in the possession of a councilman there who is the partner of Alonso Ramos, a merchant here in Mexico City. . . .

Source: On the Internet and in Kenneth Mills, William B. Taylor, and Sandra Lauderdale Graham, eds., *Colonial Latin America: A Documentary History* (Wilmington, DE: Scholarly Resources), 125–126.

4. SOR JUANA INÉS DE LA CRUZ, "THE REPLY TO SOR PHILOTHEA" (1691)

Sor Juana de la Cruz (1651–1695) was born near Mexico city to an unmarried criollo mother—that is someone of Spanish descent in the colonies who might have some amount of Amerindian blood. Sor Juana was highly religious and highly intellectual from a very young age, learning Latin, Greek, literature, and many other topics. At sixteen she entered a convent and while there wrote poetry and essays, which showed both her extensive knowledge and her love of learning. Her wide-ranging spirit got her into trouble with the leaders of the Catholic Church, who had once marveled at her brilliant mind. They chastised her, making her discard her books and repent her sinful ways as religious officialdom based in Europe still shaped policy in the colonies—as it had done for two centuries by that time. Sor Juana justified herself in the excerpt that follows, but after ending her studies, she died of the plague while tending to its victims. How does Sor Juana's story fit into the history of empire?

I hereby state that before I was three years old my mother sent me and one of my sisters, who was older than I, to one of those schools called Amigas, where we could learn to read. I followed her with affection and mischief. When I saw she was receiving lessons the desire to learn to read caught fire in me so much that I tried to trick the teacher (so I thought) by telling her that my mother had instructed her to give me lessons too. She did not believe it because it wasn't believable; yet, to reward my clever charm, she gave them to me. I continued going and she continued teaching me, no longer as a jest, because the experiment changed her mind. And I learned to read so quickly that I already knew how to by the time my mother found out; for the teacher had kept her in the dark about it in order to delight her completely and to get a reward all together. I kept quiet thinking that I would be whipped for having done this without her leave. The woman who taught me (God bless her) is still alive, and she can vouch for what I say.

I remember that in those days, because I had the sweet-tooth that is normal at that age, I would abstain from eating cheese because I had heard that it turned people into dunces. The desire to acquire knowledge was stronger in me than the desire to eat, even though the latter desire is so strong in children. Later on, when I was six or seven years old, and already knowing how to read and write along with all the other skills that women learn such as embroidery and sewing, I heard that in Mexico City there was a University and there were Schools where people studied the sciences. As soon as I heard this I began to kill my mother by constantly and naggingly begging her to dress me in boy's clothes and to send me to live with some relatives of hers in Mexico City so that I could study by enrolling in the University. She refused, and she was quite right, but I assuaged my desire by reading many kinds of books belonging to my grandfather, notwithstanding the punishment and scolding intended to stop me. So, when I came to Mexico people were amazed, not so much by my intelligence as by my memory and the facts that I had acquired at an age that seemed hardly enough just to be able to learn to speak.

I began to study Latin grammar, and I think I did not have even twenty lessons. I applied myself so intensely that since this is true about women, and even more so in the bloom of my youth, that we value so highly the natural look of our hair I would cut off four to six finger lengths of it, measuring up to where it reached before and imposing a rule on myself that, if I did not know whatever I had planned to learn. . . . I entered a religious order because, although I was aware that that lifestyle had certain things (I'm talking about incidental not official ones), or rather, many things that were abhorrent to my character given my total rejection of marriage it was the least objectionable and the most respectable one I could choose with regard to my desire to safeguard my salvation. In the face of this primary concern (surely it is the most important one) all the stubborn little impertinences of my nature gave way and bowed: that is, wanting to live alone; wanting not to have any obligatory duties that would hinder my freedom to study;

being free from community noises that would interrupt the peace and quiet of my books. . . . I thought I was fleeing myself, but wretch that I am!I brought my self with me, and I brought my greatest enemy into this disposition of mine, about which I am unable to figure out if it is a gift or a punishment from Heaven. When all the pious ceremonies involved in a religious lifestyle were extinguishing or blocking my studious nature, it exploded like gunpowder, and I proved the truth of the saying privatio est causa appetitus [deprivation is the cause of desire].

I returned to my studious task (I misspeak, for I never stopped); nay, I mean, I continued reading and reading more, studying and studying more, with only books themselves for a teacher. For me studying was a restful break during the moments left over from my duties. It is well known that studying those lifeless letters is hard, that they lack a teacher's lively voice and explanations; yet I suffered all that difficulty very gladly for the love of reading. Oh, if it had only been for the love of God which was the correct choice how deserving I would have been! Even so, I strived with all my might to raise my sights and to direct them toward his service, because the goal I sought was to study theology; for it seemed to me, Catholic that I am, a pitiful incapacity on my part not to know in this lifetime everything that can be learned by natural methods about the divine mysteries. Being a nun and not a laywoman, I thought it my duty given my religious status to profess letters. This is especially true since I was a daughter of the likes of St. Jerome and St. Paula. How degenerate it would be for an idiot daughter to descend from such learned parents! I argued with myself about this, and I thought I was right. Unless I was flattering and applauding my own propensity (and that's most likely) by relying on the logical proposition that my own pleasure was obligatory. I proceeded in this way, as I've said, always directing the path of my studies toward the summit of holy Theology. In order to reach it, it seemed to me necessary to ascend the ladder of the sciences and the humanities, for how can one who does not first know the ancillary fields possibly understand the queen of the sciences? Without logic, how could I possibly know the general and specific methods by which the Holy Scriptures are written? Without rhetoric, how could I possibly understand its figures, tropes, and phrasing? Without the natural sciences, what about so many questions pertaining to the multiple natures the animals used in biblical sacrifices, in which so many symbols have already been explained, with many more unexplained? If Saul was cured by the sound of David's harp, was it by virtue of the natural power of music, or the supernatural power God chose to infuse in David? Without arithmetic could one possibly comprehend the computation of so many years, days, months, hours, and weeks like those found in Daniel and still more, the understanding of which requires knowing the natures, concordances, and properties of numbers? Without geometry, how could one possibly measure the Holy Ark of the Covenant and the holy city of Jerusalem, whose mysterious measurements form a cube in all its dimensions, and in which the proportional distribution of all its parts is so marvelous?

Source: Sor Juana Inés de la Cruz (1691) "Answer by the poet to the most illustrious Sister Filotea de la Cruz," William Little, trans. (Santa Fe College, 2008). Copyright 2008. Santa Fe College, http://dept. sfcollege.edu/hfl/hum2461/pdfs/sjicanswer.pdf (accessed October 28, 2015).

5. SHEIKH MAHMUD HOSSON, MULLA ABDUL GHAFUR, AND OTHERS, PETITION AGAINST THE EAST INDIA COMPANY (1700)

Late in the seventeenth century, when the Mughal empire was at the height of its power, the British East India Company was itself establishing footholds along the South Asian coast. It was just one of a handful of European companies staking out trading opportunities. In addition, the Company continued the practice of seizing ships and their contents to make up for the English trade deficit—an imbalance that existed because it lacked goods of its own to sell. The British position was weak: In 1689 allies of the Mughal empire soundly defeated Company troops in a sixteen-month siege, during which British forces were reduced to starvation. Piracy continued and even increased in the 1690s, causing prominent South Asian merchants huge losses. Here merchants and other Surat notables describe to the Mughal authorities the thievery and duplicity of the British, who would soon be describing themselves as the world's most "civilized" people and who hanged individuals at home for the theft of an article of clothing. Can you explain this paradox, especially in light of the merchants' petition?

That in the time of Salabat Khan, Governor of Surat, one of the English Company's ships seized a ship of Abdul Ghafur's coming from Mocha hither. Upon notice thereof [the] said Abdul Ghafur complained to Salabat Khan, at which time Mr. [John] Child, a great villain, was President of the English Company who presently after got away from Surat and fled to Bombay. . . . [O]ut of his great clemency and love [the emperor Aurangzeb] did pardon them [the East India Company] and ordered the Sidi to quit Bombay. Then they requested a new farman to carry on their trade in Surat as formerly, which the Mughal [emperor] granted them.

During the space of one year the Company of English behaved themselves very civilly but then they began again to take and seize the merchants' ships of Surat and notwithstanding their agreement made before the Mughal [emperor] to deliver back all the ships' goods etc. taken by them, they shamefully and dishonorably put off the merchants from time to time for six years and upwards until the time of Amanat Khan [and] his coming [i.e., being appointed] governor of Surat, when they paid to several merchants some 30 percent, some 40 percent, and to some others (who in a manner forced them) 50 percent.

But one year after they had made peace in I'timad Khan's time they took nine ships of Abdul Ghafur's and several other merchants' ships out of which they took the goods etc. and returned the empty hull. Again they also took [the] ship Ganj-i-sawai belonging to the Mughal [emperor] within ten hours' sail of Bombay and delivered back the ship empty; they took also another ship full laden belonging to Hosson Hamdon [elsewhere, Ammadan]. Near Bombay [they] also [took] another ship laden belonging to Abdul Nabi, Secretary, and another also called the Quedah Merchant coming from Bengal to Surat, Hosson Hamdon's ship. And the Quedah Merchant they fitted up in order to commit further piracies which they kept [doing] on the coasts of Malabar. But hearing that their king was sending out some ships of war with some persons to do justice here they sold the two ships, since which they have committed no piracy. In this time the Company of English have robbed and taken from several merchants of Surat to the amount of eighty lakh of rupees and have committed several villainies aboard the respective ships taken by them by which [they] have almost ruined the trade and port of Surat.

This that we have here declared we whose names are underwritten do swear to be true and now we hope and pray to God that we shall have justice done us.

Source: "Surat Merchants, Clerics, and Port Officials Petition against the East India Company," British Library, India Office Records E/3/57 no. 7071, Copy of a Declaration or Demand of Several Merchants, 30 May 1700, in *The English East India Company at the Height of Mughal Expansion: A Soldier's Diary of the 1689 Siege of Bomba and Related Documents*, Margaret R. Hunt and Philip J. Stern, eds. (Boston: Bedford/St. Martin's, 2016), 173–174.

6. LADY MARY WORTLEY MONTAGU, LETTER (1717)

Lady Mary Wortley Montagu (1689–1762) was married to the British ambassador to the Ottoman Empire in 1716 and the couple spent two years there. Introduced to the intimacies of the harem, Montagu believed that Ottoman women were the freest in the world. In contrast, they chided her for her corsets, which they interpreted as a punishment European husbands used against their wives. Montagu observed all around her with great interest, especially noting the Ottoman habit of taking a bit of cowpox and inoculating their children with it to prevent the deadly smallpox disease. At this time, many European travelers were amazed at the sophistication of peoples in distant lands and imitated their clothing, bathing habits, and manners. Like Montagu they kept diaries and sent letters recording their impressions. Mary Montagu went further, inoculating her own children and causing inoculation for smallpox to be introduced in the British royal courts. Knowledge moved in multiple directions worldwide.

A propos of Distempers, I am going to tell you a thing that I am sure will make you wish your selfe here. The Small Pox so fatal and so general amongst us is here entirely harmless by the invention of engrafting (which is the term they give it). There is a set of old Women who make it their business to perform the Operation. Every Autumn in the month of September, when the great Heat is abated, people send to one another to know if any of their family has a mind to have the small pox. They make partys for this purpose, and when they are met (commonly 15 or 16 together) the old Woman comes with a nutshell full of the matter of the best sort of small-pox and asks what veins you please to have open'd. She immediately rips open that you offer to her with a large needle (which gives you no more pain than a common scratch) and puts into the vein as much venom as can lye upon the head of her needle, and after binds up the little wound with a hollow bit of shell, and in this manner opens 4 or 5 veins. The Grecians have commonly the superstition of opening one in the Middle of the forehead, in each arm and on the breast to mark the sign of the cross, but this has a very ill Effect, all these wounds leaving little Scars, and is not done by those that are not superstitious, who chuse to have them in the legs or that part of the arm that is conceal'd. The children or young patients play together all the rest of the day and are in perfect health till the 8th. Then the fever begins to seize 'em and they keep their beds 2 days, very seldom 3. They have very rarely above 20 or 30 in their faces, which never mark, and in 8 days time they are as well as before their illness. Where they are wounded there remains running sores during the Distemper, which I don't doubt is a great releife to it. Every year thousands undergo this Operation, and the French Ambassador says pleasantly that they take the Small Pox here by way of diversion as they take the Waters in other Countrys. There is no example of any one that has dy'd in it, and you may beleive I am very well satisfy'd of the safety of the Experiment since I intend to try it on my dear little Son. I am Patriot enough to take pains to bring this usefull invention into fashion in England, and I should not fail to write to some of our Doctors very particularly about it if I knew any one of 'em that I thought had Virtue enough to destroy such a considerable branch of their Revenue for the good of Mankind, but that Distemper is too beneficial to them not to expose to all their Resentment the hardy wight that should undertake to put an end to it. Perhaps if I live to return I may, however, have courage to war with 'em. Upon this Occasion, admire the Heroism in the Heart of your Freind, etc.

Source: Widely available on the Internet.

7. THOMAS BLUETT, *SOME MEMOIRS OF THE LIFE OF JOB, THE SON OF SOLOMON, THE HIGH PRIEST OF BOONDA IN AFRICA; WHO WAS A SLAVE ABOUT TWO YEARS IN MARYLAND; AND AFTERWARDS BEING BROUGHT TO ENGLAND, WAS SET FREE, AND SENT TO HIS NATIVE LAND IN THE YEAR 1734* (1734)

Ayuba Suleiman Diallo (1701–1773) was born into a prominent Fulbe family in what is today Senegal. Diallo's grandfather had founded the town in which he lived, while his father served as an important Muslim leader. In general, Africans themselves determined who would be enslaved and who not. While selling slaves himself and buying paper, he was picked up by people from a competing ethnic group and sold to a slaver. Taken to Maryland, Ayuba Suleiman Diallo, now called Job, was caught after running away from his owner's tobacco plantation and jailed. Job's intellignd learning were impressive to locals and a translator was brought in. A visiting British judge sought him out and eventually took him to England, where he was feted and eventually funded for a return passage to his African community. This is an excerpt from Diallo's story, which ends—improbably—with his release.

Mr. Vachell Denton sold JOB to one Mr. Tolsey in Kent Island in Maryland, who put him to work in making Tobacco; but he was soon convinced that JOB had never been used to such Labour. He every Day shewed more and more Uneasiness under this Exercise, and at last grew sick, being no way able to bear it; so that his Master was obliged to find easier Work for him, and therefore put him to tend the Cattle. JOB would often leave the Cattle, and withdraw into the Woods to pray; but a white Boy frequently watched him, and whilst he was at his Devotion would mock him, and throw Dirt in his Face. This very much disturbed JOB, and added to his other Misfortunes; all which were increased by his Ignorance of the English Language, which prevented his complaining, or telling his Case to any Person about him. Grown in some measure desperate, by reason of his present Hardships, he resolved to travel at a Venture; thinking he might possibly be taken up by some Master, who would use him better, or otherwise meet with some lucky Accident, to divert or abate his Grief. Accordingly, he travelled thro' the Woods, till he came to the County of Kent, upon Delaware Bay, now esteemed Part of Pensilvania; altho' it is properly a Part of Maryland, and belongs to my Lord Baltimore. There is a Law in force, throughout the Colonies of Virginia, Maryland, Pensilvania, &c. as far as Boston in New England, viz. That any Negroe, or white Servant who is not known in the County, or has no Pass, may be secured by any Person, and kept in the common Goal, till the Master of such Servant shall fetch him. Therefore JOB being able to give no Account of himself, was put in Prison there.

This happened about the Beginning of June, 1731. when I, who was attending the Courts there, and had heard of JOB, went with several Gentlemen to the Goaler's House, being a Tavern, and desired to see him. He was brought into the Tavern to us, but could not speak one Word of English. Upon our Talking and making Signs to him, he wrote a Line or two before us, and when he read it, pronounced the Words Allah and Mahommed; by which, and his refusing a Glass of Wine we offered him, we perceived he was a Mahometan, but could not imagine of what Country he was, or how he got thither; for by his affable Carriage, and the easy Composure of his Countenance, we could perceive he was no common Slave.

When JOB had been some time confined, an old Negroe Man, who lived in that Neighbourhood, and could speak the Jalloff Language, which JOB also understood, went to him, and conversed with him. By this Negroe the Keeper was informed to whom JOB belonged, and what was the Cause of his leaving his Master. The Keeper thereupon wrote to his Master, who soon after fetch'd him home, and was much kinder to him than before; allowing him a Place to pray in, and some other Conveniencies, in order to make his Slavery as easy as possible. Yet Slavery and Confinement was by no means agreeable to JOB, who had never been used to it; he therefore wrote a Letter in Arabick to his Father, acquainting him with his Misfortunes, hoping he might yet find Means to redeem him. This Letter he sent to Mr. Vachell Denton, desiring it might be sent to Africa by Captain Pike; but he being gone to England, Mr. Denton sent the Letter inclosed to Mr. Hunt, in order to be sent to Africa by Captain Pike from England; but Captain Pike had sailed for Africa before the Letter came to Mr. Hunt, who therefore kept it in his own Hands, till he should have a proper Opportunity of sending it. It happened that this Letter was seen by James Oglethorpe, Esq; who, according to his usual Goodness and Generosity, took Compassion on JOB, and gave his Bond to Mr. Hunt for the Payment of a certain Sum, upon the Delivery of JOB here in England. Mr. Hunt upon this sent to Mr. Denton, who purchas'd him again of his Master for the same Money which Mr. Denton had formerly received for him; his Master being very willing to part with him, as finding him no ways fit for his Business.

He lived some time with Mr. Denton at Annapolis, before any Ship could stir out, upon account of the Ice that lay in all the Rivers of Maryland at that Time. In this Interval he became acquainted with the Reverend Mr. Henderson, a Gentleman of great Learning, Minister of Annapolis, and Commissary to the Bishop of London, who gave JOB the Character of a Person of great Piety and Learning; and indeed his good Nature and Affability gain'd him many Friends besides in that Place.

In March, 1733 he set sail in the William, Captain George Uriel Commander; in which Ship I was also a Passenger. The Character which the Captain and I had of him at Annapolis, induced us to teach him as much of the English Language as we could, he being then able to speak but few Words of it, and those hardly intelligible. This we set about as soon as we were out at Sea, and in about a Fortnight's Time taught him all his Letters, and to spell almost any single Syllable, when distinctly pronounced to him; but JOB and my self falling sick, we were hindered from making any greater Progress at that Time. However, by the Time that we arrived in England, which was the latter End of April, 1733 he had learned so much of our Language, that he was able to understand most of what we said in common Conversation; and we that were used to his Manner of Speaking, could make shift to understand him tolerably well. During the Voyage, he was very constant in his Devotions; which he never omitted, on any Pretence, notwithstanding we had exceeding bad Weather all the time we were at Sea. We often permitted him to kill our fresh Stock, that he might eat of it himself; for he eats no Flesh, unless he has killed the Animal with his own Hands, or knows that it has been killed by some Mussulman. He has no Scruple about Fish; but won't touch a bit of Pork, it being expresly forbidden by their Law. By his good Nature and Affability he gained the good Will of all the Sailors, who (not to mention other kind Offices) all the way up the Channel shewed him the Head Lands and remarkable Places; the Names of which JOB wrote down carefully, together with the Accounts that were given him about them. His Reason for so doing, he told me, was, that if he met with any Englishman in his Country, he might by these Marks be able to convince him that he had been in England.

On our Arrival in England, we heard that Mr. Oglethorpe was gone to Georgia, and that Mr. Hunt had provided a Lodging for JOB at Limehouse. After I had visited my Friends in the Country, I went up on purpose to see JOB. He was, very sorrowful, and told me, that Mr. Hunt had been applied to by some Persons to sell him, who pretended they would send him home; but he feared they would either sell him again as a Slave, or if they sent him home would expect an unreasonable Ransom for him. I took him to London with me, and waited on Mr. Hunt, to desire leave to carry him to Cheshunt in Hartfordshire; which Mr. Hunt comply'd with.

He told me he had been apply'd to, as JOB had suggested, but did not intend to part with him without his own Consent; but as Mr. Oglethorpe was out of England, if any of JOB's Friends would pay the Money, he would accept of it, provided they would undertake to send him home safely to his own Country. I also obtained his Promise that he would not dispose of him till he heard farther from me.

JOB, while he was at Cheshunt, had the Honour to be sent for by most of the Gentry of that Place, who were mightily pleased with his Company, and concerned for his Misfortunes. They made him several handsome Presents, and proposed that a Subscription should be made for the Payment of the Money to Mr. Hunt. The Night before we set out for London from Cheshunt, a Footman belonging to Samuel Holden, Esq; brought a Letter to JOB, which was, I think, directed to Sir Byby Lake. The Letter was delivered at the African House; upon which the House was pleased to order that Mr. Hunt should bring in a Bill of the whole Charges which he had been at about JOB, and be there paid; which was accordingly done, and the Sum amounted to Fifty-nine Pounds, Six Shillings, and eleven Pence Half-penny. This Sum being paid, Mr. Oglethorpe's Bond was deliver'd up to the Company. JOB's Fears were now over, with respect to his being sold again as a Slave; yet he could not be persuaded but that he must pay an extravagant Ramson, when he got home. I confess, I doubted much of the Success of a Subscription, the Sum being great, and JOB's Acquaintance in England being so small; therefore, to ease JOB's Mind, I spoke to a Gentleman about the Affair, who has all along been JOB's Friend in a very remarkable Manner. This Gentleman was so far from discouraging the Thing, that he began the Subscription himself with a handsome Sum, and promised his further Assistance at a dead Lift. Not to be tedious: Several Friends, both in London and in the Country, gave in their charitable Contributions very readily; yet the Sum was so large, that the Subscription was about twenty Pounds short of it; but that generous and worthy Gentleman before mentioned, was pleased to make up the Defect, and the whole Sum was compleated.

I went (being desired) to propose the Matter to the African Company; who, after having heard what I had to say, shew'd me the Orders that the House had made; which were, that JOB should be accommodated at the African House at the Company's Expence, till one of the Company's Ships should go to Gambia, in which he should be sent back to his Friends without any Ransom. The Company then ask'd me, if they could do any Thing more to make JOB easy; and upon my Desire, they order'd, that Mr. Oglethorpe's Bond should be cancelled, which was presently done, and that JOB should have his Freedom in Form, which he received handsomely engross'd with the Company's Seal affixed; after which the full Sum of the whole Charges (viz. Fifty-nine Pounds, Six Shillings, and eleven Pence Half-penny) was paid in to their Clerk, as was before proposed.

JOB's Mind being now perfectly easy, and being himself more known, he went chearfully among his Friends to several Places, both in Town and Country, One Day being at Sir Hans Sloan's, he expressed his great Desire to see the Royal Family. Sir Hans promised to get him introduced, when he had Clothes proper to go in. JOB knew how kind a Friend he had to apply to upon occasion; and he was soon

cloathed in a rich silk Dress, made up after his own Country Fashion, and introduced to their Majesties, and the rest of the Royal Family. Her Majesty was pleased
to present him with a rich Gold Watch; and the same Day he had the Honour to dine
with his Grace the Duke of Mountague, and some others of the Nobility, who were
pleased to make him a handsome Present after Dinner. His Grace, after that, was
pleased to take JOB often into the Country with him, and shew him the Tools that
are necessary for Tilling the Ground, both in Gardens and Fields, and made his Servants shew him how to use them; and afterwards his Grace furnished JOB with all
Sorts of such Instruments, and several other rich Presents, which he ordered to be
carefully done up in Chests, and put on Board for his Use. 'Tis not possible for me to
recollect the many Favours he received from his Grace, and several other Noblemen
and Gentlemen, who shewed a singular Generosity towards him; only, I may say
in general, that the Goods which were given him, and which he carried over with
him, were worth upwards of 500 Pounds; besides which, he was well furnished with
Money, in case any Accident should oblige him to go on Shore, or occasion particular Charges at Sea. About the latter End of July last he embark'd on Board one of the
African Company's Ships, bound for Gambia; where we hope he is safely arrived, to
the great Joy of his Friends, and the Honour of the English Nation.

Source: Thomas Bluett, *Some Memoirs of the Life of Job, the Son of Solomon, the High Priest of Boonda in Africa; Who Was a Slave About Two Years in Maryland; and Afterwards Being Brought to England, Was Set Free, and Sent to His Native Land in the Year 1734* (London: Richard Ford,1734), 19–33.

8. JORGE JUAN AND ANTONIO DE ULLOA, *VOYAGE TO SOUTH AMERICA* (1748)

*Antonio de Ulloa y was a Spanish scientist, government official, and author who col-
laborated with Jorge Juan, mathematician, scientist, and naval expert, in the discovery
of platinum. The pair of well-born scientists made their discovery while on a French geo-
desic trip to South America, where along with their several scientific breakthroughs they
observed the geography and local life in the cities of Central America and along the west
coast of South America. They took special notice of social structure during their nine-year
stay abroad and were keen observers of the social differences among people in Spanish-
held cities. For travelers at the time, the minute class and racial divisions among the population were a major characteristic of the Spanish colonies as they had taken shape some
two hundred and fifty years after the first incursions into the Western Hemisphere. The
two scientists published their observations after Ulloa had been captured on the return
voyage, confined in London, and eventually released. As for Juan, one of his assignments
after the voyage was spying on British industry for Spain. Some travelers were actually
providing military and economic information. To whom might this account be useful?*

The commonalty may be divided into four classes, Spaniards or Whites, Mestizos,
Indians or Natives, and Negroes, with their progeny. These last are not propor-
tionally so numerous as in the other parts of the Indies; occasioned by it being

something inconvenient to bring Negroes to Quito, and the different kinds of agriculture being generally performed by Indians.

The name of Spaniard here has a different meaning from that of Chapitone or European, as properly signifying a person descended from a Spaniard without a mixture of blood. Many Mestizos, from the advantage of a fresh complexion, appear to be Spaniards more than those who are so in reality; and from only this fortuitous advantage are accounted as such. The Whites, according to this construction of the word, may be considered as one sixth part of the inhabitants.

The Mestizos are the descendants of Spaniards and Indians, and are to be considered here in the same different degrees between the Negroes and Whites, as before at Carthagena; but with this difference, that at Quito the degrees of Mestizos are not carried so far back, for, even in the second or third generations, when they acquire the European colour, they are considered as Spaniards. The complexion of the Mestizos is swarthy and reddish, but not of that red common in the fair Mulattos. This is the first degree, or the immediate issue of a Spaniard and Indian. Some are, however, equally tawny with the Indians themselves, though they are distinguished from them by their beards: while others, on the contrary, have so fine a complexion that they might pass for Whites, were it not for some signs which betray them, when viewed attentively. Among these, the most remarkable is the lowness of the forehead, which often leaves but a small space between their hair and eye-brows; at the same time the hair grows remarkably forward on the temples, extending to the lower part of the ear. Besides, the hair itself is harsh, lank, coarse, and very black; their nose very small, thin, and has a little rising on the middle, from whence it forms a small curve, terminating in a point, bending towards the upper lip. These marks, besides some dark spots on the body, are so constant and invariable, as to make it very difficult to conceal the fallacy of their complexion. The Mestizos may be reckoned a third part of the inhabitants.

The next class is the Indians, who form about another third; and the others, who are about one sixth, are the Casts. These four classes, according to the most authentic accounts taken from the parish register, amount to between 50 and 60,000 persons, of all ages, sexes, and ranks. If among these classes the Spaniards, as is natural to think, are the most eminent for riches, rank, and power, it must at the same time be owned, however melancholy the truth may appear, they are in proportion the most poor, miserable and distressed; for they refuse to apply themselves to any mechanic business, considering it as a disgrace to that quality they so highly value themselves upon, which consists in not being black, brown, or of a copper-colour. The Mestizos, whose pride is regulated by prudence, readily apply themselves to arts and trades, but chuse those of the greatest repute, as painting, sculpture, and the like, leaving the meaner sort to the Indians. They are observed to excel in all, particularly painting and sculpture; in the former a Mestizo, called Miguel de Santiago, acquired great reputation, some of his works being still preserved and highly valued, while others were carried even to Rome, where they were honoured with the unanimous applauses of the vertuosi. They are remarkably ready and excellent at imitation, copying being indeed best adapted to their phlegmatic genius. And what renders their exquisite performances still more admirable is, that they are destitute of many of the instruments and tools requisite to perform them with any tolerable degree of accuracy. But, with these talents, they are so excessively indolent and slothful, that, instead of working, they often loiter about the streets during the whole day. The Indians, who are generally shoemakers, bricklayers, weavers, and the like, are not more industrious. Of these the most active and tractable are the barbers and phlebotomists, who, in their respective callings, are equal to the most expert hands in Europe. The shoemakers, on the other hand, distinguish themselves by such supineness and sloth, that very often you have no other way left to obtain the shoes you have bespoke, than to procure materials, seize on the Indian, and lock him up till they are finished. This is indeed partly owing to a wrong custom of paying for the work before it is done; and when the Indian has once got the money, he spends it all in chicha[[a highly intoxicating beer]] so that while it lasts he is never sober. . . .

Source: Jorge Juan and Antonio de Ulloa, *Voyage to South America* (London: Lockyer Davis, 1772), I: 261–267.

9. MARY JEMISON, AUTOBIOGRAPHY (1825)

In the 1750s, Native Americans seized fifteen-year-old Mary Jemison (1743–1833) and her family from their home in western Pennsylvania. Senecas then adopted her to compensate a family that had lost a male relative in the French and Indian War after a battle with George Washington's troops. Dickewamis, as Jemison was renamed, ultimately settled in western New York with the Senecas, remaining there into old age with no interest even when in close proximity with whites in rejoining them. In the 1820s, she gave her story to a white editor who sprinkled it with barbs against Native Americans. Nonetheless, her appreciation of their customs and her life with them clearly comes through. The account presented here begins with the aftermath of her captivity. What reasons do you find in the text for Jemison's refusal to leave her captors?

At night we arrived at a small Seneca Indian town, at the mouth of a small river, that was called by the Indians, in the Seneca language, She-nan- jee, where the two Squaws to whom I belonged resided. There we landed, and the Indians went on, which was the last I ever saw of them. Having made fast to the shore, the Squaws left me in the canoe while they went to their wigwam or house in the town, and returned with a suit of Indian clothing, all new, and very clean and nice. My clothes, though whole and good when I was taken, were now torn in pieces, so that I was almost naked. They first undressed me and threw my rags into the river, then washed me clean and dressed me in the new suit they had just brought, in complete Indian style, and then led me home and seated me in the center of their wigwam.

    I had been in that situation but a few minutes before all the Squaws in the town came in to see me. I was soon surrounded by them, and they immediately set up a most dismal howling, crying bitterly, and wringing their hands in all the agonies of grief for a deceased relative. Their tears flowed freely, and they exhibited all the signs of real mourning. At the commencement of this scene one of their number began, in a voice somewhat between speaking and singing, to recite some words to the following purport, and continued the recitation till the ceremony was ended; the company at the same time varying the appearance of their countenances, gestures and tone of voice; so as to correspond with the sentiments expressed by their leader:

"Oh our brother! Alas ! He is dead—he has gone; he will never return! Friendless he died on the field of the slain, where his bones are yet lying unburied! Oh, who will not mourn his sad fate? No tears dropped around him; oh, no! No tears of his sisters were there! He fell in his prime, when his arm was most needed to keep us from danger! Alas! he has gone! and left us in sorrow, his loss to bewail : Oh where is his spirit? His spirit went naked, and hungry it wanders, and thirsty and wounded it groans to return! Oh, helpless and wretched, our brother has gone! No blanket nor food to nourish and warm him; nor candles to light him, nor weapons of war:—Oh, None of those comforts had he! But well we remember his deeds! The deer he could take on the chase! The panther shrunk back at the sight of his strength; His enemies fell at his feet! He was brave and courageous in war! As the fawn he was harmless: his friendship was ardent: his temper was gentle: his pity was great! Oh! our friend, our companion is dead! Our brother, our brother, alas! he is gone! But why do we grieve for his loss? In the strength of a warrior, undaunted he left us, to fight by the side of the Chiefs! His war-whoop was shrill! His rifle well aimed laid his enemies low: his tomahawk drank of their blood: and his knife flayed their scalps while yet covered with gore! And why do we mourn? Though he fell on the field of the slain, with glory he fell, and his spirit went up to the land of his fathers in war! Then why do we mourn? With transports of joy they received him, and fed him, and clothed him, and welcomed him there; Oh friends, he is happy; then dry up your tears! His spirit has seen our distress, and sent us a helper whom with pleasure we greet. —Dickewamis has come: then let us receive her with joy! She is handsome and pleasant! Oh! she is our sister, and gladly we welcome her here. In the place of our brother she stands in our tribe. With care we will guard her from trouble; and may she be happy till her spirit shall leave us."

In the course of that ceremony, from mourning they became serene—joy sparkled in their countenances, and they seemed to rejoice over me as over a long-lost child. I was made welcome amongst them as a sister to the two Squaws before mentioned, and was called Dickewamis, which being interpreted, signifies a pretty girl, a hand-some girl, or a pleasant good thing. That is the name by which I have ever since been called by the Indians.

I afterwards learned that the ceremony I at that time passed through, was that of adoption. The two Squaws had lost a brother in Washington's war, sometime in the year before, and in consequence of his death went up to Fort Pitt, on the day on which I arrived there, in order to receive a prisoner or an enemy's scalp, to supply their loss.

It is a custom of the Indians, when one of their number is slain or taken prisoner in battle, to give to the nearest relative to the dead or absent, a prisoner, if they have chanced to take one, and if not to give him the scalp of an enemy. . . .

It was my happy lot to be accepted for adoption; and at the time of the ceremony I was received by the two Squaws to supply the place of their brother in the family; and I was ever considered and treated by them as a real sister, the same as though I had been born of their mother.

During my adoption I sat motionless, nearly terrified to death at the appearance and actions of the company, expecting every moment to feel their vengeance, and suffer death on the spot. I was, however, happily disappointed, when at the close of the ceremony the company retired, and my sisters went about employing every means for my consolation and comfort.

Being now settled and provided with a home, I was employed in nursing the children, and doing light work about the house. Occasionally I was sent out with the Indian hunters, when they went but a short distance, to help them to carry their game. My situation was easy; I had no particular hardship to endure. But still the recollection of my parents, my brothers and sisters, my home, and my own captivity, destroyed my happiness, and made me constantly solitary, lonesome and gloomy.

My sisters would not allow me to speak English in their hearing; but remembering the charge that my dear mother gave me at the time I left her, whenever I chanced to be alone I made a business of repeating my prayer, catechism, or something I had learned, in order that I might not forget my own language. By practicing in that way I retained it till I came to Genesee Flats, where I soon became acquainted with English people with whom I have been almost daily in the habit of conversing.

My sisters were diligent in teaching: me their language, and to their great satisfaction I soon learned so that I could understand it readily, and speak it fluently. I was very fortunate in falling, into their hands; for they were kind good-natured women; peaceable and mild in their dispositions; temperate and decent in their habits, and very tender and gentle towards me. I have great reason to respect them, though they have been dead a great number of years.

The town where they lived was pleasantly situated on the Ohio, at the mouth of the Shenanjee: the land produced good corn; the woods furnished a plenty of game, and the waters abounded with fish. Another river emptied itself into the Ohio, directly opposite the mouth of the Shenan-jee. We spent the summer at that place, where we planted, hoed, and harvested a large crop of corn of an excellent quality. . . .

I had then been with the Indians four summers and four winters, and had become so far accustomed to their mode of living, habits and dispositions, that my anxiety to get away, to be set at liberty, and leave them, had almost subsided. With them was my home; my family was there, and there I had many friends to whom I was warmly attached in consideration of the favors, affection and friendship with which they had uniformly treated me, from the time of my adoption. Our labor was not severe, and that of one year was exactly similar, in almost every respect, to that of the others, without that endless variety that is to be observed in the common labor of the white people. Notwithstanding the Indian women have all the fuel and bread to procure, and the cooking to perform, their task is probably not harder than that of white women, who have those articles provided for them; and their cares certainly are not half so numerous, nor as great. In the summer season we planted, tended and harvested our corn, and generally had all our children with us, but had no master to oversee or drive us, so that we could work as leisurely as we pleased. . . .

Our cooking consisted in pounding our corn into samp or hommany, boiling the hommany, making now and then a cake and baking it in the ashes, and in boiling or roasting our venison. As our cooking and eating utensils consisted of a hommany block and pestle, a small kettle, a knife or two, and a few vessels of bark or wood, it required but little time to keep them in order for use.

Spinning, weaving, sewing, stocking-knitting, and the like, are arts which have never been practiced in the Indian tribes generally. After the revolutionary war I learned to sew, so that I could make my own clothing after a poor fashion; but the other domestic arts I have been wholly ignorant of the application of since my captivity. In the season of hunting it was our business, in addition to our cooking, to bring home the game that was taken by the Indians, dress it, and carefully preserve the eatable meat, and prepare or dress the skins. Our clothing was fastened together with strings of deer skin, and tied on with the same.

In that manner we lived, without any of those jealousies, quarrels, and revengeful battles between families and individuals, which have been common in the Indian tribes since the introduction of ardent spirits amongst them.

The use of ardent spirits amongst the Indians, and the attempts which have been made to civilize and christianize them by the white people, has constantly made them worse and worse, increased their vices, and robbed them of many of their virtues; and will ultimately produce their extermination. I have seen, in a number of instances, the effects of education upon some of our Indians, who were taken when young, from their families, and placed at school before they had had an opportunity to contract many Indian habits, and there kept till they arrived to manhood; but I have never seen one of those but what was an Indian in every respect after he returned. Indians must and will be Indians, in spite of all the means that can be used for their cultivation in the sciences and arts.

One thing only marred my happiness, while I lived with them on the Ohio, and that was the recollection that I had once had tender parents, and a home that I loved. Aside from that consideration, or, if I had been taken in infancy, I should have been contented in my situation. Notwithstanding all that has been said against the Indians, in consequence of their cruelties to their enemies—cruelties that I have witnessed, and had abundant proof of—it is a fact that they are naturally kind, tender and peaceable towards their friends, and strictly honest; and that those cruelties have been practiced only upon their enemies, according to their idea of justice.

Source: Mary Jemison, *A Narrative of the Life of Mary Jemison . . .* , James E. Seaver, ed. (London: Wilson and Sons, 1826), 32–45 passim. I have omitted remarks of the editor of Jemison's story and updated spelling. Also available at https://archive.org/stream/narrativeoflifeo00seav/narrativeoflifeo00seav_djvu.txt.

10. ROBERT CLIVE, LETTER ON THE BATTLE OF PLASSEY (1757) AND PARLIAMENTARY TESTIMONY ON CUSTOMS IN INDIA (1772)

The British East India Company has been called a political institution—a company state—because it had its own armies composed of British, South Asian, and other European soldiers and because it collected taxes for different regions in Bengal in northeast India. It was not recognized as an independent nation, but it behaved like one. In 1757, at a time when Britain had only shaky control of bits of the subcontinent, the forces of the British East India company, led by Robert Clive, defeated the Nawab (or ruler) of Bengal, who had protested the expansion of the Company's fortifications in the region. From that point on, the British were able to field large armies, as they increased their taxing powers, and to move southward to defeat competing rulers of South Asian states. Clive justified the takeover as follows: "The inhabitants, especially of Bengal, in inferior stations, are servile, mean, submissive, and humble. In superior stations, they are luxurious, effeminate, tyrannical, treacherous, venal, cruel." Given that situation, he argued without seeing the contradiction, the British should take over a region whose talented and active population had created such wealth. For many, the Battle of Plassey marked the beginning of the British control—limited as it was at the time—of South Asia. There was simultaneously the flowering of a belief that its lazy people did not deserve the wealth that their talent had created. Describe the interconnections among peoples and nations that appear in this brief account.

I gave you an account of the taking of Chandernagore in my last letter; the subject of this address is an event of much higher importance, no less than the entire overthrow of Nabob Suraj-ud-Daulah, and the placing of Meer Jaffier on the throne. I intimated in my last how dilatory Suraj-ud-Daulah appeared in fulfilling the articles of the treaty. This disposition not only continued but increased, and we discovered that he was designing our ruin by a conjunction with the French.

About this time some of his principal officers made overtures to us for dethroning him. At the head of these was Meer Jaffier, then *Bukhshee* to the army, a man as generally esteemed as the other was detested. As we had reason to believe this disaffection pretty general, we soon entered into engagements with Meer Jaffier to put the crown on his head. All necessary preparations being completed with the utmost secrecy, the army, consisting of about one thousand Europeans and two thousand sepoys, with eight pieces of cannon, marched from Chandernagore on the 13th and arrived on the 18th at Cutwa Fort. The 22nd, in the evening, we crossed the river, and landing on the island, marched straight for Plassey Grove, where we arrived by one in the morning.

At daybreak we discovered the Nabob's army moving towards us, consisting, as we since found, of about fifteen thousand horse and thirty-five thousand foot, with upwards of forty pieces of cannon. They approached apace, and by six began to attack with a number of heavy cannon, supported by the whole army, and continued to play on us very briskly for several hours, during which our situation was of the utmost service to us, being lodged in a large grove with good mud banks. To succeed in an attempt on their cannon was next to impossible, as they were planted in a manner round us, and at considerable distances from each other. We therefore remained quiet in our post. . . .

About noon the enemy drew off their artillery, and retired to their camp. We immediately sent a detachment, accompanied by two field-pieces, to take possession of a tank with high banks, which was advanced about three hundred yards above our grove, and from which the enemy had considerably annoyed us with some cannon managed by Frenchmen. This motion brought them out a second time; but on finding them make no great effort to dislodge us, we proceeded to take possession of one or two more eminences lying very near an angle of their camp. They made several attempts to bring out their cannon, but our advance field-pieces played so warmly and so well upon them that they were always driven back. Their horse exposing themselves a good deal on this occasion, many of them were killed, and among the rest four or five officers of the first distinction, by which the whole army being visibly dispirited and thrown into some confusion, we were encouraged to storm both the eminence and the angle of their camp, which were carried at the same instant, with little or no loss. On this a general rout ensued; and we pursued the enemy six miles, passing upwards of forty pieces of cannon they had abandoned, with an infinite number of carriages filled with baggage of all kinds. It is computed there are killed of the enemy about five hundred. Our loss amounted to only twenty-two killed and fifty wounded, and those chiefly sepoys.

Source: Oliver J. Thatcher, ed., *The Library of Original Sources* (Milwaukee: University Research Extension Co., 1907), Vol. VII: *The Age of Revolution*, 59–64.

11. JAMES COOK, DIARY OF HIS FIRST VOYAGE (1768–1771)

Exploration of the seas continued in the eighteenth century, notably the three voyages searching out the intricacies of the Pacific Ocean made by Captain James Cook (1728–1779), who had begun his naval career on coal-laden ships from Newcastle, England, to London. At the age of 27, Cook joined the navy and continued to gain experience of the seas and build expertise in mapping, especially the east coast of Canada during the French and Indian War. Between 1768 and 1771, he led an expedition to the Pacific that produced detailed knowledge of New Zealand (as in the diary excerpt that follows), the east Coast of Australia, and the Great Barrier Reef— all of these putting Britain at the head of European powers claiming these territories. Between 1772 and 1775, Cook traveled the southern Pacific, bringing back further knowledge of the icy dangers of the Antarctic seas and making him in some people's eyes the greatest ocean-going explorer. His final voyage covered both north and south Pacific, although on this trip he unwisely inserted himself in the politics of local people and was killed. Soon after, colonization of Australia and New Zealand began.

If the settling of this country should ever be thought an object worthy the attention of Great Britain, the best place for establishing a colony would be either on the banks of the Thames, or in the country bordering upon the Bay of Islands. In either place there would be the advantage of an excellent harbour; and, by means of the river, settlements might be extended, and a communication established with the inland parts of the country: vessels might be built of the fine timber which abounds in these parts, at very little trouble and expence, fit for such a navigation as would answer the purpose. I cannot indeed exactly assign the depth of water which a vessel intended to navigate this river, even as far up as I went with the boat, should draw, because this depends upon the depth of water that is upon the bar, or flats, which lie before the narrow part of the river, for I had no opportunity to make myself acquainted with them; but I am of opinion, that a vessel which should draw not more than twelve feet would perfectly answer the purpose.

When we first arrived upon the coast of this country, we imagined it to be much better peopled than we afterwards found it, concluding that the inland parts were populous from the smoke that we saw at a considerable distance from the shore; and perhaps that may really be the case with respect to the country behind Poverty Bay, and the Bay of Plenty, where the inhabitants appeared to be more numerous than in other places. But we had reason to believe, that, in general, no part of the country but the sea coast is inhabited; and even there we found the people but thinly scattered, all the western coast from Cape Maria Van Diemen to Mount Egmont being totally desolate; so that upon the whole the number of inhabitants bears no proportion to the extent of country. . . .

The dispositions both of the men and women seemed to be mild and gentle; they treat each other with the tenderest affection, but are implacable towards their enemies, to whom, as I have before observed, they never give quarter. It may perhaps, at first, seem strange, that where there is so little to be got by victory, there should so often be war; and that every little district of a country inhabited by people so mild and placid, should be at enmity with all the rest. But possibly more is to be gained by victory among these people than at first appears, and they may be prompted to mutual hostilities by motives which no degree of friendship or affection is able to resist. It appears, by the account that has already been given of them, that their principal food is fish, which can only be procured upon the sea coast; and there, in sufficient quantities, only at certain times: the tribes, therefore, who live inland, if any such there are, and even those upon the coast, must be frequently in danger of perishing by famine. Their country produces neither sheep, nor goats, nor hogs, nor cattle; tame fowls they have none, nor any art by which those that are wild can be caught in sufficient plenty to serve as provision. If there are any whose situation cuts them off from a supply of fish, the only succedaneum of all other animal food, except dogs, they have nothing to support life, but the vegetables that have already been mentioned, of which the chief are fern root, yams, clams, and potatoes: when by any accident these fail, the distress must be dreadful; and even among the inhabitants of the coast, many tribes must frequently be reduced to nearly the same situation, either by the failure of their plantations, or the deficiency of their dry stock, during the season when but few fish are to be caught. These considerations will enable us to account, not only for the perpetual danger in which the people who inhabit this country appear to live, by the care which they take to fortify every village, but for the horrid practice of eating those who are killed in battle; for the hunger of him who is pressed by famine to fight, will absorb every feeling, and every sentiment which would restrain him from allaying it with the body of his adversary. It may however be remarked, that, if this account of the origin of so horrid a practice is true, the mischief does by no means end with the necessity that produced it: after the practice has been once begun on one side by hunger, it will naturally be adopted on the other by revenge. . . .

The situation and circumstances, however, of these poor people, as well as their temper, are favourable to those who shall settle as a colony among them. Their situation sets them in need of protection, and their temper renders it easy to attach them by kindness; and whatever may be said in favour of a savage life, among people who live in luxurious idleness upon the bounty of Nature, civilization would certainly be a blessing to those whom her parsimony scarcely furnishes with the bread of life, and who are perpetually destroying each other by violence, as the only alternative of perishing by hunger. . . .

But these people, from whatever cause, being inured to war, and by habit considering every stranger as an enemy, were always disposed to attack us when they were not intimidated by our manifest superiority. At first, they had no notion of any superiority but numbers; and when this was on their side, they considered all our expressions of kindness as the artifices of fear and cunning, to circumvent them, and preserve ourselves: but when they were once convinced of our power, after having provoked us to the use of our fire-arms, though loaded only with small shot; and of our clemency, by our forbearing to make use of weapons so dreadful except in our defence; they became at once friendly, and even affectionate, placing in us the most unbounded confidence, and doing every thing which could incite us to put equal confidence in them. It is also remarkable, that when an intercourse was once established between us, they were very rarely detected in any act of dishonesty.

Source: John Hawkesworth, ed., *An Account of the Voyages Undertaken by the Order of His Present Majesty for Making Discoveries in the Southern Hemisphere* (London: Strahan and Cadell, 1773), 3: 444, 445, 446, 447. Widely available online.

12. POTEMKIN, MEMORANDUM ON THE ANNEXATION OF THE CRIMEA (1783)

Meanwhile, the Russians had fanned out in all directions overland. While pushing across to the Pacific Ocean, they simultaneously pressed upon the Afghans, Persians, and Tatars to the south. Many of these people were Muslims, heavily involved in trading networks, including the capture and sale of Russians as slaves across the border. Gradually, the Russians annexed Tatar areas, including the Crimea in 1783 and later Georgia in 1801. Through multidirectional continental expansion the

Russians created one of the most ethnically diverse of all modern states and showed that empire was not just a result of oceanic conquest. The announcement of Catherine's annexation of the Crimea that same year cites the unruliness of the people and the need to ensure peace in the region for their own benefit. Her chief advisor, skilled military leader Grigory Potemkin (1739–1791), cites different reasons for the annexation. What imperial values does this document contain?

The Crimea, by its position, creates a breach in our borders. Whether the Turks have to be watched along the Bug or on the Kuban' side, we always have to worry about the Crimea. Here we can clearly see why the present khan [of the Crimea] does not please the Turks: it is because he will not let them enter through the Crimea into our very heart, so to speak. Now, just imagine that the Crimea is yours and no longer a thorn in your side; suddenly our frontier situation becomes splendid: along the Bug the Turks adjoin us directly and therefore have to deal with us themselves and not use others as a cover. Here we can see every step they take. And as for the Kuban' side, in addition to a dense series of forts, manned with garrisons, the numerous Don [Cossack] Host is always in readiness. The security of the population of the Novorossiia guberniia will then be beyond doubt; navigation on the Black Sea will be free; as it is now, your ships have difficulty in leaving port and find it still harder to enter. In addition, we shall rid ourselves of the difficulties of maintaining the forts we now have in remote outposts in the Crimea. Most Gracious Sovereign! My unbounded devotion to you compels me to speak out: disregard envy, which is powerless to hinder you. It is your duty to exalt the glory of Russia. Look what others have acquired without opposition: France took Corsica; the Austrians [*tsesartsy*], without war, took more from the Turks in Moldavia than we did. There are no powers in Europe that would not divide Asia, Africa, and America among themselves. The acquisition of the Crimea can neither strengthen nor enrich you, but it will give you security. It will be a heavy blow, to be sure, but to whom? To the Turks! a still more compelling reason for you to act. Believe me, you will acquire immortal fame such as no other sovereign of Russia ever had. This glory will open the way to still further and greater glory: with the Crimea will come domination of the Black Sea; it will be in your power to blockade the Turks, to feed them or to starve them. To the [Crimean] khan you may grant anything you choose in Persia; it will keep him happy. He will offer you the Crimea this winter; the population will gladly submit a petition to this effect. Just as the annexation will bring you glory, so will posterity shame and reproach you if continued disturbances lead it to say: "She had the power to act but would not or let the moment slip by." If gentle is thy rule, then Russia needs a paradise. Kherson of Taurida [Crimea]! You were the source of piety for us; now behold how Catherine II shall again bring you the peace of a Christian rule.

Source: *A Source Book for Russian History from Early Times to 1917*, George Vernadsky et al., eds., 3 vols. (New Haven: Yale University Press, 1972), 2: 411.

REVIEW QUESTIONS

1. Describe the variety of attitudes toward people and products from distant lands in the seventeenth and eighteenth centuries.
2. Describe the movement of ideas, products, and techniques across empires during the early modern period.
3. Describe the ways in which empires and states are interacting in these centuries.
4. The Spanish invasion of the Americas, their importation of slaves from Africa, their intermingling with local peoples, and the arrival of fortune hunters from other parts of the world produced a great mixture of ethnicities and races. See https://nativeheritageproject.com/2013/06/15/las-castas-spanish-racial-classifications/. What imperial values and structures can you decipher from this chart of racial and ethnic classifications?

CHAPTER 5

Revolt Against Empire

From the fifteenth into the twentieth century, people globally revolted against imperial encroachments on their land and livelihoods and against attacks on their way of life. In the Western Hemisphere, Native Americans rose up against white invasions and settlements. Pueblo Indians across the sixteenth century resisted Spanish efforts to change their beliefs and their mounting demands for tribute such as their labor and the harvest in corn. In 1622, Opechancanough, brother of Powhatan who had led the Algonquins and established a consortium of northeastern Native Americans, had had enough of the greedy English tobacco-growers: he waged war against them, killing a third of the Jamestown community. He persisted, leading a final revolt in the 1640s, when he was captured by the English and shot in the back while a prisoner. Simultaneously, there were revolts against the encomienda system in South America, in which Native Americans along with their land were awarded to Spanish occupiers.

In the Caribbean and Brazil slaves escaped the tentacles of the exacting life on sugar plantations to set up "maroon" communities of their own as far from the center of colonial life as possible. The word "maroon" comes from the word *cimarrones*, which means mountaineer in Spanish. Because slaves on a plantation or in a distinct region often came from the same area in Africa and because many had served in armies back home, their military skills were considerable. In 1655, Jamaican maroons rose up against the new British rulers, who had taken the sugar island from the Spanish. Their struggles against Britain continued for a century and a half. Among maroon communities in Brazil, the most successful was Palmares, which thrived between c. 1602 and 1695, when it was defeated by an alliance of the Dutch and the Portuguese. This community, also known as Quilombo, had an estimated 11,000 to 30,000 escaped slaves, free blacks, and soldiers who had deserted. The Jamaican and Brazilian communities are but two of the most celebrated maroon settlements.

The tradition of resistance these uprisings represented fueled widespread revolts in the late eighteenth and early nineteenth centuries across the Western

Hemisphere and beyond it. Additionally, colonists, slaves, and some among the imperial conquerors had seen examples of different, less oppressive ways of life, inspiring further resistance. Examples of how other peoples enjoyed freedom, religious toleration, free trade, or public education reached the Atlantic world, providing an impetus to reform and revolt there. Another innovation in Europe and the wider European world was the coffee house or café, where people congregated to discuss politics and transact business over coffee, chocolate, and even tea. Like those products, the coffee house was a foreign enterprise that first started in the Ottoman Empire; it fostered the development of an informed public. As in the Ottoman Empire, the coffee house could be subversive because new ideas and criticisms of the monarch and government officials spread to a wider audience along trade routes. The Atlantic world was awash in new ideas.

One particular topic emerged across empires to stir discussion. As the European powers built ever more powerful fleets and efficient weaponry to fight both indigenous peoples and one another, they raised taxes, causing further anger. The French and Indian War (1754–1763), during which both British and French governments incurred enormous debts, was one such war, but rulers found the costs of imperial contests among virtually all contenders a cause for higher taxes. These taxes affected the vast majority of colonial subjects, although in different ways.

The examples of more efficient government run by capable officials found in places across the globe, among which China was primary in the eighteenth century, also awakened thinkers to call for more "enlightened" rule. Spain took this call to mean more rational rule, especially more efficient taxation policies, both for those in Spain itself and in its colonies. It thus instituted the "Bourbon Reforms," with those applicable to the colonies increasing taxes. It also created opportunities for Spanish officials to thrive at the benefit of other inhabitants, including the creoles or those of Spanish blood born in the colonies. Even as continental trade increased, those born in the Spanish colonies of whatever race or ethnicity felt reforms as a weight rather than the benefit of enlightened rule. Descendants of the Inca, for one, felt that it was time to restore their ancient empire, and revolts became common.

Britain likewise imposed new taxes on the colonies and prohibited additional westward expansion because it would push Native Americans to additional, costly resistance. These new rules outraged North American colonists, many of whom wanted the right to move westward for more land. Others focused on the rights of Englishmen to approve taxation now that the French had been pretty much ousted from the region; these rights the British government seemed to ignore. The spirit of revolt grew, and by 1776 the North American colonies launched an all-out uprising against the British Empire. They succeeded in large part because of the ready assistance of Britain's competitors for empire: France and Spain were both eager to thwart British global advance. Soon thereafter the French Revolution erupted, as the monarchy went bankrupt because of its huge expenditures on winning U.S. independence. Both the United States and French revolutionaries added to the vocabulary of rights, freedom, and opportunity that shaped subsequent efforts against empire.

Enslaved, conquered, or otherwise aggrieved peoples shared the goal of rights, freedom, and social and economic improvement in the face of empire. Beginning in the1780s, Haitians, both slaves and free blacks, fought for more than a decade for personal freedom and rights and eventually for freedom from the French. They set up a constitutional government, following the path of the French and Americans before them, at first freeing slaves, then re-enslaving them, and finally declaring personal freedom for everyone. Then the Spanish colonies in Latin America broke away from their European masters, again spurred on by a variety of grievances according to their station in life. In 1810, Catholic priest Miguel Hidalgo y Costilla roused thousands of New Spain's poor under the banner of the Virgin of Guadelupe to contest the privileges and wealth of the Spanish elite. Others took up the challenge for an end to the oppression of African slaves and Native Americans. Soon thereafter a creole aristocrat, Simon Bolivar, having witnessed the splendor of Napoleon's France, became a revolutionary leader combatting Spanish rule. By 1830, most of the Spanish territories in the new world had freed themselves from empire. During the age of revolution, a range of new nations emerged while others felt threatened: As France and Britain lost territories, in the nineteenth century they expanded in other regions with increased energy. The new United States set out to take Native American territory and to expand its influence globally. Many parts of the world came under attack from the empire-builders, even those like the new U.S. citizens, who both revolted from their fellow countrymen in Britain and once "free" set out to take over even more land. Spanish colonizers also revolted against fellow Spaniards, contributing, as in the U.S. case, to the chaos that empires brought with them.

1. VOLTAIRE, *ESSAI SUR LES MOEURS ET L'ESPRIT DES NATIONS [ESSAY ON THE CUSTOMS AND THE SPIRIT OF NATIONS]* (1756)

Europeans continued to have complicated reactions to and interactions with distant peoples and societies. In a fantastical novel, French jurist Montesquieu showed Persian visitors to Paris aghast at the status of absolutist kings and the superstitions of the Catholic Church. French philosopher, novelist, and critic Voltaire set some of his novels in the Middle East, suggesting that despite an element of trickery and greed among people there, greater possibilities existed for a more enlightened government .than in Europe. He decorated his home with Chinese statuary and wrote often about Chinese emperors and other rulers as models of Enlightenment. In other words, for Voltaire the rest of the world could be an example for Europe, in part because its rulers were not such bigoted do-nothings. Simultaneously in attempts to be a balanced author, Voltaire infused his books with examples of human folly and evil that existed around the world. However, providing examples of bad government in Europe and good government elsewhere, Voltaire fanned the flames of revolt and revolution generally. This passage from his writings describes Mehmed II, conqueror of Constantinople. For what purposes is Voltaire using the global knowledge brought about by imperial activity?

All Turkish histories inform us that Mehmed was the best raised prince of his day. . . . He spoke Greek, Arab, Persian; he understood Latin; he drew; he knew all that one could of geography and mathematics; he loved painting. No connoisseur of the arts but knows that he brought from Venice the famous Gentile Bellini and rewarded him, as Alexandre paid Apelles, with gifts and with his friendship. He presented him with a gift of a crown of gold, a necklace of gold, of 3,000 ducats of gold, and sent him home with honor. I can't help but mention among improbable takes, that of the slave that one claims Mehmed had beheaded to show Bellini the effect of muscles and skin on a head separated from its body. These barbarisms that we inflict on animals, humans do not inflict on other humans except in a vengeful fury or in what is called the law of warfare. Mehmed was often bloody and ferocious, like all conquerors who have ravaged the world; but why impute to him such improbable cruelty? To what good do we multiply horrors? Philip of Commines, who lived at the same time as this sultan, vows that on his deathbed he asked God's pardon for having taxed his subjects. Where are the Christian monarchs who show such repentence?

He was only twenty-two years old when he became sultan; and from that moment on he prepared to place himself on the throne of Constantinople too, especially since the capital was divided on whether or not to eat unleavened bread and on whether to pray in Greek or Latin.

(1453) Mehmed began by blockading the city from the European side and the Asian side. Finally, from the first days of April, the countryside was covered with soldiers, some 300,000 according to exaggerated accounts, and the strait of Propontis by some three hundred galleys and two hundred smaller ships.

One of the strangest sights and most remarked is how he used part of his fleet. He could not enter the city's harbor, blocked by very strong iron chains and besides that well defended. In a single night, he had a long road of greased pines made into a ship's birth; then he had machines and eighty galleys along with seventy others moved from the straits and rolled along the planks. All of this work was accomplished in a single night . . . and served as a battery for cannons. . . .

Beginning in May, they assaulted the city, which believed itself the capital of the world: it was very badly fortified and hardly better defended. . . .

[In the end] the Turcs entered . . . mastered the upper city, which was separated from the lower. The emperor was killed among the crowd; and Mehmed II made Constantine's palace that of the sultans and Saint-Sophia church his principle mosque.

Is one more filled with pity or with indignation when one reads . . . that the sultan "gave orders to set the city alight and gave the particular sign of their detestable superstition." This impious cry was the name of God, "Allah," which Muslims utter in all of their battles. The actual detestable superstition was that of the Greeks, who took refuge in Saint-Sophia church, believing in the prediction that an angel would descend into the church to defend it.

Source: Voltaire, *Textes sur l'Orient. 1. L'Empire Ottoman et le Monde Arabe*, Jean-Pierre Jackson, ed. Paris: Presses Universitaire de France, 2005), 121–123. Excerpt taken from Voltaire, *Oeuvres completes*, 1875. Bonnie G. Smith translation.

2. JOHN ADAMS, "INSTRUCTIONS OF THE TOWN OF BRAINTREE MASSACHUSETTS ON THE STAMP ACT" (1765)

Unlike the comparatively tight governmental structures in the Spanish empire, those of the British in North America had varied from place to place because colonial charters for Maryland or Pennsylvania, for example, were given to individuals of differing values and mindsets. Moreover, living on individual small farms, the population of Britain's North American colonies was more scattered than the highly urbanized population of Spain's colonies. In the thirteen British colonies, small communities developed traditions of self-rule and participation, so that when Parliament tried to impose standard taxes from a distance to pay for the French and Indian War, opposition came from many sides, beginning with attacks on the Stamp Act of 1765. John Adams, a lawyer (and later the second president of the United States), crafted this set of objections to the Act, which levied taxes on all sorts of legal and other transactions. In so doing he helped build a line of attack for colonists on the imperial project of which they were a part. Thus other townships followed, sending their criticisms to the authorities and publicizing them. What is Adams' critique of Britain's imperial project?

. . . We can no longer forbear complaining, that many of the measures of the late ministry, and some of the late acts of Parliament, have a tendency, in our apprehension, to divest us of our most essential rights and liberties. We shall confine ourselves, however, chiefly to the act of Parliament, commonly called the Stamp Act, by which a very burthensome, and, in our opinion, unconstitutional tax, is to be laid upon us all; and we subjected to numerous and enormous penalties, to be prosecuted, sued for, and recovered, at the option of an informer, in a court of admiralty, without a jury.

We have called this a burthensome tax, because the duties are so numerous and so high, and the embarrassments to business in this infant, sparsely-settled country so great, that it would be totally impossible for the people to subsist under it, if we had no controversy at all about the right and authority of imposing it. Considering the present scarcity of money, we have reason to think, the execution of that act for a short space of time would drain the country of its cash, strip multitudes of all their property, and reduce them to absolute beggary. And what the consequence would be to the peace of the province, from so sudden a shock and such a convulsive change in the whole course of our business and subsistence, we tremble to consider. We further apprehend this tax to be unconstitutional. We have always understood it to be a grand and fundamental principle of the constitution, that no freeman should be subject to any tax to which he has not given his own consent, in person or by proxy. And the maxims of the law, as we have constantly received them, are to the same effect, that no freeman can be separated from his property but by his own act or fault. We take it clearly, therefore, to be inconsistent with the spirit of the common law, and of the essential fundamental principles of the British constitution, that we should be subject to any tax imposed by the British Parliament; because we are not represented in that assembly in any sense, unless it be by a fiction of law, as insensible in theory as it would be injurious in practice, if such a taxation should be grounded on it.

But the most grievous innovation of all, is the alarming extension of the power of courts of admiralty. In these courts, one judge presides alone! No juries have any concern there! The law and the fact are both to be decided by the same single judge, whose commission is only during pleasure, and with whom, as we are told, the most mischievous of all customs has become established, that of taking commissions on all condemnations; so that he is under a pecuniary temptation always against the subject. . . . We have all along thought the acts of trade in this respect a grievance; but the Stamp Act has opened a vast number of sources of new crimes, which may be committed by any man, and cannot but be committed by multitudes, and prodigious penalties are annexed, and all these are to be tried by such a judge of such a court! . . . We cannot help asserting, therefore, that this part of the act will make an essential change in the constitution of juries, and it is directly repugnant to the Great Charter itself; for, by that charter, "no amerciament shall be assessed, but by the oath of honest and lawful men of the vicinage;" and, "no freeman shall be taken, or imprisoned, or disseized of his freehold, or liberties of free customs, nor passed upon, nor condemned, but by lawful judgment of his peers, or by the law of the land." So that this act will "make such a distinction, and create such a difference between" the subjects in Great Britain and those in America, as we could not have expected from the guardians of liberty in "both."

As these, sir, are our sentiments of this act, we, the freeholders and other inhabitants, legally assembled for this purpose, must enjoin it upon you, to comply with no measures or proposals for countenancing the same, or assisting in the execution of it, but by all lawful means, consistent with our allegiance to the King, and relation to Great Britain, to oppose the execution of it, till we can hear the success of the cries and petitions of America for relief.

We further recommend the most clear and explicit assertion and vindication of our rights and liberties to be entered on the public records, that the world may know, in the present and all future generations, that we have a clear knowledge and a just sense of them, and, with submission to Divine Providence, that we never can be slaves. . . .

Source: *The Works of John Adams*, C. F. Adams, ed., 10 vols. (Boston: Little, Brown, 1850–1856), 3: 465.

3. ADAM SMITH, "THE COST OF EMPIRE" FROM *THE WEALTH OF NATIONS* (1776)

Adam Smith, a Scottish philosopher born in 1723, first became known for advocating attention to the welfare of the community based on the empathy that humans show toward one another. After that he became legendary as a teacher and for his promotion of free trade, the division of labor, and rational behavior according to economic self-interest that appeared in his classic work The Wealth of Nations. *In it, Smith additionally*

discussed the burgeoning British Empire and the costs such an empire entailed. His ratio-
nal stand was at odds with the proponents of expansion at all costs, and he cited the
aims of finding gold as foolish from the point of view of economics. The Spanish gold and
silver mines had now run out and there was little in the way of economic development to
show in a country that had declared bankruptcy several times. Nonetheless, he noted the
momentous significance of the discovery of the "New World" and the Cape of Good Hope
route to India in this age of thinking about what globalization and empire meant.

Of the advantages which Europe has derived from the discovery of America.

Those advantages may be divided, first, into the general advantages which
Europe, considered as one great country, has derived from those great events; and,
secondly great events; and secondly, into the particular advantages which each
colonizing country has derived from the colonies which particulars belong to it, in
consequence of the authority or dominion which it exercises over them.

The general advantages which Europe, considered as one great country, has
derived from the discovery and colonization of America, consist, first, in the
increase of its enjoyments; and, secondly, in the augmentation of its industry.

The surplus produce of America, imported into Europe, furnishes the inhabitants of this great continent with a variety of commodities which they could not
Otherwise have possessed, some for convenience and use, some for pleasure, and
some for ornament, and thereby contributes to increase their enjoyments.

The discovery and colonization of America, it will readily be allowed, have
contributed to augment the industry, first, of all the countries which trade to it
directly; such as Spain, Portugal, France, and England; and, secondly, of all those
which, without trading to it directly, send, through the medium of other countries,
goods to it of their own produce; such as Austrian Flanders, and some provinces
of Germany, which, through the medium of the countries before mentioned, send
to it a considerable quantity of linen and other goods. All such countries have evi-
dently gained a more extensive market for their surplus produce, and must consequently have been encouraged to increase its quantity.

But, that those great events should likewise have contributed to encourage
the industry of countries, such as Hungary and Poland, which may never, perhaps, have sent a single commodity of their own produce to America, is not,
perhaps, altogether so evident. That those events have done so, however, cannot
be doubted. Some part of the produce of America is consumed in Hungary and
Poland, and there is some demand there for the sugar, chocolate, and tobacco, of
that new quarter of the world. But those commodities must be purchased with
something which is either the produce of the industry of Hungary and Poland,
or with something which had been purchased with some part of that produce.
Those commodities of America are new values, new equivalents, introduced into
Hungary and Poland to be exchanged there for the surplus produce of those countries. By being carried thither they create a new and more extensive market for
that surplus produce. They raise its value, and thereby contribute to encourage its
increase. Though no part of it may ever be carried to America, it may be carried to

other countries which purchase it with a part of their share of the surplus produce of America; and it may find a market by means of the circulation of that trade which was originally put into motion by the surplus produce of America.

Those great events may even have contributed to increase the enjoyments, and to augment the industry of countries which not only never sent any commodities to America, but never received any from it. Even such countries may have received a greater abundance of other commodities from countries of which the surplus produce had been augmented by means of the American trade. This greater abundance, as it must necessarily have increased their enjoyments, so it must likewise have augmented their industry. A greater number of new equivalents of some kind or other must have been presented to them to be exchanged for the surplus produce of that industry. A more extensive market must have been created for that surplus produce, so as to raise its value, and thereby encourage its increase. The mass of commodities annually thrown into the great circle of European commerce, and by it various revolutions annually distributed among all the different nations comprehended within it, must have been augmented by the whole surplus produce of America. A greater share of this greater mass, therefore, is likely to have fallen to each of those nations, to have increased their enjoyments, and augmented their industry. . . .

The particular advantages which each colonizing country derives from the colonies which particularly belong to it, are of two different kinds; first, those common advantages which every empire derives from the provinces subject to its dominion; and, secondly, those peculiar advantages which are supposed to result from provinces of so very peculiar a nature as the European colonies of America. . . .

The discovery of America, and that of a passage to the East Indies by the Cape of Good Hope, are the two greatest and most important events recorded in the history of mankind. Their consequences have already been very great: but, in the short period of between two and three centuries which has elapsed since these discoveries were made, it is impossible that the whole extent of their consequences can have been seen. What benefits, or what misfortunes to mankind may hereafter result from those great events, no human wisdom can foresee. By uniting, in some measure, the most distant parts of the world, by enabling them to relieve one another's wants, to increase one another's enjoyments, and to encourage one another's industry, their general tendency would seem to be beneficial.

In the meantime, one of the principal effects of those discoveries has been to raise the mercantile system to a degree of splendor and glory which it could never otherwise have attained to. It is the object of that system to enrich a great nation rather by trade and manufactures than by the improvement and cultivation of land, rather by the industry of the towns than by that of the country. But, in consequence of those discoveries, the commercial towns of Europe, instead of being the manufacturers and carriers for but a very small part of the world (that part of Europe which is washed by the Atlantic ocean, and the countries which lie round the Baltic and Mediterranean seas), have now become the manufacturers for the numerous and thriving cultivators of America, and the carriers, and in some respects the manufacturers too, for almost all the different nations of Asia,

Africa, and America. Two new worlds have been opened to their industry, each of them much greater and more extensive than the old one, and the market of one of them growing still greater and greater every day. . . .

Source: Adam Smith, *An Inquiry into the Nature and Causes of the Wealth of Nations* (London: T. Nelson and Sons, 1852 [1776]), 243–259 passim. Widely available on the Internet.

4. FUKANG'AN, LAMA KYIRON HUTUKTU, AND PANCHEN LAMA REPRESENTATIVE, "29 REGULATIONS FOR REORGANIZING TIBET" (1792)

One common characteristic of empire was "reorganizing" conquered peoples and territories, especially in the eighteenth-century era when rational government was much discussed. Conquerors usually announced that their system of doing things was better, although some, such as the Spanish in Aztec and Inca lands, simultaneously recognized the effectiveness of the governments already in place there. Still, although original systems of taxation, communication, transportation, and law enforcement functioned very well, conquerors often wanted standardization across their holdings and laws that reflected their own values. This was part of a move toward more efficient bureaucratization across the imperial world that blossomed in the eighteenth century. Changing laws also displayed imperial power as did imperial ceremonials or decrees on dress and other behaviors. Such was the case in the Manchu Empire's "reorganization of Tibet" that even covered the rules for selecting the Dalai Lama. The Chinese already had an admired system of educated rule, yet every display of power risked an opposing reaction in the form of criticism or revolt.

1. ***Tulkus*** [reincarnated lamas] and Hutuktus [reincarnated senior lamas] are customarily determined by divinations of the Four Guardians of Dharma. Such a practice may be open to misuse, so to show the throne's favor of the **Gelugpa,** the emperor presented them with a Golden Urn. In the future, when selecting from among the identified *tulku* candidates, . . . the *tulku* candidates' names and dates of birth will be written in Manchu, Han, and Tibetan languages on metal slips and then placed in the Golden Urn. Following this procedure, a seven-day prayer session conducted by learned lamas. Then, the reincarnation will be officially confirmed before the statue of Sakyamuni in the Jokhang Temple by the Hutuktus and the Ambans in Tibet. When there is only one *tulku* candidate, a blank metal slip will be placed in the urn in addition to one with the *tulku* candidate's name. If the blank slip is drawn, that *tulku* will not be recognized as the reincarnation, and a new one shall be sought. The reincarnations of the Dalai Lama and Panchen Lama, who have a close relationship, will be confirmed in the same manner with *tulkus* candidate names and dates of birth written in Manchu, Han and Tibetan languages on metal slips.
   [. . .]

3. The Tibetan *thanka* currency is known to contain many impurities. Here-after, the government shall use pure Han silver containing no impurities to mint coins. . . . The new Tibetan coin will be imprinted with the words Qianlong Baozang [Emperor Qianlong's Treasury] on the front, with the year around its rim; the reverse side will be imprinted in Tibetan. . . .

4. There has never been a standing army in Ü-Tsang and soldiers have been drafted only when Tibet has been threatened. Improperly trained, these soldiers have become a nuisance, harming the Tibetan people instead of protecting them. With the approval of the emperor, a standing army of three thousand men will be mobilized, with one thousand soldiers to be stationed in Ü [central Tibet], one thousand soldiers in Tsang [western Tibet], five hundred soldiers in Gyantse [a town in central Tibet], and another five hundred in Dingri [near the Nepal border].
[. . .]

8. Previously, the finances of the Dalai Lama and the Panchen Lama have not been overseen by the Amban. Since the Dalai Lama and Panchen Lama are wholly engaged with their religious duties, they tend to leave the detailed financial matters largely in the hands of relatives and attendants making it difficult to prevent abuses. Thus, the emperor instructed the Amban to audit their budgets and send a report twice annually in the spring and fall. Any misappropriation of funds will be subject to immediate punishment.
[. . .]

10. The Amban shall have the same level of power and authority as the Dalai Lama and the Panchen Lama in Tibetan administrative affairs. All officials under the *kaloons* [council ministers], including the *tulkus*, shall be subordinate to the Amban regardless of their position or rank.
[. . .]

29. In Tibet, each village is required to pay taxes, land rent and tribute. In villages that lie close to the monasteries these payments are collected by monastic officials. In more distant villages secular officials are sent to collect it. Recently, it has been discovered cases in which a handful of dishonest monastic and secular officials . . . have been caught stealing tax money and land rents which have resulted government tax revenues going astray and resulting in numerous instances of tax arrears. These investigations have also uncovered the practice of taxing a year or more in advance. As well, unpaid taxes owed by absentee laborers were arbitrarily transferred to those bound to their land. Such excessive taxes and practices made the people's life extremely onerous. In the future, all tax collectors will be appointed by *chanzods* [high officials] and shall abide to the designated taxable period. Monastic and secular officials, and *zhongpons* shall collect only the taxes and rents due that year; collecting one year in advance shall be prohibited. The taxation of runaway households shall be exempted until their return.

Source: *Sources in Chinese History: Diverse Perspectives from 1644 to the Present*, David G. Atwill and Yurong Y. Atwill, eds. (Upper Saddle River: Prentice Hall, 2010), 10–11.

5. JOSÉ ANTONIO DE ARECHE, "ALL MUST DIE" (1781)

The society that sprang up on the western coast of South America where the Incas had ruled did not die out with Pizarro's conquest. Instead, parallel social structures evolved and the accomplishments of the Incas remained vivid in popular lore. People of the former Inca Empire knew their genealogy, giving descendants and other relatives inspiration to hold on to Inca history and values. Increasing the sense of oppression, Spanish officials in the eighteenth century increased both the amount of taxes and the efficiency of tax collection because of the Bourbon reforms and in general exercised a greater sense of Spanish entitlement to South American wealth. Inca descendants resisted over the centuries; between 1720 and the 1780s there were more than one hundred uprisings. In 1781, Tupac Ameru II led a widespread revolt across much of the former Inca empire—a revolt that continued even after he was captured and executed. What understanding of eighteenth century empire do you attach to this punishment?

I must and do condemn José G. Túpac Amaru to be taken out to the main public square of this city, dragged out to the place of execution, where he shall witness the execution of the sentences imposed on his wife, Micaela Bastidas; his two sons, Hipólito and Fernando Túpac Amaru; his uncle, Francisco Túpac Amaru; and his brother-in-law, Antonio Bastidas, as well as some of the principal captains and aides in his iniquitous and perverse intent or project, all of whom must die the same day.

And once these sentences have been carried out, the executioner will cut out his tongue, and he will then be tied or bound by strong cords on each one of his arms and feet in such a way that each rope can be easily tied or fastened to others hanging from the saddle straps of four horses so that, in this position, each one of these horses, facing opposite corners of the square, will pull toward his own direction; and let the horses be urged or jolted into motion at the same time so that his body be divided into as many parts and then, once it is done, the parts should be carried to the hill or high ground known as "Picchu," which is where he came to intimidate, lay siege to, and demand the surrender of this city; and let there be lit a fire which shall be prepared in advance and then let ashes be thrown into the air and a stone tablet placed there detailing his main crimes and the manner of his death as the only record and statement of his loathesome action.

His head will be sent to the town of Tinta where, after having been three days on the gallows, it shall be placed on a stake at the most public entrance to the town; one of his arms will go to the town of Tungasuca, where he was chief, where it will be treated in like manner, and the other in the capital of the province of Carabaya; one of the legs shall likewise be sent for the same kind of demonstration to the town of Libitaca in the province of Chumbivilcas, while the remaining one shall go to Santa Rosa in the province of Lampa along with an affidavit and order to the respective chief magistrates, or territorial judges, that this sentence be proclaimed publicly with the greatest solemnity. . . .

Since this traitor managed to arm himself and form an army and forces against the royal arms by making use of or seducing and leading with his falsehoods the chiefs who are the second in command in the villages, since these villages, being of Indians, are not governed by such chiefs but rather by mayors who are elected annually by the vote or nomination of the chiefs: let these same electoral communities and the chief magistrates take care to give preference to candidates who know Spanish. . . .

To this same end, it is prohibited that the Indians wear heathen clothes, especially those who belong to the nobility, since it only serves to symbolize those worn by their Inca ancestors, reminding them of memories which serve no other end than to increase their hatred toward the dominant nation; not to mention that their appearance is ridiculous and very little in accordance with the purity of our relics, since they place in different parts images of the sun, which was their primary deity; and this prohibition is to be extended to all the provinces of this southern America, in order to completely eliminate such clothing, especially those items which represent the bestialities of their heathen kings through emblems such as the unco, which is a kind of vest; yacollas, which are very rich blankets or shawls of black velvet or taffeta; the mascapaycha, which is a circle in the shape of a crown from which they hang a certain emblem of ancient nobility signified by a tuft or tassel of red-colored alpaca wool, as well as many other things of this kind and symbolism. . . .

These latter shall be erased without fail since they do not merit the dignity of being painted in such places, and with the same end in mind there shall also be erased, so that no sign remains, any portraits that might be found on walls or other solid objects; in churches, monasteries, hospitals, holy places or private homes, such duties fall under the jurisdiction of the reverend archbishops or bishops of both viceroyalties in those areas pertaining to the churches; and in their place it would be best to replace such adornments with images of the king and our other Catholic sovereigns should that be necessary.

Also, the ministers and chief magistrates should ensure that in no town of their respective provinces be performed plays or other public functions of the kind that the Indians are accustomed to put on to commemorate their former Incas; and having carried out the order, these ministers shall give a certified account to the secretaries of the respective governments. In like manner shall be prohibited and confiscated the trumpets or bugles that the Indians use for their ceremonies and which they call pututos, being seashells with a strange and mournful sound that celebrate the mourning and pitiful memorial they make for their antiquity; and there shall also be prohibited the custom of using or wearing black clothing as a sign of mourning, a custom that drags on in some provinces in memory of their deceased monarchs and also of the day or time of the conquest which they consider disastrous and we consider fortunate since it brought them into the company of the Catholic Church and the very loving and gentle domination of our kings.

With the same goal it is absolutely forbidden that the Indians sign themselves as "Incas," since it is a title that anyone can assume but which makes a lasting impression on those of their class; and it is ordered, as is required of all those who have genealogical trees or documents that prove in some way their descent, that they produce them or send them certified and without cost by mail to the respective secretaries of both viceroyalties so that the formalities may be observed by those persons responsible to their excellencies the viceroys, consulting His Majesty where necessary according to each case; and the chief magistrates are charged to oversee the fulfillment of such requirements, to seek out and discover anyone who does not observe them correctly, in order to have it done or to collect the documents with the aim of sending them to the proper authorities after giving their owners a receipt.

And so that these Indians renounce the hatred that they have conceived against the Spaniards, and that they adhere to the dress which the laws indicate, adopting our Spanish customs and speaking Castilian, we shall introduce more vigorously than we have done up to now the use of schools, imposing the most rigorous and fair penalties on those who do not attend once enough time has passed for them to have learned the language; . . . there will be established a term of four years for the people to speak fluently or at least be able to explain themselves in Castilian, the bishops and chief magistrates being required to report on all this to their respective superior governing body, and it being left up to the sovereign discretion of His Majesty to reward and honor those towns whose inhabitants have rendered, under the present circumstances, their due loyalty and faithfulness.

Finally, the manufacture of cannons of all kinds shall be prohibited under the penalty that any noble found manufacturing such items will be sentenced to ten years of prison in one of the presidios in Africa and any commoner will receive two hundred lashes as well as the same penalty for the same time period.

Source: *The Peru Reader: History, Culture, Politics*, Orin Starn, Carlos Iván Degregori, and Robin Kirk, eds. (Durham: Duke University Press, 1995), 169–173.

6. 'ABD-AL-RAHMAN 'AL-JABARTI, DIARY (1798)

Egyptians, who had become accustomed to some autonomy from the Ottomans, were of very mixed opinion at the attempt by General Napoleon Bonaparte to extend French rule into their homeland. On the one hand, during his brief hold on Egypt (July 1798–August 1799) Napoleon desecrated holy places and social order while his soldiers were abusive, drunken, and destructive murderers, who in their everyday behavior insulted Egyptian values. On the other, some found the French armies infinitely better trained and more motivated than their own defenders. Writer and scholar 'Abd-al-Rahmân 'al Jabarti shows what it was like to be invaded and overtaken. He also captured some of these complicated reactions to Napoleon's attempt to take Egypt for France. Mohammed Ali, a soldier who helped the British drive Napoleon's forces from the region, soon became Egypt's ruler, taking from the French some of his ideas for reform. Explain 'al-Jabarti's reactions to the French.

The Ghuzz [a name for Turkish tribal groups of fighters], the soldiers, and the Mamluks gathered on the two banks, but they were irresolute, and were at odds with one another, being divided in opinion, envious of each other, frightened for their lives, their well-being, and their comforts; immersed in their ignorance and self-delusion, arrogant and haughty in their attire and presumptuousness; afraid of decreasing in number, and pompous in their finery, heedless of the results of their action; contemptuous of their enemy, unbalanced in their reasoning and judgment. They were unlike the other group, that is the French, who were a complete contrast in everything mentioned above. They acted as if they were following the tradition of the Community (of Muhammad) in early Islam and saw themselves as fighters in a holy war. They never considered the number of their enemy too high, nor did they care who among them was killed. Indeed they considered anyone who fled a traitor to his community, and an apostate to his faith and creed. They follow the orders of their commander and faithfully obey their leader. Their only shade is the hat on their head and their only mount their own two feet. Their food and drink is but a morsel and a sip, hanging under their arms. The baggage and change of clothing hang on their backs like a pillow and when they sleep they lie on it as is usual. They have signs and signals among themselves which they obey to the letter. . . .

That same day they [the French] also announced that lamps should be lit all night in the streets and markets. Each house was required to have a lamp as well as every third shop. The people were to sweep, splash water, and clean the streets of the rubbish, filth, and dead cats. This was in spite of the fact that the streets and houses where the French lived, were full of filth, infected earth mixed with bird feathers, the entrails of animals, garbage, the stench of their drinks, the sourness of their alcoholic beverages, their urine and excrement, such that a passer-by was obliged to hold his nose. . . .

And on that day the French looted the property of the soldiers of the galleon who had served the Amirs [chieftains]. They also plundered the caravanserai of ʿAli Bey which was situated on the bank of the Bulaq and another at al-Jamaliyya, seizing their wares and those of their partners, on the pretext that they had fought against them on the side of the Mamluks, and escaped with them (the Mamluks). . . .

On that day they ordered the inhabitants of the Citadel to vacate their homes and move into town and live there. Thus the inhabitants left the Citadel and the French brought up cannons which they positioned in various places. They further demolished some buildings and erected walls. Thus they pulled down the high places and raised up the low places. They built on the foundations of Bab al–ʿAzab [gates to the citadel in Cairo] in al-Rumayla and changed its features and disfigured its beauties and wiped out the monuments of scholars and the assembly rooms of sultans and great men and took what works of art were left on its great gates and in its magnificent sitting-rooms (iywan) such as arms, shields, axes, helmets, and Indian lances and balls with chains of the warriors (ukar al-fidawiyya). They demolished the palace of Yusuf Salah al-Din and the council halls of kings and sultans which had high supports and tall pillars, as well as the mosques and chapels (zawaya) of religious orders and shrines. They disfigured the Great Mosque, the lofty distinguished one which was built by the man of glorious deeds,

Muhammad ibn Qalawun al-Malik al-Nasir. They removed its *minbar* (pulpit), wrecked its *iywan*, took its wood, shook its pillars, and removed its iron stool near its praying area (*maqsura*), a wondrously wrought work in which the Sultan used to pray. Thus they behaved as the enemies of the religion would behave but "Our trust is in God alone, and He is an excellent protector." . . .

On that day they told the people to desist from burying the dead in cemeteries close to dwellings, such as the cemeteries of al-Azbakiyya, and al-Ruwayʻi and to bury them only in graveyards far (from the populated areas). Those who had no vaults in the cemetery should bury their dead in the vaults of the Mamluks. And when they buried someone they were required to increase the depth of the graves. They further ordered people to hang out their clothing, furnishings, and bedding on their roofs for several days and to fumigate their houses with fumes which would remove the putrescence. All this was out of fear, as they claimed, of the smell and contagion of the plague. The French said that the putrescence is imprisoned in the depths of the earth. When winter sets in and the depths of the earth become cold because of the flow of the Nile, the rain, and the dampness, what is imprisoned in the earth comes out with its rotten vapors and the air becomes rotten, so epidemic and plague occur.

As for the French it is their custom not to bury their dead but to toss them on garbage heaps like the corpses of dogs and beasts, or to throw them into the sea. Among the other things which they said is that when someone becomes sick they must inform the French who then send an authorized representative to examine him and to find out whether he has the plague or not. Then they decide what to do with him. . . .

To the administrators of affairs (managers), the astronomers, scholars, and scientists in mathematics, geometry, astronomy, engraving and drawing, and also to the painters, scribes, and writers they [the French] assigned al-Nasiriyya quarter and all the houses in it, such as the house of QasimBey, the Amir of the Pilgrimage known as AbuSayf, and the house of HasanKashifJarkas which he founded and built to perfection, having spent upon it fantastic sums of money amounting to more than a hundred thousand dinars. When he had completed plastering and furnishing it, the French came and he fled with the others and left all that it contained, not having enjoyed it for even a whole month. The administrators, astronomers, and some of the physicians lived in this house in which they placed a great number of their books and with a keeper taking care of them and arranging them. And the students among them would gather two hours before noon every day in an open space opposite the shelves of books, sitting on chairs arranged in parallel rows before a wide long board. Whoever wishes to look up something in a book asks for whatever volumes he wants and the librarian brings them to him. Then he thumbs through the pages, looking through the book, and writes. All the while they are quiet and no one disturbs his neighbor. When some Muslims would come to look around they would not prevent them from entering. Indeed they would bring them all kinds of printed books in which there were all sorts of illustrations and *cartes* (*kartat*) [maps] of the countries and regions, animals, birds, plants, histories of the ancients, campaigns of the nations, tales of the prophets including pictures of them, of their miracles and wondrous deeds, the events of their respective peoples and such things which baffle the mind. I have gone to them many times and they have shown me all these various things and among the things I saw there was a large book containing the Biography of the Prophet, upon whom be mercy and peace. In this volume they draw his noble picture according to the extent of their knowledge and judgment about him. He is depicted standing upon his feet looking toward Heaven as if menacing all creation. In his right hand is the sword and in his left the Book and around him are his Companions, may God be pleased with them, also with swords in their hands. In another page there are pictures of the Rightly Guided Caliphs. On another page a picture of the Midnight Journey of Muhammad and al-Buraq and he, upon whom be mercy and peace, is riding upon al-Buraq from the Rock of Jerusalem. Also there is a picture of Jerusalem and the Holy Places of Mekka and Medina and of the four Imams, Founders of the Schools and the other Caliphs and Sultans and an image of Islambul [another name for Istanbul] including her Great Mosques like Aya Sofya and the Mosque of Sultan Muhammad. In another picture the manner in which the Prophet's Birthday is celebrated and all the types of people who participate in it (are shown); also (there are) pictures of the Mosque of Sultan Sulayman and the manner in which the Friday prayers are conducted in it, and the Mosque of Abi-iAyyub al-Ansari and the manner in which prayers for the dead are performed in it, and pictures of the countries, the coasts, the seas, the Pyramids, the ancient temples of Upper Egypt including the pictures, figures, and inscriptions which are drawn upon them. Also there are pictures of the species of animals, birds, plants and herbage which are peculiar to each land. The glorious Qur'an is translated into their language! Also many other Islamic books. I saw in their possession the *Kitab al-Shifa'* of Qadi Iyad, which they call *al-Shifa al-Sharif* and *al-Burda* by Abu Siri, many verses of which they know by heart and which they translated into French. I saw some of them who know chapters of the Qur'an by heart. They have a great interest in the sciences, mainly in mathematics and the knowledge of languages, and make great efforts to learn the Arabic language and the colloquial. In this they strive day and night. And they have books especially devoted to all types of languages, their declensions and conjugations as well as their etymologies. They possess extraordinary astronomical instruments of perfect construction and instruments for measuring altitudes of wondrous, amazing, and precious construction. And they have telescopes for looking at the stars and measuring their scopes, sizes, heights, conjunctions, and oppositions, and the clepsydras [an ancient water clock] and clocks with gradings and minutes and seconds, all of wondrous form and very precious, and the like.

In a similar manner they assigned the house of Ibrahim Katkhuda al-Sinnari and the house of the former KatkhudaZayn al-Fiqar and neighboring houses to the studious and knowledgeable ones. They called this *al-Madaris* (the Schools) and provided it with funds and copious allowances and generous provisions of food and drink. They provided them with a place in the house of the above-mentioned

HasanKashif and built in it neat and well-designed stoves and ovens, and instruments for distilling, vaporizing, and extracting liquids and ointments belonging to medicine and sublimated simple salts, the salts extracted from burnt herbs, and so forth. In this place there are wondrous retorts [vessels] of copper for distillation, and vessels and long-necked bottles made of glass of various forms and shapes, by means of which acidic liquids and solvents are extracted. All this is carried out with perfect skill and wondrous invention and the like.

Source: Shmuel Moreh, trans., *Napoleon in Egypt: Al-Jabarti's Chronicle of the French Occupation, 1798* (New York: Markus Wiener, 1975), 36, 66, 70–71, 109–111.

7. MIRZA ABU TALEB KHAN, "VINDICATION OF THE LIBERTIES OF THE ASIATIC WOMEN" (1801)

Mirza Abu Taleb Khan, a writer and sometimes civil servant employed by the British, traveled to Britain at the end of the eighteenth century. At the time, the British East India Company was accelerating its inroads on the power of the Mughals; it also fought the new South Asian states springing up from Mughal decline. The hope was to make up for the loss of its North American colonies. Even as he was being observed and feted by the cream of English and Anglo-Irish society, Abu Taleb was watching them and making comparative judgments about South Asian government, society, and values. Before returning home in 1802, he published a rebuttal to all the criticisms he had heard of the situation of women in Asia—in part gaining confidence from the talk about rights, reform, and revolution current in his day. He proposed that in fact women in Europe had far fewer rights than did women in Asia. The criticism against South Asians that Abu Taleb outlines nonetheless became the imperial powers' justification for denying independence to colonies and in our own times for invading entire countries by the West: that is, takeover would halt the abuse of women in Asia and the Middle East despite the unequal pay, lack of political power, and violence against women in Western countries. Such debates unfolded alongside the turmoil of imperial advance. Where does Abu Taleb's writing fit in the ideology of empire?

One day, in a certain company, the conversation turned upon Liberty, in respect of which the English consider their own customs the most perfect in the world. An English lady, addressing herself to me, observed, that the women of Asia have no liberty at all, but live like slaves, without honour and authority, in the houses of their husbands; and she censured the men for their unkindness, and the women, also, for submitting to be so undervalued. However much I attempted, by various ways, to undeceive her, (and in truth, said I, the case is exactly the reverse, it is the European women who do not possess so much power), yet it did not bring conviction to her mind. She however began to waver in her own opinion; and falling into doubt, requested of me to write something on the subject, the purport of which she might comprehend at one view, and be enabled to distinguish the truth from falsehood. Since the same wrong opinion is deeply rooted in the minds of all other

Europeans, and has been frequently before this held forth, I considered it necessary to write a few lines concerning the privileges of the female sex, as established, both by law and custom, in Asia and in Europe; omitting whatever was common to both, . . .

First, "Their power over the property and children of the husband, by custom"; for the men of Asia consider the principal objects of marriage, after the procreation of their species for the worship of God, two things,—the one to have their money and effects taken care of, and the other to have their children brought up; so that they themselves, being left entirely disengaged of these concerns, may turn their whole endeavours to the attainment of their various pursuits. The chief part, therefore, of whatever wealth they acquire, they give in charge to their wives; and thus the women have it in their power to annihilate in one day the products of a whole life. Although this seldom happens, yet it is often the case, where the husband having amassed a large fortune in youth and power, has delivered it in charge to his wife, and requires it back in his old age and necessity, she does not allow him more than sufficient for his daily support, and lays the rest up, in a place of security, for the sake of her children. . . .

Third, "Their authority over their servants"; for the servants of the male apartments, the keeping and changing of whom are in the hands of the husband, through fear of exposing themselves to the displeasure or complaints of the wife, when she finds a proper opportunity, by their committing some fault, which servants are continually doing, are more obedient to her than to their own master; . . .

Seventh, "Their share in the children, by law." For if a divorce happens, the son go to the father, and the daughters to the mother; contrary to the custom here, where, if a divorce takes place, the mother, who for twenty years may have toiled and consumed herself in bringing up her children, has to abandon all to the father, and, full of grief and affliction, leave his house.

Eighth, "The ease, both by law and custom, with which the wife may separate herself from her husband, when there may be a quarrel between them, without producing a divorce." Thus the wife, in an hour's time after the dispute, sets off with the children and her property to the house of her father. . . .

Besides these eight, as above noticed, of the superior advantages the Asiatic women enjoy over the European, there are many others, here omitted for brevity's sake. . . .

Source: *The Asiatic Annual Register, or a View of the History of Hindustan, and of the Politics, Commerce, and Literature of Asia for the Year 1801* (London: Debrett, Cadell, and Davies, 1802), Miscellaneous Tracts, 102, 105.

8. HAITIAN CONSTITUTION OF 1801 (1801)

Toussaint Louverture (1742–1803), hero of the uprising on French sugar colony Saint- Domingue (present-day Haiti), was a former slave who freed himself to become a slave owner in his own right. At the time there were uprisings among slaves in Africa and Muslim attempts there to stop the enslavement of Muslims. Free Haitian blacks like Toussaint had also lobbied in France for more rights even before the French Revolution, but as revolution broke out in France, uprisings against slave owners quickly erupted across Haiti—the richest of the Caribbean sugar producers. Toussaint Louverture emerged as its leader and his efforts were helped by the fact that many slaves were military men, captured in battle by their wartime enemies and sold in the Atlantic markets. They had much in common and even fought together, successfully in the case of the Haitian Revolution. On the crossroads of Atlantic trade, Haitians were well aware of other uprisings, the existence of maroon communities, and the drift of Enlightenment political ideas, including the appearance of written constitutions to uphold the rule of law. The constitution that follows was one of several the Haitians proposed. It was written by committee and approved by Toussaint Loverture, whose hope for a good relationship with the Emperor Napoleon was dashed when the French invaded, captured Toussaint, and imprisoned him until his death from the bad conditions. The French, however, did not succeed in restoring their control but instead were defeated by disease and the Haitian troops, not to mention the complex interventions of other empires such as Britain. In 1804, Haitians finally became independent of France. Describe and evaluate the tenets of this constitution.

The deputies of the departments of the colony of Saint-Domingue, united in a Central Assembly, have decided on and laid out the constitutional foundation of the regime of the French colony of Saint-Domingue, which are as follows:

Title 1: Of the Territory
Article 1. Saint-Domingue in its entirety, and Samana, la Tortue, la Gonâve, les Cayemites, l'Île-à-Vache, La Saône, and other adjacent islands, form the territory of a single colony, which is part of the French empire, but submitted to particular laws.
Article 2. The territory of this colony is divided into departments, districts, and parishes.

Title 2: Of Its Inhabitants
Article 3. There can be no slaves on this territory; servitude is abolished within it forever. All men are born, live and die there free and French.
Article 4. All men, whatever their color, are eligible for all positions.
Article 5. There exist no distinctions other than those based on virtues and talents and no superiority other than that granted by the law to the exercise of a public function. The law is the same for all, whether it punishes or protects.

Title 3: Of Religion
Article 6. The Catholic, Apostolic and Roman religion is the only one that is publicly professed. . . .
Article 8. The governor of the colony will assign to each minister of the religion the extent of his spiritual administration, and these ministers can never, under any pretext, form a body within the colony.

Title 4: Of Morals
Article 9. The civil and religious institution of marriage encourages the purity of morals, and therefore those spouses who practice the virtues their status demands of them will always be distinguished and specially protected by the government.
Article 10. Divorce will not be allowed in the colony.
Article 11. The status and the rights of children born in marriage will be fixed by laws meant to spread and maintain social virtues and encourage and cement familial ties.

Title 5: Of Men in Society
Article 12. The Constitution guarantees individual liberty and security. No one can be arrested except by virtue of a formally expressed order, emanating from an administrator that the law grants the right to arrest and to detain in a publicly designated location.
Article 13. Property is sacred and inviolable. All persons, either by themselves or through their representatives, are free to dispose of and administer what is recognized as belonging to them. Anyone who attacks this right commits a crime against society and is guilty toward the person whose property they have troubled.

Title 6: Of Cultivation and Commerce
Article 14. Since the colony is essentially agricultural, it cannot be allowed to suffer even the slightest interruption in the work of cultivation.
Article 15. Each plantation is a factory that requires the union of cultivators and workers; it is the peaceful refuge of an active and faithful family, where the owner of the property or his representative is of necessity the father.
Article 16. Each cultivator and worker is a part of the family and receives a portion of its revenues. All change in residency on the part of cultivators leads to the ruin of cultivation. . . .
Article 17. Since the introduction of cultivators is indispensable to the reestablishment and the growth of crops, it will take place in Saint-Domingue; the Constitution charges the governor to take appropriate measures to encourage and favor this increase in the number of hands, to stipulate and balance various interests, and to assure and guarantee the execution of the respective obligations that will be the result of this introduction.
Article 18. Since the commerce of the colony consists entirely in the exchange of the commodities and products of its territory, the introduction of those of the same kind as its own is and will remain prohibited.

Title 7: Of Legislation and Legislative Authority
Article 19. The administration of the colony will be determined by laws proposed by the governor and pronounced by an assembly of inhabitants, who will meet at fixed dates in the center of the colony, under the title of the Central Assembly of Saint-Domingue. . . .
Article 24. The Central Assembly votes on the adoption or the rejection of the laws that are proposed by the governor; it votes on regulations that have been made

and on the application of laws that are already in place, on abuses to be corrected, on improvements to be pursued in all aspects of the services of the colony.

Article 25. On the basis of the report of the tax receipts and spending presented to it by the governor, the Central Assembly determines, if necessary, the amount, the length, and the mode of collection of the tax, and its increase or decrease; these reports will subsequently be printed. . . .

Title 8: Of the Government

Article 27. The administrative reins of the colony are confided to a governor who will correspond directly with the government of the metropole for everything relative to the interests of the colony.

Article 28. The Constitution names as governor the citizen Toussaint Louverture, the general-in-chief of the army of Saint-Domingue and, in consideration of the important services he has rendered the colony, in the most critical circumstances of the revolution, and on the request of its thankful inhabitants, the reins [of government] are confided to him for the rest of his glorious life.

Article 29. In the future, each governor will be named for five years and will be allowed to continue every five years if he has overseen a good administration.

Article 30. To affirm the tranquility that the colony owes to the firmness, activity, and tireless zeal and rare virtues of General Toussaint Louverture, and as a sign of the unlimited confidence of the inhabitants of Saint-Domingue, the Constitution attributes to him the exclusive right to choose the citizen who, in the unfortunate event of his death, will replace him. This choice will be secret. . . .

Article 31. The citizen chosen by General Toussaint Louverture to take over the reins of the government will take an oath before the Central Assembly, at his death, to execute the Constitution of Saint-Domingue, and to remain attached to the French government.

Source: Adapted from Laurent Dubois and John D. Garrigus, eds., *Slave Revolution in the Caribbean, 1789–1804: A Brief History with Documents* (Boston: Bedford/St. Martin's, 2006), 167–170.

9. DRUMMER VARGAS, DIARY (1817)

Ordinary people from all walks of life participated in the struggle for independence from colonialism; often they were positioned in the colonial system in complex ways. U.S. women, whose families were "colonizers" of the New World, nursed, clothed, and fed troops in the field fighting for independence as if they were among the colonized. In South America they did likewise. Women's position could be equally intricate: Manuela Saenz had close connections to the independence leadership of the cause as the lover of Simon Bolivar, saving Bolivar from several assassination attempts after gaining advanced knowledge through her extensive social and political networks. Yet Bolivar was in general not sympathetic to the cause of indigenous people or slaves whom he needed as allies. On the Latin American battlefields slaves of African heritage and Native Americans joined forces with the poor and even the wealthy creoles to fight the pro-Spanish royalist forces. In this diary, an orphaned drummer from the former Inca lands, directed to this army of guerilla fighters by his brother—a priest—describes the resolve of his fellow combatants in the struggle against the royalists. Eventually guerillas and regular armed forces led by upper-class generals San Martin and Bolivar joined to win freedom. These freedom fighters had diverse interests. How do you understand the use of the term "a mericano" in this passage?

September 19, 1817

In the action fought on this day, we lost five soldiers and fourteen Indians dead. Of the fourteen Indians, one died in the following manner. He and eleven others were trying to escape down a cliff, and the others had all fallen, when out stepped a well-armed royalist. The royalist took aim at the Indian, kneeling at the cliff edge, but his shot missed.

The Indian rose, saying: "Please, let me go. I'm a man just like you, with a wife and children. I'm here by force, not because I wanted to come to attack you. Think how pleasing it would be to God, and how much my whole family and I will remember you in our prayers, if you spare my life. So please let me go."

"Get moving," ordered the royalist, grabbing hold of the Indian, "and I'll ask my superior officer to spare your life." The Indian implored the soldier repeatedly to let him go, because he had a large family with many small children, but the soldier only held on to him more tightly. At that point, the Indian saw three more royalist soldiers approaching.

"If you won't have mercy," he said, "then we'll die together," and wrapping his arms around his captor, with a powerful shove, the Indian dove off the cliff, pulling the royalist with him. Some of our Indians watched all this happen and, sending word to Commander Lira, a bunch of them went to the bottom of the cliff and found both men sorely wounded but still alive. The royalist had no skin left on his face and a broken leg, but our Indian was in even worse shape, having lost the skin on his face and the entire left side of his body. Both were still able to talk, and that is how the Indian related what he had said to his captor before jumping. The wounded royalist begged us in the name of God and the *Patria* to finish him off, because he knew that he could never recover, and the pain was unbearable. After shouting these things, though, he calmed down and begged our forgiveness, saying that rage had been his undoing.

Hearing all this, Commander Lira said he'd send the soldier to be treated at Palca, and that he should beg God, not us, for forgiveness, but the soldier didn't listen, and now he was saying that he, too, had fought for the *Patria*, and please, in the name of the *Patria*, to kill him or at least give him a knife to do it himself. The Indian laughed at him, saying this was his reward for not letting go. Lira told the soldier that they would kill him, as he requested, but that he should wait until they could carry him to Morochata where there was a priest to hear his confession. The soldier angrily asked Lira why, if we believed so much in confession, we didn't have a chaplain with us, and other insulting things. He was getting delirious. So

Lira finally gave the order to put him out of his misery, and a few well-aimed club blows quickly did so.

Lira sent the Indian to Morochata but he died on the way. He was from a place called Huacaplaza on the Yani hacienda, Morochata, and his name was Mariano Mamani. Consider the energy and determination of this *a mericano* who, to win a free and independent *Patria* for his posterity, finding himself unarmed, took an enemy soldier with him when he died. For this reason, Commander Lira carefully explained to all our Indians what *Patria* meant, why Independence from Spain mattered, and exactly how it would benefit our posterity.

Source: José Santos Vargas, *Diario de un commandante de la independencia American, 1814–1825* (Mexico City: Sieglo Veintiuno, 1982) as translated in *Latin American Independence: An Anthology of Sources*, Sarah Chambers and John Charles Chasteen, eds. And trans. (Indianapolis: Hackett, 2010), 154–155.

10. AUGUSTIN DE ITURBIDE, PLAN OF IGUALA (1821)

As we have noted, revolutions are often the work of people with divergent goals, and the Latin American revolutionary uprisings against Spanish rule were no different. Having begun with the activism of Catholic clergy allied with the poor in 1810, members of the upper class descendants of the colonizers, inspired by ideas of better government, self-rule, and improvement in their social and economic status, launched more organized military campaigns against royal forces. It was difficult to get the upper classes to make common cause with people they believed to be far beneath them in value—colonized Indians, slaves, and those of mixed race. Gradually even so lofty a leader as Bolivar was forced to promise an improvement in life for ordinary people and slaves. In Mexico, leaders Agustin Iturbide—a wealthy landowner—and Vicente Guerrero—from a wealthy family but a soldier in the people's army—carved out a constitution for an independent state, which Guerrero only agreed to sign after rights were given to all, regardless of caste. The Spanish viceroy signed the agreement in the summer of 1821. What passages in this document indicate a search for unity?

ART. 1. The Mexican nation is independent of the Spanish nation, and of every other, even on its own Continent.

ART. 2. Its religion shall be the Catholic, which all its inhabitants profess.

ART. 3. They shall be all united, without any distinction between Americans and Europeans.

ART. 4. The government shall be a constitutional monarchy.

ART. 5. A junta shall be named, consisting of individuals who enjoy the highest reputation in the different parties which have shown themselves.

ART. 6. This junta shall be under the presidency of his Excellency the Count del Venadito, the present Viceroy of Mexico.

ART. 7. It shall govern in the name of the nation, according to the laws now in force, and its principal business will be to convoke, according to such rules as it shall deem expedient, a congress for the formation of a constitution more suitable to the country.

ART. 8. His Majesty Ferdinand VII shall be invited to the throne of the empire, and in case of his refusal, the Infantes [princes] Don Carlos and Don Francisco de Paula.

ART. 9. Should his Majesty Ferdinand VII and his august brothers decline the invitation, the nation is at liberty to invite to the imperial throne any member of reigning families whom it may select.

ART. 10. The formation of the constitution by the congress, and the oath of the emperor to observe it, must precede his entry into the country.

ART. 11. The distinction of castes is abolished, which was made by the Spanish law, excluding them from the rights of citizenship. All the inhabitants of the country are citizens, and equal, and the door of advancement is open to virtue and merit.

ART. 12. An army shall be formed for the support of religion, independence, and union, guaranteeing these three principles, and therefore it shall be called the army of the three guarantees.

ART. 13. It shall solemnly swear to defend the fundamental bases of this plan.

ART. 14. It shall strictly observe the military ordinances now in force.

ART. 15. There shall be no other promotions than those which are due to seniority, or which shall be necessary for the good of the service.

ART. 16. This army shall be considered as of the line.

ART. 17. The old partisans of independence who shall immediately adhere to this plan, shall be considered as individuals of this army.

ART. 18. The patriots and peasants who shall adhere to it hereafter, shall be considered as provincial militiamen.

ART. 19. The secular and regular priests shall be continued in the state in which they now are.

ART. 20. All the public functionaries, civil, ecclesiastical, political, and military, who adhere to the cause of independence, shall be continued in their offices, without any distinction between Americans and Europeans,

ART. 21. Those functionaries, of whatever degree and condition, who dissent from the cause of independence, shall be divested of their offices, and shall quit the territory of the empire, taking with them their families and their effects.

ART. 22. The military commandants shall regulate themselves according to the general instructions in conformity with, this plan, which shall be transmitted to them.

ART. 23. No accused person shall be condemned capitally by the military commandants. Those accused of treason against the nation, which is the next greatest crime after that of treason to the Divine Ruler, shall be conveyed to the fortress of Barrabas, where they shall remain until the congress shall resolve on the punishment which ought to be inflicted on them.

ART. 24. It being indispensable to the country that this plan should be carried into effect, in as much as the welfare of that country is its object, every individual of the army shall maintain it, to the shedding (if it be necessary) of the last drop of his blood.

Town of Iguala, 24th February, 1821.

Source: *From Appendix 1 of Iturbide, Agustin. Memoirs of Agustin De Iturbide* (Washington, DC: Documentary Publications, 1971) sdct.

11. GOVERNOR ARTHUR PHILIP OF AUSTRALIA, LETTER TO UNDER-SECRETARY NEPEAN (1788)

Driven by their defeat at Yorktown in 1781, the British fanned out across the globe to found new settlements and find new sources of profit to replace all they had lost. Only a few decades after Cook had charted both Australia and New Zealand and described their inhabitants and natural features, King George commissioned Captain Arthur Philip to settle Botany Bay in Australia in 1786. There were other reasons beyond pride lost in Britain's imperial defeat and continuing imperial ambition: for one, its jails were full to overflowing and prisoners could no longer be shipped off to North American colonies such as Georgia. Captain Philip thus arrived in Australia with some 1,000 passengers and crew, almost 800 of them convicts. As with other of Britain's settler colonies, supplies were wanting because of overly optimistic (and ignorant) government understanding of climate, the availability of resources, the conditions for farming, the number and attitudes of local residents, and the suitability of different sites where settlement was supposed to take place. Here is one of Captain Philip's reports on the complicated situation—a report that hardly predicted the hundreds of thousands of British subjects who joined the effort to take over Australia and New Zealand from their inhabitants by 1850.

My Dear Sir,

You will see by my letters to Lord Sydney that this colony must for some years depend on supplies from England.

The *Sirius* will be sent to the northward for live stock as soon as we can spare her carpenters; and from what Monsieur la Perouse said to Captain Hunter, one of the Isles des Navigateurs is the most likely to furnish us with what we want. But though these Islands supply two or three ships very abundantly, they will afford but very little towards the support of this colony, the situation of which I have particularly pointed out in my letter to Lord Sydney. . . .

The Lieutenant-Governor has about four acres of land in cultivation. I have from eight to ten in wheat and barley. The officers will be able to raise sufficient to support the little live stock they have, and which is all that can be expected from them. All the corn raised this year and the next will be saved for seed, and if necessity should oblige us to use it, it would be only a few days' support for the colony; and from the rats and other vermin the crops are very uncertain.

This country is subject to very heavy storms of thunder and lightning, several trees having been set on fire, and some sheep and dogs killed in the camp since we landed.

All the provisions we have to depend on until supplies arrive from England are in two wooden buildings which are thatched. I am sensible of the risk but have no remedy.

The greatest part of the stock brought from the Cape is dead, and from the inattention of the men who had the care of the cattle, those belonging to Government and two cows belonging to myself are lost. As they have been missing three weeks, it is probable they are killed by the natives. All my sheep are dead and a few only remain of those purchased for Government. The loss of two cows and four bulls falls very heavy. The horses do very well.

With respect to any resources that the Cape of Good Hope might afford, I have only to observe that the strong westerly winds that prevailed all the year between the Cape and the southern extremity of this country would render a passage to the Cape very tedious if attempted to the southward, and little less so if ships go to the northward. Batavia and our own settlements are at a great distance; and when the transports are sailed I shall have only the *Sirius* to employ on a service of this kind; and as I should not think myself at liberty to send either to the Cape or the East Indies unless in a case of the greatest necessity, it would in all probability then be too late. I mention these circumstances just to show the real situation of the colony, and I make no doubt but that supplies will arrive in time, and on which alone I depend. The provisions sent to support this colony for two years being put on board three ships, was running a very great risk, for had they separated and afterwards been lost the consequence is obvious, for this country at present does not furnish the smallest resource except in fish, and which has lately been so scarce that the natives find great difficulty in supporting themselves. Any accident of this kind will be guarded against, of course; and soldiers or convicts when sent out will be put on board the ships with provisions to serve them for two years after they land; and in our present situation I hope few convicts will be sent out for one year at least, except carpenters, masons, and bricklayers, or farmers, who can support themselves and assist in supporting others. Numbers of those now here are a burthen and incapable of any kind of hard labour, and, unfortunately, we have not proper people to keep those to their labour who are capable of being made useful.

Officers decline the least interference with the convicts, unless when they are immediately employed for their (the officers) own conveniency or when they are called out at the head of their men; the saying of a few words to encourage the diligent when they saw them at work, and the pointing out the idle when they could do it without going out of their way, was all that was desired. The convicts were then employed in clearing the ground on which the officers were encamped, and this they refused; they did not suppose they were sent out to do more than garrison duty, and these gentlemen (that is, the majority of the officers) think the being obliged to sit as members of the Criminal Court an hardship, and for which they are not paid, and likely think themselves hardly dealt by, in that Government had not determined what lands were to be given to them. But I presume an additional force will be sent out when the necessity of making detachments in order to cultivate lands in the more open country is known, and from four to six hundred men, will, I think, be absolutely necessary.

If fifty farmers were sent out with their families they would do more in one year in rendering this colony independent of the mother country *as to provisions* than a thousand convicts. There is some clear land which is intended to be cultivated, at some distance from the camp, and I intended to send out convicts for that purpose, under the direction of a person that was going to India in the *Charlotte*, transport, but who remained to settle in this country, and has been brought up a farmer, but several of the convicts (three) have been lately killed by the natives, and I have been obliged to defer it until a detachment can be made.

The natives are far more numerous than they were supposed to be. I think they cannot be less than fifteen hundred in Botany Bay, Port Jackson, and Broken Bay, including the intermediate coast. I have traced thirty miles inland, and the having lately seen smoke on Lansdown Hills, which are fifty miles inland, I think leaves no doubt but there are inhabitants in the interior parts of the country.

Lists of what articles are most wanted will be sent by the Commissary, and I am very sorry to say that not only a great part of the clothing, particularly the women's, is very bad, but most of the axes, spades, and shovels the worst that ever were seen. The provision is as good. Of the seeds and corn sent from England part has been destroyed by the weevil; the rest is in very good order.

The person I have appointed Provost-Marshal is likewise very useful in superintending the carpentry; the person sent out by the contractor, who assists the Commissary in the delivery of provisions, one that was clerk of the *Sirius*, a master smith, and two farmers, are very useful people, and I beg leave to recommend them to Government. The granting them lands would draw their attention from their present occupations.

A convict who fled to the woods after committing a robbery returned after being absent eighteen days, forced in by hunger; he had got some small support from the people, and the few fish left by accident on the beach after hauling the seine, and had endeavoured to live amongst the natives, but they could but give him but little assistance; he says they are now greatly distressed for food, and that he saw several dying with hunger. It is possible that some of the natives at this time of year might find it easier to support themselves on birds and such animals as shelter themselves in the hollow trees, than on fish; but then, I think, they would not go to the top of the mountains, where at present it must be very cold. I intend going to Lansdown or Carmarthen Hills as soon as the weather permits, if it is possible, and which will explain what is at present a mystery to me—how people who have not the least idea of cultivation can maintain themselves in the interior part of this country. When I went to the westward, in hopes of being able to reach the mountains, we carried six days' provisions, and proceeded five days to the westward; returning we were very short of provisions, and our guns only procured us two scanty meals.

I shall conclude with saying that I have no doubt but that the country will hereafter prove a most valuable acquisition to Great Britain, though at present no country can afford less support to the first settlers, or be more disadvantageously placed for receiving support from the mother country, on which it must for a time depend. It will require patience and perseverance, neither of which will, I hope, be wanting . . . .

Source: Historical Records of Australia, Vol. I, pp. 9–32, reproduced in Gwendoln H. Swinburne, *A Source Book of Australian History* (London: G. Bell and Sons, 1919). Online access http://gutenberg .net.au/ebooks/e00094.html.

12. JAMES MONROE, SEVENTH ANNUAL ADDRESS TO CONGRESS (THE MONROE DOCTRINE) (1823)

As European imperial control appeared mostly to evaporate in the Western Hemisphere, the new nations were left to struggle to build stable organizations, infrastructure, and flourishing economies. The hemisphere was thus ripe for interference, including take-overs, by the foreign empires that had intervened in virtually all the revolutions in order to weaken their imperial rivals. It was apparent that Britain, for example, was increasingly active. In this atmosphere U.S. President James Monroe issued the Monroe Doctrine in 1823. The proclamation announced that foreign interference in the vast region would not be tolerated, even though the young nation was hardly in a military position to enforce such a prohibition. Britain, however, was mighty on the seas and made clear its own willingness to block its rivals from establishing a new stake either in North or South America, thus serving as an enforcer of the Monroe Doctrine. Over the course of the nineteenth century Great Britain forged a new kind of "business" or informal imperialism based on facilitating its own trade, manufacturing, and financial capabilities, especially in South America. The United States came gradually to do the same alongside its dispossession and colonial rule of Native Americans.

. . . At the proposal of the Russian Imperial Government, made through the minister of the Emperor residing here, a full power and instructions have been transmitted to the minister of the United States at St. Petersburg to arrange by amicable negotiation the respective rights and interests of the two nations on the northwest coast of this continent. A similar proposal has been made by His Imperial Majesty to the Government of Great Britain, which has likewise been acceded to. The Government of the United States has been desirous by this friendly proceeding of manifesting the great value which they have invariably attached to the friendship of the Emperor and their solicitude to cultivate the best understanding with his Government. In the discussions to which this interest has given rise and in the arrangements by which they may terminate the occasion has been judged proper for asserting, as a principle in which the rights and interests of the United States are involved, that the American continents, by the free and independent condition which they have assumed and maintain, are henceforth not to be considered as subjects for future colonization by any European powers. . . .

It was stated at the commencement of the last session that a great effort was then making in Spain and Portugal to improve the condition of the people of those countries, and that it appeared to be conducted with extraordinary moderation. It need scarcely be remarked that the results have been so far very different from what was then anticipated. Of events in that quarter of the globe, with which we have so much intercourse and from which we derive our origin, we have always been anxious and interested spectators. The citizens of the United States cherish sentiments the most friendly in favor of the liberty and happiness of their fellow-men on that side of the Atlantic. In the wars of the European powers in matters relating to themselves we have never taken any part, nor does it comport with our policy to do so. It is only when our rights are invaded or seriously menaced that we resent injuries or make preparation for our defense. With the movements in this hemisphere we are of necessity more immediately connected, and by causes which must be obvious to all enlightened and impartial observers. The political system of the allied powers is essentially different in this respect from that of America. This difference proceeds from that which exists in their respective Governments; and to the defense of our own, which has been achieved by the loss of so much blood and treasure, and matured by the wisdom of their most enlightened citizens, and under which we have enjoyed unexampled felicity, this whole nation is devoted. We owe it, therefore, to candor and to the amicable relations existing between the United States and those powers to declare that we should consider any attempt on their part to extend their system to any portion of this hemisphere as dangerous to our peace and safety. With the existing colonies or dependencies of any European power we have not interfered and shall not interfere. But with the Governments who have declared their independence and maintain it, and whose independence we have, on great consideration and on just principles, acknowledged, we could not view any interposition for the purpose of oppressing them, or controlling in any other manner their destiny, by any European power in any other light than as the manifestation of an unfriendly disposition toward the United States. In the war between those new Governments and Spain we declared our neutrality at the time of their recognition, and to this we have adhered, and shall continue to adhere, provided no change shall occur which, in the judgement of the competent authorities of this Government, shall make a corresponding change on the part of the United States indispensable to their security.

The late events in Spain and Portugal shew that Europe is still unsettled. Of this important fact no stronger proof can be adduced than that the allied powers should have thought it proper, on any principle satisfactory to themselves, to have interposed by force in the internal concerns of Spain. To what extent such inter-position may be carried, on the same principle, is a question in which all inde-pendent powers whose governments differ from theirs are interested, even those most remote, and surely none of them more so than the United States. Our policy in regard to Europe, which was adopted at an early stage of the wars which have so long agitated that quarter of the globe, nevertheless remains the same, which is, not to interfere in the internal concerns of any of its powers; to consider the government de facto as the legitimate government for us; to cultivate friendly rela-tions with it, and to preserve those relations by a frank, firm, and manly policy, meeting in all instances the just claims of every power, submitting to injuries from none. But in regard to those continents circumstances are eminently and conspicuously different.

It is impossible that the allied powers should extend their political system to any portion of either continent without endangering our peace and happiness; nor can anyone believe that our southern brethren, if left to themselves, would adopt it of their own accord. It is equally impossible, therefore, that we should behold such interposition in any form with indifference. If we look to the comparative strength and resources of Spain and those new Governments, and their distance from each other, it must be obvious that she can never subdue them. It is still the true policy of the United States to leave the parties to themselves, in hope that other powers will pursue the same course. . . .

Source: http://www.ourdocuments.gov/doc.php?flash=true&doc=23&page=transcript. Widely available on the Internet, including Yale Project Avalon.

REVIEW QUESTIONS

1. Describe the changes desired by writers and activists in the realm of political, economic, and social structures.
2. What challenges did heads of governments and officials, including officials in revolutionary governments, face in revolutionary and post-revolutionary times?
3. What were the attitudes and concerns of ordinary people during this period of imperial change?
4. Toussaint Louverture is variously represented in painting and engravings but most often in his general's uniform. See http://slaveryandremembrance.org/people/search/ and then scroll to the page for Toussaint Louverture. What does this portrait of Toussaint Louverture, produced during his lifetime, say about how the artist wanted him to be remembered and how he wanted to appear to the public?

CHAPTER 6

Confrontation, Industrialization, and Imperial Knowledge, c. 1815–1870

Empires continued to face off in the nineteenth century over territory and trade, laying the groundwork for intense colonization by 1900. In 1815 a coalition of Britain, Austria, Russia, and Prussia finally blocked French imperial expansion on the European continent and in the Mediterranean region. Meanwhile, the British East India Company used resources to make additional conquests against the Mughal Empire and independent states in India to compensate for its losses in North America. With its armies composed of South Asians and a variety of European and British soldiers, the Company fought smaller states across the subcontinent, finally taking control of several including those of Mysore in 1799. Britain then tried to make military inroads in Central Asia to stop the descent of Russia into the region even as that empire made conquests in the Caucasus. In general, complex politics weakened local authority and made it easier for imperial powers to play one rival group against another and often to take over an area with little effort. Afghani ethnic and kin groups, however, successfully fought off numerous attempts to conquer what is present-day Afghanistan, including two major invasions in the nineteenth century, several more in the twentieth, and another in the twenty-first. Between 1853 and 1856 the Russian and Ottoman empires clashed in the Crimean War, with Britain and France joining the weakening Ottomans to halt the progress of an expanding Russia. They aimed to prop up the government in Constantinople that was seriously indebted to them.

As with the Afghanistan invasion, which took a high toll in European lives, so too the costs of slavery to empires mounted. Industrialization depended on slave production of sugar and other foodstuffs in Western Hemisphere empires—boosting the energy of factory and other workers—and cotton to clothe people more cheaply. In 1831 slaves in Jamaica rebelled once more against their masters, destroying millions of dollars in crops and real estate and killing fourteen owners and overseers. This toll was added to the more than 2,000 slaves on the island who escaped each year, again increasing the costs of owning slaves. That same year Nat Turner's rebellion in Virginia took the lives of five dozen owners of slaves, followed by harsh retribution. With cotton and other products created by slaves counting for two-thirds of U.S. exports, abolitionists nonetheless wanted to destroy the imperial system of slavery. Under economic threats, rising deaths, and humanitarian concerns, Britain abolished slavery in imitation of some Latin American new nations. Soon France and Denmark followed suit. Russia abolished serfdom in 1861, judging that its defeat in the Crimean War was due to armies composed of ill-equipped serf conscripts. Ultimately both the United States and, two decades after that, Brazil outlawed slavery. Imperial powers used their sponsorship of abolition to justify further conquest across the globe.

As imperial profits from the slave trade weakened, empires promoted themselves as a benefit to humanity. Some African leaders, who had thrived on the trade, redirected their armies towards enslavement of competing or non-Muslim ethnic groups at home to use as plantation labor growing export commodities for the new European and U.S. industries. Other expansion was imperceptible, as military, scientific, and industrial intelligence gatherers circled the globe, either as individuals or as part of teams, with both dependent on local facilitators. British forays into Central Asia were preceded by caravans of spies, including government officials, disguised as pilgrims and tourists and accompanied by an entourage of interpreters, map-makers, suppliers, and scholars. These gathered information about harbors, roads, and natural impediments to advance the cause of empire as had the ocean-borne information-gatherers before them. Others went to sand-covered areas of Asia to find hidden treasures to stock imperial museums or to fill their own collections and coffers.

Still others among these were scientists, who might provide political intelligence in addition to their findings about mineral, plant, and other natural resources. Charles Darwin, who advocated a theory of evolution and declared the superiority of white men as a scientific fact, was only one such scientist. In addition to providing useful information on animal life, fauna, and climate, he laid the groundwork for a pseudo-scientific rationale for racism, military build-up, and imperial conquest. The superior, white races needed to prepare themselves, some of Darwin's followers claimed, to fight off the savages, who were always on the lookout to defeat the forces of civilization. Such preparations came to involve everything from team sports, military drill, and weapons buildup to prenatal care for women so that they would have more fit children and better schooling, more medicine, and sufficient food to ensure fitness. Empire was a powerful force in the policies of the nation-state though somewhat less obviously so in everyday life as people came to take products from around the world for granted.

As the legal abolition of slavery in the West proceeded during these years, racism thus gained a stronger "scientific" rationale alongside the moral one, justifying new forms of imperial servitude and exploitation under empires. Agents for owners of sugar, coffee, and other plantations swooped down on different regions, especially South and East Asia and Sub-Saharan Africa, to find workers—mostly male—to serve as indentured servants. They were promised "good," temporary jobs in the colonial holdings of the Caribbean, the Pacific islands and other regions to entice them away from their communities. The reality was usually dramatically different, with harsh living and working conditions. Often it was difficult for these men to return home, and some few did not want to because of relationships they might have established in their new jobs. They became part of the vast global diaspora of former slaves, merchants, indentured workers and their offspring, and opportunity seekers who peopled this increasingly interconnected world of empires. Migrant workers created a rich hybrid global culture wherever they settled, bring order from the imperial disruption of relationships and lives. Apologists for imperialism, however, announced that the shabby appearance and living conditions of these workers was an indication of their savagery and inferiority—not of the bondage in which they were held. Indentured workers were also seen by some as better than actual slaves, indicating that economic progress held the key to freedom.

The new United States moved across the Pacific to open Japan to its trade and influence. It also moved westward and to the south on the North American continent, driving out indigenous peoples with lethal force. Between 1817 and 1850 thousands of Seminole, Chickasaw, Chocktaw, Creek, and other Native Americans were driven from the southeastern regions of the United States so that the white Americans could have their lands and the resources on them, including gold. In addition, the United States expanded into Mexican territory and between 1846 and 1848 fought a war allowing it to seize Utah, Nevada, Arizona, New Mexico, and California and to grow stronger through conquest. This annexation also involved the violent seizure of Native American lands and resources. The justification for this seizure, as for others, included the moral superiority of freedom-loving whites, the idea that Native Americans had no civilization or culture, and the notion that the United States simply had a God-given right to the entire continent. In fact, the military might of the Apache empire in the first half of the century was directed toward Mexico and thus weakened the Mexican state enough that U.S. forces could defeat it in the Mexican-American War.

Older empires faced challenges. China unsuccessfully faced off with the British over the issue of opium, which the British were smuggling into the empire. Although weak in trade goods, the British were strong militarily and made significant inroads on Chinese sovereignty using improved weapons and steampowered boats from its modernizing industries. Revivalist religions weakened both China and the Ottomans. In China, the Taiping Rebellion in the middle of the century promised a spiritualized kingdom amid job losses caused by the military defeat in the Opium wars. Some sixty million Chinese perished in the struggle against the Qing. Faced with Islamic revivalism and the loss of control over the holy places of Mecca and Medina, the Ottoman Empire tried to strengthen itself through reform of its administration and laws. Even as the Mughal Empire in India collapsed entirely amid an uprising against British rule in 1857 after a century of being undermined by other empire builders, the Ottomans were losing markets and trade advantages because of European industrialization and a general inability to keep up economically. The European powers had begun building railroads and undertaking or financing other infrastructure projects, leaving the Ottomans financially beholden to them and hardstrapped to pay their bills. Uneven Ottoman modernization also involved upgrading cities, which added to a burden of indebtedness. Simultaneously, some local businesspeople modernized their operations, buying up large tracts of land and setting up plantations for growing cotton and other crops that were in demand. Poor farmers became day laborers or even beggars, which added to the social dislocation of the Ottoman and Mughal empires in modern times.

Industrialization that had begun after c. 1750 gave the Europeans and Americans the upper hand in the form of increasingly powerful weaponry and dramatic innovations in transportation and communications. In the eighteenth century French engineers devised the interchangeability of parts for guns, making them repairable on distant battlefields. After that, guns themselves improved in accuracy, speed, and firepower, with the nineteenth-century invention of the repeater, later called the machine gun, giving the well-armed forces of imperial armies an advantage over local defenders. The chemical industry also improved to provide effective medicines such as quinine. These overcame tropical diseases, which had formed an invisible barrier to penetration of vast areas such as sub-Saharan Africa. The way was prepared for a huge spurt in imperial expansion beginning in the last third of the century.

1. SIR ROBERT WILSON, *A SKETCH OF THE MILITARY AND POLITICAL POWER OF RUSSIA* (1817)

Sir Robert Wilson, a British general and a governor of Gibraltar in the 1840s, had vast experience fighting Napoleon and observing Russia as liaison officer during Napoleon's invasion of that huge country in 1812. His book on the status of Russia, produced shortly after that empire and a coalition including Britain had defeated an expansionist France, saw Russia as poised for greater power in the form of access to the seas and ultimately a competitor to Britain. Later pro-imperial British officials cited the book as justification for interventions in Central Asia and the Ottoman Empire, but in fact the British had already increased their attention to South and Central Asia once the thirteen North American colonies had slipped from their grasp. During these decades, armies, including the colonial military, benefited from French engineer Honoré Blanc's invention of interchangeable parts for guns, allowing their easy repair near the battlefield—even one in distant lands. Explain why Britain or its officials might see distant Russia as a danger.

Thus here, as on the *Swedish*, *Polish*, and *Moldavian* frontier, invulnerable herself, she [Russia] stands ready to strike and to wound; to hurl her thunder over Asia whenever her policy deems the moment expedient: for her routes of march to all the points which attract her, are now but marches of a few days.

The distance is to Trebisond, but *eighty* miles; to the western bank of the Euphrates, not above *ninety*; to Arzroum, *one hundred*; to Sinope, *two hundred and seventy*; to Scutari, opposite Constantinople, a little more than *five hundred*; across the *Isthmus* of Asia Minor to Alexandretta (a seaport town opposite *Cyprus* in the *Mediterranean*), and only *sixty* miles from *Aleppo*, little more than *four hundred*; and to the Red Sea from thence not *five hundred*.

Here, then she is moreover posted with *perfect* communications, with a *sea* road for the transport of her stores and magazines, awaiting but a signal to advance, and make herself *mistress of those communications along which the Turks in Europe must receive their Asiatic reinforcements. . . .*

Russia has descended from the mountains! She is no longer struggling against the hostility of *nature* and *barbarians* in the regions of the Caucasus. . . .

To reach *Tchiran*, the capital of the Shah, the columns have to march only *three hundred* miles; and by the navigation of the Caspian they can be disembarked within *one hundred!* Thus an army might sail from the *Baltic* through an internal navigation from Petersburgh to Astraean, and landing on the southern shore of the Caspian, pitch their tents within *four hundred* miles of the Persian Gulf; from whence the voyage to *Bombay* is only from *twenty-four* to *thirty* days, in both Monsoons; and to Madras, but *eight* or *ten* days longer in the S. W. Monsoon. . . .

The fact is, that *Russia*, after posting *thirty thousand* men of appropriate force, with artillery, &c. in Finland, *eighty thousand* on the frontier of Gallicia, *sixty thousand* in Moldavia, *thirty thousand* on the frontier of Armenia, as many in Persia, and leaving a reserve of *one hundred thousand* men to sustain these armies, possesses still a disposable force of above *two hundred thousand* infantry, *eighty thousand* cavalry, and *one thousand two hundred* guns better horsed for service than any artillery or cavalry in the world[1];—an army, than which, there is none more brave, and with which *no other* can march, starve, or suffer physical privations and natural inclemencies. She has moreover a population equal to the needed supply, and to a great portion of whom the habits and sufferings of war are familiar; while no power in Europe can raise, equip or maintain their forces, with such disdain of the price of blood[2]. . . .

Alexander now wields the huge sceptre of Russia, and displays an ability equal to the task. . . .

Now he appears only in the character (and his enemies triumph in the result) of a conqueror. . . .

Whether he will profit by the positions and present superiority of *Russia*, to accomplish other projects long assigned to her system of policy, must interest all governments, not excepting the *government of the East Indies;* whose attention may also be more excited by the information, that *General Yermoloff*, the governor of the *Caucasus* line, who probably at this very moment has reached the *capital of* PERSIA. . . .

---

[1]The militia would perform the garrison duties, if all the regular troops were required on emergency in the field. Her *defensive* means, indeed, are so great and various, as to be incalculable.

[2]The actual pay of a *Russian* soldier is not much above half a crown a month

These reports and plans had convinced *Napoleon*, that the expedition to *India* was practicable; and it is a *positive fact*, that he had resolved on sending an united *Russian* and *French* force on that expedition, in case Russia had been compelled to make peace on his terms.

Source: Sir Robert Wilson, *A Sketch of the Military and Political Power of Russia* (New York: Kirk and Mercein, 1817), 144–154. Editorial notes deleted from the source.

2. CHEROKEE WOMEN, "PETITION" (1818)

Citizens of the young United States and those migrating to the country were as eager as other imperialists to take over the land and other resources of local peoples—in this case the Native Americans of the North American continent. These ambitions in part had caused the U.S. revolt against Britain in 1776, when that empire tried to keep the "Americans" contained so as not to stir up Native Americans. By the early nineteenth century, some Native Americans were settled farmers, had converted to Christianity, and were well-educated, but this made no difference in North America as it had made no difference elsewhere when it came to simply taking the land of others. By the nineteenth century, British industrialization of textile production made growing cotton profitable as sugar had helped other empires and their people make money—both of these driving land hunger and imperial expansion. As in China and the Ottoman Empire, some Native Americans urged spiritual revival and a return to traditional spiritual beliefs. Others confronted the legislation, treaties, and edicts confiscating Native American land in the first third of the century and forcing Cherokees and other tribes in the Southeast United States from their homes. Protests were nonstop, this one from the active council of Cherokee women who possessed land for domestic farming and their other enterprises. In 1835 the largest dispossession to that date, driving tens of thousands of Cherokees from Georgia to the other side of the Mississippi, took place so that whites could prosper instead. Analyze the argument of the Cherokee women and explain why their argument was ineffective.

Beloved Children,

We have called a meeting among ourselves to consult on the different points now before the council, relating to our national affairs. We have heard with painful feelings that the bounds of the land we now possess are to be drawn into very narrow limits. The land was given to us by the Great Spirit above as our common right, to raise our children upon, & to make support for our rising generations. We therefore humbly petition our beloved children, the head men & warriors, to hold out to the last in support of our common rights, as the Cherokee nation have been the first settlers of this land; we therefore claim the right of the soil.

We well remember that our country was formerly very extensive, but by repeated sales it has become circumscribed to the very narrow limits we have at present. Our Father the President advised us to become farmers, to manufacture our own clothes, & to have our children instructed. To this advice we have attended in every thing as far as we were able. Now the thought of being compelled to remove the other side of the Mississippi is dreadful to us, because it appears to us that we, by this removal, shall be brought to a savage state again, for we have, by the endeavor of our Father the President, become too much enlightened to throw aside the privileges of a civilized life.

We therefore unanimously join in our meeting to hold our country in common as hitherto.

Some of our children have become Christians. We have missionary schools among us. We have heard the gospel in our nation. We have become civilized & enlightened, & are in hopes that in a few years our nation will be prepared for instruction in other branches of sciences & arts, which are both useful & necessary in civilized society.

There are some white men among us who have been raised in this country from their youth, are connected with us by marriage, & have considerable families, who are very active in encouraging the emigration of our nation. These ought to be our truest friends but prove our worst enemies. They seem to be only concerned how to increase their riches, but do not care what becomes of our Nation, nor even of their own wives and children.

Source: Theda Purdue and Michael D. Green, eds., *The Cherokee Removal: A Brief History with Documents* (Boston: Bedford/St. Martins, 2005), 131–133.

3. ADDRESS OF THE HONORABLE S. F. AUSTIN, DELIVERED AT LOUISVILLE, KENTUCKY (1836)

Latin American revolutionaries created widespread instability by achieving independence. In particular, Mexico's sparsely settled lands across the Rio Grande seemed especially vulnerable. The Commanche Empire, finding itself squeezed by the forced migration of Native Americans from the East Coast, attacked these Mexican lands to gain resources. Traders from the western region of the United States migrated temporarily once a year to gain furs, silver, and other goods. To fill up its population, Mexico allotted lands to some of these, including the Austin family who eventually created a state within the Mexican federation and by 1835 declared Texas an independent nation. In 1845, the United States annexed Texas, as U.S. adventurers flooded the other Mexican territories. Sam Austin justified Texan independence in this speech, which resembled justifications given by other empire builders: The territory had ineffective government, causing widespread chaos and confusion that only whites could remedy.

But a few years back Texas was a wilderness, the home of the uncivilized and wandering Comanche and other tribes of Indians, who waged a constant warfare against the Spanish settlements. These settlements at that time were limited to the small towns of Bexar, (commonly called San Antonio) and Goliad, situated on the western limits. The incursions of the Indians also extended beyond the Rio Bravo del Norta, and desolated that part of the country.

In order to restrain these savages and bring them into subjection, the government opened Texas for settlement. Foreign emigrants were invited and called to that country. American enterprise accepted the invitation and promptly responded to the call. The first colony of Americans or foreigners ever settled in Texas was by myself. It was commenced in 1821, under a permission to my father, Moses Austin, from the Spanish government previous to the Independence of Mexico, and has succeeded by surmounting those difficulties and dangers incident to all new and wilderness countries infested with hostile Indians. These difficulties were many and at times appalling, and can only be appreciated by the hardy pioneers of this western country, who have passed through similar scenes.

The question here naturally occurs, what inducements, what prospects, what hopes could have stimulated us, the pioneers and settlers of Texas, to remove from the midst of civilized society, to expatriate ourselves from this land of liberty, from this our native country, endeared to us as it was, and still is, and ever will be, by the ties of nativity, the reminiscences of childhood and youth and local attachments, of friendship and kindred? Can it for a moment be supposed that we severed all these ties—the ties of nature and of education, and went to Texas to grapple with the wilderness and with savage foes, merely from a spirit of wild and visionary adventure, without guarantees of protection for our persons and property and political rights? No, it cannot be believed. No American, no Englishman, no one of any nation who has a knowledge of the people of the United States, or of the prominent characteristics of the Anglo-Saxon race to which we belong—a race that in all ages and in all countries wherever it has appeared has been marked for a jealous and tenacious watchfulness of its liberties, and for a cautious and calculating view of the probable events of the future—no one who has a knowledge of this race can or will believe that we removed to Texas without such guarantees, as free born, and, enterprising men naturally expect and require. The fact is, we had such guaranteed; for, in the first place the government bound itself to protect us by the mere act of admitting us as citizens, on the general and long established principle, even in the dark ages, that protection and allegiance are reciprocal—a principle which in this enlightened age has been extended much further; for its received interpretation now is, that the object of government is the well being, security, and happiness of the governed, and that allegiance ceases whenever it is clear, evident, and palpable, that this object is in no respect effected.

But besides this general guarantee, we had others of a special, definite, and positive character—the colonization laws of 1823, '24, and '25, inviting emigrants generally to that country, especially guaranteed protection for person and property, and the right of citizenship.

When the federal system and constitution were adopted in 1824, and the former provinces became states, Texas, by her representative in the constituent congress, exercised the right which was claimed and exercised by all the provinces, of retaining within her own control, the rights and powers which appertained to her as one of the unities or distinct societies, which confederated together to form the federal republic of Mexico. But not possessing at that time sufficient population to become a state by herself, she was with her own consent, united provisionally with Coahuila, a neighbouring province or society, to form the state of COAHUILA AND TEXAS, "until Texas possessed the necessary elements to form a separate state of herself." I quote the words of the constitutional or organic act passed by the constituent congress of Mexico, on the 7th of May, 1824, which establishes the state of Coahuila and Texas. This law, and the principles on which the Mexican federal compact was formed, gave to Texas a specific political existence, and vested in her inhabitants the special and well defined rights of self-government as a state of the Mexican confederation, so soon as she "possessed the necessary elements." Texas consented to the provisional union with Coahuila on the faith of this guarantee. It was therefore a solemn compact, which neither the state of Coahuila and Texas, nor the general government of Mexico, can change without the consent of the people of Texas.

In 1833 the people of Texas, after a full examination of their population and resources, and of the law and constitution, decided, in general convention elected for that purpose, that the period had arrived contemplated by said law and compact of 7th May, 1824, and that the country possessed the necessary elements to form a state separate from Coahuila. A respectful and humble petition was accordingly drawn up by this convention, addressed to the general congress of Mexico, praying for the admission of Texas into the Mexican confederation as a state. I had the honor of being appointed by the convention the commissioner or agent of Texas to take this petition to the city of Mexico, and present it to the government. I discharged this duty to the best of my feeble abilities, and, as I believed, in a respectful manner. Many months passed and nothing was done with the petition, except to refer it to a committee of congress, where it slept and was likely to sleep. I finally urged the just and constitutional claims of Texas to become a state in the most pressing manner, . . . owning to the almost total want of local government of any kind, . . . and the consequent anarchy and discontent that existed in Texas. It was my misfortune to offend the high authorities of the nation—my frank and honest exposition of the truth was construed into threats."

At this time (September and October, 1833), a revolution was raging in many parts of the nation, and especially in the vicinity of the city of Mexico. I despaired of obtaining anything, and wrote to Texas, recommending to the people there to organize as a state de facto without waiting any longer. This letter may have been imprudent, . . . I was arrested at Saltillo, two hundred leagues from Mexico, on my way home, taken back to that city and imprisoned one year, three months of the time in solitary confinement, without books or writing materials, in a dark dungeon of the former inquisition prison. At the close of the year I was released from confinement, but . . . [i]t was nine months after my arrest before I was officially informed of the charges against me. . . . The constitutional requisites were not observed, my constitutional rights as a citizen were violated, the people of Texas were outraged by this treatment of their commissioner, and their respectful, humble and just petition was disregarded.

These acts of the Mexican government, taken in connexion with many others and with the general revolutionary situation of the interior of the republic, and the absolute want of local government in Texas, would have justified the people of Texas in organizing themselves as a State of the Mexican confederation, and if attacked for so doing in separating from Mexico. They would have been justifiable in doing this, because such acts were unjust, ruinous and oppressive, and because self-preservation required a local government in Texas suited to the situation and necessities of the country, and the character of its inhabitants. Our forefathers in '76 flew to arms for much less. They resisted a principle, "the theory of oppression," but in our case it was the reality—it was a denial of justice and of our guarantied rights—it was oppression itself.

    . . . It is well known that Mexico has been in constant revolutions and confusion, with only a few short intervals, ever since its separation from Spain in 1821. This unfortunate state of things has been produced by the effects of the ecclesiastical and aristocratical party to oppose republicanism, overturn the federal system and constitution, and establish a monarchy, or a consolidated government of some kind. In 1834, the President of the Republic, Gen. Santa Anna, who heretofore was the leader and champion of the republican party and system, became the head and leader of his former antagonists—the aristocratic and church party. With this accession of strength, this party triumphed. The constitutional general Congress of 1834, which was decidedly republican and federal, was dissolved in May of that year by a military order of the President . . . ; and a new, revolutionary, and unconstitutional Congress was convened by another military order of the President. This Congress met on the 1st of January, 1835. It was decidedly aristocratic, ecclesiastical and central in its politics. . . . It accordingly, by a decree, deposed the constitutional Vice President, Gomez Farias, who was a leading federalist, without any impeachment or trial, or even the form of a trial, and elected another of their own party, Gen. Barragan, in his place. By another decree it united the Senate with the House of Representatives in one chamber, and thus constituted, it declared itself invested with full powers as a national convention. In accordance with these usurped powers, it proceeded to annul the federal constitution and system, and to establish a central or consolidated government. . . .

    The present position of Texas is an absolute Declaration of Independence—a total separation from Mexico. This declaration was made on the 7th of November last. It is as follows:

    "Whereas Gen. Antonio Lopez de Santa Anna, and other military chieftains, have by force of arms, overthrown the federal institutions of Mexico, and dissolved the social compact which existed between Texas and the other members of the Mexican Confederacy, now the good people of Texas, availing themselves of their natural rights, SOLEMNLY DECLARE,

    "1st. That they have taken up arms in defence of their rights and liberties, which were threatened by encroachments of military despots, and in defence of the republican principles of the federal constitution of Mexico, of 1824.

    "2d. That Texas is no longer morally or civilly bound by the compact of union; yet stimulated by the generosity and sympathy common to a free people, they offer their support and assistance to such of the members of the Mexican Confederacy as will take up arms against military despotism.

"3d. That they do not acknowledge that the present authorities of the nominal Mexican Republic, have the right to govern within the limits of Texas."

Source: Yale Law School, The Avalon Project. http://avalon.law.yale.edu/19th_century/texind01.asp (accessed November 9, 2015).

4. COMMISSIONER LIN, LETTER TO QUEEN VICTORIA (1839)

In order to pay for tea, porcelain, textiles, and other commodities from China, the British had to find saleable goods to raise money from consumers. For all the fanfare around the Industrial Revolution, European goods were shoddy in comparison to those from Asia and found few buyers in the region. Opium, however, was one commodity the Chinese would buy, and British merchants made fortunes in directing Indians to produce and process poppies and then export the resulting opium to users in China. The merchants would then have funds to buy tea and other Chinese products the British could not live without. Opium abuse alarmed the Chinese government, and the opium trade was made illegal. The British smuggled and otherwise forced it into the empire. The Qing Empire was weakening and tasked the official Lin Zexu with preventing further trade in opium; Lin Zexu also issued this protest to Queen Victoria. Further, he destroyed entire shiploads of the drug, leading to the Opium War of 1839–1842. The British, determined to protect their market, ultimately defeated the Chinese and in the Treaty of Nanjing forced the government to open more ports to trade and to allow the victors greater access to the empire and its wealth. This case demonstrates that profit remained a major driver of empire. Explain China's objections to Britain's support of illegal drugs and analyze the ways in which empires are intertwined in this particular case.

Lin, high imperial commissioner, a president of the Board of War, viceroy of the two Keäng provinces, &c., Tang, a president of the Board of War, viceroy of the two Kwang provinces, &c., and E., a vice-president of the Board of War, lieut.-governor of Kwangtung, &c., hereby conjointly address this public dispatch to the queen of England for the purpose of giving her clear and distinct information (on the state of affairs) &c.

It is only our high and mighty emperor, who alike supports and cherishes those of the Inner Land, and those from beyond the seas—who looks upon all mankind with equal benevolence—who, if a source of profit exists anywhere, diffuses it over the whole world—who, if the tree of evil takes root anywhere, plucks it up for the benefit of all nations;—who, in a word, hath implanted in his breast that heart (by which beneficent nature herself) governs the heavens and the earth! You, the queen of your honorable nation, sit upon a throne occupied through successive generations by predecessors, all of whom have been styled respectful and obedient. Looking over the public documents accompanying the tribute sent (by your predecessors) on various occasions, we find the following: "All the people of my country, arriving at the Central Land for purposes of trade, have to feel grateful to the great emperor for the most perfect justice, for the kindest treatment," and other words to that effect. Delighted did we feel that the kings of your honorable nation so clearly understood the great principles of propriety, and were so deeply grateful for the heavenly goodness (of our emperor):—therefore, it was that we of the heavenly dynasty nourished and cherished your people from afar, and bestowed upon them redoubled proofs of our urbanity and kindness. It is merely from these circumstances, that your country—deriving immense advantage from its commercial intercourse with us, which has endured now two hundred years—has become the rich and flourishing kingdom that it is said to be!

But, during the commercial intercourse which has existed so long, among the numerous foreign merchants resorting hither, are wheat and tares, good and bad; and of these latter are some, who, by means of introducing opium by stealth, have seduced our Chinese people, and caused every province of the land to overflow with that poison. These then know merely to advantage themselves, they care not about injuring others! This is a principle which heaven's Providence repugnates; and which mankind conjointly look upon with abhorrence! Moreover, the great emperor hearing of it, actually quivered with indignation, and especially dispatched me, the commissioner, to Canton, that in conjunction with the viceroy and lieut.-governor of the province, means might be taken for its suppression!

Every native of the Inner Land who sells opium, as also all who smoke it, are alike adjudged to death. Were we then to go back and take up the crimes of the foreigners, who, by selling it for many years have induced dreadful calamity and robbed us of enormous wealth, and punish them with equal severity, our laws could not but award to them absolute annihilation! But, considering that these said foreigners did yet repent of their crime, and with a sincere heart beg for mercy; that they took 20,283 chests of opium piled up in their store-ships, and through Elliot, the superintendent of the trade of your said country, petitioned that they might be delivered up to us, when the same were all utterly destroyed, of which we, the imperial commissioner and colleagues, made a duly prepared memorial to his majesty;—considering these circumstances, we have happily received a fresh proof of the extraordinary goodness of the great emperor, inasmuch as he who voluntarily comes forward, may yet be deemed a fit subject for mercy, and his crimes be graciously remitted him. But as for him who again knowingly violates the laws, difficult indeed will it be thus to go on repeatedly pardoning! He or they shall alike be doomed to the penalties of the new statute. We presume that you, the sovereign of your honorable nation, on pouring out your heart before the altar of eternal justice, cannot but command all foreigners with the deepest respect to reverence our laws! If we only lay clearly before your eyes, what is profitable and what is destructive, you will then know that the statutes of the heavenly dynasty cannot but be obeyed with fear and trembling!

We find that your country is distant from us about sixty or seventy thousand miles, that your foreign ships come hither striving the one with the other for our trade, and for the simple reason of their strong desire to reap a profit. Now, out of the wealth of our Inner Land, if we take a part to bestow upon foreigners from afar, it follows, that the immense wealth which the said foreigners amass, ought properly speaking to be portion of our own native Chinese people. By what principle of reason then, should these foreigners send in return a poisonous drug, which involves in destruction those very natives of China? Without meaning to say that the foreigners harbor such destructive intentions in their hearts, we yet positively assert that from their inordinate thirst after gain, they are perfectly careless about the injuries they inflict upon us! And such being the case, we should like to ask what has become of that conscience which heaven has implanted in the breasts of all men?

. . . Of the products which China exports to your foreign countries, there is not one which is not beneficial to mankind in some shape or other. There are those which serve for food, those which are useful, and those which are calculated for re-sale; but all are beneficial. Has China (we should like to ask) ever yet sent forth a noxious article from its soil? Not to speak of our tea and rhubarb, things which your foreign countries could not exist a single day without, if we of the Central Land were to grudge you what is beneficial, and not to compassionate your wants, then wherewithal could you foreigners manage to exist? And further, as regards your woolens, camlets, and longells, were it not that you get supplied with our native raw silk, you could not get these manufactured! If China were to grudge you those things which yield a profit, how could you foreigners scheme after any profit at all? Our other articles of food, such as sugar, ginger, cinnamon, &c., and our other articles for use, such as silk piece-goods, chinaware, &c., are all so many necessaries of life to you; how can we reckon up their number! On the other hand, the things that come from your foreign countries are only calculated to make presents of, or serve for mere amusement. It is quite the same to us if we have them, or if we have them not. . . .

Your honorable nation takes away the products of our central land, and not only do you thereby obtain food and support for yourselves, but moreover, by re-selling these products to other countries you reap a threefold profit. Now if you would only not sell opium, this threefold profit would be secured to you: how can you possibly consent to forgo it for a drug that is hurtful to men, and an unbridled craving after gain that seems to know no bounds! Let us suppose that foreigners came from another country, and brought opium into England, and seduced the people of your country to smoke it, would not you, the sovereign of the said country, look upon such a procedure with anger, and in your just indignation endeavor to get rid of it? Now we have always heard that your highness possesses a most kind and benevolent heart, surely then you are incapable of doing or causing to be done unto another, that which you should not wish another to do unto you! We have at the same time heard that your ships which come to Canton do each and every of them carry a document granted by your highness' self, on which are written these words "you shall not be permitted to carry contraband goods;" this shows that the laws of your highness are in their origin both distinct and severe, and we can only suppose that because the ships coming here have been very numerous, due attention has not been given to search and examine; and for this reason it is that we now address you this public document, that you may clearly know how stern and severe are the laws of the central dynasty, and most certainly you will cause that they be not again rashly violated!

Suppose the subject of another country were to come to England to trade, he would certainly be required to comply with the laws of England, then how much more does this apply to us of the celestial empire! . . . Pause and reflect for a moment: if you foreigners did not bring the opium hither, where should our Chinese people get it to re-sell? . . . Therefore it is that those foreigners who now import opium into the Central Land are condemned to be beheaded and strangled by the new statute, and this explains what we said at the beginning about plucking up the tree of evil, wherever it takes root, for the benefit of all nations.

. . . Now we, the high commissioner and colleagues, upon making a duly prepared memorial to the great emperor, have to feel grateful for his extraordinary goodness, for his redoubled compassion. Any one who within the next year and a half may by mistake bring opium to this country, if he will but voluntarily come forward, and deliver up the entire quantity, he shall be absolved from all punishment for his crime. If, however, the appointed term shall have expired, and there are still persons who continue to bring it, then such shall be accounted as knowingly violating the laws, and shall most assuredly be put to death! On no account shall we show mercy or clemency! This then may be called truly the extreme of benevolence, and the very perfection of justice!

. . . Let your highness immediately, upon the receipt of this communication, inform us promptly of the state of matters, and of the measure you are pursuing utterly to put a stop to the opium evil. Please let your reply be speedy. Do not on any account make excuses or procrastinate. A most important communication.

P. S. We annex an abstract of the new law, now about to be put in force.

> "Any foreigner or foreigners bringing opium to the Central Land, with design to sell the same, the principals shall most assuredly be decapitated, and the accessories strangled; and all property (found on board the same ship) shall be confiscated. The space of a year and a half is granted, within the which, if any one bringing opium by mistake, shall voluntarily step forward and deliver it up, he shall be absolved from all consequences of his crime."

This said imperial edict was received on the 9th day of the 6th month of the 19th year of Taoukwang, at which the period of grace begins, and runs on to the 9th day of the 12th month of the 20th year of Taoukwang, when it is completed.

Source: *Chinese Repository*, Vol. 8 (February 1840), 497–503.

5. MOHAN LAL, *THE LIFE OF DOST MOHAMMED KHAN, WITH HIS POLITICAL PROCEEDINGS TOWARDS THE ENGLISH, RUSSIAN AND PERSIAN GOVERNMENTS* (1846)

The British and Russians were pushing in many directions, including Central Asia, to expand their empires and like all modern empires jostled one another in the competition for imperial domination. Other rivals in the region were Persia and China, though both were considerably weakened by the mid-nineteenth century. Central Asia itself had fallen on very hard times, allowing the Russians in particular to build a chain of forts toward its heartland. In the middle of the many local disputes was Dost Mohammed Khan (1793–1863) who participated in a power struggle among various clans and factions within clans, eventually becoming Emir of Afghanistan from 1826–1839 and again from 1845 until his death. He was deposed once, when the Sikhs attacked his kingdom followed by the British assaulting it. He allied temporarily with Russia, and later in life he formed an alliance with Britain against Persia and neighboring clans wanting to overthrow him. The tempestuous, fragmented, and lethal politics, with European and non-Europeans aiming to control this pivotal region where clans competed too, has continued to this day. So has Afghani skill in undermining would-be invaders.

When Dost Mohammed and Fatah were informed of the hostile movements of Shah Shuja, they raised a large army, and under the royal shadow of Shah Mahmud and of Shah Zadah Kam Ran, set out to oppose Shah Shuja. Dost Mohammed volunteered to be the head of the advanced guard, and was accompanied by his stepbrother Purdil Khan, and also by Nur Mohammed Khan, the brother of Khowajah Mohammed Khan, who was slain in the late battle of Tahkal, in Peshavar. The very moment he had reached Kalat i Ghilzai, Nur Mohammed Khan went over to Shah Shuja, and Ata Mohammed Khan Nurzai and Yahya Khan Bamzai, who were commanders of large bodies of troops, fled towards Dehlah and Murghab.

At the time these sad desertions took place, and the leader of the advanced guard remained alone, Shuja would not have hesitated a moment to seize and destroy him (Dost Mohammed) by surprise, but he knew his brave heart and wise head, and therefore avoided a skirmish with him. It is said by the people that at this crisis Dost Mohammed was afraid of Shah Shuja, because he was deserted and alone, and the Shah was afraid of the talents and heroism of Dost, lest he might cause dissension among his followers. These fears, entertained on both sides, prevented an immediate contest, and afforded a favourable opportunity to Dost Mohammed Khan to retrace his steps and join his brother Fatah Khan.

On the approach of Shuja's army, Mahmud Shah, being aided only by Fatah Khan and Dost Mohammed, found himself too weak to fight with Shah Shuja, and therefore in this low spirit he fled to Girishk.

After some time Dost Mohammed and Fatah Khan left Girishk and went to Sabzvar, where they remained for three months. During their sojourn in this place they were informed that Shah Shuja had left Qandhar for Kabul. . . .

Meanwhile Dost Mohammed and Fatah Khan heard that two large caravans were to pass near Khashrod, one from Qandhar to Persia, and the other from the latter country to the former. On this they placed themselves on the road of the caravans, and the very moment they encountered with them every article fell into the possession of these noble highway-men. They gained plenty of money by this plunder from the merchants. Immediately after this they raised an army and prepared themselves to attack Qandhar.

Dost Mohammed and Fatah Khan met no opposition on the line of their march to Qandhar, which place they fortunately took with little trouble. . . . After arranging the government affairs of Qandhar, Dost Mohammed and Fatah Khan proceeded to take Kabul, under favour of the name of Shah Mahmud. They succeeded in gaining possession of this capital, and sent Mohammed Azim Khan towards Peshavar to oppose Shah Shuja.

While Mohammed Azim Khan was encamped at Balabagh to intercept the progress of Shah Shuja, Dost Mohammed and Fatah Khan were strengthening themselves and weakening their adversaries in Kabul. Among them was the Mir Alam Khan, whom they confined and treated with barbarous cruelty. Shah Shuja, at the head of twenty-five thousand men, proceeded from Peshavar to Kabul. When the royal army reached Jalalabad, Mohammed Azim Khan, finding himself unable to oppose his Majesty, left the highway and took shelter in the different skirts of the Sufaid Koh.

No sooner had the above-mentioned intelligence reached Dost Mohammed and Fatah Khan [than] they marched down to Surkhab to bring Mahmud Shah with them. These three enterprising men had no more than three thousand soldiers, and knew the strength of the army they were going to fight with; but Dost Mohammed's bravery, mingled with policy, was always depended upon, and generally productive of the results of victory. On their arrival in the vicinity of the Lukhi of Surkhab, they thought that if the Durrani chiefs should cause the release of the Mir Alam Khan, he would probably succeed in joining Shah Shuja, and desertions might take place among the followers on both sides. To prevent this anticipated misfortune, Dost Mohammed and Fatah Khan murdered the poor prisoner.

Now Dost Mohammed and Fatah Khan held a council of war with their subordinate chiefs in the presence of Shah Mahmud, and stated that it was most contrary to the rules of policy and of war to appear in the open field with a small force of three thousand before a monarch or enemy of twenty-five thousand well mounted cavalry and well equipped infantry. The only thing they think now advisable to preserve warlike fame and gain honour is to avoid a general action, and then with determined spirit to attack the enemy by surprise. . . . They also added that, though the enemy exceeded them in power and number of men, none of them ought to be disheartened and go over to him, believing that the victory would always attend his army, because such conduct would not only cause a disgraceful name for the man himself who should do so, but would also dishearten the rest of their followers.

These counsels of Dost Mohammed Khan were applauded by Mahmud Shah, Fatah Khan, and the chiefs, on which they left everything of peace and war to his sound and wise management. . . . He made a long march under cover of the darkness of night, and about five in the morning he attacked the Sardar Madad Khan, Azam Khan, and Ghafur Khan, who commanded ten thousand foot and horse, and had been sent as an advanced brigade. Persons who were present in the field of battle told me that it was out of the power of any man's tongue to describe the matchless alacrity, prowess, and steadiness of Dost Mohammed Khan in this grand battle. In one moment he was seen making a havoc in the lines of the enemy, and then, forcing his way back, he was observed to encourage his followers to fight; and another time he was perceived to restore order among the undisciplined soldiers. Madad Khan and Azam Khan, commanding the opposite forces, now felt the narrowness of their situation, and at the same time were panic-struck to see that Dost Mohammed was causing great slaughter in their army, which was already much reduced in number and in power. At length Dost Mohammed Khan routed and dispersed the enemy, who suffered exceedingly. . . .

When the report of the defeat of the strong royal force under Madad Khan, &c. &c., by a small body of troops under the personal command of Dost Mohammed Khan reached the camp of Shah Shuja, it not only incensed his Majesty, but alarmed him much, and made him proceed in person to check the progress of Dost Mohammed Khan. Shah Shuja had still fifteen thousand good soldiers under the command of the celebrated Akram Khan, who made the King believe that Shah Mahmud's forces were only three thousand men, and that they would not stand before him; and also that Dost Mohammed would soon lose the name of victorious, which he lately obtained in consequence of the ill management of Madad Khan. It appears that Akram Khan was either jealous, or had foolish brains to suppose that he could beat an army headed by Dost Mohammed Khan, who was never once known to leave a field of battle without gaining the victory, except some foresighted policy had induced him to do so. . . . I heard from several credible people in Afghanistan that at this time of the war Shah Shuja said confidentially to his minister, that while Dost Mohammed is not captured, the victory is not to be expected; and while he is alive the crown will not be on his (Shuja's) head.[3] The forces on both sides were arrayed in the field, those of Shah Shuja commanded by the Sardar Akram Khan, and those of Shah Mahmud were guided by the personal and heroic directions of Dost Mohammed Khan. A battle ensued, and after a severe conflict the Sardar Akram Khan was killed, with many hundreds of Shuja's army. Some say that the deceased was cut down by Dost himself; and others add that he had received a ball from some of his own followers. The fall of such a high nobleman in the field, with so many hundred followers, produced an alarming feeling in the forces of Shuja. His Majesty was also himself frightened, and at last compelled to flee. All the rest of his followers also dispersed.

---

[3] This appears to be a wonderful and true prophecy.

Shah Mahmud and Fatah Khan, happy in their success, and proud of the victory gained by their brave adherent Dost Mohammed Khan, returned to Kabul, and Mahmud was placed on the throne and acknowledged as King of Afghanistan. Fatah Khan, the elder brother of Dost Mohammed Khan, was appointed prime minister of the Shah, and he gave the charge of various important situations to his brothers. Since the qualifications for conducting war, unshaken courage and persevering generalship, as well as the talents for administering the affairs of the realm, prudent foresight and sound policy, were shining on the forehead of Dost Mohammed Khan, Mahmud Shah and the Vizir considered his presence with themselves of much value, and consequently he was selected as next person to the Vazir, but in reality he was first in everything.

Source: Mohan Lal, *The Life of Dost Mohammed Khan, with his Political Proceedings Towards the English, Russian and Persian Governments* (London: Longman, Brown, Green and Longmans, 1846), 67–70.

6. DECREES FROM THE OTTOMAN *TANZIMAT* (1856)

Meanwhile, some other empires worked to fortify themselves in the face of European empires' growing industrial and military might and the activism of their increasingly intrusive colonial offices. The Ottomans had witnessed the calming of their pirate allies in the Mediterranean and the inroads on Algeria by the French and more generally by the British. Reform seemed called for, as Egypt on its own undertook the modernization of Cairo as a cosmopolitan center of business, trade, and up-to-date infrastructure such as railroads. Also facing attacks from Islamic reformers pushing for the creation of committed Islamic states, the Sultan's government announced a series of decrees toward modernization. These decrees are collectively called the Tanzimat: The first, issued in 1839, guaranteed life and fortune and the regularization of taxation and government service; this one, issued in 1856 after the Ottomans' successful alliance with Britain and France in the Crimean War, gave further guarantees to non-Muslim populations. It thus seemed to offer a more "Western" sense of citizenship. Describe the guarantees offered by these reforms and their potential appeal to people in the Ottoman Empire. What might the drawbacks be?

It being now my desire to renew and enlarge still more the new Institutions ordained with the view of establishing a state of things conformable with the dignity of my Empire and the position which it occupies among civilized Nations, . . . it is my desire to augment its well-being and prosperity, to effect the happiness of all my subjects, who in my sight are all equal, and equally dear to me, and who are united to each other by the cordial ties of patriotism, and to insure the means of daily increasing the prosperity of my Empire. I have therefore resolved upon, and I order the execution of the following measures. The guarantees promised . . . in conformity with the Tanzimat, to all the subjects of my Empire, without distinction of classes or of Religion, for the security of their persons and property and the preservation of their honour, are to-day confirmed and consolidated, and efficacious measures shall be taken in order that they may have their full and entire effect.

All the Privileges and Spiritual Immunities granted by my ancestors . . . to all Christian communities or other non-Mussulman persuasions established in my Empire under my protection, shall be confirmed and maintained. Every Christian or other non-Mussulman community shall be bound . . . to examine into its actual Immunities and Privileges, and to discuss and submit to my Sublime Porte the Reforms required by the progress of civilization and of the age. . . . The Patriarchs, Metropolitans, Archbishops, Bishops, and Rabbins shall take an oath on their entrance into office according to a form agreed upon in common by my Sublime Porte and the spiritual heads of the different religious communities. The ecclesiastical dues, of whatever sort or nature they be, shall be abolished and replaced by fixed revenues of the Patriarchs and heads of communities. . . .

The Property, real or personal, of the different Christian Ecclesiastics shall remain intact; the Temporal Administration of the Christian or other non-Mussulman communities shall, how-ever, be placed under the safeguard of an Assembly to be chosen from among the members, both ecclesiastics and laymen, of the said communities.

In the towns, small boroughs, and villages, where the whole population is of the same Religion, no obstacle shall be offered to the repair, according to their original plan, of buildings set apart for Religious Worship, for Schools, for Hospitals, and for Cemeteries. . . .

Each Sect, in localities where there are no other Religious Denominations, shall be free from every species of restraint as regards the public exercise of its Religion. In the towns, small boroughs, and villages where different sects are mingled together, each community, inhabiting a distinct quarter, shall, by conforming to the above-mentioned ordinances, have equal power to repair and improve its Churches, its Hospitals, its Schools, and its Cemeteries. . . . My Sublime Porte will take energetic measures to ensure to each sect, whatever be the number of its adherents, entire Freedom in the exercise of its Religion.

Every distinction or designation tending to make any class whatever of the subjects of my Empire inferior to another class, on account of their Religion, Language, or Race, shall be for ever effaced from the Administrative Protocol. The laws shall be put in force against the use of any injurious or offensive term, either among private individuals or on the part of the authorities. As all forms of Religion are and shall be freely professed in my dominions, no subject of my Empire shall be hindered in the exercise of the Religion that he professes, nor shall be in any way annoyed on this account. No one shall be compelled to change their Religion.

The nomination and choice of all Functionaries and other Employés of my Empire being wholly dependent upon my Sovereign will, all the subjects of my Empire, without distinction of nationality, shall be admissible to public employments, and qualified to fill them according to their capacity and merit, and conformably with rules to be generally applied.

All the subjects of my Empire, without distinction, shall be received into the Civil and Military Schools of the Government, if they otherwise satisfy the conditions as to age and examination which are specified in the Organic Regulations of the said Schools. Moreover, every community is authorised to establish Public Schools of Science, Art, and Industry. Only the method of instruction and the choice of Professors in schools of this class shall be under the control of a Mixed Council of Public Instruction, the members of which shall be named by my Sovereign command.

All Commercial, Correctional, and Criminal Suits between Mussulmans and Christian or other non-Mussulman subjects, or between Christians or other non-Mussulmans of different sects, shall be referred to Mixed Tribunals.

The proceedings of these Tribunals shall be public: the parties shall be confronted, and shall produce their witnesses, whose testimony shall be received, without distinction, upon an oath taken according to the religious law of each sect. . . .

Penal, Correctional, and Commercial Laws, and Rules of Procedure for the Mixed Tribunals, shall be drawn up as soon as possible, and formed into a Code. Translations of them shall be published in all the languages current in the Empire. . . .

The organization of the Police in the capital, in the provincial towns, and in the rural districts, shall be revised in such a manner as to give to all the peaceable subjects of my Empire the strongest guarantees for the safety both of their persons and property.

The equality of Taxes entailing equality of burdens, as equality of duties entails that of rights, Christian subjects, and those of other non-Mussulman sects, as it has been already decided, shall, as well as Mussulmans, be subject to the obligations of the Law of Recruitment. The principle of obtaining substitutes, or of purchasing exemption, shall be admitted. A complete law shall be published, with as little delay as possible, respecting the admission into and service in the Army of Christian and other non-Mussulman subjects. . . .

As the Laws regulating the purchase, sale, and disposal of Real Property are common to all the subjects of my Empire, it shall be lawful for Foreigners to possess Landed Property in my dominions, conforming themselves to the laws and police regulations, and bearing the same charges as the native inhabitants, and after arrangements have been come to with Foreign Powers. The Taxes are to be levied under the same denomination from all the subjects of my Empire, without distinction of class or of Religion. . . . The Laws against Corruption, Extortion, or Malversation shall apply, according to the legal forms, to all the subjects of my Empire, whatever may be their class and the nature of their duties.

Steps shall be taken for the formation of Banks and other similar Institutions, so as to so effect a reform in the monetary and financial system, as well as to create Funds to be employed in augmenting the sources of the material wealth of my Empire. Steps shall also be taken for the formation of Roads and Canals to increase the facilities of communication and increase the sources of the wealth of the country. Everything that can impede commerce or agriculture shall be abolished. To accomplish these objectives means shall be sought to profit by the science, the art, and the funds of Europe, and thus gradually to execute them.

Source: Edward Hertslet, *The Map of Europe by Treaty*, 4 vols. (London: Butterworths, 1875–1891), II: 1243–1249.

7. PRINCE ALEKSANDR BARIATINSKII, LETTER TO GRAND DUKE MIKHAIL NIKOLAEVICH, VICEREGENT OF THE CAUCASUS (1862)

The Russian empire worked to absorb regions of the Ottoman and Persian empires in the first half of the nineteenth century, as Wilson predicted it would. After decades of fighting, the Imam Shamil (1797–1871), a leader in the northern Caucasus so powerful and respected that Russian author Lev Tolstoy wrote a novella about him, was finally defeated. Russians faced the problem of ruling over a people so united in their Muslim faith that the task appeared impossible. Prince Bariatinskii wrote this letter to the tsar's new official over the Caucasus, providing advice from information he had gleaned while leading Russian forces in the region. At the end of the letter, he advises the resettlement of local Muslims from the region to the Ottoman Empire— a resettlement that actually occurred thereafter. Describe the Russian government's approach to religious and cultural difference in its empire.

On the basis of these observations, . . . I believe it is important to win the greatest possible devotion of the territory to the government, and to administer each nationality with affection and complete respect for its cherished customs and traditions. The administrator, in my view, may only prepare the ground and point the way to improvements, but he must permit each nationality to contribute its share to general national progress consistent with its own particular conditions. In this respect the education of native women is, of course, of prime importance. Because of her influence upon the family as a repository of the national manners and customs, a woman has an equal effect on the habits of the child, the adult, and the aged, and therefore she alone can change for the better the domestic customs that are the primary basis for general improvement.

This is why, in a territory where a need is felt for a transformation of customs, attention should be given first of all to increasing the number of schools for women.

. . .

The problem of such a transformation is more difficult among Moslem peoples, since their civil organization rests on the foundations of Mohammedanism, and all their rules are therefore at odds with the civil principles of Christian government.

Eradication of the [Moslem] clergy's influence must therefore precede all other measures. Yet direct action on our part can only strengthen the people's fanaticism. Hence, it is necessary in this area to find also some means, derived and formed within their midst, which, gradually undermining the importance of the Mullahs, would in time destroy the authority of the Koran.

It was to this end that I restored the power of the khans as a force inimical to the theocratic principle. Although the khans recognize the Shariat, they seek to give precedence to the Adat, a law based on custom and consequently admitting of change. The Adat, based on the rights of the different estates, is extremely onerous, and if—with the decline of the Shariat—the people will no longer be protected against the oppression of the khans, they will, naturally, prefer to see the introduction of our civil laws.

. . .

To conclude my survey, permit me, for the sake of greater clarity, to submit to Your Imperial Highness a brief recapitulation of the topics on which I expressed my views and which I regard as the cornerstones of the welfare and happiness of the peoples entrusted to your care:

1. Education of women
2. Eradication of the Shariat
3. Restoration of Christianity
4. Means of communication
5. Irrigation
6. Colonization

. . .

We have conquered Shamil and, with him, all of the eastern Caucasus. The subjugation of the western Caucasus will be different because here we are not fighting with an established society and an administrative hierarchy. . . .

There is no doubt that the enemy we are trying to dislodge will defend himself with stubborn fury. But, in my opinion, the desirable outcome can be facilitated by reaching an agreement with the Porte concerning the installation of Shamil on Turkish lands which he should be allowed to colonize with voluntary exiles from the Caucasus. In this manner, we shall soon be rid of malcontents, fanatics, and the entire theocratic party, and we shall pacify simultaneously both European philanthropists and our own conscience, while providing the Circassians with a way out of the present desperate situation. We shall avoid bloodshed, Turkey will acquire an excellent addition to her population, and Shamil, along with gratitude to the emperor, will find fulfillment of his cherished aspirations. . . .

Source: *A Source Book for Russian History from Early Times to 1917*. Vol. 3: *Alexander II to the February Revolution*. George Vernadsky et al., eds. (New Haven: Yale University Press, 1972), 608–609.

8. U.S. COMMODORE MATTHEW PERRY, DIARY ACCOUNTS (1854)

The march of empire continued, albeit in different forms. Sometimes expansion gave warning to neighboring countries: After the Opium Wars the Japanese feared being defeated as had China, even swallowed up. For several hundred years the Japanese government had closed itself off to much, though not all, contact with foreign powers. The young United States, involved in whaling, trade with China and other Asian ports, and increasing oceanic ventures, picked up Japanese victims of shipwrecks with no place to deposit them and sought out convenient locations for repairing ships and resupplying them. From the first colonies, North Americans believed themselves more worthy than peoples of cultures from which they wanted to make profits. In the summer of 1853 a U.S. fleet under the command of Commodore Matthew Perry, outfitted with the latest steamships, made a well-organized if brief show of its superiority—notably its technology and military drill—to gain access to the country. The fleet then sailed off, to return six months later with even more ships to receive the Japanese government's response to the U.S. demand for access to Japan's ports and people. Perry succeeded in getting Japanese officials' attention with the new industrial products it gifted to them, but they hedged on giving full access to the country. This document presents a picture of Perry's determination to succeed despite Japanese stalling. How would you categorize this letter in tone, given that it is being addressed to the Emperor of Japan?

United States Flag-ship Powhatan,
Yedo Bay, off the town of Yoku-hama, March 1, 1854.

YOUR EXCELLENCY: In presenting for the consideration of your highness the accompanying draught of a treaty, which, in all its essential features, is identical with that at present subsisting between the United States and China, I again venture to urge upon the Imperial government of Japan the importance of establishing a friendly understanding with the nation which I have the honor on this occasion to represent. . . .

I have in a former communication remarked that the President of the United States entertains the strongest desire, and cherishes a most fervent hope, that the mission which he has intrusted to my charge may result in the accomplishment of a treaty mutually beneficial, and tending to avert, by timely negotiation, the consequences that would otherwise grow out of collisions certain to arise, should the present undefined relations between the two countries much longer continue.

In the increasing number of American ships almost daily passing and repassing the territories of Japan, the President is apprehensive of the occurrence of some further act of hostility towards the unoffending citizens of the United States who may be thrown by misfortune upon your shores, and hence his wish to establish a treaty of friendship, which shall give assurance of the discontinuance of a course of policy, on the part of the Japanese, altogether at variance with the usages of other nations, and no longer to be tolerated by the United States.

As an evidence of the friendly intentions of the President, and to pay the highest honor to his Imperial Majesty, he has sent me in command of a number of ships—to be increased by others which are to follow—not only to bear to his Majesty the letter which I have already presented, but to evince, by every suitable act of kindness, the cordial feelings entertained by him towards Japan.

That there might be sufficient time allowed for a full consideration of the just and reasonable demands of the President, I took upon myself to withdraw the ships in July last from the coast; and have now, after an absence of seven months, returned, in the full expectation of a most satisfactory arrangement.

Another proof of the friendly disposition of the President has been given in his sending for exhibition to the Imperial court, three of the magnificent steamers of the United States, of which there are many large and small in America; and he has also sent, for presentation to the Emperor, many specimens of the most useful inventions of our country.

Therefore, after all these demonstrations of good will, it would be strange if the Japanese government did not seize upon this very favorable occasion to secure a friendly intercourse with a people anxious to prevent, by wise and prudent foresight, all causes of future misunderstanding and strife.

It will be observed that there is no western nation so intimately connected with the peace and welfare of Japan as the United States, a part of whose territory lies opposite the Imperial coast, and whose commerce covers the Pacific ocean and Japan seas; not less than five hundred large ships being engaged exclusively in those regions in pursuit of whales, the crews of many of which suffer for want of water and other refreshments; and it would seem nothing more than common humanity to receive those who may seek shelter in the ports of Japan with kindness and hospitality. . . .

I have adverted to these facts merely to show the advantages that would grow out of such a treaty as I now propose, and to remark again that some amicable arrangement between the two nations has become positively necessary, and for reasons already explained.

Indeed, I shall not dare to return to the United States without carrying with me satisfactory responses to all the proposals of the President, and I must remain until such are placed in my possession.

With the most profound respect,

M.C. Perry

Commander-in-Chief United States Naval Forces East India, China, and Japan Seas, and special Ambassador to Japan.

Source: Francis L. Hawks, *Narrative of the Expedition of an American Squadron to the China Seas and Japan* (New York: D. Appleton and Company, 1856), 409–410.

9. FRENCH COMMITTEE REPORT ON SENEGAL (1857)

From the beginning of modern empires, armies of local soldiers fought and preserved order alongside military forces from the imperial capital. Among the most famous were the expert "tirailleurs sénégalais" or Senegalese sharpshooters. The report that follows shows plans for enlarging a handful of men into a more systematic recruitment of large numbers of forced laborers. The French faced the problem that in the 1850s they, like most European imperialist countries, were still confined to small coastal areas and islands along the shorelines. Diseases still blocked their access to the interior, so over the centuries they depended on Africans to sell them captured men. They could not do it themselves. Because slavery had been abolished across France, it was necessary to devise an acceptable solution to their recruiting problems. Analyze this common strategy of organizing captive or subject peoples into imperial armies.

Native Troops

... it is highly desirable that the Senegalese infantry should be composed of European and native troops in equal parts. Black soldiers have always given excellent service in the colony. Among others, those who belong to the Bambara race are, it may be said, as good as white soldiers, and they have the advantage over them of being immune to all the hardships of the climate. One can thus well appreciate the value which the support of such a force might have for Senegal in a host of circumstances, especially for the garrisons up-river. This is indisputably one of the most urgent needs of the locality. The remaining companies, already much reduced in strength following successive liberations of their personnel, will soon be run down completely, when the remainder have received their discharge. The Commission attaches the greatest urgency to consideration of methods of reconstructing this force.

There are two ways in which this reconstruction might be effected. Firstly, one might consider subjecting the population of Senegal to the metropolitan law of recruitment. But we must recognise that populations unaccustomed to military service would accept such obligations only with extreme repugnance. Moreover they could hardly provide an intake of more than 25 or 30 men a year, which is clearly insufficient for present needs. The alternative method of recruitment, the most hopeful and indeed the only effective one, would be that formerly employed, which consists of going up-country to enrol captives, to whom the sum needed to purchase their freedom is given as enrolment bounty. The Commission is aware that the terms of the emancipation decree now seem to put legal obstacles in the way of such an operation. It is also aware of the moral and humanitarian reasons which led to the inclusion in this act of a prohibition of long-term contracts of service—and which indeed had already caused them to be forbidden by the previous regime. These contracts, handed over to private interests as they formerly were in the Colony, had indeed degenerated into a veritable slave trade, and could no longer be tolerated. But if they are strictly confined to the needs of military recruitment and entrusted exclusively to the hands of the administration, they cannot give rise to any abuse. What after all is their effect?—that the government restores to freedom a certain number of captives who would otherwise be doomed to almost certain death, on the sole condition that they serve the government for several years. One might add that when these men return to their homelands at the end of their military service they should become excellent agents for the diffusion into the interior of Africa of the first notions of civilisation and commerce. In view of the major political interest, supported by this humanitarian interest, in not merely maintaining but increasing the strength of the black companies in Senegal, the Commission feels quite justified in asking that all steps be taken to reconcile the requirements of existing legislation with the obvious needs of our position in Senegal.

It further recommends that these troops should be completely assimilated to troops sent from Europe in regard to pay and rations, though care should be taken that they are organised in separate units. . . .

Source: John Hargreaves, ed. and trans., *France and West Africa: An Anthology of Historical Documents* (London: Macmillan, 1969), 99–101.

10. PETITIONS TO GOVERNOR OF JAMAICA
AND COLONIAL MISSIONARY SOCIETY (1849)

Once the slave trade ended, planters besieged their governments to find new sources of labor. A system of indentured labor to staff their enterprises, with agents searching out and enlisting contract workers from South Asia, China, sub-Saharan Africa, and other parts of the world. These mostly male workers signed on for terms of two or three years or more to serve on plantations in tropical colonies in the Caribbean, South America, the Pacific, and elsewhere. Conditions were almost uniformly poor, but even then the workers, because of their substantial numbers, transformed the culture wherever they worked. They imported myths, theatrical and musical traditions, and religion. They thereby continued the process of cultural mixture and hybridity in the imperial world—a hybridity that remained long after empires disappeared. Despite the development of community, many longed to go home and constantly petitioned officials for their promised return. Imperial powers used the fact that indentured workers were technically "free" to demonstrate the civilized nature of modern empires.

. . . your Excellency's Petitioners have children and other relatives each who had been carried to the West Indies in the year 1842, and 1844 as emigrants with the promise and assurance that after the expiration of five years a free passage will be granted them to Sierra Leone, now they are there for about fourteen long years, that your Excellency's Petitioners' children and other relatives are very desirous and longing to return home to Sierra Leone, but have not the means and opportunity.

Your Excellency's Petitioners have received several letters of late from their children and other relatives in the West Indies, in which they expressed that at present they are not in good circumstances, and they are full of anxiety to return home, and the promise and assurance which had been given them ere they were carried away, that a free passage will be given is neglected, therefore they call for our help that a free passage might be granted them.

. . .

We your humbled servants or scholars beg to solicit you the gents of the committee most graciously to do us this favor and oblige us to inquire the present Governor of Sierra Leone of our returning passage to Sierra Leone, before we left Sierra Leone for Trinidad the emigration agent told us that if we do come to Trinidad and serve five years, there will be a returning of free passage for us back to Sierra Leone and from since we are here it is more than five years (and more) we went an inquire the Governor of Trinidad and the agent for our returning passage back to Sierra Leone they told us there is no returning passage back for us, From the time that we was in Trinidad we suffer much by the Planters. In the first place let us tell you about the people of Trinidad. The people of Trinidad do not care for the Sabath day as they do care for some of their holy days in their holy days they will keep it very quiet but on the Sabath they will beat drum and Tambarine even before the church door especially the Roman Catholic. We your scholars write to you the gents of the committee most expressly that through our own foolishness cause us to left our native country for Trinidad, but we are very sorry to state to you that we have repented for the day that we left Sierra Leone. To you the C.M.S. we write our fillings [feelings] to, that we are in a misserable life a life that leads to distraction . . . the planters of Trinidad ruin us very much so that we cannot have no time as to attend the morning and evening prayer but constantly at work to you the gents we beg to inform you that we are in distress and in darkness and under the shadow of death.

Source: Monica Schuler, *"Alas, Alas, Kongo": A Social History of Indentured African Immigration into Jamaica, 1841–1965* (Baltimore: Johns Hopkins University Press, 1980), 90, 92–93.

11. ANONYMOUS, CIRCULAR LETTER (1857)

The British, after losing their North American colonies, placed more effort than ever in India. Whereas in South America they engaged in business imperialism, financing projects, setting up businesses, and even directing government policies in the new nations, in South Asia they undertook actually to control its many kingdoms. First, they wanted access to taxation and other finances. Additionally, they worked to drive manufacturers of the vivid and high-quality cottons out of business because the visibly inferior British cottons—manufactured in factories—were simply less appealing to consumers around the world. Finally, the British often worked to change political regimes and ordinary practices in everyday life. One of these was the prohibition against ingesting animal fats by Muslims and Hindus. By 1857, many South Asians, including rulers, rose up against Britain's many encroachments, with soldiers in the British Indian army rebelling as well. The rumor that the British were going to introduce weapons demanding the use of pork or beef fat was given as one reason for the uprising. The British interpreted that as the main cause of the dissatisfaction, intending to show South Asians as fanatics and covering up the widespread harm that empire was doing to the subcontinent, traditional politics, and people's values. The following is a joint circular letter of grievances.

All you kings who are very steadfast in faith and men of great qualities and generous and bountiful and brave and upholders of your faith and of others, wishing you well we submit that the Almighty has given you this body in order to maintain your faith, the faith of each is evident from their religion and you are steadfast on it. The Creator has produced you kings to destroy those who seek to corrupt your faith and has given you a kingdom. It is desired that whoever has the power should kill those who corrupt your faith and those who do not have the power should think in their hearts of ways to do so and save your faith because the Shastras state that it is better to die on your faith but one should not take up another faith. This is what God has said and everyone knows this. And these English are the destroyers of faith, everyone should know this because for a long time in order to corrupt the religion of the people of Hindustan they have prepared books and have distributed them through their priests all over Hindustan and used their power to propagate books which proved their religion and this has been heard from the people who are their confidants. Witness how they have come up with schemes to spoil the religion that firstly, when a woman becomes a widow they forcibly command her to remarry and secondly, there was an ancient practice of sati so they forcibly forbade it and proclaimed a law that nobody should become sati, and thirdly, they say that if you adopt our religion this will make us happy and you will be rewarded by the government. And they say you should come to the church and listen to our religious speeches. . . .

And look at their designs that they were bent upon feeding prisoners from a common kitchen, many of whom preferred to starve than to eat that food and many said that our faith has been corrupted. When they realized that this plan has not worked, they wanted to grind bones and mix it in flour and sugar and feed it to the people. They made a powder of meat and bones and mixed it in rice and supplied it to shops and they devised all sorts of schemes for us to give up our faith. Then some Bengali thought of this suggestion that if your army accepts these things then the rest too will follow suit. The English really liked this sugges-tion and said this is a wonderful scheme, they will themselves come round. Then they told the Brahmans, etc., in their army that these bullets are laced with fat, bite them with your mouths. Seeing the loss of faith of the Pandits, the Muslim soldiers also refused to bite the bullet. The English then became bent on corrupting both their faiths and they blew from a cannon the men of any platoon who refused to bite the bullets. When the soldiers observed this tyranny, in order to save their own lives, they began to kill them and wherever they were found they were killed. There are only a few left now and they are making to dispose of them too. We all know now that if these English stay in Hindustan they will kill everyone and spoil the faith but some of our fellow believers side with them and fight for them and give them support and we say to them that know that they will not leave you or your faith either. In this scenario we ask you what you are doing to defend your faith and your lives. If your mind is the same as ours then with a little effort we can slay them all and preserve our faith and our country.

And this has been published in order to save the religion and faith and the lives of all you Hindus and Muslims. Hindus must take oath on *Ganga Tulsi Saligram* and Muslims must swear on God and the Quran and we say that the English are enemies of both, that it would be wise for the Hindus and Muslims to kill them because that way they would be able to protect their faith and religion. Hindus regard cow slaughter as a great evil and in order to prevent that all the leaders of the Muslims in the country of Hind have made a compact that the day the Hindus show eagerness to kill the English the practice of cow slaughter will be ended and if it doesn't then it will be tantamount to reneging on the Quran and eating it will be akin to eating a pig. . . . The wise ones will never accept this fraud because the promises made by the English are self-serving and meant to deceive; once they get what they want they will renege from the contract and it is evident to the high and the low. Therefore do not pay heed to what they say, you will never get another chance like this. . . .

This letter has been written unanimously by Hindus and Muslims and has been published at the Bahaduri Press, Bareilly thanks to the efforts of Maulvi Syed Qutub Shah Saheb.

Source: Mahmood Farooqui, *Besieged: Voices from Delhi 1857* (New Delhi: Viking, 2010), 23–25.

12. VICTOR HUGO, LETTER ON THE SACKING OF THE SUMMER PALACE (1861)

Treasure entered imperial countries in the nineteenth as it had in the fifteenth and sixteenth centuries. Those from the Chinese fleet of the fifteenth century and from Spanish ships in the sixteenth amazed anyone lucky enough to witness the wonders that empires brought from distant lands. By the mid-nineteenth century, critics of empire were starting to make a fuss about imperialists' destruction of magnificent works of human creativity across the globe. One of these critics was famed author Victor Hugo, author of Les Miserables. *In 1860, through a series of missteps British and French troops began looting the Chinese "Summer Palace"—an architectural marvel containing irreplaceable works of art. As the Chinese retaliated against the British and French, British representative in China Lord Elgin ordered the complete destruction of this architectural treasure. The looted contents were put on display in London and Paris, drawing in tens of thousands of spectators. Prideful imperial citizens could either marvel at the works of other cultures or at the superiority of their own nations in now possessing them. Author Victor Hugo had much to say about the event that brought such treasures to his capital.*

To Captain Butler
Hauteville House,
25 November, 1861

You ask my opinion, Sir, about the China expedition. You consider this expedition to be honourable and glorious, and you have the kindness to attach some consideration to my feelings; according to you, the China expedition, carried out jointly under the flags of Queen Victoria and the Emperor Napoleon, is a glory to be shared between France and England, and you wish to know how much approval I feel I can give to this English and French victory.

Since you wish to know my opinion, here it is:

There was, in a corner of the world, a wonder of the world; this wonder was called the Summer Palace. Art has two principles, the Idea, which produces European art, and the Chimera, which produces oriental art. The Summer Palace was to chimerical art what the Parthenon is to ideal art. All that can begotten of the imagination of an almost extra-human people was there. It was not a single, unique work like the Parthenon. It was a kind of enormous model of the chimera, if the chimera can have a model. Imagine some inexpressible construction, something like a lunar building, and you will have the Summer Palace. Build a dream with marble, jade, bronze, and porcelain, frame it with cedar wood, cover it with precious stones, drape it with silk, make it here a sanctuary, there a harem, elsewhere a citadel, put gods there, and monsters, varnish it, enamel it, gild it, paint it, have architects who are poets build the thousand and one dreams of the thousand and one nights, add gardens, basins, gushing water and foam, swans, ibis, peacocks, suppose in a word a sort of dazzling cavern of human fantasy with the face of a temple and palace, such was this building. The slow work of generations had been necessary to create it. This edifice, as enormous as a city, had been built by the centuries, for whom? For the peoples. For the work of time belongs to man. Artists, poets and philosophers knew the Summer Palace; Voltaire talks of it. People spoke of the Parthenon in Greece, the pyramids in Egypt, the Coliseum in Rome, Notre-Dame in Paris, the Summer Palace in the Orient. If people did not see it they imagined it. It was a kind of tremendous unknown masterpiece, glimpsed from the distance in a kind of twilight, like a silhouette of the civilization of Asia on the horizon of the civilization of Europe.

This wonder has disappeared.

One day two bandits entered the Summer Palace. One plundered, the other burned. Victory can be a thieving woman, or so it seems. The devastation of the Summer Palace was accomplished by the two victors acting jointly. Mixed up in all this is the name of Elgin, which inevitably calls to mind the Parthenon. What was done to the Parthenon was done to the Summer Palace, more thoroughly and better, so that nothing of it should be left. All the treasures of all our cathedrals put together could not equal this formidable and splendid museum of the Orient. It contained not only masterpieces of art, but masses of jewelry. What a great exploit, what a windfall! One of the two victors filled his pockets; when the other saw this he filled his coffers. And back they came to Europe, arm in arm, laughing away. Such is the story of the two bandits.

We Europeans are the civilized ones, and for us the Chinese are the barbarians. This is what civilization has done to barbarism.

Before history, one of the two bandits will be called France; the other will be called England. But I protest, and I thank you for giving me the opportunity! the crimes of those who lead are not the fault of those who are led; Governments are sometimes bandits, peoples never.

The French empire has pocketed half of this victory, and today with a kind of proprietorial naivety it displays the splendid bric-a-brac of the Summer Palace. I hope that a day will come when France, delivered and cleansed, will return this booty to despoiled China.

Meanwhile, there is a theft and two thieves.

I take note.

This, Sir, is how much approval I give to the China expedition.

Source: Foundation Napoleon http://www.napoleon.org/en/reading_room/articles/files/477511.asp# informations (accessed November 19, 2015).

REVIEW QUESTIONS

1. What moral arguments do officials use in their negotiations, government documents, and speeches?
2. Describe the varying economic concerns in the first decades of the nineteenth century; how do they differ from one another?
3. What arguments can be made from the documents for seeing empire as lawless and chaotic? What arguments do the documents present for empire being civilizing and orderly?
4. Between 1833 and 1834, famed artist Hiroshige depicted travelers along the Tokaido road that ran from Edo (present-day Tokyo) to other parts of the Japanese realm. See http://www.hiroshige.org.uk/hiroshige/tokaido/tokaido. htm. Click on any of the editions of "The Fifty-Three Stations of the Tokaido Road". What aspects of his woodcuts indicate that Japanese industrialization and imperial expansion might be close at hand?

CHAPTER 7

The Big Push: Imperialism at the End of the Nineteenth Century

During the last third of the nineteenth century, many of the existing imperial powers made dramatic advances in Africa, Asia, the North American continent, and the Pacific. Continuing industrial transformation, the discovery of new mineral resources, and increasing medical know-how spurred these advances. Japan and Germany joined the established imperial powers in seeking new conquests, while the United States started building its overseas empire in Hawaii, the Caribbean, Central America, and Southeast Asia. Germany and Japan modernized their governments as they entered the imperial fray. Warfare erupted but with a greater number of combatants than before.

So intense was imperial expansion in these years that the contests among competitor nations seemed to call for international agreements. In 1884–1885 Otto von Bismarck summoned a congress of the major powers to meet in Berlin to adjudicate conflicting claims in the interior of Africa, where imperial rivalry was most intense. The big push of the European powers that prompted the Berlin Conference was called "the scramble for Africa," enabled by the development of quinine that protected invaders from malaria and by the famine and weather conditions that debilitated the African (and other) populations. From all sides imperialists advanced through the continent's interior, made deals with local rulers, and fought them when thwarted. Resistance was formidable, with chiefs, heads of kingdoms, and large-scale traders dealing defeats to the Europeans, though most often coming to terms. Ever-more powerful European weaponry—especially the machine gun—gave them an advantage as did the modern steamboats that carried people and supplies into the interior.

As before, agents of imperialism had an overwhelming lust for diamonds and gold, whose sudden appearance in the south of Africa led to a vast influx of fortune seekers and increasing tensions in the region. Other entrepreneurs sought palm oil and cocoa from West Africa, set up coconut and coffee plantations in East Africa, started rubber plantations in Southeast Asia, and searched out minerals and metals in Siberia and elsewhere to supply industrial ventures in such new inventions as the bicycle, sewing machine, and automobile. Globalization allowed that where needed raw materials were missing, entrepreneurs could set up plantations in regions of the world far from their natural habitat.

Across the globe, local people facilitated these enterprises and imperial expansion, especially by participating in keeping order, collecting taxes, building roads and harbors, organizing gangs of laborers, and serving in colonial bureaucracies, albeit with far less power than their rulers. Down through the nineteenth and twentieth centuries, people from the imperial powers migrated in the millions to fill the higher ranks of bureaucracy, teach school, and serve as missionaries, and more often simply to find work or land or escape from religious persecution. The world's population was in motion as part of an increasingly modern globalization sparked by industrialization. This boosted exploitation around the world: Laborers on plantations were overworked; small landowners and artisans from India to Europe lost their livelihoods; more women turned to casual or full-time prostitution to make ends meet. One-third of all Europeans left their homes to find work abroad, while millions in the colonies signed on to indentured labor in distant lands.

There were massive political changes too. Japan undertook a modern state-building effort when its people overthrew the old ruling powers and instituted the Meiji Restoration in 1868. In part the leadership undertook modernization of government and the economy to prevent Japan from falling prey to foreign powers as had just happened to the Chinese in the series of Opium Wars that had begun in 1839. Looking at the world powers, they saw that the drive to have colonies had been part of financing European state-building. In 1894–1895 Japan defeated China and gained the island of Taiwan plus a massive monetary indemnity. In 1910, it took Korea, cementing its imperial credentials and again creating financial and business opportunities for its own citizens.

Germany also seized colonies, despite Bismarck's lack of interest in them, except as a way of buying off industrialists, who felt their own lack of influence and resented the conservative, aristocratically controlled government. Enclaves in East and West Africa and in the Pacific fell tentatively to the Germans—tentatively, because already established African elites and rulers often resisted their incursions. When Kaiser William II came to power in 1888 he made demands for additional possessions in North Africa. Meanwhile, in the beginning of the twentieth century the German military began drawing up plans for expanding across central and even eastern Europe should war among the European imperial powers provide the opportunity. Like the United States, it was adding—or dreaming of adding—both continental and oceanic resources to its empire.

Following the Civil War (1861–1865), the United States continued its conquest of Native American territory, killing innocents as well as resisters and herding these unwanted people into ever narrower reservations. The United States justified defeating Spain for control of the Caribbean islands important to the east-west passage from Atlantic to Pacific by citing its backwards, tyrannical rule that rode roughshod over the desires of local people for independence. Then the

United States, instead of giving those in Cuba, Puerto Rico, and the Philippines their freedom, used them to add to its Hawaiian conquest and expand its own overseas empire.

Although earlier colonizers had justified their theft of local people's land by pointing to their own Christianity, and although they also pointed to the savagery of those they wantonly mowed down with their new machine or "repeater" guns, the imperialists now explained that they were more advanced in science and technology. Railroad systems spread across India and stretches of Africa, speeding the extraction of wealth from local people and bringing the chaos of famine and poverty as an ingredient of their rule. Massive dams and even two spectacular canals—the Suez and the Panama—dramatically cut transoceanic travel time and costs. Moreover, U.S. army physicians made significant inroads in preventing loss of life due to malaria and yellow fever around Panama construction sites. Machinery, engineering, and hygienic measures, many claimed, proved the civilizational superiority of the imperial powers. Thus imperial propagandists promoted the belief that superior races undertook the difficult work of empire to foster their "civilizing mission." The United States advertised its superiority as it seized Cuba, Hawaii, Puerto Rico, and the Philippines from their former rulers. Piggy-backing on the independence movements that had brought about revolt in the first place, the United States then destroyed those movements, executing leaders and followers alike. The Russian tsar's officials made great attempts to Christianize and Russify their millions of Muslim subjects. As with the United States and other imperial powers, the idea was to eliminate these new subjects' culture, beliefs, and allegiances so that they could become more docile citizens, supposedly like the native-born. Histories came to enshrine the myth of imperial rule of law and colonized people's lawlessness.

Simultaneously the rush of global migration continued to staff these undertakings. Diasporas of Chinese merchants and indentured workers from Africa and Asia circled the globe, building strong familial networks back to their home country as they staffed ships and moved products. Workers from the Caribbean islands thronged to get jobs building the Panama Canal, despite the hardships and constant threat of death from dangerous machinery, avalanches of mud, and, for most of the time, unchecked diseases. In making such a voyage they followed the earlier examples of workers on the Suez Canal, who came not just from Egypt but from around the Mediterranean basin, often working with other male relatives. As before, much migration was less than voluntary: Imperialists imposed taxes that needed to be paid in cash as a way of forcing people into mines, domestic service, and plantation work. Those people also had to leave their homes for distant work sites. Under far less compulsion, adventurers such as Danish-born Christian Lautherborn moved from place to place to "make something" of themselves, as he put it. The vast spaces of North and South America were seen as especially "open" to new settlers, but so suddenly was Africa, thanks to quinine and the deadly effects of famine.

1. ANTHONY TROLLOPE, "THE DIAMOND FIELDS OF SOUTH AFRICA" (1877)

The discovery of diamond mines in South Africa caused a massive migration to the region, some of it voluntary but a lot of it forced by the British policy of imposing on Africans a range of taxes that had to be paid in actual money. Anthony Trollope (1815–1882) was a world traveler to Eygpt, Australia, the United States, and Ceylon, among other places, with South Africa being one of his destinations. Some of his voyages were as part of his work for his employer—the British postal system. He surveyed its routes across Britain and investigated its functioning in parts of the empire and in areas where there was substantial British interest. He wrote many important reports, while also writing celebrated novels and making improvements in postal service. For example, he devised the "pillar box"—that is the red mail boxes still in use in Britain, all the while being a keen observer of people and societies, possibly for use as material for his works of fiction. The following document reports on the mines, where African laborers worked far from their families and communities and where they inventively set up new relationships to substitute at least temporarily for old ones. Describe Trollope's attitudes toward those living under imperial rule.

The first known finding of a diamond in South Africa was as recent as 1867, and this diamond was found by accident and could not for a time obtain any credence. It is first known to have been seen at the house of a Dutch farmer named Jacobs, in the northern limits of the Cape Colony, and south of the Orange River. It had probably been brought from the bed of the stream or from the other side of the river. . . . At Jacobs's house it was seen in the hands of one of the children by another Boer named Van Niekerk, who observing that it was brighter and also heavier than other stones, and thinking it to be too valuable for a plaything, offered to buy it. But the child's mother would not sell such a trifle and gave it to Van Niekerk. From Van Niekerk it was passed on to one O'Reilly, who seems to have been the first to imagine it to be a diamond. . . . But it became a matter of discussion, and was at last sent to Dr. Atherstone, of Grahamstown, who was known to be a geologist and a man of science. He surprised the world of South Africa by declaring the stone to be an undoubted diamond. It weighed over 21 carats and was sold to Sir P. Wodehouse, the then Governor of the Colony, for £ 500.

In 1868 and 1869 various diamonds were found, and the search for them was no doubt instigated by Van Niekerk's and O'Reilly's success; but nothing great was done nor did the belief prevail that South Africa was a country richer in precious stones than any other region yet discovered. Those which were brought to light during these two years may I believe yet be numbered, and no general belief had been created. But some searching by individuals was continued. . . . Even then the question whether this part of South Africa was diamondiferous had not been settled to the satisfaction of persons who concern themselves in the produce and distribution of diamonds. . . . It was too good to believe,—or to some perhaps too bad,—that there should suddenly come a plethora of diamonds from among the Hottentots.

It was in 1870 that the question seems to have got itself so settled that some portion of the speculative energy of the world was enabled to fix itself on the new Diamond Fields. In that year various white men set themselves seriously to work. . . . The operations of those times are now called the "river diggings" in distinction to the "dry diggings," which are works of much greater magnitude, carried on in a much more scientific manner away from the river. . . .

The commencement of diamond-digging as a settled industry was in 1872. . . . The English came,—at the end of 1871,—just as the system of dry-digging had formed itself. . . . In September 1872, the territory of Griqualand West became a British Colony, and at that time miners from the whole district were congregating themselves at the hill, and that which was at once called the "New Rush" was established. In Australia where gold was found here or there the miners would hurry off to the spot and the place would be called this or that "Rush."

The New Rush . . . and the Kimberley mine are one and the same place. It is now within the town of Kimberley,—which has in fact got itself built around the hill to supply the wants of the mining population. Kimberley has in this way become the capital and seat of Government for the Province. As the mine is one of the most remarkable spots on the face of the earth, I will endeavor to explain it with some minuteness.

At Du Toit's Pan and Bultfontein the works are scattered. Here everything is so gathered together and collected that it is not at first easy to understand that the hole should contain the operations of a large number of separate speculators. It is so completely one that you are driven at first to think that it must be the property of one firm,—or at any rate be entrusted to the management of one director. It is very far from being so. In the pit beneath your feet, hard as it is at first to your imagination to separate it into various enterprises, the persons making or marring their fortunes have as little connection with each other as have the different banking firms in Lombard Street. There, too, the neighborhood is very close, and common precautions have to be taken as to roadway, fires, and general convenience.

. . . You are told that the pit has a surface area of nine acres; but for your purposes, as you will care little for diamondiferous or non-diamondiferous soil, the aperture really occupies twelve acres. The slope of the reef around the diamond soil has forced itself back over an increased surface as the mine has become deeper. The diamond claims cover nine acres. You stand upon the marge and there, suddenly, beneath your feet lies the entirety of the Kimberley mine, so open, so manifest, and so uncovered that if your eyes were good enough you might examine the separate Operations of each of the three or four thousand human beings who are at work there.

As you stand at the edge you will find large, high-raised boxes at your right hand and at your left, and you will see all round the margin crowds of such erections, each box being as big as a little house and higher than most of the houses in Kimberley. These are the first recipients for the stuff that is brought up out of the mine. And behind these, so that you will often find that you have walked between them, are the whims by means of which the stuff is raised, each whim being worked by two horses. Originally the operation was done by hand—windlasses which were turned by Kafirs [originally an Arab term for those not believing in Islam that became a derogatory name for Africans], and the practice is continued at some of the smaller enterprises;—but the horse whims are now so general that there is a world of them round the claim. The stuff is raised on aerial tramways,—and the method of an aerial tramway is as follows. Wires are stretched taut from the wooden boxes slanting down to the claims at the bottom, —never less than four wires for each box, two for the ascending and two for the descending bucket. As one bucket runs down empty on one set of wires, another comes up full on the other set. The ascending bucket is, of course, full of "blue. . . ."

When the world below is busy there are about 3500 Kafirs at work,—some small proportion upon the reef which has to be got into order so that it shall neither tumble in nor impede the work, nor overlay the diamondiferous soil as it still does in some places; but by far the greater number are employed in digging. Their task is to pick up the earth and shovel it into the buckets and iron receptacles. Much of it is loosened for them by blasting, which is done after the Kafirs have left the mine at 6 o'clock. You look down and see the swarm of black ants busy at every hole and corner with their picks moving and shoveling the loose blue soil. . . .

It need hardly be said that in such an operation as I have described the greatest care is necessary to prevent stealing, and that no care will prevent it. The Kafirs are the great thieves,—to such an extent of superexcellence that white superintendence is spoken of as being the only safeguard. The honesty of the white man may perhaps be indifferent, but such as it is it has to be used at every point to prevent, as far as it may be prevented, the systematized stealing in which the Kafirs take an individual and national pride. The Kafirs are not only most willing but most astute thieves, feeling a glory in their theft, and thinking that every stone stolen from a white man is a duty done to their chief and their tribe. I think it may be taken as certain that no Kafir would feel the slightest pang of conscience at stealing a diamond, or that any disgrace would be held to attach to him among other Kafirs for such a performance. They come to the Fields instructed by their chiefs to steal diamonds, and they obey the orders like loyal subjects. Many of the Kafir chiefs are said to have large quantities of diamonds, which have been brought to them by their men returning from the diggings;—but most of those which are stolen no doubt find their way into the hands of illicit dealers. I have been told that the thefts perpetrated by the Kafirs amount to twenty-five per cent on the total amount found;—but this I do not believe.

The opportunities for stealing are of hourly occurrence and are of such a nature as to make prevention impossible. These men are sharp-sighted as birds, and know and see a diamond much quicker than a white man. They will pick up stones with their toes and secrete them even under the eyes of those who are watching them. I was told that a man will so hide a diamond in his mouth that no examination will force him to disclose it. They are punished when discovered with lashes and imprisonment,—in accordance with the law on the matter. No employer is now allowed to flog his man at his own pleasure. And the white men who buy diamonds from Kafirs are also punished, when convicted, by fine and imprisonment for the simple offense of buying from a Kafir, but with flogging also if convicted of having instigated a Kafir to steal. Nevertheless, a lucrative business of this nature is carried on, and the Kafirs know well where to dispose of their plunder, though of course but for a small proportion of its value.

Ten shillings a week and their food were the regular wages here as well as elsewhere. This I found to be very fluctuating, but the money paid had rarely gone lower for any considerable number of men than the above-named rate. The lowest amount paid has been 7s. 6d. a week. Sometimes it had been as high as 20s. and even 30s. a week. A good deal of the work is supplied by contract, certain middle-men undertaking to provide men with all expenses paid at £1 a week. . . .

Perhaps the most interesting sight at the mine is the escaping of the men from their labor at six o'clock. Then, at the sound of some welcome gong, they begin to swarm up the sides close at each other's heels, apparently altogether indifferent as to whether there be a path or no. They come as flies come up a wall, only capering as flies never caper,—-and shouting as they come. In endless strings, as ants follow each other, they move, passing along ways which seem to offer no hold to a human foot. Then it is that one can best observe their costume, in which a pair of trousers rarely forms a portion. A soldier's red jacket or a soldier's blue jacket has more charms than any other vestment. They seem always to be good-humored, always well-behaved,—but then they are always thieves. And yet how grand a thing it is that so large a number of these men should have been brought in so short a space of time to the habit of receiving wages and to the capacity of bargaining as to the wages for which they will work. I shall not, however, think it so grand a thing if any one addresses them as the free and independent electors of Kimberley before they have got trousers to cover their nakedness.

I must add also that a visitor to Kimberley should if possible take an opportunity of looking down upon the mine by moonlight. It is a weird and wonderful sight, and may almost be called sublime in its peculiar strangeness.

Source: Eva March Tappan, ed., *The World's Story: A History of the World in Story, Song and Art* (Boston: Houghton Mifflin, 1914), Vol. III: *Egypt, Africa, and Arabia*, 437–457. Also on the Internet: Modern History Sourcebook, https://legacy.fordham.edu/halsall/mod/1870trollope-southafrica.asp (accessed November 19, 2015).

2. GENERAL ACT OF THE BERLIN WEST AFRICA CONGRESS (1885)

Business people and governments rushed to control African riches through colonization once the profits from slave trading had ended and disease was less of a threat. The conference at Berlin in 1884–1885, called by German Chancellor Otto von Bismarck to help calm the competition for control of rivers and territory, led to a series of agreements. These limited the use of firearms and provided that a nation had to control the coastline of a region in order to claim its interior, among other provisions. The Congress of Berlin only hastened an onslaught of new imperial ventures across the continent in order to gain the minerally and agriculturally rich African interior, not to mention the skills of its inhabitants. Still, some might call it a move toward world governance that seemed to arise from imperial competition. By this time the policy of unencumbered or "free" trade had gained many adherents. Tightly regulated and taxed trade from the early modern period in hopes of impoverishing rivals was periodically revived in practice however. On what grounds would you characterize the Congress of Berlin as an act of world governance? On what grounds would you characterize it as world disorder?

General Act of the Conference at Berlin of the Plenipotentiaries of Great Britain, Austria-Hungary, Belgium, Denmark, France, Germany, Italy, The Netherlands, Portugal, Russia, Spain, Sweden and Norway, Turkey and The United States. . . .

WISHING, in a spirit of good and mutual accord, to regulate the conditions most favourable to the development of trade and civilization in certain regions of Africa, and to assure to all nations the advantages of free navigation on the two chief rivers of Africa flowing into the Atlantic Ocean; BEING DESIROUS, on the other hand, to obviate the misunderstanding and disputes which might in future arise from new acts of occupation . . . on the coast of Africa; and concerned, at the same time, as to the means of furthering the moral and material well-being of the native populations; HAVE RESOLVED. . . .

Chapter I
Article 1

The trade of all nations shall enjoy complete freedom—

Article 5

No Power which exercises or shall exercise sovereign rights in the above mentioned regions shall be allowed to grant therein a monopoly or favor of any kind in matters of trade.

Foreigners, without distinction, shall enjoy protection of their persons and property, as well as the right of acquiring and transferring movable and immovable possessions; and national rights and treatment in the exercise of their professions.

Article 6

All the Powers exercising sovereign rights or influence in the aforesaid territories bind themselves to watch over the preservation of the native tribes, and to care for the improvement of the conditions of their moral and material well-being, and to help in suppressing slavery, and especially the slave trade. They shall, without distinction of creed or nation, protect and favour all religious, scientific or charitable institutions and undertakings created and organized for the above ends, or which aim at instructing the natives and bringing home to them the blessings of civilization.

Christian missionaries, scientists and explorers, with their followers, property and collections, shall likewise be the objects of especial protection.

Freedom of conscience and religious toleration are expressly guaranteed to the natives, no less than to subjects and to foreigners. The free and public exercise of all forms of divine worship, and the right to build edifices for religious purposes, and to organize religious missions belonging to all creeds, shall not be limited or fettered in any way whatsoever.

Article 9

Seeing that trading in slaves is forbidden in conformity with the principles of international law as recognized by the Signatory Powers, and seeing also that the operations, which, by sea or land, furnish slaves to trade, ought likewise to be regarded as forbidden, the Powers which do or shall exercise sovereign rights or influence in the territories forming the Conventional basin of the Congo declare that these territories may not serve as a market or means of transit for the trade in slaves, of whatever race they may be. Each of the Powers binds itself to employ all the means at its disposal for putting an end to this trade and for punishing those who engage in it.

Article 10

In order to give a new guarantee of security to trade and industry, and to encourage, by the maintenance of peace, the development of civilization in the countries mentioned in Article 1, and placed under the free trade system, the High Signatory Parties to the present Act, and those who shall hereafter adopt it, bind themselves to respect the neutrality of the territories, or portions of territories, belonging to the said countries . . .

Article 12

In case a serious disagreement originating on the subject of, or in the limits of, the territories mentioned in Article 1, and placed under the free trade system, shall arise between any Signatory Powers of the present Act, or the Powers which may become parties to it, these Powers bind themselves, before appealing to arms, to have recourse to the mediation of one or more of the friendly Powers.

In a similar case the same Powers reserve to themselves the option of having recourse to arbitration.

Article 13

The navigation of the Congo, without excepting any of its branches or outlets, is, and shall remain, free for the merchant ships of all nations equally, whether carrying cargo or ballast, for the transport of goods or passengers. It shall be regulated by the provisions of this Act of Navigation, and by the rules to be made in pursuance thereof.

In the exercise of this navigation the subjects and flags of all nations shall in all respects be treated on a footing of perfect equality, not only for the direct navigation from the open sea to the inland ports of the Congo, and vice versa, but also for the great and small coasting trade, and for boat traffic on the course of the river.

These provisions are recognized by the Signatory Powers as becoming henceforth a part of international law.

Article 34

Any Power which henceforth takes possession of a tract of land on the coasts of the African continent outside of its present possessions, or which, being hitherto without such possessions, shall acquire them, as well as the Power which assumes a Protectorate there, shall accompany the respective act with a notification thereof, addressed to the other Signatory Powers of the present Act, in order to enable them, if need be, to make good any claims of their own.

Article 35

The Signatory Powers of the present Act recognize the obligation to insure the establishment of authority in the regions occupied by them on the coasts of the African continent sufficient to protect existing rights, and, as the case may be, freedom of trade and of transit under the conditions agreed upon.

Source: Widely available on the Internet, e.g., http://africanhistory.about.com/od/eracolonialism/l/bl-BerlinAct1885.htm.

3. HAMAD BIN MUHAMMAD BIN JUMAH BIN RAJAB BIN MUHAMMAD BIN SA'ĪD AL-MURGHABĪ (TIPPU TIP), *AUTOBIOGRAPHY* (1907)

Tippu Tip (1837–1905)—his common name in the West and in Africa—was a trader in slaves, ivory, and other commodities in eastern and central Africa. Of Swahili-Arab extraction, he forged his own empire in the eastern Congo, even as he served as a governor of an eastern district of Belgium's holdings. He was also an agent for the sultan of Zanzibar in East Africa, with all of these pursuits bringing him a great fortune and showing the intertwined nature of empire. Tippu Tip was a player but also a broker in the complicated imperial world, aiding Europeans such as David Livingstone in their illnesses and misfortunes but also fighting those who might contest his power. He used his wealth to establish vast clove plantations, profiting from these, his interactions with Europeans, and his network of trading stations. In this part of his narrative, translated from Tippu Tip's account of his life and put into the form of a biography, he follows a long train of ivory purchases at low prices with his ascent to a sultanship over a wide region. What are Tippu Tip's goals and values and how does he fit into the carving up of Africa?

The caravan got under way with its new booty, and after four days' march reached a town called Msange, on the borders of Utetera. The name Msange signifies, in the author's opinion, a settlement of men belonging to various tribes who had joined together here on the frontier to keep off common enemies. It was thus not a wholly Watetera town, though these seemed to form the majority.

After the travellers had made themselves at home on the camping-ground assigned to them, a relative of the Sultan, named Ribwe, visited them, who struck Tippoo Tib by his exceptionally large build. To him Tippoo Tib again dished up his well-prepared tissue of lies as to his relationship with the Sultan, and recounted in a touching way how year by year, not shrinking from war or privations, he had journeyed in order to see the relatives of his much-loved mother.

Ribwe, whom the vast knowledge of the stranger must have fully convinced, was so touched by this proof of his kinsman's affection that he at once sent his new cousin 300 goats and 20 elephants' tusks, and informed the Sultan, who lived four marches away, of the joyful discovery. Kassongo, equally convinced, at once sent envoys to fetch Tippoo Tib. He did not require much pressing, and hastened to the capital, which was of moderate size, and inhabited only by Kassongo and his wives; it was, however, completely surrounded by larger towns. Kassongo himself, the holder of an important tract between Lomami and Sankurru, was an old man of eccentric habits. The only beings that he regarded as his social equals were the sun and the elephant. He considered both these as Sultans like himself. He demonstrated his respect for the sun by never looking at the sunrise or the sunset, for he considered it improper to watch the toilet of his royal brother. His regard for his brothers the elephants he displayed by never eating their flesh or touching their tusks.

If one may believe Tippoo Tib, Kassongo voluntarily resigned the sovereignty over the whole country in his favour the very morning after his arrival. Extraordinary as this may seem, yet it appears to have been the truth that our traveller with his clumsy artifice found credence, and at once became ruler of the country. To the simple Shensis, who till then had scarcely come into contact with civilized tribes, it must have seemed inexplicable how a stranger come from afar should on his first entry into the country be acquainted with the whole genealogy of the Sultan's family. Moreover, it stood Tippoo Tib in very good stead that he had had the opportunity at Mkahuja of making prisoners of several hundreds of Watetera. These he brought back to his adopted grandfather as a present, and was thus enabled to show his family feelings in a most disinterested fashion, and so destroy any possible doubt of the genuineness of his blood-relationship. So he became Sultan of Utetera, in full legal sovereignty. He exercised justice and exacted heavy penalties from all who committed offences. He also appointed subordinate rulers, who had to pay him heavy tributes. Kassongo's conscientious attitude towards the elephants turned particularly to his advantage. As the succession in the office of ruler did not bind him to share the scruples of his kinsman, he could take all the ivory for himself, and if he does not exaggerate, within a fortnight he had acquired 200 tusks, of a weight of 374^ frasilas.

In other respects, too, he did not, in his activity as Sultan, forget his business as a merchant. He sent out his uncle Bxishir bin Habib to trade in Ukusu, a district lying to the west. As usual, this commercial journey degenerated into a plundering expedition, and Bushir, together with ten Zanzibaris and fifty Wanyamwezi, paid for the attempt with their lives. They were one and all devoured by the cannibal natives. This again was the signal for a great campaign, conducted by Tippoo Tib himself. Even old Kassongo would not be held back from taking part in the expedition. In spite of all representations to the contrary, he insisted on not parting from his long-lost great-nephew; after having lost his two sisters he would not survive their grand-son. If Tippoo Tib was doomed to die now, he would at least share his fate.

The advance was made with a large force. Tippoo Tib declares they had in a few days got together 100,000 men. . . . Killing and burning, as usual, they marched from place to place, and the cruelties elsewhere practiced were enhanced by all the male prisoners being devoured, at which the victors developed a hearty appetite, two of them eating up a whole man. Tippoo Tib endeavoured to put a stop to these doings—less out of love for his neighbor than because the sickening smell of the slaughtered human flesh upset him. The Manjema, however, paid little heed to his representations. "If," they replied, "we are not to eat men's flesh, do you refrain from goat's flesh." In face of this reasonable argument things remained as they were. After two months the claims of justice were satisfied, the natives who were left paid an indemnity of sixty tusks as a mark of submission, and the victori-ous army withdrew.

Tippoo Tib's absence from Utetera had been utilized by Mkahuja to avenge himself for the defeat inflicted on him. He had raided a village on the frontier, plundering in the usual manner. Thus our hero on returning from one campaign had at once to undertake another. Old Kassongo again accompanied him. This time it was more serious, for the enemy was strong, yet he was overcome within forty days. A large territory was subjugated and much booty in ivory and goats secured.

The supply of ivory now came in very copiously, for the conquered districts had to surrender all the tusks they had. Pange showed himself a very trusty sub-ject, who paid his tribute regularly.

So Tippoo Tib spent several years occupied with the duties of a ruler in his own territory and with expeditions, partly peaceful, partly warlike, into the coun-try round.

Source: Heinrich Brode, *Tippoo Tib: The Story of His Career in Central Africa Narrated from His Own Accounts*, H. Havelock, trans. (London: Edward Arnold, 1907), 89–93.

4. MOKSHODAYANI MUKHOPADHYAY, "THE BENGALI BABU" (1882)

There were many ways to counter imperial rule beyond direct confrontation and resistance. In the verse that follows, the daring woman poet, Mokshodayani Mukho-padhyay, mocks the self-importance of the local Indian colonial official who served British interests. She also responds to the general call for the improvement of women at a time when local people (the "babu") were doing the pivotal work of enforcing imperial rule, thus cutting costs by paying them far less than they would a British officer. Identifying with the imperial ruler, local officials could thus be said to betray their own people because many came to appreciate aspects of imperial culture— including the constant harping about customs pertaining to women—and even to prefer them. The author criticizes the steady contempt and condescension imperialists and those local people who served empire showed the population at large. Both the poem and the behavior of the local Indian officials sparked outrage, although for different reasons. Explain the critique of the Indian who works for the English.

Who's that rushing through his breakfast and bath?
The Bengali babu! He's terribly pressed:
The sahib will scold him, should he be late
So he's got to get ready, and bustles about.
There he comes, decked in trousers and jacket!
On his head a pith helmet, tied round with a scarf,

Alas, there goes our Bengali babu!
He slaves away from ten till four,
Carrying his servitude like a pedlar's wares.
A lawyer or magistrate, or perhaps a schoolmaster,
A subjudge, clerk, or overseer:
The bigger the job, the greater his pride;
The baby thinks he's walking on air.
Red in the face from the day's hard labor,
He downs pegs of whiskey to relax when he's home.
He's transported with pride at the thought of his rank—
But faced with a sahib, he trembles in fear!
Then he's obsequious, he mouths English phrases,
His own tongue disgusts him, he heaps it with curses.
The babu's learned English, he swells with conceit
And goes off in haste to deliver a speech.
He flounders while speaking, and stumbles and stutters,
But he's speaking in *English:* you must come and hear.

Alas, there goes our Bengali babu!
The lackey's livery is shed when he's home.
Bare-chested in slippers, he's a sight to be seen;
The baby speaks a patter of Bengali and English
But he berates the English with all his heart.
These sports are but nocturnal; wiping his mouth, in the morning
The babu is respectful and sober again.

Source: Susie Tharu and K. Lalita, eds., *Women Writing in India, 600 BS to the Early Twentieth Century* (London: HarperCollins, 1991), 219–221.

5. JULES FERRY, DEBATE IN THE
CHAMBER OF DEPUTIES (1884)

Among citizens in expanding imperial nations there was hot debate about the value of the conquest and the high cost of empire by the 1880s. Some objected to the oppression and violence involved; others saw no value in ruling areas so far from the mainland when mass politics at home were becoming so complicated. Jules Ferry (1832–1893), twice French prime minister and the politician who gave France free, compulsory education, was a strong advocate of expansion. France itself had some of the most accomplished surveyors of the world, not to mention a history of relationships around the globe, including North America, Asia, Africa, and the Pacific. The debate was never one-sided, as many objected to facing the constant resistance from the colonized and competitors. Ferry saw advantages to colonies from many perspectives, as shown in this speech to the French legislature in 1884. The French followed his lead. What were Ferry's arguments?

I will say that the policy of colonial expansion is a political and economic system . . . that one can connect to three sets of ideas: economic ideas; the most far-reaching ideas of civilization; and ideas of a political and patriotic sort.

In the economic realm, I lay before you considerations, supported by statistics, that justify the policy of colonial expansion, as seen from the perspective of a need, felt more and more urgently by the industrialized population of Europe and especially the people of our rich and hardworking country of France: the need for outlets [for exports]. Is this a fantasy? Is this a concern [that can wait] for the future? Or is this not a pressing need, one may say a crying need, of our industrial population? I merely express in a general way what each one of you can see for himself in the various parts of France. Yes, what our major industries, irrevocably steered by the treaties of 1860-1 into exports, lack more and more are outlets. Why? Because next door Germany is setting up trade barriers; because across the ocean the United States of America have become protectionists, and extreme protectionists at that; because not only are these great markets . . . shrinking, becoming more and more difficult of access, but these great states are beginning to pour into our own markets products not seen there before. This is true not only for our agriculture, which has been so sorely tried . . . and for which competition is no longer limited to the circle of large European states. . . . Today, as you know, competition, the law of supply and demand, freedom of trade, the effects of speculation, all radiate in a circle that reaches to the ends of the earth. . . . That is a great complication, a great economic difficulty; . . . an extremely serious problem. It is so serious, gentlemen, so acute, that the least informed persons must already glimpse, foresee, and take precautions against the time when the great South American market that has, in a manner of speaking, belonged to us forever will be disputed and perhaps taken away from us by North American products. Nothing is more serious; there can be no graver social problem; and these matters are linked intimately to colonial policy.

Gentlemen, we must speak more loudly and more honestly! We must say openly that indeed the higher races have a right over the lower races. . . .

I repeat, that the superior races have a right because they have a duty. They have the duty to civilize the inferior races. . . . In the history of earlier centuries these duties, gentlemen, have often been misunderstood; and certainly when the Spanish soldiers and explorers introduced slavery into Central America, they did not fulfill their duty as men of a higher race. . . . But, in our time, I maintain that European nations acquit themselves with generosity, with grandeur, and with sincerity of this superior civilizing duty.

I say that French colonial policy, the policy of colonial expansion, the policy that has taken us under the Empire [the Second Empire, of Napoleon III], to Saigon, to Indochina, that has led us to Tunisia, to Madagascar—I say that this policy of colonial expansion was inspired by . . . the fact that a navy such as ours cannot do without secure harbors, defenses, supply facilities on the high seas. . . .

Gentlemen, these are considerations that merit the full attention of patriots. The conditions of naval warfare have greatly changed. . . . And that is why we needed Tunisia; that is why we needed Saigon and Indochina; that is why we need Madagascar . . . and why we shall never leave them! . . . Gentlemen, in Europe such as it is today, in this competition of the many rivals we see rising up around us, some by military or naval improvements, others by the prodigious development of a constantly growing population; in a Europe, or rather in a universe thus constituted, a policy of withdrawal or abstention is simply the high road to decadence! In our time nations are great only through the activity they deploy; it is not by spreading the peaceable light of their institutions . . . that they are great, in the present day.

Spreading light without acting, without taking part in the affairs of the world, keeping out of all European alliances and seeing as a trap, an adventure, all expansion into Africa or the Orient-for a great nation to live this way, believe me, is to abdicate and, in less time than you may think, to sink from the first rank to the third and fourth.

Source: From Jules François Camille Ferry, "Speech Before the French Chamber of Deputies, March 28, 1884," *Discours et Opinions de Jules Ferry,* ed. Paul Robiquet (Paris: Armand Colin & Cie., 1897), 199–201, 210–211, 215–218.

6. LILIUOKALANI, *HAWAII'S STORY BY HAWAII'S QUEEN* (1896)

The United States embarked on oceanic expansion toward the end of the nineteenth century after building its transcontinental holdings by conquering native peoples. Cooperating with businessmen and missionaries to depose the queen and ruling family of Hawaii, it annexed the islands. Almost simultaneously the U.S. government helped encourage uprisings against Spain across Cuba, Puerto Rico, and the Philippines. Ultimately America contributed to the chaos of empire and the Spanish defeat. Though promising independence, the United States quickly replaced Spanish power either with a direct takeover as in the case of the Philippines or in enforcing more indirect rule as in the case of Cuba and Puerto Rico. Deposed queen of Hawaii Lili-uokalani gives her account of U.S. methods to force her from power there. Imperial coercion was at odds with the growing European and U.S. rhetoric of rights and fair play. Explain how the contradictions seemed to be problematic for Queen Liliuoka-lani but not for the agents of the United States.

FOR the first few days nothing occurred to disturb the quiet of my apartments save the tread of the sentry. On the fourth day I received a visit from Mr. Paul Neumann, who asked me if, in the event that it should be decided that all the principal parties to the revolt must pay for it with their lives, I was prepared to die? I replied to this in the affirmative, telling him I had no anxiety for myself, and felt no dread of death. He then told me that six others besides myself had been selected to be shot for treason, but that he would call again, and let me know further about our fate. . . .

About the 22d of January a paper was handed to me by Mr. Wilson, which, on examination, proved to be a purported act of abdication for me to sign. . . . For myself, I would have chosen death rather than to have signed it; but it was represented to me that by my signing this paper all the persons who had been arrested, all my people now in trouble by reason of their love and loyalty towards me, would be immediately released. Think of my position,—sick, a lone woman in prison, scarcely knowing who was my friend, or who listened to my words only to betray me, without legal advice or friendly counsel, and the stream of blood ready to flow unless it was stayed by my pen.

My persecutors have stated, and at that time compelled me to state, that this paper was signed and acknowledged by me after consultation with my friends whose names appear at the foot of it as witnesses. Not the least opportunity was given to me to confer with any one; but for the purpose of making it appear to the outside world that I was under the guidance of others, friends who had known me well in better days were brought into the place of my imprisonment, and stood around to see a signature affixed by me. . . .

Then the following individuals witnessed my subscription of the signature which was demanded of me: William G. Irwin, H. A. Widemann, Samuel Parker, S. Kalua Kookano, Charles B. Wilson, and Paul Neumann. . . .

So far from the presence of these persons being evidence of a voluntary act on my part, was it not an assurance to me that they, too, knew that, unless I did the will of my jailers, what Mr. Neumann had threatened would be performed, and six prominent citizens immediately put to death. I so regarded it then, and I still believe that murder was the alternative. Be this as it may, it is certainly happier for me to reflect to-day that there is not a drop of the blood of my subjects, friends or foes, upon my soul.

Source: Liliuokalani, Queen of Hawaii. *Hawaii's Story by Hawaii's Queen* (Boston: Lee and Shepard, 1898), Chapter XLIV, "Imprisonment—Forced Abdication."

7. FADHMA AMROUCHE, *MY LIFE STORY* (1890)

By the 1890s the French had positioned themselves to rule Algeria after decades of combat to take control of the region. As tens of thousands of immigrants arrived from all parts of Europe, they took the best lands for farming and other enterprises from local residents. Jules Ferry announced that part of French imperial expansion included a "civilizing mission" based on education in French culture and values. For some, access to such education could lead to greater, albeit still limited, opportunity within the racist imperial culture. Especially if education entailed living on French premises, there could be protection from a bad family or social situation, as in the case of Fadhma Amrouche from the Berber ethnic group. As in the early Spanish empire, women were especially adept at taking advantage of institutions such as courts, churches, and schools to protect their families. Many of these children— Amrouche among them—had very mixed experiences of these institutions. How would you characterize Fadhma Amrouche's experience of the French?

My mother was left on her own at the age of twenty-two or twenty-three, with two children, the elder one five or six and the younger one three. She was very beautiful, with a clear pink complexion and blue-grey eyes, rather short and stocky, with broad shoulders, a strong chin and a low, obstinate forehead. But she was young and foolish. In her own courtyard there lived a young man from the same family as her old husband. She fell in love with him. And the inevitable happened. She became pregnant and the young man denied that he was the father of the child. . . . On the night of my birth my mother was all alone with her two small children: there was no one at hand to assist her or to go for help. She delivered herself and bit through the umbilical cord. The next day one old woman brought her a little food.

When I was nine days old my mother tied me warmly to her breast, for it had been snowing, and set out, with a child in each hand, to lodge a complaint with the public prosecutor against my father. She wanted him to recognise me and give me his name. He refused because he was engaged to a girl from the village who came from a powerful family; they threatened to kill him if he abandoned this girl and he was afraid!

The world is a cruel place and "the child of sin" becomes the scapegoat of society, especially in Kabylia [a mountainous region near the Algerian coast inhabited by Berbers]. I cannot count the blows I received. What endless bullying I suffered! If I ventured into the street, I would risk being knocked down and trampled upon.

My mother took fright. What was she to do with me? How was she to protect me from people's cruelty? She could not keep me shut up, but she was afraid that if I went out I would be killed and, in the eyes of the law, the blame would fall on her.

She heard that at Ouadhias [a town in the Kabylia region] there was a convent of the White Sisters, who took in little girls and looked after them. She thought that if she entrusted me to these nuns she would have no more worries on my account; no one would hurt me any more. Nevertheless, she held out for a long time as she loved me, I was her child. She had refused to give me to the magistrate's wife, who was childless and had wanted to adopt me . . . , but seeing that I was still a victim of ill-treatment, she decided to take me to the White Sisters. . . .

From this whole period of my life, I can only recall the tune of *Ave Maria Stella* and the impression of the chapel, all lit up, with the officiating priest holding out the monstrance. (For a long time after I had left Ouadhias, I wondered what all that meant.) But, most of all, I am haunted by a terrible picture: that of a tiny girl standing against the wall of a corridor: the child is covered with filth, dressed in sackcloth, with a little mug full of excrement hung around her neck. She is crying. A priest is walking towards her; the nun who is with him explains that she is a wicked little girl who has thrown her comrades' thimbles into the privy and so has been made to climb down into it to retrieve them: she is covered with the contents of the cesspool, which also fill the mug.

In addition to this punishment, the child was also flogged till she bled: when my mother came the following Wednesday, she found me still covered with the marks from the whip.

And so I left the Sisters of Ouadhias. . . .

In the autumn, the *kaïd* [a North African governor or chief] sent for my mother and said, "Your daughter Fadhma is a burden to you, take her to Fort-National where a school for girls has just been opened, she will be happy and treated well, and the Administrator will take her under his wing. You will have nothing more to fear from your first husband's brothers." My mother held out for a long time . . . the village people, who still considered me the child of sin, were disapproving. In October or November 1886, she agreed to give me up. Once again she took me on her back and we set out. I cannot recall this journey; I can only remember that as we climbed down towards the river we picked arbutus berries to eat–I can still see the red fruit. This brings us to the end of the first part of my childhood. . . .

The orphanage of Taddert-ou-Fella, which owes its name to the nearby village, was founded between 1882 and 1884. At this same time, the first schools in Greater Kabylia were opened, one in Beni-Yenni, with M. Verdy in charge, one in Tamazirth, under M. Gorde, and one in Tizi-Rached under M. Maille. . . .

When I arrived at the school I was still very young and I cannot remember much of my first two years there. I was very impressed when I was taken to the headmistress. My mother had first gone to see the Administrator to put me in his care. This wasn't M. Sabatier, who had been elected Deputy, but his successor, M. Demonque. The commune was still responsible for the school expenses. I saw a tall woman, dressed all in black; she seemed terribly sad to me. She had recently lost her only son from typhoid and her husband had died some little time before. They came from Aveyron where they had been ruined when phylloxera destroyed all the vines. Since the death of her husband and son, Mme Malaval had devoted herself wholeheartedly to her school. When I arrived the dormitory was full. There were some really big girls who were put in charge of the smaller ones. My memories are vague up to 1888. In October of that year, I was put up into the big girls' class: there were four of us little ones: Alice, Ines, Blanche and myself,

Marguerite. We had all been given French names, as there were too many Fadh-mas, Tassadits and Dabhias. . . .

For a long time the school at Taddert-ou-Fella was considered a show-place and we were visited by a succession of members of the French government, includ-ing Jules Ferry, and often tourists came simply out of curiosity, like the Grand Duke George of Russia. . . .

The years went by, the seasons, summers and winters. In 1891 I in turn passed my school certificate. I was fairly good at the subjects I liked. I was top in French history, but I hated geography—I could never remember all the Departments and Districts, whereas I can still remember in detail all the kings of France, who married whom, who succeeded whom, and all about the French Revolution and the Napoleonic era. I loved French, except when I had to explain proverbs and maxims. . . .

People were beginning to demand the emancipation of Muslim women. At that time school was compulsory for boys; if a pupil played truant, the father and son were sentenced to three days in prison and a fine of fifteen francs. So boys attended school regularly. But, alas! nothing similar was enforced for girls. There was no secular teaching for them, with the exception of our school which unfor-tunately soon had to close. . . .

Mme Malaval refused to obey; she kept the orphanage going for six months out of her own savings; she moved heaven and earth, writing to members of the government and any influential persons who might help her. Eventually she got her way in 1893. It was decided that the Taddert-ou-Fella Orphanage should be taken over by the State and renamed "The Taddert-ou-Fella Normal School."

February was over and we were into March when, one morning, I saw the Mother Superior of Tagmount arriving. She told me that she had submitted my application to the Mother General, who wanted to see me. . . .

I wasn't sure at first if I should go with her, but then I got dressed and left with her. . . . I was taken to a tall, dark nun with a rather severe expression who told me to go to the Hospital at Ai'th-Manegueleth, saying she had sent me, and to ask for Mother Saint-Matthew. But before that she asked me if we had been taught any-thing about religion at school. I told her, no, not a word, as it was a lay school and supposed to be non-sectarian.

The day I arrived, I entered by "the corridor" where I found the janitor, a gnome-like creature.

He went to fetch a nun who took me to Mother Saint-Matthew. I remem-ber my surprise at finding myself in the presence of a young woman of pleasant appearance as the name Matthew had for some reason made me expect someone old and shrivelled up.

Mother Saint-Matthew told me that she had been warned to expect me by the Mother General, Mother Salome. I would be fed, all my expenses paid and, in addition, would earn ten francs a month. I accepted and went back to let my brother know of the arrangements before he returned home. Then I followed the nun who was to take me in hand. I went with her to a room on a lower level on the other side of the main building.

There I found creatures of all ages; with few exceptions they had all been patients in the hospital and still had scars and sores visible on their bodies. When I was asked what my name was, and replied "Marguerite," I was told that I had no right to a Christian name as I hadn't been baptised, and so I became "Fadhma from Tagmount." That already put a damper on my spirits. . . .

I still have a confused and painful impression of that period of my life. Everyone kept talking about God, everything had to be done for the love of God, but you felt you were being spied upon, everything you said was judged and reported to the Mother Superior. I thought I was going to be back in the friendly atmosphere of Taddert-ou-Fella but I was disappointed and baffled. When I mentioned that there was some good to be found in all religions, it was considered blasphemous. . . .

The prayers had been translated into Kabyle: the *Ave Maria*, "Our Father," the *Credo*, and the nuns pegged away at drumming these expressions into our rebellious heads. And I couldn't help smiling when I heard the nuns' way of pronouncing the Kabyle language. . . .

Easter was approaching. During Holy Week we went to the service at the monastery every day. . . . I liked these Holy Week services because of the liturgical chants and the organ music. As for the Catholic religion, I don't think I was ever truly convinced. But I believe sincerely in God. When the Fathers declared that only those who had been baptized would go to heaven, I didn't believe them. I thought of my mother, of all that she had suffered, the three months a year she spent fasting (for besides Ramadan, she imposed supplementary fasts on herself), of the heavy loads of water she took it upon herself to carry to the mosque in all weathers and I thought, "Is it possible that my mother will not go to heaven?"

Source: Fadhma A. M. Amrouche, *My Life Story: The Autobiography of a Berber Woman*, translated and with an introduction by Dorothy S. Blair (New Brunswick, NJ: Rutgers University Press, 1989). First published by Librairie Francois Maspero, Paris, 1968), 3–18, 43–48.

8. CHRISTIAN LAUTHERBORN, LETTER TO HIS SISTER AND BROTHER-IN-LAW (1889)

The Dane Christian Lautherborn had worked on a cotton farm in the United States and then, seeking a more challenging life, moved to East Africa where the Germans were trying to gain a foothold. While there, he ran plantations and planned the reconstruction of towns and cities and established himself as a fair and accomplished citizen. Before that, Lautherborn's life in Africa was in fact more challenging, given the violence and confusion brought by imperial invaders. He arrived at a time when the range of competitors for influence and especially property in East Africa was wide: a variety of Arab and African local notables, the Sultan of Zanzibar, the British, French missionaries, the Germans, and ordinary African and Arab inhabitants of the region. Shifting, unstable alliances among these led to confrontations. As Lautherborn arrived, local notable Bushiri aimed to drive out those he saw as competitors for influence—specifically the Germans. He wreaked havoc in the region, until his final stand, which Lautherborn describes to his sister and brother-in-law back in Denmark.

. . . But now a little bit about Bushiri. When I last wrote we had recaptured the two, stolen cannons, and he had withdrawn to his camp and was quiet. Now and then he would steal a couple of Negroes and sell them. When, however, Wissmann's soldiers had trained for a couple of weeks, they paid a little visit to Bushiri's camp on 8th May 1889, which cost him more than a hundred of his people's lives. He also just barely got away himself. How is not known, since his donkey was captured and he is so heavy, he can only move with difficulty. It is believed that he was carried away. Our soldiers found many things of great value and about 6000 rupees, which Bushiri had received as ransom for an English missionary he had captured. After everything usable was taken out, the entire camp was set on fire. One hour later a large pile of ashes was the only trace of Bushiri's camp. A couple of captured Arabs and Negroes were brought back. The next day one of the Arabs was hung, because our Black mason recognized him as the one who had cut off his hands. The rebels in Pangani also had to give up after a two hour battle, when we attacked them on 8th July 1889. They had stretched a thick rope over the Pangani River to block the boats. Commander Wissmann, however, had two flat-bottomed steamships equipped with revolving cannons, with which he steamed into the river. Naturally the rope broke when the ship sailed against it. When the shells began to fall among the rebels, it was not long before they retreated and we went ashore as victors. Now all is quiet there, and the Arabs have come back to ask for peace, which has been granted. However, we keep a sharp eye on them, because no one trusts them anymore. My cotton plantation is completely ruined; all the buildings are burned down, the animals are slaughtered, and all equipment broken up. There will be work for me, when I begin again, which I believe will be in a couple of months. Tanga has also been recaptured. There is only one station more, but it will not be long before that also belongs to us. . . .

Here in Bagamoyo, where I am now, everything is peaceful. The burned down town is rising from its ashes. I have had, during this time, very pleasant work, laying out the streets and clearing building sites. We will not use anymore the African construction style, with its three feet wide streets, twisting into so many turns that one has to tie the end of a piece of string to something when one goes into the town and unwind it in order to find the way out. Bagamoyo will be laid out in a new, European style with wide, straight streets. It really looks beautiful with the palm leaf covered houses in a straight line and the wide streets, completely clean and even as a macadamized road back home. The natives looked askance at the wide streets, when we first measured them out, and thought that they were too difficult to keep clean. But when I said that each man had to sweep in front of his door, so that it would all be clean, they opened their eyes wide and said, *"Mzunga hapa kazi ingi"* (Now the Europeans are here, so we must work). But they know there is no way around it and do the work without complaining.

Now I am tired of writing. In my next letter I will write about plant growth and the animal world here. I will also write about the Arabs' slave hunting and a little more about the people's lives here.

Source: *The Practical Imperialist: Letters from a Danish Planter in German East Africa 1888–1906*, Jane L. Parpart and Marianne Rostgaard, eds. (Leiden: Brill, 2006), 91, 94.

9. WILLIAM II, KAISER OF GERMANY, SPEECH TO THE NORTH GERMAN REGATTA ASSOCIATION (1901)

In 1871, Chancellor Otto von Bismarck presided over the creation of a unified Germany after waging a series of successful wars bringing all the German states except Austria together into a single empire. Despite the activities of German businessmen world-wide, Bismarck was not an enthusiast for all-out imperial venture, instead adding a very few colonies and using Berlin as a center for global diplomacy among the powers. All that changed in 1888, when the young Kaiser (Emperor) William II came to power and fired Bismarck, preliminary to expanding Germany's global presence. He challenged France's claims to North Africa and built the German navy's capacity to influence worldwide events and claim territory. This talk is known as the Kaiser's "Place in the Sun" speech, made at a time of massive armed build-up and German incursions into additional faraway lands. Germany's business ventures at the time into the Ottoman empire may be seen as preliminary expansionist moves.

In spite of the fact that we have no such fleet as we should have, we have conquered for ourselves a place in the sun. It will now be my task to see to it that this place in the sun shall remain our undisputed possession, in order that the sun's rays may fall fruitfully upon our activity and trade in foreign parts, that our industry and agriculture may develop within the state and our sailing sports upon the water, for our future lies upon the water. The more Germans go out upon the waters, whether it be in races or regattas, whether it be in journeys across the ocean, or in the service of the battle-flag, so much the better it will be for us.

For when the German has once learned to direct his glance upon what is distant and great, the pettiness which surrounds him in daily life on all sides will disappear. Whoever wishes to have this larger and freer outlook can find no better place than one of the Hanseatic cities. . . . We are now making efforts to do what, in the old time, the Hanseatic cities could not accomplish, because they lacked the vivifying and protecting power of the empire. May it be the function of my Hansa during many years of peace to protect and advance commerce and trade! . . .

As head of the empire I therefore rejoice over every citizen, whether from Hamburg, Bremen, or Lübeck, who goes forth with this large outlook and seeks new points where we can drive in the nail on which to hang our armor. Therefore, I believe that I express the feeling of all your hearts when I recognize gratefully that the director of this company who has placed at our disposal the wonderful ship which bears my daughter's name has gone forth as a courageous servant of the Hansa, in order to make for us friendly conquests whose fruits will be gathered by our descendants!

Source: C. Gauss, *The German Kaiser as Shown in His Public Utterances* (New York: Charles Scribner's sons, 1915), 181–183.

10. JAN SMUTS, LETTER TO W. T. STEAD (1902)

Trained in philosophy and the law, Jan Smuts (1870–1950) was a white Afrikaner— that is, a person of European, particularly Dutch heritage, raised to speak Afrikaans. During the Boer War he took up military service against the British and then served as a general on the British side during World War I and a field marshall in World War II, all the while reading philosophy, as he saw it, to sharpen his mind. Smuts became prime minister of South Africa after World War I, but remained comparatively quiet from the early twentieth century on as the South African government progressively took away rights and property from local black citizens. In this letter to prominent British journalist W. T. Stead, Smuts suggests that most of the destruction attributed to the white forces were actually the result of there being black Africans among the troops. He also claimed that whites easily understood the less developed "native mind." When Smuts opened up in this letter, his positions were very clear.

. . . That point is the incontestable fact that, in spite of all official assurances to the British people, the fighting forces of the British army in South Africa contain a very large element of armed Natives and Coloured people. All the irregular corps and mobile columns, on which the bulk of the active warfare in South Africa has devolved, contain a very large proportion of armed Natives; indeed some of them consist almost entirely of Natives. I was surprised to find, during my march through the Orange Free State in August of last year, that in the many encounters I had with British columns, not a single dead or wounded British soldier fell into our hands, but in all cases armed Kaffirs or Coloured Cape boys. When I arrived in the Cape Colony I was—at first somewhat to my astonishment—informed by the inhabitants that all the crack columns . . . consisted very largely of armed Natives, but I very soon found out that such was but too truly the case. . . .

I do not say that it is positively contrary to the rules of international law to employ armed barbarians under white officers in a war between two white Christian peoples. But it is certainly shocking to the moral sense of all civilized people; it is even more shocking when one considers the numerical disproportion of the two peoples engaged in this struggle; and it is most shocking of all from the point of view of South African history and public policy. I do not speak of the Boer wounded who have fallen into the hands of these armed fiends and have subsequently been found mutilated and tortured to death in the most awful forms which the insensate fury of their racial passions could suggest. I do not even speak of those poor women and children whose cruel violation has followed in the wake of the British columns. For these are but exceptions, and a policy must be judged by its natural and not by its exceptional consequences. But I refer to the way in which the public conscience of South Africa, both Boer and British, has been shocked by this enlistment of coloured combatants. The peculiar position of the small white community in the midst of the very large and rapidly increasing coloured races and the danger which in consequence threatens this small white community and with it civilization itself in South Africa, have led to the creation of a special code of morality as between the white and coloured races which forbids interbreeding, and of a special tacit understanding which forbids the white races to appeal for assistance to the coloured races in their mutual disputes. This understanding is essential to the continued existence of the white community as the ruling class in South Africa, for otherwise the coloured races must become the arbiter in disputes between the whites and in the long run the predominating political factor or "casting vote" in South Africa. That this would soon cause South Africa to relapse into barbarism must be evident to everybody.

Source: *Selections from the Smuts Papers*, K. Hancock and J van der Poel, eds. (Cambridge: Cambridge University Press, 1966), II, 483–484.

11. STORIES OF JAPANESE HEROES
OF EMPIRE: NOGI MARESUKE

Biographies of high-ranking imperial leaders and accomplished adventurers filled newspapers, attracted full life histories, and led to their images being used on posters, now made colorful by modern printing technology. These stories were adapted for children too so that they might become "baby imperialists," as a British ABC primer also showed. Often stories emphasized the ways in which empire builders brought order from savage disorder. Imperialist responsibility for disorder was downplayed; instead the violence empire builders used was seen as cleansing and ultimately civilizing. The brief vignette presented here takes a moment in the life of Nogi Maresuke, a general in the Japanese war against China (1894–1895) from which the Japanese took Taiwan and other islands and the Liaodong Peninsula. The victory was a big step forward for the Japanese empire.

In the twenty seventh year of the Meiji era [1894], Maresuke, Commander of the First Brigade, left Tokyo for the front in China. When he attacked Kinshujo, he always stood at the head of his army, and directed it with vigour and strength. The morale of his troops was thus stirred up; and after terrible struggles, he and his men eventually occupied Kinshujo. It was the end of November. The vast field of Manchuria was entirely covered with snow; and yet the commander himself never wore any special material for protection against the cold.

Shortly after the occupation, a staff-officer received material for protection against cold from the father land. He at once brought one of them to the commander.

"What is it?" enquired the commander, looking at him.

"A material for protection against cold," replied the staff-officer, respectfully. "Pray put it on first. I'm intending to distribute them among the other officers."

"What about soldiers?" demanded Maresuke, anxiously.

"There is none for them, sir," replied the subordinate officer.

"How could the officers wear them, when the men have none to put on?". . .

Maresuke left it untouched. All the other officers under him followed his noble example.

The men soon heard of this.

Some were moved to tears. . . .

Source: Tadashige Matsumoto, *Stories of Fifty Japanese Heroes* (Tokyo: Koseikaku, 1929), 351–352.

12. SERGEI WITTE, *MEMOIRS* 1921

Sergei Witte (1849–1915) launched Russia on the path to modernization when he sponsored the building of the Trans-Siberian Railroad and reforms lightening the peasantry's ties to the lands by allowing them free movement. In the course of his career, he also made treaties with China allowing the Trans-Siberian to pass through Manchuria in order to reach Vladivostok more directly. However, he criticized further intrusions by Russia into the region and the empire's failure to treat Japan more favorably, thus causing, he believed, the Russo-Japanese War of 1904–5 in which Russia was defeated. His support for a parliament led to his dismissal from the government, but his loyalty to its well-being led him to oppose Russia's entry into World War I. At the time it was published (1921), Witte's revelations explained a great deal about Russia's positioning in the Far East. Explain the entanglements that Witte notes, endorses, and opposes.

. . . [For the coronation of Emperor Nicholas II in May 1896,] China sent Li Hung-chang. This was the most outstanding of [China's] statesmen, occupying at that time the highest office in China, and so the dispatch of Li Hung-chang to the coronation was meant to indicate the particular gratitude of China to our young emperor for the service he had rendered China in preserving the integrity of Chinese territory, and likewise for the assistance we had rendered China in her financial affairs.

In the meantime our great Trans-Siberian railway had almost reached Trans-Baikalia, and it became imperative to decide the further route the railroad should follow. Quite naturally, I conceived the idea of continuing the road straight across to Vladivostok, cutting across Mongolia and northern Manchuria. This would speed up its construction considerably. In this way the Trans-Siberian would become a real transit line, an artery of worldwide importance, connecting Japan and the entire Far East with Russia and Europe. . . .

I met with Li Hung-chang, and we reached an agreement on all points, setting forth the following principles for a secret pact with China:

1. The Chinese Empire would grant us permission to build a railroad across its territory along a straight line between Chita and Vladivostok; but the management of this railroad must be entrusted to a private company. Li Hung-chang absolutely refused to accept my proposal that the road should be constructed by the treasury, or that it should belong to the treasury and the state. For that reason we were forced to form the Chinese Eastern

Railway Company, which of course was and still is completely in the hands of the government. . . .

2. Furthermore, a strip of land for the railroad should be alienated to us, as necessary for railway operations. Within this alienated strip we would be sovereign in this respect: that since the territory belonged to us, we would have complete jurisdiction in it, with our own police force and our own guards, i.e. what later comprised the so-called protective guard of the Chinese Eastern Railroad. . . .

On the other hand, we would bind ourselves to defend Chinese territory from any aggressive action on the part of Japan. . . .

A treaty with Japan was also signed in Moscow. . . . I consider that this was a felicitous treaty. By this treaty Russia and Japan arranged for a division of influence in Korea, with Russia obtaining the preponderant influence.

Japan's representatives willingly agreed to this treaty. By this treaty we could keep military instructors and several hundred of our soldiers in Korea, so that in military and financial matters, as regards the management of state finances, Russia was accorded considerable, one might say dominant, rights; thus, by the treaty, we appointed a financial counselor to the Korean emperor, which was equivalent to the appointment of a minister of finance. But influence in Korea was shared by Japan as well as by Russia; Japan could likewise have its industrial companies and carry on trade there; Russia had no special financial privileges that were not accorded to Japan as well, and so forth. In general, as I have already said, I consider this a felicitous treaty. . . .

[In December, 1897, a Russian naval squadron entered the harbor of Port Arthur, and on March 15, 1898, an agreement was signed with China for the twenty-five-year "lease" of the Kwantung region of the Liaotung Peninsula. . . .] This seizure of the Kwantung region [by Russia] . . . was an act of unexampled perfidy.

Several years before our seizure of the Kwantung region we had forced the Japanese to leave it, and, under the pretext that we could not tolerate a violation of China's integrity, we concluded a secret defensive alliance with China against Japan, through which we obtained very considerable advantages in the Far East. Then, after a very short interval, we ourselves occupied a part of the region we had compelled the Japanese after their victory to abandon, on the ground that we could not tolerate any violation of the integrity of the Chinese Empire. . . .

Our seizure of the Kwantung region made such an overwhelming impression on Japan that Count Murav'ev, fearing an armed conflict with Japan, yielded to her demands and withdrew our military instructors and our military forces from Korea; . . .

Military as well as financial and economic influence in Korea passed from our agents to agents of Japan.

As a result, in order to pacify Japan, an agreement with Japan was concluded on April 13, 1898, by which we clearly yielded dominant influence in Korea to Japan. Japan understood this and was pacified for the moment. . . .

In the summer of 1902 the sovereign emperor went to Revel' to attend naval maneuvers. In June the German emperor came for the maneuvers. When the maneuvers were over, the following interesting incident took place, revealing the frame of mind of the German emperor. When his yacht was bearing off and the usual farewell signals were being exchanged, the German emperor gave the following signal: the admiral of the Atlantic Ocean salutes the admiral of the Pacific Ocean. The sovereign was greatly embarrassed for an answer to this salute. I do not know how His Majesty replied, but I know for a fact that the German emperor sent to ours a message that, if translated into ordinary language, meant; I aim to seize or acquire a dominant position in the Atlantic Ocean, and I advise you and will give you my support to obtain a dominant position in the Pacific Ocean.

Source: Sergei Witte, *Memoirs*, Abraham Yarmolinsky, trans. (Garden City, NY: Doubleday, Page and Co., 1921), 85–86, 89–90, 97–98.

REVIEW QUESTIONS

1. Describe the different relationships to empire of Liliuokalani, Mokshodayani Mukhopadhyay, and Fadhma Amrouche in the late nineteenth century.
2. Compare the visions of African politics expressed in the Berlin Conference, the autobiography of Tippu Tip, and the letters of Lautherborn and Smuts.
3. Compare the differing economic and political appraisals of empire expressed by Trollope, Ferry, William II, and Witte.
4. Germany, Japan, and the United States jumped into the waters of oceanic expansion late in the nineteenth century, with Grover Cleveland facing the demand that Hawai'i be annexed after the planters had overthrown Liliuokalani's regime. Cleveland was against empire, however, while the press stirred things up. What role does the press seem to be playing in U.S. expansion according to this drawing, which itself appeared in the press? https://www.loc.gov/resource/ppmsca.28987/

CHAPTER 8

Increased Expansion, Increased Resistance

In the quest for resources, imperial rivalries and violence intensified as the twentieth century opened. Colonial bureaucracies aimed for ever more efficient extraction of goods and raw materials to aid industry and thus boost national wealth, no matter what the cost to ordinary people. In addition, governments increasingly focused on strategic positioning around the world so that they could advance their holdings and militarily protect them. Building battleships was one key to this positioning. Leaders of nation-states came to realize that an expanding empire built national pride and solidarity when citizens came to see their nation and themselves as superior to those they ruled. In their view global power yielded emotional patriotism, preventing criticism of government policies. Public holidays centered on celebrations of empire, while newspapers, magazines, and music halls promoted the deeds of explorers and conquerors of distant lands. Imperial rivals also sponsored world fairs, attended by hundreds of thousands. Even at these supposedly educational events, nations with empires competed to show not only their mastery of the latest technology but also their command of foreigners, often by recreating the everyday life in "exotic villages" within their empires. Many participants from the colonies, however, rebelled against the ways in which they were made into "savages."

Some colonized individuals profited from colonial regimes and learned to protect themselves by using imperial institutions to their benefit. In Africa colonizers chose local chiefs and officers to staff a vast system of control. Other local people built up industries, shipping capacity, and a variety of economic tools that competed with those of their colonizers. In general, however, the colonizers had the most control of plantation economies, new mining ventures, transportation systems, and the military. By ever-improved rail and steamship, resources speeded out of the region and away from those who did the work of growing crops on plantations and digging for precious metals, minerals, and raw materials for industry. As in the Belgian Congo, imperialists drove local people to the limit of endurance and punished those who did not fill work quotas with whippings, amputations, and even death. Impoverishment and suffering increased not just because of the natural disasters hitting many African, Asian, and South American regions late in the nineteenth century but also because of the rising greed of empires in the face of increased worldwide competition. The situation put everyone on edge.

Local resistance increased, and colonial powers used all available fire-power to crush it. The British slaughtered Mahdist resisters to their rule in the Sudan in 1884–1885. The French suppressed university students in Indochina who opposed their domination and executed many young activists. In the early twentieth century, resistance became ever fiercer. In 1900, the Boxers in China rose up against foreign incursions, specifically though not exclusively murdering missionaries and other Christians for causing the bad weather conditions that had brought on famine. To other Chinese reformers, Manchu rule had become utterly destructive of the actual Chinese people. The imperial powers united to crush these rebels. In 1911–1912 Sun Yat-sen (1866–1925), who had been educated in Hawaii, led a coalition to overthrow the weakened and discredited Manchu rulers of the Qing Empire after several decades of revolutionary strug-gle on his part. When the Herero in Southwest Africa refused to surrender their lands to the Germans in 1904–5, some were killed outright, while the rest were driven from their pasturage lands to areas where they and their flocks simply starved. The United States brutally repressed Filipinos demanding their inde-pendence in the Filipino-American War (1899–1902) and in the guerilla war-fare that followed. Tens of thousands of Filipinos died not only on the battlefield but from the starvation and disease that accompanied American occupation and repression on the islands.

Reform-minded groups—both in the colonies and among the colonizers—protested, made inquiries, and publicized abuses, especially as rebellions, warfare, colonial competition, and exploitation of ordinary people mounted. New religious movements promised salvation, and some predicted the coming of a savior or a utopian world. On the explicitly political level, some anti-imperial advocates developed a pan-Islam program for uniting Muslims against imperial exploita-tion. Africans and African-Americans drew together in a series of Pan-African conferences to discuss ways of publicizing not only the many harms done to their people but also the centuries of African accomplishment. The possibility that Africans could unite across ethnic groups and even continents grew. Alongside pro-imperial groups in the home countries building support for empire, angry or religious people became outspoken anti-colonial activists. Resistance became multifaceted, reaching beyond the local level.

The colonized developed an array of organizations aimed at overthrowing imperial regimes or at least at gaining more rights. In 1885, after the brutal sup-pression of the Indian Uprising of 1857–1858, activists in India formed the Indian National Congress—a political group that evolved into a powerful political party that remains a major force in India to this day. Later, in part instigated by the British to subdue the influence of the Congress, the Muslim League came into being. The idea behind the League was that given the Hindu majority in the Congress there should be a distinct bloc to represent Muslim interests. Resistance to empire now took as many forms as empire itself, and some established empires succumbed. Arabs and Armenians within the Ottoman Empire formed political action groups, demanding recognition and publicizing their cause widely. Secret and open nationalist societies took shape in southeastern Europe to gain independence from both Ottoman and the Hapsburg empires.

While resistance proliferated, empires increased their competition with one another. Imperial European powers weakened the Ottomans by supporting various of the Balkan groups that aimed for greater or complete independence, but those same powers also fought among themselves for territory and position. In 1898, the French and British faced off over control of the upper Nile at Fashoda in the Sudan but ultimately avoided war when the French withdrew their forces. In the same year, the United States was helping freedom fighters defeat Spain, even as that North American power moved to replace Spanish rule with its own domination. The British fought Dutch settlers in South Africa in the South African War of 1899–1902, leading many in Britain itself to question their government's methods, such as the use of concentration camps. Meanwhile Germany confronted the French in North Africa in 1905 and 1911 in an attempt to drive them from Morocco. Seven imperial powers ganged up to put down the Boxer Rebellion, weakening the Qing Empire still further.

Simultaneously, artists, musicians, and intellectuals came to appreciate the accomplishments of people in other parts of the world and to imitate them despite official racist propaganda. Besides imitation in the arts, the diets and homes of most urban peoples were often dependent on the variety of fruits and vegetables and the energizing products such as coffee, tea, chocolate, tobacco, and sugar (to name a few) from around the world. Rubber tires on bicycles, wagons, and the growing number of automobiles were some of the products built from resources culled from colonized people's lands. The dependence on supposedly inferior foreign peoples only pumped up patriotism in denial of that dependence.

Amid this interdependence, in the fast-paced struggle for more of everything, empire showed itself as entailing chaos, destruction, and confusion. It became a war of nerves and weapons. As nationalists who had long chafed under Ottoman and Habsburg rule pulled away, especially in the Balkans, and then fought one another, Armenians on the other side of the Ottoman Empire made demands for reform. Like those resisting elsewhere, they were massacred in a series of brutal pogroms. Arab reformers also wanted recognition of their distinct role within the Ottoman Empire, while a rising group of Turkish nationalists in the empire, the Young Turks, combatted Arab demands for a confederation-style government. This competition for Ottoman lands caused further weakening. For a time after their uprising in 1908 the Young Turks gained control of the sultan's government. The growing contingent of diverse activists brought tensions to a fevered pitch and made the competition among empires explosive until world war erupted in 1914.

1. JAMAL AL-DIN AL-AFGHANI,
"PLAN FOR ISLAMIC UNITY" (1884)

Colonized peoples devised plans to combat their oppression and to overcome the divide and rule programs of the imperialists. In these turn-of-the-century years, they produced plans to unify all Muslims, Hindus, or people of African descent or to modernize themselves economically or culturally in order to create independent societies. Among these reformers was Jamal al-Din al-Afghani (c. 1839–1897), who restlessly went from region to region in the Middle East with a program to unite all people around adherence to Islam. Although he was born in Iran and a Shia, al-Afghani claimed to be born in Afghanistan and thus a Sunni. The purpose, one might suppose as he traveled across India, Central Asia, and the Ottoman Empire, was to demonstrate how one lived a life without local thinking or religious sectarianism. He wanted Muslims of all stripes to unite and thus be strong and influential, a vision of unity that did not agree with leaders in the region who benefited from rivalries.

"Obey Allah and His Messenger and do not quarrel with one another, lest you fail and die." (Quran 8:48)
The dominions of Islam stretched between the furthest point west to Tonkin, on the borders of China, in a breadth between Fezzan in the north and Sarandib south of the Equator. Muslims inhabited [these] continuous and contiguous lands, which they ruled invincibly. Great kings reigned over them and administered most of the globe with their swords. None of their armies was routed, none of their flags was lowered and none of their words was contradicted. . . . Their cities were well populated and solidly constructed, competing with the world's cities in the industry of the inhabitants and their originality. . . . [When] their Abbasid Caliph spoke, the Chinese Emperor would obey him and the greatest Kings in Europe would tremble.

The Muslim navies ruled unrivalled in the Mediterranean Sea, the Red Sea, and the Indian Ocean, being predominant there until recently; their opponents had to yield to the power that defeated them. Muslims abound nowadays in those lands inherited from their forefathers; their number is no less than 400 millions. Individually, their hearts are replete with the tenets of their religion; they are more courageous than their neighbors and better prepared to die. In this, they are the strongest people in their contempt for worldly life and the most unconcerned with vain glories, since the Koran reached them. . . . Every Muslim perceives himself personally involved whenever a group of Muslims is subjugated by foreigners.

This has been the case [both] formerly and nowadays. However, the Muslims have come to a halt, retarded in knowledge and industry, after having been teachers to the world. Their countries started losing the lands on their periphery, although their religion forbids them to yield authority to their opponents. . . . [C]onflict among their princes had caused disunity, so that Muslims failed to oppose the aggression of their enemies. . . . This is what happened to the Muslim princes, along with shameful losses brought about by their disunity in wars in which no nation could have competed with them [otherwise]. However, corruption penetrates the souls of those princes, over time. . . . This is what brought down the Muslims of Spain and destroyed the pillars of the Timurid [Mughal] Sultanate in India, erasing its remains. The British established their government there on this Sultanate's ruins. . . . Agreement and co-operation for strengthening Islamic rule are among the pillars of the Islamic religion; belief in them is a basic doctrine for Muslims, requiring neither a teacher to preach it, nor a book to confirm it. . . . Were it not for their misguided princes, eager for domination, Muslims east and west, north and south, would have joined a common appeal. For preserving their rights, the Muslims need only to turn their thoughts towards their own defense and agree on common action, when necessary, and merge their hearts in a joint feeling about the dangers threatening their nation.

Looking at the Russians, one notices three characteristics. They are lagging in the arts and sciences behind the rest of Europe's nations, their lands have no natural resources (if there are, nobody can exploit them for industry), and they are abjectly poor. None the less, focusing their thoughts on the defense of their nation, agreeing on its development, and joining their hearts have created a state capable of shaking the whole of Europe. The Russians do not own factories required for most instruments of war, which does not prevent them from obtaining them; the arts of war are less developed in Russia, which does not prevent them hiring officers from other nations to instruct their armies—so that their military forces have acquired awesome strength and an aggressive power feared by European states.

So what has prevented us from resembling others in a matter which is simple for us and which we strongly desire—to preserve our nation's honor, to grieve for what hurts it, and to co-operate to defend a total union against whomsoever attacks it? Those responsible for preventing the movement of thoughts and the rise in enthusiasm are [the princes] sunk in luxury, seeking succulent food and soft bedding . . . who have become a yoke on the necks of Muslims, barring these lions from rising to attack—rather, rendering them a prey to foxes. There is no refuge except in Allah.

O people, descendants of the brave and the noble, has the tide turned against you and has the time for despair come? No, no, may Allah forbid the loss of hope! From Edirne to Peshawar, there is an uninterrupted sequence of Islamic states, united in the religion of the Koran, numbering no less than 50 millions, distinguished by courage and bravery. Should these not agree between themselves on defense and attack, as have all the other nations? Were they to agree between themselves, this would be no innovation [bida'], for co-operating is one of the pillars of their religion. Has apathy stricken their senses, so that they are insensitive to one another's needs? Should not each consider his brother with the Koranic precept of "the Muslims are brethren," so that they set up together the union to stem the waves threatening them from all sides?

I am not implying that one person ought to rule all [Muslims]; this is difficult, perhaps. I do hope, however, that the Koran would be their ruler and religion the focal point of their union; that every leader would do his utmost to preserve the others, since his own life and survival depends on them. Not only is this a pillar of religion, but a necessity, also. The time for an agreement has come! The time for an agreement has come!

Source: Jamal al-Din al-Afghani, "Islamic Union" (from *al-Urwah al-Wuthqa*) in Jacob Landau, *The Politics of Pan-Islam: Ideology and Organization* (Oxford: Clarendon Press, 1990), appendix B, 318–320, as reproduced with American spellings and brackets in *The Middle East and Islamic World Reader*, Marvin Gettleman and Stuart Schaar, eds. (New York: Grove Press, 2003), 98–99.

2. DAVID STARR JORDAN, "IMPERIAL DEMOCRACY" (1898)

Citizens in imperial nations like the United States were also vocal in their protests. David Starr Jordan, a scientist, became the founding president of Stanford University after being tapped to be president of Indiana University at age 34. For Starr, the "control of nation by nation" was like slavery: "each has industrial and civil good as its avowed purpose and each has brute force as its method."[1] Thus Starr gave many lectures—the excerpt presented here is one he gave to students at Stanford in 1898—describing the ways in which imperialism would cause the nation to decay. He saw patriotism as being a feeling that necessitated taking on another nation and making a big central government to do so. Instead he preferred a democratic United States based on a strong individual of character and talent developed in the homeland, not in military adventures. Those conquered, he also believed, would always remain inferior. There were thus various and complex arguments against empire worldwide. What were Jordan's main disagreements with imperialism?

. . . There are three main reasons for opposing every step toward imperialism. First, dominion is brute force; second, dependent nations are slave nations; third, the making of men is greater than the building of empires.

As to the first of these: The extension of dominion rests on the strength of arms. Men who cannot hold town meetings must obey through brute force. In Alaska, for example, our occupation is a farce and scandal. Only force can make it otherwise. Only by force can the masses of Hawaii or Cuba be held to industry and order. To furnish such power, we shall need a colonial bureau, with its force of extra-national police. A large army and navy must justify itself by doing something. Army and navy we must maintain for our own defense, but beyond that they can do little that does not hurt, and they must be used if they would be kept alive. Even warfare for humanity falls to the level of other wars, and all wars according to Benjamin Franklin, are bad, some worse than others. The rescue of the oppressed is only accomplished by the use of force against the oppressor. The lofty purposes of humanity are forgotten in the joy of struggle and the pride of conquest.

---

[1]David Starr Jordan, *Imperial Democracy* (New York: D. Appleton, 1901), viii.

It is not true that the government "which is best administered is best." That is the maxim of tyranny. That government is best which makes the best men. In the training of manhood lies the certain pledge of better government in the future. The civic problems of the future will be greater than those of the past. They will concern not the relations of nation to nation, but of man to man. The policing of far-off islands, the herding of baboons and elephants, the maintenance of the machinery of imperialism are petty things beside the duties which the higher freedom demands. To turn to these empty and showy affairs, is to neglect our own business for the gossip of our neighbors. Such work may be a matter of necessity; it should not be a source of pride. The political greatness of England has never lain in her navies nor the force of her arms. It has lain in her struggles for individual freedom. . . . The pomp of imperialism, the display of naval power, the commercial control of India and China,—all these are as the "bread and circuses" by which the Roman emperors held the mob from their thrones. They keep the people busy and put off the day of final reckoning. . . .

National ambitions, national hopes, national aggrandizement—all these may become public nuisances. Imperialism, like feudalism, belongs to the past.

Source: David Starr Jordan, *Imperial Democracy* (New York: D. Appleton, 1901), 31, 33–34, 36.

3. MALAN BOXER PROCLAMATION (1900)

Other forces of resistance emerged. Drought and famine struck northern China as it had struck parts of Asia, Africa, and Latin America late in the nineteenth century. The conditions further weakened resistance to imperial takeover, but the Boxers—a group that practiced martial arts and spiritual strengthening to ward off enemies— began attacking Chinese Christians, missionaries, and foreign officials as the cause of China's problems. They sent placards from village to village to raise awareness that foreigners were at the root of all evils in the Qing Empire and stirred up rebellion across the region. Eight of the imperial powers sent troops to slaughter the Boxers and to take further control of the still weakening Chinese empire. The joint occupation was an example of increasing global cooperation among empires to seize resources, even as they became increasingly competitive. What are the Boxers' grievances and what in their opinion will restore Chinese well-being?

Public Notice of Malan Village the Kan Army (Wanping County in Beijing Suburb)

Since the Xianfeng reign [1851–1861], Catholics have been conspiring with foreigners; causing chaos in China; squandering the state's revenue; tearing down temples and monasteries; destroying Buddhist statues; and taking over people's graveyards. Such evil acts have aroused hatred far and wide. They have also caused swarms of locusts and droughts which harm the trees and plants. Our country is no longer harmonious and the Chinese people are no longer secure. This has angered Heaven.

Blessed by the great god in Heaven, all the spirits have descended to set up an altar. They will teach our young men how to support the Qing, eliminate the foreigners, and implement virtuous principles on behalf of Heaven. We want to contribute to the country so that it will be at peace; and to help the peasants so that the villages and neighborhoods are safe. In the end, misfortune will come to an end while prosperity returns. Yet, we worry that ignorant people and hooligans will use the support of the foreigners to mistreat the weak. All such behavior should be reported to the local leaders to be dealt with publicly and in accordance with the laws and regulations. It is forbidden to resolve the matter in a purely selfish manner. The eyes of the gods are as sharp as lightening and will see those who are pursuing the cases purely with selfish motives and will punish them accordingly.

The false methods perpetrated by the deluded foreign missionaries have angered Heaven who has ordered the spirits to descend to the divine altar in order to teach the youth. The meaning of Yihetuan (Boxer) is as follows: *yi* means benevolent and *he* means unified. Benevolence and unity keep villages and neighborhoods peaceful and harmonious. Virtue is the foundation of living. Agriculture is the means by which we make a living. Buddhism is the religion that we should follow. Public matters should not to be handled with selfish aims of revenge. It is not allowed to mistreat the poor and the weak. No one should mistake wrong for right.

Source: *Sources in Chinese History: Diverse Perspectives from 1644 to the Present*, David G. Atwell and Yurong Y. Atwill, eds. (Upper Saddle River, NJ: Prentice Hall, 2009), 105.

4. ZITKALA-SA, ESSAY (1900)

Zitkala-Sa (Red Bird, 1876–1938) was a Sioux author, sent as a child along with others from her Native American community to a white missionary school where she was renamed Gertrude and after her marriage became Gertrude Simmons Bonnin. The idea behind this renaming and then reprogramming was to give Native Americans knowledge of "civilization" and to prepare them for low-level work in the U.S. economy. Zitkala-Sa wanted more, keeping the values of her own culture but also learning to play the violin and piano and to become an author. She rejected the "menial" future white Americans wanted for her. In addition to writing her memoir of this experience, Zitkala-Sa wrote many Native American stories and co-produced the first Native American opera and founded the National Council of American Indians in 1926—two years after passage of the law granting many Native Americans the rights to citizenship. Resistance and adaptation joined one another in many a life. What is your evaluation of this educational system?

Iron Routine

A loud-clamoring bell awakened us at half-past six in the cold winter mornings. From happy dreams of Western rolling lands and unlassoed freedom we tumbled out upon chilly bare floors back again into a paleface day. We had short time to jump into our shoes and clothes, and wet our eyes with icy water, before a small hand bell was vigorously rung for roll call.

There were too many drowsy children and too numerous orders for the day to waste a moment in any apology to nature for giving her children such a shock in the early morning. We rushed downstairs, bounding over two high steps at a time, to land in the assembly room.

A paleface woman, with a yellow-covered roll book open on her arm and a gnawed pencil in her hand, appeared at the door. Her small, tired face was coldly lighted with a pair of large gray eyes.

She stood still in a halo of authority, while over the rim of her spectacles her eyes pried nervously about the room. Having glanced at her long list of names and called out the first one, she tossed up her chin and peered through the crystals of her spectacles to make sure of the answer "Here."

Relentlessly her pencil black-marked our daily records if we were not present to respond to our names, and no chum of ours had done it successfully for us. No matter if a dull headache or the painful cough of slow consumption had delayed the absentee, there was only time enough to mark the tardiness. It was next to impossible to leave the iron routine after the civilizing machine had once begun its day's buzzing; and as it was inbred in me to suffer in silence rather than to appeal to the ears of one whose open eyes could not see my pain, I have many times trudged in the day's harness heavy-footed, like a dumb sick brute.

Once I lost a dear classmate. I remember well how she used to mope along at my side, until one morning she could not raise her head from her pillow. At her deathbed I stood weeping, as the paleface woman sat near her moistening the dry lips. Among the folds of the bedclothes I saw the open pages of the white man's Bible. The dying Indian girl talked disconnectedly of Jesus the Christ and the paleface who was cooling her swollen hands and feet.

I grew bitter, and censured the woman for cruel neglect of our physical ills. I despised the pencils that moved automatically, and the one teaspoon which dealt out, from a large bottle, healing to a row of variously ailing Indian children. I blamed the hard-working, well-meaning, ignorant woman who was inculcating in our hearts her superstitious ideas. Though I was sullen in all my little troubles, as soon as I felt better I was ready again to smile upon the cruel woman. Within a week I was again actively testing the chains which tightly bound my individuality like a mummy for burial.

The melancholy of those black days has left so long a shadow that it darkens the path of years that have since gone by. These sad memories rise above those of smoothly grinding school days. Perhaps my Indian nature is the moaning wind which stirs them now for their present record. But, however tempestuous this is within me, it comes out as the low voice of a curiously colored seashell, which is only for those ears that are bent with compassion to hear it.

Source: Gertrude Simmons Bonnin/Zitkala-Sa, "School Days of an Indian Girl," *Atlantic Monthly*, Vol. 0085, No. 58 (February 1900), 190.

5. ROGER CASEMENT, CORRESPONDENCE
AND REPORT FROM HIS MAJESTY'S COUNSEL
AT BOMA RESPECTING THE ADMINISTRATION OF THE
INDEPENDENT STATE OF THE CONGO (1903)

Britain, like the United States, did not lack citizens critical of empire. Emily Hobhouse had studied and publicized the death rate in concentration camps into which the British had forced the Boers and Africans. Missionaries published pictures of Africans whose hands had been amputated for not producing enough rubber. Others circulated images of starving humans in India, for whom the government had refused to provide food during famine. Reformers and pacifists took up the humanitarian cause and conducted investigations. The Irish nationalist Roger Casement had first gone to the Congo in 1890, working for the African International Association—a group intended to cover King Leopold's rapacious treatment of the Congo and its inhabitants. Casement joined the British government, ultimately producing the report that follows. Critics of the report said that it drew attention from the horrors of empire across Africa more generally to focus all outrage on the Congo instead of opposing abuse everywhere. What is your opinion of this assessment?

"It used to take ten days to get the twenty baskets of rubber—we were always in the forest and then when we were late we were killed. We had to go further and further into the forest to find the rubber vines, to go without food, and our women had to give up cultivating the fields and gardens. Then we starved. Wild beasts— the leopards—killed some of us when we were working away in the forest, and others got lost or died from exposure and starvation and we begged the white men to leave us alone, saying we could get no more rubber, but the white men and their soldiers said: "Go! You are only beasts yourselves, you are only nyama (meat)." We tried, always going further into the forest, and when we failed and our rubber was short, the soldiers came to our towns and killed us. Many were shot, some had their ears cut off; others were tied up with ropes round their necks and bodies and taken away. The white men sometimes at the posts did not know of the bad things the soldiers did to us, but it was the white men who sent the soldiers to punish us for not bringing in enough rubber."

"We said to the white man: 'We are not enough people now to do what you want of us. Our country has not many people in it and we are dying fast. We are killed by the work you make us do, by the stoppage of our plantations, and the breaking up of our homes.'

. . . We fled because we could not endure the things done to us. Our Chiefs were hanged and we were killed and starved and worked beyond endurance to get rubber."

Q.: "How do you know it was the white men themselves who ordered these cruel things to be done to you? These things must have been done without the white men's knowledge by the black soldiers."

A. (P.P.): "The white men told their soldiers: 'You kill only women; you cannot kill men. You must prove that you kill men.' So then the soldiers when they killed us" (here he stopped and hesitated, and then pointing to the private parts of my bulldog—it was lying asleep at my feet) he said: "then they cut off those things and took them to the white men, who said: 'It is true, you have killed men.'"

Source: *Correspondence and Report from His Majesty's Counsel at Boma Respecting the Administration of the Independent State of the Congo.* Cd 1933 [Command Paper no. 1933] (London: Harrison and Sons, 1904), 60–61.

6. COUNT SHIGENOBU OKUMA, "THE RISE OF JAPAN WAS NOT UNEXPECTED" (1904)

In 1904–5, Japan defeated Russia in a war over territory in East Asia. The Russians had been expanding for some five centuries in the region and believed that claiming further rights in Manchuria, around Korea, and other adjacent lands was natural. The Japanese saw Russian expansion not only as a menace to their safety but as an incursion into areas to which they had a more legitimate natural right. While Europeans were stunned by the defeat of a member of their Great Power constellation, colonized peoples and others struggling to escape the imperial grip were elated and actually galvanized to action. For their part, the Japanese felt that their triumph resulted from decades of reform, hard work, and modernization in addition to their innate, superior values. How does this Japanese leader compare his nation's imperial success with the situation of European powers?

. . . The recent development and prosperity of the Japanese Empire is no sudden and unexpected event which has come before the world without any adequate cause or reason for its coming into existence. It is the necessary outcome of certain causes well known to all who have studied our national history. . . .

Any nation, no matter what its constitution or form of Government may be, will prosper so long as it keeps itself swimming with the great current of human thought: to attempt to stem the current or swim against it, involves national ruin. . . .

At the end of the Middle Ages, we find the people of Spain and Portugal full of a vigorous spirit of adventure: the discovery of America, the circumnavigation of the Cape of Good Hope, the opening of the new trade routes to India, were all due to their energy, and brought them into intimate relations with the peoples of the Far East. Spanish settlements were to be found in every quarter of the globe, and the name of Spain was feared and respected over the whole continent of Europe. But her ruin soon came. The whole extent of her power scarcely covered two centuries of pleasant but profitless dreams. . . .

The same phenomenon may be observed in the case of Holland, more distinctly still in that of Turkey. Turkey was a great power in the fifteenth century . . . but the Renaissance and Revival of Learning, which her arrival at Constantinople brought to Western Europe, she rejected for herself. She turned her back deliberately on the modern civilization and culture that was coming. . . .

Russia is now following the bad examples of these countries: the same poison is at work in her political and social system. . . .

If now you will turn to the history of Japan, you will be able to see at a glance why it is that this Empire has always been so successful in all her undertakings. It is because our nation has always acted from the beginning on the principle . . . of . . . adopting what is good from every country, and entering into an honorable rivalry in culture and civilization with all nations throughout the world.

This is the fundamental principle which accounts for the rise of Japan in the world; she has never hesitated to adopt anything that she has found to be good; she has ever tried to swim with the tide of human progress; she has never shrunk from any sacrifice in eradicating what she has found to be bad. The voice of the people can make itself heard in . . . a liberal form of governmental administration . . . illuminated and guided by knowledge sought throughout the world, has rendered possible the granting of a wise and just Constitution and Body of Laws, and Representative Government co-existent with a large measure of local autonomy, the execution of Juridical Reforms, the abolition of vexatious restrictions on commerce and the free development of every form of national life. . . .

For more than thirty years, the Government of Japan has devoted a very large amount of attention and energy to the question of education, and the best training that could be procured has been given with a generous hand to students of political, social and military affairs, as well as for those preparing themselves for humbler but no less important walks of life in commerce, industry, and agriculture. . . .

The Japanese people . . . has no mean skill in agriculture, industry, and commerce, and if you will take the trouble to investigate the statistical tables of progress throughout the Empire, you will find that the national wealth has increased six or seven fold during the last thirty years, and that if you compare the present wealth of the country with what it was at the conclusion of the Japan-China War ten years ago. . . . The utilization of the Chinese War indemnity added immensely to the permanent wealth of the nation. . . .

The origin of our modern Japanese development must not be sought in the opening of the country half a century ago. If you read her history for the last two thousand five hundred years you will find that her people have always possessed in a very high degree the power of assimilation. Japan came into contact first with the civilization of China, and assimilated it, without any trouble. When some years later the Buddhism of India invaded Japan through China, her native Shinto found a way to make room amicably for the new-comer. . . .

During the 216 years of her seclusion from the world, Japan was quietly developing her internal resources, and her treasures of national literature and vigor. . . .

When peace shall have crowned the efforts which Japan is making in the present war, the effect upon herself will be that she will be able to make still greater progress in the paths of civilization, and that the true spirit of the Japanese nation will have more room to display itself. Japan has never been an advocate of war, and will never draw her sword from its sheath unless compelled to do so by the pressure of foreign powers. We are fighting now for peace and not for war; and when peace is secured we shall be only too glad to put by the sword and devote ourselves to the promotion of the higher interests of our country.

I think, Gentlemen, that if you will study the history of the country, you will find that the present eminence of our country . . . has its roots in the past. . . . I hope, too, that many foreigners may be induced to devote attention to the history of Japan. They will then understand that the present war is not one of race against race or religion against religion, but that the victory of Japan means the fusion into one harmonious whole of the civilizations of East and West.

Source: Shigenobu Okuma, "The Rise of Japan Was Not Unexpected," in *The Russo-Japanese War Fully Illustrated* (Tokyo: Kinkodo, 1904), 347–350, 352–354.

7. MARGARETHE VON ECKENBRECHER, "STORMY WEATHER" (1908)

Margarethe von Eckenbrecher (1875–1955) settled in German Southwest Africa with her husband in 1902. It was a territory she believed to be her own by rights, even after Germany lost the colony as a result of World War I. Early in the twentieth century the Herero ethnic group in Southwestern Africa refused to turn over to Germany the lands, on which its herds of cattle traditionally grazed. They thus rose up against German confiscations, ordered and executed with grim brutality. Ultimately the Herero were defeated and forced from their lands into starvation, while the von Eckenbrecher family lost some of its property and returned to Germany. Later, having divorced her husband in 1913, Margarethe von Eckenbrecher returned with her sons to a region she believed her own. She wrote her memoir of life in Southwest Africa, including an account of the Herero. Assess von Eckenbrecher's account of the situation in Southwest Africa.

. . . [W]e were discussing a journey we had been planning with the deputy chief, Joshua, when he broke in with, "I have a feeling that you will not get far. Stay here."

"What makes you think that?"

"You white people shouldn't think that you are safe here, in the country of the black people. It is written up there in the clouds: Our Lord God will send a terrible war which will devastate the land and kill the whites." We regarded these words as boasts and foolish gossip.

A song by my poetically inclined washerwoman, Emma, made me sit up and listen, "You poor white people. You will die in this country after all. You little child, it's not your fault that you were born here. But you also must die. I am crying and my son is crying, but there is nothing we can do."

"Emma, what are you singing about?"

"Oh nothing, Madam, I am singing what my silly thoughts tell me. You should not listen."

And yet another occasion: "Madam, do you sleep well?"

"Yes, thank you, very well."

"I'm sorry."

"Why?"

"It would be better if you did not sleep well. Put some pebbles between your ribs. You must not sleep deeply."

Samuel, Emma's son, who had accompanied us to Gui-Gams months before, came onto the veranda one day and stared at me. "Why are you looking at me like that?"

"Oh Madam, I am looking at the ones marked by death." I took note of this and discussed it with Ertmann and my husband who were getting ready for a major journey. "Would you not rather stay here?"

"Heaven forbid, no."

"All the same, these things have the ring of hidden warnings. I cannot interpret them." . . .

We were all conscious of the fact that there had been a search for weapons and ammunition at several large Herero settlements the year before and that the efforts had been successful. The Hereros, habitually violent and overbearing, had become even more arrogant. A few behaved in an insubordinate manner towards us whites. At their settlements, where one used to receive a friendly welcome, one now got an ice-cold reception. The possibility of a revolt was in the air. With so few troops in the north, now seemed to be the most opportune moment in time. If the Hereros were considering an uprising at all, it had to be soon. We made all sorts of guesses.

Even the government received warnings. However, it also took a very optimistic viewpoint. It was indeed fortunate that the troops designated to return home had not yet embarked for the voyage when the revolt of the Bondelzwarts broke out. . . .

[My husband] had been gone half a day, when a messenger from Omaruru appeared in front of our house, on horseback and dripping with perspiration. He had to deliver draft papers. All the reserves were being called up. . . . There were rumours of large gatherings, mysterious messages and lively traffic between all the settlements.

I had no choice but to have my husband called back. My most trust-worthy messenger reached him and Themis returned by the evening of the second day. He just had enough time to barricade a window in the bedroom and to move some items of furniture, so that I could at least not be shot from the window while I was asleep. He had to stay at the station day and night in order to be able to defend it if the need arose.

I myself, on the other hand, was left to my fate, completely alone in the house with my small child.

I was really upset by the harshness of that order. We, the wives of the settlers, irrespective of our social standing, shared the fate of our husbands in times of peace. We suffered with them, even hunger and thirst. Like our husbands, we put all our strength at the service of the colony. Our children were born under the most difficult conditions. We had to endure more in the colony than would have been conceivable in Germany—and now, in the hour of danger, my husband was taken away from me.

Ten days and ten nights I stayed alone with no one except my nine-year-old servant Isaac, whom I put up in the kitchen so that someone could at least hold the child for me once in a while.

During the day, I had to do all the chores, including my husband's. At night I was left to my own devices. Several times my dogs barked fiercely. I got up thinking that a hyena or some other predator was disturbing the livestock. Because I saw nothing, I turned back. The next morning Isaac showed me fresh footprints in the sand round the house and in the garden. Whether kaffirs or Hereros, they had certainly tried to steal something. The lambs got lost, a calf disappeared mysteriously. I was powerless. And my husband was just twenty minutes away and could not help me.

Nevertheless, things were going to get even worse. At midday on 13 January, two Hereros, whom I knew quite well, arrived with their servants. They wanted to sell a sheep to me. I noticed that the men, six in all, were armed. Two carried guns, the servants had knobkerries. Even in times of peace it happens that one is visited by armed people. But then they lean their weapons on the outside wall of the house as an indication of their peaceful intentions. This time, however, they kept holding them in their hands.

I was not in the mood to buy the sheep. There was no money in the house and we had run out of suitable articles for exchange long ago. They asked for two shirts. In order to get rid of the fellows, I agreed. Since I was completely unsuspecting, I thought no evil when they followed me into the house. We soon came to an agreement and we talked like always after concluding even the smallest business deal. The conversation revolved round the impending revolution.

Geert Afrika, the oldest of the Hereros, asked me, "Do you think it is right that the Hereros want to start a war against the whites?" I answered truthfully that it would be an extremely foolish enterprise in my opinion, because the white man would win under any conditions whatever.

"And what do you think will happen?"

"If you are that imprudent and do start, then a lot of blood will be shed, you will lose land and livestock, and your lives will be in the hands of the white man."

Then another fellow said, "Oh, don't you worry. We are the servants of the white man. The lion who sleeps does not know when danger approaches."

Thereupon they all grinned and, at a casually dropped word from Geert Afrika, two people stood in front of each of the two doors in order to cut off the exit unobtrusively. All at once I became aware of the danger and the seriousness of my position.

Geert Afrika stepped right up close to me, laughing and shouting in my face, "Now we'll have the real talk about the war, you'll see." My heart was beating violently. I forced myself to be calm. There was no help at hand, if I did not help myself. I pulled myself together, "You come to do business with me and you don't know how to behave towards a white woman? Make way, you scoundrel." I pushed past him and went to the door. There I had expected resistance. However, both of the fellows were so surprised that they moved aside without waiting for the push I had intended to give them. In no time the door flew open towards the outside—I was outside.

There I was safe. There they could do nothing to me because the place was crowded with Bergdamaras. They would not have dared to shoot inside either. A blow of the knobkerrie is silent, however. That was what I had expected.

I stopped in front of the store. Geert came out grinning. He lifted his floppy hat, "This time the madam was clever. She was cleverer than we were. It doesn't matter. The time is near when she will hear from me again." . . .

Never in my life have I felt so utterly deserted as I did at that moment. And yet, I had to be grateful that I had been alone at the time when the Hereros came. If my husband had been there, they would probably have clubbed him to death mercilessly inside the house.

Source: *Women Writing Africa: The Southern Region*, M. J. Daymond et al., eds. (New York: Feminist Press, 2003), 148–152.

8. PETITION OF THE NATIVE AND COLOURED WOMEN OF THE PROVINCE OF THE ORANGE FREE STATE, "PETITION" (1912)

The Boers, descendants of the original Dutch settlers of southern Africa, established the Orange Free State in 1854 after waging war against established African kingdoms. When the British conquered them in the Boer War in 1902, the Orange Free State became part of Britain's South African colony. In the 1890s, before their defeat, the Boers had enacted a "Pass law" decreeing that all African women had to carry government registration cards that would allow police to check their movements. In effect, police, employers, and officials used these cards to restrict local women's general access to the public sphere and to limit their ability to find jobs freely. Far from being uninstructed and passive, as colonial officials declared women to be—and wanted them to be—African women in the Orange province of British South Africa organized a petition and undertook demonstrations against the law during which they burned their passes. The result was immediate imprisonment, but the activism established a tradition of women's protest against Boer and British violence against local peoples. Describe their arguments against the pass laws.

(a) It renders them liable to interference by any policeman at any time, and in that way deprives them of that liberty enjoyed by their women-folk in other Provinces.

(b) It does not afford them that protection which may, peradventure, have been contemplated by the legislators, but on the other hand it subjects them to taxation, notwithstanding the sex to which they belong—a policy which was unknown in the late South African Republic, and is unknown in the history of British Rule.

(c) It has a barbarous tendency of ignoring the consequences of marriage in respect of natives, especially the right of parents to control their children, a right which parents ought to exercise without interference from out-side; and the effect of its operation upon the minds of our children is that it inculcates upon them the idea that as soon as they become liable to comply with the requirements of this law, their age of majority also com-mences, and can, therefore, act independently of their parents.

(d) It is an effective means of enforcing labour, and as such, cannot have any justification whatever on the ground of necessity or expediency.

(e) It lowers the dignity of women and throws to pieces every element of respect to which they are entitled; and for this reason it has no claim to recognition as a just, progressive and protective law, necessary for their elevation in the scale of civilization; moreover it does not improve their social status.

(f) It can only have one ground for its existence in that Statute Book—namely, that it is a most effective weapon the governing powers could resort to make the natives and coloured women in the Province of the Orange Free State ever feel their inferiority, which is only another way of perpetuating oppression regarless of the feelings of those who are gov-erned; whereas the essence of justice is "Do unto others as you would be done by."

1. Your petitioners are the only women in the whole of the Union who are subjected to such an oppressive law; the women in the other provinces are not subjected to any Pass Laws.

Source: Native and Coloured Women of the Province of the Orange Free State, "Petition," 1912 from the National Archives of South Africa, Pretoria, Transvaal Archives Depot, National Archives Reposi-tory [Ref: GG1542 50/284], as reproduced in M. J. Daymond et al., eds., *Women Writing Africa: The Southern Region* (New York: Feminist Press, 2003), 159–161.

9. QIU JIN, AN ADDRESS TO TWO HUNDRED MILLION FELLOW COUNTRYWOMEN (ND)

Reforming the lives of women rippled through global ideas, imperial thought, and nation-building across the centuries. Imperial powers in Europe as well as the United States pointed to the condition of women in colonies or areas they wanted to colonize as inferior to women's condition among "civilized" nations. This was the imperialists' rationale for conquest and colonization. Some Western feminists, however, pointed to facts showing that in many instances women had more rights outside the "West." Still, the conviction somehow grew that those in imperial countries were better off despite their poverty, lack of rights, and the persistent violence against them. In China, reformers picked up on the need to improve women's condition to make their country as strong as the West and Japan. Reformers such as Qiu Jin (1875–1907) traveled to Japan to gain an education and to become more informed politically. Returning to China, Qiu Jin was eventually executed for her activism. What does Qiu Jin believe women need to do to help strengthen China's empire?

Alas! The greatest injustice in this world must be the injustice suffered by our female population of two hundred million. If a girl is lucky enough to have a good father, then her childhood is at least tolerable. But if by chance her father is an ill-tempered and unreasonable man, he may curse her birth: "What rotten luck: another useless thing." Some men go as far as killing baby girls while most hold the opinion that "girls are eventually someone else's property" and treat them with coldness and disdain. In a few years, without thinking about whether it is right or wrong, he forcibly binds his daughter's soft, white feet with white cloth so that even in her sleep she cannot find comfort and relief until the flesh becomes rotten and the bones broken. What is all this misery for? Is it just so that on the girl's wedding day friends and neighbors will compliment him, saying, "Your daughter's feet are really small"? Is that what the pain is for? . . .

Dear sisters, you must know that you'll get nothing if you rely upon others. You must go out and get things for yourselves. In ancient times when decadent scholars came out with such nonsense as "men are exalted, women are lowly," "a virtuous woman is one without talent," and "the husband guides the wife," ambitious and spirited women should have organized and opposed them. When the second Ch'en ruler popularized footbinding, women should have challenged him if they had any sense of humiliation at all. . . . Men feared that if women were educated they would become superior to men, so they did not allow us to be educated. Couldn't the women have challenged the men and refused to submit? It seems clear now that it was we women who abandoned our responsibilities to ourselves and felt content to let men do everything for us. As long as we could live in comfort and leisure, we let men make all the decisions for us. . . .

When we heard that men liked small feet, we immediately bound them just to please them, just to keep our free meal tickets. As for their forbidding us to read and write, well, that was only too good to be true. We readily agreed. Think about it, sisters, can anyone enjoy such comfort and leisure without forfeiting dearly for it? It was only natural that men, with their knowledge, wisdom, and hard work, received the right to freedom while we became their slaves. . . .

I hope that we all shall put aside the past and work hard for the future. Let us all put aside our former selves and be resurrected as complete human beings. Those of you who are old, do not call yourselves old and useless. If your husbands want to open schools, don't stop them; if your good sons want to study abroad, don't hold them back. Those among us who are middle-aged, don't hold back your husbands lest they lose their ambition and spirit and fail in their work. After your sons are born, send them to schools. You must do the same for your daughters and, whatever you do, don't bind their feet. As for you young girls among us, go to school if you can. If not, read and study at home. Those of you who are rich, persuade your husbands to open schools, build factories, and contribute to charitable organizations. Those of you who are poor, work hard and help your husbands. Don't be lazy, don't eat idle rice. These are what I hope for you. You must know that when a country is near destruction, women cannot rely on the men any more because they aren't even able to protect themselves. If we don't take heart now and shape up, it will be too late when China is destroyed.

Sisters, we must follow through on these ideas!

Source: *Chinese Civilization and Society. A Sourcebook*, Patricia Buckley Ebrey, ed. (New York: The Free Press, 1981), 247–248. *Translated by Nancy Gibbs.*

10. RUDYARD KIPLING,
"THE WIDOW AT WINDSOR" (1892)

Rudyard Kipling was born in Mumbai (Bombay), India where his father was a professor of art. Although his family sent him to England for his education, he was seen as unfit for university and returned to India to become a journalist. In this capacity Kipling came to view people in India, including its soldiers, children, and ordinary folks, as complicated and human. These complications became the stuff of his poetry and fiction such as "Kim" and "Jungle Book," which grew in popularity in the 1890s and thereafter. He celebrated the entry of the United States into the overseas imperial system, urging its citizens to "Take Up the White Man's Burden" in one of his most famous (and presently criticized) poems (1899). Yet Kipling was full of paradox, writing "Recessional" in 1897, which sentimentally foresaw the demise of empires such as the British as part of a cycle of rise and fall. Before that, however, he wrote "The Widow at Windsor," describing the downside of empire, especially for soldiers. His work thus echoed the complex feelings about empire—both pro and con and in-between—prevalent at the turn of the century. Note that he drops the "h" at the beginning of words and occasionally a "d" or "f" at the end to capture the accent of ordinary soldiers. What are Kipling's attitudes toward the British Empire?

'AVE you 'eard o' the Widow at Windsor
With a hairy gold crown on 'er 'ead?
She 'as ships on the foam—she 'as millions at 'ome,
An' she pays us poor beggars in red.
(Ow, poor beggars in red!)

There's 'er nick on the cavalry 'orses,
There's 'er mark on the medical stores—
An' 'er troopers you'll find with a fair wind be'ind
That takes us to various wars.
(Poor beggars!—barbarious wars!)

Then 'ere's to the Widow at Windsor,
An' 'ere's to the stores an' the guns,
The men an' the 'orses what makes up the forces
O' Missis Victorier's sons.
(Poor beggars! Victorier's sons!)

Walk wide o' the Widow at Windsor,
For 'alf o' Creation she owns:
We 'ave bought 'er the same with the sword an' the flame,
An' we've salted it down with our bones.
(Poor beggars!—it's blue with our bones!)

Hands off o' the sons o' the Widow,
Hands off o' the goods in 'er shop,
For the Kings must come down an' the Emperors frown
When the Widow at Windsor says "Stop"!
(Poor beggars!—we're sent to say "Stop"!)

Then 'ere's to the Lodge o' the Widow,
From the Pole to the Tropics it runs—
To the Lodge that we tile with the rank an' the file,
An' open in form with the guns.
(Poor beggars!—it's always they guns!)

We 'ave 'eard o' the Widow at Windsor,
It's safest to let 'er alone:
For 'er sentries we stand by the sea an' the land
Wherever the bugles are blown.
(Poor beggars!—an' don't we get blown!)

Take 'old o' the Wings o' the Mornin',
An' flop round the earth till you're dead;
But you won't get away from the tune that they play
To the bloomin' old rag over'ead.
(Poor beggars!—it's 'ot over'ead!)

Then 'ere's to the sons o' the Widow,
Wherever, 'owever they roam.
'Ere's all they desire, an' if they require
A speedy return to their 'ome.
(Poor beggars!—they'll never see 'ome!)

Source: Widely available on the Internet.

11. SUN YAT-SEN, THE PURPOSE OF OUR REVOLUTION[2] (1905)

Even as Kipling wrote his poems questioning empires and yet praising them, Sun Yat-sen (1866–1925) was championing the conversion of the deteriorating Qing empire into a modern Chinese nation by overthrowing the rule of foreigners of the Manchu dynasty.

---

[2]This is the editorial that appeared in the first issue of The People (Min pao), the organ of The Alliance for Chinese Revolution (Chung-kuo ko-ming t'ung-meng hui), on November 17, 1905. Translated from a photographed copy of the original that appears in The Pictorial Biography of Dr. Sun Yat-sen (Kuo-fu hua-chuan) (Taipei, 1954) by Lo Chia-lun, p. 43.

Foreign states, as we have seen, also sought to gain territory, resources, or other benefits from the empire's decline. On the one hand, Sun became a medical doctor, testifying to his belief in Western science; on the other by the 1890s he abandoned science to launch a series of Western-style revolutions to bring China a nationalist (non-Manchu), democratic, and capitalist-oriented government. After a series of failed revolutions, in 1912 he and his allies caused the Qing emperor to abdicate, as Sun briefly became president in the midst of chaos. Here is his editorial in the inaugural edition of The People (1905) describing his program around which people should unify in the cause of China's rebirth.

As I see it, the progress of the Euro-American society can be expressed in terms of three main ideas, namely, nationalism, democracy, and people's livelihood. Nationalism came about after the fall of the Roman Empire and in due course gave birth to the rise of national states. In each of the national states all power was concentrated in the hands of one man, namely, the king, whose autocratic conduct and abuse of power resulted in unbearable suffering by the people and, in time, paved the way for the rise of the principle of democracy. Towards the end of the eighteenth century and early in the nineteenth century, absolute monarchies fell one after another and were replaced by constitutional governments. As the Western world became more and more enlightened, intellectual achievement progressed side by side with material prosperity at such a pace that what once took one millennium to achieve was then attained in one century. Economic problems persisted, however, and the persistence of these problems gave birth to the principle of people's livelihood. One might even say that the twentieth century is the century of the principle of people's livelihood. These three principles—nationalism, democracy, and people's livelihood—formulated to serve the needs of the people, have taken turns to play a central role in the development of the Euro-American society and have in fact been primarily responsible for pushing its civilization ahead. All ideologies, whether on a personal or group basis, are merely elaborations or ramifications of these three basic principles.

While it is clear that there should be no delay in beginning our national and democratic revolution in view of the present circumstances, such as thousands of years of autocratic rule, oppression by an alien people,[3] and intensified encroachment of China by foreign powers, it should also be kept in mind that the causes of social revolution which have accumulated for a long time in Europe and the United States and which have not become serious in China should also be given adequate attention. . . . While we are concentrating on the principles of nationalism and democracy, we should by no means neglect the principle of people's livelihood. A man who walks on a low ground cannot see very far; it is indeed sad to see that people travel all around the world, buy the most beautiful clothes they can find simply because they happen to be fashionable, and never ask themselves whether they really fit. We do not deny that these people are seriously concerned with the welfare of China; yet they argue persistently that to build a strong China, we have to imitate Europe and the United States. They do not realize that strong as the Western powers are, their people remain poor. Labor strikes are frequent, and

[3]The Manchus.

the anarchists and the socialists have become increasingly active. In the near future a social revolution is bound to take place. Even if we did succeed in imitating Europe and the United States by successfully completing our political revolution, there is no assurance that there will not be a second or social revolution sometime in the future. In short, there is serious doubt as to whether we can achieve our own goals by following a path which has been traveled by others. The seeds of evils in the Euro-American society were sown several decades ago, and such evils cannot be easily disposed of even after they have been discovered. If we can foresee these evils before they occur and prevent their occurrence by practicing the principle of people's livelihood, we can kill two birds with one stone and thus complete political and social revolution at the same time. The day will arrive when we will look over our shoulder and find Europe and America lagging behind.

China is the largest country in the world, and the Chinese can be compared favorably with any other people in intelligence and native ability. Yet this country has been in a long slumber and has refused to wake up. Meanwhile everything about and around her has gone from bad to worse. Fortunately, under the impact of the drastic change of events in recent years, she is now opening her eyes; in fact, she is fighting hard to rejuvenate herself so once more she can become strong. As long as she remains in a fighting mood, she may achieve in five years what normally takes a decade. To be sure, we need leaders. Since our country is so large, there is bound to be a small group of selfless people who are not only capable of assuming leadership but also know the most appropriate methods to push our progress ahead, methods that comform with the unique situation in China as well as with the general trend of the world. These are men of foresight and vision who believe that they have a great duty to perform. It is in this spirit that this publication, *The People*, is founded. It is hoped that revolutionary ideas, however strange or radical they may sound, will become commonplace after they have been made familiar. Once an idea becomes commonplace, it will not be long before it can be put into practice. The very appearance of this publication is witness to the soundness of this statement.

Source: *China in Transition: 1517–1911*, Dun J. Li, ed. (New York: Van Nostrand Reinhold co., 1969), 317–319.

12. WASSILY KANDINSKY, *CONCERNING THE SPIRITUAL IN ART* (1911)

In the late nineteenth century and early in the twentieth, painting in Europe and the United States increasingly stopped trying to present a realistic depiction of life. Instead, it became hazy and looked only approximately real—if one squinted. Early in the twentieth century, Russian-born artist Wassily Kandinsky produced paintings that had no relationship to reality. His work marked the beginning of "abstract" art. Kandinsky proclaimed that his abstract art was based on that in Africa and represented not savagery but a higher, "spiritual" form of reality. The French composer Claude Debussy wrote that compared to the music of Southeast Asia "Our

own music is not much more than a barbarous kind of noise more fit for a travel-
ing circus."[4] Thus, others in sculpture, music, and dance began moving away from
Western traditions to take up forms from around the world, making it unclear who
had the superior culture. How does Kandinsky's writing challenge imperialists' pro-
paganda about the "civilizing mission" behind conquest?

Every work of art is the child of its age and, in many cases, the mother of our emotions. It follows that each period of culture produces an art of its own which can never be repeated. Efforts to revive the art-principles of the past will at best produce an art that is still-born. It is impossible for us to live and feel, as did the ancient Greeks. In the same way those who strive to follow the Greek methods in sculpture achieve only a similarity of form, the work remaining soulless for all time. Such imitation is mere aping. Externally the monkey completely resembles a human being; he will sit holding a book in front of his nose, and turn over the pages with a thoughtful aspect, but his actions have for him no real meaning.

There is, however, in art another kind of external similarity which is founded on a fundamental truth. When there is a similarity of inner tendency in the whole moral and spiritual atmosphere, a similarity of ideals, at first closely pursued but later lost to sight, a similarity in the inner feeling of any one period to that of another, the logical result will be a revival of the external forms which served to express those inner feel-ings in an earlier age. An example of this today is our sympathy, our spiritual relation-ship, with the Primitives. Like ourselves, these artists sought to express in their work only internal truths, renouncing in consequence all consideration of external form.

Source: Wassily Kandinsky, *Concerning the Spiritual in Art*, M. T. H. Sadler, trans. (London: Constable and Company, 1914), 1.

REVIEW QUESTIONS

1. What visions for imperial improvement do activists, reformers, and thinkers present?
2. Some speakers and authors critique the internal policies of their own societies. What different standards are they using?
3. To what extent do words convey the violence of the times? In what ways to they fall short?
4. When early in the twentieth century the Herero resisted the German take-over of their lands, many were shot, while tens of thousands of others were driven into the desert to die. See the image at https://en.wikipedia.org/wiki/Herero_and_Namaqua_genocide#/media/File:Herero_chained.jpg. Does this image represent the beginning of genocide, punishment for disobedience to imperial rule, or something else? How should this image be interpreted in the context of Germany's drive for empire?

---

[4]Claude Debussy, *Debussy in Music*, Richard Langham Smith, ed. and trans. (New York: Knopf, 1977), 278–279.

CHAPTER 9

World War I and Its Aftermath

The imperial world was in turmoil on the eve of World War I (1914–1918)—the first of a string of disastrous global killing sprees to save, perpetuate, or expand empires. Competition among the imperial powers set the stage for war, while the global connections created since the fifteenth century accounted for war's worldwide reach. There also were seemingly localized outbreaks of violence whose global implications many recognized. The Boxer Uprising in China brought in the military from eight imperial powers, but the fall of the Qing led to decades of competition internally for influence and externally for dominion. The Mexican Revolution that began in 1910 challenged the informal imperialism that took land from agricultural families and gave it to U.S. and other business interests. In Mexico, several factions attacked the government of Porfirio Diaz and other officials who had sold off many peasant holdings to U.S. business interests. These interests led the U.S. government to intervene at various moments in the war to crush reformers in their bloody, ten-year struggle. In the Balkans, secret societies, individual activists, and ethnic groups had fought against the Ottoman military and police for decades, while independent countries like Serbia struck out against both the Austrian and Ottoman empires in order to gain meaningful political freedom. The last of a series of conflicts in the region—World War I—began in 1914.

World War I engaged the globe, as imperial powers divided into two competing sides that simultaneously sought more territories and craved greater security from the widespread uprisings and land grabs threatening that security. The idea was that gaining more territory would provide a show of force and legitimacy and yield more resources with which to handle political and economic challenges. These challenges included the costs of crushing rebellions and of administering ever more distant and diverse territory. The Allies—Britain, France, and Russia—struggled to protect (or expand) their empires; they were later joined by Italy and faraway empires including Japan and the United States. The Central Powers of Germany, Austria-Hungary, and the Ottoman Empire also had imperial preservation and some expansion in mind, with Germany in particular eager to push into central and eastern Europe and Austria-Hungary and Russia into the Balkans. Thus the war was fought on these, a variety of terrains, including the homelands of many of the Middle Eastern, African, and European combatants. Like empires, the war was additionally oceanic, consisting of battleship and submarine clashes.

Slaughter, devastation of property, and the collapse of livelihoods in World War I was global as well, affecting not just Europe but broad swaths of the Middle East and Africa and bringing in soldiers and forced laborers from around the world. The number of colonized people enlisted or forced into working for the war effort numbered in the millions. On the western front on the European continent, they were often those sent first into battle, leading to their immediate slaughter by machine guns. In Africa, war disrupted village life and even annihilated tracts of farm and grazing land. In the Ottoman Empire, even as the British and French worked to undermine Muslim loyalty from within because of their craving for more land in the Middle East, Muslims under the Ottomans often responded to the Sultan's call for jihad (or holy war) against the European infidels. Yet many had mixed feelings: In Egypt, for example, subjects of the British were torn about which master to support—the British who oppressed them at the time or the Ottomans who had oppressed them in the past. World War I was imperial violence on an entirely new scale.

World War I brought colonizer and colonized up close to one another, not only in the trenches but on civilian terrain. The experience was varied. Soldiers from Asia and Africa were often prevented from marching through European villages and cities, as their presence suggested that the empire was not strong enough to fight on its own. Some colonized soldiers gave up religious and other traditions to fight as loyal soldiers of the British or French; others found the so-called civilized values of the imperial powers a sham. Mass slaughter, to their minds, was the height of barbarism, not civilization. In the dead of winter, some soldiers from the imperial powers empathized with soldiers from tropical regions, searching out warm clothing and other items that would lessen their hardship. Others, however, expressed only bigotry and their feelings of racial superiority. Civilians were also conflicted: Rumors that African soldiers were determined to rape all white women ran wild, even as those same soldiers were pushed to the most menial or most dangerous positions despite being notoriously expert sharpshooters.

From the perspective of morale-building, World War I did few, if any, favors. The victors were awash in debt, except for the United States, which entered the war only at its end and which profited handsomely selling goods to the combatants. The economies of other regions outside the theater of war also picked up. India and Australia, for example, did thriving export business. Otherwise Britain, France, Germany, Austria, and Hungary were emotionally depleted, their political systems and populations traumatized. In that psychic state, the belief arose that war for empire had been a sacred undertaking. Politicians and the public advertised battlefield deaths for territory and other gain as holy sacrifices. There was a sanctification of this war of conquest and of all who participated in it.

The aftermath of imperial war—this "holy" war— was thus more imperialism, instability, violence, and struggle, both by the colonizers and against them, continuing down to our own time and related to these earlier developments. At the end of World War I, four empires—Ottoman, German, Austro-Hungarian, and Russian— had fallen apart or were torn apart by the victors. The future of some of their territories was resolved in the form of the mandate system. In this settlement, Ottoman and German territories were divided among Britain, France, and a few other empires and nations. In 1917, the Bolsheviks, who were communists in their beliefs, worked hard to keep the Russian Empire intact and to a great extent eventually succeeded in doing so despite civil war and the invasion by the allies at war's end in 1918. That said, like the tsarist empire they took over, the Bolsheviks hoped to change the culture of its diverse peoples by persuasion or by force into a uniformly communist one. Across the imperial world, the end of the war brought more killing in the name of empire and simultaneous attempts to create movements that could lead to independence. Exhausted, shell-shocked, and bankrupt, the victorious allies presided over a peace conference that was one of greedy revenge and whose outcome was the creation of a League of Nations. Its remit was to monitor the newly expanded empires and ensure world tranquility through negotiation of disagreements. Needless to say, the violence of empire continued and, some would say, increased.

1. ZACHARY STOYANOFF (ZAHARI STOYANOV), AUTOBIOGRAPHY (1913)

What was it like to be fighting to free one's people from an empire? Tupac Ameru had unified people over the extensive territory of the former Inca Empire controlled by Spain. Some two centuries later, in the 1870s, former shepherd Zahari Stoyanov gradually involved himself in plots to free the far smaller territory of what is present-day Bulgaria from the grip of the Ottoman Empire. Stoyanov's biography shows small groups of networked freedom-fighters trying to rouse villagers, among whom many Turks lived, to join them—often unsuccessfully and with great suffering. He describes the strong hand of the Ottomans clamping down on anyone suspected of trying to weaken the empire: The uprising of April 1876 was brutally suppressed and the town of Panagyurishte burned to the ground. Over the decades before World War I, captured activists were imprisoned, tortured, and executed. Eventually, revolutionaries such as Stoyanov created the disturbances in the Balkans that brought the Ottomans into World War I. By 1918, the series of uprisings, including Armenians, the Young Turks, Balkan activists, and others contributed to the Ottoman defeat in World War I and allowed it to be divided up. What sense of the health of the Ottoman Empire in the late nineteenth century does this testimonial convey?

On the way [to meet local leader Benkovski] my guide, who was one of the couriers, told me that he had just returned from a mission to Tirnovo, the First Revolutionary Division, where he assured me that the preparations were far more advanced than in our district.

As we were making our way along the path which follows the mountain stream leading to Banya, we were challenged by a stranger who suddenly appeared from behind a tree and levelled his musket at us. Following the established brigand custom we fell flat on our faces, and the only answer given by us was the click of our revolvers as we cocked them. However, my guide suspected that we might have fallen in with the Revolutionary sentinels, and to a second inquiry he gave a reply which proved satisfactory.

Panaghyurishte and the surrounding villages . . . had long since ceased to form part de facto of the Ottoman Empire. All the functions of the police, the tax-gatherers, the law courts and the municipality had been for some time practically taken over by the Revolutionary Committee. I will maintain that at that time a traveller could journey in the Fourth District, especially in its western portions, with greater ease and security on the strength of a safe-conduct from one of the Revolutionary Committees than with any number of passports granted by the Government of his Ottoman Majesty.

The police section of the Panagyurishte Committee had organized a system of patrols and sentinels, whose duties were to observe any one entering or leaving the village, and to meet the secret couriers from other Revolutionary centers. Their orders were to stop any one who had not the proper password, unless they could satisfy themselves that they were harmless.

About midnight, as we were nearing Banya, we were again stopped by sentries. This time, in reply to the question: "Who goes there?" we answered at once, "Your brother Bulgarians from Panagyurishte." At once three hardy mountaineers rushed out to meet us, the barrels of their guns glistening in the moonlight. They overwhelmed us with questions, and sighed with satisfaction when we assured them that the day was now close at hand. "It wasn't our turn to keep guard tonight," said one of the three, "but what are we to do at home? One can't either work or sleep during these times."

We had been informed at Panaghyurishte that the house to which I was to be taken was that of Pope Grouyou, the village priest, and accordingly we went thither. The door was opened, not as I expected by a burly insurgent, but by the pope's daughter, a young girl of eighteen. I was told that ever since the beginning of the agitation this girl had given up all her usual occupations to assist in making cartridges and embroidering the banner. We found neither the pope nor Benkovski at home, but were told they were expected to return almost immediately.

Not having slept for several days, I began to doze by the fire, and eventually fell asleep. I have a recollection of the good wife carefully covering me up with a rug, muttering to herself, "Poor fellow! he's dripping with perspiration; we mustn't let him catch cold."

How long I slept or what happened round me, I cannot say. Suddenly I felt some one shaking me roughly, and heard myself addressed unceremoniously: "Get up and let's see who you are, who make so free in other people's houses."

Half-dazed, I got up, and was surprised to see a tall stranger, dressed in a kind of military costume, armed with two revolvers and a dagger, and with a knapsack and field-glass slung from his shoulders. Moreover, looming behind him I could see ten or fifteen armed figures who were apparently keeping guard. "Who are you—can't you speak?" the stranger repeated.

"I'm a workman, sir," I stammered, "looking out for a job."

"Don't frighten the lad; he's come specially to meet you," said the pope's wife.

"Oh! it's you, is it?—then you may sit down," said the stranger. Then, turning round, "To your posts on guard round the house, my lads! Some coffee, old lady, and see that my horse gets his feed!"

While Benkovski gave his orders, I was able to steal a glance at him. He was from twenty-eight to thirty years of age, tall and slender, very upright, with a long neck and rather thin face, a long reddish moustache, and light grey eyes with a most piercing look.

After throwing his waterproof cloak on the ground—the only adjustment of his toilet which suggested itself to him, for he always kept his heavy revolvers, dagger, and cartridge-belt on him—he turned to me with the words: "Well, then, let's see where you've been and what you've been doing." So saying, he finished his coffee and immediately ordered another cup. I gave him a full account of all I had done, and showed him the statistics I had collected. Somehow mention was made of my credentials signed by Yoloff, and Benkovski asked at once to see the letter.

"These people can't be made to understand," he grumbled, "that it isn't with grammars and spelling-books that our country can be freed!" and, crumpling up my precious letter, which was to me as the apple of my eye, he threw it into the fire. "Haven't been educated in Europe, have you?" he asked with a suspicious look at me. . . .

He was annoyed because Yolofi, in signing the letter, had described himself as "Chief Agitator for Western Thrace," a title which Benkovski arrogated to himself. I could soon see that the relations between these brother "apostles," who had crossed the frozen Danube together not to dispute about precedence but to give their lives for their country, were much strained, and when Benkovski found that I had not been educated in Europe he began to launch out openly against Yolofi, and to accuse him of failing to carry out his duties as an "apostle."

But in discussing the preparations for the revolt Benkovski showed his mastery of every detail of the subject. Once he opened his mouth there was no stopping him; he seemed to be reading it all out of a book. "I shan't be satisfied," he said, "until I see five thousand flintlocks in front of me" (this was his favorite expression). From time to time he complained that his throat was sore from constant speaking and that he had not slept ten hours during the preceding ten days: he swallowed cup after cup of black coffee, saying it was the only thing which kept him alive.

It was settled that I should go back to Panagyurishte and from thence to Firdop, where I was to try and found a Committee. . . . Benkovski was to go to Yetren and thence to return to Panagyurishte, where the general meeting was to be summoned. He was afraid that some treachery might cause the revolt to break out prematurely before we were fully ready, and for this reason he was anxious to hurry on our preparations. Yolofi was at that time in the villages round Giopsa, and he had also been warned to make haste.

I left Benkovski at the house of Pope Grouyou and went with my guide towards Panagyurishte.

Source: Zachary Stoyanoff, *Pages from the Autobiography of a Bulgarian Insurgent*, M. W. Pottee, trans. (London: E Arnold, 1913), 95–100. Spelling modernized in text.

2. PROCLAMATION OF THE YOUNG TURKS (1908)

The Ottoman Empire had promulgated a constitution in 1876 calling for elections and a parliament. The Sultan canceled its operation two years later. Within the Otto-man army were military men who had become familiar not just with modern mili-tary techniques but with the strength of representative government, which was seen as more effective than rule by an imperial clique. As more regions peeled away from the Ottoman empire with assistance from competing empires, in 1908, a group call-ing itself the "Young Turks" rose up against the traditional rule of the Ottoman sultan and his administration. They issued a proclamation tightening imperial order but also favoring economic modernization. The reforms received approval from public opinion in some Western countries. The declaration, signaling a weakened Ottoman state, led Bulgaria to declare its independence and the Austro-Hungarian Empire to seize Bosnia. As Young Turk leadership advocated restoration of the constitutional monarchy simultaneously with recognition of Turkish domination over a multiethnic empire, other groups within the Ottoman Empire demanded reforms on their behalf. The question their takeover raised, as it led to snowballing claims to autonomy, was whether the Ottoman Empire could survive the agitation of all ethnic and regional groups in imitation of the Young Turks. Of what benefit is the Young Turks' constitu-tion to the Ottoman Empire?

1. The basis for the Constitution will be respect for the predominance of the national will. One of the consequences of this principle will be to require without delay the responsibility of the minister before the Chamber, and, consequently, to consider the minister as having resigned, when he does not have a majority of the votes of the Chamber.
2. Provided that the number of senators does not exceed one-third the number of deputies, the Senate will be named as follows: one-third by the Sultan and two-thirds by the nation, and the term of senators will be of limited duration.
3. It will be demanded that all Ottoman subjects having completed their twentieth year, regardless of whether they possess property or fortune, shall have the right to vote.
4. It will be demanded that the right freely to constitute political groups be inserted in a precise fashion in the constitutional charter. . . .
7. The Turkish tongue will remain the official state language. Official corre-spondence and discussion will take place in Turkish. . . .

9. Every citizen will enjoy complete liberty and equality, regardless of nationality or religion, and be submitted to the same obligations. All Ottomans, being equal before the law as regards rights and duties relative to the State, are eligible for government posts, according to their individual capacity and their education. Non-Muslims will be equally liable to the military law.
10. The free exercise of the religious privileges which have been accorded to different nationalities will remain intact. . . .
17. All schools will operate under the surveillance of the state. In order to obtain for Ottoman citizens an education of a homogenous and uniform character, the official schools will be open, their instruction will be free, and all nationalities will be admitted. Instruction in Turkish will be obligatory in public schools. In official schools, public instruction will be free. Secondary and higher education will be given in the public and official schools indicated above; it will use the Turkish tongue. Schools of commerce, agriculture, and industry will be opened with the goal of developing the resources of the country.
18. Steps shall also be taken for the formation of roads and railways and canals to increase the facilities of communication and increase the sources of the wealth of the country. Everything that can impede commerce or agriculture shall be abolished.

Source: *Civilization since Waterloo*, Rondo Cameron, ed. (Paris, 1912), 40–42.

3. W. E. B. DUBOIS, *THE NEGRO* (1915)

W.E.B. Dubois (1868–1963) was a brilliant African-American who instead of being relegated to a menial place in U.S. society became highly educated thanks to encouragement and financial support from outside his family. Dubois was a college professor, journalist, and globally oriented political activist. Among the theories that he fostered in the political realm was Pan-Africanism, which thrived before, during, and after World War I in response to the racism that justified imperialism and that haunted African American lives in the United States. The idea behind Pan-Africanism held that to re-establish their independence and rights, Africans above all needed unity. Beginning in 1900, several Pan-African worldwide meetings served to initiate that unity. Besides activism on behalf of Pan-Africanism, Dubois published a series of major works, among them The Negro *(1915), which provided a story opposing that used by racist whites to justify taking black peoples' lands and keeping them in complete subservience. To this end, whites held that "Negro" was a scientifically established inferior "race" and that Africa as a whole lacked any kind of civilization or accomplishment. It was more or less "empty." In Dubois's ideas, we find a history forcefully countering that of the imperialists. What are his major arguments?*

Primarily Africa is the Land of the Blacks. The world has always been familiar with black men, who represent one of the most ancient of human stocks. Of the ancient world gathered about the Mediterranean, they formed a part and were viewed with no surprise or dislike, because this world saw them come and go and play their part with other men. Was Clitus the brother-in-law of Alexander the Great less to be honored because he happened to be black? Was Terence less famous? The medieval European world, developing under the favorable physical conditions of the north temperate zone, knew the black man chiefly as a legend or occasional curiosity, but still as a fellow man—an Othello or a Prester John or an Antar.

The modern world, in contrast, knows the Negro chiefly as a bond slave in the West Indies and America. Add to this the fact that the darker races in other parts of the world have, in the last four centuries, lagged behind the flying and even feverish footsteps of Europe, and we face to-day a widespread assumption throughout the dominant world that color is a mark of inferiority.

The result is that in writing of this, one of the most ancient, persistent, and widespread stocks of mankind, one faces astounding prejudice. That which may be assumed as true of white men must be proven beyond peradventure if it relates to Negroes. One who writes of the development of the Negro race must continually insist that he is writing of a normal human stock, and that whatever it is fair to predicate of the mass of human beings may be predicated of the Negro. It is the silent refusal to do this which has led to so much false writing on Africa and of its inhabitants. Take, for instance, the answer to the apparently simple question "What is a Negro?" We find the most extraordinary confusion of thought and difference of opinion. There is a certain type in the minds of most people which, as David Livingstone said, can be found only in caricature and not in real life. When scientists have tried to find an extreme type of black, ugly, and woolly-haired Negro, they have been compelled more and more to limit his home even in Africa. At least nine-tenths of the African people do not at all conform to this type, and the typical Negro, after being denied a dwelling place in the Sudan, along the Nile, in East Central Africa, and in South Africa, was finally given a very small country between the Senegal and the Niger, and even there was found to give trace of many stocks. As Winwood Reade says, "The typical Negro is a rare variety even among Negroes."

As a matter of fact we cannot take such extreme and largely fanciful stock as typifying that which we may fairly call the Negro race. In the case of no other race is so narrow a definition attempted. A "white" man may be of any color, size, or facial conformation and have endless variety of cranial measurement and physical characteristics. A "yellow" man is perhaps an even vaguer conception.

In fact it is generally recognized to-day that no scientific definition of race is possible. Differences, and striking differences, there are between men and groups of men, but they fade into each other so insensibly that we can only indicate the main divisions of men in broad outlines. As Von Luschan says, "The question of the number of human races has quite lost its *raison d'être* and has become a subject rather of philosophic speculation than of scientific research. It is of no more importance now to know how many human races there are than to know how many angels can dance on the point of a needle. Our aim now is to find out how ancient and primitive races developed from others and how races changed or evolved through migration and inter-breeding."

The mulatto (using the term loosely to indicate either an intermediate type between white and black or a mingling of the two) is as typically African as the black man and cannot logically be included in the "white" race, especially when American usage includes the mulatto in the Negro race.

It is reasonable, according to fact and historic usage, to include under the word "Negro" the darker peoples of Africa characterized by a brown skin, curled or "frizzled" hair, full and sometimes everted lips, a tendency to a development of the maxillary parts of the face, and a dolichocephalic head. This type is not fixed or definite. The color varies widely; it is never black or bluish, as some say, and it becomes often light brown or yellow. The hair varies from curly to a wool-like mass, and the facial angle and cranial form show wide variation.

It is as impossible in Africa as elsewhere to fix with any certainty the limits of racial variation due to climate and the variation due to intermingling. In the past, when scientists assumed one unvarying Negro type, every variation from that type was interpreted as meaning mixture of blood. To-day we recognize a broader normal African type which, as Palgrave says, may best be studied "among the statues of the Egyptian rooms of the British Museum; the larger gentle eye, the full but not over-protruding lips, the rounded contour, and the good-natured, easy, sensuous expression. This is the genuine African model." To this race Africa in the main and parts of Asia have belonged since prehistoric times.

The color of this variety of man, as the color of other varieties, is due to climate. Conditions of heat, cold, and moisture, working for thousands of years through the skin and other organs, have given men their differences of color. This color pigment is a protection against sunlight and consequently varies with the intensity of the sunlight. Thus in Africa we find the blackest men in the fierce sunlight of the desert, red pygmies in the forest, and yellow Bushmen on the cooler southern plateau.

Next to the color, the hair is the most distinguishing characteristic of the Negro, but the two characteristics do not vary with each other. Some of the blackest of the Negroes have curly rather than woolly hair, while the crispest, most closely curled hair is found among the yellow Hottentots and Bushmen. The difference between the hair of the lighter and darker races is a difference of degree, not of kind, and can be easily measured. If the hair follicles of a China-man, a European, and a Negro are cut across transversely, it will be found that the diameter of the first is 100 by 77 to 85, the second 100 by 62 to 72, while that of the Negro is 100 by 40 to 60. This elliptical form of the Negro's hair causes it to curl more or less tightly.

There have been repeated efforts to discover, by measurements of various kinds, further and more decisive differences which would serve as really scientific determinants of race. Gradually these efforts have been given up. To-day we realize that there are no hard and fast racial types among men. Race is a dynamic and not a static conception, and the typical races are continually changing and developing, amalgamating and differentiating. . . .

The known history of Songhay covers a thousand years and three dynasties and centers in the great bend of the Niger. There were thirty kings of the First Dynasty, reigning from 700 to 1335. During the reign of one of these the Songhay kingdom became the vassal kingdom of Melle, then at the height of its glory. In addition to this the Mossi crossed the valley, plundered Timbuktu in 1339, and separated Jenne, the original seat of the Songhay, from the main empire. The sixteenth king was converted to Mohammedanism in 1009, and after that all the Songhay princes were Mohammedans. Mansa Musa took two young Songhay princes to the court of Melle to be educated in 1326. These boys when grown ran away and founded a new dynasty in Songhay, that of the Sonnis, in 1355. Seventeen of these kings reigned, the last and greatest being Sonni Ali, who ascended the throne in 1464. Melle was at this time declining, other cities like Jenne, with its seven thousand villages, were rising, and the Tuaregs (Berbers with Negro blood) had captured Timbuktu.

Sonni Ali was a soldier and began his career with the conquest of Timbuktu in 1469. He also succeeded in capturing Jenne and attacked the Mossi and other enemies on all sides. Finally he concentrated his forces for the destruction of Melle and subdued nearly the whole empire on the west bend of the Niger. In summing up Sonni Ali's military career the chronicle says of him, "He surpassed all his predecessors in the numbers and valor of his soldiery. His conquests were many and his renown extended from the rising to the setting of the sun. If it is the will of God, he will be long spoken of."

Sonni Ali was a Songhay Negro whose father was a Berber. He was succeeded by a full-blooded black, Mohammed Abou Bekr, who had been his prime minister. Mohammed was hailed as "Askia" (usurper) and is best known as Mohammed Askia. He was strictly orthodox where Ali was rather a scoffer, and an organizer where Ali was a warrior. On his pilgrimage to Mecca in 1495 there was nothing of the barbaric splendor of Mansa Musa, but a brilliant group of scholars and holy men with a small escort of fifteen hundred soldiers and nine hundred thousand dollars in gold. He stopped and consulted with scholars and politicians and studied matters of taxation, weights and measures, trade, religious tolerance, and manners. In Cairo, where he was invested by the reigning caliph of Egypt, he may have heard of the struggle of Europe for the trade of the Indies, and perhaps of the parceling of the new world between Portugal and Spain. He returned to the Sudan in 1497, instituted a standing army of slaves, undertook a holy war against the indomitable Mossi, and finally marched against the Hausa. He subdued these cities and even imposed the rule of black men on the Berber town of Agades, a rich city of merchants and artificers with stately mansions. In fine Askia, during his reign, conquered and consolidated an empire two thousand miles long by one thousand wide at its greatest diameters; a territory as large as all Europe. The territory was divided into four vice royalties, and the system of Melle, with its semi-independent native dynasties, was carried out. His empire extended from the Atlantic to Lake Chad and from the salt mines of Tegazza and the town of Augila in the north to the 10th degree of north latitude toward the south.

It was a six months' journey across the empire and, it is said, "he was obeyed with as much docility on the farthest limits of the empire as he was in his own palace, and there reigned everywhere great plenty and absolute peace." The University of Sankore became a center of learning in correspondence with Egypt and

North Africa and had a swarm of black Sudanese students. Law, literature, grammar, geography and surgery were studied. Askia the Great reigned thirty-six years, and his dynasty continued on the throne until after the Moorish conquest in 1591.

Meanwhile, to the eastward, two powerful states appeared. They never disputed the military supremacy of Songhay, but their industrial development was marvelous. The Hausa states were formed by seven original cities, of which Kano was the oldest and Katsena the most famous. Their greatest leaders, Mohammed Rimpa and Ahmadu Kesoke, arose in the fifteenth and early sixteenth centuries. The land was subject to the Songhay, but the cities became industrious centers of smelting, weaving, and dyeing. Katsena especially, in the middle of the sixteenth century, is described as a place thirteen or fourteen miles in circumference, divided into quarters for strangers, for visitors from various other states, and for the different trades and industries, as saddlers, shoemakers, dyers, etc.

Source: W. E. B. Dubois, *The Negro* (New York: Holt, 2015), 6–9, 30–32. Project Gutenberg: http://www.gutenberg.org/files/15359/15359-h/15359-h.htm (accessed September 4, 2015).

4. TWO LETTERS FROM INDIAN SOLDIERS
ON THE WESTERN FRONT (1915)

Soldiers from colonized countries served in the armies of World War I combatants just as they had served for centuries in a variety of military roles. They suffered greatly in the war on whatever front they served yet they fought with tenacity and skill, conducting themselves as loyal troops. Their service was politically complicated however. The Ottoman emperor, for example, called Muslims to jihad against the infidel Allied Powers—among them Britain. This meant that Muslim soldiers were torn among several possible outcomes: triumph of the Muslim sultan; triumph of the British imperialists; triumph of Indian nationalists. Whatever their political and religious allegiances, World War I was one of the most destructive of soldiers' lives and bodies in history because of the unprecedented firepower all sides mustered. In addition, colonized soldiers of whatever region often saw their imperial masters unhinged and uncivilized but much celebrated at home. In contrast, colonial troops received little or no recognition at the time, one reason many then joined anti-colonial movements. Explain these different visions of the war.

Ratna Singh Bisht (Garhwali) to Jot Singh Bisht (Garhwal District, UP)

[Garhwali]

Brighton Hospital 21st June 1915

On the 12th May, I was wounded, and came into the Brighton Hospital. I was struck by bullets in both legs—in the left thigh, and the right knee. I am easier now but cannot yet walk. I shall get all right, for God protected the bone. The fight is still raging, and the number of killed is beyond counting. Mothers' good sons do not turn their back to the enemy in battle. Reverence is paid to seven generations of those whose fathers were engaged in war. Such a war has never been before, and never will be again. For a year has passed, and the war is still going on. Hundreds of thousands of corpses are strewn on the ground; the line of battle is 900 miles long; but in England *lakhs* of armies are collecting, so don't have any anxiety. The Hindustani soldiers who will come here will have a second birth [meaning "will die"]. So I have no hope of returning. May the true Narayan [Vishnu] have mercy on us.

Mohammad Ali Bey (Deccani Muslim) to Lance Dafadar Ranjit Singh (Depot, 20th Deccan Horse, Neemuch, Mindasok, Gwalior, Central India)

20th Deccan Horse [Urdu?]

France [June 1915?]

My friend, tell everyone at the Depot that this is the time to show one's loyalty to the Sirkar, to earn a name for oneself. To die in the battlefield is glory. For a thousand years one's name will be remembered. The British Army is now pressing the Germans very hard. It is our destiny to conquer. As for those who are frightened of the fighting and trouble, it were better for them to die. We have all got to die some day. Why should one trouble oneself and be a coward. Government is now testing men of all nationalities, and is watching what men are making pretexts. It is the duty of everyone now to sacrifice one's life and property for the Government and to show one's courage. Let the man at the Depot know what I have written. If you people do not show your loyalty to the Sirkar at this juncture, the Sirkar will not overlook it, and there will be no prosperity for your children. My friend, you should try and get your relatives and friends to enlist and to take part in the war. What are the Germans in the face of the Indian troops? They do nothing but run away in front of us. Our artillery fire has upset all the plans of the Germans. Perhaps the Germans are now thinking of making peace, but Britain and France wish to crush the Germans utterly and set their flags flying over Berlin. It is the desire of everyone to take vengeance on the Germans for the loss of our comrades and to drink their blood. . . . Judged impartially the Germans are not the equals of the Indian troops.

Source: *Indian Voices from the Great War: Soldiers' Letters, 1914–1918.* David Omissi, ed. (London: Macmillan, 1999), 71, 73.

5. NAR DIOUF AND IBRAHIMA THIAM, ORAL TESTIMONY (1982)

The French, like the British and Germans, depended extensively on colonial troops not just during World War I but across their empires to suppress resistance and generally to maintain order. World War I brought uneven recognition for their efforts. In oral interviews decades later, these two Senegalese veterans remembered

*the changing political attitudes and behaviors of colonial officials after the war.
Many officials became more trigger-happy and suspicious, especially given the
growing appeal of Pan-Africanism and communism among both veterans and
workers. The wartime experience changed these veterans and made them more
confident and informed politically, helping to build support for work actions and
for independence movements thereafter.*

I received many lasting things from the war. I demonstrated my dignity and courage, and [I] won the respect of the people and the [colonial] government. And
whenever the people of the village had something to contest [with the French]—
and they didn't dare do it [themselves] because they were afraid of them—I used
to do it for them. And many times when people had problems with the government, I used to go with my decorations and arrange the situation for [them].
Because whenever the *Tubabs* saw your decorations, they knew that they [were
dealing with] a very important person. . . . And I gained this ability—of obtaining
justice over a *Tubab*—from the war.

[For example], one day a *Tubab* came here [to the village]—he came from the *service de génie* (he was a kind of doctor)—to make an examination of the people. So he
came here, and there was a small boy who was blind. And [the boy] was walking, [but]
he couldn't see, and he bumped into the *Tubab*. And the *Tubab* turned and pushed
the boy [down]. And when I saw that, I came and said to the *Tubab*: "Why have you
pushed this boy? [Can't] you see that he is blind?" And the *Tubab* said: "Oh, *pardon,
pardon*. I did not know. I will never do it again, excuse me!" [But] before the war, [no
matter what they did], it would not have been possible to do that with a *Tubab*. . . .

The war changed many, many things. At first, when we joined the army, when
you had an argument or a problem with a "white" man, what happened? You were
wrong; you were [always] wrong. But later, those things changed. [Then] they
looked into the matter and determined who was wrong or right. [But] before that
time, the "black" man didn't mean anything. So that [change] was something [very
important]. [And] the respect we gained [from] the war [continued] increasing;
it never [diminished]. [And this] respect [continued] increasing day to day—up
until [it culminated in] the Independence Day.

Source: Joe Lunn, *Memoirs of the Maelstrom: A Senegalese Oral History of the First World War* (Portsmouth, NH: Heinemann, 1999), 199, 232–233.

6. BUCHI EMECHETA, *THE LITTLE SLAVE GIRL* (1980)

*Toward the end of World War I, a lethal strain of influenza ["felenza" in the excerpt
from the novel presented here] virus struck down people in the prime of life across
empires. Diseases traveling globally continued and even accelerated with technological improvements in transportation and the demands of wartime. Unlike earlier outbreaks, this "flu" seemed less virulent when contracted by the very old or the very
young. Instead, those in the prime of life were its major victims. As influenza spread*

from continent to continent, the pandemic increasingly disrupted entire societies. For example, killing off young, vigorous men in Africa left women to tend large animals and do other "men's work." Or, with families unhinged by the war, a brother might easily sell his sister for funds that would support him in the postwar consumer society. The story told in the novel is that of Buchi Emecheta's mother, who was in fact sold in this way. How does the narrator depict the course of the influenza epidemic and people's reaction to it?

"*Pom! Pom! Pom!* The rumours that have been going round are true. *Pom!* There is a kind of death coming from across the salty waters. It has killed many people in Isele Azagba, it is creeping to Ogwashi, it is now coming to us. They call it Felenza. It is white man's death. They shoot it into the air, and we breathe it in and die. *Pom! Pom. . . .*"

People, some on the verge of eating their evening meal, some still thudding their yam for the meal in their wooden mortars, listened helplessly as the gongman went round Ibuza with his unwelcome news. The town's runner must have returned. He must have told his tale of woe to the diokpa, the oldest man, then there must have been consultation among the elders and it must have been decided that the whole town should be warned. Everybody felt a kind of chill; not that an epidemic was anything new to the people of Ibuza, but at least previously they had always known what measures to take to avert mass disaster. They had experienced diseases like smallpox, which was so feared that they gave it the name of "Nna ayin"—"Our Father"—for at that time smallpox meant death; they knew that to stop it spreading throughout the villages any victim had to be isolated, so when somebody was attacked he would be taken into the bush and left there to die. All his worldly possessions would be burned, and no one would be allowed to mourn for him. So much feared was smallpox.

But this felenza was a new thing that the "Potokis" had shot into the air, though everyone wondered why.

"We have done them no wrong," people said. "They came to places like Benin and Bonny, bought healthy slaves from our people and paid us well. And this is how they thank us."

Rumour had it that some Europeans had been killed in Benin (Okwuekwu was one of those who carried the rumour when he returned from Idu with the copper charms for his daughter); but they had had their revenge at the time by killing many of the people there and exiling the rightful king of Idu. Why send them this kind of death now? The people of Ibuza pondered, speculated and hoped that it would never come to them, for where were they to run to?

But soon it came to Ogwashi, and within days men started dropping down dead on their farms. Death was always so sudden that the relatives were too shocked to cry.

Ojebeta's father, the strong man Okwuekwu Oda, was one of the first to be hit. She remembered that morning he had come to where she was still sleeping by the wood fire: it was the harmattan season and mornings inside the hut were chilly at that time of year.

"You did not take the *adu* I brought you from the farm yesterday," he said to her. "Here it is. Roast it for your morning meal."

She had scrambled up and greeted him with his praise names that meant "your father's wealth is the greatest"—"*Aku nna yi ka.*" He had returned her greeting, enquiring how she was that morning and whether she had slept well. She had nodded. As she watched her mother fill his pipe for him and light it she heard her say:

"If the head is so bad, stay at home today."

Her father had snapped: "Cowards fear death. It can catch up with you anywhere, whether you're lying down on your sleeping mat or digging in your farm. I don't want to die lying down like a crochety old man. I am going to the farm. Besides, who told you headaches mean felenza?"

With that he stalked out puffing angrily at his pipe as he went, smoke from the pipe following him like a line of mist.

That was the last time Ojebeta saw her father on his feet; she could still hear his footfall as he marched away in indignation. He came back in the evening, but carried by some people. He had died. Felenza had killed him on his farm.

After that it seemed to Ojebeta's young mind that the whole world was dying, one by one.

Source: Buchi Emecheta, *The Slave Girl* (New York: George Braziller), 24–26

7. MAP SHOWING THE SYKES-PICOT AGREEMENT (1916)

Even as the British enlisted various Arab ethnic groups to aid them in fighting the Central powers, the Allies were busy planning to expand their empires at war's end

CREDIT: Royal Geographical Society

at the expense of these same communities of fighters. The British promised Arabs that allying with them in the war would guarantee their independence at the war's end, but they simultaneously produced the map showing the Sykes-Picot agreement that divided the Middle East into British-controlled areas (marked B plus lands running along the east and south of the B area) and French ones (marked A plus lands to the north of the A area). The map paid no heed to actual political divisions in the region nor to the fact that many areas had already been self-governing under the Ottomans. The Allies had in mind gaining additional territories in this devastating war and imposing their rule as they had elsewhere in the world. They especially needed and craved Middle Eastern wealth. What is your opinion of this division of the Middle East?

8. THE SYRIAN CONGRESS, "RESOLUTION OF THE GENERAL SYRIAN CONGRESS AT DAMASCUS" (1919)

The Allies promised leaders of Greater Syria, part of the Ottoman Empire before World War I, that in exchange for their military and other support during the war the region would become independent at its end. In fact, that support materially helped the Allies across the Middle East until the Ottomans, alongside the other Central Powers, were defeated in the fall of 1918. The Balfour Declaration of 1917, however, had already promised Palestine to the Jewish people in order to get their support too. At the Paris Peace Conference in Paris in 1919, Middle Eastern leaders attended to watch their promised reward of independence unfold. In addition, representatives of Greater Syria met to issue a statement about that independence. Instead of fulfilling their promises, however, Britain and France obtained control of much of the Middle East, with France gaining the right to rule over most of Greater Syria. This resolution was passed in July 1919 just after the League of Nations was promulgated in June of 1919. Evaluate this resolution of the Greater Syria Congress.

We, the undersigned, members of the General Syrian Congress assembled in Damascus on the 2nd of July, 1919, and composed of delegations from the three zones, namely the southern, eastern, and western, and furnished with credentials duly authorizing us to represent the Moslem, Christian and Jewish inhabitants of our respective districts, have resolved to submit the following as defining the aspirations of the people who have chosen us to place them before the American section of the Inter-Allied Commission. With the exception of the fifth clause, which was passed by a large majority, the Resolutions which follow were all adopted unanimously:—

1. We desire full and absolute political independence for Syria. . . .
2. We desire the Government of Syria to be a constitutional monarchy based on principles of democratic and broadly decentralized rule which shall safeguard the rights of minorities, and we wish that Amir Faisal who has striven so nobly for our liberation and enjoyed our full confidence and trust be our King.
3. In view of the fact that the Arab inhabitants of Syria are not less fitted or gifted than were certain other nations (such as the Bulgarians, Serbs, Greeks and

Rumanians) when granted independence, we protest against Article XXII of the Covenant of the League of Nations which relegates us to the standing of insufficiently developed races requiring the tutelage of a mandatory power.

4. If, for whatever reason that might remain undisclosed to us, the Peace Conference were to ignore this legitimate protest, we shall regard the mandate mentioned in the Covenant of the League of Nations as implying no more that the rendering of assistance in the technical and economic fields without impairment of our absolute independence. We rely on President Wilson's declaration that his object in entering the War was to put an end to acquisitive designs for imperialistic purposes. In our desire that our country should not be made a field for colonization, and in the belief that the American nation is devoid of colonial ambitions and has no political designs on our country, we resolve to seek assistance in the technical and economic fields from the United States of America on the understanding that the duration of such assistance shall not exceed twenty years.

5. In the event of the United States finding herself unable to accede to our request . . . we would seek [assistance] from Great Britain, provided always that it will not be allowed to impair the unity and absolute independence of our country and that its duration should not exceed the period mentioned in the preceding clause.

6. We do not recognize to the French Government any right to any part of Syria, and we reject all proposals that France should give us any assistance. . . .

7. We reject the claims of Zionists for the establishment of a Jewish commonwealth in that part of southern Syria which is known as Palestine and we are opposed to Jewish immigration into any part of the country. We do not acknowledge that they have a title, and we regard their claims as a grave menace to our national, political, and economic life. Our Jewish fellow-citizens shall continue to enjoy the rights and to bear the responsibilities which are ours in common.

8. We desire that there should be no dismemberment of Syria and no separation of Palestine or the coastal region in the west or the Lebanon from the mother country. . .

10. The basic principles proclaimed by President Wilson in condemnation of secret treaties cause us to enter an emphatic protest against any agreement to provide for the dismemberment of Syria. . . .

The lofty principles proclaimed by President Wilson encourage us to believe that the determining consideration in the settlement of our own future will be the real desires of our people; and that we may look to President Wilson and the liberal American nation, who are known for their sincere and generous sympathy with the aspirations of weak nations, for help in the fulfilment our hopes. . . .

Source: J. C. Hurewitz, *Diplomacy in the Near and Middle East: A Documentary Record, 1914–1956*, vol. 2 (New York: D. Van Nostrand, 1956), 63–64.

9. COVENANT OF THE LEAGUE OF NATIONS, ARTICLE 22 (1919)

The League of Nations was established in 1919–20 with great expectations on the part of some that it would right many of the world's wrongs or monitor the progress toward human rights and fair treatment. The institution was weak from the outset because Russia and Germany were excluded and the United States, whose president had helped inspire it, refused to join. Still, Woodrow Wilson had announced as a war aim "the self-determination of peoples," which seemed to signal the end of imperial powers. Instead of independence for non-Europeans, there was a new form of colonialism in the form of mandates. Although the mandates talk in terms of tutelage and oversight by the League of these mandates, in fact Britain and France put down with incredible violence any resistance to their rule in the region. They also saw the Middle East, like other colonies, as a region to be stripped of its resources. By this time, access to oil had become important to further modernization in Europe and the United States. The League virtually guaranteed the Allies' right to it. The apportionment of land in the mandate system provoked outcries wherever the mandate system was instituted, substituting rule by the victors over the Ottoman lands and the colonies of Germany. The new rulers used the League of Nations to smother this extension of their empires in the language of the civilizing mission and readiness to rule. What aspects of this Covenant would raise the most objections from inhabitants of mandates and former colonies?

To those colonies and territories which as a consequence of the late war have ceased to be under the sovereignty of the States which formerly governed them and which are inhabited by peoples not yet able to stand by themselves under the strenuous conditions of the modern world, there should be applied the principle that the well-being and development of such peoples form a sacred trust of civilisation and that securities for the performance of this trust should be embodied in this Covenant.

The best method of giving practical effect to this principle is that the tutelage of such peoples should be entrusted to advanced nations who by reason of their resources, their experience or their geographical position can best undertake this responsibility, and who are willing to accept it, and that this tutelage should be exercised by them as Mandatories on behalf of the League.

The character of the mandate must differ according to the stage of the development of the people, the geographical situation of the territory, its economic conditions and other similar circumstances.

Certain communities formerly belonging to the Turkish Empire have reached a stage of development where their existence as independent nations can be provisionally recognized subject to the rendering of administrative advice and assistance by a Mandatory until such time as they are able to stand alone. The wishes of these communities must be a principal consideration in the selection of the Mandatory.

Other peoples, especially those of Central Africa, are at such a stage that the Mandatory must be responsible for the administration of the territory under conditions which will guarantee freedom of conscience and religion, subject only to the maintenance of public order and morals, the prohibition of abuses such as the slave trade, the arms traffic and the liquor traffic, and the prevention of the establishment of fortifications or military and naval bases and of military training of the natives for other than police purposes and the defence of territory, and will also secure equal opportunities for the trade and commerce of other Members of the League.

There are territories, such as South-West Africa and certain of the South Pacific Islands, which, owing to the sparseness of their population, or their small size, or their remoteness from the centres of civilisation, or their geographical contiguity to the territory of the Mandatory, and other circumstances, can be best administered under the laws of the Mandatory as integral portions of its territory, subject to the safeguards above mentioned in the interests of the indigenous population.

In every case of mandate, the Mandatory shall render to the Council an annual report in reference to the territory committed to its charge.

The degree of authority, control, or administration to be exercised by the Mandatory shall, if not previously agreed upon by the Members of the League, be explicitly defined in each case by the Council.

A permanent Commission shall be constituted to receive and examine the annual reports of the Mandatories and to advise the Council on all matters relating to the observance of the mandates.

Source: Covenant of the League of Nations. Avalon Project Yale University: http://avalon.law.yale.edu/20th_century/leagcov.asp (accessed September 3, 2015) or Covenant of the League of Nations, Champaign, IL : Project Gutenberg. http://self.gutenberg.org/articles/eng/Covenant_of_the_League_of_Nations (accessed September 3, 2015).

10. JOHN AND ALICE DEWEY, *LETTERS FROM CHINA AND JAPAN* (1920)

People in the Middle East were not alone in protesting their postwar colonization; the Chinese were outraged too. John Dewey was a famed professor, celebrated for his understanding of the crucial connection between public education and democracy. Spending his sabbatical in Japan in the fateful year of 1919 as the aftermath of war was being arranged in Paris, he went to Beijing on May 1 of that year, just as Chinese students were about to protest against imperialism and inequality. In particular they objected to the outcome of a war supposedly directed against oppression that handed over the Shandong province to Japan. In Chinese eyes, Japan was thus rewarded for invading and decimating a chunk of their country. They also wanted greater democracy and a major reform of the family, where fathers ruled like autocrats and where women were often so debased that they committed suicide. Here is Dewey's view of China just as the student movement was about to take its stand against empire. What is Dewey's view of the imperial situation in East Asia?

May 13, 1919

All the mineral resources of China are the prey of the Japanese, and they have secured 80 per cent of them by bribery of the Peking government. Talk to a Chinese and he will tell you that China cannot develop because she has no transportation facilities. Talk to him about building railroads and he tells you China ought to have railroads but she cannot build them because she cannot get the material. Talk to him about fuel when you see all the weeds being gathered from the roadsides for burning in the cook stoves, and he tells you China cannot use her mines because of the government's interference. There are large coal mines within ten miles of this city with the coal lying near the surface and only the Japanese are using them, though they are right on the bank of the Yangste River. The iron mines referred to are near the river, a whole mountain of iron being worked by the Japanese, who bring the ocean ships up the river, load them directly from the mines, the ore being carried down the hill, and take these ships directly to Japan, and they pay four dollars a ton to the Chinese company which carries on all the work.

The last hope of China for an effective government passed away with the closing of the Peace Conference, which has been working hard here for weeks. . . . Despair is deeper than ever, and they all say that nothing can be done. We have gone round recommending many ways of getting at the wrong impressions that prevail in our country about them, such as propaganda, an insistence upon the explanation of the differences between the people and the government. But the reply is, "We can do nothing, we have no money." Certainly the Chinese pride has been grounded now. An American official here says there is no hope for China except through the protection of the great powers, in which Japan must join. Without that she is the prey of Japan. Japanese are buying best bits of land in this city for business, and in other cities. Japan borrows money from other nations and then loans it to China on bleeding terms. The cession of Shantung has, of course, precipitated the whole mess and some Chinese think that is their last hope to so reduce them to the last extremity that rage will bring them to act. The boycott of Japanese goods and money has begun, but many say it will not be persistently carried out. The need for food and clothes in China keeps everybody bound by the struggle for a livelihood, and everything else has to be forgotten in the long run.

The protests of the Faculty on behalf of the students seem to have been received by the government in good part. Students here are in trouble also to some extent and there is a probability of a strike of students in all the colleges and middle schools of the country. The story at St. John's here is very interesting. It is the Episcopalian mission school, and one of the best. Students walked to Shanghai, ten miles, on the hottest day to parade, then ten miles back. Some of them fell by the way with sunstroke. On their return in the evening they found some of the younger students going in to a concert. The day was a holiday, called the Day of Humiliation. It is the anniversary of the date of the twenty-one demands of Japan,

and is observed by all the schools. It is a day of general meetings and speechmak-
ing for China. These students stood outside of the door where the concert was to
be held and their principal came out and told them they must go to the concert.
They replied that they were praying there, as it was not a time for celebrating by
a concert on the Day of Humiliation. Then they were ordered to go in first by
this principal and afterwards by the President of the whole college. Considerable
excitement was the result. Students said they were watching there for the sake of
China as the apostles prayed at the death of Christ and this anniversary was like
the anniversary of the death of Christ. The President told them if they did not go
in then he would shut them out of the college. This he did. They stood there till
morning and then one of them who lived nearby took them into his house. Therefore St. John's College is closed and the President has not given in.

I fancy the Chinese would be almost ready to treat the Japanese as they did
the treacherous minister if it were not for the reaction it would have on the world
at large. They do hate them and the Americans we have met all seem to feel with
them. Certainly the apparent lie of the Japanese when they made their splurge in
promising before the sitting of the Peace Conference to give back the German
concessions to China is something America ought not to forget. All these, and the
extreme poverty of China is what I had no idea of before coming here. . . .

The students' committees met yesterday and voted to inform the government
by telegraph that they would strike next Monday if their four famous demands
were not granted—or else five—including of course refusal to sign the peace
treaty, punishment of traitors who made the secret treaties with Japan because
they were bribed, etc. But the committee seemed to me more conservative than
the students, for the rumor this A.M. is that they are going to strike to-day anyway.
They are especially angered because the police have forbidden them to hold open-
air meetings—that's now the subject of one of their demands—and because the
provincial legislature, after promising to help on education, raised their own salaries and took the money to do it with out of the small educational fund. In another
district the students rioted and rough-housed the legislative hall when this happened. Here there was a protest committee, but the students are mad and want
action. Some of the teachers, so far as I can judge, quite sympathize with the boys,
not only in their ends but in their methods; some think it their moral duty to urge
deliberate action and try to make the students as organized and systematic as possible, and some take the good old Chinese ground that there is no certainty that
any good will come of it. To the outsider it looks as if the babes and sucklings who
have no experience and no precedents would have to save China—if. And it's an
awful if. It's not surprising that the Japanese with their energy and positiveness feel
that they are predestined to govern China.

I didn't ever expect to be a jingo, but either the United States ought to wash its
hands entirely of the Eastern question, and say "it's none of our business, fix it up
yourself any way you like," or else it ought to be as positive and aggressive in calling
Japan to account for every aggressive move she makes, as Japan is in doing them.
It is sickening that we allow Japan to keep us on the defensive and the explanatory,

and talk about the open door, when Japan has locked most of the doors in China already and got the keys in her pocket. I understand and believe what all Americans say here—the military party that controls Japan's foreign policy in China regards everything but positive action, prepared to back itself by force, as fear and weakness, and is only emboldened to go still further. Met by force, she would back down. I don't mean military force, but definite positive statements about what she couldn't do that she knew meant business. At the present time the Japanese are trying to stir up anti-foreign feeling and make the Chinese believe the Americans and English are responsible for China not getting Shantung back, and also talking race discrimination for the same purpose. . . .

The question which is asked oftenest by the students is in effect this: "All of our hopes of permanent peace and internationalism having been disappointed at Paris, which has shown that might still makes right, and that the strong nations get what they want at the expense of the weak, should not China adopt militarism as part of her educational system?"

Source: John and Alice Dewey, *Letters from China and Japan* (New York: E. P. Dutton, 1920), 171–181, 280–282.

11. SAROJINI NAIDU, "THE AGONY AND SHAME OF THE PUNJAB" (1920)

Everyone was trigger happy at the end of the war and never more so than across empires. In Europe, some armies refused to disband and went rampaging. In Britain, for example, returning soldiers trashed university classrooms, while in Germany civilians, especially politically minded ones, were hunted down. Russians fought a deadly civil war. Across empires, imperial armies were similarly on edge, while many colonial soldiers returning home had been politicized. When pilgrims gathered at a shrine in Amritsar in order to hear a militant speaker, the British Indian army massacred some 1,600 worshippers and wounded thousands more—men, women, and children alike—because they were said to constitute an insurrectionary mob. Terrorists, the colonial administration called the pilgrims and activists, and then declared martial law, during which even more violence against Indians took place. From London, where she had been sent on an official delegation, beloved poet and later leader of the India National Congress Sarojini Naidu gave the following speech, which caused loud objections right afterward in Parliament. What would members of Parliament—that is, the imperial leadership—have found so objectionable in Sarojini Naidu's speech?

I speak to you today as standing arraigned because of the blood-guiltiness of those who have committed murder in my country. I need not go into the details. But I am going to speak to you as a woman about the wrongs committed against my sisters. Englishmen, you who pride yourselves upon your chivalry, you who hold more precious than your imperial treasures the honour and chastity of your women, will you sit still and leave unavenged the dishonour, and the insult and agony inflicted upon the veiled women of the Punjab?

The minions of Lord Chelmsford, the Viceroy, and his martial authorities rent the veil from the faces of the women of the Punjab. Not only were men mown down as if they were grass that is born to wither; but they tore asunder the cherished Purdah, that innermost privacy of the chaste womanhood of India. My sisters were stripped naked, they were flogged, they were outraged. These policies left your British democracy betrayed, dishonored, for no dishonor clings to the martyrs who suffered, but to the tyrants who inflicted the tyranny and pain. Should they hold their Empire by dishonoring the women of another nation or lose it out of chivalry for their honor and chastity? The Bible asked, "What shall it profit a man to gain the whole world and lose his own soul?" You deserve no Empire. You have lost your soul; you have the stain of blood-guiltiness upon you; no nation that rules by tyranny is free; it is the slave of its own despotism.

Source: Sarojini Naidu, "The Agony and Shame of the Punjab," in Padmini Sengupta, *Sarojini Naidu: A Biography* (London: Asia Publishing House, 1966), 161–162.

12. MUSTAFA KEMAL (ATATÜRK), SPEECH TO THE ASSEMBLY (1925)

Mustafa Kemal was a modernizing Turkish general and determined leader of Ottoman troops during World War I. A major player in holding off the Allied attacks at Galipoli, Kemal's reputation soared as he tried to hold Anatolia and other regions together to form a postwar Turkish state. The competition was stiff because even after the war had ended British and American forces remained in the region trying to grab Constantinople and surrounding areas for their own empires. When they finally withdrew their troops, Kemal was instrumental in creating a new Turkey—one that was secular, unified, and militarily strong. Here is a speech he gave as President of Turkey in 1923. What changes is he specifically advocating to convert the Ottoman Empire into a nation-state?

"The object of the revolution which we have already put on a secure footing, and which we are still carrying on, is to give to the citizens of the Republic a social organization completely modern and progressive in every sense. It is imperative for us to discard every thought that does not fall in line with this true principle. All absurd superstitions and prejudices must be rooted out of our minds and customs. Only thus can we cause the light of truth to shine upon all the people."

Referring to the practice of some Moslems of praying at the graves of their departed priests and of tying bits of cloth in the grilled windows of their tombs to remind them of their petitions, the Ghazi said:—

"It is shameful for a civilized nation to expect help from the dead. Let the worthy occupants of those tombs rest in the happiness which they have found in a religious life. I can never tolerate the existence, in the bosom of a civilized Turkish society, of those primitive-minded men who seek material or moral well-being under the guidance of a sheik, possibly blind and hostile to the clear light of modern science and art.

"Comrades, gentlemen, fellow countrymen! You well know that the Republic of Turkey can never be a country of dervishes and sheiks and their disciples. *The only true congregation is that of the great international confraternity of civilization.* To be a real man it is necessary to do what civilization commands. The leaders of the *tekkés* (Moslem cloisters, shrines, or "monasteries") will comprehend this truth, which will lead them voluntarily to close those institutions as having already fulfilled their destiny.

"It is my duty to my conscience and to history to set forth openly what I have seen and felt. The Government of the Republic possesses a bureau of religious affairs. This department includes a numerous staff of imams (priests), muftis (chief priests), and scribes. These functionaries are required to have a certain standard of knowledge, training, and morality. But I know that there are also persons who, without being entrusted with such functions, continue to wear priestly garb. I have met many among them who are unlearned, or even illiterate. Yet they set themselves up as guides for the nation! They try to prevent direct contact between the Government and the people. I should like to know from them from what and from whom they have received the qualities and attributes which they arrogate to themselves. . . .

"It is said that we Turks have a national costume. However that may be, whatever we wear is certainly not of our own invention. The fez is of Greek origin. Very few of us would be able to say what constitutes a national costume. For example, I see in this crowd a man who is wearing a fez wound round with a green turban. He has on a vest with sleeves, and over that a coat like my own. I cannot see what he is wearing below that. What sort of clothing is that anyway? How can a civilized man consent to make himself ridiculous in the eyes of everyone by decking himself out in such outlandish garb? All employees of the Government, and all our fellow citizens, will have to reform such anachronisms in their dress. . . .

"By her great achievements the Turkish nation has proved that she is a nation essentially revolutionary and new. Even before these last few years we had entered upon the path of progress. But all our efforts to advance remained relatively futile. The reason we failed was that we did not pursue our purpose with method. It must be clearly recognized, for instance, that human society is made up of the two sexes. Is it possible for one half of society to progress while the other half is neglected? It is imperative that man and woman march together along the way of progress at the same time and in the same step. We may note with satisfaction that we at last appreciate this necessity. Let us look straight at this question, then, and face the consequences with courage. . . .

"I close with these beautiful verses from our great poet, Namuk Kemal Bey:—

'This nation cannot die. If the impossible should come to pass, that she should die, the earth itself could not sustain the weight of her casket.'"

Source: Mustafa Kemal, "An Exhortation to Progress," Reprinted in *The Living Age*, October 31, 1925.

REVIEW QUESTIONS

1. Describe reactions of colonized peoples and their allies to World War I and the social and economic conditions that followed it.
2. Describe reactions to the peace settlements following the war.
3. Describe the speakers, authors, and official documents that contain more positive evaluations of and solutions for the prewar and postwar situation.
4. See "The Colors and Color Party of the 4th Battalion, King's African Rifles at Bombo, Uganda" at http://www.iwm.org.uk/collections/item/object/205266384. In your opinion, what is the aim of this photograph meant to be? What did the visible use of troops from colonized countries in World War I (and World War II), as shown in this image, tell us about imperialism? Has their presence been acknowledged in your other history books?

CHAPTER 10

Imperial Expansion Amid Economic Downturn in the Interwar Years

During the 1920s and 1930s, imperial governments, business people, adventurers, and the military presided over the reconfiguration of empires and the expansion of some far beyond their pre–World War I boundaries. The Japanese moved farther into the Asian mainland, the Germans into central and eastern Europe, the Italians into Africa, and European and other Jews into Palestine, which, taken from the Ottomans, had become a new part of the British Empire. The Bolsheviks kept the old Russian Empire relatively intact, waging war to block the independence of Asian and European colonized peoples after the Russian Revolution and the peace settlement made in Paris. The establishment of the USSR in 1923 encompassed much of the old Russian Empire and would grow. The United States kept up its interventionist policies as part of its business imperialism and sent troops to countries in the Western Hemisphere, even as it announced its "isolation" from the affairs of the world by refusing to join the League of Nations. Meanwhile, the French, British, Japanese, and others among the Allies exploited their new holdings or "mandates" taken from the defeated Ottoman and German empires. In the Middle Eastern mandates, oil was becoming an increasingly lucrative commodity fueling automobiles, ships, and airplanes and heating homes.

As empires took freedoms and profits from local people across their empires, nationalist ideologies and independence movements grew stronger. The wartime settlement, alongside the prewar ramping up of violence against these non-free people, strengthened anti-imperial political philosophies and sometimes factionalized, if highly active nationalist and pro-independence groups. Right after the war, Egyptians, Syrians, Turks, Chinese, and others rebelled against the rampant greed of the imperial powers, especially against the British and French who had emphatically promised independence in exchange for much-needed assistance during the war. After the British army committed the massacre of pilgrims and unarmed nonviolent protesters at Amritsar India in 1919, its government ordered the use of airplanes to strafe striking or activist civilians in both India and Iraq in the 1920s as still another instance of maintaining "order" and instilling "civilized" values.

Even in the face of such violence, resistance to empire grew and was vocal, as soldiers returned from fighting in World War I. Veterans were full of horror at the barbarism of Europeans, adding to the determination of movements for national liberation from Western savagery. The Indian National Congress metamorphosed from a movement of elites calmly seeking reform to one of the masses demanding liberation. Its leading advocate, Mohandas Gandhi, drew support from millions with his doctrine of civil disobedience and soul-force (satyagraha), thus adding traditional concepts to ideas of nationalism. In large stretches of Africa, wartime fighting, forced labor, and recruitment of soldiers had gutted societies, while in the mandates such as Greater Syria, the Allies had inflicted famine as a way of spurring revolt against the Ottomans. When it came to protests in the Middle East, these were based not just on theories of rights and independence. Instead, the legacy of starvation spurred intense hatred for imperialists, which only added to the hatred stemming from the duplicity involved in the mandate system from its very beginning.

Theories of liberation circled the globe. One inspiration to many was the apparent success of working people's activism in the Bolshevik revolution of 1917, which was proclaimed a triumph for the oppressed. Many anti-colonial activists embraced Communist programs and ideals during the 1920s and 1930s and spent time training for revolution against imperialists in Moscow. The Bolsheviks undertook energetic recruitment and training of these would-be organizers. Pan-Arab and pan-Islamic thinking also grew in importance as unifying, anti-imperialist programs. Pan-Africanism spread among the activist leadership from the Caribbean, the United States, and Africa as still another way of combatting imperialism and setting up new, more just societies. African leaders-in-the-making flocked to global cities such as London and Paris to merge their ideas, gain higher education, establish networks, and build organizational skills. These leaders were sometimes attracted to socialism and Marxism but also to liberal, democratic ideals. They developed global networks to achieve African economic development and political freedom.

One often shared belief was that if colonies were to become strong and independent nations, some kind of "modernization" of women would be necessary. In China, for example, where the imperial powers made inroads in terms of business imperialism and in influencing politics there, reformers urged the patriarchal family to become more egalitarian as the family in the West was seen to be. Similar debates occurred in India, but as in some other colonies there was a gender spin: Men would be independent citizens while women maintained customs from South Asia's non-Western heritage. In some regions of Africa the "modern girl" was seen to be a credit to her race and eventually the foundation of liberation. Women's activism in the colonies advanced, often combining feminism and nationalism and leading women to be strong and public advocates for liberation from colonialism. They participated in work stoppages and outright protests, in some cases with lethal consequences as in the "Women's War" of 1929.

In this tumult of revolutionary ideas, there was also continuing tumult in people's everyday lives. Alongside the catastrophic destruction and loss of life in the war, a global influenza epidemic killed additional tens of millions of healthy people, followed by a collapse of commodity prices in the 1920s. Colonial production of raw materials and food had increased to make up for the wartime shortfall in European agriculture and the need of armies to be well fed. As a result of the economic collapse, life in the colonies became ever more difficult, especially as the depression in commodities merged with an industrial and financial depression in the more industrialized parts of the world. Loans were called in on farmers who had borrowed for motorized heavy equipment during the war and for those who were expanding industrial production and investment too. The imperial powers increased their taxes levied on their colonies to help balance budgets and ensure prosperity for the metropole, insisting on gold as payment, not commodities. By the mid-1930s strikes and other labor action by miners, railroad workers, and producers of commodities rocked the imperial world, especially in Asian and African colonies.

In this steaming cauldron of suffering and conflicting ambitions, those who were militarily strong and who wanted to be even stronger increasingly preyed on the world. The Japanese, Germans, and Italians saw more empire as an answer to problems, joining Britain, France, and the United States in ferocious efforts to extend their grip on the world. That grip was military, financial, and based on a shared idea of their own superiority. Leaders in these nations felt that the gender order had disintegrated during the war and that this weakened the nation. To remedy this weakness, men should become revirilized—that is, made more physically fit and militaristic—so that they could lead in imperial conquest while fathering the next generations of conquerors. The aggressive imperialist powers were thus driven by the belief that conquest would restore their superiority—a racial superiority that entitled them to confiscate the world's resources. Adolf Hitler took imperial racism to new heights of greed, destruction, and death. As in earlier imperial thought, though even more extreme, the murder and suffering of inferior peoples of the globe was necessary for the vitality of superior civilizations.

1. KHWAJA HASAN NIZAMI, "CREATING THE MODERN MUSLIM WOMAN" (1922)

Khwaja Hasan Nizami (1878–1955) was born into a leading Muslim family in Delhi and became a journalist and literary figure promoting better understandings and practice of Islam in a modernizing colonial society. He wrote, among other topics, about women's updating their lives by learning to converse and become more enlightened in their social practices. They would thus be better arrangers of sturdy Muslim marriages. His essays appeared at a time when Muslim women in the Middle East were developing strong feminist movements and allying themselves with nationalist organizations. His wife, Laina Batu, Nazimi claimed, embodied these capacities, as she gave her own reactions to his observations after many of his magazine articles. At the same time, Mustafa Kemal legislated the education of Turkish women and "modern clothing" for them. Still, imperialists continued to cite women's backwardness as a reason to keep people in their colonies without rights and tightly governed.

The custom of the seclusion of women has its source in mystical thought. There used to be mystical orders of people in the East who contemplated in solitude and lived in seclusion. The magnetism and power of influence that they developed by seclusion was in itself a marvel. This gave power to their gaze, power in their word, and influence in their atmosphere. This custom of seclusion was then imitated by the kings and people of high rank.

They had two ways of veiling themselves when away from home. One was to put a covering over the back of the head, which was made to hang down in front, so that the eyes could be half-covered; and the other was to put a veil over the face. . . . Every prophet of Beni Israel had this. In the Hindu race also many orders of Buddhists and yogis wore a mantle over the head. The veil which the kings used, which was called *Makna*, later became customary in the East, and ladies of high rank wore what is called in Turkish the *Yashmak*. . . .

Behind all these different customs of veiling the head and face lies mystical significance. Man's form is considered by Sufis as consisting of two parts: the head and the body; the body for action and the head for thought. Since the head is for thought its radiance is incomparably greater than that of the body, and the hairs are as rays of that radiance in a physical form. It is a constant outpouring of light that one observes in man's life. Every action of looking, or breathing, or speaking, steals much of the radiance out of man's life. By preserving this radiance the mystic develops within himself the influence, power, and magnetism that, in the average person, are wasted. . . .

The custom of the seclusion of mystics remains only in the mystical orders, but one finds the seclusion of women prevalent in the East. . . .

However, it is not true that this custom was the outcome of the teaching of the Prophet. . . . In one place it is told that when some coarse dances were going on among the peasants of his land, he said that women must be clad properly. In the other place [it is said] that when the ladies of the Prophet's household were returning home after taking care of the Prophet and his army during a battle, they were disinclined to look at the battlefield and to show themselves to their enemies, and the only thing that could be advised by the Prophet was that now that peace had been made, if they did not like to show themselves, they might veil their faces. . . .

The task of woman as a mother is of a greater importance than that of a man in any position. . . . During the period before motherhood very great care must be taken, for any word spoken to her reaches the depth of her being, and it re-echoes in the soul of the child. If a word made her bitter at the time or cross at a moment, it can create bitterness or crossness in the child. Especially during that period woman is more sensitive and susceptible to all impressions, beautiful or ugly. . . . Having this in consideration, the custom of seclusion has been kept in the East, and still exists among certain communities.

No doubt there is another side to consider: that home and state are not two separate things. Home is the miniature of the state; and if woman performs a part equally important at home, why must she not perform an equally important part in the out-ward life? No doubt these ancient customs, even with their psychological importance, often make an iron bar before the progress of the generality. Life in the world is a constant battle, and a hard battle if one has any delicacy of feeling, any refinement of manner. . . . From the first moment any child, whether boy or girl, opens his eyes in the world, he seeks the protection of woman. Woman, as his mother, sister, daughter, friend, or wife, in every form, is the source of his happiness, comfort, and peace. How-ever he may undertake to do it—whether by means of a crude custom such seclusion in the East or by some other means—to guard a woman against the hard knocks that fall on every soul living in this world of selfishess is the first duty of a thoughtful man.

Source: Khwaja Hasan Nizami, "Creating the Modern Muslim Woman," *The Sufi Message of Hazrat Imayat Khan*, vol. XIII, online http://wahiduddin.net/mv2/III/III_1_3.htm. Reprinted in *Islam in South Asia in Practice*, Barbara Metcalf, ed. (Princeton: Princeton University Press, 2009), 334–336.

2. MOHANDAS GANDHI, ANSWERS TO INTERVIEW QUESTIONS FROM DREW PEARSON (1924)

Mohandas Gandhi (1869–1948), born in colonial India to prosperous Jain [a religion based on doing no harm and self-renunciation] parents, felt their pacifist influence in his lifelong political activism. Training as a lawyer in England, he took a post in South Africa and experienced the colony's harsh discrimination first-hand. He organized South Asians there and then returned to colonial India during World War I, where he reinvigorated the Indian Congress Party, demanding that both English goods and Western values be boycotted. Why, he asked, did South Asians respect England and the United States, the latter of which was even more materialistic and warlike than the former? He urged the mass audiences who attended his rallies to cherish and uphold their tradition of spirituality and respect for life. After giving interviews such as the one with American journalist Drew Pearson presented here, Gandhi led demonstrations based on civil disobedience against British imperial institutions—for example the British monopoly on Indian salt—for which he was repeatedly jailed and his supporters beaten in a show of Western "civilization." His movement would become more radical in its demands in the next decades. Explain the appeal of Gandhi's political thought as expressed in this document.

MG: I still believe it possible for India to remain within the British Empire. I still put implicit faith in non-violence, which, if strictly followed by India, will invoke the best in the British people. My hope for the attainment of swaraj by non-violence is based upon an immutable belief in the goodness which exists deep down in all human nature.

I have always maintained that India had no quarrel with the Eng-lish. Jesus denounced the wickedness of the Scribes and Pharisees, but he did not hate them. So we need not hate Englishmen, though we hate the system they have established. They have given India a system based upon force, by which they can feel secure only in the shadow of their forts and guns. We Indians, in turn, hope by our conduct to demonstrate to every Englishman that he is as safe in the remotest corner of India as he professes to feel behind the machine gun.

DP: What do you mean by swaraj?

MG: A full partnership for India with other parts of the Empire, just the same as Canada, South Africa and Australia enjoy. Nor shall we be satisfied until we obtain full citizens' rights throughout the British Dominions for all the King's subjects, irrespective of caste, colour or creed.

DP: I asked Mr. Gandhi if he still believed in boycotting the Councils.

MG: Yes, I still believe that we should not participate in the Councils until Britain suffers a change of heart and acts squarely with us. However, I do not wish to express any opinion on the action of the Nationalist party in participating in the Councils, until I have talked with the leaders. This I have already started to do.

DP: When asked if imprisonment had changed his views on politics and religion, Mr. Gandhi replied:

MG: They have undergone no change, but have been confirmed by two years of solitude and introspection. I have been experimenting with myself and friends by introducing religion into politics, and now I believe they cannot be divorced. Let me explain what I mean by religion. It is not Hinduism, which I prize most highly, but the religion which transcends Hinduism—the basic truth which underlies all the religions of the world. It is the struggle for truth—for self-expression. I call it the truth-force—the permanent element in human nature, constantly struggling to find itself, to know its Maker. This is religion.

I believe that politics cannot be divorced from religion. My politics can be summed up in two words—non-violent non-co-operation. And the roots of non-co-operation are buried in the religions of the world. Christ refused to co-operate with the Scribes and Pharisees. Buddha fearlessly refused to co-operate with the arrogant priesthood of his day. Mahomed, Confucius, most of our great prophets have been non-co-operators. I simply and humbly follow in their footsteps.

Non-co-operation means nothing less than training in self-sacrifice. And this again was practised by the great teachers of the world. Strength does not come from physical capacity. It comes from indomitable will. I have ventured to place before India the ancient law of self-sacrifice—the obedience to the strength of the spirit.

By non-violence I do not mean cowardice. I do believe that, where there is only a choice between cowardice and violence, I would advise violence. But I believe that forgiveness adorns a soldier. And so I am not pleading for India to practise non-violence because she is weak, but because she is conscious of her power and strength. The rishis, who discovered the law of non-violence, were greater geniuses than Newton. Having themselves known the use of arms, they realized their uselessness and taught a weary world that its salvation lay not through violence, but through non-violence.

Therefore, I respectfully invite Americans to study carefully the Indian National Movement and they will therein find an effective substitute for war.

DP: Before his imprisonment Mr. Gandhi was a most severe critic of modern civilization and I asked if his views had suffered any change.

MG: They remain unchanged. My opinion of modern civilization is that it is a worship of materialism, resulting in the exploitation of the weak by the strong. American wealth has become the standard. The United States is the envy of all other nations. Meanwhile, moral growth has become stunted and progress measured in pounds, shillings and pence.

This land of ours, we are told, was once the abode of the gods. But it is not possible to conceive of gods inhabiting a land which is made hideous by the smoke and din of mill chimneys and factories, and whose roadways are traversed by rushing engines, dragging cars crowded with men who know not for the most part what they are after, do not care, and whose tempers do not improve by being uncomfortably packed together like sardines in boxes. Factories have risen on the corpses of men, women, and children to create what we call civilization.

Source: Mohandas Gandhi, "Anwers to Drew Pearson's Questions," *The Collected Works of Mohandas Gandhi*, vol. 23 (Ahmedabad: Navajivan Trust, 1963), 195–197.

3. CALVIN COOLIDGE, INTERVENTION IN NICARAGUA (1926)

With the spread of business imperialism, governments justified controlling other nations through military and other kinds of intervention in sovereign states instead of occupying and then colonizing them. The United States became increasingly active in this kind of intervention in foreign governments on the grounds that U.S. citizens had property in those foreign nations or that U.S. citizens were endangered. Another justification for military intervention was that the foreign nation would not engage in trade. The Opium War in 1839–1842 was waged on such grounds and thereafter opening trade also justified warfare or the threat of it—as in the case of the United States threatening Japan in the 1850s. By the twentieth century such intervention in other governments' affairs became a constant feature of U.S. policy, especially in the Western Hemisphere. The countries of the Caribbean, Central America, and Mexico were especially vulnerable. Nicaragua is just one example, as President Calvin Coolidge's justification of yet another use of force (an earlier one was 1911–1912) there shows. What explanation does this document provide of business imperialism?

While conditions in Nicaragua and the action of this government pertaining thereto have in general been made public, I think the time has arrived for me officially to inform the Congress more in detail of the events leading up to the present disturbances and conditions which seriously threaten American lives and property, endanger the stability of all Central America, and put in jeopardy the rights granted by Nicaragua to the United States for the construction of a canal.

It is well known that in 1912 the United States intervened in Nicaragua with a large force and put down a revolution, and that from that time to 1925 a legation guard of American Marines was, with the consent of the Nicaragua government, kept in Managua to protect American lives and property. In 1923 representatives of the five Central American countries, namely, Costa Rica, Guatemala, Honduras, Nicaragua, and Salvador, at the invitation of the United States, met in Washington and entered into a series of treaties.

These treaties dealt with limitation of armament, a Central American tribunal for arbitration, and the general subject of peace and amity. The treaty last referred to specifically provides in Article II that the governments of the contracting parties will not recognize any other government which may come into power in any of the five republics through a coup d'etat, or revolution, and disqualifies the leaders of such coup d'etat, or revolution, from assuming the presidency or vice-presidency. . . .

The United States was not a party to this treaty, but it was made in Washington under the auspices of the secretary of state, and this government has felt a moral obligation to apply its principles in order to encourage the Central American states in their efforts to prevent revolution and disorder. . . .

In October 1924 an election was held in Nicaragua for president, vice-president, and members of the Congress. This resulted in the election of a coalition ticket embracing Conservatives and Liberals. Carlos Solorzano, a Conservative Republican, was elected president, and Juan B. Sacasa, a Liberal, was elected vice-president. This government was recognized by the other Central American countries and by the United States. . . .

Notwithstanding the refusal of this government and of the other Central American governments to recognize him, General Chamorro continued to exercise the functions of president until Oct. 30, 1926. In the meantime a revolution broke out in May on the east coast in the neighborhood of Bluefields and was speedily suppressed by the troops of General Chamorro. However, it again broke out with considerable more violence. The second attempt was attended with some success, and practically all of the east coast of Nicaragua fell into the hands of the revolutionists. . . .

Repeated requests were made of the United States for protection, especially on the east coast, and on Aug. 24, 1926, the secretary of state addressed to the secretary of the navy the following communication:

I have the honor to suggest that war vessels of the Special Service Squadron proceed as soon as possible to the Nicaraguan ports of Corinto and Bluefields for the protection of American and foreign lives and property in case that threatened emergencies materialize. The American chargé d'affaires at Managua has informed the department that he considers the presence of war vessels at these ports desirable, and the American consul at Bluefields has reported that a warship is urgently needed to protect life and property at that port. An attack on The Bluff and Bluefields is expected momentarily.

At the request of both parties; Marines were landed at Corinto to establish a neutral zone in which the conference could be held. Doctor Sacasa was invited to attend this conference but refrained from doing so and remained in Guatemala

City. . . . I understand that at this conference General Chamorro offered to resign and permit the Congress to elect a new designate to assume the presidency. The conference led to no result, since, just at the time when it seemed as though some compromise agreement would be reached, the representatives of Doctor Sacasa suddenly broke off negotiations. . . .

The Nicaraguan constitution provides in Article 106 that in the absence of the president and vice-president the Congress shall designate one of its members to complete the unexpired term of president. As President Solorzano had resigned and was then residing in California, and as the vice-president, Doctor Sacasa, was in Guatemala, having been out of the country since November 1925, the action of Congress in designating Señor Díaz was perfectly legal and in accordance with the constitution. Therefore, the United States government on Nov. 17 extended recognition to Señor Díaz. . . .

Immediately following the inauguration of President Díaz, and frequently since that date, he has appealed to the United States for support, has informed this government of the aid which Mexico is giving to the revolutionists, and has stated that he is unable solely because of the aid given by Mexico to the revolutionists to protect the lives and property of American citizens and other foreigners. . . .

As a matter of fact, I have the most conclusive evidence that arms and munitions in large quantities have been, on several occasions since August 1926, shipped to the revolutionists in Nicaragua. Boats carrying these munitions have been fitted out in Mexican ports, and some of the munitions bear evidence of having belonged to the Mexican government. It also appears that the ships were fitted out with the full knowledge of and, in some cases, with the encouragement of Mexican officials and were in one instance, at least, commanded by a Mexican naval reserve officer.

At the end of November, after spending some time in Mexico City, Doctor Sacasa went back to Nicaragua, landing at Puerto Cabezas, near Bragmans Bluff. He immediately placed himself at the head of the insurrection and declared himself president of Nicaragua. He has never been recognized by any of the Central American republics nor by any other government, with the exception of Mexico, which recognized him immediately. As arms and munitions in large quantities were reaching the revolutionists, I deemed it unfair to prevent the recognized government from purchasing arms abroad, and, accordingly, the secretary of state notified the Díaz government that licenses would be issued for the export of arms and munitions purchased in this country. It would be thoroughly inconsistent for this country not to support the government recognized by it while the revolutionists were receiving arms and munitions from abroad.

During the last two months the government of the United States has received repeated requests from various American citizens, both directly and through our consuls and legation, for the protection of their lives and property. The government of the United States has also received requests from the British chargé at Managua and from the Italian ambassador at Washington for the protection of their respective nationals. . . .

For many years numerous Americans have been living in Nicaragua, developing its industries and carrying on business. At the present time there are large investments in lumbering, mining, coffee growing, banana culture, shipping, and also in general mercantile and other collateral business. . . . In the present crisis such forces are requested by the Nicaraguan government, which protests to the United States its inability to protect these interests and states that any measures which the United States deems appropriate for their protection will be satisfactory to the Nicaraguan government.

There is no question that if the revolution continues, American investments and business interests in Nicaragua will be very seriously affected, if not destroyed. The currency, which is now at par, will be inflated. American as well as foreign bondholders will undoubtedly look to the United States for the protection of their interests. . . .

Manifestly, the relation of this government to the Nicaraguan situation and its policy in the existing emergency are determined by the facts which I have described. The proprietary rights of the United States in the Nicaraguan canal route, with the necessary implications growing out of it affecting the Panama Canal, together with the obligations flowing from the investments of all classes of our citizens in Nicaragua, place us in a position of peculiar responsibility. . . .

The United States cannot, therefore, fail to view with deep concern any serious threat to stability and constitutional government in Nicaragua tending toward anarchy and jeopardizing American interests, especially if such state of affairs is contributed to or brought about by outside influences or by any foreign power. It has always been and remains the policy of the United States in such circumstances to take the steps that may be necessary for the preservation and protection of the lives, the property, and the interests of its citizens and of this government itself. In this respect I propose to follow the path of my predecessors.

Consequently, I have deemed it my duty to use the powers committed to me to ensure the adequate protection of all American interests in Nicaragua, whether they be endangered by internal strife or by outside interference in the affairs of that republic.

Source: *Record,* 69 Cong., 2 Sess., pp. 1324–1326.

4. GOLDA MEIR, *MY LIFE* (1977)

Golda Meir (1898–1978) was the fourth prime minister of Israel. Born in Kiev, Ukraine, she emigrated with her family to the United States and spent her teenage years in Milwaukee and Denver, where she became involved in activism and studying political thought. In 1921, she emigrated with her husband to Palestine, working with him on a kibbutz and continuing her Zionist political activities. An accomplished speaker, she traveled widely to raise money and gain support for the Zionist movement but failed to gain assistance from other nations for the Jews persecuted by Hitler and by anti-Semites globally. Nonetheless, she became an expert politician both locally and internationally, and though called the only "man" at certain tough political moments, she noted having cried at the founding of the state of Israel in

1948. Golda Meir supported the consolidation and expansion of Israel's borders and, as in the passage that follows, had no qualms about Israel's hold over what had been Palestinian territory. Still, as prime minister she engaged in many sessions to find a settlement to Middle Eastern questions and particularly to stabilizing the status of Israel. How does Meir explain Jewish settlement in Palestine?

I was in my very early twenties, doing exactly what I wanted to do, physically fit, full of energy and together with the people who meant most to me—my husband, my sister, my best friend. I had no children to worry about, and I didn't really care whether we had an icebox or not, or if the butcher wrapped our meat in pieces of newspaper he picked up off the floor. There were all kinds of compensations for these small hardships, like walking down the street on our first Friday evening in Tel Aviv and feeling that life could hold no greater joy for me than to be where I was—in the only all-Jewish town in the world, where everyone from the bus driver to our land-lady shared, in the deepest sense, not only a common past, but also common goals for the future. These people hurrying home for the Sabbath, each one carrying a few flowers for the table, were really brothers and sisters of mine, and I knew we would remain bound to each other for all our lives. Although we had come to Palestine from different countries and from different cultures and often spoke different languages, we were alike in our belief that only here could Jews live as of right, rather than suf-ferance, and only here Jews could be masters, not victims, of their fate. So it was not surprising that for all the petty irritations and problems, I was profoundly happy. . . .

. . . [I]n 1901, the Jewish National Fund had already been formed by the Zion-ist movement for the exclusive purpose of buying and developing land in Palestine in the name of the entire Jewish people. And a great deal of the Jewish-owned land in Palestine was bought by the "people"—the bakers, tailors and carpenters of Pinsk, Berlin and Milwaukee. As a matter of fact, ever since I was a little girl, I can remember the small tin blue collection box that stood next to the Sabbath candles in our living room and into which not only we but our guests dropped coins every week, and this blue box was likewise a feature in every Jewish home we visited. The truth is, from 1904 on it was with these coins that the Jewish people began to buy extensive tracts of land in Palestine.

Come to think of it, I am more than a little tired of hearing about how the Jews "stole" land from Arabs in Palestine. The facts are quite different. A lot of good money changed hands, and a lot of Arabs became very rich indeed. Of course, there were other organizations and countless individuals who also bought tracts. But by 1947 the JNF alone—millions of filled blue boxes—owned more than half of all the Jewish holdings in the country. So let that libel, at least, be done with.

About the time that we came to Palestine a number of such purchases were carried out in the Emek—despite the fact that much of the area consisted of the kind of deadly black swamps that inevitably brought malaria and blackwater fever in their wake. Still, what mattered most was that this pestilential land could be bought, though not cheaply; much of it, incidentally, was sold to the Jewish National Fund by a single well-to-do Arab family that lived in Beirut.

The next step was to make this land arable. In the nature of things, private farmers did not and could not interest themselves in a backbreaking and dangerous project which would obviously take years before it showed any profit. The only people who could possibly undertake the job of draining the Emek swamps were the highly motivated pioneers of the Labor Zionist movement, who were prepared to reclaim the land, however difficult the circumstances and regardless of the human cost. What's more, they were prepared to do it themselves, rather than have the work done by hired Arab laborers under the supervision of Jewish farm managers. The early settlers of Merhavia were such people, and many of them lived to see the Emek become Israel's most fertile and loveliest valley, dotted by flourishing villages and collective settlements.

Source: Golda Meir, *My Life* (New York: G. P. Putnam's Sons, 1975), 81, 83–84.

5. TU BIN TRAN, MEMOIR (1920)

Tu Bin Tran was an impoverished worker who became increasingly active politically during the interwar years because of the oppression of people living under French rule in Indochina. His memoir describes the hopeless lives that many, including himself, led as they signed on to work on rubber plantations, in his case the Phu Rieng plantation in Indochina. Like many peasants and urban workers during these years he came to be influenced by communist theories and the political organizing spreading across Asia. In the aftermath of the Bolshevik Revolution, Communist agents fanned out to different regions to help teach workers principles of solidarity and of collective action. This passage from Tu Bin Tran's memoir describes abortive resistance to treatment on the plantation in 1927 and 1928—both direct action and slowdowns—and the horrific punishment that followed. The memoir as a whole also reflects his gradual education into communism because he cites class consciousness and capitalism. As in Tran's case, oppression under empire failed to draw ordinary people to imperial "civilizing ways" but instead made them flock to communism. What evidence of imperialists' civilizing mission do you find in this document?

The First Battles (1927–1928)

All those things gave us the feeling we had stumbled into a corner of hell. . . . The two hundred or so of us, having reached this place, would have to close ranks to oppose them and protect each other until we could escape their wickedness. . . .

The owners of the Michelin company were applying a policy of brutal whippings. The manager was a certain Triai, a captain in the Foreign Legion, a French soldier. I should also make it clear that the manager, the assistant manager, and all the overseers were recruited from among the mercenary troops.

This Triai was very big, very strong, and his face was as cold and fierce as that of a jail keeper. He never cursed, he only beat. . . .

The overseers commonly beat workers who had just arrived in order to intimidate them. . . .

One youth with an upset stomach did not get into a straight line soon enough and Triai sprang toward him, drew back his leg and kicked the youth, rupturing his spleen. The incapacitated youth lay writhing at his feet. Straight-faced as if nothing had happened, he gave a sign to his subordinates. Valentin and Monte then came over and struck out with their rods, at once striking us and counting out the number of workers in a loud voice.

When they reached me, I raised both arms to protect my head and spoke up quickly: "The contract forbids beatings. Why are you beating us?" . . .

Triai was standing nearby, and when he heard me protest he seemed astonished. . . .

Suddenly he struck me hard on the head with his rod and shouted: "Donnez la cadeuille! (Let him feel the club.)" At once French and Vietnamese overseers alike began caning me from left and right and kicking me with their hobnailed boots. As the rain of blows fell, the scene grew twice as riotous as before. I was beaten by Triai and Monte themselves. At the beginning I was still standing, encircling my head with my arms to protect it. After they beat me to the ground, I drew myself up into a ball, using my legs to protect my stomach and chest. The two of them kept raining down blows. . . .

By then I had passed out. I have no idea how much longer they continued beating me. When I came to, I found myself in a dark house with my legs held apart by shackles. I felt as if every spot on my whole body had been hit. When I felt gently with my hands, I discovered that I had wet, sticky blood all over me. . . .

Before we realized it, we had been at Phu-rieng for over half a year. Around Village 1, Village 2, and Village 3 vast areas of the jungle had been cleared out. The bright red earth gleamed vermillion in the sun. Here and there rubber saplings transplanted from the nursery had put out deep green shoots. How many of us had departed this life to create that scene! Our compatriots had died like sand, like dust, and their flesh and bones had decayed and become a part of that vermillion earth.

After the passage of a half year, we also had more experience in methods of struggle with the capitalist masters. I do not know who started it, but a new form of struggle appeared: We would pass the word to slow the tempo of our work. At the time the workers did not really recognize this as a form of struggle, nor did they call it a slowdown. They simply said, "Why should we knock ourselves out working for them?"

One person was assigned to look out for the French foreman and the Vietnamese foreman who tagged along with him. Whenever they were looking the other way, we worked indifferently. Hoes rose and fell, but no one bothered to scoop up the dirt. They just left it wherever it fell. Knives chopped on wood for hours without felling a single tree. The overall productivity of the plantation fell perceptibly. The overseers grew increasingly upset, yet there was no way they could keep a close enough watch on things. Whenever they happened to be at a particular place, we worked fine there. But as soon as they left, the workers passed the word to slow down again.

As we gradually gained experience, we began to tell each other how to kill rubber saplings. These saplings were brought from the nursery and planted in small, skillfully woven bamboo baskets. We would dig the soil out of the basket, use a small knife to cut nearly half way through the main root, then plant it carefully in the hole. The root would become waterlogged. A week later the root would rot. Gradually the tree would lose its leaves, and even if it lived it would be weak and would have to be dug up and replaced with another tree. The French did not become suspicious, as we only slit the root of about one tree in three.

Source: Tu Bin Tran, *Red Earth: Memoir of a Life on a Colonial Rubber Plantation* (Athens: Ohio University Center for International Studies, 1985), 33–35, 42.

6. TESTIMONY OF MILITARY ON KILLING
OF IGBO WOMEN (1929)

One solution to the European imperial powers' need to replenish their treasuries was increasing the exploitation of colonized people. As part of that solution, officials devised new taxes to impose across their empires. At the same time many veterans in the colonies had returned from the war disillusioned, and as the influenza epidemic traveled the world it seemed as if an entire generation of the young was being struck down. Such was the case in colonial Nigeria, where the British government decided to take a head count of women Africans who had previously been exempt from taxation in preparation for taxing them and their businesses. The women, already upset that their men had died from the flu and reeling from the extra work this meant in order to support their families, rebelled against the head count and mustered thousands of women living at great distance from one another to protest—this in days without phones. They painted their bodies, waved branches and decorated themselves with them, and even stripped naked. African officials working for the British realized that this protest was serious; the British involved ordered that the unarmed women be shot down. Back home, few British citizens cared; violence across the empire was now ordinary and often considered the only way to deal with savages.

I ordered my leading section of six men to fire two rounds rapid and they did so. One or two figures were seen to drop but the remainder took no notice whatever and continued to advance. Meantime I had signalled [*sic*] up my Lewis gun . . . [and] gave the order to the Lewis gun to fire. The first burst went over the heads of the crowd; that was not intentional, . . . as the men had been ordered to fire at the crowd. The third burst found the mark and I at once ordered to stop fire. The crowd also stopped. The first two bursts had no effect. The crowd continued shouting, waving their arms and sticks and then they slowly withdrew. The distance was stepped out later and the distance where they were stopped was sixty yards from us. When I stopped two or three more casualties had been caused by the Lewis gun; that was what stopped them. The platoon then advanced and began burning down the house of the chief under the orders of the District officer. While we were doing this we heard the noise of another crowd coming towards us and we advanced to meet it. I had my Lewis gun section in front. They were also decked out in green leaves and were waving sticks. They had the same hostile attitude as the other mob. I brought the Lewis gun section into action and gave the order to fire. It fired one burst of seven rounds which caused casualties and stopped the crowd; a few people dropped. There were two dead. They withdrew but still kept shouting. We advanced and then told them to disperse.

At the outskirts of Opobo station the road was blocked by about 300 women and they were carrying sticks, bricks and lumps of mud. I told the driver of the motor lorry to go full speed ahead through them and they cleared to either side of the road and threw the sticks, mud and bricks at the lorry. The driver of the lorry told me that they were shouting that they smelt blood and they did not mind the soldiers coming. . . .

At the time the crowd were [sic] pressing against the light bamboo fence, they were all shouting and waving sticks. I estimated the crowd at 400 women of all ages; there were no children; some were nearly naked wearing only wreaths of grass round their heads, waist and knees and some were wearing tails made of grass. . . . Some abused me in English and one took off her loin cloth and told me that I was the son of a pig and not of a woman. I was told that the others were speaking in native dialect were telling the soldiers to cut their throats. . . . Each time a new batch of women arrived the frenzy of the mob increased.

Source: Mark Matera, Misty L. Bastian, and Susan Kingsley Kent, *The Women's War of 1929* (New York: Palgrave Macmillan, 2012), 175–176, 207.

7. A. NICOUÉ, *LE PHARE DU DAHOMEY* (1933)

The Great Depression, erupting alongside events like the Women's War, had devastating effects on colonies almost everywhere. Having been made into laborers on single crop plantations, workers had their wages cut because of the drastic drop in commodity prices. Those with smaller farms or traders in these commodities were badly off too, as their income fell drastically. In the past, African farmers had engaged in multi-crop farming, but "modernization" projects saw these as backwards because they supported an individual family instead of producing crops to be sold on the market. During the Great Depression, the imperial powers raised taxes on the colonies instead of recognizing the horrendous hardship of hard times and thus reducing them. The idea was that the metropole needed the taxes and the colonies were there to pay for the needs of whites. Here newspaper editor Nicoué reports his confrontation over taxes and the need to pawn children—that is, give them over as collateral until a debt is paid—with the new Governor-General Coppet in Dahomey, which was taken over by the French in 1894. The highest ranks of colonized peoples like those in more ordinary positions continued to challenge the hypocrisy of imperial rule and the chaos it brought to their lives. How do the positions of newspaper editor Nicoué and Governor-General Coppet clash?

One by one M. de Coppet shook hands with all who were presented to him, and had a friendly word for each. . . .

[C]onfident in the future, [he] said that the difficulties will be over in a relatively short time, maintaining that the recently enacted law for the fiscal protection of oilseeds will bring about a considerable improvement in the country. . . .

M. Rogeau, District Commissioner of Great Popo, whom we have always mistakenly regarded as a negrophil administrator, had the *cynical face* to declare that "if the taxes are not coming in it is because of the ill-will of the natives, who have plenty of money but refuse to pay, in hope of forcing a reduction in the rate of taxation."

M. Nicoué, our Editor-in-chief, was an eye-witness of this *odious declaration* by M. Rogeau.

M. Nicoué felt his crinkly hair standing on end; but out of respect he kept quiet and waited for a suitable moment to refute this lying assertion, which shows us as disloyal people. . . .

M. de Coppet spoke somewhat as follows—attempts having already been made to poison his opinions:
"I am very happy to come to your country. I have come to help as well as to command. I am told that you are showing ill-will in paying your taxes. You must know that it is your duty to pay your taxes on time. Almost all the West African colonies have already set a good example, it is only you who have not completed payment …" and so on.

M. Nicoué asked to speak, and was allowed to do so.

M. NICOUÉ: Your Excellency, just now an Administrator told you that we have plenty of money, and fail to pay our taxes through ill-will. I beg you not to believe this statement, and to get the impression on your first day that the Dahomean people are refractory. On the contrary, we make a virtue of respect and obedience. We have always paid our poll-tax gladly, ever since it was imposed. If today the administration finds us in arrears, this is solely on account of the economic crisis, which has struck Dahomey extremely acutely.

THE GOVERNOR: But it is not only Dahomey that has been hit by the crisis. It exists everywhere, even in France, and yet people pay their taxes.

M. NICOUÉ: The proof that the crisis has struck Dahomey more seriously than other colonies is that several firms have closed their factories in Dahomey while continuing business in other colonies. . . . Our distress is due above all to monoculture.

THE GOVERNOR: But Senegal also depends on a single crop, and yet its people have already paid their taxes.

M. NICOUÉ: Senegal has the benefit of a preferential export duty which we do not have. There is a 50 per cent reduction of customs duty on exports of groundnuts. If we had money, we would not be *forced to pledge our own children as security before paying tax.*

THE GOVERNOR: That is not so. You are not forced to pledge your children as security in order to pay tax.

M. NICOUÉ: When we have sold our property and our lands, when we are being thrashed and imprisoned, our only hope of securing peace is to pawn our children to some better-off person. These children remain with the creditor for periods between five and fifteen years. You will know this for yourself, Your Excellency, once you are established in Porto Novo, and have made some journeys in the country. Events will confirm the truth of what I say.

Source: John Hargreaves, *France and West Africa: An Anthology of Historical Documents* (London: Macmillan, 1969), 254–256.

8. ADOLF HITLER, SPEECH (1937)

Adolf Hitler, who became dictator of Germany in 1933, built a vast empire until his downfall in 1945. Like other modern conquerors, he saw his victims as inferior and menacing, however. Hitler's explanation for German dominance differed greatly from that of the early conquerors of the Incas and Aztecs. While the Spanish sought to conquer in order to convert those they colonized—as well as to exploit their labor and wealth—Hitler sought to annihilate them through genocide and starvation. The Spanish saw their mission as a moral one; Hitler explained his as scientifically determined. There were those across Europe, according to Hitler—Jews, Roma and Sinti, homosexuals, and the disabled—who were not fit to live because they were biologically inferior. Their biological inferiority made them dangerous, especially should they intermarry with white Germans: By intermarrying, the Jews, for example, were waging world war to destroy the superior German race. Germany's imperial expansion under Hitler rested on the idea of preserving purity of race through conquest of distant peoples, including those as far off as the Pacific Ocean border of the Russian Empire. There would then be room for an empire of pure-blooded Germans to thrive. This excerpt comes from a speech commemorating Hitler's ascent to power, January 30, 1933. How has imperial ideology changed over the centuries, as evidenced in this statement of Hitler?

The main plank in the National Socialist program is to abolish the liberalistic concept of the individual and the Marxist concept of humanity and to substitute therefore the folk community, rooted in the soil and bound together by the bond of its common blood. A very simple statement; but it involves a principle that has tremendous consequences.

This is probably the first time and this is the first country in which people are being taught to realize that, of all the tasks which we have to face, the noblest and most sacred for mankind is that each racial species must preserve the purity of the blood which God has given it. And thus it happens that for the first time it is now possible for men to use their God-given faculties of perception and insight in the understanding of those problems which are of more momentous importance for the preservation of human existence than all the victories that may be won on the battlefield or the successes that may be obtained through economic efforts. The greatest revolution which National Socialism has brought about is that it has rent asunder the veil which hid from us the knowledge that all human failures and mistakes are due to the conditions of the time and therefore can be remedied, but that there is one error which cannot be remedied once men have made it, namely the failure to recognize the importance of conserving the blood and the race free from intermixture and thereby the racial aspect and character which are God's gift and God's handiwork. It is not for men to discuss the question of why Providence created different races, but rather to recognize the fact that it punishes those who disregard its work of creation.

Unspeakable suffering and misery have come upon mankind because they lost this instinct which was grounded in a profound intuition; and this loss was caused by a wrong and lopsided education of the intellect. Among our people there are millions and millions of persons living today for whom this law has become clear and intelligible. What individual seers and the still unspoiled natures of our forefathers saw by direct perception has now become a subject of scientific research in Germany. And I can prophesy here that, just as the knowledge that the earth moves around the sun led to a revolutionary alternation in the general world-picture, so the blood-and-race doctrine of the National Socialist Movement will bring about a revolutionary change in our knowledge and therewith a radical reconstruction of the picture which human history gives us of the past and will also change the course of that history in the future. And this will not lead to an estrangement between the nations; but, on the contrary, it will bring about for the first time a real understanding of one another. At the same time, however, it will prevent the Jewish people from intruding themselves among all the other nations as elements of internal disruption, under the mask of honest world-citizens, and thus gaining power over these nations.

Source: http://www.hitler.org/speeches/01-30-37.html accessed March 28, 2017.

9. JOMO KENYATTA, *FACING MOUNT KENYA* (1937)

Jomo Kenyatta (c. 1891/4–1978), was born in present-day Kenya, which at the time was a British colony. Raised by his extended family after his father's early death, Kenyatta received an education at a British mission and became a carpenter. He began to engage in politics and in the 1930s traveled to London to present the cause of the Kikuyu ethnic group to which he belonged. In England he met a range of politicians, artists, and academics while also studying at the London School of Economics. His thesis at the LSE became the celebrated book, Facing Mount Kenya *(1938)— an appreciation of Kikuyu politics and culture that outlined the Kikuyu Constitution and the democratic nature of Kikuyu rule destroyed by the British. Returning home, Kenyatta went on to participate in the liberation and Pan African movements in Kenya, which as in Algeria faced lethal resistance from whites. Amid the Mau Mau uprising, Kenyatta was imprisoned, to be released only in 1961. After independence in 1963, he became prime minister and then president and forged a dynasty of family and friends that grew wealthy and that dominated the nation into the twenty-first century. How does Kenyatta see Africans and non-Africans in relation to one another? What political values does Kenyatta's ethnic group hold?*

I know that there are many scientists and general readers who will be disinterestedly glad of the opportunity of hearing the Africans' point of view, and to all such I am glad to be of service. At the same time, I am well aware that I could not do justice to the subject without offending those "professional friends of the African" who are prepared to maintain their friendship for eternity as a sacred duty, provided only that the African will continue to play the part of an ignorant savage so that they can monopolise the office of interpreting his mind and speaking for him. To such people, an African who writes a study of this kind is encroaching on their preserves. He is a rabbit turned poacher.

But the African is not blind. He can recognize these pretenders to philanthropy, and in various parts of the continent he is waking up to the realisation that a running river cannot be dammed for ever without breaking its bounds. His power of expression has been hampered, but it is breaking through, and will very soon sweep away the patronage and repression which surround him. . . .

The Gikuyu System of Government

The Gikuyu system of government prior to the advent of the Europeans was based on true democratic principles. But according to the tribal legend, once upon a time there was a king in Gikuyuland, named Gikuyu, a grandchild of the elder daughter of the founder of the tribe. He ruled many moons and his method of governing was tyrannical. . . .

After King Gikuyu was dethroned, the government of the country was at once changed from a despotism to a democracy which was in keeping with the wishes of the majority of the people. This revolution is known as *itwika*, derived from the word *twika*, which means to break away from and signified the breaking away from autocracy to democracy. This achievement was celebrated all over the country; feasting, dancing and singing went on at intervals for a period of six moons which preceded the new era of government by the people and for the people. In order to run the new government successfully, it was necessary to have a constitution, so during this time of festivities a revolutionary council, *njama ya itwika*, was formed to draft the constitution. . . .

Every village appointed a representative to the Council, which took the responsibility of drafting the new constitution. . . . At the first meeting of the *njama ya itwika* it was decided that in order to maintain harmony in the government of the country, it was necessary to make a few rules which would act as the guiding principles in the new government; and the following rules, which afterwards became law, were made:

1. Freedom for the people to acquire and develop land under a system of family ownership.
2. Universal tribal membership, as the unification of the whole tribe, the qualification for it to be based on maturity, and not on property. . . .

3. Socially and politically all circumcised men and women should be equally full members of the tribe, and thereby the status of a king or nobleman should be abolished. . . .

8. All men and women must get married, and that no man should be allowed to hold a responsible position other than warrior, or become a member of the council of elders (*kiama*) unless he was married and had established his own homestead. And that women should be given the same social status as their husbands.

9. Criminal and civil laws were established and procedure clearly defined. . .

Source: Jomo Kenyatta, *Facing Mt. Kenya: The Tribal Life of the Gikuyu* (New York: Random House, 1965 [1938]), xviii, 179–182.

10. JAPANESE STATEMENT TO THE LEAGUE OF NATIONS (1932)

Japanese businesses had expanded into the northeast Chinese province of Manchuria, while Russians had also built railroads in collaboration with the Chinese across the region. Japan saw Russia encroaching on its ambitions to control the territory and in 1931, used the pretense of the sabotage of its train by the Chinese—a train which the Japanese army itself had actually blown up—to justify invading and taking over the province. This was called the Mukden incident. After the invasion, the Japanese renamed Manchuria the state of "Manchukuo," installed the last Qing emperor, Puyi, as puppet head of state, and ruled it from behind the scenes. Japanese colonists poured into the area, and the press went wild with enthusiasm for expansion. The League of Nations censured Japan's aggression, with the Japanese themselves subsequently withdrawing from the League. In their defense, the Japanese cited a new menace: the Soviet Union, even though Russians had been in the area for centuries. The Japanese ambassador's statement to the League uses a familiar imperialist argument: that the region to be conquered was disorganized or badly ruled and that a more highly civilized and modern government was needed. As usual, it was the chaos of imperial aggression that had caused the disorder in the first place. What specific charges does the Japanese ambassador level at China?

The [report by the League on the invasion of Manchukuo] has brought a strong light to bear upon the conditions prevailing in China which representatives of her Government throughout the world have long sought to cover, to excuse and to condone. There are many parts and passages in the Report which we regard as entirely correct and accurate. Our principal disagreement with the Report, in the sections dealing with the disordered condition of China, is where it occasionally expresses optimism for the rehabilitation of the country. We, too, have hope, but it is not for the immediate future, for a country in China's condition of disorganization, as Chinese history shows, cannot recover quickly. . . .

Japan is a loyal supporter of the League of Nations. In conformity with the principles of peace, on which the League is founded, we have striven to avoid war for many years under provocations that, prior to the drafting of the Covenant, would certainly have brought it about. Our adherence to the Covenant has been a guiding principle in our foreign policy for the thirteen years of the League's existence, and we have been proud to participate in the advancement of its noble project. No open- minded person who has observed our long and earnest patience in our relations with China can contend to the contrary.

Our Government was still persisting earnestly in efforts to induce the Chinese Government at Nanking and that of Chang Hsueh-liang at Mukden, to see the light of reason when the incident of September 18th, 1931, took place. We wanted no such situation as has developed. We sought in Manchuria only the observance of our treaty rights and the safety of the lives of our people and their property. We wanted from China the right to trade, according to existing treaties, free from unwarranted interference and molestation. But our policy of patience and our efforts at persuasion were misinterpreted by the Chinese people. Our attitude was regarded as weakness, and provocations became persistently more unbearable.

A Government which had its beginning as a result of aid obtained from Soviet Russia, in arms, men and money (seven or eight years ago) and which is still imbued with what are called "revolutionary" principles, was not content to injure our trading interests in China proper, but extended its campaign against us into Manchuria with the avowed purpose of driving us out of that territory—territory which we, through war with Russia, had returned to the Manchu Dynasty twenty-seven years ago. That our rights and interests were assailed, and even, in some Leases, the persons of Japanese subjects attacked, are facts established by record. That we acted in self-defense is clear and warranted. . . .

Our Government was in no such position with regard to Manchuria, because it did not expect the incident of September 18th, 1931, to take place. Our Government had no knowledge of the trouble until after it occurred. But, on learning of it, we informed the League. It must be well noted, in this connection, that, prior to the incident, we had been making every effort to negotiate and bring about better understanding and feelings in Manchuria, and had not abandoned until the last moment the hope that our efforts would be crowned with success. Our Government also hoped subsequently to check the developments and limit their scope in the affected territory, but too many elements were active in opposition. Chinese military forces were mobilized at Chinchow and rebel armies . . . assembled in other parts of the country.

Later, in October, 1931, Japan proposed to enter into direct negotiations with China, with a view to arriving at a pacific settlement of the controversy. Our Government was insistent on this point. But the Council of the League failed to countenance it, and China, encouraged by the attitude taken by the League, turned a deaf ear to this proposal, thus stiffening and complicating the situation. What followed is well known. At the same time, the boycott—which had been going on in China before the incident—was greatly, intensified, thereby provoking, on the one hand, further ill-feelings in Japan and, on the other hand, adding fuel to the mob psychology in China.

The Chinese Representative spoke before the Council the other day of the legalization of the boycott. If that is admitted, it is sure to create a very serious situation. In point of fact, the statement he made in that sense provoked a fresh outbreak of the boycott in many parts of China (as related at length in the communication made by our delegation yesterday to the League).

The boycott, as we see it in China, is a great hindrance to the promotion of international peace and co-operation. It creates circumstances which threaten the good understanding between nations, on which peace depends. It therefore deserves a thorough consideration on the part of the League, one of whose primary duties lies in the elimination of possible causes of friction between nations.

While the situation was developing in Manchuria, efforts were made in Europe and America to rally what is called "world opinion" against Japan. The craft of propaganda . . . encouraged Chinese leaders to take an uncompromising attitude towards us. It encouraged them to believe that Western countries would interfere and save them from the consequence of their anti-foreign policies as they were applied to Japan and her interests. . . .

In dealing with China, Japan is dealing with a State in a menacing condition. The actual menace to us not only existed prior to the incident of September 18th, 1931, but was being intensified by the activities of the Kuomintang Party and officials of the Nanking Government. . . . Against such a party and Government, and against their declared policy and active efforts to terminate our interests and treaties in Manchuria, we have acted in defense. We have acted also with a view to promoting and preserving peace. Because our action came as the result of an incident does not alter the general fact. It had to come sooner or later. The menace to Japan was actual. If her rights and interests in Manchuria were violated, the sufferer would be none but Japan.

With regard to the recognition of Manchoukuo there is this to say. The new government had the sympathy of all Japanese people. We saw in it the solution of a problem which had troubled us for forty years. We saw in it the termination of hostile incitement from China Proper. We saw the advent of a civil Government, composed of reasonable men who understood the strategic and economic importance of the territory to Japan. We saw the promise of peace for the future. We wanted peace. We did not, and we do not, want Manchuria. We wanted only the preservation of our rights and interests there. Here at hand, was the solution, the prompt recognition of Manchoukuo; and our Government, in giving that recognition, acted in response to the demands of the Japanese people and the appeals of Manchoukuo. . . .

Since the proclamation of the Republic in China, Governments have been short-lived. They have risen and fallen in quick succession. And now what do we see? A National Government that had its beginning in the Russian movement to "sovietize" China. . . . I might even say that communism is to-day eating into the very heart of China. . . .

Our action in recognizing the State of Manchoukuo was the only and the surest way for us to take in the present circumstances. In the absence of any other means of stabilizing conditions in that territory—where we have interests, both strategic and economic, which we cannot sacrifice—we had no other recourse. . . .

Source: Japanese Delegation to the League of Nations, *Japan's Case in the Sino-Japanese Dispute as Presented before the Special Session of the Assembly of the League of Nations* (Geneva: League of Nations, 1933), 12–21 passim. Also available at Internet Archive http://archive.org/details/japanscasein sino00leag/japanscaseinsino00leag_djvu.txt

11. HAILE SELASSIE, *APPEAL TO THE LEAGUE OF NATIONS* (1936)

As an institution of world governance, the League of Nations was meant to adjudicate disputes among its members. In the fall of 1935, following the lead of Adolf Hitler, who had denounced the Treaty of Versailles that year and then remilitarized the Rhineland the next, Italian dictator Benito Mussolini sent troops into Ethiopia. With both Italy and Ethiopia members of the League, the emperor Haile Selassie urged the international body to support its autonomy, as Italian troops used their superior weaponry ultimately to defeat the Ethiopians in December 1936. Although the League had imposed minimal sanctions on Italy with its first attacks in 1935, by the summer of 1936 it lifted them with signs of the Italian victory. While Italians celebrated the advance of their empire, Selassie's remarks in retrospect seem prophetic: "It is us today," he warned, "It will be you tomorrow." Italy along with Germany and Japan proceeded to expand further, taking over ever more territory. How do the accusations of Ethiopia against Italy differ from those of Japan against China?

"I, Haile Selassie I, Emperor of Ethiopia, am here today to claim that justice which is due to my people, and the assistance promised to it eight months ago, when fifty nations asserted that aggression had been committed in violation of international treaties.

There is no precedent for a Head of State himself speaking in this assembly. But there is also no precedent for a people being victim of such injustice and being at present threatened by abandonment to its aggressor. Also, there has never before been an example of any Government proceeding to the systematic extermination of a nation by barbarous means, in violation of the most solemn promises made by the nations of the earth that there should not be used against innocent human beings the terrible poison of harmful gases. . . .

It is not only upon warriors that the Italian Government has made war. It has above all attacked populations far removed from hostilities, in order to terrorize and exterminate them.

It was at the time when the operations for the encircling of Makalle were taking place that the Italian command, fearing a rout, followed the procedure which it is now my duty to denounce to the world. Special sprayers were installed on board aircraft so that they could vaporize, over vast areas of territory, a fine, death-dealing rain. Groups of nine, fifteen, eighteen aircraft followed one another so that the fog issuing from them formed a continuous sheet. It was thus that, as from the end of January, 1936, soldiers, women, children, cattle, rivers, lakes and pastures were drenched continually with this deadly rain. In order to kill off systematically all living creatures, in order to more surely to poison waters and pastures, the Italian command made its aircraft pass over and over again. That was its chief method of warfare.

Ravage and Terror

The very refinement of barbarism consisted in carrying ravage and terror into the most densely populated parts of the territory, the points farthest removed from the scene of hostilities. The object was to scatter fear and death over a great part of the Ethiopian territory. These fearful tactics succeeded. Men and animals succumbed. The deadly rain that fell from the aircraft made all those whom it touched fly shrieking with pain. All those who drank the poisoned water or ate the infected food also succumbed in dreadful suffering. In tens of thousands, the victims of the Italian mustard gas fell. It is in order to denounce to the civilized world the tortures inflicted upon the Ethiopian people that I resolved to come to Geneva. None other than myself and my brave companions in arms could bring the League of Nations the undeniable proof. The appeals of my delegates addressed to the League of Nations had remained without any answer; my delegates had not been witnesses. That is why I decided to come myself to bear witness against the crime perpetrated against my people and give Europe a warning of the doom that awaits it . . .

From the outset of the dispute, the Ethiopian Government has sought a settlement by peaceful means. It has appealed to the procedures of the Covenant. The Italian Government desiring to keep strictly to the procedures of the Italo-Ethiopian Treaty of 1928, the Ethiopian Government assented. It invariably stated that it would faithfully carry out the arbitral award even if the decision went against it.

In October, 1935. the 52 nations who are listening to me today gave me an assurance that the aggressor would not triumph, that the resources of the Covenant would be employed in order to ensure the reign of right and the failure of violence.

. . . Counting on the faith due to treaties, I had made no preparation for war, and that is the case with certain small countries in Europe.

Forced to Mobilize

On October 3rd, 1935, the Italian troops invaded my territory. A few hours later only I decreed general mobilization. In my desire to maintain peace I had, following the example of a great country in Europe on the eve of the Great War, caused my troops to withdraw thirty kilometres so as to remove any pretext of provocation.

War then took place in the atrocious conditions which I have laid before the Assembly. . . . In December, 1935, the Council made it quite clear that its feelings were in harmony with those of hundreds of millions of people who, in all parts of the world, had protested against the proposal to dismember Ethiopia.

What have become of the promises made to me as long ago as October, 1935? I noted with grief, but without surprise that three Powers considered their undertakings under the Covenant as absolutely of no value. Their connections with Italy impelled them to refuse to take any measures whatsoever in order to stop Italian aggression. . . . As soon as any measure which was likely to be rapidly effective was proposed, various pretexts were devised in order to postpone even consideration of the measure.

Finally a statement has just been made in their Parliaments by the Governments of certain Powers, amongst them the most influential members of the League of Nations, that since the aggressor has succeeded in occupying a large part of Ethiopian territory they propose not to continue the application of any economic and financial measures that may have been decided upon against the Italian Government. . . .

I have heard it asserted that the inadequate sanctions already applied have not achieved their object. At no time, and under no circumstances could sanctions that were intentionally inadequate, intentionally badly applied, stop an aggressor. This is not a case of the impossibility of stopping an aggressor but of the refusal to stop an aggressor.

I ask the fifty-two nations, who have given the Ethiopian people a promise to help them in their resistance to the aggressor, what are they willing to do for Ethiopia? And the great Powers who have promised the guarantee of collective security to small States on whom weighs the threat that they may one day suffer the fate of Ethiopia, I ask what measures do you intend to take?

. . . .What reply shall I have to take back to my people?"

Source: Widely available on the Internet.

12. IMPERIAL ARMY DRAFT, "THE GREATER EAST ASIA CO-PROSPERITY SPHERE" (1942)

During the Meiji Restoration of 1868 establishing an organized nation-state under an emperor and parliament, Japan began conquering an overseas empire. The idea was that such actions would prevent other imperial powers from gobbling it up. These seemingly piecemeal conquests evolved into more ambitious plans in the 1920s and 1930s, as businesses and the military started moving into Manchuria and the main cities of China. Spies, dirty tricks, and outright violence by the Japanese disrupted the already challenged Nationalist government in China, even as it motivated the Japanese public to support Japanese dreams of an even greater empire. As this situation evolved in the 1930s, the Japanese government devised a series of ever more all-encompassing visions of imperial expansion, this one from 1942 found in draft form. Describe Japanese imperial ambitions as announced in this document.

The Form of East Asiatic Independence and Co-Prosperity.

The states, their citizens, and resources, comprised in those areas pertaining to the Pacific, Central Asia, and the Indian Oceans formed into one general union are to be established as an autonomous zone of peaceful living and common prosperity on behalf of the peoples of the nations of East Asia. The area including Japan, Manchuria, North China, lower Yangtze River, and the Russian Maritime Province, forms the nucleus of the East Asiatic Union. The Japanese empire possesses a duty as the leader of the East Asiatic Union.

The above purpose presupposes the inevitable emancipation or independence of Eastern Siberia, China, Indo-China, the South Seas, Australia, and India.

Regional Division in the East Asiatic Union and
The National Defense Sphere for The Japanese Empire.

In the Union of East Asia, the Japanese empire is at once the stabilizing power and the leading influence. To enable the empire actually to become the central influence in East Asia, the first necessity is the consolidation of the inner belt of East Asia; and the East Asiatic Sphere shall be divided as follows for this purpose:

The Inner Sphere—the vital sphere for the empire—includes Japan, Manchuria, North China, the lower Yangtze Area and the Russian Maritime area.

The Smaller Co-Prosperity Sphere—the smaller self-supplying sphere of East Asia—includes the smaller co-prosperity sphere, plus Australia, India, and island groups in the Pacific. . . .

For the present, the smaller co-prosperity sphere shall be the zone in which the construction of East Asia and the stabilization of national defenses are to be aimed at. After their completion there shall be a gradual expansion toward the construction of the Greater Co-Prosperity Sphere.

Source: "Draft of Basic Plan for Establishment of Greater East Asia Co-Prosperity Sphere," in *Sources of Japanese Tradition*, Ryusaku Tsunoda et al. (New York: Columbia University Press, 1958), 801–802.

REVIEW QUESTIONS

1. Which authors propose to live with empire and which have nothing but scorn? Describe their differences.
2. Describe the grievances of the colonized in these years and compare them to earlier charges against empire.
3. What are the visions of empire described by the Japanese, Hitler, and Coolidge? Compare their reasons for imperial action.
4. From being a lawyer attired in tailored English suits, Mohandas Gandhi began to dress differently in the 1920s as a leader of the Indian nationalist movement. What do his change of dress and his taking up of spinning indicate to you? What differing reactions would people at the time have had to this change? http://www.abc.net.au/news/2014-04-05/mahatma-mohandas-gandhi/3935842

CHAPTER 11

World War II and the Growing Call for Independence

World War II was yet another war caused by clashing ambitions in the drive for empire, enlisting and destroying more of the world's peoples and property than ever before. Japan's invasion of China in 1937 began the hostilities; German aggression followed, picking off Austria and Czechoslovakia in eastern Europe in 1938 after first marching troops into the demilitarized Rhineland in 1935. Germany's annexations of 1938 were followed by its invasion of Poland in 1939, which united France and Great Britain in an effort to block further conquest of former Habsburg lands. Meanwhile, just before the attack on Poland, Germany and the Soviet Union allied, each of them eager to claim as much as possible of east-central Europe. Yet Soviet and German ambitions themselves clashed when Germany invaded the USSR in 1941. At that point the Soviets joined with Britain and France; after Japan bombed Pearl Harbor and the Philippines in December 1941, the United States also joined the coalition. World War II continued until 1945, when the Allies dominated by Britain, the Soviet Union, and the United States achieved their victory over the expansionist Axis powers of Germany, Japan, and Italy. The cost in human life has been estimated to be as high as 100 million people, killed in the name of imperial ambition and the racist ideologies supporting that ambition. Far more civilians than soldiers were killed in this war; from then on, the safest place during wartime was the battlefield. Had imperial chaos reached its limit?

Colonized peoples fought in imperial armies and served as forced laborers as they had thirty years earlier in World War I, and imperial governments declared war against the Axis in the name of their colonies. Africans were conscripted to build roads, carry supplies, and give up their livelihoods, produce, equipment, and other resources on behalf of their masters. Two million Indian men, mostly from the northwest of the colony, served in the Middle East and African theaters of war. They were the lucky ones among the Indian population, for British officials forced the sale of locally produced Indian grain and its transport to the armies and to the granaries in Britain. Prime Minister Winston Churchill was so racist in his attitude toward Indians that he turned a deaf ear when his own ministers pointed to the consequences of stripping India of its crops. He also refused U.S., Australian, and other offers to send excess grain to India, saying that ordinary Indians were already over-stuffed with food. At least three million people died in the resulting famine.

The Japanese professed to liberate Europe's colonies while simultaneously forcing civilians in Southeast Asia, for example, into forced labor and the women of the region into prostitution to serve the military. The devastation of many parts of the world was horrific, not only killing civilians but dramatically affecting their lives by stripping away resources, not to mention human dignity. The Atlantic Charter of 1941, signed by U.S. President Franklin D. Roosevelt and British Prime Minister Winston Churchill, affirmed "the right of all peoples to choose the form of government under which they will live." Most of the western European imperial powers announced that this affirmation did not pertain to people in the colonies however. Manipulating colonized peoples, imperial combatants promised freedom for co-operation, but colonized people had heard all this before. In addition, the racial ideologies that empire had fostered allowed imperialists, whose superiority scientists were said to have proven, to run rampant over those people whom scientists deemed "inferior." The earlier genocide inflicted by European and other imperial powers was ratcheted up during World War II and in its aftermath as the deliberate killing of the so-called racially worthless took the lives of millions— Jews, Slavs, Roma and Sinti, and gays in Europe, Indians in Bengal, and many East and Southeast Asians. Many see Churchill's pronouncements against the population of India as another manifestation of imperial racism.

Colonized people were increasingly aware of the cost of that imperial racism not just to themselves but to the competing empires. France, the Netherlands, and Belgium were so drained from securing their colonies that they could hardly match Germany's and Japan's onslaughts. As a result, Japan scooped up colonies in Southeast Asia and the Pacific, while Germany moved into both eastern and western Europe and then the Middle East and North Africa as well. Sensing weakness and organizing for independence, Indian nationalists during the war called on Britain to leave South Asia immediately; some even met with Hitler and fielded their own army to fight alongside the Japanese against the British. Southeast Asian activists co-operated with the Japanese to cast off European rule. The imperial grip was disintegrating in the Middle East and Africa too, as organizing among local people flourished.

The war drained winners and losers alike, so that the immediate aftermath of war saw the collapse of Germany's, Japan's, and Italy's empires, the decolonization of India in 1947, and a successful Communist revolution in China in 1949 that rejected Western influence. The Atlantic Charter initially seemed to be fulfilling its aims and allowing peoples to choose their political destiny. At the end of the war, Indian soldiers, businessmen, and workers, for example, were finally so enraged at the dishonest thievery by the British that they staged strikes and protests even as the British continued to mow them down. It became apparent to

British leaders—to some, even during the war—that India had reached the breaking point and that the British would have to leave. Britain itself was bankrupt and owed a huge debt to India for resources it had plundered and even for those that it had bought without paying. Consolidating these early achievements of independence, the United Nations was formed at the end of the war and passed a Charter and Declaration of Human Rights that endorsed free choice in the form of government and the enforcement of rights for all people. By this time, such efforts at governance seemed a standard reaction to orgies of imperial violence, allowing empires to catch their breath.

Simultaneously with moves toward world governance, postwar nation-building, and independence, however, the Allies still hoped to hold onto remaining empires or expand them. Once critical of imperialists, the Soviet Union extended its control farther into eastern Europe. The Apartheid regime in South Africa became more repressive, while the French, British, and Dutch fought tenaciously to keep many of their other colonies. As these contradictory moves took place—freedom for some, recolonization for others—the United States turned its attention away from ending colonialism and toward winning another conflict—the Cold War. Given superpower distractions, some empires seized the moment to crush new attempts at independence. The imprisonment, torture, and slaughter of Kenyans, Algerians, Vietnamese, and South Africans—to name a few—resulted, often appearing to be an interlocking effort.

1. MUHAMMAD ALI JINNAH, "DIVIDE INDIA; CREATE PAKISTAN" (1940)

Muhammad Ali Jinnah (1876–1948) was a prosperous lawyer in Bombay who before World War I joined the Muslim League, inspired in part by the British to form a counterweight to the Hindu-dominated Indian National Congress. For the British, the rationale behind sponsoring a second reformist group in the Raj was to divide and conquer—that is, keeping two of the major religious groups from joining forces. Increasingly, Muslims came to see themselves as potentially second-class citizens in an independent India, which looked ever more likely as World War II strained Britain's resources and its capacity to rule. At the time of this speech, Jinnah was president of the All-India Muslim League, lobbying for an independent "Pakistan" ("land of the pure") for Muslims, separate from India, which would be predominately Hindu. Although Muslims and Hindus, not to mention many other religious groups, had lived in relative peace before this, the stoking of tensions as the war unfolded made for widespread violence as Muslims, Sikhs, Hindus, and others organized paramilitary groups. What differences does Jinnah see among the peoples of the Asian subcontinent?

The problem in India is not of an inter-communal character but manifestly of an international one, and it must be treated as such. If the British Government are really in earnest and sincere to secure peace and happiness of the people of this subcontinent, the only course open to us all is to allow the major nations separate homelands by dividing India into "autonomous national states." There is no reason why these states should be antagonistic to each other. On the other hand the rivalry and the natural desire and efforts on the part of one to dominate the social order and establish political supremacy over the other in the government of the country will disappear. It will lead more towards natural good-will by international pacts between them, and they can live in complete harmony with their neighbors. This will lead further to a friendly settlement all the more easily with regard to minorities by reciprocal arrangements and adjustments between Muslim India and Hindu India, which will far more adequately and effectively safeguard the rights and interests of Muslims and various other minorities.

It is extremely difficult to appreciate why our Hindu friends fail to understand the real nature of Islam and Hinduism. They are not religions in the strict sense of the word, but are, in fact, different and distinct social orders, and it is a dream that the Hindus and Muslims can ever evolve a common nationality, and this misconception of one Indian nation has gone far beyond the limits and is the cause of most of your troubles and will lead India to destruction if we fail to revise our notions in time. The Hindus and Muslims belong to two different religious philosophies, social customs, literatures. They neither intermarry nor interdine together and, indeed, they belong to two different civilizations which are based mainly on conflicting ideas and conceptions. Their aspects on life and of life are different. It is quite clear that Hindus and Muslims derive their inspiration from different sources of history. They have different epics, different heroes, and different episodes. Very often the hero of one is a foe of the other and, likewise, their victories and defeats overlap. To yoke together two such nations under a single state, one as a numerical minority and the other as a majority, must lead to growing discontent and final destruction of any fabric that may be so built up for the government of such a state.

The present artificial unity of India dates back only to the British conquest and is maintained by the British bayonet, but the termination of the British regime, which is implicit in the recent declaration of his Majesty's Government, will be the herald of the entire break-up with worse disaster than has ever taken place during the last one thousand years under Muslims. Surely that is not the legacy which Britain would bequeath to India after 150 years of her rule, nor would Hindu and Muslim India risk such a sure catastrophe.

Muslim India cannot accept any constitution which must necessarily result in a Hindu majority government. Hindus and Muslims brought together under a democratic system forced upon the minorities can only mean Hindu *raj*. Democracy of the kind with which the Congress High Command is enamored would mean the complete destruction of what is most precious in Islam.

Muslims are not a minority as it is commonly known and understood. One only has to look round. Even today, according to the British map of India, 4 out of 11 provinces, where the Muslims dominate more or less, are functioning notwithstanding the decision of the Hindu Congress High Command to . . . prepare for civil disobedience. Muslims are a nation according to any definition of a nation, and they must have their homelands, their territory and their state. We wish to live in peace and harmony with our neighbors as a free and independent people. We wish our people to develop to the fullest our spiritual, cultural, economic, social and political life in a way that we think best and in consonance with our own ideals and according to the genius of our people. Honesty demands and the vital interests of millions of our people impose a sacred duty upon us to find an honorable and peaceful solution, which would be just and fair to all. But at the same time we cannot be moved or diverted from our purpose and objective by threats or intimidations. We must be prepared to face all difficulties and consequences, make all the sacrifices that may be required of us to achieve the goal we have set in front of us.

[This is] the task that lies ahead of us. Do you realize how big and stupendous it is? Do you realize that you cannot get freedom or independence by mere arguments? The intelligentsia in all countries in the world have been the pioneers of any movements of freedom. What does the Muslim intelligentsia propose to do? I may tell you that unless you get this into your blood, unless you are prepared to take off your coats and are willing to sacrifice all that you can and work selflessly, earnestly and sincerely for your people, you will never realize your aim. Friends, I therefore want you to make up your mind definitely and then think of devices and organize your people, strengthen your organization and consolidate the Muslims all over India. I think that the masses are wide awake. They only want your guidance and your lead. Come forward as servants of Islam, organize the people economically, socially, educationally and politically and I am sure that you will be a power that will be accepted by everybody.

Source: *Some Recent Speeches and Writings of Mr. Jinnah*, Jamil-Ud-Din Ahmad, ed. 3rd ed. (Lahore: Sh. M. Ashraf, 1943), 152–156, as reproduced in *The Middle East and Islamic World Reader*, Marvin Gettleman and Stuart Schaar, eds. (New York: Grove Press, 2003), 136–138.

2. MOHANDAS GANDHI, QUIT INDIA DECLARATION (1942)

The India National Congress and the Muslim League had for decades petitioned for rights and, eventually, for independence from Great Britain. On the eve of World War II the British had promised that those rights would soon be realized. Yet when war broke out in 1939, Britain not only postponed the implementation of those rights but simultaneously issued an Indian declaration of war on Britain's European enemies. During the course of the war some two million South Asian men were mobilized, taxes raised there, and agricultural and other resources confiscated for the war effort. Some thus protested British rule even more, including Subhas Chandra Bose who organized the Indian National Army that allied itself with Japan. Supporting non-violence, Mohandas Gandhi in contrast called for a strike in 1942 with the aim of forcing Britain to "Quit India." The British imprisoned those leading and participating in the strike, only strengthening the opposition to imperialism and the demands for independence. What is Gandhi's attitude toward the British?

There are people who ask me whether I am the same man that I was in 1920, or whether there has been any change in me. You are right in asking that question. Let me, however, hasten to assure that I am the same Gandhi as I was in 1920. I have not changed in any fundamental respect. I attach the same importance to nonviolence that I did then. If at all, my emphasis on it has grown stronger. There is no real contradiction between the present resolution and my previous writings and utterances.

Occasions like the present do not occur in everybody's and but rarely in anybody's life. I want you to know and feel that there is nothing but purest *Ahimsa* [the idea of doing no harm] in all that I am saying and doing today. The draft resolution of the Working Committee is based on *Ahimsa*, the contemplated struggle similarly has its roots in *Ahimsa*. If, therefore, there is any among you who has lost faith in *Ahimsa* or is wearied of it, let him not vote for this resolution. . . .

Ours is not a drive for power, but purely a nonviolent fight for India's independence. In a violent struggle, a successful general has been often known to effect a military coup and to set up a dictatorship. But under the Congress scheme of things, essentially non-violent as it is, there can be no room for dictatorship. A non-violent soldier of freedom will covet nothing for himself, he fights only for the freedom of his country. The Congress is unconcerned as to who will rule, when freedom is attained. The power, when it comes, will belong to the people of India, and it will be for them to decide to whom it should be entrusted. . . .

I know how imperfect our *Ahimsa* is and how far away we are still from the ideal, but in *Ahimsa* there is no final failure or defeat. . . . I believe that in the history of the world, there has not been a more genuinely democratic struggle for freedom than ours. I read Carlyle's *French Revolution* while I was in prison, and Pandit Jawaharlal has told me something about the Russian revolution. But it is my conviction that inasmuch as these struggles were fought with the weapon of violence they failed to realize the democratic ideal. In the democracy which I have envisaged, a democracy established by nonviolence, there will be equal freedom for all. Everybody will be his own master. It is to join a struggle for such democracy that I invite you today. Once you realize this you will forget the differences between the Hindus and Muslims, and think of yourselves as Indians only, engaged in the common struggle for independence.

Then, there is the question of your attitude toward the British. I have noticed that there is hatred toward the British among the people. The people say they are disgusted with their behavior. The people make no distinction between British imperialism and the British people. To them, the two are one. This hatred would even make them welcome the Japanese. It is most dangerous. It means that they will exchange one slavery for another. We must get rid of this feeling. Our quarrel is not with the British people, we fight their imperialism. The proposal for the withdrawal of British power did not come out of anger. It came to enable India to play its due part at the present critical juncture. It is not a happy position for a big country like India to be merely helping with money and material obtained willy-nilly from her while the United Nations [at the time, another name for the Allied Powers] are conducting the war. We cannot evoke the true spirit of sacrifice and valor, so long as we are not free. I know the British Government will not be able to withhold freedom from us, when we have made enough self-sacrifice. We must, therefore, purge ourselves of hatred. Speaking for myself, I can say that I have never felt any hatred. As a matter of fact, I feel myself to be a greater friend of the British now than ever before. One reason is that they are today in distress. My very friendship, therefore, demands that I should try to save them from their mistakes.

As I view the situation, they are on the brink of an abyss. It, therefore, becomes my duty to warn them of their danger even though it may, for the time being, anger them to the point of cutting off the friendly hand that is stretched out to help them. People may laugh, nevertheless that is my claim. At a time when I may have to launch the biggest struggle of my life, I may not harbor hatred against anybody.

Source: Shriman Narayan, ed., *The Selected Works of Mahatma Gandhi*, vol. 6, *The Voice of Truth* (Ahmedabad-14, India: Navajivan Publishing House, 1968), 50–54.

3. CH'OE IL-RYE, TESTIMONY OF A COMFORT WOMEN ON SEX SLAVERY DURING THE WAR POST–WORLD WAR II

Empires have always included the sexual engagement of conquering men and subjected women. In the case of Spanish and Inca and Aztec women, there were some partnerships in which princesses and other women with high social standing continued to wield social prestige and to hold political standing valuable to the Spanish. In the majority of cases, women in conquered societies were of lower standing, though their relationships could benefit their families. The history of the so-called comfort women of World War II shows the extreme side of imperial abuse, as Korean, Chinese, and other women in conquered regions were enslaved in military brothels. Many of these brothels passed to the Allied forces occupying East Asia at the war's end in 1945. The situation was abusive and ultimately so traumatic and humiliating to most of the women survivors that it was many decades before they would speak of this wartime aspect of empire. This is the account of Ch'oe Il-rye. What is the role of imperial rule in her story?

My family lived in the remote countryside in South Chŏlla Province where one could hardly see a car pass by. I did not know about schools or studying. My father was an agricultural laborer. My mother died of an illness after she gave birth to my younger sister. We were very poor, and I worked as a maid for a neighbor. It was in 1932, when I was sixteen years old, that two men in military uniforms [believed to be Japanese] abducted me from near a village well. The soldiers took me to a nearby city [possibly Kwangju], where we stayed for about a month so that they could gather more women. When we set out on the road, there were about thirty women riding in several trucks passing through Taejŏn, Seoul, and P'yŏngyang.

Upon the arrival of my group of five girls at a remote unpopulated battlefront in Manchuria on a very cold winter day, I watched the soldiers build their barracks using plywood and tent materials. A few yards away from their own large barracks, they built separate living quarters for us women. Metal wire fences surrounded the buildings, and two sentinels stood at the entrance to guard the barracks. At first, my group of five women was accommodated in one room, but later we were assigned to individual rooms. They also gave us new names. Mine was Haruko, and all five of us got along very well. The military provided us with meals and seasonal clothing.

A month or so after our arrival, a soldier came to conduct medical tests on us by drawing blood from the ear. After the test, a high-ranking officer summoned me to have sex. Until then I had no knowledge about the male sexual organ, let alone about coitus. The officer raped me, and I tried to accept everything as my fate. I recall that about thirty of us women resided scattered across the huge military compound. We gathered together for weekly medical examinations on a weekday when we did not serve soldiers.

For thirteen years, from 1932 to 1945, I labored as *wianbu*, serving only officers most of the time. Officers sent their men to fetch me to their places. My colleagues and I also worked as nurses and washerwomen for the soldiers. We would send off soldiers to battle, tend the wounded, and attend the funerals of those killed in combat, wearing black hats and kimonos. Sometimes, some of my colleagues and I became "serving women," which afforded us an opportunity to consume alcoholic drinks with the soldiers. There was no regular payment, but I was able to save a very large amount of money (about 1,000 yen) by accumulating the occasional tips of 2 to 3 yen given by some officers.

Toward the end of the war, when life became harder, without enough food to go around, an officer whom I served regularly told me to flee without telling the other women. He provided me with three white identification cards and explained to me in detail how to run away. I followed his instructions and was able to make it. By the time I arrived in Seoul, Korea was liberated. Then I returned to my hometown right away.

Source: C. Sarah Soh, *The Comfort Women: Sexual Violence and Post-Colonial Memory in Korea and Japan* (Chicago: University of Chicago Press, 2008), 125–127.

4. HO CHI MINH, DECLARATION OF VIETNAMESE INDEPENDENCE (1945)

Ho Chi Minh (1890–1969) was born in French colonial Indochina, receiving a classical education but setting out in his twenties to work on ships sailing the oceans. Traveling everywhere, including to the United States and Europe, Ho soon became a revolutionary and then a Communist after a stay in the Soviet Union in the 1920s. First and foremost, however, Ho was an anti-colonial leader, fighting the French control of Indochina as well as Chinese attempts to conquer the country in 1945. In that year, Ho declared Vietnamese independence, networking with a number of countries in hopes of achieving that end. After the 1954 defeat at Dien Bien Phu of the returning French, who expected to reclaim their empire easily after World War II, the Geneva Conference of great powers divided the country in two. Ho led the North Vietnamese attempt to reunify North and South, though he died before the United States had been driven from the south in 1975 and the unification fulfilled. Here is his Declaration of Independence. Note the references to founding values of the very countries seen by the Vietnamese and others as imperialist. In what ways does Ho's "Declaration" resemble other statements founding nations?

"All men are created equal. They are endowed by their Creator with certain inalienable rights; among these are Life, Liberty, and the pursuit of Happiness."

This immortal statement was made in the Declaration of Independence of the United States of America in *1776*. In a broader sense, this means: All the peoples on the earth are equal from birth, all the peoples have a right to live, to be happy and free.

The Declaration of the French Revolution made in *1791* on the Rights of Man and the Citizen also states: "All men are born free and with equal rights, and must always remain free and have equal rights."

Those are undeniable truths.

Nevertheless, for more than eighty years, the French imperialists, abusing the standard of Liberty, Equality, and Fraternity, have violated our Fatherland and oppressed our fellowcitizens. They have acted contrary to the ideals of humanity and justice.

In the field of politics, they have deprived our people of every democratic liberty.

They have enforced inhuman laws; they have set up three distinct political regimes in the North, the Center, and the South of Vietnam in order to wreck our national unity and prevent our people from being united.

They have built more prisons than schools. They have mercilessly slain our patriots; they have drowned our uprisings in rivers of blood.

They have fettered public opinion; they have practised obscurantism against our people. To weaken our race they have forced us to use opium and alcohol.

In the field of economics, they have fleeced us to the backbone, impoverished our people, and devastated our land.

They have robbed us of our rice fields, our mines, our forests, and our raw materials. They have monopolized the issuing of banknotes and the export trade.

They have invented numerous unjustifiable taxes and reduced our people, especially our peasantry, to a state of extreme poverty.

They have hampered the prospering of our national bourgeoisie; they have mercilessly exploited our workers.

In the autumn of 1940, when the Japanese Fascists violated Indochina's territory to establish new bases in their fight against the Allies, the French imperialists went down on their bended knees and handed over our country to them.

Thus, from that date, our people were subjected to the double yoke of the French and the Japanese. Their sufferings and miseries increased. The result was that from the end of last year to the beginning of this year, from Quang Tri province to the North of Vietnam, more than two million of our fellow citizens died from starvation. On March 9, the French troops were disarmed by the Japanese. The French colonialists either fled or surrendered showing that not only were they incapable of "protecting" us, but that, in the span of five years, they had twice sold our country to the Japanese.

On several occasions before March 9, the Vietminh League [understood by the French to be Communist] urged the French to ally themselves with it against the Japanese. Instead of agreeing to this proposal, the French colonialists so intensified their terrorist activities against the Vietminh members that before fleeing they massacred a great number of our political prisoners detained at Yen Bay and Caobang.

Notwithstanding all this, our fellowcitizens have always manifested toward the French a tolerant and humane attitude. Even after the Japanese putsch of March 1945, the Vietminh League helped many Frenchmen to cross the frontier, rescued some of them from Japanese jails, and protected French lives and property.

From the autumn of 1940, our country had in fact ceased to be a French colony and had become a Japanese possession.

After the Japanese had surrendered to the Allies, our whole people rose to regain our national sovereignty and to found the Democratic Republic of Vietnam.

The truth is that we have wrested our independence from the Japanese and not from the French.

The French have fled, the Japanese have capitulated, Emperor Bao Dai has abdicated. Our people have broken the chains which for nearly a century have fettered them and have won independence for the Fatherland. Our people at the same time have overthrown the monarchic regime that has reigned supreme for dozens of centuries. In its place has been established the present Democratic Republic.

For these reasons, we, members of the Provisional Government, representing the whole Vietnamese people, declare that from now on we break off all relations of a colonial character with France; we repeal all the international obligation that France has so far subscribed to on behalf of Vietnam and we abolish all the special rights the French have unlawfully acquired in our Fatherland.

The whole Vietnamese people, animated by a common purpose, are determined to fight to the bitter end against any attempt by the French colonialists to reconquer their country.

We are convinced that the Allied nations, which at Tehran and San Francisco have acknowledged the principles of self-determination and equality of nations, will not refuse to acknowledge the independence of Vietnam.

A people who have courageously opposed French domination for more than eight years, a people who have fought side by side with the Allies against the Fascists during these last years, such a people must be free and independent.

For these reasons, we, members of the Provisional Government of the Democratic Republic of Vietnam, solemnly declare to the world that Vietnam has the right to be a free and independent country—and in fact is so already. The entire Vietnamese people are determined to mobilize all their physical and mental strength, to sacrifice their lives and property in order to safeguard their independence and liberty.

Source: Ho Chi Minh, *Selected Writings (1920–1969)* (Hanoi: Foreign Languages Publishing House, 1973), 53–56.

5. UNITED NATIONS, UNIVERSAL DECLARATION OF HUMAN RIGHTS (1948)

The initial alliance of Britain, the United States, the USSR, and the Free French joined by dozens of other smaller nations was called the United Nations—an organizational name later given to collective body of states that came to replace the League of Nations. Established in 1945, just at the end of World War II, the United Nations aimed to end conflict on a global scale through negotiation and to protect the well-being of the world's people. There were internal problems in achieving these goals: Nations such as Britain wanted their empires restored even though colonized peoples wanted freedom; the USSR and the United States were engaged in an increasingly lethal cold war—lethal because they fought one another in proxy wars in Korea, Vietnam, and other regions of the world. Still, hope was alive, and pushed by reformers, the UN was able to issue a Universal Declaration of Human Rights that was supposed to override the ethos of imperialism and provide just global governance for all. That is, it aimed to eradicate the idea that some people—those in the metropole—were worthy of rights and decent treatment and that the colonized or formerly colonized were not worthy of rights. What tenets in this document provide for world governance and address the ills of empire?

Preamble

Whereas recognition of the inherent dignity and of the equal and inalienable rights of all members of the human family is the foundation of freedom, justice and peace in the world,

Whereas disregard and contempt for human rights have resulted in barbarous acts which have outraged the conscience of mankind, and the advent of a world in which human beings shall enjoy freedom of speech and belief and freedom from fear and want has been proclaimed as the highest aspiration of the common people,

Whereas it is essential, if man is not to be compelled to have recourse, as a last resort, to rebellion against tyranny and oppression, that human rights should be protected by the rule of law,

Whereas it is essential to promote the development of friendly relations between nations,

Whereas the peoples of the United Nations have in the Charter reaffirmed their faith in fundamental human rights, in the dignity and worth of the human person and in the equal rights of men and women and have determined to promote social progress and better standards of life in larger freedom,

Whereas Member States have pledged themselves to achieve, in co-operation with the United Nations, the promotion of universal respect for and observance of human rights and fundamental freedoms,

Whereas a common understanding of these rights and freedoms is of the greatest importance for the full realization of this pledge,

Now, Therefore THE GENERAL ASSEMBLY proclaims THIS UNIVERSAL DECLARATION OF HUMAN RIGHTS as a common standard of achievement for all peoples and all nations, to the end that every individual and every organ of society, keeping this Declaration constantly in mind, shall strive by teaching and education to promote respect for these rights and freedoms and by progressive measures, national and international, to secure their universal and effective recognition and observance, both among the peoples of Member States themselves and among the peoples of territories under their jurisdiction.

Article 1.
All human beings are born free and equal in dignity and rights. They are endowed with reason and conscience and should act towards one another in a spirit of brotherhood.

Article 2.
Everyone is entitled to all the rights and freedoms set forth in this Declaration, without distinction of any kind, such as race, colour, sex, language, religion, political or other opinion, national or social origin, property, birth or other status. Furthermore, no distinction shall be made on the basis of the political, jurisdictional or international status of the country or territory to which a person belongs, whether it be independent, trust, non-self-governing or under any other limitation of sovereignty.

Article 3.
Everyone has the right to life, liberty and security of person.

Article 4.
No one shall be held in slavery or servitude; slavery and the slave trade shall be prohibited in all their forms.

Article 5.
No one shall be subjected to torture or to cruel, inhuman or degrading treatment or punishment.

Article 6.

Everyone has the right to recognition everywhere as a person before the law.

Article 7.

All are equal before the law and are entitled without any discrimination to equal protection of the law. All are entitled to equal protection against any discrimination in violation of this Declaration and against any incitement to such discrimination.

Article 8.

Everyone has the right to an effective remedy by the competent national tribunals for acts violating the fundamental rights granted him by the constitution or by law.

Article 9.

No one shall be subjected to arbitrary arrest, detention or exile.

Article 10.

Everyone is entitled in full equality to a fair and public hearing by an independent and impartial tribunal, in the determination of his rights and obligations and of any criminal charge against him.

Article 11.

(1) Everyone charged with a penal offence has the right to be presumed innocent until proved guilty according to law in a public trial at which he has had all the guarantees necessary for his defence.

(2) No one shall be held guilty of any penal offence on account of any act or omission which did not constitute a penal offence, under national or international law, at the time when it was committed. Nor shall a heavier penalty be imposed than the one that was applicable at the time the penal offence was committed. . . .

Article 12.

No one shall be subjected to arbitrary interference with his privacy, family, home or correspondence, nor to attacks upon his honour and reputation. Everyone has the right to the protection of the law against such interference or attacks.

Article 13.

(1) Everyone has the right to freedom of movement and residence within the borders of each state.

(2) Everyone has the right to leave any country, including his own, and to return to his country.

Article 14.

(1) Everyone has the right to seek and to enjoy in other countries asylum from persecution.

(2) This right may not be invoked in the case of prosecutions genuinely arising from non-political crimes or from acts contrary to the purposes and principles of the United Nations.

Article 15.

(1) Everyone has the right to a nationality.

(2) No one shall be arbitrarily deprived of his nationality nor denied the right to change his nationality.

Article 16.

(1) Men and women of full age, without any limitation due to race, nationality or religion, have the right to marry and to found a family. They are entitled to equal rights as to marriage, during marriage and at its dissolution.

(2) Marriage shall be entered into only with the free and full consent of the intending spouses.

(3) The family is the natural and fundamental group unit of society and is entitled to protection by society and the State.

Article 17.

(1) Everyone has the right to own property alone as well as in association with others.

(2) No one shall be arbitrarily deprived of his property.

Article 18.

Everyone has the right to freedom of thought, conscience and religion; this right includes freedom to change his religion or belief, and freedom, either alone or in community with others and in public or private, to manifest his religion or belief in teaching, practice, worship and observance. . . . .

Article 19.

Everyone has the right to freedom of opinion and expression; this right includes freedom to hold opinions without interference and to seek, receive and impart information and ideas through any media and regardless of frontiers.

Article 20.

(1) Everyone has the right to freedom of peaceful assembly and association.

(2) No one may be compelled to belong to an association.

Article 21.

(1) Everyone has the right to take part in the government of his country, directly or through freely chosen representatives.

(2) Everyone has the right of equal access to public service in his country.

(3) The will of the people shall be the basis of the authority of government; this will shall be expressed in periodic and genuine elections which shall be by universal and equal suffrage and shall be held by secret vote or by equivalent free voting procedures.

Article 22.

Everyone, as a member of society, has the right to social security and is entitled to realization, through national effort and international co-operation and in accordance with the organization and resources of each State, of the economic, social and cultural rights indispensable for his dignity and the free development of his personality.

Article 23.

(1) Everyone has the right to work, to free choice of employment, to just and favourable conditions of work and to protection against unemployment.

(2) Everyone, without any discrimination, has the right to equal pay for equal work.

(3) Everyone who works has the right to just and favourable remuneration ensuring for himself and his family an existence worthy of human dignity, and supplemented, if necessary, by other means of social protection.

(4) Everyone has the right to form and to join trade unions for the protection of his interests.

Article 24.

Everyone has the right to rest and leisure, including reasonable limitation of working hours and periodic holidays with pay.

Article 25.

(1) Everyone has the right to a standard of living adequate for the health and well-being of himself and of his family, including food, clothing, housing and medical care and necessary social services, and the right to security in the event of unemployment, sickness, disability, widowhood, old age or other lack of livelihood in circumstances beyond his control.

(2) Motherhood and childhood are entitled to special care and assistance. All children, whether born in or out of wedlock, shall enjoy the same social protection.

Article 26.

(1) Everyone has the right to education. Education shall be free, at least in the elementary and fundamental stages. Elementary education shall be compulsory.

Technical and professional education shall be made generally available and higher education shall be equally accessible to all on the basis of merit.

(2) Education shall be directed to the full development of the human personality and to the strengthening of respect for human rights and fundamental freedoms. It shall promote understanding, tolerance and friendship among all nations, racial or religious groups, and shall further the activities of the United Nations for the maintenance of peace.

(3) Parents have a prior right to choose the kind of education that shall be given to their children. . . .

Source: United Nations, http://www.un.org/en/universal-declaration-human-rights/ accessed March 22, 2017.

6. BIBI INDER KAUR, "I SPREAD MY WINGS": EXPERIENCE OF THE PARTITION OF INDIA (1947)

Amid a series of uprisings and protests against the empire, the struggling British government let go of its hold on India in 1947. Other tensions had taken shape across the twentieth century among the various religious groups, with the British having emphasized differences among Muslims and Hindus when in fact, the Indian population comprised many religions. Once independence became inevitable due to the strength of liberation movements, the weak British establishment supported the formation of two nations as opposed to one unified state—a plan that fostered rivalries, the seizure of property, kidnapping of women and children, physical violence, and murder. As the August 15, 1947, date for the creation of two distinct nations— India and Pakistan—approached, suffering mounted and continued even into the 1950s because of civilian violence among competing factions in the society. The toll in deaths, rapes, and ruined lives was horrific—in the millions. Yet there were mixed experiences: For Bibi Inder Kaur the broken regional borders provided the opportunity for her to get advanced degrees and excellent jobs against her husband's will and community traditions—both of which had been weakened while overcoming the perils of escape had strengthened her. What sense of Partition do you find in this document?

How Partition affected men and women . . . You see . . . men . . . either they were killed or they escaped. Both ways they were . . . spared. If they died the problems died with them; if they survived they were resettled, they earned their daily bread and carried on. [But the women] were either left behind and treated like outcastes, often raped and brutalised—I mean if she came, she came with a guilty conscience, with the stigma of having been "soiled." And even if they were kept back and sent on later, the younger ones were never the ones to be returned. . . .

You see, we had never really thought of leaving Karachi . . . but after '47 we saw that our neighbours were looking at us differently, looking askance at us. Where my husband's clinic was, that was the place where they started kill-ing Sikhs. Their intentions took practical shape. But you can't blame them alone, people here also misbehaved. Now the way things happened in Rawalpindi, our original place . . . the way the Muslims slaughtered children, women . . . in Pindi Muslims were in the majority, they started attacking. After a while things cooled down a bit. But as soon as Partition happened the "work" that had been started by the Muslims was picked up here . . . we were no less. We also raped women, we also murdered and burnt houses here. It was a question of action and reaction.

. . . It was my husband who left me, really speaking, I always tried to keep some sort of relationship going with him. But I wasn't too unhappy because I had my job, a future. In a way I was glad that this obstacle had been removed. Partition provided me with the opportunity to get out of the four walls of my house. I had the will power, the intelligence, Partition gave me the chance. In Karachi I would have remained a housewife. Personally I feel Partition forced many people into taking the initiative and finding their own feet.

Source: Rita Menon and Kamla Bhasin, *Boundaries and Borders in India's Partition* (New Delhi: Kali for Women, 1999), 207–210, 214–215.

7. MAO ZEDONG, ADDRESS TO THE CHINESE PEOPLE'S POLITICAL CONSULTATIVE CONFERENCE (1949)

The son of prosperous Chinese peasants, Mao Zedong (1893–1976) spent his youth studying and engaging in student politics, including the May Fourth Movement of 1919. Farming was hardly his passion and he was coming to hate the arrogance of imperial powers slicing off parts of China for exploitation. By the mid-1930s he had become head of China's Communist Party, even as the Party itself faced attempts to destroy it by the Kuomintang or Nationalists, who were the heirs to the Qing dynasty in 1911–1912. After a massacre by the Kuomintang, Mao led the Communists out of the cities and into rural areas, as he developed his ideas of communism based on the force of the peasantry instead of the industrial workers. During the Japanese invasion late in the 1930s and throughout World War II, Mao joined with the Kuomintang to rid China of Japan's imperially minded armies. As opponents of the imperial powers—whether Japan, Germany, the United States, or Britain, which had slowly taken over Chinese ports and finance—the Communists struggled after the war against the Nationalists with their imperial connections. Here is Mao's speech on the eve of cre-ating a Communist regime in China after defeating the Nationalists. Evaluate this speech as one against the imperial domination of China by other world powers.

[O]ur work will go down in the history of mankind, demonstrating that the Chi-nese people, comprising one quarter of humanity, have now stood up. The Chinese have always been a great, courageous and industrious nation; it is only in modern times that they have fallen behind. And that was due entirely to oppression and exploitation by foreign imperialism and domestic reactionary governments. For over a century our forefathers never stopped waging unyielding struggles against domestic and foreign oppressors. . . . [N]ow we are proclaiming the founding of the People's Republic of China. From now on our nation will belong to the community of the peace-loving and freedom-loving nations of the world and work courageously and industriously to foster its own civilization and well-being and at the same time to promote world peace and freedom. Ours will no longer be a nation subject to insult and humiliation. We have stood up. Our revolution has won the sympathy and acclaim of the people of all countries. We have friends all over the world. . . .

Our state system, the people's democratic dictatorship, is a powerful weapon for safeguarding the fruits of victory of the people's revolution and for thwart-ing the plots of domestic and foreign enemies for restoration, and this weapon we must firmly grasp. Internationally, we must unite with all peace-loving and freedom-loving countries and peoples, and first of all with the Soviet Union and the New Democracies, so that we shall not stand alone in our struggle to safeguard these fruits of victory and to thwart the plots of domestic and foreign enemies for restoration. As long as we persist in the people's democratic dictatorship and unite with our foreign friends, we shall always be victorious.

The people's democratic dictatorship and solidarity with our foreign friends will enable us to accomplish our work of construction rapidly. We are already con-fronted with the task of nation-wide economic construction. We have very favour-able conditions: a population of 475 million people and a territory of 9,600,000 square kilometres. There are indeed difficulties ahead, and a great many too. But we firmly believe that by heroic struggle the people of the country will surmount them all. The Chinese people have rich experience in overcoming difficulties. If our forefathers, and we also, could weather long years of extreme difficulty and defeat powerful domestic and foreign reactionaries, why can't we now, after vic-tory, build a prosperous and flourishing country? As long as we keep to our style of plain living and hard struggle, as long as we stand united and as long as we persist in the people's democratic dictatorship and unite with our foreign friends, we shall be able to win speedy victory on the economic front.

An upsurge in economic construction is bound to be followed by an upsurge of construction in the cultural sphere. The era in which the Chinese people were regarded as uncivilized is now ended. We shall emerge in the world as a nation with an advanced culture.

Our national defence will be consolidated and no imperialists will ever again be allowed to invade our land. Our people's armed forces must be maintained and devel-oped with the heroic and steeled People's Liberation Army as the foundation. We will have not only a powerful army but also a powerful air force and a powerful navy.

Let the domestic and foreign reactionaries tremble before us! Let them say we are no good at this and no good at that. By our own indomitable efforts we the Chinese people will unswervingly reach our goal. . . .

Hail the founding of the People's Republic of China!

Source: *Selected Works of Mao Tse-tung*, vol. 5 (Beijing: Foreign Languages Press, 1977), 16–18. Also in Michael H. Hunt, *The World Transformed 1945 to the Present: A Documentary Reader* (Boston: Bedford St. Martins, 2004).

8. PEOPLE'S COURT IN PRAGUE, INDICTMENT OF MILADA HORÁKOVÁ (1950)

Imperial rulers often terrorize segments of a governed population to whip up loyalty, fear, or both among the conquered masses. Such was the case of Milada Horáková (1901–1950), who was accused of being the leader of a widespread and danger-ous terrorist organization in postwar Czechoslovakia and was executed. Guided by Soviet advisors, Horáková's trial in 1950 was the largest show trial in eastern Europe to that time and it occurred just a few years after Stalinists had taken over the Czech government. Far from having a terrorist past, Horáková had studied law in Prague, received her doctorate in 1927, lobbied for feminist reform, and been captured and sentenced to death by the Nazis early in World War II. Her death sentence commuted by the Germans, Horáková was freed from prison when the Soviets liberated Czecho-slovakia. She returned to being a democratic politician—a fatal mistake. She was condemned to death, as seen in the charge that follows, for attempting to undermine the "paradise" that would replace a backwards, corrupt society—a charge empires often launched against the conquered. Einstein, Churchill, and Eleanor Roosevelt— among others—worked to save her life, without success.

The trial of Dr. Milada Horakova and her twelve companions in the state court in Prague, May 31–June 8, 1950. . . . Here, facing the working people, on the bench of the accused are those who followed the shameful road of the bourgeoisie, of the criminals who joined against the people of this republic in order to thrust a dagger in their back. The traitors of the republic sit here fully unmasked. The trial of the enemies of the people took place in front of the working people of the whole republic. They were representatives of the class which lost its battles on the open stage, and now it no longer returns as a political force, but as a political under-world which is preparing a new Munich and a war against its own people. This trial however is not only ending as the unmasking of those obscure figures, but also of the gentlemen whom February blew to the West.

This trial reveals Messers Zenki and Ripka, Hais and Majer and all the rest . . . as professional agents of the American, English or French imperialists, as agents [selling] the main, now American, goods, war. After the war, the West-ern imperialists tried to penetrate into the Czechoslovak Republic over the bridge which was built for them by Messers Zenkl, Sramek, Lettrich and their companions.

Then in February '48 this bridge collapsed. Messers Zenkl, Ripka and Lettrich ran away from under it and pulled Monsignor Sramek and Hala out of the toilet of the Zatec airport, prepared to fly away on a French plane.

After February the rats crawled into their holes, and as a number of trials showed, they continued in the underground dancing according to the American whistle.

But the objective situation is not favorable to the gauleiters and little Hitlers. Our camp, the world camp of peace, democracy and socialism, led by the powerful Soviet Union, grows and becomes more powerful every day. We are fighting, and we are fighting for peace. We are building socialism. The accused wanted to stand in the way of this building. They are preparing war. They long for . . . closed factories, for Zenkl's beggars, [Zenkl was mayor of Prague before the war], for . . . pacts with the bourgeoisie, for the occupants. . . .

We advise the traitors at home and abroad: keep your hands off the republic. . . . I call on the working people to be ever watchful. May they learn from this case . . . to recognize the enemy, those . . . who prepare the new war, the servants of the aggressors. The people of our republic are not only building paradise on earth; they also will defend this paradise against the forces of the old, mean world which is condemned to destruction.

Source: Wilma Iggers, *Women of Prague: Ethnic Diversity and Social Change from the Eighteenth Century to the Present* (New York: Berghahn, 1995), 300–301.

9. FRANTZ FANON, *BLACK SKIN, WHITE MASKS* (1952)

Born in the French Caribbean, Frantz Fanon (1925–1961) professed to believe, like many colonized people, in European promises that imperial rule would bring civilization and uniform standards of rights. Fanon learned otherwise when he served in the French army during World War II and when he attended medical school in Paris. After becoming a psychiatrist, Fanon started writing sharp analyses of the situation of colonized people, people of color, and their rulers. From his own experience and that of his patients, he came to see the ways in which values such as a belief in the superiority of whites and their culture infected blacks. He also proposed that colonized peoples needed to drive whites out of their minds with violence because that was the way in which whites had gotten control of all aspects of black society, including its politics, economy, and culture. Fanon's books, written over the course of his very short life, became a powerful inspiration to decolonizers and reformers around the world: The Black Power movement in the United States adopted some of his ideas to counter the non-violent civil rights movement. What is your assessment of Fanon's thought in this passage?

Professor D. Westermann, in *The African Today* (p. 331), says that the Negroes' inferiority complex is particularly intensified among the most educated, who must struggle with it unceasingly. Their way of doing so, he adds, is frequently naïve: "The wearing of European clothes, whether rags or the most up-to-date style; using European furniture and European forms of social intercourse; adorning the Native language with European expressions; using bombastic phrases in speaking or writing a European language; all these contribute to a feeling of equality with the European and his achievements."

On the basis of other studies and my own personal observations, I want to try to show why the Negro adopts such a position, peculiar to him with respect to European languages. Let me point out once more that the conclusions I have reached pertain to the French Antilles; at the same time, I am not unaware that the same behavior patterns obtain in every race that has been subjected to colonization.

And then the occasion arose when I had to meet the white man's eyes. An unfamiliar weight burdened me. The real world challenged my claims. In the white world the man of color encounters difficulties in the development of his bodily schema. Consciousness of the body is solely a negating activity. It is a third-person consciousness. The body is surrounded by an atmosphere of certain uncertainty. I know that if I want to smoke, I shall have to reach out my right arm and take the pack of cigarettes lying at the other end of the table. The matches, however, are in the drawer on the left, and I shall have to lean back slightly. And all these movements are made not out of habit but out of implicit knowledge. A slow composition of my *self* as a body in the middle of a spatial and temporal world—such seems to be the schema. It does not impose itself on me; it is, rather, a definitive structuring of the self and of the world—definitive because it creates a real dialectic between my body and the world.

For several years certain laboratories have been trying to produce a serum for "denegrification"; with all the earnestness in the world, laboratories have sterilized their test tubes, checked their scales, and embarked on researches that might make it possible for the miserable Negro to whiten himself and thus to throw off the burden of that corporeal malediction. Below the corporeal schema I had sketched a historico-racial schema. The elements that I used had been provided for me not by "residual sensations and perceptions primarily of a tactile, vestibular, kinesthetic, and visual character," but by the other, the white man, who had woven me out of a thousand details, anecdotes, stories. I thought that what I had in hand was to construct a physiological self, to balance space, to localize sensations, and here I was called on for more.

"Look, a Negro!" It was an external stimulus that flicked over me as I passed by. I made a tight smile.

"Look, a Negro!" It was true. It amused me.

"Look, a Negro!" The circle was drawing a bit tighter, I made no secret of my amusement.

"Mama, see the Negro! I'm frightened!" Frightened! Frightened! Now they were beginning to be afraid of me. I made up my mind to laugh myself to tears; but laughter had become impossible.

I could no longer laugh, because I already knew that there were legends, stories, history, and above all *historicity*, which I had learned about from Jaspers. Then, assailed at various points, the corporeal schema crumbled, its place taken by a racial epidermal schema. In the train it was no longer a question of being aware of my body in the third person but in a triple person. In the train I was given not one but two, three places. I had already stopped being amused. It was not that I was finding febrile coordinates in the world. I existed triply; I occupied space. I moved toward the other . . . and the evanescent other, hostile but not opaque, transparent, not there, disappeared. Nausea. . . .

I was responsible at the same time for my body, for my race, for my ancestors. I subjected myself to an objective examination, I discovered my blackness, my ethnic characteristics; and I was battered down by tom-toms, cannibalism, intellectual deficiency, fetichism, racial defects, slave-ships, and above all else, above all: "Sho' good eatin.'"

On that day, completely dislocated, unable to be abroad with the other, the white man, who unmercifully imprisoned me, I took myself far off from my own presence, far indeed, and made myself an object. What else could it be for me but an amputation, an excision, a hemorrhage that spattered my whole body with black blood? But I did not want this revision, this thematization. All I wanted was to be a man among other men. I wanted to come lithe and young into a world that was ours and to help to build it together.

Source: Frantz Fanon, *Black Skin, White Masks*, Charles Lam Markmann, trans. (New York: Grove Press, Inc., 1967), 23–25, 110–113.

10. NGUGI WA THIONG'O, *IN THE HOUSE OF THE INTERPRETER: A MEMOIR* (2012)

Mau Mau was a widespread group composed of members of the Kikuyu ethnic group in the east of Africa who right after World War II actively opposed British rule. Also called the Land and Freedom Army, Mau Mau participants took part in oaths and rituals to cement their determination to regain their lands in present-day Kenya that the British had been seizing during the first half of the twentieth century. On these lands, settlers had then set up coffee and other plantations on which once land-holding Kenyans were forced to work. Mau Mau protested this situation in the 1950s, and the British responded by forcing Kenyans into concentration camps where they were deprived of food, shelter, and medical treatment in addition to being tortured and even castrated. Celebrated author Ngũgĩ wa Thiong'o (b. 1938) describes returning from boarding school to find his family's home destroyed and his mother and siblings relocated. In 1960, the Kenyan independence movement won the right to self-government, while activists brought legal proceedings against the British government for their genocidal treatment, its victims in the hundreds of thousands. What psychological aspects of British imperialist tactics appear in "villagization"?

I

It's the end of my first term at boarding school, and I'm going home. It's April. When I first left Limuru for Alliance High School in January, it was in the last car of a goods train into which I had been smuggled, my sole company then being workmen's tools and clothes. Now I travel third class, with schoolmate Kenneth Wanjai. It's very crowded, standing room only, and our school uniform of khaki shirts, shorts, and blue ties marks us as different from the general passengers, all black Africans, their clothes in different stages of wear and tear. Their haggard faces belie the animated voices and occasional laughter. On getting off at Limuru railway station, I linger on the platform and look around me to savor the moment of my return. The goods shed, the tea kiosk, the waiting room, and the outside toilets marked for Europeans only, Asians only, and Africans, minus the qualifying only, still stand, silent weather-beaten witnesses of time that has passed since the station first opened in 1898.

Wanjai and I part company for our different destinations, he in his father's car, and I alone, on foot. Then it hits me: I'm going home to my mother. Soon, very soon, I'll be with my sisters and younger brother. I have news to share with them: I was among the top of my class. No doubt my mother will ask me if that was the best I could have done, or her variation, were you number one, and I will have to confess that another boy, Henry Chasia, was ahead of me. As long as you tried your best, she will surely tell me with pride. I am going to bask in her sunny smile, which always carries warmth and depth of care. I enjoy her reaction in advance.

I lift my wooden box by the handle with my right hand. It's not very heavy, but it dangles and keeps on hitting against my legs. After a time, I change hands; it's worse on the left side, so I lift it onto my shoulder. I keep up the pattern: right hand, left hand, right shoulder, left shoulder, and back to the right hand. My progress is slow. I walk past the African marketplace, which looks deserted, a ghostly place, except for a pack of stray dogs, chasing and fighting over a female in heat. But the memory of my childhood interactions with the place floods back: my brother's workshop; people massing outside the Green Hotel to hear news; my falling off Patrick Mūrage's bike. I stagger up the slope toward the Indian shopping center. Almost two years back, my brother, Good Wallace, ran down this very slope, barely escaping a hail of police bullets, but I refuse to let memories of pain interfere with my first homecoming as an Alliance student. Instead, I conjure up images from my Limuru youth that are more in tune with my triumphant mood.

Onesmus Kīhara Warūirū immediately comes to my mind. Kīhara, an incredible cyclist and showman to boot, loved climbing this slope. People used to stand aside and cheer him in wonder and admiration as he cycled up the hill to take mail and parcels to the Indian shopping center. No other cyclist had ever managed to climb the hill all the way without once getting off his bike and pushing it. Kīhara was our bike hero, possessor of superhuman endurance.

I'm so engrossed in these thoughts that I forget to take note of the landscape around me. But instinct suddenly tells me that I have gotten home . . . or where home should be. I stop, put down the box, and look around me. The hedge of ashy leaves that we planted looks the same, but beyond it our homestead is a rubble of burnt dry mud, splinters of wood, and grass. My mother's hut and my brother's house on stilts have been razed to the ground. My home, from where I set out for Alliance only three months ago, is no more. Our pear tree is still standing, but like the ashy hedge, it's a silent witness. Casting my eyes beyond, I suddenly realize the whole village of homesteads has disappeared. The paths that had crisscrossed the landscape, linking the scattered dwellings into a community, now lead from one mound of rubble to another, tombs of what has been. There is not a soul in sight. . . .

13

Villagization, the innocuous name the colonial state gave to the forced internal displacement, was sprung on the Kenyan people in 1955, in the middle of my first term at Alliance, but living within the walls of the school, I had not heard about the agents of the state bulldozing people's homes or torching them when the owners refused to participate in the demolition. Mau Mau suspects or not, everybody had to relocate to a common site. In some regions, the state forced people to dig a moat around the new collective settlement, leaving only one exit and entrance. The whole of central Kenya was displaced, and the old order of life destroyed, in the name of isolating and starving the anticolonial guerrillas in the mountains.

The mass relocation was followed by forced land consolidation. A person or families who owned parcels of land in different locations would have them joined together into a contiguous piece but had no choice over the location of this consolidated land. People in the mountains and the concentration camps were not there to verify their claims. It was a mass fraud, often giving land from the already poor to the relatively rich, and from the families of guerrilla fighters to those loyal to the colonial state.

The division between the loyal and everyone else was reflected in the architecture of the new village. The loyal occupied corner houses of corrugated iron roofs with ample space between them, while those deemed disloyal, the majority of the landless and poor, lived in mud-walled grass-thatched round huts, with hardly any space between them. The loyal household was likely to be Christian, relatively wealthy, better educated, with the nuclear family of father, mother, and children left intact. The peasant and worker households were usually just mothers and children.

The new villages were the rural equivalent of the concentration camps, where thousands were still being held, with more additions every year, since the Declaration of Emergency in 1952. The inmates of the concentration camps were mostly men, those in the concentration villages mostly women and children. These two sets of concentration had many features in common.

The most visible of these features was the watchtower, usually built on the highest ground, and from which the Union Jack fluttered its symbol of conquest and control. Under constant surveillance, the inmates of the camp and the village, loyal or not, were likely to be stopped and searched at any time of day or night. For all practical purposes, the line between the prison, the concentration camp, and the village had been erased.

Source: Ngugi wa Thiong'o, *In the House of the Interpreter: A Memoir* (New York: Pantheon Books, 2012), 3–5, 36–38.

11. GENERAL FERNAND GAMBIEZ, TESTIMONY IN THE MILITARY TRIAL OF GENERALS CHALLE AND ZELLER, (1961)

Officials who opposed decolonization even tried to overthrow imperial governments. The French army, after its defeat at the beginning of World War II and at the postwar battle of Dien Bien Phu (1954), staked its reputation on keeping Algeria as part of the French empire. It had slaughtered an uprising of activists there at the war's end and engaged in an incredibly savage effort to squash another uprising that began in 1954. Outnumbered and outgunned, the Algerian FLN or National Liberation Front went to the court of public opinion, describing to the global press the atrocities committed by the French army against suspects including women, who were raped with broken bottles, burned on their breasts and genitals with cigarettes, and otherwise tortured. Buttressed by rising opposition in France itself, a new government led by war hero Charles de Gaulle began winding the war down, holding a vote in January 1961 on whether Algeria should become independent. In the face of the overwhelmingly positive vote, French generals plotted to overthrow the government through coups in Algiers and Paris, which resulted in the arrest and trial of two of them (the others escaped). Following is testimony from the head of the armed forces in Algeria, who had no part in the plan, outlining the army's feelings of betrayal because of decolonization.

What remains is that the army of Algeria . . . did not fully accept state politics. However, it applied it and made itself its instrument, not with enthusiasm but with loyalty. From the politics of what was called "French Algeria" it undertook without too much trouble what was called "self-determination." In the majority it had disapproved of the reversal of the French community in January 1960 (the mounting of the barricades); it then accepted "Algerian Algeria" and hoped that there was time to construct it. . . . But the process was speeded up. . . . November 4 General de Gaulle was heard speaking of the "Algerian Republic." . . . The army was troubled but remained disciplined, enough anyway not to lose its sang-froid during the riots of December to permit the success of the "referendum of January 1961."

But the progress continued to be uneven, the problem to solve greater, and the day would come when in the mountainous areas, in the deep wilds, the flags had to be lowered, leaving the population in fear and without protection. . . .

Then in the hearts and minds of some the feeling grew that one could not and should not accept that. This was called anxiety, the sickness of the army. This was not unknown either to me or the government. But I thought that the spirit of discipline would prevail and that the appreciation for the task yet to be done would remain strong.

And so it was for the great majority. A colonel Dufour leaving with his flag, a captain and his assistants joining the maquis [resistance movement] for an impossible adventure. These were isolated cases. But certain units, the parachutists who believed themselves the last bastion of warrior virtues of our race, of military honor, and the [Foreign] Legion which thought Algeria was the reason for its being, were more sensitive than others of the evolution of the situation. Unaware, perhaps unconscious in some of the units, they believed themselves destined, designed for a great destiny. Their intoxication was so profound that they did understand that they were not "the entire army."

. . . [However] among 85 military units of the Battalion, only two followed their commanders' orders to participate in the insurrection. . . .

Anxiety and malaise of the Army of Algeria for sure! Despair at not being able to keep the happy promises of 1958: France survives and will survive, the army survives and will survive. . . . Without any doubt. But as commander-in-chief of this army, I know and have the right to say that the many dashed hopes do not allow one to believe in the possibility of leading the Army in rebellion.

Those who have believed in that possibility have made an immense and unpardonable error, even if they thought they were acting from an unreasonable love of their country, of our country.

Source: Maurice Faivre, *Conflits d'authorités Durant la guerre d'Algérie. Nouveaux inédits* (Paris: L'Harmattan, 2004), 188–189. Donald R. Kelley and Bonnie G. Smith trans.

12. EMMA MASHININI, *STRIKES HAVE FOLLOWED ME ALL MY LIFE* (1989)

While other empires and systems of racial oppression appeared to be struggling, the Apartheid regime in South Africa fortified itself after World War II. It increasingly took lands owned by blacks and drove ever more of them into overcrowded ghettoes with substandard living conditions called "townships." Strict segregation laws were enforced with brutality, and those who protested them were often tortured and then murdered. Nonetheless, under this regime, activism prevailed in the form of union organizing, worker protest, and student resistance. There were also many African organizations that operated along ethnic lines and other political parties, such as the African National Congress, that struggled for a better future. Union leader Emma Mashinini organized successfully to achieve a shorter workday and insurance for workers in the 1950s and 1960s. She became one of the thousands of protesters in South Africa who experienced multiple arrests, imprisonment, torture, and worse.

It had been announced that I had been seen accompanied by police and that my offices were being ransacked. Several young men came to say, "What are you doing to Emma?" And even though the police said, "Get away, get away," they still came, just to show that they were with me. And when I walked out of the lift with the police carrying all the books and was taken to the cars, the people did not go into the lift, but instead they followed us. They were singing and chanting, "*Siphe Amandla Nkosi Okunge Sabi*"—"God Give Us Courage"—about fifty of them, black and white, singing "Give her strength, Lord, not to be scared. Give her strength, Lord, for her to stand up and face whatever they are going to expose her to."

I was strengthened by these people, and all the goodbyes, the waving at me, and the good things they were saying, that there will come a day when all this will be over, one day. Right in front of the car they were standing, and they sang the national anthem and chanted, "*Amandla Ngawethu*"—"The power is ours" and I was raising my clenched fist back.

We went to John Vorster Square, where I was put into a room, and there I was interrogated and harassed and given a number. And after some time I was called in by other policemen, who were looking through all the books and things which had been collected from my home.

"You're fat, Kaffir meid," one said to me. "You're a nuisance and a trouble-maker." And afterwards he said to me, in Afrikaans, "Are you a commie?"

Well, my understanding of that was, "Are you a communicant?" because I saw some Bibles and I thought he meant was I communicant of the Church. So I said yes.

And he said, "Well, I'm not going to give you the damned Bible, because you are a Communist and you admit it."

I was shocked, and all by myself, and it seemed everyone had an insult for me, that everyone who walked past had a word of insult to say to me. I was just in the centre of a mess. Who was I to argue over anything and say I misunderstood and that the last thing I was was a commie? That is how they work. They put you in a room, and confine you there so that you must just think you are the only person who is arrested and detained. They don't want you to be exposed to the knowledge that there are other people who are detained as well.

As fate would have it, with all the shock, I kept needing to go to the toilet, and time and time again I had to say to this lady, "Now I want to go to the toilet."

But this time when I went, just before we turned into the toilet, we passed the lift, and it stopped, and someone walked out and said, "Hello, Emma." It was Neil Aggett. I wanted to respond, to say hello back to him, but the relief of finding I was not the only one who was arrested took it away from me, and I could not bring out even that one word. . . .

The cell was a very small cell. There was a toilet, there was a basin to wash. The toilet was a proper flush toilet, very clean. Extremely clean. There was a bed, and there were sheets on the bed. The window was right next to the door. It was a very small window. Through it somebody in the corridor could see you, but they had put Elastoplast on the other side so you could not see out.

I was cold. Everything was taken. I had a gold chain which my daughters had given me for my fiftieth birthday. That was taken. Everything was removed, up to my rings. I sat in that place with nothing to read. Just with myself. The bare me.

It was a prison where there seemed to be whites only. A prison of black people would not have been so clean. They would not have bothered. It was November, mid-summer in Pretoria, but I was very, very cold.

I had no visits, no interrogation, no word from anybody whatsoever. All I had was people talking behind shut doors. The white prisoners who were there were the ones who would bring the food. They were criminals and they were not allowed to open the door. They put the plate just on the doorstep until the police-woman decided to come, open the door, and push the food in. At times, when the plate had been there for some time, you could hear them talk amongst themselves. "You know, that plate has been there for some time. It is now cold."

I was able to count the days by my meals and by dark and light, by how many nights, how many getting ups. I was able to count that day onwards to day fourteen.

On my fourteenth day, when the policewoman came to open the door for me and brought my food in, she said would I like to go and have a bath. I thought that this meant I was going home.

After my bath, when she was locking me in, I said to her, "Am I not going home?" She said to me, "Didn't you see the newspapers—that you are charged with another section?"—as though I could get a newspaper. Yet I think she was not doing this to spite me but was unaware of the system, of her own system.

Now I think that was the most heartbreak I had. The heartache was even greater than when I was actually removed from home, because I was now being held under Section 6. I kept telling myself, Section 6 is one of the worst sections. You can remain in prison for an indefinite time. It depends on the government.

When the policewoman told me that she'd read from the newspapers that I was being transferred from Section 22 to Section 6, I really felt this was very bad for me, because I had known people who were there for a very long time. And now this hope of saying I would be out of prison within two weeks had gone; it was like being detained for the first time. Section 6 meant complete isolation and solitary confinement, . . .

Source: Emma Mashinini, *Strikes Have Followed Me All My Life: A South African Autobiography* (New York: Routledge, 1991), 53–54, 61–62. Also in Hilda L. Smith and Berenice A. Carroll, *Women's Political and Social Thought* (Bloomington: Indiana University Press, 2000).

REVIEW QUESTIONS

1. What aspects of imperial thought and behavior found in the documents does the Declaration of Human Rights seem to address?
2. In what ways did World War II change people's minds about empire; in what ways did opinions and behavior remain the same?
3. Compare people's accounts of their lives under war and empire during this period.
4. Find a "socialist realist" poster of Mao Zedong and Chinese peasants on the web and describe the various elements in the composition of this poster. Then explain the importance of such depictions to ending foreign domination of China and making the Chinese Revolution a reality.

CHAPTER 12

The Rise of Free Nations
and the Afterlife of Empire

By the mid-1950s, activists were determined to form independent nations across the weakened imperial world. In the Gold Coast, strikers and other activists against British rule led to the creation of the independent and multiethnic Republic of Ghana in 1957, helping decolonization to snowball across the African continent. There were differences in the processes of decolonization. Egypt appeared to have gained its independence from Britain in 1923, but it was only after Gamal Abdel Nasser (1918–1970) nationalized the Suez Canal in 1956 and faced off against a British, French, and Israeli invasion that it was fully liberated. Although Ghana, Morocco, and Tunisia became independent nations relatively peacefully because fewer whites had made these regions their homeland, in the case of settler colonies such as Indochina, Algeria, and Kenya the white settlers participated alongside government troops in devastating wars in which hundreds of thousands were killed. The tools in these wars, besides incessant military operations, were confinement in concentration camps, confiscation of property, and outright murder. Because the world was globalizing through technology such as communication satellites and television, independence leaders often took their causes to a global citizenship. People around the world could view images of torture, read about the use of chemical warfare against civilians, and imagine that armed forces from World War II were still slaughtering innocent women and children. Liberation fighters often had citizens globally on their side, except where the United States played the Cold War card: It often launched persuasive propaganda that those who wanted freedom were in fact part of a worldwide Communist conspiracy.

The resulting independence had mixed consequences, just as it had had along the course of nation-building such as in the United States almost two centuries earlier. Many postcolonial leaders were eager to provide the newly free citizens with benefits they had seen the colonial powers enjoy: education, large hydroelectric power projects, modern sanitation, airports, and other signs of economic prosperity, to name a few. The costs of such benefits, however, were overwhelming, especially because the course of world wars and the economic depression had taken their toll. The colonial powers devised a system whereby they had taken as many economic and human resources from their colonies as possible and had let infrastructure decay over the course of economic depression and total war. Newly independent nations had already been stripped bare, coming to freedom with little in the way of modern transportation, water and sewer systems, industry, schools and institutions of higher education, and up-to-date health care structures.

Additionally the new nations had to tack between the Cold War superpowers, who now conducted their struggle in emerging independent countries such as Korea, Vietnam, and eventually Afghanistan. In 1955, President Sukarno (1901–1970) of newly independent Indonesia summoned a meeting of new nations and regimes, leading them to a declaration of non-alignment, which was often difficult to attain. The United States, the Soviet Union, and the revived European nations might aid the former colonies but often with strings of loyalty, even obedience, attached. More than that, funds were often designated for the purchase of military goods, not the building of schools, hospitals, and infrastructure, or providing other beneficial ingredients of nation-building. Equally, successful leaders of independence movements often rewarded their allies, their families, or themselves with control of these funds, as kinship ties had been the only, often weak protection under colonialism. As decolonization unfolded, the former imperial powers were forced to deal with counter-trends. Newly independent countries formed consortia such as OPEC (Organization of Petroleum Exporting Countries, 1961) to consolidate their power over raw materials.

Having ravaged the colonies for funds, people, and raw materials, the former imperial powers received a flood of migrants from newly independent countries, both because living conditions, including wars and civil wars, were problematic, even life-threatening, and because Europe itself needed a large pool of labor for postwar rebuilding. Colonial officials also returned home, bringing imperial values, including racism, and techniques for ruling inferiors back with them. As this occurred, the former powers faced the challenge of living with diversity at home instead of brutalizing those who were different in distant colonies. As Frantz Fanon, a psychiatrist and anti-colonial activist from the French Caribbean, had witnessed, racism was on full display in imperial metropoles.

Amid the combat and migratory turmoil, new nations established themselves nonetheless and authors began writing about both the colonial and the postcolonial experience. Works of art flowed from their pens and appeared on their canvases, and a modern world literature flourished amid the remnants of colonialism. Many of these works reported the trauma of the colonial experience or the racist behavior that still flowed from colonial ideology. Nonetheless, many of these works were also infused with great wit and even humor, gaining a worldwide readership. Creativity abounded, not just fiction but in theories demanding the rewriting of history, political thought, anthropology, and literary criticism. A new term, "post-colonialism," demanded that the condition of the world and its peoples be rewritten in the light of what colonialism had meant for the past five hundred years of human experience. In some instances, this theory came to inspire governmental policy and political thought further. Although independence leaders took some of their ideas from liberal ideas of national autonomy and individual rights, others saw things differently. Frantz Fanon, for example, came to produce analyses of decolonization that were based in the violence necessary in order for the "wretched of the earth" to become free. Freedom included "decolonization" of the mind. For many, however, learning the imperialists' language and culture and even excelling at such imperialist sports as soccer were their dream. Postcolonial studies critical of empire flourished in universities around the world even as imperial culture kept many parts of the world in its grip.

Legacies of colonialism, especially its violence, persisted even as many regions emerged as independent nations. Well into the 1980s, secret forces and state police harassed, tortured, and murdered anti-colonial protestors in South Africa, not to mention those who perpetuated the impoverishment and malnutrition of Asians and many other Africans through corruption and sweatshop labor. By1994, a combination of persistent local and global protest had brought down the brutal apartheid regime in South Africa, with President Nelson Mandela supporting the policy of reconciliation. Violence also persisted in Palestine, where Israeli forces defeated local resisters and supporters of a Palestinian state. This conflict persists and has even escalated to this day. Imperialists stoked religious and ethnic tensions: the British among Sikhs, Muslims, and Hindus; the Belgians and others among Hutus and Tutsis in the former Congo. These tensions and their continuing violence were also part of colonialism's aftermath. The legacy of inferior, even inhuman treatment also resonates among Uyghurs in China and Native Americans in North, South, and Central America, as the Zapatista proclamation makes clear. Alongside the problematic, even inhumane, remains of empire are those who live with hope that institutions of world governance and cooperation can alleviate the hatred, inequalities, and greed that are also empire's children.

1. PRESIDENT SUKARNO OF INDONESIA, SPEECH AT THE OPENING OF THE BANDUNG CONFERENCE (1955)

In an atmosphere of Cold War when newly independent nations were under pressure to choose sides, these governments that replaced imperial ones were also hard pressed for funds. The USSR and the United States competed for allegiance of the new nations by offering funds for weapons (or the weapons themselves), infrastructure such as dams, and the necessities of life such as food. As this pressure took shape, President Sukarno (1901–1970) of Indonesia, a politician who had worked with several governments to eliminate the Dutch from his country, summoned the heads of state of what was coming to be called the Third World to talk about the situation. (The term "Third World" was first used as a flattering term indicating the freedom fighters composed of ordinary people during the French Revolution. As such, they were far better than the corrupt and privileged clergy and aristocracy and represented a more

*egalitarian and just future. Today, people take it as a slur.) Sukarno's talk at Band-
ung was a primer in outlining the forms of colonialism, which he and his allies knew
all too well. From this meeting emerged statements of solidarity with one another
and of the intention to remain "unaligned" in the face of U.S. and USSR pressure.
The meeting stirred people around the world because the formerly oppressed and
enslaved appeared far more noble in their attitudes toward global well-being than
the power-seeking USSR, United States, and their allies. What dangers did Sukarno
see as menacing the world and how did he propose to overcome them?*

This twentieth century has been a period of terrific dynamism. Perhaps the last
fifty years have seen more developments and more material progress than the
previous five hundred years. Man has learned to control many of the scourges
which once threatened him. He has learned to consume distance. He has learned
to project his voice and his picture across oceans and continents. He has probed
deep into the secrets of nature and learned how to make the desert bloom and
the plants of the earth increase their bounty. He has learned how to release the
immense forces locked in the smallest particles of matter. . . .

We are living in a world of fear. The life of man today is corroded and made
bitter by fear. Fear of the future, fear of the hydrogen bomb, fear of ideologies.
Perhaps this fear is a greater danger than the danger itself, because it is fear which
drives men to act foolishly, to act thoughtlessly, to act dangerously. . . .

All of us, I am certain, are united by more important things than those which
superficially divide us. We are united, for instance, by a common detestation of
colonialism in whatever form it appears. We are united by a common detestation
of racialism. And we are united by a common determination to preserve and sta-
bilize peace in the world. . . .

We are often told "Colonialism is dead." Let us not be deceived or even
soothed by that. I say to you, colonialism is not yet dead. How can we say it is
dead, so long as vast areas of Asia and Africa are unfree.

And, I beg of you do not think of colonialism only in the classic form which
we of Indonesia, and our brothers in different parts of Asia and Africa, knew.
Colonialism has also its modern dress, in the form of economic control, intellectual control, actual physical control by a small but alien community within a
nation. It is a skillful and determined enemy, and it appears in many guises. It does
not give up its loot easily. Wherever, whenever and however it appears, colonialism is an evil thing, and one which must be eradicated from the earth. . . .

Not so very long ago we argued that peace was necessary for us because an
outbreak of fighting in our part of the world would imperil our precious independence, so recently won at such great cost.

Today, the picture is more black. War would not only mean a threat to our
independence, it may mean the end of civilization and even of human life. There is
a force loose in the world whose potentiality for evil no man truly knows. Even in
practice and rehearsal for war the effects may well be building up into something
of unknown horror.

Not so long ago it was possible to take some little comfort from the idea that the clash, if it came, could perhaps be settled by what were called "conventional weapons"—bombs, tanks, cannon and men. Today that little grain of comfort is denied us for it has been made clear that the weapons of ultimate horror will certainly be used, and the military planning of nations is on that basis. The unconventional has become the conventional, and who knows what other examples of misguided and diabolical scientific skill have been discovered as a plague on humanity.

And do not think that the oceans and the seas will protect us. The food that we eat, the water that we drink, yes, even the very air that we breathe can be contaminated by poisons originating from thousands of miles away. And it could be that, even if we ourselves escaped lightly, the unborn generations of our children would bear on their distorted bodies the marks of our failure to control the forces which have been released on the world.

No task is more urgent than that of preserving peace. Without peace our independence means little. The rehabilitation and upbuilding of our countries will have little meaning. Our revolutions will not be allowed to run their course. . . .

What can we do? We can do much! We can inject the voice of reason into world affairs. We can mobilize all the spiritual, all the moral, all the political strength of Asia and Africa on the side of peace. Yes, we! We, the peoples of Asia and Africa, 1,400,000,000 strong, far more than half the human population of the world, we can mobilize what I have called the Moral Violence of Nations in favor of peace. We can demonstrate to the minority of the world which lives on the other continents that we, the majority are for peace, not for war. . . .

So, let this Asian-African Conference be a great success! Make the "Live and let live" principle and the "Unity in Diversity" motto the unifying force which brings us all together—to seek in friendly, uninhibited discussion, ways and means by which each of us can live his own life, and let others live their own lives, in their own way, in harmony, and in peace.

Source: *Africa-Asia Speaks from Bandong* (Jakarta: Indonesian Ministry of Foreign Affairs, 1955), 19–29. Available at Modern History Sourcebook, http://www.fordham.edu/halsall/mod/1955sukarno-bandong.html

2. GAMAL ABDEL NASSER, SPEECH ON THE NATIONALIZATION OF THE SUEZ CANAL (1956)

Gamal Abdel Nasser (1918–1970) was a leader of the group of military officers that ousted the British puppet King Farouk in 1952–3. After massive non-violent protests between 1919 and 1922, Britain had awarded Egypt limited independence in 1922 but installed puppet rulers, kept control of Sudan (ruled in principle by Egypt), and ran the Suez Canal. As a youth before World War II, Nasser had participated in anti-British demonstrations, and one of the first acts of his seizure of entire power in 1956 was the nationalization of the Suez Canal. The act took away Britain's last vestige of authority—control of the canal—which Nasser justified in the speech presented here. Britain, France, and Israel invaded Egypt to regain the canal, calling Nasser another Hitler as they did so but even then failing to get U.S. support. Nasser became a hero to most people in the Arab world. What problems does Nasser aim for Egypt to overcome?

Citizens,

We shall not let imperialists or exploiters dominate us. We shall not let history repeat itself once more. We have gone forward to build a strong Egypt. We go forward towards political and economic independence. We go forward towards national economy for the sake of the whole people. We go forward to work. But, whenever we look behind, we do so to destroy the traces of the past, the traces of slavery, exploitation and domination.

Today, citizens, rights have been restored to their owners. Our rights in the Suez Canal have been restored to us after 100 years.

Today, we actually achieve true sovereignty, true dignity and true pride. The Suez Canal Company was a state within a state. It was an Egyptian Joint Stock Company, relying on imperialism and its stooges.

The Suez Canal was built for the sake of Egypt and for its benefit. But it was a source of exploitation and the draining of wealth.

As I said a short while ago, it is no shame to be poor and to work for the building of my country. But it is shameful to suck blood. They used to suck our blood, our rights and take them.

Today, when we regain our rights, I say in the name of the people of Egypt that we shall defend these rights and shall hold fast. We shall sacrifice our lives and our blood in defending them. We shall make up for the past.

Today, when we build the edifice of our dignity, freedom and pride, we feel that it will not be completely sound until we eradicate domination, humiliation and submission. The Suez Canal constituted an edifice of humiliation.

Today, citizens, the Suez Canal Company has been nationalised. This order has been published in the Official Journal. It has become a matter of fact.

Citizens, today we say our wealth has been restored to us.

Citizens; Today, the Suez Canal income is estimated at £E. 35 million or 100 million dollars per annum or 500 million dollars in five years. We shall not seek the 70 million dollar American aid.

Today, fellow-countrymen, by our sweat, our tears, the souls of our martyrs and the skulls of those who died in 1856, a hundred years ago during the corvee, we are able to develop this country: We shall work, produce and step-up production despite all these intrigues and these talks. Whenever I hear talk from Washington, I shall say "Die of your fury."

We shall build up industry in Egypt and compete with them. They do not want us to become an industrial country so that they can promote the sale of their products and market them in Egypt. I never saw any American aid directed towards industrialization as this would cause us to compete with them. American aid is everywhere directed towards exploitation.

On entering upon the fifth anniversary of the Revolution, as I said at the beginning of my speech, we feel stronger, more resolute and faithful than during the former years.

On embarking upon the fifth year of the Revolution, as Farouk was expelled on July 26, 1952, the Suez Canal Co. will depart on the very same day. We are conscious of accomplishing glories and achieving true dignity. Sovereignty in Egypt will belong only to her sons.

We shall march forward united . . . one nation confident in itself, its motherland and its power, one nation relying on itself in work and in the sacred march towards construction, industrialization and creation . . . one nation . . . a solid bloc to hold out treason and aggression and resist imperialism and agents of imperialism.

In this manner, we shall accomplish much and feel dignity and pride and feel that we are building up our country to suit ourselves. . . . We build what we want and do what we want with nobody to account to.

Turning Towards Force

When we obtain our usurped and stolen rights, we shall turn towards strength. We shall become stronger each year, and, God willing, next year we shall become more powerful with increased production, work and factories.

Now, while I am speaking to you, fellow countrymen, brothers of yours are taking over the administration and the management of the Canal Company, the Egyptian Canal Company not the foreign Canal Company. They are taking over the Canal Company and its facilities for the direction of navigation in the Canal, the Canal which is situated in the territory of Egypt, cuts through the territory of Egypt, is a part of Egypt and belongs to Egypt. We now perform this task to compensate for the past and build up new edifices for pride and dignity.

May God guide you and peace be with you.

Source: *The Suez Canal Problem, 26 July–22 September 1956*, U.S. Department of State Publication No. 6392 (Washington, DC: Government Printing Office, 1956), 25–28.

3. STATUTE OF THE ORGANIZATION OF THE PETROLEUM EXPORTING COUNTRIES (1961)

For centuries, European and other empires had exploited the human and natural resources of areas they conquered. In the twentieth century oil became a driver of imperial and other financial enterprises, as the development of the mandate system in the Middle East shows. From the beginning of the twentieth century, British, Dutch, French, and U.S. oil companies made inroads into oil exploration and development around the world. Once decolonization took hold in the 1950s and 1960s, Western governments tried to keep a stranglehold on the oil business even in countries like Saudi Arabia and Iran, neither of them actually colonized by European powers. In Iran, the United States government used its power to oust a prime minister who wanted to raise the royalties from oil paid to his government. In 1961, the oil-producing nations of Iran, Iraq, Kuwait, Saudi Arabia, and Venezuela joined to create OPEC, and in 1973 and 1979 the Arab nations of OPEC struck at Western nations supporting Israel with embargos on oil and drastic increases in petroleum prices. What transformation does the OPEC statement aim to accomplish?

Article 1

A. The principal aim of the Organization shall be the coordination and unification of the petroleum policies of Member Countries and the determination of the best means for safeguarding their interests, individually and collectively.

B. The Organization shall devise ways and means of ensuring the stabilization of prices in international oil markets with a view to eliminating harmful and unnecessary fluctuations.

C. Due regard shall be given at all times to the interests of the producing nations and to the necessity of securing a steady income to the producing countries; an efficient, economic and regular supply of petroleum to consuming nations; and a fair return on their capital to those investing in the petroleum industry.

Article 3

The Organization shall be guided by the principle of the sovereign equality of its Member Countries. Member Countries shall fulfil, in good faith, the obligations assumed by them in accordance with this Statute.

Source: Statute of OPEC. http://www.opec.org/opec_web/static_files_project/media/downloads/publications/OPEC_Statute.pdf (accessed January 19, 2016).

4. FIDEL CASTRO, "SECOND DECLARATION OF HAVANA" (1962)

Fidel Castro (b. 1926) spent his university years as a committed anti-Communist. A young lawyer from a prosperous family, he was pro-business and a liberal, but he joined the forces that overthrew the U.S.-backed dictatorship of Fulgencio Batista in 1959—a foundation of American business imperialism. The United States attempted to assassinate Castro and when asked by his government for support it refused. In a Cold War atmosphere, Castro turned to the Soviet Union, nationalized businesses, and clamped down on dissent, especially after the United States launched an attempted invasion at the Bay of Pigs in 1961—the turning point that created Cuba as a Soviet client and a socialist state. From then on, Castro became an important mouthpiece for Communism and anti-imperialist causes, making him a hero in the minds of millions in Latin America and the Third World. This is one of his most important speeches after the Bay of Pigs and the full pivot to Communism. What is Castro's analysis of the history of empire?

What is Cuba's history but that of Latin America? What is the history of Latin America but the history of Asia, Africa, and Oceania? And what is the history of all these peoples but the history of the cruelest exploitation of the world by imperialism?

At the end of the last century and the beginning of the present, a handful of economically developed nations had divided the world among themselves, subjecting two thirds of humanity to their economic and political domination.

Humanity was forced to work for the dominating classes of the group of nations which had a developed capitalist economy.

The historic circumstances which permitted certain European countries and the United States of North America to attain a high industrial development level put them in a position which enabled them to subject and exploit the rest of the world. . . .

The discovery of America sent the European conquerors across the seas to occupy and to exploit the lands and peoples of other continents; the lust for riches was the basic motivation for their conduct. . . .

Since the end of the Second World War, the Latin American nations are becoming pauperized constantly. The value of their capita income falls. The dreadful percentages of child death rate do not decrease, the number of illiterates grows higher, the peoples lack employment, land, adequate housing, schools, hospitals, communication systems and the means of subsistence. . . . Latin America, moreover, supplies cheap raw materials and pays high prices for manufactured articles.

Like the first Spanish conquerors, who exchanged mirrors and trinkets with the Indians for silver and gold, so the United States trades with Latin America. To hold on to this torrent of wealth, to take greater possession of America's resources and to exploit its long-suffering peoples: this is what is hidden behind the military pacts, the military missions and Washington's diplomatic lobbying. . . .

The ruling classes are entrenched in all positions of state power. They monopolize the teaching field. They dominate all means of mass communication. They have infinite financial resources. Theirs is a power which the monopolies and the ruling few will defend by blood and fire with the strength of their police and their armies.

The duty of every revolutionary is to make revolution. We know that in America and throughout the world the revolution will be victorious. But revolutionaries cannot sit in the doorways of their homes to watch the corpse of imperialism pass by. . . . Each year by which America's liberation may be hastened will mean millions of children rescued from death, millions of minds freed for learning, infinitudes of sorrow spared the peoples. Even though the Yankee imperialists are preparing a bloodbath for America they will not succeed in drowning the people's struggle. They will evoke universal hatred against themselves. This will be the last act of their rapacious and caveman system. . . .

Source: James Nelson Goodsell, *Fidel Castro's Personal Revolution in Cuba: 1959–1973* (New York: Alfred A. Knopf, 1975), 264–268.

5. ENOCH POWELL, "RIVERS OF BLOOD SPEECH" (1968)

The aftereffects of empire rippled around the world. These included wars of libera-tion and civil wars in newly liberated nations, not to mention the grinding poverty in the new nations that had been pillaged by the colonial powers before achieving independence. To escape danger and find opportunity people migrated in all direc-tions, many of them entering the nations that had once ruled over them. Britain saw influxes first from the Caribbean followed by immigrants from East Asia, South Asia, and various new nations in Africa. Britons reacted in various ways, employ-ing nurses and doctors in menial hospital tasks, for example, to cut health care costs. While some profited economically from migrant labor, others profited politically by building popular support for anti-immigrant and racist programs. Across Europe and the United States, racist, anti-foreigner political parties blossomed. Enoch Powell (1918–1988), a member of Parliament, gave his speech at a Conservative Party meeting. While it ruined his hopes of being a member of a future Conservative cabinet, ordinary people took to the streets to support his anti-immigrant and racist ideas. How, according to Powell, were the British victims of decolonization?

. . . While, to the immigrant, entry to this country was admission to privileges and opportunities eagerly sought, the impact upon the existing population was very different. For reasons which they could not comprehend, and in pursuance of a decision by default, on which they were never consulted, they found themselves made strangers in their own country.

They found their wives unable to obtain hospital beds in childbirth, their chil-dren unable to obtain school places, their homes and neighbourhoods changed beyond recognition, their plans and prospects for the future defeated; at work they found that employers hesitated to apply to the immigrant worker the standards of discipline and competence required of the native-born worker; they began to hear, as time went by, more and more voices which told them that they were now the unwanted. They now learn that a one-way privilege is to be established by act of parliament; a law which cannot, and is not intended to, operate to protect them or redress their grievances is to be enacted to give the stranger, the disgruntled and the agent-provocateur the power to pillory them for their private actions.

In the hundreds upon hundreds of letters I received when I last spoke on this subject two or three months ago, there was one striking feature which was largely new and which I find ominous. All Members of Parliament are used to the typi-cal anonymous correspondent; but what surprised and alarmed me was the high proportion of ordinary, decent, sensible people, writing a rational and often well-educated letter, who believed that they had to omit their address because it was dangerous to have committed themselves to paper to a Member of Parliament agreeing with the views I had expressed, and that they would risk penalties or repri-sals if they were known to have done so. The sense of being a persecuted minority which is growing among ordinary English people in the areas of the country which are affected is something that those without direct experience can hardly imagine.

I am going to allow just one of those hundreds of people to speak for me:

"Eight years ago in a respectable street in Wolverhampton a house was sold to a Negro. Now only one white (a woman old-age pensioner) lives there. This is her story. She lost her husband and both her sons in the war. So she turned her seven-roomed house, her only asset, into a boarding house. She worked hard and did well, paid off her mortgage and began to put something by for her old age. Then the immigrants moved in. With growing fear, she saw one house after another taken over. The quiet street became a place of noise and confusion. Regretfully, her white tenants moved out.

"The day after the last one left, she was awakened at 7am by two Negroes who wanted to use her 'phone to contact their employer. When she refused, as she would have refused any stranger at such an hour, she was abused and feared she would have been attacked but for the chain on her door. Immigrant families have tried to rent rooms in her house, but she always refused. Her little store of money went, and after paying rates, she has less than £2 per week. "She went to apply for a rate reduction and was seen by a young girl, who on hearing she had a seven-roomed house, suggested she should let part of it. When she said the only people she could get were Negroes, the girl said, "Racial prejudice won't get you anywhere in this country." So she went home.

"The telephone is her lifeline. Her family pay the bill, and help her out as best they can. Immigrants have offered to buy her house—at a price which the prospective landlord would be able to recover from his tenants in weeks, or at most a few months. She is becoming afraid to go out. Windows are broken. She finds excreta pushed through her letter box. When she goes to the shops, she is followed by children, charming, wide-grinning piccaninnies. They cannot speak English, but one word they know. "Racialist," they chant. When the new Race Relations Bill is passed, this woman is convinced she will go to prison. And is she so wrong? I begin to wonder."

The other dangerous delusion from which those who are wilfully or otherwise blind to realities suffer, is summed up in the word "integration." To be integrated into a population means to become for all practical purposes indistinguishable from its other members.

Now, at all times, where there are marked physical differences, especially of colour, integration is difficult though, over a period, not impossible. There are among the Commonwealth immigrants who have come to live here in the last fifteen years or so, many thousands whose wish and purpose is to be integrated and whose every thought and endeavour is bent in that direction.

But to imagine that such a thing enters the heads of a great and growing majority of immigrants and their descendants is a ludicrous misconception, and a dangerous one.

We are on the verge here of a change. Hitherto it has been force of circumstance and of background which has rendered the very idea of integration inaccessible to the greater part of the immigrant population—that they never conceived or intended such a thing, and that their numbers and physical concentration meant the pressures towards integration which normally bear upon any small minority did not operate.

Now we are seeing the growth of positive forces acting against integration, of vested interests in the preservation and sharpening of racial and religious differences, with a view to the exercise of actual domination, first over fellow-immigrants and then over the rest of the population. The cloud no bigger than a man's hand, that can so rapidly overcast the sky, has been visible recently in Wolverhampton and has shown signs of spreading quickly. The words I am about to use, verbatim as they appeared in the local press on 17 February, are not mine, but those of a Labour Member of Parliament who is a minister in the present government:

"The Sikh communities' campaign to maintain customs inappropriate in Britain is much to be regretted. Working in Britain, particularly in the public services, they should be prepared to accept the terms and conditions of their employment. To claim special communal rights (or should one say rites?) leads to a dangerous fragmentation within society. This communalism is a canker; whether practised by one colour or another it is to be strongly condemned."

All credit to John Stonehouse for having had the insight to perceive that, and the courage to say it.

For these dangerous and divisive elements the legislation proposed in the Race Relations Bill is the very pabulum they need to flourish. Here is the means of showing that the immigrant communities can organise to consolidate their members, to agitate and campaign against their fellow citizens, and to overawe and dominate the rest with the legal weapons which the ignorant and the ill-informed have provided. As I look ahead, I am filled with foreboding; like the Roman, I seem to see "the River Tiber foaming with much blood."

That tragic and intractable phenomenon which we watch with horror on the other side of the Atlantic but which there is interwoven with the history and existence of the States itself, is coming upon us here by our own volition and our own neglect. Indeed, it has all but come. In numerical terms, it will be of American proportions long before the end of the century.

Only resolute and urgent action will avert it even now. Whether there will be the public will to demand and obtain that action, I do not know. All I know is that to see, and not to speak, would be the great betrayal.

Source: Reprinted in *The Telegraph*, November 6, 2007.

6. PHILIP CAPUTO, *A RUMOR OF WAR* (1979)

After decades of resistance to French rule, Vietnam was one of the three independent nations that emerged from the colony of Indochina after World War II; the others were Laos and Cambodia. Initially at war's end, France fought hard to keep the colony under its control, until in 1954 the forces of the Viet Minh under Ho Chi Minh defeated French troops in the battle of Dien Bien Phu. Cold War politics came into play in the final settlement, when Vietnam was divided in two, with one half more oriented toward the Communist world and the other a U. S. client state dominated by large landowners and the Catholic church. Still, outrage at foreign domination and the new division of territory provoked resistance both from oppressed peasants in South Vietnam and from the revolutionary forces in North Vietnam—each of these groups determined to unify the countries under control of the North. The United States increasingly raised its commitment to the South Vietnamese establishment, and despite the U.S. dropping of more bombs on the region than were dropped in all of World War II, Viet Minh forces caused U.S. troops to withdraw from Saigon in 1975, creating a fully independent and unified Vietnam. The war itself was a true horror for the Vietnamese people as well as for the foreign soldiers sent to fight it. Philip Caputo served in the war and described the circumstances that made some U.S. soldiers go insane and others worry constantly about doing so. What message do you take away from Caputo's account of the war?

Out there, lacking restraints, sanctioned to kill, confronted by a hostile country and a relentless enemy, we sank into a brutish state. The descent could be checked only by the net of a man's inner moral values, the attribute that is called character. There were a few—and I suspect Lieutenant Cally was one—who had no net and plunged all the way down, discovering in their bottommost depths a capacity for malice they probably never suspected was there.

Most American soldiers in Vietnam—at least the ones I knew—could not be divided into good men and bad. Each possessed roughly equal measures of both qualities. I saw men who behaved with great compassion toward the Vietnamese one day and then burned down a village the next. They were, as Kipling wrote of Tommy Atkins, neither saints "nor blackguards too/But single men in barricks most remarkable like you." That may be why Americans reacted with such horror to the disclosures of U.S. atrocities while ignoring those of the other side: the American soldier was a reflection of themselves.

. . . I did not go crazy, not in the clinical sense, but others did. The war was beginning to take a psychological toll. Malaria and gunshot and shrapnel wounds continued to account for most of our losses, but in the late summer the phrases *acute anxiety reaction* and *acute depressive reaction* started to appear on the sick-and-injured reports sent out each morning by the division hospital. To some degree, many of us began to suffer "anxiety" and "depressive" reactions. I noticed, in myself and in other men, a tendency to fall into black, gloomy moods and then explode out of them in fits of bitterness and rage. It was partly caused by grief, grief over the deaths of friends. I thought about my friends a lot; too much. That was the trouble with the war then: the long lulls between actions gave us too much time to think. I would brood about Sullivan, Reasoner, and the others and feel an emptiness, a sense of futility. They seemed to have died for nothing; if not for nothing, then for nothing tangible.

. . . In the dry season, even the nights in Vietnam are hot, seldom any cooler than eighty or eighty-five degrees; and it was hot on the night Harris woke up Olson and told him it was his turn to go on watch.

"Screw you," Olson said. "I ain't going on post."

"Get up, Olson. You're my relief. I gotta get a little sleep."

"Screw it and screw you, Harris. I gotta get a little sleep myself."

"Olson, I hate your guts. I oughtta kill you, you shitbird."

Olson stood up and leveled his rifle at Harris. "You ain't got the balls to kill me."

"Olson, you shitbird, I gotta automatic rifle pointed at your fuckin' head. All I gotta do is give a little trigger squeeze and I'll blow your head off."

A few other marines, who were later witnesses at the court-martial, stood watching the confrontation. Perhaps they thought nothing would happen.

"Like I said, Harris, you ain't got the balls to do it." And that was the last thing Olson ever said. Harris pumped five or six rounds into Olson's skull at point-blank range.

Source: Philip Caputo, *A Rumor of War* (New York: Holt, Rinehart and Winston, 1979), xviii–xix, 201, 203.

7. AYATOLLAH RUHOLLAH KHOMEINI, "THE UPRISING OF KHURDAD" (1979)

Ayatollah Ruhollah Khomeini (1900–1989) was a learned Islamic cleric (ayatollah) who led a revolution in 1978–1979 that overthrew Shah Mohammad Reza Pahlavi and established Iran as an Islamic republic. In 1963, the Shah, as a client of the United States and Great Britain, announced a series of reforms that in the view of Khomeini would Westernize Iran. When Khomeini spoke out forcefully against them, he was arrested. Tens of thousands of outraged Iranians protested, and as they did so the Shah's police shot them down. Released and in exile, Khomeini himself used "modern" technology to bring his speeches to the discontented Iranian masses via cassettes. Yet once their backing brought him to power, he urged Iranians not to fall for the modern ways of the West that would put them under the yoke of Western neo-imperialism. This speech commemorates those who were massacred in 1963 even as it also aims to free Iran from the grip of the West. What is the relationship of Khomeini's speech to the history of empire?

Those who are ignorant must be guided to a correct understanding. We must say to them: "You who imagine that something can be achieved in Iran by some means other than Islam, you who suppose that something other than Islam overthrew the Shah's regime, you who believe non-Islamic elements played a role—study the matter carefully. Look at the tombstones of those who gave their lives in the movement of Khurdad 15 [the Persian calendar date of the uprising]. If you can find a single tombstone belonging to one of the non-Islamic elements, it will mean they played a role. And if, among the tombstones of the Islamic elements, you can find a single tombstone belonging to someone from the upper echelons of society, it will mean that they too played a role. But you will not find a single tombstone belonging to either of those groups. All the tombstones belong to Muslims from the lower echelons of society: peasants, workers, tradesmen, committed religious scholars. Those who imagine that some force other than Islam could shatter the great barrier of tyranny are mistaken. As for those who oppose us because of their opposition to Islam, we must cure them by means of guidance, if it is at all possible; otherwise, we will destroy these agents of foreign powers with the same fist that destroyed the Shah's regime.

Your opponents, oppressed people, have never suffered. In the time of the *taghut* [secularism or non-worship of Allah], they never suffered because either they were in agreement with the regime and loyal to it, or they kept silent. Now you have spread the banquet of freedom in front of them and they have sat down to eat. Xenomaniacs, [that is,] people infatuated with the West, empty people, people with no content! Come to your senses; do not try to westernize everything you have! Look at the West, and see who the people are in the West that present themselves as champions of human rights and what their aims are. Is it human rights they really care about, or the rights of the superpowers? What they really want to secure are the rights of the superpowers. Our jurists should not follow or imitate them. You should implement human rights as the working classes of our society understand them. Yes, they are the real Society for the Defense of Human Rights. They are the ones who secure the well-being of humanity; they work while you talk; for they are Muslims and Islam cares about humanity. You who have chosen a course other than Islam—you do nothing for humanity. All you do is write and speak in an effort to divert our movement from its course.

But as for those who want to divert our movement from its course, who have in mind treachery against Islam and the nation, who consider Islam incapable of running the affairs of our country despite its record of 1400 years—they have nothing at all to do with our people, and this must be made clear. How much you talk about the West, claiming that we must measure Islam in accordance with Western criteria! What an error! It was the mosques that created this Revolution, the mosques that brought this movement into being. The *mihrab* [an alcove or niche in the wall of a mosque] was a place not only for preaching, but also for war—war against both the devil within and the tyrannical powers without. So preserve your mosques, O people. Intellectuals, do not be Western-style intellectuals, imported intellectuals; do your share to preserve the mosques!

Source: Modern History Sourcebook http://legacy.fordham.edu/halsall/mod/1979khom1.asp (accessed December 30, 2015).

8. FADWA TUQAN, *MOUNTAINOUS JOURNEY* (1985)

Fadwa Tuqan (1917–2003) was a Palestinian poet, born into a wealthy and accomplished family of ten children. Her brothers were poets and prime ministers, while she expressed the constraints put on women and girls, even as her brother Ibrahim taught her the art of poetry for which she became famous. Her views on the repression of women made her appear sympathetic to Western imperial values, causing Arabs to heap criticism on her. In her early years she focused almost exclusively on the personal aspects of life. How, she asked, could she write about large political issues when, like all the women in her family, she was confined to the household? Tuqan increasingly focused on the pain inflicted by both British and Israeli occupation, not just on Palestinian identity but on the history of the land and its peoples. This focus brought the scorn of those Westerners and Israelis with whom Arab critics said she identified. This excerpt is a reaction in her diary to the Israeli invasion of her city, Nablus, in the Six-Day War of 1967. What kind of role, if any, do you see for the poet or artist in the life of empire?

19

The general atmosphere in the Arab countries portends evil. I have no sense of stability nor any confidence in the future. There is already an element of let-down and loss of morale. These are inner sentiments.

The news is announcing Israeli mobilization on the Syrian border and Abd al-Nasser is signing a joint defence treaty with Syria. The tension increases every day. Abd al-Nasser requests U Thant to remove the United Nations forces from the armistice line. Abd al-Nasser announces the closing of the Straits of Tirân.

Israel will not stand by with folded arms. There is a strange smell in the air.

20

Abd al-Nasser holds a news conference in which he says: "If Israel wants war we say welcome, we are ready."

Suddenly and unexpectedly King Hussein flies to Cairo. Everyone is in suspense.

21

King Hussein adds his signature to that of Egypt and Syria on the joint defence treaty. I am filled with inner despair and fear of a fresh defeat that might rob the Arab people again of their resolution. They lost their self-confidence at the time of the 1948 disaster.

22

I had a telephone call summoning me to an immediate, urgent meeting with my "foreign friend." I left for Jerusalem at once. He advised me to quit Nablus for Amman or Beirut, as war was inevitable and coming sooner than I imagined.

"I'll die on my doorstep," I told him, "rather than flee to another country. Unthinkable!"

"I'm afraid for you," he replied. "I respect your stand, but remember you do not own yourself. You belong to others and that is your lot. That's your destiny. You must remain for the others."

"For me that means escape. And I will never run away!"

In his estimation the carnage was going to be terrible between Nablus resistance fighters and the Israeli army.

I thought to myself: what resistance will there be in a city whose inhabitants have been stripped of arms for nineteen years?

I returned to Nablus, my heart heavy with foreboding. I tried to persuade my sister to leave for Amman, but she refused, declaring: "I'll live or die with you."

23

The Arab lands have been humiliated.... We were defeated.... We lost the war.... Our grief is insupportable ... the wind plays with the white flags on our roofs. We have been occupied by the Israeli army.... The shock has removed us from the realms of reality....

I am sick unto death with grief!

24

Seven days after the occupation of the city, my foreign friend surprised me with an unexpected visit. I was sick and feverish.

He came to reassure himself about me and ask if I was in need of anything.... I thanked him with tears in my eyes. His grief was also profound and sincere.

25

One month of occupation has gone by. I am unable to write one line of poetry.

26

Another month has gone by and I have written nothing.... Silence ... continual silence ... however, it is a conscious silence, aware and vigilant, not a silence of absence and emptiness.

27

The chain of silence has been broken; I have written five poems. I feel somewhat at ease.

I shall write, I shall write a lot. I feel I have been for some time living moment by moment in a drama, moved by every act in it. All of a sudden I, myself, am a poem, burning with anguish, dejected, hopeful, looking beyond the horizon!

Source: Fadwa Tuqan, *A Mountainous Journey: An Autobiography*, Olive Kenny, Naomi Shihab Nye, and Salma Khadra Jayyusi, trans., and Salma Khadra Jayyusi, ed. (St. Paul: Graywolf Press, 1985), 189–191.

9. TSITSI DANGAREMBGA, *NERVOUS CONDITIONS* (1988)

Novelist and filmmaker Tsitsi Dangarembga grew up in colonial Southern Rhodesia— now Zimbabwe. A superior student, for a while she studied medicine in England and worked across Europe as a writer of novels and drama. The title of her first novel, Nervous Conditions, *refers to Frantz Fanon's comment: "The condition of the native is a nervous condition." In it, Dangarembga crafts a coming-of-age story full, not only of the aches of growing up but also of the sensibility of those young people living in a world where whiteness was prized. On the cusp of Rhodesian independence first as the white-dominated Republic of Rhodesia and then as the new nation of Zimbabwe, the teenaged heroine is torn between the values of her own culture and those of the "modern" West and the white people who, even a distance away from her village, subtly influence its inhabitants. She strives to make her family proud but also to fulfill her desire to use her mind in new, challenging ways, especially as her cousin Nyasha suffers a breakdown. Describe the author's opinion of Englishness or whiteness in this passage.*

I did not want to stay at the mission, where there was too much that reminded me of Nyasha, and where she was. It was difficult to accept that this thing had happened, particularly difficult because I had no explanation. If you had asked me before it all began, I would have said it was impossible. I would have said it was impossible for people who had everything to suffer so extremely.

I may have no explanation, but my mother had. She was very definite.

"It's the Englishness," she said. "It'll kill them all if they aren't careful," and she snorted. "Look at them. That boy Chido can hardly speak a word of his own mother's tongue, and you'll see, his children will be worse. Running around with that white one, isn't he, the missionary's daughter? His children will disgrace us. You'll see. And himself, to look at him he may look all right, but there's no telling what price he's paying." She wouldn't say much about Nyasha. "About that one we don't even speak. It's speaking for itself. Both of them, it's the Englishness. It's a wonder it hasn't affected the parents too."

She went on like this for quite a while, going on about how you couldn't expect the ancestors to stomach so much Englishness. She didn't mention Nhamo, but I was beginning to follow her trend of thought. I knew she was thinking about him and I could see she considered me a victim too: "The problem is the Englishness, so you just be careful!"

It was a warning, a threat that would have had disastrous effects if I had let it. When you're afraid of something it doesn't help to have people who know more than you do come out and tell you you're quite right. Mother knew a lot of things and I had regard for her knowledge. Be careful, she had said, and I thought about Nyasha and Chido and Nhamo, who had all succumbed, and of my own creeping feelings of doom. Was I being careful enough? I wondered. For I was beginning to have a suspicion, no more than the seed of a suspicion, that I had been too eager to leave the homestead and embrace the "Englishness" of Sacred Heart. The suspicion remained for a few days, during which time it transformed itself into guilt, and then I had nightmares about Nhamo and Chido and Nyasha two nights in a row. That should tell you how much my mother's words disturbed me: I had not had a nightmare since the first time I went to the mission. But term-time was fast approaching and the thought of returning to Sacred Heart filled me with pleasure. The books, the games, the films, the debates—all these things were things I wanted. I told myself I was much more sensible than Nyasha, because I knew what could or couldn't be done. In this way, I banished the suspicion, buried it in the depths of my subconscious, and happily went back to Sacred Heart.

I was young then and able to banish things, but seeds to do grow. Although I was not aware of it then, no longer could I accept Sacred Heart and what it represented as a sunrise on my horizon. Quietly, unobtrusively and extremely fitfully, something in my mind began to assert itself, to question things and refuse to be brainwashed, bringing me to this time when I can set down this story.

Source: Tsitsi Dangarembga, *Nervous Conditions* (London: Women's Press, 1988), 202–204.

10. NELSON MANDELA, "NEW YEAR MESSAGE FROM THE ANC PRESIDENT NELSON ROLIHLAHLA MANDELA TO THE PEOPLE OF SOUTH AFRICA FOR 1992" (1991)

While much of Africa was decolonizing in the 1950s and 1960s, South African whites of Dutch and British origin tightened their hold over Africans in the country. As the Apartheid system strengthened during these decades, the land available to Africans was reduced even more than it had been previously, and black Africans themselves were pushed into small "townships" where living conditions were poor and oppressive and where opportunity hardly existed. Opposition came from groups of protesters and from many organizations, among them the African National Congress, one of whose leaders was the lawyer Nelson Mandela (1918–2013). After traveling to Europe, Mandela was arrested in 1962, allegedly for leaving the country, and sentenced to five years in prison; in 1964 he was tried for inciting uprisings and sentenced to life in prison. Protest only increased in South Africa and international firms and organizations came to boycott the country because of its increasingly violent attacks on blacks. In 1990, Mandela was set free, giving the following speech two years later. In 1994 he became the country's first democratically elected president, clinging to his credo of reconciliation despite the torture, mutilation, rape, and murder of Africans by white colonial forces. What in this speech explains Nelson Mandela's reputation as an exceptional politician, different from most other global political leaders?

Fellow South Africans,

A New Year is upon us. A New Year that, in the last decade of this century, could usher in a new era of hope for all South Africans. While we have achieved a great deal, we should not, however, mark this New Year in a spirit of self congratulation, but rather as an occasion for calm and sober reflection. We need to take stock of the tasks and challenges that still lie ahead. Yet it is an index of the advances we have made that the opportunity to set South Africa firmly on the road to democracy is with us.

1991 saw many new developments, including the formation of the Patriotic Front. We can all justly take pride in the success of the first meeting of the Convention for a Democratic South Africa, CODESA, which brought together the overwhelming majority of political parties, organisations and formations in our country. The commonly agreed objective of CODESA, subscribed to by all but two of the participants, is the attainment of a non-racial democracy.

The tragedy of South Africa is that CODESA comes after eighty years of costly struggles by the majority of South Africans who had been excluded from the so-called "national convention" that took place in 1909. After the innumerable missed opportunities of the past eight decades, CODESA represents a promising window of opportunity for all South Africans to map out the future of our country together.

As 1991 draws to a close, there remains the painful, fruitless and tragic bloodshed that has been the source of so much grief in Natal and other parts of the country. There is little merit today in attempting to determine who fired the first shot. But it is abundantly clear that no one—other than those who wish to preserve the apartheid order—benefits from the continuation of this bloodletting.

During Christmas and New Year, dedicated to peace and goodwill to all, I appeal to all the leaders of our people, be they in the civics, the mass movement, the trade unions, women's or youth organisations, cultural or educational bodies, the churches or in business, to spare no effort to make the Peace Accord work and bring peace into our lives. For the sake of our children, for the future of our country, and to ensure that the democratic order so many have sacrificed so much to achieve is not still-born, the killing must stop now. Not another life should be lost in this futile violence.

As we enter the New Year, we cannot forget those of our fellow citizens whose lot is the despair of homelessness, hunger and poverty. Millions of our people are still denied fundamental human rights–shelter, food and the right to a full and productive life. The future we seek to build will be seriously flawed if it cannot address this national problem. The ANC has its own proposals to resolve the socio-economic problems afflicting the people of our country. I would appeal to others to give the matter the priority it deserves.

We realise that many South Africans are deeply concerned about the future, particularly the question of creating a vibrant and growing economy. The speed with which we can achieve this is dependent on progress made towards fundamental change. We have proposed, and the world has endorsed, the phased lifting of sanctions. The achievements to date have enabled us to lift people-to-people sanctions, and the benefits are there for all to see and enjoy—in cricket and other sports, in the cultural sphere and in tourism. The establishment of a democratic constitution would allow for all remaining sanctions, including financial sanctions, to be lifted and enable us to take our place with pride in the international community. Investors are keenly interested in the progress we make. If we accomplish these goals, the world is open to us.

This New Year will be the first that many who have engaged in struggle will observe outside prison. I take this opportunity to renew my heartfelt, warm welcome to these former political prisoners. I embrace these comrades, fully confident that they will find their rightful place in the ranks of the struggle they have served with such distinction, even while they were behind bars. The release of the majority of political prisoners, fought for and won by the people of South

Africa, supported by millions throughout the world, is a great victory. But it is not complete, for outstanding patriots like Robert McBride, Mthetheleli Mncube and Mzondeleli Nondula are among the over 400 political prisoners who still remain in jail and on death row.

The harsh reality is that irrespective of the numbers that we, through our collective strength and efforts, can release from apartheid's jails, no one in South Africa can be truly free as long as the racist constitutional order remains in place. In our view, the foundations laid at CODESA make it possible for an Interim Government of National Unity to be established to oversee the transition process and supervise free and fair elections for a Constituent Assembly, on the basis of one person, one vote. A democratic constitution is, therefore, one of our priority goals to be achieved for this coming year.

1992 can be the year in which our country takes this giant step, which is necessary to realise our goal of democracy and win international acceptance. But all this can be achieved through our actions alone. For the sake of our country and our future, we dare not fail!

Let us begin this New Year by resolving not to perpetuate distinct racial, ethnic and language groups, which are the legacy of apartheid, but to act as fellow South Africans, ready and willing to work together. Let us seize this opportunity to make a new beginning by creatively harnessing what is best in our past to build for the future. There is a role and place for everyone in our country. Let us set aside narrow sectoral and party political interests to serve the greater national interest that will guarantee a future of peace, stability and prosperity for all.

To the extent that we all do this, 1992 can indeed become a Happy and Prosperous New Year.

Source: Nelson Mandela website, http://db.nelsonmandela.org/speeches/pub_view.asp?pg=item&Item ID=NMS071&txtstr=index accessed March 28, 2017

11. SUBCOMANDANTE INSURGENTE MARCOS, "THE WORD AND THE SILENCE" (1995)

In 1994, a group called the Zapatista movement in the state of Chiapas rose up against the Mexican government. Their charge against the government was that it was a mere extension of imperial policies that had begun some five hundred years earlier. Their spokesperson was Subcomandante Marcos, an anonymous figure who put out scores of documents explaining the oppression of indigenous people. Subcomandante Marcos showed through statistics and details that the vast indigenous resources in oil and other natural products were siphoned off from traditional lands even as the people themselves became ever more impoverished, ill, and uneducated. Named after Emiliano Zapata, the assassinated indigenous leader of the Mexican Revolution that began in 1910, the Zapatistas saw themselves as representing not just the Mayan people but all those whose well-being had been destroyed by successive *and varying forms of imperial oppression. For them, specifically, the oppression began on October 12, 1492. What is the importance of this pronouncement?*

To the people of Mexico
To the peoples and governments of the world
Brothers and sisters:

Today we are remembering our oldest elders, those who initiated the long struggle of resistance against the arrogance of Power and the violence of money. They, our ancestors, taught us that a people with pride are a people who do not surrender, who resist, who have dignity. They taught us to be proud of the color of our skin, of our language, of our culture. More than 500 years of exploitation and persecution have not been able to exterminate us. We have resisted since that time because history has been made with our blood. The noble Mexican nation rests on our bones. . . .

Today we are a fundamental part of a country whose governing officials have a foreign vocation and look with disdain and repugnance at our past. . . . They have already tried to exterminate us. Different doctrines and many different ideas have been used to cover ethnocide with rationality.

Today, the thick mantle with which they try to cover their crime is called neoliberalism, and it represents death and misery for the original people of these lands, and for all those of a different skin color but with a single indigenous heart that we call Mexicans.

Today, the conquerors continue to persecute the indigenous who are rebellious. Today, the modern invaders of our lands live in the supreme government. They pursue the indigenous people, who cover themselves with the flag of the red five-pointed star, the flag of the Zapatista National Liberation Army. But they pursue not only the Zapatistas: death decreed by Power pursues all the indigenous of Mexico, including those with fair skin. Our brothers and sisters in Guerrero suffer the intolerance of the viceroy who is supported by the central power; our brothers and sisters in Tabasco suffer the imposition of drug trafficking and its dirty money; in Veracruz, Oaxaca, Hidalgo, and San Luis Potosí the blood of the dark ones is pursued by political bosses disguised as government officials. . . . The arrogant one thinks that he has won and that there are no people with dignity left under our Mexican skies. . . .

But the color of the skin does not define the indigenous person: dignity and the constant struggle to be better define him. Those who struggle together are brothers and sisters, regardless of the color of our skin or the language that we learned as children.

What matters is the national flag, the one that acknowledges the indigenous foundation of a nation that until now has condemned them to despair. . . . What matters is the land that sustains us in history and prevents us from abandoning ourselves. What matters is the sky that is carried on our shoulders, the sky that today weighs greatly but will heal our vision. What matters are Mexicans, and not those who sell us by knocking on foreign doors.

What matters is our eldest elders who received the word and the silence as a gift in order to know themselves and to touch the heart of the other. Speaking and listening is how true men and women learn to walk. . . . When we are silenced, we remain very much alone. Speaking, we heal the pain. Speaking, we accompany one another. Power uses the word to impose his empire of silence. We use the word to renew ourselves. Power uses silence to hide his crimes. We use silence to listen to one another, to touch one another, to know one another.

This is the weapon, brothers and sisters. We say, the word remains. We speak the word. We shout the word. We raise the word and with it break the silence of our people. We kill the silence, by living the word. Let us leave Power alone in what the lie speaks and hushes. Let us join together in the word and the silence which liberate.

Five hundred and three years ago today, October 12, the word and the silence of Power begin to die.

Five hundred and three years ago today, October 12, our word and our silence began to resist, to fight, to live. Today, 503 years later, we are still here. There are more of us and we are better. We are of many colors, and many are the languages that speak our word.

Today there is no shame in our heart because of the color of our skin or our speech.

Today we say we are indigenous, and we say it like giants.

Today, 503 years after death from a foreign land arrived to bring us silence, we resist and we speak.

Today, 503 years later, we live. . . .

Long live the indigenous Mexicans!

Democracy!

Liberty!

Justice!

Source: Subcomandante Marcos, *Our Word Is Our Weapon: Selected Writings*, Juana Ponce de León, ed. (New York: Seven Stories Press, 2001), 83–85: Stephen Allen kindly provided this reference.

REVIEW QUESTIONS

1. Describe the remnants and reverberations of empire found in the documents.
2. How do leaders evaluate informal empire and create policies in light of the Cold War?
3. What are the different solutions found in the documents to the continuing issue of empire?
4. See https://www.wikiart.org/en/diego-rivera/the-blood-of-the-revolutionary-martyrs-fertilizing-the-earth-1927. What elements in this painting from 1927 depicting the murder of two leaders of the Mexican Revolution give it post-imperial importance? In what ways would the memory of empire be important to analyze?
5. See http://www.wikiwand.com/en/El_Mahalla_El_Kubra. Describe the attitudes of crowds to Nasser and explain Egyptians' and other Arabs' attitudes towards him. Why were his actions important worldwide?

Bibliography

General Histories of Imperialism and Empire

Burbank, Jane, and Frederick Cooper. *Empires in World History: Power and the Politics of Difference.* Princeton: Princeton University Press, 2011.

Chanda, Nayan. *Bound Together: How Traders, Preachers, Adventurers, and Warriors Shaped Globalization.* New Haven: Yale University Press, 2007.

Fernández-Armesto, Felipe. *Pathfinders: A Global History of Exploration.* New York: W. W. Norton, 2006.

Frankopan, Peter. *Silk Roads: A New History of the World.* New York: Alfred A. Knopf, 2016.

Hart, Jonathan. *Empires and Colonies.* Cambridge: Polity Press, 2008.

Kent, Susan Kingsley. *A New History of Britain since 1688: Four Nations and an Empire.* New York: Oxford University Press, 2017.

McNeill, John Robert. *Mosquito Empires: Ecology and War in the Greater Caribbean, 1620–1914.* New York: Cambridge University Press, 2010.

Northrop, Douglas. *An Imperial World: Empires and Colonies since 1950.* Upper Saddle River, NJ: Pearson, 2010.

Reinhard, Wofgang. *A Short History of Colonialism.* Manchester: Manchester University Press, 2011.

Rieber, Alfred J. *The Struggle for the Eurasian Borderlands: From the Rise of Early Modern Empires to the End of the First World War.* New York: Cambridge University Press, 2014.

Streets-Salter, Heather, and Trevor R. Getz. *Empires and Colonies in the Modern World: A Global Perspective.* New York: Oxford University Press, 2015.

Chapter 1

Alpers, Ned. *The Indian Ocean in World History.* New York: Oxford University Press, 2014.

Brook, Timothy. *The Troubled Empire: China in the Yuan and Ming Dynasties.* Cambridge, MA: Harvard University Press, 2010.

Brummett, Palmyra Johnson. *Mapping the Ottomans: Sovereignty, Territory, and Identity in the Early Modern Mediterranean.* New York: Cambridge University Press, 2015.

Carrasco, Davíd, and Scott Sessions. *Daily Life of the Aztecs: People of the Sun and Earth,* 2nd ed. Indianapolis: Hackett, 2008.

Dale, Stephen F. *The Garden of Eight Paradises: Babur and the Culture of Empire in Central Asia, Afghanistan and India (1483–1830)*. Leiden: Brill, 2004.

Dale, Stephen F. *The Muslim Empires of the Ottomans, Safavids, and Mughals*. New York: Cambridge University Press, 2010.

Faroqhi, Suraiya. *The Ottoman Empire and the World Around It*. London: I. B. Tauris, 2006.

Levathes, Louise. *When China Ruled the Seas: The Treasure Fleet of the Dragon Throne, 1405–1433*. New York: Oxford University Press, 1994.

Rossabi, Morris. *The Mongols: A Very Short Introduction*. New York: Oxford University Press, 2012.

Varlik, Nükhet. *Plague and Empire in the Early Modern Mediterranean World: The Ottoman Experience, 1367–1600*. Cambridge: Cambridge University Press, 2016.

Chapter 2

Alchon, Suzanne Austin. *A Pest in the Land: New World Epidemics in a Global Perspective*. Albuquerque: University of New Mexico Press, 2003.

Austen, Ralph. *Trans-Saharan Africa in World History*. New York: Oxford University Press, 2010.

Barr, Juliana. *Peace Came in the Form of a Woman: Indians and Spaniards in the Texas Borderlands*. Chapel Hill: University of North Carolina Press, 2007.

Lamana, Gonzalo. *Domination without Dominance. Inca-Spanish Encounters in Early Colonial Peru*. Durham: Duke University Press, 2008.

Lane, Kris. *The Colour of Paradise: The Emerald in the Age of Gunpowder Empires*. New Haven: Yale University Press, 2010.

Lane, Kris. *Quito 1599: City and Colony in Transition*. Albuquerque: University of New Mexico Press, 2002.

Matthew, Laura E. *Memories of Conquest: Becoming Mexicano in Colonial Guatemala*. Chapel Hill: University of North Carolina Press, 2012.

Newitt, Malyn. *A History of Portuguese Overseas Expansion, 1400–1668*. New York: Routledge, 2005.

Powers, Karen Vierira. *Women in the Crucible of Conquest: The Gendered Genesis of Spanish American Society*. Albuquerque: University of New Mexico Press, 2005.

Sahin, Kaya. *Empire and Power in the Reign of Süleyman: Narrating the Sixteenth-Century Ottoman World*. New York: Cambridge University Press, 2013.

Schwartz, Stuart. *All Can Be Saved: Religion Tolerance and Salvation in the Iberian Atlantic World*. New Haven: Yale University Press, 2009.

Smith, Roger C. *Vanguard of Empire: Ships of Exploration in the Age of Columbus*. New York: Oxford University Press, 1993.

Vilches, Elvira. *New World Gold: Cultural Anxiety and Monetary Disorder in Early Modern Spain*. Chicago: University of Chicago Press, 2010.

Chapter 3

Ali, Omar. *Malik Ambar: Power and Slavery Across the Indian Ocean*. New York: Oxford University Press, 2016.

Crowley, Roger. *Empires of the Sea: The Siege of Malta, the Battle of Lepanto, and the Contest for the Center of the World*. New York: Random House, 2009.

Games, Alison. *The Web of Empire: English Cosmopolitans in the Age of Expansion, 1560–1660*. New York: Oxford University Press, 2008.

Kupperman, Karen. *The Jamestown Project*. Cambridge, MA: Harvard University Press, 2007.

Lunsford, Virginia West. *Piracy and Privateering in the Golden Age Netherlands*. New York: Palgrave Macmillan, 2004.

McDonnell, Michael. *Masters of Empire: Great Lakes Indians and the Making of America*. New York: Hill and Wang, 2015.

Purdue, Peter. *China Marches West: The Qing Conquest of Central Asia*. Cambridge, MA: Harvard University Press, 2005.

Pritchard, James S. *In Search of Empire: The French in the Americas, 1670–1730*. Cambridge: Cambridge University Press, 2004.

Riello, Giorgio, and Roy Tirthankar, eds. *How India Clothed the World: The World of South Asian Textiles, 1500–1850*. Leiden: Brill, 2009.

Struve, Lynn, ed. *Voices of the Ming-Qing Cataclysm: China in Tigers' Jaws*. New Haven: Yale University Press, 1993.

Weiss, Gillian. *Captives and Corsairs: France and Slavery in the Early Modern Mediterranean*. Stanford: Stanford University Press, 2011.

Chapter 4

Anderson, Jennifer L. *Mahogany: The Costs of Luxury in the Early Americas*. Cambridge, MA: Harvard University Press, 2012.

Carney, Judith, and Nicholas Rosomoff. *In the Shadow of Slavery: Africa's Botanical Legacy in the Atlantic World*. Berkeley: University of California Press, 2011.

Dukes, Paul. *A History of the Urals: Russia's Crucible from Early Empire to the Post-Soviet Era*. London: Bloomsbury, 2015.

Fenn, Elizabeth A. *Encounters at the Heart of the World: A History of the Mandan People*. New York: Hill and Wang, 2014.

Ibsen, Pernille. *Daughters of the Trade: Atlantic Slavers and Interracial Marriage on the Gold Coast*. Philadelphia: University of Pennsylvania Press, 2015.

McLynn, Frank. *Captain Cook: Master of the Seas*. New Haven: Yale University Press, 2011.

O'Toole, Rachel Sarah. *Bound Lives: Africans, Indian, and the Making of Race in Colonial Peru*. Pittsburgh: University of Pittsburgh Press, 2012.

Owens, Sarah E., and Jane E. Mangan, eds. *Women of the Iberian Atlantic*. Baton Rouge: Louisiana State University Press, 2012.

Rothschild, Emma. *The Inner Life of Empire: An Eighteenth Century History*. Princeton: Princeton University Press, 2012.

Stern, Philip J. *The Company-State: Corporate Sovereignty and the Early Modern Foundation of the British Empire in India*. New York: Oxford University Press, 2011.

Schaffer, Simon, Lissa Roberts, Kapil Raj, and James Delbourgo, eds. *The Brokered World: Go-Betweens and Global Intelligence, 1770–1820*. Sagamore Beach: Science History Publications, 2009.

Taylor, Jean. *The Social World of Batavia: Europeans and Eurasians in Batavia*. 2nd ed. Madison: University of Wisconsin Press, 2009.

Chapter 5

Brown, Vincent. *The Reaper's Garden: Death and Power in the World of Atlantic Slavery*. Cambridge, MA: Harvard University Press, 2008.

Dubois, Laurent. *A Colony of Citizens: Revolution and Slave Emancipation in the French Caribbean, 1787–1804*. Chapel Hill: University of North Carolina Press, 2004.

Elliott, J. H. *Empires of the Atlantic World: Britain and Spain in America, 1492–1830*. New Haven: Yale University Press, 2007.

Grandin, Greg. *The Empire of Necessity: Slavery, Freedom, and Deception in the New World*. New York: Metropolitan Books, 2014.

Grimshaw, Patricia, Marilyn Lake, Ann McGrath, and Marian Quartly. *Creating a Nation, 1788–1990*. Ringwood, Victoria: McPhee Gribble, 1994.

Jasanoff, Maya. *Liberty's Exiles: American Loyalists in the Revolutionary World*. New York: Knopf, 2011.

Pagden, Anthony. *The Burdens of Empire: 1539 to the Present*. New York: Cambridge University Press, 2015.

Rodriguez O., Jaime. *"We Are Now the True Spaniards": Sovereignty, Revolution, Independence, and the Emergence of the Federal Republic of Mexico, 1808–1824*. Palo Alto: Stanford University Press, 2012.

Rucker, Walter. *Gold Coast Diasporas: Identity, Culture, and Power*. Bloomington: Indiana University Press, 2015.

Van Young, Erik. *The Other Revolution: Popular Violence, Ideology, and the Mexican Struggle for Independence 1810–1821*. Palo Alto: Stanford: Stanford University Press, 2001.

Chapter 6

Adas, Michael. *Dominance by Design: Technological Imperatives and America's Civilizing Mission*. Cambridge, MA: Harvard University Press, 2006.

Burton, Antoinette, ed. *The First Anglo-Afghan Wars: A Reader*. Durham: Duke University Press, 2014.

Brower, Benjamin. *A Desert Named Peace: The Violence of French Empire in the Algerian Sahara, 1844–1902*. New York: Columbia University Press, 2005.

Carter, Marina, and Khal Torabully. *Coolitude: An Anthology of the Indian Labour Diaspora*. London: Anthem Press, 2002

Delay, Brian. *War of a Thousand Deserts: Indian Raids and the U.S.-Mexican War*. New Haven: Yale University Press, 2008.

Doyle, Dan. *The Cause of All Nations: An International History of the American Civil War*. New York: Basic Books, 2015.

Ehrenberg, Ralph E., and Herman Viola. *Mapping the World with Lewis and Clark*. Washington, DC: Levenger/Library of Congress, 2015.

Golden, Peter B. *Central Asia in World History*. New York: Oxford University Press, 2008.

Halsey, Stephen R. *Quest for Power: European Imperialism and the Making of Chinese Statecraft*. Cambridge, MA: Harvard University Press, 2015.

Lowe, Lisa. *The Intimacies of Four Continents*. Durham: Duke University Press, 2015.

Rowe, William T. *China's Last Empire: The Great Qing*. Cambridge, MA: Harvard University Press, 2009.

Sergeev, Evgeny. *The Great Game, 1856–1907: Russo-British relations in Central and East Asia*. Baltimore: Johns Hopkins University Press, 2013.

Wright, Donald R. *The World and a Very Small Place in Africa: A History of Globalization in Niumi, The Gambia*. Armonk, NY: M. E. Sharpe, 2004.

Chapter 7

Dash, Mike. *Late Victorian Holocausts: El Nino Famines and the Making of the Third World*. London: Verso, 2001.

Johannes Fabian. *Out of Our Minds: Reason and Madness in the Exploration of Central Africa*. Berkeley: University of California Press, 2000.

Kennedy, Dane. *The Last Blank Spaces: Exploring Africa and Australia.* Cambridge, MA: Harvard University Press, 2013.

Matsuda, Matt K. *Pacific Worlds: A History of Seas, Peoples, and Cultures.* Cambridge: Cambridge University Press, 2012.

McCullough, David. *The Path between the Seas: The Creation of the Panama Canal 1870–1914.* New York: Simon and Schuster, 1977.

Osborn, Emily Lynn. *Our New Husbands Are Here: Households, Gender and Politics in a West African State from the Slave Trade to Colonial Rule.* Athens: Ohio University Press, 2011.

Osborne, Myles, and Susan Kingsley Kent. *Africans and Britons in the Age of Empire, 1660–1980.* London: Routledge, 2015.

Parpart , Jane L., and Marianne Rostgaard, eds. *The Practical Imperialist: Letters from a Danish Planter in German East Africa 1888–1906.* Leiden: Brill, 2005.

Robinson, David. *Muslim Societies and French Colonial Authorities in Senegal and Mauritania, 1880–1920.* Athens: Ohio University Press, 2000.

Çelik, Zeynep, Julia Clancy-Smith, and Frances Terpak, eds. *Walls of Algiers: Narratives of the City through Text and Image.* Los Angeles: Getty Research Institute, 2009.

Chapter 8

Anderson, Warwick. *Colonial Pathologies: American Tropical Medicine, Race, and Hygiene in the Philippines.* Durham: Duke University Press, 2006.

Goswami, Manu. *Producing India: From Colonial Economy to National Space.* Chicago: University of Chicago Press, 2010.

Hajdarpasic, Edin. *Whose Bosnia? Nationalism and Political Imagination in the Balkans, 1840–1914.* Ithaca: Cornell University Press, 2015.

Harp, Stephen L. *A World History of Rubber: Empire, Industry, and the Everyday.* Hoboken: Wiley-Blackwell, 2015.

Hunt, Nancy Rose. *A Nervous State: Violence, Remedies, and Reverie in Colonial Congo.* Durham: Duke University Press, 2016.

Jonas, Raymond. *The Battle of Adwa: African Victory in the Age of Empire.* Cambridge, MA: Harvard University Press, 2011.

Mir, Farina. *The Social Space of Language: Vernacular Culture in British Colonial Punjab.* Berkeley: University of California Press, 2010.

Mishra, Pankaj. *From the Ruins of Empire: The Intellectuals Who Remade Asia.* New York: Farrar, Straus, and Giroux, 2012.

Steinmetz, George. *The Devil's Handwriting: Precoloniality and the German Colonial State in Qingdao, Samoa, and Southwest Africa.* Chicago: University of Chicago Press, 2007.

Sunseri, Thaddeus. Vilimani: Labor Migration and Rural Change in Early Colonial Tanzania 1884–1915. Portsmouth, NH: Heinemann 2002.

Chapter 9

Gerwarth, Robert, and Erez Manela. *Empires at War, 1911–1923.* New York: Oxford University Press, 2014.

Gingeras, Ryan. *Mustafa Kemal Atatürk: Heir to an Empire.* New York: Oxford University Press, 2016.

Henry, Todd A. *Assimilating Seoul: Japanese Rule and the Politics of Public Space in Colonial Korea, 1910–1945.* Berkeley: University of California Press, 2014.

Kim, Janice C. H. *To Live to Work: Factory Women in Colonial Korea, 1910–1945*. Stanford: Stanford University Press, 2009.

McQuilton, John. *Rural Australia and the Great War: From Tarrawingee to Tangambalanga*. Carleton: Melbourne University Press, 2001.

Omissi, David, ed. *Indian Voices of the Great War: Soldiers' Letters, 1914–1918*. London: Macmillan Press, 1999.

Page, Melvin, ed. *Africa and the First World War*. New York: St Martin's Press, 1987.

Susan Pederson. *The Guardians: The League of Nations and the Crisis of Empire*. New York: Oxford University Press, 2015.

Eugene Rogan. *The Fall of the Ottomans: The Great War in the Middle East*. New York: Basic Books, 2015.

Satia, Priya. *Spies in Arabia: The Great War and the Cultural Foundations of Britain's Covert Empire in the Middle East*. New York: Oxford University Press, 2009.

Varma, D. C. *Indian Armed Forces in Egypt and Palestine, 1914–1918*. New Delhi: Rajesh Publications, 2004.

Chapter 10

Ayala, César J. *American Sugar Kingdom: The Plantation Economy of the Spanish Caribbean, 1898–1934*. Chapel Hill: University of North Carolina Press, 1999.

Bush, Barbara. *Imperialism, Race and Resistance: Britain and Africa, 1919–1945*. New York: Routledge, 1999.

Driscoll, Marc. *Absolute Erotic, Absolute Grotesque: The Living, Dead, and Undead in Japan's Imperialism, 1895–1945*. Durham: Duke University Press, 2010.

Lopez, Kathleen. *Chinese Cubans: A Transnational History*. Chapel Hill: University of North Carolina Press, 2013.

Matera, Marc. *Black London: The Imperial Metropolis and Decolonization in the Twentieth Century*. Berkeley: University of California Press, 2015.

Matera, Marc, Misty L. Bastian, and Susan Kingsley Kent. *The Women's War of 1929: Gender and Violence in Colonial Nigeria*. New York: Palgrave Macmillan, 2012.

Northrop, Douglas. *Veiled Empire: Gender and Power in Stalinist Central Asia*. Ithaca: Cornell University Press, 2004.

Ochonu, Moses E. *Colonial Meltdown: Northern Nigeria in the Great Depression*. Athens: Ohio University Press, 2009.

Schwarz, Bill. *The White Man's World*. New York: Oxford University Press, 2011.

Sinha, Mrinalini. *Specters of Mother India: The Global Restructuring of an Empire*. Durham: Duke University Press, 2006.

Zarrow, Peter. *After Empire: The Conceptual Transformation of the Chinese State, 1885–1924*. Stanford: Stanford University Press, 2012.

Chapter 11

Anderson, David Anderson, *Histories of the Hanged: The Dirty War in Kenya and the End of Empire*. New York: W. W. Norton, 2005.

Brown, Carolyn, Timothy Parsons, and Ahmad Sikainga. *Re-Centering Africa in the History of the Second World War*. Cambridge: Cambridge University Press, 2015.

Burleigh, Michael. *Small Wars, Faraway Places: Global Insurrection and the Making of the Modern World, 1945–1965*. New York: Viking, 2013.

Fontaine, Darcie. *Decolonizing Christianity: Religion and the End of Empire in France and Algeria, 1940–1965. Cambridge: Cambridge University Press, 2016.*

Khan, Yasmin. *The Great Partition: The Making of India and Pakistan*. London: Yale University Press, 2007.

Khan, Yasmin. *The Raj at War: A People's History of India's Second World War*. London: Bosley Head, 2015.

Menon, Ritu. *No Woman's Land: Women from Pakistan, India, and Bangladesh Write on the Partition of India*. New Delhi: Women Unlimited, 2004.

Mitter, Rana. *Forgotten Ally: China's World War II, 1937–1945*. Boston: Houghton Mifflin Harcourt, 2013.

Mukerjee, Madhusree. *Churchill's Secret War: The British Empire and the Ravaging of India during World War II*. New York: Basic Books, 2010.

Shepard, Todd. *Voices of Decolonization: A Brief History with Documents*. Boston: Bedford St Martins, 2015.

Snyder, Timothy. *Bloodlands: Europe Between Hitler and Stalin*. New York: Basic Books, 2010.

Soh, C. Sarah. *The Comfort Women: Sexual Violence and Post-Colonial Memory in Korea and Japan*. Chicago: University of Chicago Press, 2008.

Spector, Ronald. *In the Ruins of Empire: The Japanese Surrender and the Battle for Postwar Asia*. New York: Random House, 2008.

Chapter 12

Bailkin, Joanna. *Afterlife of Empire*. Berkeley: University of California Press, 2012.

Cooper, Frederick. *Africa since 1940: The Past of the Present*. Cambridge: Cambridge University Press, 2002.

Garavini, Giuliano. *After Empires: European Integration, Decolonization, and the Challenge from the Global South, 1957–1986*. Oxford: Oxford University Press, 2012.

Lee, Christopher J. *Making a World After Empire: The Bandung Movement and Its Political Afterlives*. Athens: Ohio University Press, 2010.

Menchu, Rigoberta. *I, Rigoberta Menchu: An Indian Woman in Guatemala*. London: Verso, 1993.

Shepard, Todd. *The Invention of Decolonization: The Algerian War and the Remaking of France*. Ithaca: Cornell University Press, 2006.

Sherman, Daniel, *French Primitivism and the Ends of Empire, 1945–1975*. Chicago: University of Chicago Press, 2011.

Wenzel, Jennifer. *Bulletproof: Afterlives of Anticolonial Prophecy in South Africa and Beyond*. Chicago: University of Chicago Press, 2009.

White, Luise. *Unpopular Sovereignty: Rhodesian Independence and African Decolonization*. Chicago: University of Chicago Press, 2015.

Worger, William H., Nancy L. Clark, and Edward Alpers, eds. *Africa and the West: A Documentary History*. Vol. 2: *From Colonialist to Independence, 1875 to the Present*. New York: Oxford University Press, 2010.

Topical Index

Five Pillars, 29
in India, 44–45
Pan-Islam, 244–246
rivalries among Muslims, 35–37
rivalry with Catholicism, 11
Israel, 343–358
Italo-Ethiopian Treaty of 1928, 312
Italy, 311–313

Japan
begins overseas expansion, 9, 214–215
bombing of Pearl Harbor, 315
capture of European colonies in World
War II, 316
defeats China 1894–1895, 9
expansion 1920s and 1930s, 289
in French Indochina, 324
Greater East Asian Co-Prosperity
Spher, 313–314
heroic stories of empire, 237–238
invasion of China 1937, 315
invasion of Manchuria, 308–311
Korean Expedition, 87–88
Meiji Restoration, 215
movement of businesses and spies into
China, 313
Mukden incident, 308–309
United States demands access to
204–206
victory over Russia, 251–253

Kenya
concentration camps, 336
Kikuyu heritage and system of government, 306–308
Land and Freedom Army
(Mau Mau), 336
postwar independence movements
crushed 317
as settler colony, 2
villagization, 336–338
violent independence struggle, 343
Korea
cold war menace, 344
defeat of Japanese invasion 1592, 87–88
taken over by Japan, 9
proxy war in, 325
sex slavery in World War II, 321–322

USSR backed military action in, 14
U.S. troops in, 14
Kuwait, 350

Labor Zionist Movement, 300
land-based empires, 1, 4–5, 8
Laos, 354
Latin American pauperization, 351
League of Nations, 13, 281–282, 308–310,
311–313
Lebanon, 3, 14
legal structures, 135–136, 157–158,
172–173, 175–177
Lepanto, battle of, 10, 85–87
little ice age, 19

Malta, battle of, 10
Mamluk Sultanate, 38–39
Manchuria-Manchuko, 308–311
mandates, 289, 290
marital alliances of victors and
vanquished, 93
maroon communities in Western
Hemisphere 153
medicine, 136–137
Merv, 27–28
Mayan people, 363–365
Mexico
business imperialism in, 3
agreement on new governmental
structure 1821, 175–177
independence struggle, 155, 175
Mexican Revolution 1910, 264
Mexican Revolution remembered
363–365
role of go-betweens and alliances in
Spanish conquest of, 68–69
Texas complaints against, 189–193
Middle East, 6
migration, 177–180, 189–193, 215, 344, 352
military
British, 183
combat in Central Asia, 197–200
experience of World War I, 265
fighting in East Africa, 233–234
France plan for African troops, 206–207
Indian soldiers in World War I,
274–275
in Women's War of 1929, 302–303

advance across West Asia and North
Africa, 42
attack on Mamluk regime in Egypt,
38–39
beginnings and expansion, 3
blocks eastern Mediterranean, 5
in Caucasus, 4
versus Christians in Mediterranean, 92
defeats Byzantine Empire, 24
defeats Mamluk sultanate, 38
develops fleet, 4
expands in Middle East, 26
fleet in Gujarat, 83–84
gunpowder use, 26
Islamic power of, 4
letter threatening Persians, 35–37
move into Asia Minor, 24
nationalist activists, 266–269
naval development, 79–80
non-Muslim peoples in, 4
occupation of Constantinople, 34–35
powers eager to seize its lands, 4
program of Young Turks, 269–270
reform efforts, 185
religious rights in, 200–202
rule of law in, 10
skill of horsemen, 17
in southeastern Europe, 4
status of Jews and Christians in, 10
takes to the sea, 26
Tanzimat reforms, 202
territories given to Britain and France
postwar, 13
travel descriptions, 119–121
use of cannons, 17
weakened by European industrialization, 185–186

Pan-African movement, 242,
270–274, 290
Pan-Arab movement, 290
Pan-Islam movement, 242, 244–246, 290
Pakistan, 317–319
Palestine, 257–258, 258–259, 298–300, 345
Persian Empire, 4, 35–37 (see also Iran)
pilgrimage, 28–30, 80–81
piracy, 7, 127, 135–136
Philippines, 9, 10, 242
Poland, 10, 315

Portugal
acquisition of geographic knowledge,
47–49
in Atlantic islands and along African
coast, 5
Columbus studies geography in, 5
create caravel, 17
competition with Muslim traders, 54
establishment of plantations on Atlantic
islands, 47
in Indian Ocean, 2
naval battles with Ottomans 79–84
origins of empire, 5
population problems, 89–90
praise of Prince Henry, 49
reach Malacca and Macau, 5, 54
rounds southern Africa to Indian
Ocean, 5
sugar production in Brazil, 100–102
use of spies, 45
post-colonial culture, 23, 344–345
precious metals, 7, 217–220
Protestantism, 91
proxy wars, 325

race, 3, 21, 141–143, 265, 270–274
racism, 184, 305–306, 316, 344, 352
religious conversion, 305
Rhodes, Battle of, 10
rise and fall of empires, 9
Roman Empire, 1
rule of law, U.S. discrimination against
imperial subjects, 10
Russia
Bolsheviks keep empire intact post-
World War I, 289
Bolshevik Revolution, 266, 320
British assessments of Russian strength,
186–188
business imperialism, 3
clash with Japan, 8
conquest in Caucasus, 203–204
English charter companies for trade
with, 97
expansion across Asia, 7, 105, 150
fur trading 105
justification for Crimean
annexation, 151
peasant migration to Siberia, 8